y Times.

S is the PALLADIUM of all the Civil, Political and RELIG

OCTOBER 20, 1822.   CE 7d.

CTURES.

...entitled to be free? Convinced ourselves of a national political truth, that where the public press shrinks from its bounden duty, liberty is in the direst danger; and that, if annihilated or invaded, the same press is the only remaining means of its recovery, the only surviving hope of the people—we determined, instead of being discouraged and laying upon our oars, instead of being idle lookers on, to apply our utmost strength with that renovated and glowing ardour, worthy of the cause so near and dear to our hearts; and to have nothing more to wish or hope for, in aid of our earnest and ardent exertions, than the favouring and auspicious gale of public encouragement.

Our motive, then, for instituting THE SUNDAY TIMES is explained. Of the merit of the *particulars* of the mode we have adopted for attaining our purpose, the public will best judge. It it may not be improper to make a few observations on that province of our undertaking. With respect to the selection of our *title*, we wish to observe, that the Times themselves having so materially changed from what they were when the press was free and honest, it became necessary that the very face of our Paper should announce our intention to keep pace with the variation of their aspect; we therefore thought no title would better express such intention, than that which we have adopted; an appellation which, as it will apply to all future periods, will continue to remind both ourselves and our readers, of the necessity of conforming to the demands of the existing moment, and of making those demands the index and impulsion of our conduct. Of the detail of our other arrangements, we shall leave our readers to judge. We have only to add, that not only seeing an opening for the expression of our own free and unbiassed sentiments on the present state of men and measures, and on foreign and domestic politics, but an *imperious call* for a firm, stanch, and resolute assertion of public freedom, we resolved to exert ourselves to answer to that call, and to execute to the best of our zeal and talents, a task more requisite to the liberation and happiness of mankind, than any other. To this task we set down with an honest and ardent zeal; and shall hope to persevere in it to the satisfaction and advantage of our country and the world.

ASPECT OF PUBLIC AFFAIRS.

In directing our attention to this painful and heart-rending subject, we feel an awful presentiment that damps our spirits, and almost induces us to lay down our pen in despair. If we glance our eye to the state of foreign politics, we are appalled with the sickening view of our unnatural alliance with a combination of Despots, assembling in Congress to consult and devise how they shall most effectually subdue the spirit of liberty, and rivet the chains of the people of Europe. If we turn from the contemplation of this disgusting scene, to the internal state of our country, an endless and unvarying succession of almost general distress presents itself to our view. Bankruptcy, beggary, and calamity, with giant strides, stalk through this once-smiling and flourishing country; while the weight of taxation, and an obstinate adherence on the part of Ministers to the same profligate waste of the national resources, and the same corrupt system to which are to be attributed all our reverses, precludes all rational hope of returning prosperity. Such is the moment when we have embarked in the cause of the...

...moment the Royal Conspiracy will be broken up. Then the example they themselves have set, will be followed by the people of all countries; their HOLY ALLIANCE will be succeeded by a HOLY ALLIANCE OF NATIONS; and their rods of iron be converted into so many golden standards of liberty. There is a chance in favour of mankind, over and above the probable effect of the clear notions and lively sense of freedom and the rights of men, which are quickening and spreading in all directions, and promise, if nations are but true to themselves, to liberate the world they illumine; and whether the present conspiration, about to be re-acted at Verona, break to pieces, or not, by virtue of its own frail materials, it cannot long endure; any more than it can be rent asunder, without shaking the peace of Europe to its foundation, and involving this devoted Empire in the greatest of all possible dangers.

With respect to our own country, its distresses and sufferings (thanks to the despotic profligacy of Ministers) are great enough, Heaven knows, without the additional scourge of a new state of Continental hostilities, or those losses and inconveniences from which England could not protect herself, even if some secret and subtle motive should determine her Cabinet to be the neutral spectator of a second contest between the legions of tyranny, and the phalanxes of freedom. But that neutrality would be unnatural; because where the views and chief interests of the parties are the same, coalition and good faith are rather necessaries than virtues, and comprise all their merit in their *prudence*. The British Government will not desert the Continental Conspiracy, nor will Spain and Portugal be so untrue to themselves, as to divide their political energies. Happily both for one and the other of these regenerated countries, their Sovereigns are what FREDERICK THE THIRD, of Prussia, pronounced the Statholder and some other Chief Magistrates to be, the Servants of the States, at the head of which they are stationed. And fortunately will it be for the present Holy Confederates, if they adopt with respect to the Peninsula, the maxim of the same wise Sovereign, that he had no right, or title, to interfere in the internal affairs of other nations. Had England made so just and wise a rule the guide of her conduct, how different had been her situation at this moment from that in which she is placed! Withdrawing our eyes, for an instant, from the deplorable state of the Continent; from the daily infraction of the Constitution of France by her overbearing Ministers, her enslaved Press, and her Military Cordon; the base and arbitrary policy of the Austrian and Prussian Governments, in excluding every liberal sentiment from the future system of education prescribed for their Universities; the unfeeling indifference with which the Tyrant of Russia observes the murderous barbarities committed by the Turks upon a people struggling for a liberation to which, by the laws of GOD, and the claims of Christianity and common justice, they are entitled; the secret encouragement given to that most infamous of all possible practices, the Slave Trade, and the very object of the Holy Congress at Verona (a Congress so holy, that his Holiness himself, it seems, is not holy enough to form one of its members); turning our eyes from these painful and disgusting vexations and terrific objects, what do we see at home? Is the picture of England's political condition less offensive, less distressful, less mortifying and alarming? Does Ireland present a more favorable scene? If the evils that overwhelm this country, and have been enumerated till the tongue of complaint has become weary of its task, exhibit the most frightful omens of the future, is there any better prospect in the present condition of the sister kingdom? Have not the privations and miseries, the penury and oppressions of the lesser island, grown out of the poli...

THE PEARL OF DAYS

THE PEARL OF DAYS.

A Sabbatarian handbill of February 1885 which was supplied at the rate of two shillings a thousand.

THE PEARL OF DAYS

An Intimate Memoir of
The Sunday Times

1822-1972

HAROLD HOBSON · PHILLIP KNIGHTLEY
LEONARD RUSSELL

Hamish Hamilton
LONDON

First published in Great Britain
by HAMISH HAMILTON LTD *1972*
90 Great Russell Street London WC*1*

SBN 241 02266 5

Printed in Great Britain by
WESTERHAM PRESS LTD
Westerham in the county of Kent

Contents

Illustrations

Facsimiles in text: Matrimony (p. 5); newspaper stamps (p. 6); The Independent Observer and The Weekly Dispatch (p. 12); E. Johnson's British Gazette (p. 13); Lloyd's penny Sunday Times (p. 15), the latter three items by courtesy of the Cambridge University Press, from Stanley Morison's 'The English Newspaper'; the death of George IV (p. 17); the Duke of Cumberland and the Reform Bill (p. 21); weekly newspaper stamps return (p. 24); Queen Victoria, Prince Albert, and an announcement of their wedding supplement (p. 26); the Queen and the Tories (p. 27); repeal of the Corn Laws (p. 29); the Duke of Wellington's funeral (p. 32); 'Nicholas Nickleby' (p. 37); handbill for 'Fortescue' (p. 43); Baroness Lehzen etc (p. 46); death of the Prince Consort (p. 47); Franco-Prussian war (p. 49); death of Queen Victoria (p. 55); 'Watch on the Rhine' advertisement (p. 100); message from Lord Stamfordham (p. 113); the first Sunday Times crossword puzzle (p. 158); general strike front page (p. 169); the battered OMS advertisement (p. 171). The title-pages of the various parts of the book also have appropriate facsimiles.

Acknowledgments

One of the three authors of this book is reminded of the famous remark about Churchill: 'Winston has written a book about himself and called it "The World Crisis" '. This particular author is very conscious that he has introduced himself into the narrative too frequently, but he pleads in extenuation that the work does not attempt to be an orthodox newspaper history. Besides, he is by now too well aware of the truth of a remark made to him recently by Mr James Moran, the printing historian, who said, out of his large experience, that books on printing and journalism teem with mistakes and contradictions. It seemed best, then, in his own part of the book at least, to try to stick to things he knew about.

Even so, all three authors have had a good deal of help, though no blame must be attached to anyone but themselves for mistakes or misinterpretations. The complete list of helpers is too long to give here, but mention must be made of the following, all of whom work, or have worked, for The Sunday Times:

General research: Fred Brazier, Stella Frank. Picture research: Doris Bryen. Art work and design: Edwin Taylor, Rosalind Newcomen, Gillian Crampton-Smith.

Donald McCormick gave much assistance with the story of Ian Fleming and the Mercury service; and Nicholas Carroll supplied some cuttings and other information about his grandmother, who owned The Sunday Times in the 1880s. Mr and Mrs Will Sandford, Roger Wilding and other veterans of the Camrose era, including George Darker, are thanked for their reminiscences. To two people outside The Sunday Times thanks are also due. John Carter CBE, gave authoritative assistance on Sir Edmund Gosse's involvement with T. J. Wise, and James Moran sorted out problems of early newspaper printing and production.

Quotations from books are usually acknowledged throughout this work in footnotes, but special mention must be made of the guidance derived from Stanley Morison's 'The English Newspaper' (Cambridge), A. J. P. Taylor's masterly volume in the Oxford History of England, 'English History, 1914–1945', and from a history-book from the United States, Alfred F. Havighurst's 'Twentieth-Century Britain' (Row, Peterson & Co). Insufficiently acknowledged help (or even totally unacknowledged help) came from Russell Braddon's 'Roy Thomson of Fleet Street' (Collins) and Evan Charteris's 'Life and Letters of Sir Edmund Gosse' (Heinemann, 1931).

Inevitably, newspapers nowadays being volatile engines, there could be some degree of change at The Sunday Times before this book is in print. Members of the staff therefore hold their specified posts 'at the time of writing', which is – May 1, 1972.

H. H.
P. K.
L. R.

Punch.

Standfirst

The drawing for the wood engraving is by Thackeray, who does a caricature of himself reading The Sunday Times. Beside him is Douglas Jerrold of Punch, and they hear the third gentleman addressing the lady on the iniquities of that magazine, which she has been reading. The caption, which is forgettable, is of record length even for the early days of Punch.

Standfirst

> **STANDFIRST** Brief few sentences to introduce a news story or feature, set in distinctive type at top. See also *blurb, precede*.[1]

'The Sunday paper is one of the features of the age,' says Mr Finsbury in 'The Wrong Box'. But it was hardly a respectable phenomenon then, in 1889, and much less so in 1822, when The Sunday Times was born.

True, it was respectable enough when that unsung heroine, Mrs E. Johnson, of Ludgate Place, Ludgate Hill, began the whole thing by founding E. Johnson's British Gazette, and Sunday Monitor in about 1779. This sober and successful journal had nothing of the magazine element in it, if we except a column of Christian discourse on the front page, and might have been a daily paper of the time, such as The Morning Post, published on a Sunday. Across nearly two hundred years the wily charm of Mrs Johnson survives in an announcement she made about 'the Original Sunday Newspaper' after it had been going along very nicely for a dozen years: 'Four thousand Papers are published every Sunday morning in the Cities of London, Westminster etc which circumstance must give a most pleasing sensation to all Advertising Customers.'

Other Sunday papers came along, and the more serious among them, including The Observer, followed Mrs Johnson's example and produced a conventional seventh-day paper. But the pattern ended and the mould was smashed at about the time of Waterloo. The innovator was an Irish barrister named Robert Bell, who obtained control of The Weekly Dispatch, which had been founded in 1801 (d. 1961 as The Sunday Dispatch), and started a new trend; he introduced into it long reports of sexual crimes, murders, and so on, combining this kind of sensationalism with serious, if radical, attention to current problems, and varying his columns still further by engaging the most famous sporting writer of the time, Pierce Egan. The radical opinions of The Dispatch, The Sunday Times and most of the other Sunday papers survived the disapproval of the authorities. As Stanley Morison says, 'the

---

1. Harold Evans: 'Editing and Design, Book Three, News Headlines'. London: Heinemann, 1972.

xiii

Sunday press was one of the greatest of the forces lying behind the Reform Bill'; and for nearly a century, in part as a result of Bell's revolution, even the most respectable of Sunday papers excited feelings of disapproval and suspicion among many people.

Robert Bell's impact seems to have been felt by both The Observer and The Sunday Times. The Observer abandoned the seventh-day paper formula, and The Sunday Times never attempted it. Although both were classed as political papers, to distinguish them from Sunday family journals in which the magazine element prevailed, or purely sporting Sunday publications, they came to rely heavily on certain ingredients of Bell's formula, including the crude satisfactions of the crime report, and The Observer, under William Clement, went on to make a big thing of illustrating murder cases with wood engravings.

In those days there had to be some sacrifice of ideals if a political paper was to survive the handicaps laid on it by Government. Thus there was the stamp tax, imposed originally to lay restraint on all newspaper enterprise and so keep the lower classes in the dark. There was a duty on paper – about a farthing a sheet. There was a tax of 3s 6d on each advertisement, and there were relatively few advertisements.

So if the proprietor charged seven pence a copy – which was the price of the original four-page Sunday Times – the cost of printing, the duties, the trade discounts and the distribution charges amounted to something like 5½d a copy. No wonder, as he would be doing extremely well in the 1820s if he sold 7,000 copies, he had to look to the Tories or Whigs for financial support. (The proprietor and editor of The Sunday Times of 1822, Henry White, insisted that he was innocent of venality, but that may have been because he was loathed by the Tories and was too radical for the Whigs.) It was all a murky business, and so it remained until advertising increased and the various duties – the 'taxes on knowledge' – were removed in the middle of the nineteenth century.

Since then experience has shown that the most successful papers have been those with strong editors enjoying continuity of office. There was little continuity of either editorship or ownership in the nineteenth-century Sunday Times. It was frequently sold off to some new proprietor, and for thirteen years from 1864 it was even without an editor at all – the records are silent about the precise details of this conductorless orchestra.

Then in 1887 an Englishwoman known as 'Princess Midas', from the fortune she had made out of prospecting for gold in

Victoria, Australia, and for striking it rich with the Midas mine, bought the paper, with the intention of reducing its relatively extensive coverage of the arts and extending its news. It is true that her very grandson, Nicholas Carroll, has been on the present paper for more than twenty years, but there is no continuity here either: his appointment happened fortuitously.

A second woman proprietor, a member of the Sassoon family, controlled The Sunday Times at the same time as her husband owned its rival, The Observer. Here again was ambiguity: the first Lord Camrose[1] says that there was 'great rivalry between them, resulting sometimes in keen personal disagreement', whereas the financial journals of the time anticipated a merger and the truth seems to have been that the husband, Frederick Beer, was an ailing, withdrawn figure who gave his ambitious but scatterbrained wife a free hand with both papers.

So the nineteenth-century record is one of interest without significance, with the paper sometimes reminding one of Hazlitt's famous crack about The Times after it had replaced the hand-press with the steam-press – 'That prodigious prosing paper, which seems to be written as well as printed by a steam-engine.'

By the turn of the century, the shabby and boring years were continuing. The paper was still a commercial pawn, and on the outbreak of the first world war, with a circulation of only 30,000, its principals were a mysterious quartet – a German financier, Hermann Schmidt; Sir Basil Zaharoff, the notorious, and even then legendary, international munitions agent; Cecil Rhodes's ally Dr Jameson (of the Jameson Raid), who had been Prime Minister of the Cape Colony; and the chairman of the Conservative party, Sir Arthur Steel-Maitland, MP.

Schmidt was interned and a year later the paper was bought by two ambitious Welshmen, Mr W. E. Berry and Mr J. Gomer Berry, of Ewart, Seymour & Co. Ltd, Windsor House, Kingsway, a firm which published a weekly paper called Boxing. It had found respectability at last; William Berry was buying it for keeps, and to put it on a sound footing, not as a way of seeking political advancement. He surmised that he was a professional with something outstanding to offer Fleet Street, and he was right. Over the years the first Viscount Camrose showed himself the greatest newspaperman since Northcliffe, a formidable combination of the adventurous and the cautious, a proprietor who disdained to

---

1. It is always to the first Viscount Camrose that this book refers.

advertise himself in his own newspapers, such as Beaverbrook did, but who yet had his own magnetism. The other brother, Gomer Berry, enacted for many years – too many for his comfort – the rôle that Harold Rothermere played to his brother Alfred Northcliffe: the man who looked after the books and was in charge of the advertising.

The Sunday Times now began to rise in the world. If the dingy years were over, it was the stingy ones which began; with Gomer watching over the till, with a perky little editor named Leonard Rees, who sported an eyeglass and made a great thing of playing bridge at the Savile Club and who seemed to aspire to be taken for a peppery colonel, but who under it all was a shrewd editor with a sound provincial background and training and a remarkable eye for talent. Sir Edmund Gosse, an underrated figure today, James Agate, Ernest Newman, Desmond MacCarthy, and Dilys Powell were all brought on to the paper by him.

Soon its new offices in the Strand were a striving, cheerful, parsimonious place, with Dickensian characters in every corner, such as the invincible cockney Mr Hake, the circulation manager of Boxing, who had been brought over to sell The Sunday Times. The autocratic Leonard Rees was the little god of 186 Strand, but everyone knew that elsewhere in the building there was Jehovah himself, Mr William, soon to be Sir William, as handsome then as a Roman gladiator, with peculiarly searching eyes and of such commanding stature and presence that nearly everyone in the office trembled if they were summoned. It was never, however, as bad as they thought it would be. He was a just man.

From Boxing and other publications he had learned something about type and editing, and he began, very cautiously, to improve the content and appearance of The Sunday Times, even getting hot about the use and abuse of such minutiae as the 'half-double', a rule which in those days – we are in the early twenties now – was used to separate news stories. Opinion, criticism, leading articles – for the moment he left these mainly to Rees: they were comparatively easy to organise, and he knew that many a paper has foundered from having too heavy a load of abstractions. What he himself wanted, despite the soothsaying of J. L. Garvin in The Observer, was hard news. For the first time in its history the news side of the paper was taken in hand, and the post-mortems could be very severe. One news editor, quite unfitted for his job, went mad under the strain.

The result was that The Sunday Times became at last a good,

lively alert *newspaper* as well as a respected journal of opinion. Weaknesses, however, remained. Certain areas of it were strangely unsophisticated and remained so for a long time. Its permanent staff was fantastically small, and the paper was bundled together on Saturdays with casual editorial help at two guineas a day. It was without a single whole-time foreign correspondent and equally had no diplomatic, Services or certain other specialists of its own. But it began to make money, and when Camrose formed the great Allied Newspapers chain in 1923 it became (and remained), as used to be said ruefully around the sparsely populated office, one of his chief milch-cows for the company's profits.

Conditions improved when Camrose bought the tottering Daily Telegraph in 1928. From 1930 The Sunday Times was housed in The Telegraph's splendid new offices in Fleet Street and shared its plant (from 1933) and services. But stinginess remained. If it went so far as to appoint a diplomatic correspondent – he was a sub-editor on The Telegraph – he was paid only two guineas for darting about Whitehall on Saturdays.

It must have been about now that Arnold Bennett wrote in his Journal that The Sunday Times had 'the edge on The Observer'; and it was Camrose's attention to detail (as well as J. L. Garvin's ever-increasing devotion to Delphic utterance and growing abandonment of an editor's mundane duties) which helped The Sunday Times to pull comfortably ahead of its always respected rival. Unspectacularly, doggedly, Camrose made progress with his two national papers and consolidated his whole vast empire, which included, as well as Allied Newspapers, which was the largest newspaper chain in the country, the Northcliffe-founded magazine group, the Amalgamated Press, owned today – with accretions – by the International Publishing Corporation.

All the same, Camrose in these relatively early days had a defect as a proprietor. In the papers under his immediate control he was insufficiently open-minded. He had picked up one of the most objectionable characteristics of Northcliffe, Rothermere, and Beaverbrook, in that he was apt not to allow any public man or movement of which he deeply disapproved to be mentioned favourably even in a signed article. There was no tangible black-list, but his entourage knew and his editors knew, and the word went down the line, resulting in suppression even worse than he might have intended because of the zeal of subordinates.

This was the kind of thing which helped to give the press lords of the time a bad name. Camrose himself – at this stage at any rate –

would rarely allow another newspaper or even a weekly journal (not to mention branded goods of any kind) to be mentioned by name in his two main papers – it was always 'a weekly journal' or 'a newspaper report'. His brother Lord Kemsley was not jealous in that way – 'let us be big about it' he used to say – but he had the same attitude as the other press lords to public characters of whom he disapproved (Aneurin Bevan was one), and he continued this form of censorship in The Sunday Times and only moderated it after the war under pressure from new men on his staff and out of fear of the advances being made, in a changed world, by the liberal Observer. He didn't believe in the political man-hunt, like Northcliffe; it was rather a shutter of silence.

It was this kind of thing which gave substance to Randolph Churchill's attacks on the press lords in The Spectator in the 1950s, though the admirable but preposterous Randolph reserved his real philippics for gutter-press practices of which The Sunday Times was never guilty (his references to the 'electronic suppressors' of The Times were a joking but unsuccessful attempt to intimidate Sir William Haley into reviewing his books or otherwise giving him publicity).

The second phase of The Sunday Times was drawing to a close, if we allow the first phase to extend over the undistinguished period of 1822–1915. For at the beginning of 1937 the Berry brothers divided their empire, for family reasons, and thereafter went it alone. Camrose took The Daily Telegraph and the Amalgamated Press, Kemsley The Sunday Times and Allied Newspapers.

This was of course the run-up to the war, when Hitler and Mussolini were disturbing the peace, and everything – including their speeches – seemed to happen on a Saturday. It was a bad time for an inexperienced proprietor such as Lord Kemsley to take the stage. There was a new editor of The Sunday Times, too: W. W. Hadley, a provincial journalist of the best kind who had been editor of The Merthyr Times, the Berrys' home-town paper, and had said of the schoolboy William, when judging an essay competition, 'This boy must become a journalist'.

William began in Hadley's office at the age of fourteen, and when Hadley was out of a job in 1930 because of the disappearance of The Daily Chronicle, whose political correspondent he had been, Camrose invited him to join The Sunday Times, at 58, 'to help with the Letters', a page in the paper around which Rees had erected a mystique. Hadley had just about absorbed the whole rite of making-up what was an undeniably trivial feature when Rees died practically at his desk.

After a long probationary period Hadley became accepted as editor, and he used to claim, thirty years later, that he was the only editor of a national paper who had never actually been appointed to his job. He became Lord Kemsley's Elder Statesman, and together, encouraged by Neville Chamberlain, Kemsley and Hadley naïvely pursued a German propaganda plan for Anglo-German press rapprochement which ended on the eve of the war with Lord K (he was always called Lord K or K in the office) paying an injudicious visit to Hitler.

It was a bad start. But if Lord K had failed in this first attempt to draw attention to himself and become a national figure like the other press lords, he had the war years, when the fire of all newspapers was damped down, to meditate on his post-war hopes and plans.

They were ambitious plans. Urged on by Ian Fleming, who used to meet him socially during the war, he foresaw a brave future for the Kemsley regional papers, the old Allied chain to which he gave his name in 1943, two years later ordering that under the title-block on the front page of every paper in the group the words 'A Kemsley Newspaper' must appear, a command which caused Lord Camrose to write, enigmatically: 'He is, perhaps, more a believer in personal journalism than I am.' (Kemsley also believed in a daily Biblical text in all his newspapers – in The Sunday Times it appeared at the foot of the leader columns.) The Kemsley sons, of which there were five (a sixth was killed in action in the war) were to help in this regional renaissance and also make The Daily Sketch into a successful picture paper, while Lord K himself recruited new talent for The Sunday Times and fashioned it, with Hadley and a few new trusties, into one of the world's great newspapers.

It is easy to be unjust to Lord K. Some of those who knew him outside the office thought he was too grand by half and on the wrong side of the division between a puritan and a prude. Certainly he had a monumental sense of his own importance, but he was never really at ease anywhere outside his own domain, where his writ ran and his foibles were obeyed but not resented. (Stalin had an Aunt Anna who wrote an artless little book about their family; but Stalin discovered 'impermissible familiarity' in it and sent her off to solitary imprisonment for ten years. Lord K always seemed afraid of impermissible familiarity outside his own office.) With his carnation, his pearl tie-pin and his homburg hat, of a peculiarly out-of-date style (you can see its fellow in the Museum of Costume at Bath *c.* 1912), he looked like some Edwardian grandee mixed with a suspicion of Groucho Marx. Indeed, some of the younger things in society called him 'Groucho' behind his back, and when he heard of it he was cut to the quick. So much so that when an innocent member of his editorial staff proposed at the Tuesday morning conference that The Sunday Times interview Groucho, who was coming to London, he got his bewildered head bitten off.

All the same, if you had met Lord K for a few minutes at an air-port terminal or somewhere, and had broken down his automatic reserve and exchanged a few words with him, you would have realised, despite the utter ordinariness of his knowledge and opinions, that here was a man with a steam-roller personality. After a glance or two you could not have failed to identify him, for when he travelled one of his servitors would be near carrying a brief-case labelled, in big black letters, VISCOUNT KEMSLEY. (He was always insistent on the formal use of titles in the paper: only barons were lords – otherwise you were always a viscount, an earl, and so on.)

He could, despite everything, be a great if elephantine charmer, and somewhere in his Victorian mind and formal, middle-class personality was a wild electric fibre of romanticism, some vivid gambler's instinct which occasionally set him off on a course which appalled his entourage yet in the end could yield big journalistic dividends. His 'let us be big about it' sometimes meant that he was off on one of these sprees. Nobody could restrain him then. What-ever it was must be put in hand without the waste of a second, and those rash enough to utter platitudes about thinking it over or sleeping on it would be trampled down and left as corpses while he stampeded on scattering havoc like a whirlwind. In other words, though he was by no means the equal of his brother as a news-paperman, he was capable of very successful intuitions, and those are the things that men live by in journalism.

He wasn't tradition-bound. He didn't want to embalm the paper, as The Times was embalmed after Northcliffe and before Lord Thomson took it over. He was all for experiment, for having something new in appearance or content every week. But this experimentation took a formal shape. Delane's classic dictum that the press lives by disclosure – 'whatever passes into its keeping becomes a part of the knowledge and history of our times' – left him unconvinced, supposing he had ever heard of it; and dis-

closures of a personal nature, however valid, made him uncomfortable.

If he talked of having more news in the paper, as he often did, he
would be thinking of harmless columns about foreign affairs,
traditionally a very respectable subject. Crime stories – that is,
reports or sketches of big cases, for speculative stories such as
crime reporters engage in were not allowed – were mere sordidness
to him in the context of The Sunday Times. Encouraged by his
formal approach to journalism, there were always sober old gentlemen around the office who were apt to take the life out of the paper
by suppressing its sharpest or most interesting disclosures: not
necessarily because they feared libel or untruth but in the sacred
cause of 'responsible' journalism. To such 'serious' journalists, and
even more to Lord K himself, disclosure became tainted by
vulgarity, even when it was disclosure of comparatively trivial
matters. He proved once more that it is fatal for a newspaperman
to think too much about respectability and responsibility.

He was at his worst when some article in the paper evoked
letters of protest; he would censure the writer automatically as if he
had done something blameworthy in starting a controversy. It was
said in the office, ruefully, that if any regular contributor had
possessed an enemy knowledgeable enough to send three or four
letters of criticism a week, under assumed names, for a space of six
successive weeks, he could have got the poor man or woman run
off the paper.

In the first number of The Sunday Times poor Henry White
grandiloquently promised to unfold the secret springs by which
the Government was actuated. It was an honourable ambition
even if he didn't manage to live up to it. Lord K, however, wasn't
interested in nosing about for secret springs. His instinctive
attitude was rather that of the man about town in Stevenson's
novel who had the opportunity of resolving the strange story of Dr
Jekyll and Mr Hyde but averted his eyes on principle, on the
ground that once you started a question it was like starting a
stone: 'You sit quietly on top of a hill; and away the stone goes,
starting others; and presently some bland old bird (the last you
would have thought of) is knocked on the head in his own back
garden, and the family have to change their name. No, sir, I make
it a rule of mine: the more it looks like Queer Street, the less I ask.'

Perhaps it was compassion which made Lord K reluctant to
start a question which might lead to embarrassment for someone,
even a highly disapproved politician on the wrong side of the

House; more likely he thought it was all a bit vulgar and ungentle-manly. He preferred to preserve a princely reserve and occupy his time in consorting with the eminent, thinking of them all as possible recruits for the leader page of his paper, where articles by 'big names' were the pillars which largely supported the whole editorial structure. It was not a successful architecture. As eminent public men are busy on their own account and not usually practised, like professional journalists, in quick writing, there would sometimes be delays in delivery with consequent loss of topicality. Worse, the eminent in whatever profession are apt to do their true work in private and indulge in blameless nothings about it in public. This was something Lord K never tumbled to; if you had offered him the choice between the finest and sharpest reporter's profile of some big name and a mild public relations exercise signed by the big name himself he would have thought it mad to have preferred the profile. It was this passion for the emptily impressive which frequently made Ian Fleming, one of Lord K's advisers, sigh with exasperation. One Tuesday at the editorial conference he was asked by a courtier of Lord K's, 'Don't you think we had a good paper on Sunday?' 'As a matter of fact,' said Ian, fitting another Morland special into his cigarette-holder and laconically summarising the whole business, 'no. Too many bishops.'

You couldn't have too many bishops or ambassadors for Lord K. He once met Lewis Douglas, then US ambassador in London, at some reception and was astounded to hear from him that he was writing an article for The Sunday Times; it turned out that it was on fishing, Mr Douglas's favourite pastime. First thing next morning Lord K, mortified at not having been told about it, summoned the executive who had commissioned the article and mingled severe reproaches at this lèse-majesty with joyful congratulations on their having hauled in yet another ambassador, and such a big fish as the American one at that.

These elevated attitudes had certain commercial drawbacks. In the days of Lord Camrose there had been expansion at Allied Newspapers, but with Lord K in control of the group the shrinkage was creeping but deadly. When The Daily Graphic was sold in December, 1952, the big daily newspaper room at Kemsley House fell ominously silent. In November, 1955, The Sunday Chronicle was merged with The Empire News, and in the same month The Daily Dispatch title was purchased by The News Chronicle. Control was given up of the three Glasgow papers, and by the middle of 1959, when Roy Thomson took over, The Sunday Graphic and The Empire News were seen to be doomed.

Yet when all the weaknesses of Lord K have been admitted it has to be acknowledged that, as far as The Sunday Times was concerned, he did just what he set out to do. After the war, that is to say, he surrounded himself with a little band of bright young men, kept them on a tight chain, exposed them regularly to his own enthusiasm, paid them generously, and took the paper nearly to the million mark without sacrifice of quality. This had never been done before with a quality Sunday newspaper – it has never been matched since for that matter – and the first credit must go to this extraordinary man, who in some mysterious way, and in a sufficiently agreeable manner (for he rarely savaged his protégés and could indeed be jovial in a formidable, headmasterly way) set them off on a crusade.

Chief of these young men was Denis Hamilton, brought down by Lord K from his Middlesbrough paper after the war, in which at an impossibly early age he had commanded a battalion and won the DSO, to become his personal editorial assistant. Because Hamilton is an outstanding natural newspaperman he was soon editorial director of the whole group. Hadley was still editor of The Sunday Times, unflappable, gentle, enjoyably ironic, but he was an old man and withdrawn from much that was going on in the world. Without objection from him, Hamilton took over the search for the serials and special series which became so important to the paper, and when Hadley retired in 1950, full of years and warm affection for both the Berrys, Hamilton retained very intimate connections with The Sunday Times.

But he was not, and did not want to be, its next editor. That was a Fellow of All Souls, H. V. Hodson, who came relatively late to journalism, to which he brought a razor-sharp mind of a scientific bent. In the disorder of newspaper life he remained the detached and calm academic, just as unflappable as his predecessor but infinitely more aware of modern movements and particularly, as an inheritor of the traditions of Lord Milner's Kindergarten, of the problems of the Commonwealth and emergent nations. Of this devotion to the Commonwealth Lord Kemsley naturally approved. But Hodson had to work hard on the editor-in-chief, which was Lord K's title and his brother's in his time, before The Sunday Times was allowed to express liberal views on certain social questions. Hodson recalls in 1972 his struggle with the patriarch:

I had to get the famous leader on homosexuality past K, who saw every word of every leader in proof or by teleprinter. My success in this was one of my great achievements on the ST. The price I had to pay was to use opprobrious terms like 'perversion' instead of neutral ones. The upshot is interesting. The leader gave rise to a great flow of letters. K, who with all his prejudices knew when he was on a good thing journalistically, agreed that we should have a follow-up article at the top of the leader page. ('Big names'!). I recommended John Wolfenden, as a former headmaster who was now vice-chancellor of a modern university (Reading). He wrote a wise article. Could it be a coincidence that he was later chosen to head the Wolfenden Committee?

Hodson was a man of independent mind, but he had never worked as it were on the factory floor, and in disposition he was never a natural citizen of Lord K's vast and creaking empire, with all its baffling links with the great Withy Grove plant and offices in Manchester, where the northern edition of the paper was printed. Early in his career as editor, in the course of some Saturday night disagreement on the telephone with Lord Kemsley at Dropmore, his country home in Buckinghamshire, to which the first edition of the paper was sent by despatch rider, Hodson had to 'consider his position'. Lord K was startled – this kind of thing never happened. He changed the subject and never referred to the incident again. It cast a cloud over his week-end at Dropmore, which had teleprinters in the library, menservants to hand his lordship bits of agency tape on a silver salver, a terrific décor by Lady Kemsley, grounds of nearly 200 acres, 36 bedrooms, and fifteen or twenty bridge-playing guests (bridge and canasta were Lord K's great joy, and after the war he was enthusiastic about the appointment to The Sunday Times as bridge correspondent of a relatively unknown MP named Iain Macleod).

Hodson was still editor when, in 1959, out of the blue, Roy Thomson, of The Scotsman and Scottish Television Ltd, the little guy with the pebble-glasses who, as Beaverbrook had said condescendingly, owned a lot of little Canadian papers, took over Kemsley Newspapers down to the last typewriter ribbon.

No one on The Sunday Times at first gave credit to the rumours – or, at any rate, no one would believe that The Sunday Times itself was included in the deal. How could Lord Kemsley possibly part with his darling? He was like Maurice Baring who, in the war, when the paper was difficult to get hold of, had addressed a despairing ballade to Desmond MacCarthy with the recurring line 'I cannot live without The Sunday Times'.

The night that the deal with Thomson was announced, but without any mention of The Sunday Times, two members of its staff, husband and wife, dined in Wilton Crescent with the Neville Berrys – Neville was Kemsley's able second son. The party was rather a constrained one – it included Lionel Fraser, the merchant banker who represented Lord K in the take-over, and the Reginald Maudlings – and Neville indicated to his guests from the start that he could not talk about the thing which was uppermost in everyone's mind. But the pair from The Sunday Times, who had known Lord Kemsley for a long time, and liked him, continued to assume, when the deal was sketchily touched on in a word with Neville at the door, that though Roy Thomson might have acquired wonderful properties in Manchester and Middlesbrough and Glasgow and goodness knows where else he had not got The Sunday Times. It could not be. Lord Kemsley would not allow it.

But he had. He had sold out, for family reasons among others, without telling a single director other than those who belonged to his own clan. Props of the place like Michael Renshaw, the advertisement director, and Eric Cheadle, the general manager, who had been with Lord K since they were young men, were left abandoned to the new master, without contracts, though pressure initiated by Denis Hamilton resulted in their being given them by Roy Thomson on the day they first met him officially. Before this, at his very first meeting with Thomson, Cheadle had put out a feeler and received a bleak answer. Cheadle said that he would very much like to notch up fifty years with one company, and what about a contract? Thomson replied: 'I don't believe in contracts. If a guy's good he'll stay with me. If he's no good he's out.'

On the editorial side no one said it was a betrayal but everyone thought so. It seemed impossible that no longer would Lord K's maharajah's Rolls-Royce, with the black glass windows and the royal headroom, draw up at his private entrance in Coley Street.

It was all over, though. Lord Kemsley took his cheque for £5 million, along with his editor-in-chief's chair and desk, as a sort of historical monument, went out of the back door (he also took the Rolls-Royce waiting there), and was heard of no more. While his coevals like Lord Beaverbrook and the first Lord Camrose had remained to the end of their lives the sole masters of their businesses, the awesome, unpredictable overlords whom no one dare cross or contradict, 'whose word was law and whose nod was fate', he abdicated suddenly. It was the end of the third phase in the history of The Sunday Times.

There was some skirmishing before the fourth phase truly opened. For example, a little later on there was another party at the Neville Berrys. This time Roy Thomson himself was there. There were other guests, including Sir Arthur Bryant, who had a long friendship with the Kemsley family, and the same pair from The Sunday Times. Christabel Berry had conceived the idea that her Neville – the Kemsley sons were staying on for the time being – should be put in charge of The Sunday Times. It was not a very likely notion, and Roy Thomson was non-committal. He was non-committal about everything, in fact, except for a remark, made privately to one of The Sunday Times people, that economies were necessary and he thought Ian Fleming would have to go.

Ian Fleming had joined Kemsley Newspapers just after the war as foreign manager, and as well as acting as adviser to Lord K and urging him to get rid of the old pros around the place, substituting for them sophisticated young men and women, he had created a vastly expensive foreign news service called Mercury, which had been practically dismantled even before Thomson took over. Fleming had his James Bond novels to fall back on, and his connection with the newspaper meant very little to him financially. But he was devoted to The Sunday Times, if not to the other Kemsley publications, and he didn't want to leave it completely. With all his extensive friendships and contacts he had never met Thomson, but he was gloomy about him after a friend of his, recently staying at a health farm, had found himself on a massage table next to Thomson. 'I wouldn't,' said Fleming's friend, 'like to have any money in a business run by a man with a belly like that.' After their second evening at the Neville Berrys The Sunday Times pair were even more gloomy than Ian Fleming.

The sun soon came out, however, particularly when Roy Thomson, with the diplomatic Denis Hamilton at his elbow, began by taking The Sunday Times conference. He didn't talk like a man who was going to sack everyone. He gave no indication that he proposed to run the paper on a tiny budget, as was his habit, or so rumour said, with his Canadian papers and The Scotsman. He merely kept saying how good The Sunday Express was and turning over The Sunday Times in a bewildered way. At last he ventured the opinion that the paper needed more 'want ads' and much more news from New York.

The Sunday Times executives listened indulgently. To some of them at this first meeting he looked like a Canadian rotarian who very likely owned a small canning factory. But they liked him. They liked his wisecracks and his strong good sense. They were even *determined* to like him, to make up for the way in which Lord Kemsley had let them down.

Soon everyone was getting on excellently with him, including Ian Fleming and H. V. Hodson, and there was no feud with his editor, no mutual and implacable dislike, as there had been between him and the editor of The Scotsman when he took it over. But though he gave up praising The Sunday Express, seeming merely to yearn for it silently, he evidently came to believe that taking the conference might seem to interfere with his principle of freedom for his editors, and Hamilton became its chairman. And the magic million a week was reached.

At this point one of the top men on The Sunday Times fell ill and was away, on and off, for a long time. When he came back permanently he found the whole place changed. There was a new building – or, rather, a rebuilding of the old Kemsley House – a new editor, a new spirit everywhere. The old corridors had been narrow and devoid for years of much human traffic and everyone had a little cubby-hole to himself. There were few corridors or cubby-holes now. The editor had an elegant room designed by Lord Snowdon, otherwise it was mostly a plain of open-plan offices tenanted among others by a small army of editorial recruits and troupes of secretarial girls.

The new editor was Denis Hamilton, who had taken the job, reluctantly, to launch a great plan of Thomsonian expansion, made possible by the installation of expensive new plant at 200 Grays Inn Road, put in rapidly when it was no longer physically possible to print The Sunday Times at The Daily Telegraph in Fleet Street. H. V. Hodson had moved on to one of the great country houses of England, Ditchley, to become provost of the Anglo-American Foundation.

Thomson was certainly getting his 'want ads', otherwise personal advertisements, by now and the whole paper was booming. It had gone up to 48 pages. Plans were well advanced, too, for Thomson's own particular contribution to Sunday journalism, the colour magazine – still determinedly called the colour supplement by many people. It was his own baby, the child of his North American experience, and he was dandling it and nourishing it and trying, with daily lunches and evening receptions, to get advertising agents to go for it, at £2,000 the colour page.

To help him in the hard-sell there had come into being a grand and very expensive marketing division. 'Just one brilliant editor,' said Mr Hugh Cudlipp feelingly in 1971, and no doubt thinking of his unfortunate experiences in the launching of The Sun, 'is worth far more than all the eggheads and market research gremlins in the world.' The marketing division seems to have justified itself all the same, but it remained a somewhat metaphysical conception to journalists of the old school in Thomson House.

Denis Hamilton was the leader of the editorial side. It was easier for him than it had been for Hodson or indeed for any other previous twentieth-century editor. He was a powerful member of the board of directors of Thomson Newspapers, and if there was anything he wanted, and he particularly wanted extra staff, he got it without, as his predecessor had had to do, pitching a hard-luck story to the chairman. On the other hand, the programme needed someone of his subtlety. Apart from the colour magazine, for which he was responsible to Roy Thomson, there was the Business News section. With William Rees-Mogg, who had come from The Financial Times to be financial editor, and was now political and deputy editor, he kept a tight hold on its planning, refusing to be influenced by the offbeat views of some of the younger spirits around. Business News was a success from the start. The colour magazine was not.

With the magazine there was early trouble with the newsagents about discounts. It was (and is) printed on colour presses by an outside firm and distributed independently (at considerable expense) to newsagents, who had to join it up with the paper itself, and they understandably wanted something more for doing this and for delivering the whole package – the question was just how much. Again, the advertising agents, for all the pressure put on them, remained cool, and the advance bookings of advertisements were only fair. Worst of all, the first issue of the magazine disappointed those who wanted something less original, and Hamilton had to answer personally more than a thousand letters from indignant readers. The following Sunday the paper was frank and rueful about the disappointment.

There was shock and despair in the office, but number two was better, and thereafter it improved rapidly. In time the advertisements came along handsomely too.

It had been laid down from the first that the magazine was to complement the more serious approach of the paper itself by appealing to the young. This it did, and does, and in this lies its character and its chief secret. Nevertheless, it was a fearsome start in one way and another, and Roy Thomson's revolution in British journalism was only achieved with the writing-off of more than £800,000 in development charges. Yet it was cheap at the price if one remembers The Daily Mirror magazine, which cost four or five times that and after only a few months sank without trace.

The Sunday Times was now in the middle of its most successful period to date, with a circulation – the magazine had put on some 130,000 – approaching the 1,400,000 mark, with newly tapped areas of classified and displayed advertising contributing to a paper which often rose to 64 pages, and with Hamilton's newest invention, the Insight team, now famous on both sides of the Atlantic. Equally notable, the paper, for the first time in its history, had become a real political force under William Rees-Mogg.

The profits were approaching the level of £1,500,000 a year when, in January, 1967, Roy Thomson crowned his career, started in this country at an age when most men are thinking of retiring, by taking over The Times. The merger aroused the concern of the Monopolies Commission: 'as a result of the editorial link with The Sunday Times, The Times might speak with the same voice on major matters as The Sunday Times.' Denis Hamilton, who became editor-in-chief of both papers, gave his assurance that his two editors, William Rees-Mogg and Harold Evans, would be free to put forward opposing views, and in the event the commission's fears that The Sunday Times would become the seventh-day paper of The Times have proved utterly unfounded.

So it was that Harold Evans came in at an extremely difficult time for a new editor – difficult, that is to say, for his own reputation. The paper was riding so high that a great effort would be needed to improve it. Not that Evans was either daunted by the prospect or extravagantly confident: after a day or two of panic he settled down to do his best and hope for the best. From that day to this he has been unremittingly modest, cool-headed, courageous and successful.[1]

---

1. Maurice Wiggin's light-hearted summing-up of the last three editors of the paper: 'H. V. Hodson, the scholarly editor who looked after the cultural section and leader page so well; Denis Hamilton, the great innovator and adventurer who expanded all our horizons; and now Harold Evans, the human dynamo who is steering *The Sunday Times* into the unimaginable future with the panache of a Sioux chief steering a birchbark canoe down the rapids of the Grand Canyon, standing up and laughing, waving his paddle, while some of his crew crouch under the gunwales, deep in prayer.'

The contrasts in temperament between Hamilton and Evans are strikingly reflected in their style as editors. It was Hamilton who spotted Evans originally and persuaded him to come south in 1966 to become his assistant. A year later Hamilton recommended him to the board of Times Newspapers as his successor on The Sunday Times. There were other candidates to be considered, from outside the office as well as from in, but the choice finally fell on Evans, who was then 38, because he was so strongly supported by the younger members of the staff – people newly recruited since Lord K's day and innocently unaware that in the autocracy of old it would have been unthinkable for any weight to be given to their feelings.

Denis Hamilton is an enigma and a mass of contradictions. To his intimate friends on one day he can be as brisk as a soldier sniffing victory, radiating confidence and superiority over the enemy in every hair of his military moustache, and on the next as languorous and remote as the dreaming poet; or tortured and tortuous and then disarmingly frank and straightforward.

Politically and otherwise he is (as was said of Barnes of The Times) a constitutionalist: a preserver of the *status quo*, a worrier about modern trends in general and the bitchiness of the younger school of journalists in particular. He is no great student of politics – like many sensible journalists he stands aside from party.

The eighteenth-century actor Macklin once boxed the prompter's ears because 'he interrupted me in my Grand Pause'. With his friends and associates Hamilton's grand pauses are famous, particularly on the telephone, when sometimes the conversation suddenly falls down dead; he is not an outstandingly articulate man (voluble spellbinders never seem to have what it takes inside newspaper offices), though very good at the informal speech.

He is a great delegator, unwilling to concern himself, as he puts it, with the 'nuts and bolts' of things; his executives were there to do their jobs and to take the consequences if they failed. This endeared him to The Sunday Times people, the older of whom had rarely breathed such an air of freedom. He was certainly never a writing editor – in his five years in the chair at The Sunday Times he never wrote a single leader or book review, nothing, perhaps, except articles on Nasser and John Kennedy and an obituary tribute to Ian Fleming which illustrated the curious friendship that grew up between these two very different people, the one a man of conscience, the other a lovable scoffer.

Not unexpectedly, considering his long years as Lord Kemsley's right-hand man, when the most chaotic situations could occur, Hamilton is a sympathetic smoother of ruffled dignities and outraged susceptibilities, the one who is never too busy to send the note of congratulation or condolence: and anyway he is a man of good will who *likes* people to be happy and who shows old-world courtesy and sympathy to those around him. And at the root of his complex personality (sometimes over-eager to impress, sometimes almost painfully modest) is his greatest strength: his brooding intuitions, his unspoken hunches, things that only rarely take verbal form, which combined with his formidable patience have largely helped to make him the success he is. All else apart, to his long-term nurturing of friendships and contacts we owed the great Tutankhamun exhibition in London. Sir William Haley, who does not believe in waiting to see nice things carved on a man's gravestone, has called him one of the great journalists of the twentieth century.

This style is certainly different from Harold Evans's. Evans isn't a constitutionalist, he is a radical and a reformer and a campaigner, the W. T. Stead of our time. There was some trace of paternalism in Hamilton as editor, a remnant of Lord K's authoritarianism, and it made his relations with some of the *jeunes féroces* of the paper uneasy. With Evans they were in sympathy immediately; and he has the respect and admiration of one or two of them who are sufficiently way out to belong to what is called the Free Communications group and who will argue with him that editorial control of newspapers should pass to editorial and production staffs. He listens but won't think of it, and Lord Thomson would interpose the proverbial dead body anyway.

For the time being, in any case, Evans is a sufficient innovation in himself, a new man who has broken old rules and shown himself indifferent to many traditional aspirations. Under him the paper has returned to its radical historical position or rather origin.

Before he came to Gray's Inn Road he was editor of The Northern Echo, which has been for a long time a power in Yorkshire, Northumberland and Durham and was Stead's paper into the bargain before Stead came to London. He is no delegator, like Hamilton. Far from it. He knows the theory and practice of journalism inside out, as his newspaper manuals prove, and he yearns to do it all himself and be for ever where the action is – even at an office party he will be waking things up by dodging about helping the waitresses pour out the drinks.

Evans, as Pepys was always saying, is 'with child' at the spectacle of life in all its variousness. There was an editor of The Standard, the nineteenth-century morning paper, of whom a colleague said that if, in his younger days, he had been sent out on a story and seen St Paul's on fire, he would have done nothing about it because it wasn't his business at the time. How different from Mr Evans. 'The fire was put out by Mr Harold Evans, 40, editor of a Sunday paper, who was on the scene in advance of the firemen and is now in hospital recovering from slight burns after writing a 5,000-word report on the incident. He is instituting an enquiry into the organisation of the London Fire Brigade.'

Blazingly blue-eyed, a tiny tornado, with a mind so quick that nobody over fifty can keep up with it, and a rapid flow of speech unsubject to the Wavell-like silences of his predecessor, he is a paragon of steady temper, even when he is turning things upside down, as he too frequently does. His young staff love him, but whether they really appreciate the greatest of all his qualities, his courage, may be doubted. For they live in a time when writs for libel hold no terrors. It was different in the days of Camrose and Kemsley, when a man could hardly commit a greater crime than have the paper threatened with a libel action, no matter if the complaint was entirely without justification or serious intention.

When Robert Harling, who was introduced to the paper as typographical adviser by Ian Fleming just after the war and was in its inner councils, told Lord K that a newspaper wasn't doing its job unless it had a few writs for libel hanging about, he was smiled at as a licensed jester, and the truth of his remark went unrecognised. Evans the campaigner would have understood. This is where his courage comes in. In all his big inquiries he is at the centre of things, and it is his own head which is on the block. Libel lawyers can guide an editor part of the way, but after that there usually opens out an uncharted danger area where only courage, combined with a realistic judgment of the reliability of the exposure, can steel him to go on.

The first major inquiry organised by Harold Evans was the Kim Philby affair: it demonstrated startlingly and for the first time the full extent of the damage done to the West by Philby. It involved Evans in difficult and protracted negotiations, and a less resolute man might have given it up.

There was also a Sunday Times book about Philby, written by three members of the staff. It has so far brought in more than £40,000 in royalties, and of this over £15,000 was shared among the three authors, with £20,000 to the paper (which was the cost of the original investment in the serial plus an insignificant profit) and the rest divided up, in varying proportions, among those who were in on the original enquiry. When the news arrived in the office late one Thursday afternoon that the book had been chosen by the US Book of the Month Club, and therefore would be a great financial success, a party with champagne was laid on immediately in the Insight room. Evans joined the crowd, most of whom were participants in the bonanza, and as he jumped on to a table-top to say something the telephone rang. 'Answer it,' he said in the hush. 'It's Kim Philby wanting a cut.' They were prophetic words, for the success of the serial and the book gave Philby the idea of writing his own memoirs, from which he hoped, unsuccessfully, for a large cut from The Sunday Times.

In The Spectator, of March 1, 1968, the late Donald McLachlan, first editor of The Sunday Telegraph, was acute enough to realise that something new and journalistically important was afoot in all this:

> The interesting aspect of the transaction is that the newspaper not only covers the cost of obtaining an important serial but also makes a profit. As I understand it, *Philby* was written by its authors in their working time and at their normal salary. They had assistance from colleagues at home and abroad. It was, therefore, in staff terms an expensive enterprise. However, by producing the kind of articles that are wanted by *The Sunday Times*, in its present drive for a two million circulation, the team also collected enough material for a book which would more than pay for those costs. A Sunday newspaper may well think twice about paying £15,000 down for serial material that will raise its circulation for three or four weeks, when it can get suitable material written by a few of its own staff and keep all book, newspaper, film and television rights.

Since then there have been five or six co-operative books of this kind. Practically all have been big money-makers, and three of them have in addition become famous and enduring – 'Do You Sincerely Want to be Rich?', 'The Strange Voyage of Donald Crowhurst', and 'The Secret Lives of Lawrence of Arabia'.

Harold Evans had, as has been said, a happy but, paradoxically, a difficult inheritance when he took over. But in times of unparalleled trouble in the newspaper industry, and despite the sharpest rises in price in the history of The Sunday Times, he has increased its circulation while extending its quality and reputation. Of Sir James Molloy, the editor created in 'Trent's Last Case' by the inventor of the clerihew (and E. C. Bentley of The Daily Telegraph wrote an occasional leader for The Sunday Times under Lord Camrose) it was said as it could be said of Evans: 'He was respected by his staff as few are respected in a profession not favourable to the growth of the sentiment of reverence.'

All this, from the first editor Henry White to Harold Evans, is the prologue to an informal memoir of The Sunday Times. It is not a newspaper history based on the archives, or a social history of 150 years. Just a memoir, compounded among other things of recollection, observation and deduction.

PART I

The Obscure Years

1822–1915

The Obscure Years

I

It had been getting steadily colder all through the week. The Sunday of November 18, 1827, had been foggy but comparatively mild: the thermometer registered 50 degrees. The next day the temperature had dropped to 49, and it continued to fall until the following Saturday, when at noon it reached freezing point.

The first snow of the winter, which promised to be severe, was in the air as a young man, who was probably commercially-minded, unreligious, and Radical in his views, hurried along the slippery pavements to the printing office of The Sunday Times at 76 Fleet Street, carrying in his pocket an eloquent advertisement for the front page of that newspaper's next issue, for which he was prepared to pay the considerable sum of 7s with an additional 2s because of the prominent position he was expecting the advertisement to occupy.

Not all this money went into the coffers of the paper. There were a Government duty on newsprint, a stamp duty of 4d which had been only a penny in the days of Addison and Steele, and a tax of 3s 6d on each and every advertisement. It is not surprising that the young man, who was in his middle twenties, had to pay seven pence for his Sunday paper.

The Sunday Times was not, of course, the only Sunday paper in existence at this time. There were sixteen or seventeen others, including The Observer. Our prospective advertiser, therefore, had presumably exercised a rational choice in his selection of where to place his advertisement. He may have been influenced by the paper's vigorously democratic outlook. It believed firmly, even stridently, in at least an approach to social and racial equality. It was in favour of abolishing slavery, differing in this from many religious and conscientious men like Mr Gladstone, who spoke in the House of Commons in its defence. It was convinced that the upper classes were wicked and degenerate and it enjoyed printing arbitrary little paragraphs hinting at unmentionable evils.

Only the previous Sunday, for example, in relation to nothing at all, it had remarked sententiously, 'It is said that in the novel of "Flirtation", just announced, and reported to be from the pen of the Duke of Argyll's sister, some of the fashionable ladies of the day are severely and amusingly handled; not, however, in a spirit of mere wanton satire, but with a moral purpose. We trust this is true; as it is obvious that no good can be effected in the circles of the great, except by one who moves in them, and who is acquainted with all their obliquities.'

It looked sourly on the riches of the church. If the Archbishops of France could exist on £1,000 a year, why should there be English bishoprics worth £30,000?

On the other hand, it disliked royalty even more than the aristocracy or ecclesiastics. It was glad to hear that the death of the Duchess of Buccleuch had made the young Duke one of the richest men in the country, 'because in a Monarchial Government we think a few such overgrown rich men are of great use in maintaining the balance of power between the Prince and the peasant.' Heading its gossip column 'On Dits', it showed already that partiality for French which has marked certain sections of the paper through Clement Scott down to more recent days.

As he mounted the narrow stairs towards the counting-house, fingering both the advertisement and the money he had brought with him to pay for it, and not very far, doubtless, from the little back room where the editor, like Mr Pott of The Eatanswill Gazette, prepared his thunderbolts, the young man was probably actuated by more worldly considerations than a sympathy for the paper's advanced views on social questions and its zeal for the reform of the wealthy. Naturally enough he wanted a large public for what he had to say, a public that would include many young women of attractive disposition. For what he had brought with him was in fact a proposal of marriage. He had come to the right place. His advertisement procured no fewer than ninety-nine replies.

At that period The Times sold about 7,000 copies a day, but its readership was nearly ten times that because of the system of illegal lending – a newshawker might make seventy or eighty lendings of the paper at the rate of 1d an hour. The sale of the Sunday papers varied from 1,000 to 15,000. The Sunday Times then claimed to be the most popular of the lot, but ten years or so later, as we shall see, it was well down the field. It could be received within 170 miles of London post free on Sunday morning. Other

SUNDAY, NOVEMBER 25, 1827.

MATRIMONY.—A Private Gentleman, aged 24 intirely independent, whose disposition is not to be exceeded has lately lost chief of his family by the hand of Providence, which has occasioned discord amongst the remainder, under circumstances most disagreable to relate. To any female of respectability, who would study for domestic comforts, and willing to confide her future happiness to one in every way qualified to render the marriage state desirable, as the advertiser is in affluence. Many very happy marriages have taken place through means similar to this now resorted to, and it is hoped no one will answer this through impertinent curiosity, but should this meet the eye of any agreable lady who feels desirous of meeting with a sociable, tender, kind, and sympathising companion, they will find this advertise-ment worthy of notice. Honor and secresy may be relied on. As some little security against idle applications, it is requisite that letters may be addressed (post paid) A. Z., care of Mr. Foster, stationer, 68, Lea-denhall-street, with real name and address, which will meet with most respectful attention.

MEDICAL PUPIL.—WANTED, by a general Practitioner in the country, a Youth, of good education, as an APPRENTICE. Premium moderate.—Apply, post paid, to Mr. Michell, surgeon, Trowbridge, Wilts.

TO PARENTS and GUARDIANS.—A Medical Man, residing in the City, and practising the three branches of the Profession, is in immediate want of an APPRENTICE; who will be treated as one of the family, and will be allowed to attend the hos-pitals the three last years of his time.—For particulars inquire of Mr. Hattley, chemist, Fore-street, or of Mr. Rogers, chemist, Cheapside.

BELGRAVE-SQUARE.—HOUSES, in Belgrave-square are now to be PURCHASED, or LET on LEASE; the terms of which may be obtained of Mr. George Basevi, the Architect, 17, Saville-row, Burlington-gardens.

HIGHGATE-PARK HAMILTONIAN SCHOOL —No Vacations.—DR. DUNCAN has the satisfaction to an-nounce to the public, that Mr. Hamilton has most successfully in-troduced his excellent system of education into this school. The profi-ciency of pupils in this establishment is guaranteed in one half year to be equal to those of a similar age in two years, who are studying the classics and modern languages on the system usually adopted, con-sequently allowing sufficient time for acquiring knowledge of paramount importance to youth designed for Mercantile pursuits. Terms vary with the age of the pupils from 20 to 30 guineas per annum.

A private gentleman who passed into folklore (see page 10).

Sunday papers were printed in two impressions, on Sunday and Monday, and advertisements appeared in one impression only, unless specially paid for. In The Sunday Times they appeared automatically in every copy sold. These claims appeared beneath the title-block, which was in Gothic letters, and so remained for well over a century.

The common, excited talk of London at this time was of the battle of Navarino, in which the Turkish fleet had been destroyed. But more domestic happenings had also been taking place, their tameness partly disguised by the relish with which the penny-a-liners of The Sunday Times recorded them. There was the alarm-ing fact that 147 peers, including six dukes and five marquesses, were without issue. At Greenwich Hospital Andrew Brown, an inmate, sang two capital songs, and died a few hours later: which is hardly surprising, since he was 105 years and nine months old.

Newspaper stamps (applied as postmarks) were reduced from 4d each to 1d, in September, 1836, and after December of that year had the newspaper's name on them, to prevent papers buying too many (to give a false idea of their circulation) and then selling them off at a discount. The duty was repealed in 1855.

On Wednesday, November 21, Liston, the favourite of Charles Lamb, had opened at Drury Lane in a comedy called 'Forget and Forgive'. The drama critic of The Sunday Times found the play fairly amusing, though he thought the plot was complicated but without any real excitement. The same night the Warwick mail was robbed of £20,000 in bank notes. Several Manchester gentlemen formed a company for a service of carriages driven by steam for carrying passengers and parcels on the road between Manchester and London at a speed of twelve miles an hour. This was a prodigious rate of progress which might have interested our visitor, for there were certain circumstances which might make it desirable for him to leave London (or anywhere else he might be staying) as quickly as possible.

On the Sunday of November 25, 1827, his advertisement duly appeared. That day the paper carried advertisements (book advertising and patent medicine advertising brought in most of the revenue) of Sir Walter Scott's 'Chronicles of the Canongate'; houses for sale in Belgrave Square; a cure for gout without medicine; a school in Highgate that had no vacations; a shop which had 2,000 of 'the most splendid, useful, and fashionable cloaks' for sale at prices ranging from 30s to ten guineas. Port and sherry were offered at 2s a bottle, and champagne, 'the cheapest in town', at 5s 6d, whilst Ree's 'Compound Essence of Cubebs' guaranteed 'the most safe, speedy, and certain remedy ever discovered for cure of gonorrhea, gleets, seminal weakness, and pains in the loins'.

Notwithstanding the attractiveness of these advertisements for the high-living and comparatively well-to-do, it was the young man's contribution which, on a bitterly cold but fairly bright morning, with last night's snow still lying in the streets, held pride of place. It was printed at the head of the third column on the front page, immediately below the rubric, 'London, Sunday, November 25, 1827'. No doubt he read it with the eagerness and admiration felt by all young authors when they see their own compositions in print, even if they have had to pay for publication. And indeed it was quite a polished production. In the minute type known as minion, about twelve words to a line in a column scarcely two inches wide, it read:

MATRIMONY – A Private Gentleman, aged 24, intirely independent, whose disposition is not to be exceeded has lately lost chief of his family by the hand of Providence, which has occasioned discord amongst the remainder, under circumstances most disagreable to relate. To any female of respectability, who would study for domestic comforts, and willing to confide her future happiness to one in every way qualified to render the marriage state desirable, as the advertiser is in affluence. Many very happy marriages have taken place through means similar to this now resorted to, and it is hoped no one will answer this through impertinent curiosity, but should this meet the eye of any agreable lady who feels desirous of meeting with a sociable, tender, kind, and sympa-thising companion, they will find this advertisement worthy of notice. Honor and secresy may be relied on. As some little security against idle applications, it is requisite that letters may be addressed (post paid) A. Z., care of Mr. Foster, stationer, 68, Leadenhall-street, with real name and address, which will meet with most respectful attention.

The young man had chosen for the insertion of his advertisement a rather dull and uninspired issue of the paper. The leader writer, in particular, was completely out of form. A week before he had been in tremendous fettle, thundering away in the highly-coloured, patriotic rhetoric which was to characterise the political writing of The Sunday Times for the greater part of the nineteenth century. His subject then had been the defeat of the Turks at Navarino, a sea battle in which the British fleet sank the whole of the Turkish fleet and secured the independence of Greece, which had been subject to Turkey. 'The Ottoman', he wrote,

has received a lesson he will long remember. If Mahmoud, like the regal Persian, should call at some future day for the records of his reign, Navarin's bloody noon will dash the volume from his hands. Never since the day of Lepanto, and the Muscovite triumph at Tchesine, has the sun sunk on the Aegean and witnessed such a scene of havoc. It was a stirring sight to see the Christian chivalry united in one holy cause, and pouring on the ruthless infidel their combined thunder. The Mussalman ravened with a tiger's thirst for blood, and he has been saturated. But for this blow the fate of Greece was sealed.

There were people even then who complained that a style like this was a mere inflation of the language. They said that a better form of writing was being evolved in the universities. They pointed with admiration to the conciseness of Dean Gaisford of Christ Church who, when Lord Liverpool, with profuse compliments, offered him the Regius Professorship of Greek, replied, 'My Lord, I have received your letter, and accede to the contents. Yours, T.G.'; and to a complaining parent, 'Dear Sir – Such letters as yours are a great annoyance to your obedient servant, T. Gaisford.' But the lessons of such terseness took a long time to sink down to the world of journalism.

But on November 25 the leader writer had nothing more exciting to discuss than the debts of the late Duke of York, the legal decisions of Lord Erskine, and the new Turnpike Act. His eloquence was altogether muted, his interest obviously exhausted. The front page of The Sunday Times at that time consisted of four columns of advertisements and of one of bankruptcies. The second page was led by a summary of foreign news, snipped from mailed copies of foreign papers, brief replies to correspondents, a note on a Brazilian mining company, and theatrical advertisements. Mr and Mrs Wynne were to give themselves a benefit in 'Rob Roy' at the Surrey Theatre; at the Royal Coburg Theatre (which subsequently became the Old Vic) there was to be presented the next night, and during the week, 'A New National Drama, in Two Acts, called Britons at Navarino, or the Destruction of the Turko-Egyptian Fleet. The whole to conclude with the popular and interesting Melo-drama of the Heart of Midlothian, or the Lily of St Leonard's.' After that followed the time of high water at London Bridge, and then, three-quarters of the way down the first column, and under the Gothic heading of Sunday Times, a couple of closely printed columns of the for once desultory editorials.

No effort was made to present any of the contents attractively. They all had single-line titles and were unsigned. There seems to have been no systematic arrangement; the death of the Bishop of Winchester, who had had a stroke as he was getting out of bed on a visit to friends, is recorded in three separate and unrelated articles.

It was an age of transition. Steam was nearly on the way in but stage-coaches still bugled their way down long dusty roads and through sleepy villages. The sound of church bells pealing across streams and meadows would continue for many years yet to have significance, and a young man who smoked a cigar and lounged in the village street on a Sunday morning whilst the vicar was preaching was considered to have touched the very limit of impious daring. Boisterous young fellows read law and drank port at dinner in the Temple; pleasure-loving youths at Oxford and Cambridge drove tandems, whilst the worthier sort read Tacitus and occasionally thrashed bargees; visiting actresses, often chaperoned by elderly relatives, played seasons in the theatres in market towns, sometimes driving the local bloods into frenzies of love and jealousy.

It was also an age of considerable brutality, from which the richest and best born were not exempted. The headmaster of Eton was the famous Dr Keate, 'with whom,' says John Morley, 'the appointed instrument of moral regeneration was the birch rod; who on heroic occasions was known to have flogged over eighty boys on a single summer day; and whose one mellow regret in the evening of his life was that he had not flogged far more.'

All these aspects of life are reflected in the four pages of The Sunday Times in which our young man inserted his advertisement. Was he interested in the list of undergraduates of the various colleges at Cambridge? Or in a Heroico-Scholastic Ballad about Rugby? It is unlikely; he was only himself a tenant-farmer at Polstead in Suffolk. He might have been amused, or set wondering in his country way, by a piece of gossip to the effect that 'at the performance of the "Clandestine Marriage" the other night, on Miss Sterling saying, "Oh that some Lord or *Duke* would pay his addresses to me," all eyes were turned to the box where the Duchess of St Albans happened to be sitting that evening. Her Grace was not in the least discomposed.' He may even have noted the case of William Dorrian, Esq, who was charged at Bow Street with indecently assaulting a soldier in the 72nd Regiment of Highlanders by holding his hand and pressing it in Holborn. 'I dashed his hand from me,' said the gallant soldier, whom The Sunday Times penny-a-liner guaranteed to be 'a fine lad', 'and was going to knock him down, but I was afraid of collecting a crowd about us.'

But if his eye wandered as far as the last column of the fourth page there was one article in that morning's issue which our seeker after a wife must have read with a slight shiver. It told how four men, J. Keaton, aged 46, E. Lowe, aged 40, J. Powell, aged 23, and C. Smith, aged 21, had last Thursday morning been hanged. Lowe, a coiner, and Powell, a dishonest shop assistant, had behaved with courage and dignity, but Smith was in a pitiful condition and could hardly be got up the steps of the scaffold.

Our advertiser can scarcely have read this unmoved: he was a murderer himself. His name was William Corder, and he had killed Maria Marten in that red barn which later became so famous in melodrama. But before he was hanged a year afterwards, Corder had months of perfect happiness with the bride whom his advertisement in The Sunday Times supplied.

II

At the time of Corder's advertisement The Sunday Times was only five years old, the creation of a controversial character named Henry White, who among other excursions into newspaper ownership had founded in 1806 The Independent Whig, also a Sunday paper, and edited it until 1821. White may or may not have been less venal than some other newspaper proprietors of his day – he was certainly fond of proclaiming his integrity and disinterestedness – but somehow one gets the impression that, as was said of Pope, he could hardly even drink tea without a stratagem. It is true that some of his little dodges were common practice at the time, yet there is more than the usual impudence in his attempts, when launching a serious, stamped newspaper, to steal readers from The Observer by calling his new Sunday journal first The New Observer and after a short interval The Independent Observer, and then when success still evaded him casting envious eyes on The Times and settling finally on the title of The Sunday Times. Stanley Morison records these ruses with his habitual detached scholarship in 'The English Newspaper':

> The editor of *The Independent Whig* left that paper at the beginning of 1821 and brought out a new Sunday journal dated February 18, 1821. He chose for the title '*The New* [device of a human eye] *Observer*', set in large egyptian capitals. In a month or two the paper was reconstructed, with new serial numeration and in the same typographical style, as '*The Independent* [same device] *Observer*' (No 1, April 21, 1821). In October 1822, as if convinced that the goodwill of the name 'Observer' was not what it had been, another change in the title was decided upon. On

Mr HENRY WHITE,

The founder and first editor of The Sunday Times.

October 20 the journal appeared with gothic lettering for its new title '*Sunday Times*' [*which lettering it carried until after the second world war*]. A notice in the interior of the paper reads '*The Sunday Times* | *The Independent Observer* is incorporated with *The Sunday Times*.' A royal device in the style of that of *The Times* was added on November 3, 1822. The typography itself, in using the egyptian capitals in the heading and in the text, drew away from *The Weekly Dispatch* style and assimilated, deliberately, one supposes, the standards of Printing House Square.

THE
Independent  Observer

"Let it be impressed upon your minds, let it be instilled into your children, that the LIBERTY OF THE PRESS is the PALLADIUM of all the Civil, Politic*
and RELIGIOUS RIGHTS of an ENGLISHMAN."

NO. LXXXIV   SUNDAY OCTOBER 6. 1882.   PRICE SEVEN PENCE

*On October 20, 1882, Henry White's Independent Observer, formerly The New Observer, became The
Sunday Times. Below: the paper which revolutionised Sunday journalism in about 1815 (see page xiii).*

WEEKLY   DISPATCH.

VOL. 22.—No. 1204.]   SUNDAY,   SEPTEMBER 26, 1824.   [PRICE 8

PRINTED, PUBLISHED, AND EDITED BY ROBERT BELL, AT THE OFFICE, NO. 139, FLEET-STREET.

HISTORY AND POLITICS.

HOW ARE CANTING ENTHUSIASTS & FANATICS
TO BE DEALT WITH?

Having in last Sunday's DISPATCH, and in several former
numbers at various times, animadverted on the canting media
that has become almost universal throughout the kingdom;
we may be asked by some one who entertains the same dis-
gust for it, and views it in the same mischievous light that we

lyte-making Sectarians have pursued:—that of acquiring an
absolute dominion over the purse, the minds, and bodies of
their followers. Fortunately, however, the Methodists are
not yet in possession of the field of power: and we are
confident they never will be. To be sure there is no Act of
Parliament—no law to check their progress; they are at full
liberty to cant, and rant, and brawl as much as they please;
and that is the very reason why they will never gain the ascen-
dancy they aim at. If any law were passed to silence or re-

FOREIGN & COLONIAL AFFAIR

PARIS, Sept. 21.—All the pensions granted by the late King
of the Civil List, will be provisionally continued by His Maje
from the 16th instant.
According to his Majesty's intention, the Museum and ot
public places, which have been closed, will be re-opened on Fri
the 24th of this month.—The Council of State, the clergy of Pa
the clerks in the several ministerial offices, the Municipal Body,
National Guard, the Courts and Tribunals have been to-day
sensively to the Tuileries, to throw holy water on the corpse of
late king.

There is a good deal of ambiguity in the paper's early history, as
in the history of other newspapers of this time and before. All were
intentionally crippled by the taxes imposed in order to prevent
newspapers, particularly Radical newspapers, falling into the
hands of the multitude; Palmerston had the additional reason
that he dreaded the recurrence of such viciously personal journals
as the old Satirist, which was The Private Eye of the early nineteenth century. The younger Pitt thought newspapers were a
luxury which the poor could ill afford.

Paper was taxed: there was at this time a duty of 3d a pound
weight, for books as well as newspapers, and it was not repealed
until 1861. Until 1833 advertisements were taxed, down to the
very smallest, at the rate of 3s 6d each, and until 1853 at 1s 6d

E. Johnson's British Gazette, and Sunday Monitor.

Printed by E. JOHNSON, in Ludgate Place, (the Entrance between No. 4 and 5, Ludgate Hill) where LETTERS and ADVERTISEMENTS are taken in.

e Three-Pence Halfpenny.]   **S U N D A Y**, January 2, 1791.   [No. DLXXXIII.

Mrs Johnson founded the first Sunday paper, c. 1779.

each. The stamp duty on every copy of a newspaper was 4d (less 20 per cent discount) until 1836, when it was reduced to 1d; it is true that this impost allowed newspapers to be sent through the post without charge, but the concession was of little commercial value. The 1d stamp duty lingered on until 1855.

Newspapers had for a long time accepted financial assistance either from the Government of the day or the Opposition. In the latter part of the eighteenth century The Times received a Government subsidy of £300 a year as a fair reward 'for the politics of the Paper' as John Walter 1 put it. The Morning Chronicle took Government money, and so did The St James's Chronicle, The London Evening Post, The Whitehall Evening Post, and The Morning Herald. All of the London journals took

13

money probably, either from the Treasury or the Opposition; they could not have lived otherwise.

In the first quarter of the nineteenth century the system continued, but more clandestinely. Professor Arthur Aspinall has shown that The Observer, founded in 1791 and for long a Tory paper, was financed by the Whig Government as late as 1840. The practice disappeared slowly as newspapers' ordinary commercial advertising grew in volume, and it was this and nothing else which gave the Press its independence.

Henry White, that equivocal veteran of these Grub Street days, established the editorial office of The Sunday Times at 4 Salisbury Court, Salisbury Square,[1] and had the paper printed at 76 Fleet Street, now part of Chronicle House, opposite The Daily Telegraph, and once the home of The Daily Chronicle (d. 1930). Doubtless White's office communicated directly with a printing works adjoining it, and doubtless, too, there had been a printer's on the site for a long time. The area of Salisbury Square and Salisbury Court (originally the square was also the court – the courtyard of Salisbury House, residence of the bishops of Salisbury) is the original area of Fleet Street printing. Wynkyn de Worde, William Caxton's successor, and Thomas Berthelet, appointed King's printer in 1530, were two of its historic names. Samuel Richardson, the novelist and printer, lived in Salisbury Square and wrote his 'Pamela' there, and he worked at 21 Salisbury Court. It is not impossible that Henry White knew Richardson's printing office, at which Oliver Goldsmith served, for a short time, as press-corrector. Fifty years after White founded The Sunday Times Richardson's printing office belonged to Edward Lloyd, founder of the weekly Lloyd's News and The Daily Chronicle, and renowned in the nineteenth century as the father of the cheap magazine-type press. He had Richardson's lease of the premises, dated May 30, 1770, and his freeholds and leaseholds were a strange medley of properties, 'extending into Whitefriars', as a contemporary chronicler put it, 'under streets and over streets, and all devoted to the mechanical requirements of Lloyd's News and The Daily Chronicle.'

It was Edward Lloyd who published The Penny Sunday Times in the 1840s – its subtitle was 'Peoples' Police Gazette'. This unstamped publication – unstamped because it was judged a

---

1. He mistakenly called it 4 Salisbury Square in his 'Announcement of an Important Change in the Title and Form of this Paper' in The Independent Observer of October 6, 1822 (see page 1).

No connection with The Sunday Times.

magazine and not a newspaper – had no connection with The
Sunday Times. Its title was part of the cheerful brigandage of the
period, and like the publication on which Lloyd founded his
fortune, Lloyd's News (1d a copy after the taxes on knowledge
were repealed), it was magazine journalism for the masses – crime
reports, fiction disguised as true stories, society serials, riddles,
illustrated poems.

All this was after Henry White's time. In any case, White seems to have passed his journalistic prime when he founded The Sunday Times. His days of death or glory and melodramatic defiance belonged to The Independent Whig. It was in 1814 that the light of history was thrown most strongly on him, and it made him blink. Eighteen-fourteen was a troubled period in England and the world. Finding that a war with Napoleon was not in itself sufficient fully to occupy their energies, the English started a campaign against the Gurkhas of Nepal, and on the other side of the world they captured Washington; Castlereagh, the politician who of all others most horrified Shelley, went as our representative to the Congress of Vienna; the Tsar and the King of Prussia visited the Prince Regent, and London was illuminated for three nights; Wellington won the battle of Orthez, Napoleon had a series of victories in France, and Henry White was very hard up.

He also received a disturbing letter. It told him that his paper's policy of defending the Princess Caroline against the cruel and humiliating treatment given to her by her husband, the Prince Regent, was causing offence in high quarters, but that if this policy were changed it might lead to his financial advantage. White guessed rightly that this came from the household of the Prince himself, which earlier had had the hardihood to buy up The Morning Post to ensure its support for their royal master, and he replied in the indignant tones suitable to a champion of the people who regarded the trappings of the court as mere tinsel and dross.

Unfortunately The Independent Whig was behindhand with its advertisement and stamp duties when he made these highflown and melodramatic professions of his integrity. Three days later, curiously enough, he was peremptorily notified by the Stamp Office that unless he paid up the arrears the most severe legal proceedings would be taken against him. He was in a desperate situation and, not knowing what else to do, wrote to the Princess Caroline and asked her to lend him £200. He explained that this would place him above the machinations of his and her enemies, who were trying to force him either to sell his paper or submit to utter ruin.

After all, it was his zeal for the cause of the princess that had got him into trouble. It was on her behalf that he had written to the Prince Regent's household a letter whose ringing phrases Edmund Kean himself, that rising star of the provincial and London stage, would not have been ashamed, though he might have been afraid,

Sunday Times.

" A. Esq." is rather too irreverent. There is a good deal of point in his poem, but it is carelessly written; and *sleep* and *meat* put for rhymes would almost be too bad for the Bishop.

" Nervosa's Nephew." If she had not called him " a *sad dog*," we should have supposed to be " a merry one." The subject he has seized is now rather threadbare; but we should like to see him try his hand (paw we mean) at another.

" A Friend" we suspect to be an enemy, for he can hardly be fool enough not to see that the " unfair sarcasm," as he calls it, is a silly attempt on the part of an obscure self-puffing bundle of twaddle to induce us to make known that such a thing is in existence, a fact to which the poor creatures connected with it will never be able to give publicity without our benevolent aid.

" A." may recover his money by a simple summons if the debtor resides in the city of London or in the Borough of Southwark; if not, he can carry the case to the Palace Court.

The death of George the Fourth and the great exertions we have made to give our readers the fullest information on the subject compel us to omit the whole of the Poetry promised for insertion, and numerous other articles.

HIGH WATER AT LONDON BRIDGE—THIS DAY.
Morn. 35 min. after 6.—After. 59 min. after 6.

Sunday Times.

LONDON: SUNDAY, JUNE 27, 1830.

EDITION FOR COUNTRY SUBSCRIBERS.

This Edition of the Sunday Times can be received in the course of Sunday (post free) at any place within 200 miles of the metropolis. The later, or London Edition, contains Foreign and Domestic Intelligence up to a late hour on Saturday night.

DEATH OF GEORGE IV.

Our fears are realized. The highest in the land has fallen. GEORGE the Fourth, to use the simple expressive language of Scripture, " sleeps with his fathers."

His case has so long been hopeless, that the result now announced is no more than every one was prepared to hear; and the sufferings of the dying KING were known to have been so great, that it is in some degree soothing to know that these have reached their termination, though the most unfeigned regret is universally manifested, that thus only could relief approach. The Royal Family feel severely the loss of their beloved relative, and none more than his august successor, our present KING.

It was at a quarter past three o'clock that the struggle terminated. Nature quite worn out yielded to Fate, and the MONARCH breathed his last.

The latter days of the KING were for the most part less painful than those of the preceding weeks. Until the last his Majesty retained perfect mental consciousness, with a mind in harmony with his state, and in peace with all mankind.

When the first shock produced by the death had subsided, and the necessary attentions had been paid to the body, messengers were despatched with the melancholy tidings to his Royal Highness the Duke of CLARENCE, at Bushy (now our Sovereign), and the Duke of WELLINGTON, in London. The news

reached his Grace at about half-past six o'clock. He wrote immediately to Sir ROBERT PEEL, and soon after seven o'clock, the Honourable Secretary forwarded Circulars to all the Ministers, announcing the event, and requesting an instant meeting. Soon after ten o'clock, summonses were issued to all the Members of the Privy Council now in town, and who assembled in the course of the morning.

The Duke of WELLINGTON left his house in Piccadilly at nine o'clock, dressed in black, in his travelling carriage, and took the Windsor road; but we understand that his Grace is gone to Bushy to pay his respects to his present MAJESTY.

The following bulletins were issued last Sunday, and on the succeeding days :—

" June 20.—The King's rest has again been broken by the cough and expectoration, and his Majesty feels languid this morning."

" June 21.—The King's rest has been interrupted by cough with expectoration during the night. His Majesty complains less, however, this morning."

" June 22.—The King has passed a good night. His Majesty's cough and expectoration continue."

" June 23.—The King is still troubled by his cough; but it has not interrupted his rest, and his Majesty awoke refreshed this morning."

" June 24.—The King's cough continues, with considerable expectoration. His Majesty has slept at intervals in the night, but complains of great languor to-day."

" June 25.—The King has slept at intervals during the night. His cough and expectoration continue much the same; but his Majesty is more languid and weak."

These, it will be seen, held out nothing that could encourage a hope that the catastrophe so long dreaded might be averted. On Sunday, the Sacrament was administered to his MAJESTY by the Bishop of CHICHESTER; but this fact, for some reason or other, did not reach the public till Friday, when it found its way into the Court Circular. Why it should have been thought necessary to prevent its being known that the KING had received religious consolation on that day, we are at a loss to conjecture.

The KING suffered much from his cough, which was sometimes so violent as to shake his whole frame, and to threaten instant dissolution. This from time to time interrupted his rest, and otherwise distressed him, while the accompanying expectoration tended greatly to exhaust the little remaining strength of a patient so much reduced by previous affliction.

In the midst of this pain, while struggling with disease and death, the KING was not wholly withdrawn from cares of State. He had interviews with several Members of the Administration, and on these occasions his calmness, fortitude, and resignation, were the subject of great surprise. On Wednesday the Duke of WELLINGTON proceeded to the Castle, when a list of Treasury warrants and other public documents were submitted to the KING, who signified his commands that all of them should receive the royal signature. The documents had previously had their intent inscribed at the back; to this endorsement was appended the signatures of three of the Cabinet Ministers named in the Act. The Duke of WELLINGTON, Sir A. BARNARD, and Sir W. KEPPELL, being appointed by his MAJESTY, to declaim on the boards of Drury Lane. It was reasonable enough to suppose that the princess might be disposed to help him. All this is true. Yet at the same time there is something rather daunting in the spectacle of a man who has befriended a lady asking her for money. The Princess Caroline, in whom gratitude was not the most striking quality, and whose assistance to another editor who was behind with the stamp duty was in the end limited to a paltry £15, thought so too. She refused.

There were people who said that White got his deserts; he was certainly despised by both Whigs and Tories. Lord Brougham, adviser to the Princess Caroline (she appointed him her Attorney-General when she became Queen), showed himself particularly indignant with the unfortunate man. On September 25, 1814, he wrote to Earl Grey: 'As his newspapers are the very worst written in London, and the dullest as well as the most blackguard, I heartily regret such men as Coke being deceived by his flummery to patronise him. It will finish the little credit we still have among the popular newspapers if we take up the worst and most venomous after being too nice and moderate to patronise the respectable sheets.'

It seems that White wrote the princess further letters – Brougham called them 'threatening' – raising his request from £200 to £300. This made Brougham the Whig call him a common beggar, a swindler, and a blackmailer and allege that he had threatened to expose the private life of a man who had refused him money.[1]

Nevertheless, there is evidence that there was so much prejudice against The Independent Whig because of its outspoken attitude on social questions that White did not always get fair treatment. He went to prison in 1808 for describing the verdict in a murder case as 'unjust', and three years later was charged, but acquitted, on a charge of stirring up sedition in the army. White obviously did nothing to disabuse the Government of the idea that the Sunday papers were 'vehicles of treason'.

This attitude was long-lived. Sir Walter Scott had said, 'Nothing but a thoroughgoing blackguard ought to attempt the daily press', and the repute of the Sunday press was still lower. Respectable men considered White's Independent Whig and his Sunday Times degrading, vicious, and Radical. The only things that

1. 'Politics and the Press,' 1780–1850, by A. Aspinall. (Home and Van Thal, 1949.)

could legally be sold on a Sunday were milk and mackerel, but the law seems not to have been enforced against newspapers. They were sold in hairdressers', greengrocers', and pastrycooks' shops, and were a scandal to the righteous. They were supposed to spread ribaldry and atheism. They were sold even at the church door. Attempts to stop the sale of Sunday newspapers by specific enactments were made in 1799, 1820, 1833, 1834, 1835, and 1838; but they all failed.

When Arthur Pendennis joined Captain Shandon at the launching of The Pall Mall Gazette, a paper written by gentlemen for gentlemen, it was only in a state of euphoria that a sale of 10,000 copies an issue could be hoped for. Circulation was hampered by the mechanical difficulties of production, by poor communications (yet The Sunday Times could be read in Sheffield or Manchester on the day of publication), by the illiteracy of the public, by the hostile attitude of the governing classes, and by the stamp duty.

These handicaps kept down the total sale of newspapers to about 12,000,000 a year in the first quarter of the nineteenth century. This figure, however, gives no indication of how widely they were read. The Sunday Times was read in coffee-houses, pubs, subscription reading-rooms, and at Radical public meetings. In the country every alehouse had its newspaper for its patrons. Nowadays it is estimated that every copy of The Sunday Times is read by at least four people. In 1829 every copy must have been read by thirty.

III

Brougham may or may not have been right in ascribing to Henry White a despicable character, but when he casually includes The Independent Whig amongst the popular papers he was clearly saying something that was universally accepted as a fact. The Independent Whig and, from 1822, The Sunday Times were popular, not quality, papers. A consideration of what, during the first half of the century, constituted a quality reader, added to the general disreputability of Sunday publications, will explain why this was so.

The quality reader of today would, in the 1830s and for a long time afterwards, have been considered by the quality readers of the time as little better than a rake. His interest in sport and in the arts, except for the most serious poetry, would have been thought indefensibly light-minded. The fascination which entertainment holds for him would have been thought immoral. On his twenty-third birthday Gladstone wrote these revealing words: 'Nor do I now think myself warranted in withdrawing from the practices of my fellow men, except when they really involve an encouragement of sin, in which case I certainly rank races and theatres.' In the very act of declaring his solidarity with ordinary mankind, Gladstone excludes from the realm of intellectual appreciation two features of life which the quality reader of the twentieth century would never dream of foregoing. The mistake should not be made of considering that Gladstone was a particularly sanctimonious young man. On the contrary, he was a typical intellectual of the period, a representative Oxford man, brilliant in debate, overwhelmingly persuasive in argument with all classes of people, ready to plunge successfully into the deep waters of political life.

Today a man who occupies in university life a position comparable with that held by Gladstone passes much of his Sunday reading The Sunday Times and The Observer, as greatly interested in the latest films, novels, television programmes, concerts, art exhibitions, theatres, and football matches as in moral and political questions. His counterpart in 1830 would have found this attitude incomprehensible and disgusting. Such a Sunday would have seemed a sizable progress towards hell.

It is instructive to turn from this attitude of mind to The Sunday Times and to note the contents of a typical issue in May, 1833. On the front page are three columns of advertisements. Three other columns consist of roughly 6,000 words of parliamentary reports, which are continued in another 3,500 words on page two. The rest of this page is occupied by 3,000 words of leaders on the emancipation of the slaves and on a riotous meeting held during the week to canvass the setting up of a National Convention in accordance with ideas generated by the French Revolution. There are nearly 2,000 words on the death of Edmund Kean, and 2,500 of miscellaneous information. There are also advertisements for theatres.

Page three has a column of poems and theatrical reports, and a densely-massed, 10,000-word account of the police court proceedings arising out of the death of a policeman named Cully

THE DUKE OF CUMBERLAND'S BIRTH-DAY, AND THE REFORM BILL. When the news arrived in the Surrey environs of London, on Tuesday last, of the passing of the Reform Bill, in the House of Lords, on the preceding evening, it was at first intended, by the Inhabitants of several of the parishes, that a merry peal should be rung in the churches, in honour of the event; but that day being the birth-day of the Duke of CUMBERLAND, one of the most violent opponents of the Bill, it was afterwards resolved that no rejoicings of the kind should take place, in order that it should not be supposed that the bells were ringing in compliment to the anti-reform Duke of CUMBERLAND, and consequently not a rope was pulled until the following morning.

HOW TO DIMINISH THE EXPENSE OF EXPATRIATING FEMALE PAUPERS.—The Parish of St. Marylebone is said to have incurred an expense of 300l. in sending out Paupers to Van Diemen's Land. It has been suggested, that from the scarcity of females there, if, when the ship arrives, 10l. each were demanded before they were suffered to leave, the money would soon be paid by the gallant wife-coveting gentlemen of the Colony.

June 10, 1832

involved in bashing in the heads of the National Convention demonstrators. The fourth and last page has further news about anti-slavery meetings and Kean's post-mortem, about the trial of a man accused of murdering Cully, accounts of the Middlesex court sessions, a thousand-word description of the arrest and confession of the murderer of an elderly spinster named Elmes, a further 2,000 words on the court proceedings at the Mansion House and Marlborough Street involving a murder in Ireland, the robbery of a prostitute by a client, and of a client by a prostitute; and three perfunctory book reviews.

A paper like this could not have much appeal for grave men of a religious turn of mind: and the numbers of such men were increasing. G. M. Young (who made many fine contributions to the book pages of The Sunday Times in the 1930s) says that in 1810 only two gentlemen in Staffordshire held family prayers. In 1850 only two did not. The respectability engendered by the long parliamentary reports was quickly dissipated by the rest of the paper, with its consuming interest in violence, disorder, and crime, much of it supplied by the 'liners' – that curious tribe of illiterate bohemians who haunted the police-courts and other public places, made notes of the proceedings, manifolding their copy by means of blackened paper and an ivory pen, and sent these 'flimsies' to half-a-dozen papers, to be paid, if they were lucky, at the rate of a penny a line, or 1½d by the middle of the century. The paper had no correspondents abroad. A reporter or two may have frequented the House of Commons to take a shorthand note of the speeches, somebody called the sub-editor was very busy with scissors and paste boldly poaching acknow-ledged items from the London, provincial and foreign press, the 'liners' buzzed about the police-courts, one or two people in the office attended theatres and read a few books. That seems to be the sum of the professional occupations involved. That, and the writing of leading articles.

These are generally what we should call enlightened. They support the freeing of the slaves (but with a certain amount of compensation for the owners), the Great Reform Bill, and the repeal of the Corn Laws. While agreeing on the need to preserve order they are suspicious of the methods and brutality of the police in dealing with noisy crowds. They struggle to be as forceful and hard-hitting as any in The Times of the same period, without quite succeeding, they are chauvinistic, and they trounce the Tories tremendously.

IV

But the voice is not the voice of Henry White. In the autumn of 1823 he carried his resentments into private life and sold The Sunday Times to (among others) Daniel Whittle Harvey, a lawyer who was gaining some reputation as a Radical politician and who represented Colchester in the House of Commons for many years. But he, like White (and Leigh Hunt and his brother), was destined to get into trouble with the Prince Regent. For libelling him in The Sunday Times, by quoting a current saying about him, he was sentenced to three months' imprisonment and fined £200.

Harvey was an enterprising chief proprietor. From their earliest days as 'news books' newspapers had used crude illustrations, and he introduced wood engravings as early as the end of 1823. (Fifteen years later a wood engraving of the coronation of Queen Victoria was the largest which up to then had appeared in any newspaper.) He organised sporting and agricultural supplements, which were profitable for advertising and (as The Times had found) an enormous advertisement for the paper itself. He was a great believer, as has been noted, in hard-hitting leading articles, and his use in them of the editorial 'we', to give a tone of judiciousness to the whole, must have annoyed Cobbett, who had his own particular detestation of leader-writers: 'The mysterious WE that they make use of, gives men an idea that what they are reading proceeds from a little council of wise men, who have been sitting and deliberating upon what they wish to put forth. Each paragraph appears to be a sort of little order-in-council; a solemn decision of a species of literary conclave.'

When Daniel Whittle Harvey sold The Sunday Times, at a nice profit, it is said, he took up other newspaper enterprises. But these were less successful, and he became a bankrupt in 1839. No matter, he still had friends, and in the following year they came to his rescue and he was appointed Commissioner of the Metropolitan Police, a statutory office which he held until his death in 1854.

This change in the chief ownership of the paper heralded the lack of continuity in proprietorship and editorship which was to dog it throughout the rest of the nineteenth century. From Harvey it passed seemingly to a book publisher named A. J. Valpy, of Red Lion Court, who advertised in The Sunday Times and was represented by a full column on the first page of the first issue; he may well then have had some financial interest in it. From Valpy the legend is that it passed to another and more important publisher, Henry Colburn, whose publishing list included the diaries of Evelyn and Pepys and who in addition owned a select library in New Burlington Street, where he hired-out three-decker novels. In this phase of his career Colburn speculated in monthly literary periodicals as well as in The Sunday Times, but it came to an end when he impulsively sold his New Burlington Street business to his partner, Richard Bentley (who became Publisher in Ordinary to Queen Victoria), and engaged himself not to start up again in London or within twenty miles of it. But finding the lure of publishing too strong he sacrificed his guarantees and built up another fine business. Hurst and Blackett, today one of the Hutchinson group, took over the business when Colburn retired.

In his ownership The Sunday Times was edited by a veteran novelist named Gaspey, who died in harness at the age of 83.

From 1823 the paper had had a connection, managerially or financially, with the publishing and theatrical Chapmans; and from 1834 to 1852 the theatrical producer John Kemble Chapman

WEEKLY NEWSPAPER STAMPS.

	December 1837.	January 1838.	February 1838.	March 1838.	Total.	Average of 7 weeks.
Weekly Dispatch	50,000	224,000	300,000	150,000	724,000	42,588
Weekly Chronicle	304,000	178,000	137,000	132,000	651,000	38,294
Bell's Life in London	45,000	90,000	62,000	86,000	284,250	16,647
Sunday Times	65,000	80,000	50,000	50,000	215,000	12,647
Bell's Weekly Messenger	67,000	87,250	68,000	72,000	283,000	9,808
Weekly True Sun	36,000	60,000	33,000	30,000	158,000	9,294
London Dispatch	35,000	33,000	26,000	25,000	119,000	7,000
Examiner	24,350	20,580	20,625	26,400	91,965	5,469
Magnet	23,000	16,500	19,500	22,500	81,500	4,794
Observer	50,000		30,000		80,000	3,155
Patriot	20,000	25,000	20,000	15,000	60,000	4,705
Bell's New Weekly Messenger	21,750	17,000	14,500	10,750	64,000	3,764
Spectator	12,000	17,000	12,000	15,000	56,000	3,294
Satirist	14,000	12,500	12,100	16,400	55,000	3,235
Age	19,500	8,500	14,000	12,000	54,000	3,176
News and Sunday Globe	12,000	11,500	9,500	11,500	44,500	2,617
Church of England Gazette	17,000	5,000	10,000	9,500	41,500	2,441
Watchman	15,000	6,000	6,000	14,000	41,000	2,411
Atlas	5,000	15,000	8,000		28,000	1,647
United Service Gazette	5,500	7,000	8,500	6,000	27,000	1,588
Mining Journal	5,000	5,000	5,000	7,000	22,500	1,323
Court Journal	4,000	6,300	4,700	5,000	20,000	1,176
Christian Advocate	5,040	3,840	3,737	4,475	17,092	1,005
Literary Gazette	2,500	2,500		2,500	7,500	441
Champion	2,000	2,000	1,500	1,500	7,000	411

We should have contented ourselves with publishing the above return without a word of comment, but for the gross imposition practised on advertisers by some of our contemporaries who have a Monday edition as well as Sunday. Both publications are printed under one title, and the issue of stamps placed to the credit as for *one paper* only, whereas it ought to be *two*. We will take the *Bell's Weekly Messenger* as an example. In the above four months' return, that journal is made to appear as having a weekly circulation of 17,308.

THE BELL'S WEEKLY MESSENGER

publishes a Sunday and a *Monday* edition, the respective circulation of which may be stated as follows—

By the above return 17,308
Monday edition (without the Sunday advertisements) 7,500

Leaving a weekly average Sunday sale of 9,808
In the Monday edition advertisements are not inserted *unless paid for twice*. The circulation, so far as advertisers are concerned, is thus reduced nearly one half. In this respect the two editions are as much distinct as though they were published under different titles.

THE OBSERVER.

By the above return 4,705
Monday edition 1,550

Leaving a weekly average Sunday sale of 3,155
The same rule applies to all other weekly journals which issue a Monday edition

We have no wish to interfere with other papers, but we cannot allow the *Bell's Weekly Messenger* to be placed before the *Sunday Times* as having a superior circulation; our paper is published on the Saturday and Sunday, and *all* advertisements appear in both editions. To render the return of stamps of any use to advertisers, all persons bringing out a Monday edition of a Sunday paper under the same title, should be compelled to use a distinct die, "Monday edition;" this would bring their Sunday publication down to what they really ought to be, and the Sunday sale of the three papers above referred to, to something like the number mentioned.

Sunday Times.

The official weekly record of the sale of newspaper stamps, as amended by The Sunday Times, July 1, 1838, to put it above a rival (see opposite page).

was owner or part-owner. During this period one sees his superior journalistic mind at work, and his supplement on the marriage of Queen Victoria, copiously illustrated with woodcuts, was deservedly a best-seller and trebled that week's circulation. The wood engravings in the coronation and marriage issues were so large, including one of full-page size of the interior of Westminster Abbey, that probably a team of engravers were involved, the wood being cut in pieces for them to work on, after an artist had pencilled the design, and then bolted together to make a single printing surface. Chapman married the sister of Mrs Charles Kean, had twelve children, and when he died in 1857 left them and his widow to the care of Kean and his actress wife, Ellen Tree, who did their duty nobly.

In the year of Queen Victoria's coronation, 1838, Chapman was involved in a war about circulation figures which has a modern ring. The Bell's Weekly Messenger (among others) published both a Sunday and a Monday edition, the respective circulations of which were 9,808 and 7,500. The Sunday Times contended that these were really two separate papers, as advertisements in the Monday edition had to be paid for. In the same way it claimed that the poor old Observer had a true Sunday circulation of only 3,155, with 1,550 for the Monday edition. Chapman was anxious to show that as the weekly figure for his paper (which was published on Saturdays and Sundays only and not on Mondays) was 12,647, it must stand above The Bell's Weekly Messenger in the eyes of advertisers, as they had to pay nothing extra; and he seems to have had the temerity to monkey with the official list to make his point. The leader in the stamped Sunday paper field was Robert Bell's Weekly Dispatch, at 42,588 copies a week.

V

The paper continued to be savage with the Tories. With the Socialists it was equally savage, and its grammar was destroyed along with its equanimity. 'There can, we think,' it prophesied,

be little doubt that in the course of a very short time, Socialism . . . will become extinct, since in its various dens and strongholds in the more immoral parts of the country, we already discover signs and symptoms of a desire to return to the faith at least, if not to the practice, of the rest of the community. Even if these outward indications of an inward con-

VICTORIA AND ALBERT.

That every family throughout the civilized world may possess a faithful record of the most important event which takes place To-morrow (Monday), the 10th of February, the Conductors of the

SUNDAY TIMES

Will present to their subscribers on the 16th of Feb.

A Stamped

SUPPLEMENT,

GRATIS,

Containing the longest and most authentic account of

HER MAJESTY'S

MARRIAGE

With Prince Albert, and a full description of the Royal Nuptial Procession to and from the Chapel Royal, accompanied by a large

ENGRAVING,

Representing the Interior of the Chapel as it appeared when the "Queen of England" pronounced the word "Obey;" also full particulars of the Doings at Windsor Castle, Buckingham Palace, and every Town and City in the Kingdom on the evening of that eventful Day.

Sunday Times.

LONDON: SUNDAY, FEBRUARY 9, 1840.

These wood engravings of Queen Victoria and Prince Albert were among the numerous illustrations of the royal marriage which appeared in a special stamped supplement of The Sunday Times – the supplement stamp was ½d and it was in addition to the usual 1d stamp on the front of the paper itself. This panel heralded the supplement a week in advance, and is a nice little example of blurb-writing and layout. On February 16 the impressive supplement itself – it was a roaring success – contained a leading article (opposite) in the Pott and Slurk tradition, on the insults which the paper's enemies, the Tories, had offered the Queen, who herself was a declared enemy of that party. The article declares that the 'reduced grant for the royal consort' is virtually a fine on both the Queen and Prince Albert 'for not bearing allegiance to the Tory party'.

Supplement to the Sunday Times of February 16, 1840

THE QUEEN AND THE TORIES.

The royal marriage is a topic which plunges our Tory contemporaries into most amusing incongruities. The conventional language of loyalty to which they have been accustomed, the overwhelming burst of national feeling elicited by this auspicious union, the sinister and servile hope of turning Prince Albert to some account for party purposes, and the vindictiveness and virulence generated by party disappointments, blend in rare confusedness through their columns, making a mixture as strange and loathsome as that of the witches' imps around the filthy cauldron in *Macbeth*.

> "Black spirits and white,
> Blue spirits and grey,
> Mingle, mingle, mingle,
> Ye that mingle may."

There is nothing English or honest in this vibration from a crawling sycophantism that licks the dust, to a swaggering insolence that feels appalled at its own rudeness. Nor shall the faction quietly escape from its own double-dealing, and subside into a course which may be more apparently consistent, but will not have an atom more of public principle. The base metal is tested, and the rap shall be nailed to the counter. Often will the Queen's marriage be called to mind in coming years, with emotions of complacency and gratitude ; and as often shall it recall the damning record of Tory insults to her, and to the partner of her future life.

Under ordinary circumstances, and in the circles of decent society, no man would have married the woman against whom *credible* tongues had wagged in vituperations like those heaped on the Queen at the festivals of Toryism. The Prince was insulted by anticipation in the object of his affection. The venemous dastards took full advantage of her position. In their caricatures she was depicted as the female president of vicious orgies. Her chosen personal companions were described as unconscious of the difference between vice and virtue, purity and impurity. That her fair maiden name is unspotted as her bridal veil, simply arises from the fact that nobody, unconnected with the faction, puts any faith in a "winewarmed" Tory orator, or a hireling Tory journalist. That truth which she has pledged, and without which her nuptials are a mere form, has been deliberately assailed. Falsehood has been basely ascribed to her ; falsehood to statesmen, who had a right to frank dealing ; and falsehood to public obligation, demanding a scrupulous observance. The crime is not to be forgotten in a marriage compliment. It will rise up in judgment when the slanderers of the wife attempt to curry favour with the husband—an additional baseness which they seem to meditate.

The falsehoods which had been circulated about Prince Albert's religion, the insinuations of "amorous dalliance with a Papist," and other appeals to the unreasoning bigotry of a class, were thought worthy of solemn embodiment in the Peers' amendment to the Address. The word "Protestant" was thrust in her Majesty's face, because the Tory leaders had more regard for the silly ignorance of a rabid section of their followers, than for the respect due to the intellect and conscience of their Sovereign. The satisfaction of any sincere Protestant religionist, by this impertinent interpolation, was a sheer and pitiful pretence. In that fine moral sense which the Queen has repeatedly evinced, the country had an infinitely firmer security than in the faction, chicanery, and assumption of the majority that carried this suspicious and insolent addition. The stigma it attempted to fix, both on the royal bride and bridegroom, fell pointless. It recoils on the obtrusive ignorance of those who did not, or would not, know how his house has been the pillar of continental Protestantism, or how her heart is the shrine of religious conscientiousness. But faction has ever been ignorant of what is most honourable in historical fact or human feeling.

In the reduced grant for the royal consort, there was evidently a strong action upon members of the economical feelings of the constituencies. Could the vote have stood simply as an economical result, there would have been nothing reasonably offensive, either to her Majesty or her illustrious consort. Sir Robert Peel, in the name of his party, took care that this should not be the case. He pointedly disclaimed the economical ground. The reduction is virtually a fine upon the Queen and her consort for not bearing allegiance to the Tory party. For this offence they are amerced in a heavy penalty. It were needless to say how we should deprecate the disgusting sight of two parties bidding against each other for royal favour out of the public purse. But not less to be deprecated is the ostensible and ostentatious opening or closing of that purse in proportion to the acceptability of the recipient in the eyes of Toryism. We have now a patriotic Queen and her husband, with a smaller net revenue at their joint uncontrolled disposal than that of a Tory Queen-Dowager, who has not, unless she so please, any public state to maintain. Whatever may be said in praise of the economy, nothing can be said in praise of the proportion. Toryism recognises no proportion, save the proportion of subserviency to its own purposes ; for that, wherever it can reach the public money, it bestows bounties and inflicts penalties. In this way has it aimed at making Prince Albert feel its power.

The Naturalization Bill afforded an opportunity for a far grosser insult, and one more deeply and wantonly wounding to the feelings of her Majesty. On state occasions, with all their endurance and fatigue, whom should the Queen have by her but her husband ? What is there in this worn-out conventionalism of precedence, this obsolete unmeaning ceremony, this faint shadow of a shade, to deprive a youthful Queen of the support which the effete chimera allows to other wives of humbler rank ? What is there of respect or endearment to the English nation in the name of Hanover, that it should be pushed forward as a point of state, to sever those whom God hath joined ? The precedence desired by her Majesty for her husband has a valid claim at the tribunal of truth, and justice, and the human heart. It is good everywhere but in the House of Lords. There, even its consideration was deemed subservient to the convenience of Lord Lyndhurst. The bridal Majesty of England commanded to stifle its emotions, and make them wait the convenience of Lord Lyndhurst! Do the Tories dream that these things are unheeded by the people of England ? Or that they will be forgotten ? Do they think the people have no eyes, no ears, no hearts, no memories ? They are as much mistaken as if they imagine that the Queen can forget them too, and, after all their unseemly treatment, sink into the submissive slave and deceptive tool which they once vainly hoped to make her. It is as impossible as it would be to imagine, in relation to her brave and generous spirit, that appalling shout of contempt which such a submission would cause to ring around the land.

On the insulting admonitions and insinuations of some of the Tory journals we have already commented, not so much to controvert their allegations as to fix the recollection of their malignity. They are an appropriate climax to the preceding series of insults. If in private life any man dared to whisper of a bride such inuendoes as those we allude to, he would be kicked out of the house which his breath polluted ; and very properly.

Tory loyalty is described by its own professors as being

> "True as the dial to the Sun,
> Although it be not shone upon."

The similitude is, perhaps, more correct than those who retail it would have us understand. The function of the dial, its only service to man, consists in its telling the time of day. Like Toryism, it discharges its function just so long as it is in the sunshine, and no longer. Those who rely upon it are left in the lurch at every passing cloud. Every flitting shade, though it were that of an angel's wing, makes its vaunted truth vanish ; and in a cloudy day, though the clouds be fraught with heaven's blessing for earth's fruitfulness, it becomes nothing more than a bit of sullen and worthless brass.

viction of the truth of religion be altogether hypocritical, there is still one point gained – they are ashamed of the principles they formerly professed, and feel the imperative necessity of disguising them . . . In proportion, however, as they develop their cowardly and knavish system, society will discover the absolute necessity of extinguishing, at any price, so infamous a political heresy . . .

Stylistically, however, the political writers of The Sunday Times could already do better than such hysterical abuse of Socialists and Tories. One of them, Greville Brooke, who has left no memorial in the Dictionary of National Biography, which commemorates many men of lesser literary and political ability, wrote during the 1840s a weekly signed column called 'The Political Inquirer'. It is in striking contrast with the tone of the other political articles in the paper and with the bombastic, thundering style set up as a model of political controversy by The Times. It is cool, restrained, ironic, and because it is strictly controlled it is able to build up to a climax which most of the other leader writers of the period would have wasted in the vain fulminations of their opening paragraph. A typical example of Brooke's style is seen in his letter on the Corn Laws to His Grace the Duke of Buckingham on April 12, 1840:

My Lord Duke, though you state it to be your conviction that the agricultural labourer, with a large family, whose wages amount to nine shillings per week, is sufficiently well paid, there appears to be strong reason for supposing you to be in error. In the first place, the labourers themselves think very differently from Your Grace. They consider themselves to be very ill-paid, and the reasons which they give for so thinking are not unworthy of your Grace's attention.

Soberly and quietly Brooke exposes the poverty of the agricultural poor. He then, but still always distancing himself from his anger, proceeds to discuss the possible consequences of this poverty.

No doubt, as a member of an oligarchy accustomed to look down with contempt upon the humble and industrious classes, and to treat with extreme disdain all their endeavours to think and reason for themselves, your Grace supposes it to signify but little what notions the multitude get into their head, or whether their feelings towards the privileged orders be those of affectionate veneration, or of deep and rankling hatred.

In the same measured tones Brooke points to the unemployment and misery that the retention of the Corn Laws will produce in the manufacturing centres of the midlands. It is only then that he

Sunday Times.

LONDON : SUNDAY, DECEMBER 7, 1845.

TOTAL REPEAL OF THE CORN-LAWS.

It appears to be at length pretty certain that the end of the Corn-laws is rapidly approaching, and the question now is, who dealt them the fatal blow? There need not, however, be much doubt about the matter. To have watched the progress of events for the last seven or eight years, and not to be able to fix with certainty on the author of this assassination, seems to us scarcely a conceivable predicament ; and yet the *Times* asks the question. Many circumstances, and many men have, we admit, concurred in bringing us to the point at which we have now arrived. The Tory ministers have done something, the Liberal ex-ministers, have done more ; but the great agent in the business has been the Anti-Corn-law League. No one in his senses can deny this. Without the kind assistance of the League, the Corn-laws would, probably, have perished some day or another, because it is not in the nature of injustice to be everlasting; but we much fear they would have outlived the present generation, and sent many thousands and tens of thousands prematurely to their graves.

But though the Corn-laws appear to be in their last agonies, they are not actually deceased, and it will be quite as well, there-fore, for the country to treat them as living, not as dead things. Strange events are recorded in the history of mankind, unexpected revivals, mysterious resuscitations, marvels which were thought impossible, but, nevertheless, actually happened. For this reason we most earnestly hope that no breath of premature triumph will pass over the waves of agitation, and cause them to subside before they shall have wafted us fairly into port. Let parliament meet in the midst of the Anti-Corn-law tempest—let the voice of a whole nation, alarmed by the approach of gaunt famine, ring in the ears of both houses. Let town speak to town, and county call upon

begins to reveal the dramatic threat which is to be the culmination of his article :

These miserable men, with bodies and minds disordered by hunger, will be prepared to kindle and blaze forth at the throwing in of the first revolutionary brand among them. Hunger, let me inform your Grace, is as bad a reasoner, and oft-times as bad a patriot, as a member of the oligarchy itself . . . Your Grace has read the history of France for the last sixty years, and need not be told that the worst horrors of the revolution were but the natural and necessary reaction of tyrannical principles pushed to extremes.

Brooke makes one realise the extent of the agitation for free trade in corn. The trouble went back to a law of 1815 designed to keep out cheap grain. However much the squires may have benefited from this protection, it was bitterly opposed equally by the middle-class employers and the poor themselves, neither of whom wished to see slender wages expended on impossibly dear bread. In general Brooke's writing is of an order not to be matched anywhere else in the paper in its early days. Nevertheless, the position of political oracle had been pre-empted in these years by The Times; and the reputation of The Sunday Times, which by the 1860s was very considerable, had to be made in other fields of journalism.

But before this, there were other changes of ownership. After John Kemble Chapman came Samuel Benaiah Frederick. Then the real founder of the highly-successful Daily Telegraph, a printer named Joseph Moses Levy, became its chief proprietor in 1855, but finding that he had his hands full with The Telegraph, which made history in Fleet Street when he reduced its price to one penny in September, 1855, he sold his interest to E. T. Smith, the impresario and lessee of Drury Lane Theatre. Under Smith and his editor, William Carpenter, the paper gave more space to the theatre and other entertainments, to book reviews and to sporting news, with special attention to racing and boxing. Thus at a time when the removal of the 'taxes on knowledge', the appearance of The Daily Telegraph, with its emphasis on news, and the successes of William Howard Russell in the Crimean War for The Times had all resulted in a new and more enterprising spirit in Fleet Street, The Sunday Times gave up the vulgar struggle and retreated into semi-literary journalism, to become a highly respectable quality publication which disdained the old ruffian appeal of its earliest days.

The disappearance of the taxes on knowledge had another tonic effect on Fleet Street: it fathered a series of momentous developments in the printing of newspapers and the mechanical composition of type.

Newspapers were originally printed in the same way as books on wooden screw and lever presses, which could print a sheet of paper up to about royal size (20in × 25in), but were not powerful enough to do so at one operation. Two pulls of the bar were required, one for each half of the type forme.

About 1800 Earl Stanhope invented an iron version of the hand-press, and by adding a set of compound levers to the bar increased the power so that a sheet could be printed at one pull. This was a step forward but the output of the press – some 250 sheets an hour – remained much the same. By the 1820s Stanhope presses were made in five sizes – foolscap, royal, super royal, double crown and 'newspaper', with a platen (the pressing surface) of 36in × 23$\frac{1}{2}$in.

The Sunday Times was probably printed on a Columbian or an Albion, the iron hand-presses which succeeded the Stanhope, until well into the nineteenth century, and certainly at a succession of printers in or adjoining Fleet Street. Henry White printed his Independent Observer in Racquet Court, Fleet Street, and went across the road to 76 Fleet Street, and a selection of new types of which he confessed himself proud, when he started The Sunday Times. Thereafter, with that happy-go-lucky air which characterised the paper throughout the whole of the nineteenth century, it changed editorial offices frequently and was printed in Peterborough Court (now in the domain of The Daily Telegraph), Shoe Lane, St Clement's Press, Portugal Street, and by Bradbury, Agnew, of Punch. At some point, probably in the early 1860s, it would in the order of things have been printed on the cylinder press, which was invented by Frederick Koenig in 1811. In this type of press the type forme no longer made a simple movement under the platen, but the bed to which it was fastened received a continual motion to and fro, and the platen was discarded in favour of a revolving pressing cylinder. When driven by steam the new cylinder press could produce at the rate of 1,000 copies an hour.

The reasons for the retention of the hand-press (except by the very largest newspapers) were economic and social. A Koenig machine cost ten times as much as a Stanhope press, which was adequate for the small number of copies required while the reading public remained limited. But the expansion of newspapers and the development of printing techniques had been held up by the taxes on knowledge, one of which was the newspaper tax instituted in 1712. Originally it was 1d on a whole sheet (which could be folded to make four pages), but by the Newspaper Regulation Act of 1815 this was increased to fourpence a sheet, and so it remained until 1836. A sheet was to be not less than 21in × 17in.

The legal requirement that each sheet of paper carry a stamp retarded rotary printing from a reel of paper. Because of this requirement Rowland Hill abandoned his rotary press invention after 1835. The newspaper tax, as we know, was repealed in 1855, leading to the foundation of many new newspapers for the increasingly literate public. Cylinder presses replaced hand-presses and there was a revived interest in rotary techniques. A rotary press incorporates the printing surface on one cylinder, pressure being supplied by another, while paper is fed between them from a reel. It follows that a means of fitting type round a cylinder had to be devised.

Before 1855 the first rotaries were type-revolving machines,

The Duke of Wellington's funeral car.

with the type secured round a cylinder by wedge-shaped column rules. These machines were fed by sheets of paper, output being increased by adding to the number of feeding stations. The ten-feeder from Hoe of New York was capable of 20,000 impressions an hour, but it was obvious that this development could not go on indefinitely. The desideratum was a machine which could be fed by a reel of paper and which printed from a curved relief plate.

The first requirement could be met as paper was made in reels. The second took some time to achieve until the stereotyping process could be adapted to produce a curved plate. After much experiment this was achieved in the 1860s, and the way was clear for the development of the modern rotary press. William Bullock of Philadelphia made a reel-fed rotary in 1865, but the paper was cut into lengths before receiving the impression. In the Walter rotary developed at The Times before 1868 the paper was printed on the reel and cut afterwards. By 1878 Hoe had produced the 'double supplement' rotary, which had two elements built at right-angles to each other. The modern rotary installation for printing the large circulations required consists of a multiplication of units.

The development of a satisfactory typesetting machine to match that of the printing machine was a much slower process. While a large army of compositors was available the demands of the newspapers for increasing amounts of typesetting could at first be met. A mechanical composer also presented greater technical problems than the printing machine. From 1822 onwards many machines were invented, nearly all based on a simple principle. Pieces of type were stored in channels or tubes, to be released in the order required by the touch of a key. The type still had to be distributed back into the tubes after use. Some machines, such as the Hattersley, were used on provincial newspapers, but the compositors' union in London was opposed to them. The Times managed to use a Kastenbein from 1872 onwards, as it was a non-union house. From 1886 new type was cast daily for the Kastenbein, thus overcoming the need to distribute the type back into the machine. This indicated a superior approach to mechanical typesetting. What was needed was a machine which would both cast type and compose it in the order required. The solution was not to compose pieces of foundry type but matrices – the small moulds from which the relief letter on a piece of type is cast.

After a number of experiments the practical solution was worked out by Ottmar Mergenthaler, a German-born American. In 1888 he invented a machine which was virtually the basis of the modern Linotype. This stored matrices in a sloping magazine, to be released by keyboard action and assembled in words, separated by space bands. The completed justified line was brought to the orifice of a mould and there cast into a type-high slug or line of type. After casting, the matrices were distributed back into their channels automatically.

33

The first Linotypes were installed in British provincial newspapers from 1890 onwards. By 1894 the London Society of Compositors and the London Daily Newspaper Proprietors had reached an agreement on payment for Linotype composition. The Globe and The Financial Times had installed the machine a year before, and after the agreement Linotypes were used in the major newspaper offices in London including St Clement's Press, the big jobbing house associated with both The Financial Times and The Sunday Times.

There remained the problem of printing half-tone blocks by rotary methods, but it can be said that by about 1905 the larger newspapers were being produced – qualitatively if not quantitatively – in the same way as they are today.

VI

Tom Hood, the handsome, reckless, improvident, and occasionally brilliant son of the man who wrote 'The Song of the Shirt', jerked out his gold eye-glass with one of the beautiful smiles for which he was famous and leaned across his desk in the War Office in Pall Mall. He said to his fellow-clerk, Clement Scott, then scarcely twenty years old, 'Have you heard that Foard is going to resign The Sunday Times? There will be a vacancy for a dramatic critic.'

Clement Scott was immensely excited. He remembered Hood's words till the day of his death. Long after this incident in 1863 had changed the whole course of his career he declared that The Sunday Times at that period had left nearly all its rivals far behind. Its influence in the arts, especially in the theatre, had become paramount.

Thackeray had said, some time before, that no periodical could hope to attain the highest position in the world of journalism by devoting its chief powers to the relaxations of cultured men and women instead of to the stern occupations of politics and religion. It was a principal achievement of The Sunday Times in the middle of the nineteenth century to prove that Thackeray was wrong. To get an appointment on it in the 1860s was, said Scott, looking back in his old age, to secure one of the plums of the profession. Even twenty years before this time impressionable and ambitious young men had felt a thrill of emulation and pleasure when they saw a member of The Sunday Times staff going about his daily or nightly avocation. Edmund Yates, the precocious youth who was elected to the Garrick Club at the age of seventeen, and later precipitated a famous quarrel between Thackeray and Dickens, used to gaze enraptured at The Sunday Times drama critic, Stirling Coyne, whenever he saw him in the theatre in the 1840s. He, like Clement Scott, looked back in his old age upon the journalism of the middle years of the century, and found that The Sunday Times shone with more than average lustre. This naturally provoked a certain amount of jealous comment from other newspapermen. Coyne was a man of kindly disposition, but his personal habits were said not to be very cleanly. 'Stirling Coyne?' exclaimed the wag Douglas Jerrold, '*I* call him Filthy Lucre.'

From its earliest days The Sunday Times had given a good deal of attention to matters concerned with literature. But at the beginning at any rate it had little or no interest in questions of criticism. It showed this characteristically in its treatment of the death of Lord Byron in May, 1824. Barefacedly borrowing a long extract from The Times, it adopted its tone of elevated morality, and was interested in almost every aspect of Byron except his poetry. Its style and its outlook were considerably more solemn than would be found anywhere today. 'There were', it said, 'individuals more to be approved for moral qualities than Lord Byron – to be more safely followed or more tenderly beloved; but there lives no man on earth whose sudden departure from it under the circumstances in which that nobleman was cut off, appears to us more calculated to impress the mind with profound and unmingled mourning. Lord Byron was doomed to pay that price which Nature sometimes charges for stupendous intellect in the gloom of his imagination, and the intractable energy of his passions.' The article spoke of Byron's devotion to Greece and of his private entanglements; but of 'Childe Harold', 'English Bards and Scotch Reviewers' or even the 'Maid of Athens' there is not a word.

It adopted a very similar attitude towards the death of Edmund Kean nine years later. But the paper's growing interest in aesthetic concerns is shown in the fact that, whereas it dealt with Byron in a few hundred words, it devotes several thousands to Kean, without, however, recalling any of the performances that alone made him worth writing about. Nothing is said of his Othello, his Shylock, or his Richard III. Its biography begins with a highly uncharitable paragraph on one of his old friends, notes that none of his relatives was present when he died, comments on Kean's own conviction that he was the illegitimate son of the Duke of Norfolk, and dismisses his theatrical career with the remark that his performances are too well known to be discussed.

The paper then goes on to say that it does not want to speak of Kean's moral weaknesses, or to 'draw his frailties from their dread abode'. Nevertheless, when he is described 'as an excellent and most benevolent man we feel truth (to be) outraged. In what did his excellence consist? Was it his conduct as a husband or father? Alas, for the truth! He had a wretched habit of drinking . . . his affair with Mrs Cox was connected with circumstances peculiarly discreditable,' and 'a love of low society led him to offend some of his noblest patrons.' At this point, however, moral indignation retreated a little before the onset of Christian charity. After his death 'there was nothing unpleasing in his appearance. The corpse was considered a remarkably fine one. His lips were in a slight degree decomposed, but in other respects he had the appearance of one sleeping'. This enthusiasm continued into the account of the post-mortem. A layer of fat two inches thick was found in Kean's breast, and caused much surprise. The brain was the finest the surgeons had ever seen. If Kean had been a temperate man he might have lived to be a hundred instead of dying at forty-five. Between 1814 and 1833 he had been paid for the performances which were too familiar to be mentioned the sum of £176,000.

The stern sense of morality persisted even when critical judgments, of a sort, began to intrude. The literary critics of The Sunday Times at this period believed that it was their duty to maintain a high and healthy attitude towards life. They balanced the paper's crusading political convictions with a strong feeling of moral rectitude. They looked, in a sentimental and at times even mawkish way, for a literature of reassurance and simple goodness. In 1848 they welcomed the unstrenuous and optimistic Longfellow.

They felt uneasy about Dickens. 'Nicholas Nickleby' was 'the cleverest disagreeable book we have ever read'. 'Our Mutual Friend'

has all Mr Dickens's striking and well-known eccentricities, beauties, and defects. These are, in fact, more apparent than in his earlier works. As in a young face, so long as the fulness of cheek and efflorescence of complexion exercise their full sway, peculiarity of feature is not only not offensive, but may even be scarcely apparent: but, as the flesh falls in

> **NICHOLAS NICKLEBY. No. IV.**
> The fourth number is out. In talent it transcends its precursors. All we can say of Dickens's present work is, that it is the cleverest disagreeable book we ever read.
>
> *February 16, 1840*

with age, the cheekbones assume unwonted prominence, the nose looms forth in larger proportions, and a face once handsome becomes singular or it may be repulsive, so it is with an author: and now that the freshness of style is departed for ever from Mr Dickens, the peculiarities of his manner become duly more marked and impressive . . . He is a bad artist, but a delightful writer.

This is floridly put, but there is something in it. Dickens's mannerisms did grow on him as the years went by.

What is more disconcerting is the sort of literature to which unqualified admiration was given. In Blackwood's in the year of Victoria's coronation there appeared a poem, 'The Sexton's Daughter', to which The Sunday Times gave unstinted praise. Despite pressure on space, it declared, 'we . . . shall . . . make room for two more verses, which for tenderness and beauty yield to none in our language'. Then followed these remarkable lines:

> I know not – 'twas not said of yore,
> But still to me, a man, it seems
> That motherhood is something more
> Than even a father's fondness deems.
> The teaming (sic) breast has thrills,
>   'tis plain,
> More deep than e'er its partner knew,
> A mystery of hopeful pain,
> That make a greater blessing due.

It is easy enough to scoff at stuff like this from the vantage point of the present day. But Blackwood's published it, and Blackwood's was at least as intelligent a magazine as any existing in the twentieth century. The Sunday Times praised it, and the paper's cultural reputation rose steadily year by year.

Even the sporting pages show a determined effort to introduce the graces of fine writing into the paper. If the racing news could hardly be a discussion of literature there can be little doubt that the racing correspondent felt that his copy should actually be literature itself, comparable less with Hazlitt on the Gasman than with the idyllic musings of Wordsworth. By 1848 The Sunday Times was printing the stupendous number of 12,000 words an issue about racing even on a day when there was little of importance to chronicle. In this comparatively frivolous section the paper nevertheless expected its readers to be reasonably well educated and able to identify and be at home with elementary classical references. A characteristic article published on June 18, 1848, illustrates this, and shows also the paper's demagoguery even in the flowery meadows of its most luscious prose. 'Thursday last at Moulsey Hurst, like the Derby Day on the Downs, proved indeed a bumper. The weather was as favourable as could possibly be desired. It was such a day as we might imagine shone on the fair Proserpine, whilst she was gathering flowers in the Vale of Enna, or such a day as the gods themselves would have issued a special order for when they were about to celebrate a carnival on Olympus.'

After this ecstatic echo of Shakespeare's 'On such a night', the poetic-minded racing correspondent, who seems to have been interested in everything but horses, passes to elaborately phrased political reflections. 'Never perhaps on any similar occasion previously did the little town of Hampton, a place associated with the grandeur of bygone days, and the glories of departed royalty – a place where the bluff Harry was wont to revel, and where the merry monarch played many a mad prank and many a joyous gambol – a place now alas deserted by the sovereign, and preserved only for the sovereign's retainers and satellites, and yet a place how lovely, how beautiful!' And so the correspondent, his syntax broken down but his flow of eloquence and rhetoric unimpaired, goes on and on and on interminably, till he almost forgets to note – what was presumably the chief point of his article – that the Claremont Stakes was won by the favourite, Christiana, whom he calls a neat-looking filly with a good turn of speed.

What, however, first brought the intelligent middle-class public to The Sunday Times was neither the high falutin prose of its sporting columns nor the middle of the road judgments of its book reviews. It is simply the fact that the middle classes were snobs. They wanted to know where their social superiors lived and what they were up to. This put the paper into a difficulty. On principle it had no liking for aristocrats. In its earliest days it never mentioned them except with abuse, and we shall see with what acrimony it pursued them in its theatrical pages. It was never at any time prepared to follow their activities with the sedulous flattery that young readers like Edmund Yates would have desired.

The most it would do was to introduce an item of lordly gossip into columns which it fondly thought to be humorous. 'Everybody may not have heard when a bonnet is not a bonnet. Do you give it up?' 'Yes.' 'When it becomes a woman.' 'Why do cats grin in Cheshire?' 'Because it was once a county palatine, and the cats cannot help laughing whenever they think of it.' It was in such contexts that it gave its aristocratic information, even then seeking to present the nobility in an undignified light. Thus in June, 1848, it recalls that the Duchess of Charteris beat her husband in a foot race for 200 guineas, and notes that the Duchess was allowed to run with her dress pulled high above her knees.

The middle classes did not yet aspire to mingle with the nobility. They kept themselves to themselves and lived in the odour of opulent respectability. The great acting families, who could, as Edmund Yates quaintly said, have dined off gold plate had they wished, formed a little colony of their own round Brompton Square and Pelham Crescent. They preferred to dine in Bloomsbury at tables where they had the chance of meeting Dickens and Thackeray rather than to ingratiate themselves with earls and marquises. Yet the fact that they had begun to notice that their way of life was separate from that of the aristocracy is a portent. At an earlier period they would not even have considered the possibility of comparing themselves with the hereditary peerage. They now began to take a fascinated interest in what went on in the houses of the great.

Yates himself, who made a hit when he started in 1874 a brilliant weekly called The World, which put an unashamed stress on 'personal journalism', was the son of an actor who had been educated at the Charterhouse. As a youth he used to spend the weekends with his grandfather in a small house with a garden in Kentish Town. The old gentleman would have a paper sent round to him from a neighbouring tavern with his dinner beer. Yates may have found the political articles heavy going, but he took a vivid delight in The Sunday Times. In the eighteen-forties he waited eagerly for the paper and its serial. For one of these serials (there were also Harrison Ainsworth's 'Old St Paul's',[1] for which the tremendous sum of £500 was paid for the serial rights, and

---

1. Ainsworth felt he was making a great and possibly dangerous experiment 'in undertaking to publish a novel in a weekly newspaper', says James Grant in his 'Newspaper Press', 1871. He adds: 'It . . . proved injurious to his reputation.' By the 1880s serialisation of fiction in newspapers was a commonplace, and Mr Tillotson of Bolton set himself up as 'purveyor of fiction' to the provincial press.

G. P. R. James's 'The Smugglers') was by Lady Blessington, and it afforded ravishing glimpses of life in high society.

In fiction The Sunday Times allowed itself to speak of the aristocracy with a subservient adulation it would never have permitted in its columns of news and political comment. Lady Blessington presumably knew what she was writing about. She was the wife of an earl and the mistress of a count – the celebrated Alfred d'Orsay. But she wrote of the households of the socially exalted with the wondering admiration of a servant girl. She begins her novel of 'Strathern', which was in The Sunday Times in 1843, with an account of a breakfast party in a mansion near St James's Park. Her description of the room where this took place is of ecstatic particularity:

On each side of this lofty mirror were suspended some of the choicest works of the ancient masters, collected with great judgment, and at a vast expense, by the father of the present Lord Wyndermere, an acknowledged connoisseur in pictures. The curtains were of the richest satin, the precise colour of the oak bookcases, and the chairs and sofas were covered with the same material. The uncut velvet pile carpet, of a substance which prevented a footfall from being heard, was of the peculiar tint denominated Raphael green, from the preference evinced the colour by that glorious artist, and the walls were of similar hue. A *dejeuner* served on the most delicate and costly Sevres porcelain, was placed on a table, near the open window, while dumb waiters, covered with snowy damask, and piled with plates, forks, and spoons, stood near the two chairs intended for the persons who were to partake the repast. Fruit, which might be likened to the golden produce of the fabled Hesperides, if not from its bloom, at least from the enormous cost of its culture, crowned the breakfast-table, mingled with every description of cake and bread furnished by modern refinement to stimulate the sated appetite of an Epicurean.

Towards the end of 1843, when the young Edmund Yates read this vulgar epitome of gracious living, his mouth watered and he felt that he was truly being admitted into the company of the great. And there were many others like him.

But if the popularity of The Sunday Times was in part built on its serials, the real foundation of its mid-nineteenth-century reputation was its treatment of the theatre. Its influence in this respect was due less to the percipience of its criticism than to the robustness and tone of its attitude to the theatre in general. Its critics, from Stirling Coyne onwards to Foard, a hardworking barrister as well as a journalist, regarded activities in the theatre as events to be recorded rather than as artistic manifestations to be analysed.

The Editor of the

SUNDAY TIMES

Has the pleasure of announcing that on the

4th of January, 1846,

Will be Published in the Columns of that Journal,

THE FIRST NUMBER

OF

A NEW NOVEL,

ENTITLED

FORTESCUE,

WRITTEN EXCLUSIVELY

FOR THE "SUNDAY TIMES."

BY

JAMES SHERIDAN KNOWLES,

ESQ.

Orders Received by all Newsagents.

Chapman and Elcoate, Printers, Peterborough-court, and 6, Shoe-lane, Fleet-st.

It looked on the theatre as one of the principal factors in the national life, even though after the death of Kean the playhouses became less and less popular until they were revived by the breath of vitality that Tom Robertson breathed into the moribund drama with his play of 'Caste' in 1867.

The paper was equally firmly on the side of nationalism, and it was a rousing occasion when both causes came together in the week ending June 18, 1848. The previous Monday had seen the total rout of a French company at Drury Lane. Dumas's Théâtre Historique brought to London an adaptation of 'Monte Cristo' and was howled off the stage. 'We feel proud,' said The Sunday Times, (and its then proprietor John Kemble Chapman was a theatrical producer who could obviously grind an axe with the best),

in having been the first of our contemporaries to denounce the audacious attempt of the French theatrical adventurers to drive the British drama from the English stage, starve our actors, beggar our managers, drag down Shakespeare from the pedestal of genius, and set up in his place the mischievous charlatan, Alexandre Dumas.

In tub-thumping style the paper demands:

Shall the English drama be trampled upon because a worthless portion of the aristocracy chooses to give its support to foreign entertainments? Shall English art fail that French trumpery may flourish? Shall we receive with open arms the men who brutally drove our countrymen from their stage, from their factories, and from their railroads? And the public voice answered, within the walls of Drury Lane Theatre on Monday night, a triumphant No!

There then follow four thousand words of rejoicing that never in theatrical history had there been such an uproar as prevented the French from giving their ill-starred performance. This is capped by an analysis, quoted with clear approval from 'An English Actor', of the root cause of the sad condition of the English theatre at that time. It is not surprising to find its misfortunes traced to the gates of the Palace itself. 'The plain fact is, that the one great cause of the present state of the drama (however it may suit the purposes of some to blink the question) is, the want of patronage on the part of Her Most Gracious Majesty herself – her frequent visits to the foreign theatres – her continued absence from their English rivals.'

The summing up of the whole matter is on a truly exalted note:

The point on which the great weight of our opposition rests is the baneful influence it would exercise upon our social character. The profligacy and utter disregard for every religious and moral restraint which, almost without an exception, pervades the works of modern French dramatists, especially those of Alexandre Dumas, would speedily infect the minds of our youth, and we should find libertinism, infidelity, and all the vices that belong to the Dumas and George Sand school of liberal philosophy transplanted from the stage to our homes and hearths. Englishmen would no longer be English, but bastard Frenchmen.

Not only did profligacy find an unexpected new champion in Queen Victoria, but the aristocracy was also at fault. The paper was not content with vague fulminations. Unlike many news-papers it sought facts, and when it got facts it printed them. It sent someone to discover who precisely was patronising the Italian opera at Covent Garden, and then published a long Roll of Dishonour, bearing the names of those who supported foreign art. It found amongst other high-born criminals Lord and Lady Waterpark, Lady Vernon, the Duke and Duchess of Montrose, the Duke and Duchess of Beaufort, the Earl and Countess of Longford, Lady Elizabeth Pakenham, the Marquis and Mar-chioness of Sligo, the Marquis of Titchfield, Lord Burghley, and forty-three other titled traitors to British art.

VII

Clement Scott had been brought up in a deeply religious house-hold. His clergyman father preached twice a day, and three times on Sunday. The profoundly moral stand he took at a later date against the foreign drama represented by Ibsen is well known. One can well imagine with what zest he acted on Tom Hood's advice in order to join a newspaper as morally impeccable as the reformed Sunday Times. Its owner was now Edward Seale, a banker, who had reduced its price to 2d (this was in 1858 when the advertisement tax and the stamp duty had both been abolished) and appointed a Unitarian minister named Henry M. Barnett as editor. Deeply satisfied by the moral seriousness of Mr Barnett's articles, Clement Scott secured letters of recommendation from his father's influential friends, and went round to see Mr Seale at his office, a neat and even imposing establishment called The Bank. It was in Leicester Square,[1] next door to an underground dining-place known as The Shades, which in turn was attached to old Saville House, once the home of Miss Linwood's needlework museum. Scott had no idea who banked at Mr Seale's establish-ment, but he heard subsequently that Mr Seale discounted securities and lent money at very fair interest. Scott among his other recommendations presented a testimonial from a clergy-man who was also a Freemason. Seale was a Freemason too, and Scott was immediately engaged at what was then considered to be the thumping salary of two pounds a week.

---

1. On the same side as the Empire cinema stands today.

Clement Scott

This auspicious beginning, which should have kept Scott at
The Sunday Times for the next forty years, did in fact keep him
there for only two. He tried to change the paper's continuing
attitude to the French drama. He published articles showing how
much the English stage had owed to visiting French players. This
proved too much for the patriotism of Mr Seale. Scott was dismissed and went on to make his name on The Daily Telegraph.
In his place was put a worthy Bohemian, Joseph Knight, known
as 'Good Knight', not because of his moral qualities but in recognition of the fact that he was always the last to leave any pub or
club to which he had gained entrance.

VIII

Clement Scott's association with The Sunday Times in the 1860s
marked the highest point of reputation the paper achieved in the
nineteenth century. It had become a journal with a personality of
its own, combining gravity and levity and capable at times of

Joseph Knight

emotional outbursts which redeemed it from any charge of safe predictability. But now a long period of eclipse was beginning.

George Smith, founder of The Dictionary of National Biography, had started The Cornhill Magazine, with Thackeray as editor, and plunged into newspaper ownership in 1865 with The Pall Mall Gazette, a London evening paper of high literary quality which took its name from Thackeray's invention in 'Pendennis'. So in one way and another the big reviews, including The Fortnightly, and the quality daily and evening journals were pressing on the cultural margins of The Sunday Times. Against the great names they attracted – Ruskin, Mill, Leslie Stephen – The Sunday Times could set only a Bohemian boozer like Joseph Knight, a serviceable critic but no match for intellectual and literary heavyweights. Frederic Harrison wrote for The Pall Mall Gazette and Matthew Arnold's 'Friendship's Garland' first appeared in it. Swinburne, Meredith, Rossetti, Bagehot, Huxley, Pater, and George Lewes all contributed to The Fortnightly. To offset these illustrious figures The Sunday Times, which began to be handicapped by its frequent changes of editorship, and sometimes (between 1864 and 1877) had no editor at all, being directed

During the whole of the period that the court remained at Windsor Castle the name of the Baroness Lehzen invariably appeared upon the royal dinner list, and was heralded forth, accordingly, in the diurnals of the next day. Her Majesty scarcely ever stirred abroad, either on foot or on horseback, without the "old creature" being found "tacked to her apron strings." But since the Queen has been at Buckingham Palace, where her Majesty arrived from Windsor on the 10th of last January, not once has the Baroness's name figured in the Court Circular, as one of the "royal dinner party," although she "eats her mutton" daily with her royal mistress; and but once (January 25) has the "old un's" name been given by the Court Newsman as having attended her Majesty during her equestrian exercises in the Riding-house near Buckingham Palace, although the Baroness has never, upon such occasions, been absent. There may be something more in this studious attempt to keep the Baroness, just now, in the back ground with the public, than meets the eye. The Court Newsman, of course, takes his cue from the higher powers, and invariably acts "according to orders." The same observation may be applied to the singular circumstance of the Duchess of Kent never, now, appearing to dine with her Majesty. That there is still considerable coolness existing between mother and daughter—a state of things much to be regretted—our readers may rest assured. Indeed, it is the intention of the Duchess of Kent to take refuge, for a short time, at Claremont, as soon as the nuptials have been celebrated; and, as soon as the spring has farther advanced, her royal highness will proceed to the Continent. She has now commenced breaking up her establishment. Several of her domestics have been, or are in the course of being, discharged. Amongst them is her old and faithful page, Mr. Fruchet, who has just retired upon a pension.

A "grand row" is expected to take place at the dinner which is to be given in the Town-hall to-morrow, in honour of the Queen's wedding. Those toadies, who "serve the Castle," have made up their minds to "carry out" the Queen Dowager, by refusing to drink her health, unless "the rising sun," Master Albert, is first toasted immediately after the royal bride. There are certain persons who would not only "hold a candle to the devil," but drink his Satanic majesty's "good health" into the bargain, if they thought that by so doing they would conciliate the Master of the Household, and thus get an extra order for a dozen or two of larks, or a nine gallon barrel of table beer. The Mayor's in a *funk*, and well he may be, at the threatening aspect of the "congratulatory feed." We think we hear him exclaim, amidst the din which will be raised about his ears, if he does not permit Albert to play first fiddle *after* "the Queen"—

> "Full many a storm on this grey head was beat;
> And now, on my high station, do I stand,
> Like the tired watchman in his air-rock'd tower,
> Who looketh for the hour of his release:
> I'm sick of worldly broils, and fain would rest
> With those who war no more."—*Joanna Baillie.*

A JERRY SNEAK.
ALBERT TO VICTORIA.

Yes, love, I hasten back to thee,
  My fervent passion never doubt;
Ah! I am sick of Germany,
  Of slender purse, and sharp sour krout!

With you, my dear, I'd fain be dining—
  Than German fare there can't be worse,
I long to see a *sov'reign* shining;
  I'll wade thee in my *heart* and *purse!*

Let me but have a little *change*—
  A change of linen and of diet—
And all affairs you may arrange
  Just as you please—I'm very quiet!

I know that you will reign and rule—
  'Tis not for me, my gentle VIC,
When we are *harness'd*, like a *mule*
  Or *ass*, against your will to *kick*.

The *inexpressibles* you mention
  I'll never *put my foot in*, save
With your free leave, when condescension
  Inclines you to oblige your slave!

Upon the wings of love I post—
  I'm well aware it is expedient
That I, to one who "rules the roast,"
  Should be in everything obedient.

Royal Hotel, Saxe Coburg.   ALBERT.

THE QUEEN AND HER HUSBAND.

Mr. Editor—As it is in contemplation to have another "flare up," or illumination, to-morrow (Monday), no doubt great ingenuity will be displayed. Turtle doves wooing, love among the roses, "Such a getting up stairs," "Even joys are pains because they cannot last"—these and many more sayings will be to view. Allow me to recommend a quotation from *Wat Tyler*, for a transparency. "When I gaze on the proud palace, and behold one man in the blood-purpled robes of royalty, feasting at ease, and lording over millions; then turn me to the hut of poverty, and see the wretched labourer, worn with toil, divide his scanty morsel with his infants, I sicken, and, indignant at the sight, blush for the patience of humanity.

Or this: 390,000 per year for an establishment!!!
    30,000 per year for a husband!!!
    70,000 for stables!!!
    30,000 *only* for educating the people!!!!!!
Your obedient servant,   A BURNING SHAME.

Nathan Nathan, one of the children of Israel, aged 30, and *Charles Ware*, an intelligent lad, aged 13, were indicted for stealing two hats, of the value of 10s., the property of Charles Saunders, the master of Ware, a manufacturer in the Borough.—The Recorder sentenced the youth to three months' imprisonment, and Nathan to seven years' transportation.—On hearing the sentence the convict fell upon the floor, and was carried from the bar in the arms of the turnkeys.

When Prince Albert married Queen Victoria in 1840 the English distrusted him, along with the Queen's confidante, Baroness Lehzen (a 'Jerry sneak' was a henpecked husband). But by the time he died of

for these thirteen years jointly by Joseph Knight and Ashby Sterry, offered pleasant discursive articles by Ashby Sterry. They did nothing to protect the position The Sunday Times had won for itself as an authority on art and literature. Very soon even a magazine like The Cornhill had a circulation of 90,000, a figure twice that of the threepenny The Sunday Times.

On the death of E. W. Seale in 1867 his son Edmund Seale became principal proprietor until 1881. The price of the paper during these years came down from 3d to 2½d to 2d.

These were significant years in the development of Fleet Street.

ALARMING ILLNESS OF THE PRINCE CONSORT.

For some days the whole British nation has read with anxious sympathy the medical bulletins issued from Windsor Castle. A mere hint that the Prince Consort was unwell was sufficient to awaken into activity the feeling of respectful affection for her Majesty and her Consort ever present in the British heart. But this feeling has deepened into one of pain, we may say, apprehension. The public heard with pleasure that, up to Thursday, no unfavourable symptoms attended the progress of the malady with which the Prince Consort was unhappily afflicted. One day, however, brought with it a change, and the bulletin of Friday created at once a profound and painful impression. It was as follows :—

"His Royal Highness the Prince Consort passed a restless night, and the symptoms have assumed an unfavourable character during the day.

"JAMES CLARK, M.D.
"HENRY HOLLAND, M.D.
"THOMAS WATSON, M.D.
"WILLIAM JENNER, M.D.

"Windsor Castle, Dec. 13."

The bulletin of yesterday was slightly re-assuring. It was to this effect :—

"The Prince Consort has passed a quiet night, and the severity of the symptoms are a little better.
"Windsor Castle, December 14th, Nine a.m."

The favourable symptoms continued during the morning, and at half-past twelve the "Times" published the following :—

"We are happy to state that an improvement has taken place in the state of his Royal Highness the Prince Consort. The immediate cause of alarm has passed away, and hopes may be entertained for a favourable issue."

These hopes, however, were speedily to be dissipated for a telegram from Windsor, at half-past four in the afternoon, gave the following melancholy announcement :—

"The Prince is in a most critical state, and the physicians who are in attendance upon his royal highness state that another hour will decide whether he lives or dies. A special service has just been held in St. John's Church for the purpose of offering up prayers for the restoration of his royal highness's health. The greatest excitement prevails in the town."

Telegrams received later in the day brought no comfort. The last received stated—

"There is no change in the Prince's condition. He is reported to be neither better nor worse. It is impossible at present to say what may be the result. Four physicians are in attendance."

DEATH OF THE PRINCE CONSORT.

Our readers will learn with inexpressible regret that after a brief but severe illness—the details of which are given in another column—his Royal Highness the Prince Consort expired at Windsor Castle, at about eleven o'clock, on Saty day night, the 14th inst. The melancholy event will take the whole nation by surprise, and will afflict it with the deepest possible sadness. The bulletins issued during Friday and Saturday, though likely to cause anxiety, were not of a nature to create positive alarm. Yesterday afternoon, however, they assumed a more serious form, and the metropolis was kept in a state of the utmost excitement until the intelligence arrived that the illustrious patient had breathed his last. It is impossible to describe the grief and consternation which this announcement created. But one pang seemed to strike upon but one heart. The earnest affection which all classes of the population feel for her Majesty and her family, in the sudden and sore distress which has fallen upon them inspires a sorrow too deep for the mere phrases of ceremonial loyalty. Our united lamentations rise to Heaven in solemn and devout prayers that her Majesty may receive those consolations which only the Infinite and Omnipotent Spirit can communicate. It is too early to estimate at their proper value the character of the departed Prince and the place he filled in the British Empire. History will do full justice to his intelligence, his virtues, and the delicacy as well as the value of his many public services. At the present moment we can do no more than express the poignant concern with which we hear of our beloved and venerated Monarch's bereavement. The whole nation will mourn with her. This day the whole population will bow down before the mysterious heavens in humble but earnest supplications that her heart may be comforted. It would be easy to calculate some of the more momentous

typhoid fever at Windsor Castle in 1861 the Prince Consort was deeply respected, if not loved. These two pieces about his illness and death appeared side by side on December 15.

The Franco-Prussian War of 1870 was the first great animator; the chief daily papers spent – or some of them, at any rate – what was then regarded as amazing money on war correspondents and special correspondents. J. R. Robinson, the manager of The Daily News, for example, staggered his men, who included the famous Archibald Forbes, when he told them that they were to telegraph their copy and hang the cost. They presumed that he meant only pieces of it – the key news – and that their long reports would be sent by mail as usual; telegraphing was still a very costly business. 'No,' he said, 'everything.' The development of the electric tele-

graph in the early 1840s and the laying of the Atlantic cable in
1858 were at last transforming journalism.

Mr Julius Reuter was also on the scene. He came to London in
1858 and introduced himself to James Grant, editor of The
Morning Advertiser:

> I am a Prussian; and have been employed for many years as a Courier
> to several of the Courts of Europe, from the Government of Berlin; and in
> that capacity have formed personal intimacies with gentlemen connected
> with most of the European Governments. It has occurred to me that I
> might, therefore, be able to supply, by telegraph, the daily press of
> London with earlier and more accurate intelligence of importance, and,
> at the same time, at a cheaper rate than the morning journals are now
> paying for their telegraphic communications from the Continent.

He offered Grant a free service for a fortnight, at a charge of
only £30 a month if he found it successful. The Times had already
turned him down (it had, of course, to take Reuter's service later
on), but Grant and the editors of most of the other London
morning papers became delighted subscribers. So Reuter's success
in this country was rapid, and he went on to make a service available to Sunday newspapers. When The Sunday Times took it, in
the 1880s, his charge was £150 a year. It is now, with the trans-
atlantic service, more than £9,000 annually.

But this was after Edmund Seale and his associates had sold
The Sunday Times to a firm called Sylvester & Co., whose two
principal partners were a military and naval combination called
Colonel FitzGeorge and Captain FitzGeorge, RN. Unresponsive
to the wind of change which was blowing down Fleet Street, they
distinguished themselves chiefly by watering down the paper's
coverage of the arts with, as a contemporary put it, 'the smallest of
small-beer chronicles concerning the Services, mixed up with
feeble attempts at wit.' After a time Colonel FitzGeorge took full
control, and he continued as owner until about 1888, selling the
paper then in compliance, as was currently alleged, 'with the wish
of Her Majesty the Queen, who desired him to give up letters and
"live cleanly like a gentleman"'. The colonel and his brother
were the illegitimate sons of the second Duke of Cambridge (d.
1904) by Sarah Louisa Fairbrother.

At this time the little fly-by-night society and financial papers
which flourished strongly in the 1880s and 1890s often carried
gossip about The Sunday Times. On May 28, 1889, The Financial
World had this to say:

LATEST FOREIGN NEWS.

THE GERMANS BEFORE PARIS.

VERSAILLES, FEB. 16, 8.20 A.M.—There can be no doubt that the German troops will enter and probably occupy Paris militarily during the peace negotiations. The absence of any cordial expression in the Queen's speech on the successes during the war has excited disappointment and unfavourable comment here. The Germans have turned all the external works so as entirely to command Paris, and have completed their batteries. We hear that the armistice is prolonged to the 24th of February. Fuel is very much wanted in Paris. Provisions are plentiful. Cardinal Bonnechose was graciously received by the Emperor William the day before yesterday.

THE TERMS OF PEACE.

PARIS, FEB. 16.—The *Figaro* of to-day publishes a letter from Versailles, which gives fresh details of the terms of peace proposed by Prussia. These are:—"The cession of Alsace and Lorraine, and som portions of the department of the Doubs. An indemnity of a milliard and a half of thalers. Prussia to keep all the *matériel* of war acquired. Prussia will not ask for a colony, and the fleet will remain intact." The inhabitants of Metz at present in Lille have sent a protest to-day to the National Assembly against the cession of Lorraine.

PRUSSIAN REQUISITIONS.

HAVRE, FEB. 16 (EVENING).—The Prussians have exacted 300,000fr. at Bernay, under a threat to bombard the town. Prussian impositions continue in Normandy, notwithstanding the armistice.

DIEPPE, FEB. 16, 8 P.M.—An application having been made to the Emperor William at Versailles, supported by the most influential members of the department, he has reduced the war contributions for the whole of the Seine Inférieure by two-thirds. The Prussians are installed at the custom house and receive all payments. Some Prussian soldiers have arrived this afternoon, but after staying a few hours left by train.

THE GERMAN REQUISITIONS.

LILLE, SATURDAY, FEB. 18, 3.40 P.M.—At Sedan the Prussians have demanded payment of the taxes for the last quarter of 1870. On the municipality refusing to comply with this demand, they threatened to take away the leading citizens as prisoners. The Municipal Council thereupon gave way, and has contracted a loan of 210,000 francs to meet this requisition.

Sunday Times.

TOWN EDITION.

LONDON: SUNDAY, FEBRUARY 26, 1871.

The anticipations which we have indulged during the past fortnight are now, we may fairly hope, on the point of realisation. The terrible war between France and Germany has reached its termination. A terrible war, indeed, it has been—matchless not less in horror than in magnitude. But in proportion to the severities of the conflict is the joy with which the advent of peace is welcomed. The reports which reach us just before going to press with our country edition are encouragingly consistent with each other; and they are, moreover, in our own view, in thorough harmony with the probabilities of the case. We cannot, of course, undertake to say, with any pretence to certainty, what the terms of peace are; but that a preliminary treaty of peace has been signed by Count BISMARCK on the one part, and by M. THIERS, M. JULES FAVRE, and M. ERNEST PICARD on the other, can scarcely be doubted. It is alleged that the French commissioners left for Bordeaux on Friday afternoon. We presume that the sanction of the National Assembly to the convention they had agreed to would be asked on Saturday; and that on Sunday morning they would be back at Versailles, fully authorised to conclude a formal compact with the German power.

Our readers will not need to be reminded that we have never been among those who have attributed beforehand the most monstrous rapacity to Germany. We have never failed to recognise the practical severity of German discipline, the stedfastness of German purpose, and the directness and determination of German policy. But we have never believed that it would constitute any part of the tactics of Count MOLTKE or of the diplomacy of Count BISMARCK wantonly to inflict upon France superfluous humiliation and painful sacrifice. We retain these convictions. We do not, we cannot, deny that some ugly instances of cruelty have been presented in the history of this campaign. But these have been occasional and exceptional. It may be

In the Franco-Prussian War of 1870–71 the feeling of Britain was strongly against Germany, but The Sunday Times had a more lenient attitude. Some anti-German wit parodied King William of Prussia's sanctimonious messages to his consort: By right divine, my dear Augusta,/We've had another awful buster;/Ten thousand Frenchmen sent below,/Praise God from Whom all blessings flow.

The *Sunday Times* has passed through some interesting vicissitudes. Once it held the first position as a scholarly and accurate authority on music and the drama. Then it was sold in a violent hurry to three speculators [probably Sylvester & Co.]. All the old and experienced staff was got rid of, and the change was effected in so chaotic a manner that the 'liners' and ordinary newsmongers sent in copy to the old printers, while the new printers were waiting for a supply of literary pabulum that never came. The *Sunday Times* that week was a thing to make the unskilful laugh and the judicious grieve. We believe there were two or three columns left blank.

(It was in such circumstances that The Sporting Times once tore out the weekly 'Queer Story' from Labouchere's 'Truth', prefaced it with the question, 'What does "Truth" mean by this?' and filled up a yawningly empty column.)

At any rate, whether this contretemps actually did occur when the FitzGeorges took over or not, there is no doubt of the identity of the new proprietor. It was a woman, Miss Alice Cornwell (Mrs John Whiteman), the 'Princess Midas' who was born in Essex, went gold-mining in Australia, and struck it rich with the Midas mine in Sulky Gully, Ballarat. She was naturally a sensational figure in London and Australia, and in 1877 she gave birth to Sydney W. Carroll, who was associated with The Sunday Times for many years and whose real name was Whiteman. Ten years later she bought the paper as a present for the war-correspondent Phil Robinson, whom she later married. In the following extract from an interview published in Victoria in 1888 she took it all very breezily:

'It has also been announced that you have become a London news-paper proprietress?'

'Yes,' said Miss Cornwell, 'I bought out the *Sunday Times*, a Conservative paper. It would be called Liberal out here, for mostly what is called Conservative at home is Liberal in Victoria, and so *vice versa*. When I purchased the paper it was only a scissors and paste affair, with hardly any original news. After being placed under the management of Mr Phil Robinson it began to be a splendid paper, and when I left its circulation was rapidly increasing. There are six Sunday papers in London, some of them having very large circulations. Two or three elderly ladies were rather shocked at my becoming proprietress of a Sunday newspaper, until I explained that the work was nearly all done on Saturday. One of the ladies thereupon determined to take the paper but not to read it until Monday. When I go home again shortly to float some more claims the circulation is pretty sure to have more than doubled.'

It was not to be. Though the Cornwell–Robinson régime reduced the price to 1d and boldly entered the ranks of popular journalism, intending, as a contemporary chronicler put it, at once 'to knock the sleepy and expensive Observer on the head' and to fight it out with a new rival, also priced at 1d, The People, the circulation remained miserably unresponsive. Mr Robinson, by all accounts a charming writer, was also a reluctant editor, and he went off to Victoria to see Miss Cornwell and give some lectures, leaving Joseph Hatton, whose 'Journalistic London' is a useful book on the period, to occupy the editorial chair at The Sunday Times, whose offices by now were once more in Salisbury Court, where the first issue was conceived by Henry White.

Robinson came back, brimming with Antipodean news for the paper, in which gold-mines were by no means overlooked. Hatton went to Venice after writing a much-derided interview with Henry Irving, given to him as the great man walked quickly down Bond Street. And neither Robinson nor Hatton is heard of again. Nor, for that matter, is Miss Alice Cornwell, otherwise Mrs John Whiteman, otherwise Mrs Phil Robinson, formally Mrs Stannard Robinson, save for this extract from a Brighton & Hove newspaper, published probably in 1928.

There died at Hove a few days ago an old lady who had passed through eighty years of as romantic a career as any woman of her generation. Born in Essex, the opening years of her adventurous career were devoted to music. Having secured great distinction at the Royal Academy of Music, won several gold medals, and composed a number of songs and pianoforte pieces that secured considerable popularity, her interests after the death of her mother in Australia underwent a sudden and remarkable change. She turned her attention to gold-mining, and had the good fortune to discover one of the richest alluvial gold mines in the colony of Victoria. This was the Midas Mine in Sulky Gully, Ballarat. Her discovery was made in the teeth of strong local scepticism.

Just as suddenly, however, as she had entered this particular sphere of activity she deserted it for the newspaper world. Having heard that the FitzGeorge family were desirous of disposing of the *Sunday Times*, she made it her business to acquire this journal and ran it with considerable distinction for a period of five years. This experience did not complete the range of her achievements, for as Mrs Stannard Robinson she originated the Ladies' Kennel Association and, assisted by the sympathy and interest of the late Queen Alexandra, formed the first dog club to be entirely devoted to the interests of women dog-owners.

She was the mother of Sydney Carroll, the well-known writer on the theatre and film critic of the *Sunday Times*. Her sisters still alive are Lady Hutchinson (the wife of the late Sir George Thompson-Hutchinson) and Mrs Sydney Groom, the novelist.

A remarkable woman. And so, too, was the next virtual proprietor of The Sunday Times, Mrs Frederick Beer, Siegfried Sassoon's aunt, whose husband was 'proprietorially interested', as they said at the time, in The Observer. (Mr Sassoon says explicitly in his book of memoirs, 'The Old Century', 'At that time both The Observer and The Sunday Times, which in those days were rather unobtrusive and retiring newspapers, belonged to Mr Beer, whose father had been a financier.') When Rachel Beer took over The Sunday Times in 1893 it was confidently said that one paper or the other was doomed to die. Mrs Beer denied it. She explained that she wanted a penny paper into which she could inject imperial views. The Daily Telegraph and other papers had, in the 1880s, combined supporting Mr Gladstone's home policy and Disraeli's foreign one. They were jingoists, otherwise patriotic supporters of Lord Beaconsfield in sending, in 1878, a British fleet into Turkish waters to menace the advancing Russians. Mrs Beer was a jingoist. She didn't object, as Pearson's Magazine put it, to things domestic, social, theatrical and artistic enjoying their due place in The Sunday Times, but other matters were to be admitted to her columns, particularly colonial and Indian affairs. There was some predictability in the editorial outlook of both Miss Cornwell, who prospered in the Victorian goldfields, discovered three of the largest nuggets ever found there, and wanted her readers to know about Australia and gold-mining, and Rachel Beer, who had been born in Bombay, had family commercial interests in India, and was an addict of Kipling: she had a standard heading for her main leading article, 'The World's Work', with his 'What should they know of England who only England know?' beneath it. The two ladies seem to have had an eye to business, though within a few years, as we shall see, Mrs Beer was to lose her drive and her happiness.

Mr W. W. Hadley, whose memory went back a long time, believed with a good many other people of the time that the woman who was one of his predecessors in the editorial chair of The Sunday Times was also the true controller of The Observer and that Mr Beer was merely the front-man:

> She became first an occasional contributor to the *Observer*, and then its assistant editor and then – so Fleet Street believed – its editor. Her ambition still unsatisfied, she bought the *Sunday Times* in 1893 and edited it herself – this without relinquishing her position on the staff of the *Observer*. Journalists were amused by this wealthy, slapdash newcomer who edited two rival journals simultaneously and wrote articles for both with equal assurance.

It was at least one way of ending the rivalry between the two papers, which went on doggedly throughout the nineteenth century and reached a peak of obsession, as we shall see, in the 1950s.

Somebody from The Sunday Times who was alive until the spring of 1972 remembered Mrs Beer. Gus Wingrove, head printer, 1946 to 1959, was apprenticed to St Clement's Press, and as a boy he was always having to pop from the works in Portugal Street, behind the Law Courts, to the Strand with proofs for The Sunday

'Princess Midas', proprietor of The Sunday Times and Sydney Carroll's mother (see pages 50–51).

SUNDAY TIMES.

London: SUNDAY, JANUARY 27, 1901.

THE WORLD'S WORK.

"WHAT SHOULD THEY KNOW OF ENGLAND WHO ONLY ENGLAND KNOW?"

The life of our good Queen QUEEN VICTORIA. was not, after all, to be prolonged further to her people. "Worn out with more than sixty years of travail for the land," she passed away peacefully on Tuesday last. To say that the sad event has caused deep and profound grief throughout, not the British Empire only, but the whole world, has become mere commonplace. Nothing can have so much struck the newspaper reader who may have only glanced over the columns of matter which have been published about the death of the Queen than the universality and spontaneity of the feelings of sorrow, and of the warm tributes of admiration and regard it has called forth. The Speaker of the House of Commons did not exaggerate when he remarked that the Queen had passed away "without one single enemy in the world." The desire that her precious life might be spared to her people yet a few years longer was a heartfelt one, and was shared by all, high and low, rich and poor, at home and abroad. But it was not to be gratified. Queen Victoria, full of years and honour, has been gathered to her fathers ; she has left us the sweet memory of a loveable and happy character, a noble example of womanhood. Of her it may be said in degree even more truly than of her beloved Consort, we saw her—

—Through all this tract of years,
Wearing the white flower of a blameless life
Before a thousand peering littlenesses,
In that fierce light which beats upon a throne
And darkens every blot.

The great secret of of Queen Victoria's popularity was the way in which she she identified herself with her people, and shared both their joys and their sorrows. That has never been more strikingly manifested than during the last twelve months of her long and eventful life, when she showed herself so intensely sympathetic with the sufferings and losses occasioned by an unhappy and disastrous war. The kindly way in which Her Majesty exerted herself to visit the hospitals in which were gathered the sick and wounded who had returned from the war, touched a chord of affection in the hearts of her subjects, which riveted more strongly the attachment between Sovereign and people. She was herself a direct sufferer by the war, for it bereaved her of one of her own grandsons. But apart from that personal loss, there is little doubt that recent events in South Africa had laid a load upon Her Majesty's spirits which hastened the final collapse. Although the Queen's death did not come upon us without warning, the nation feels it as a staggering blow, and can hardly be said to realise yet the full extent of its bereavement. In the homes of the people the feeling is general that an old and dear friend—one who was not only a beloved Queen, but in a sense the head of the household—had passed away. For Queen Victoria was truly, as she has so often been styled, the " Mother of her People," the " Great White Mother," as her dark subjects called her. Besides the remembrance of her own sweet and queenly personality she has left us the memory of a long and glorious reign. The Victorian era will live in history as a halcyon period for the British Nation. During its course the people progressed as they never did before in all that goes

Times, whose office over a stamp-shop in the Strand consisted of merely two or three rooms with a maximum staff of five. On Saturdays he used to work three hours' overtime at 3d an hour to take proofs of the leader page to Mrs Beer. He was given 2d for his fare to Mayfair and back, and at Mrs Beer's house at 7 Chesterfield Gardens he would be met by the butler and put in the kitchen with

Opposite : Mrs Rachel Beer, by H. Thadeus Jones.

cakes. Usually he had to wait a long time for the page to be passed, for Mrs Beer was in the habit of falling asleep over it (he somehow got the impression that she drank a little too much at lunch), and the butler would often have to rouse her and remind her that the messenger was still awaiting, at which she would stir herself and tell him to send the boy back in the carriage; so Gus Wingrove, having saved the 1d given him for the return fare, would arrive back in style in an open landau with footman as well as coachman, and be greeted by ribald remarks from printers standing about outside St Clement's Press. (After this he graduated to the reading-room among the correctors of the press, who worked in Victorian times in little hutches like prison-cells, usually in perpetual gaslight, and who were notoriously susceptible to tuberculosis. A spell in the reading-room was considered an essential for all who aspired to become compositors – there is no such rule nowadays.)

Mr Beer was alive when Wingrove called but an invalid confined to his room somewhere heavenwards of that stupefying marble staircase at 7 Chesterfield Gardens which was said to have cost £20,000. It was not a happy house, Siegfried Sassoon recalled, remembering it as he knew it when he was a boy:[1]

All Auntie Rachel's unshadowed years had been before I could remember. She had married in 1887, when both she and Uncle Beer, as we called him, were well under thirty. According to my mother's account of him he was a most sweet-natured and charitable man, but after the first few years the doom of ill health descended on him, and even my earliest impression was of someone rather limp and aimless who drifted into the room with a cigar which seemed more an appurtenance than a cause of contentment to his gentle brown-bearded face. They had no children, and from the first I was aware of Auntie Rachel as a lonely rich woman with an ailing husband.

But Auntie Rachel's despair over the health of Uncle Beer did little to temper her extravagances and idiosyncrasies. She continued to take special trains everywhere, at a cost (it was wonderingly whispered) of a guinea a mile, she wasn't content to dress just her numerous footmen in brown liveries with gilt buttons showing the Beer crest of a pelican feeding its young but even had it clipped out on the back of her little black poodle Zulu. As Mr Beer grew worse, and she became haunted by dread and loneliness, she became vague and lost and late for everything, an

1. *The Old Century*, Faber, 1938.

DEATH
OF THE
EARL OF BEACONSFIELD.

With profound grief we record the death of the Earl of Beaconsfield, which took place at the deceased's house in Curzon Street, Mayfair, at half-past four o'clock on Tuesday morning.

The long struggle is over, and a gap has been made in English politics and literature by the death of Lord Beaconsfield it will be difficult to fill. His writings will certainly still be with us, and for an indefinite number of years England must feel more or less directly the effects of his domestic and foreign policy; but that strange and impressive personality, so calm in will, so active in imagination, so strong to move others without the appearance of being itself deeply stirred, is gone, and the Conservative party has lost an admired, brilliant, and trusted leader.

According to the most reliable accounts, Monday night's bulletin had indicated a decline of strength, and at two in the morning the noble earl lost consciousness. An hour later he was seized with another attack of difficulty of breathing, so serious as to induce the two physicians in attendance to summon Dr. Quain. It was then evident that the end was approaching. Lord Rowton and Lord Barrington, clasping the right hand of Lord Beaconsfield, with Sir Philip Rose and the physicians, stood by the bedside watching until the noble earl passed away, in the words of the final bulletin, "calmly, as if in sleep."

These 'Vanity Fair' cartoons of Disraeli (d. 1881) and Gladstone (d. 1898) are by the great 'Ape' (Carlo Pellegrini). Max Beerbohm never saw the Disraeli caricature but he burst out laughing.

MR. GLADSTONE.

A "STATE" OR A "PUBLIC" FUNERAL?

OFFICIAL STATEMENT.

SCENES AT HAWARDEN YESTERDAY.

FURTHER MESSAGE FROM THE PRINCE OF WALES.

SYMPATHETIC TELEGRAMS FROM ABROAD.

ANXIETY ABOUT MRS. GLADSTONE.

increasingly distraught figure whose highly fashionable clothes seemed rightly to belong to some more serene beauty. To the boy Siegfried his paternal aunt seemed in the year in which she gave up The Sunday Times, 1897, to be more absent-minded than ever (his mother put it down to those wretched sleeping draughts), 'though her amusingness and charm were always apparent. While we were showing her round the garden I picked a rose for her, and couldn't help noticing when she took it that her hand with its magnificent rings was positively grimy. When had she last taken off her rings, I wondered.' Touchingly, when Mr Beer died in 1902, shadowy to the last, she kept his park hack at livery, at a cost of some £700, until it died also. She herself lived on until 1927.

Mr Hadley said that Mrs Beer edited the paper herself. More likely she was editor-in-chief, and certainly in the early 1890s she had a working editor named Arthur à Beckett (1891–5), son of one of the founders of Punch. Arthur at this time was also assistant editor of Punch, and in an abysmally dreary and slapdash book of memoirs he explains how he combined the jobs:

> I was able to assist to edit *Punch*, and at the same time to wholly edit the *Sunday Times*. . . . On Saturdays my work commenced without exaggeration at 4 am, and without a break – for I was reading proofs at my meals – continued until 4 am the next morning. At that time the final revisions of the *Punch* proofs were prepared for press at 8 am on Sunday morning . . . after filling up odd corners – two lines here, three there, and so on – with jokes made on the spur of the moment, I completed the pages of *Punch* and sent them back to Bouverie Street by the waiting messenger. When there were no suitable jokes in the overset I supplied them, and this further exercise of my brain fairly exhausted me.

Beckett was one of those many inexplicable Victorian and Edwardian journalists who, with a notable paucity of talent, managed to float from one important job to another. He had gone from The Sunday Times, though, by the time Mrs Beer gave up in 1897. It is said that the solicitor representing Mr Beer's estate offered both The Sunday Times and The Observer to R. D. Blumenfeld for £5,000 in 1903 or so. The proposal was declined.

IX

In the earlier part of the second half of the nineteenth century the English quality press lived in a brief, disastrous state of euphoria.

All the wrong conclusions were drawn from the Education Act of 1870. It was supposed that this would greatly increase the public for intelligent newspapers, for papers that carried informed articles on foreign affairs, vigorous and closely-argued political editorials, and careful and responsible reviews of plays, operas, and concerts. It was on this assumption that cultivated morning and evening newspapers in London bided their time.

True, the Elementary Education Act did, as had been fore-seen, create a new body of readers. But they were not readers who wanted anything like The Times, The Sunday Times or The Observer. These papers were too recondite for them. The existence of this new public was first revealed by the enormous success of George Newnes's Titbits, which consisted not only of original articles but of snippets of information taken from other publications, all bright, snappy and brief. This unforeseen triumph of the partially educated inspired Alfred Harmsworth in 1896 to found The Daily Mail on the same principles, and with the same astounding success, even if his Daily Mail was by modern standards certainly not as lightweight as all that. These developments were not only a direct challenge to papers of quality; they actually altered the outlook and modified the contents and treatment of such papers. Thus the half century before the first world war was marked by the decline of the quality press, as the years after the second were notable in journalism for its resurgence.

At a time when it was more necessary than at any previous period for such papers to be at the peak of their performance, The Times made a series of blunders which culminated in the extraordinary incident of the Parnell forgeries. The Parnell letter was a plausible fake: The Times's own legal adviser, Sir Henry James, when he was asked for his opinion of the document, told the editor of the paper that its validity was doubtful. In these circumstances, and with this advice, it is astonishing that The Times should have taken the reckless step of challenging Parnell to sue it for libel. Even W. T. Stead of the Pall Mall Gazette, a man never out-standing for worldly wisdom or caution, had refused to have anything to do with the alleged Parnell letters. At first The Times hesitated to use a facsimile of the famous letter 'No. 2', which threw a shameful light on Parnell's denunciation of the Phoenix Park murders in the House of Commons. Inglis, the foremost handwriting expert of the time, was convinced that Parnell had signed this letter, though the text was admittedly in another hand. When, however, Sir Henry James revealed that he had seen the letters before, The Times, while retaining its confidence in their authenticity, decided to undertake 'a comprehensive survey of the whole course of the murder conspiracy in Ireland,' called 'Parnellism and Crime', and culminate it with publication of the letters.

Parnell cannily refused to take legal action when the 'No. 2' letter was published by The Times in facsimile and instead asked the House of Commons to appoint a select committee to inquire into its genuineness. The Government made the counter-offer, which was accepted, of a special commission, composed of three judges, to examine the charges contained in 'Parnellism and Crime'. But the expense of calling nearly 500 witnesses – a strange injustice – was ordered to fall upon The Times, and it well-nigh ruined it. Against this, the £5,000 it paid to settle a libel action tardily started by Parnell was a fleabite. The villain of the whole bizarre affair, perhaps the greatest political thriller of the nineteenth century, was a seedy Irish journalist named Richard Pigott, who forged the letters and committed suicide by shooting himself in a hotel in Madrid at the moment of his arrest.

The whole Parnell affair, which was not concluded till 1890, cost The Times more than £200,000 and – what was worse – its hitherto impeccable reputation for accuracy. But The Times was able to offset, to a large extent, its decline in journalistic acumen by introducing many refinements of professional management.

The Sunday Times was less skilful and less fortunate. It navigated these stormy waters, where a strong sense of direction was necessary, either with a hand at the rudder that was frequently changed, or even, in the Joseph Knight–Ashby Sterry period, with no hand at all. The most assiduous and intelligent reader of The Sunday Times at this period of its history and later in the nineteenth century could not gain from it a coherent picture of what the world was like nor form from its columns a sensible estimate of its artistic achievements.

Miss Cornwell lowered the price to 1d but kept it at eight pages. The only significant changes took place in the advertisements. There were more of them and they became more striking, particularly the abundant and, even then, slightly despised patent medicine advertisements, the undue prominence of which in any newspaper, then or now, is usually a sign of desperation. On April 21, 1889, half of one page was divided into three columns and headed across the entire page-width 'She Was an Angel of Mercy'. This turned out to be not Florence Nightingale but Mother Seigel of the syrup. On page 2 the most prominent feature was a column-long advertisement for 'Clark's World-famed Blood Mixture'. Yet these advertisements caught the eye as did nothing else in the paper. They were by far its most outstanding typographical features.

The editorial columns had none of this adventurous and effective vulgarity. There was no variety in typography or presentation. Nevertheless, the leading articles maintained their vigorous standard, and it is true that at the end of December, 1902, The Sunday Times was one of the first papers in the world to recognise the existence of a new force in entertainment, the cinema. But this somewhat bleak awareness of innovating aims in the artistic world was not matched by a corresponding grasp of other aspects of life. In 1903, for example, the news coverage was still scrappy and perfunctory: there seems to have been no co-ordinating hand at all in this section of the paper. Typographically, and for simple human interest for that matter, the advertisements, sometimes using double columns, and making generous use of white space (Peter Robinson, a sale at Fenwicks, State Express cigarettes), were still far ahead of any other part of the paper.

These advertisements were often illustrated with line blocks, a form of illustration arising from the impact of photography in the middle of the nineteenth century. By then it had become common practice for the surface of a wood block to be sensitised so that a photographic image could be exposed on it for the wood engraver to work on and produce a relief block. Metal could be sensitised in the same manner, and from the process emerged what is known as the line block. For the most part The Sunday Times of this period and long after did very little to illustrate its editorial columns. It could not show itself so out of date as to perpetuate the woodenness – in both senses – of the old style of engraving, and it was aloof, as were other quality newspapers, to the experiments in the 1890s and onwards with the half-tone block. The Daily Mirror, the first daily newspaper to be illustrated exclusively with mechanical blocks, appeared in 1904, but it was not until the 1920s that really satisfactory half-tones began to be printed in rotary-produced newspapers. Even as late as 1930 The Sunday Times, like The Times and The Observer, was using half-tones very sparingly: there was still a suspicion of vulgarity about them, apart from the feeling that a serious newspaper would lose its mission and become 'popular' if it used too many pictures.

Haphazard management and lack of editorial policy were

Sunday Times and Sunday Special.

[Registered at the G.P.O. as a Newspaper.]   LONDON, JANUARY 31, 1904.

Sunday Times and Sunday Special.

JANUARY 31, 1904.

AVE ATQUE VALE.

One bleak Sunday morning towards the close of the Diamond Jubilee year, 1897, a newspaper, bearing the alliterative title of "THE SUNDAY SPECIAL," quietly and unostentatiously entered the arena of Sunday journalism, with the firm but unadvertised determination to compete with formidable rivals and to beat anything save a retreat. The infant paper was on sale that Sunday morning, December 5, 1897, at many bookstalls and street corners, and an indulgent public spent their pennies out of curiosity. Patrons of other papers felt that the newcomer—no matter how shortlived its career—would furnish just that impetus which was necessary to stimulate their old friends to maintain their already high standard, and gladly they invested their coppers by way of vicarious encouragement.

By degrees the stimulus became the rival. But it was an uphill task at first, and no Royal Road was discovered; none indeed was explored. The management determined to gain their public by real worth; they backed themselves to win by the exhibition of talent, not by "talents" concealed. No placards announcing "hidden gold" were employed to further the sale, and the progress of the young journal at first was comparatively slow. The voyage of the best ship is a zigzag line of a hundred tacks, and "The Sunday Special" had to steer through the rough weather of the war and the national depression which accompanied it. But in good times and in bad times alike, the paper never lost sight or hold of its ideals, and during the past two years its ultimate triumph has been assured.

Of all the Sunday papers the old-established and popular "Sunday Times" held out as long as possible against its younger rival, until at last the continued and increasing success of "The Sunday Special" begat in the proprietors of the "Sunday Times" that discretion which is the better part of valour and occasioned the surrender now completed by the purchase of the senior paper by its prosperous junior. The question of the title of the amalgamated journals resolved itself into a conflict between sentiment and business instincts, ending in a drawn battle. The best features of both papers were to be preserved—why not both names? And so it comes about that, having due regard for the old axiom, "seniores priores," the latest "combine" is issued to-day for the first time with the joint title of both papers. In the numbers which follow there will be no departure from those principles which have invariably guided the two contracting parties in the past, and, starting with an assured circulation never yet equalled by a Sunday paper of first-class standing, the "SUNDAY TIMES AND SUNDAY SPECIAL," a paper of many parts and no Party, cannot fail to take a prominent and, in many ways, unique position among the influential organs of public opinion.

bound in the end to have a deleterious effect on The Sunday
Times. In December, 1897, a new rival, The Sunday Special,
sprang into existence and met with some success. Late in 1903 it
bought up The Sunday Times. From the conclusion of January,
1904, the two papers were merged, but although The Sunday
Special was the more prosperous of the pair the joint issue continued the name of The Sunday Times, which it was evidently
considered had by then acquired an historic value. The new editor
was, however, the editor of The Sunday Special, Leonard Rees,
and the new proprietors were the proprietors of The Sunday
Special, a company of which a German, Hermann (or George)
Schmidt, was chairman.

The change did not solve the basic journalistic problems of The
Sunday Times. Indeed, Mr Hadley thought that during the
continuance of Schmidt and his partners the paper was at the
nadir of its fortunes and merits.

We shall hear more in this book of Schmidt and his partners
(who operated until 1915), as well as of Leonard Rees. Theirs was
a rescue operation without which The Sunday Times might have
perished.

THE "SUNDAY TIMES."

The controlling interest in THE SUNDAY TIMES has been acquired by W. E. and J. Gomer Berry, of the firm of Ewart, Seymour, and Co., Limited, Windsor House, Kingsway, W.C., publishers.

June 6, 1915

The Camrose Era
1915–1936

The Camrose Era

I

James White (not our first editor Henry White) was a jovial red-faced villain with a bowler hat, a clipped moustache and a strong north-country accent: if his life had remained centred on Rochdale, where he began as a bricklayer's lad in 1878, he would probably have been recognisable as the bent sergeant-major-type who loves betting and boxing and beer and women and fiddling the accounts. He had in him, however, large ambitions, and these took him in 1907 from the Midlands to London, where he became a wheeler-dealer and dodged about on the fringes of show business, attempting at last to join the big-time by promoting a fight between Jack Johnson, the Negro, one of the greatest of all champions, and Bombardier Billy Wells (who much later struck the gong at the beginning of Rank films), a tall fair boxer with a beautiful body which was apt to prove rather frail when he encountered someone like the Frenchman Carpentier, let alone a fighter as terrible as Jack Johnson.

When the Home Secretary intervened and asked for the fight to be called off, Jimmy White was in serious financial straits: no bank would look at him, no moneylender accept his paper. He went to his friend Camrose, who as William Ewert Berry owned, with his brother James Gomer, the magazine Boxing, and begged for a monkey, a couple of hundred, a pony – anything. The Berry brothers had made a great success of Boxing; it had started with a print of 100,000 and had now reached a quarter of a million, with a doubled price for big-fight numbers; but they were still struggling, and there was little money to spare. All the same, Bill Berry liked Jimmy White, much as he may have deplored his addiction to betting, women, and whisky, and he believed in him. He went to his friends and raised £500, which White duly repaid. White let many people down, but never Bill Berry. The curious friendship between the Welsh Methodist and the Lancashire civilian sergeant-major continued and never weakened.

Not much of the wisdom of Jimmy White, who was a rough

diamond to the end, has been preserved, but he once told a crony that the smartest thing he had ever done in his early days was to become associated with boxing, for it was there that you met the boys with money to burn.

White became a financier. From Ernest Terah Hooley, a dishonest but very prominent old company promoter, he picked up the tricks of the trade, and from this apprenticeship he passed to a close association with Sir Joseph Beecham, another Lancashire man and one who had built up the Beechams pills business and spent a fortune backing the musical ventures of his son Thomas. He was persuaded that in White he had come across a financier of genius, and he knew what he was talking about, making allowance for The Times's haughty denial, published on the morning after White's death, that the man was a financier at all – 'he was looked upon rather as a particularly bold speculator, with a passion for deals on a large scale, with corresponding risks.'

At one time White must have had four millions in the kitty, but in the end they turned out to be fairy gold. He was out-manoeuvred in a Stock Exchange showdown and needed to raise £900,000 immediately. He couldn't do it. He who had despised 'moogs' all his life had been caught like a mug.

So he gave up. At 6.15 on the evening of Tuesday, June 28, 1927, he left his home at 21 Park Street and went by car to Foxhill, his house and training stables near Swindon. There he told the butler and the other servants to take the night off and not to call him until noon. At lunch-time they found him with a bottle of prussic acid near by and a sponge which had been soaked in chloroform pressed over his mouth. There was a note to his butler Williams: 'Go easy with me, old man – I'm dead from prussic acid.' There was, as somebody said, 'not a bob left'.

Sir William Berry was at the funeral. After all, James White had once been a director of The Sunday Times Ltd.[1]

II

It began, this triangular association between William Berry, James White and The Sunday Times, at the National Liberal Club in Whitehall Place.

---

1. Information from a private source.

Berry had taken to going there, but for a different reason from F. E. Smith, the first Earl of Birkenhead. According to the old story, the famous F. E. was seen to enter the club from time to time, swinging his umbrella nonchalantly and making for the washroom. He would reappear after a short interval, bid the porter a condescending good-bye, and depart. The secretary of the club came to hear of these visits, and he grew marble-eyed with annoyance: F. E. Smith was a Tory, not a Liberal, and in any case the man wasn't a member. So when F. E. made his next visit the secretary trapped him. 'I say, sir, correct me if I'm wrong, but I don't think you're a member of this club.' F. E. looked amazed. 'Club? What do you mean club? I thought it was a public lavatory!'

William Berry went there for strictly business reasons. He and his brother were by now looking round for their first newspaper, and it was a place where you heard things. Boxing and a few smaller periodicals were not enough. The brothers were eager for a bigger deal.

They were the sons of a Merthyr Tydfil estate agent and alderman, John Berry, and there was a third brother, Seymour, the eldest. All three became peers, and Seymour a tycoon who acquired huge interests in coal, iron, and steel. But when William came to London in 1898 from a decently prosperous and godfearing Welsh home he could expect little financial help from the family. He had left school at 14 and served for a year on The Merthyr Times under his patron W. W. Hadley. After other little journalistic jobs in South Wales he arrived in London. He was a reporter on The Investors' Guardian at 35s a week and was then out of work for three months, successfully hiding the fact from his parents. He went to the Commercial Press Association, again as a reporter, and while there attracted the attention of the great Alfred Harmsworth. It was at a meeting of Harmsworth Brothers (later to be bought by the Berrys and called the Amalgamated Press), and William's knowledge of company law – he was always a financier as well as a newspaper man – was already sufficient to allow him to make some suggestion about a point of procedure. Northcliffe was impressed and after the meeting, it is said, invited Berry to apply to him for a job. But the young lion may for some reason have been wary of the older lion. Nothing came of the encounter.

In any case he was soon to start – on £100 lent him by Seymour – a periodical of his own, The Advertising World, the first of its kind in this country. He wrote most of it himself, canvassed for the advertisements himself, did the lay-out himself, and when it began to make a profit he brought Gomer to London to look after the advertising and administration. He was 23 by now and may have thought it time to do his first real deal – both of the brothers had a passionate love of buying and selling newspapers. So they sold The Advertising World and started a small publishing company from which they founded Boxing in 1909. Now, some five years later, they wanted to get out of the alleys and cellars of small periodical publishing into the national sphere.

Then one day early in 1915 James White lunched with William Berry at the National Liberal Club.

White had control of the Beecham Trust and wouldn't look at any deal less than £250,000 – as he explained, a small 'un takes up as much time as a big 'un. He went into the mustard-coloured dining-room with Berry, and there was West de Wend Fenton, who had at about this time bought The Sporting Times, otherwise known as The Pink 'Un, and seen its celebrated staff walk out and start a rival paper, Town Topics. At the end of his lunch he came over to their table and said that he had an option to buy The Sunday Times. Was Bill Berry interested? Sydney Carroll, whose mother had owned the paper in the 1880s, used to say that Fenton first offered it to the Liberal Party but found them uninterested, possibly because the war was on and its chief proprietor, Hermann Schmidt, was a German who had been naturalised as a British subject but was now interned.

Carroll, a large Australian with a rasping voice, was associated with the Berrys in these early days and afterwards. He had a little group of periodicals of his own, and he was successively dramatic critic of The Sunday Times in the 1920s, film critic up to 1939, and then editor of Kemsley's Daily Sketch. Through all his life there remained something tough and rough and open-air about him, a flavour of the Australian gold-diggings; and indeed he had managed a gold mine and sold books at Cole's Arcade in Sydney, apart from starting the Open Air Theatre in Regent's Park.

At any rate, Fenton's offer must have electrified William Berry, and James White, with the Beecham Trust money behind him, immediately offered to help him out until he could make satisfactory arrangements with his bank.

It is believed that the Berrys ran into many difficulties and hindrances with the partners in The Sunday Times other than the interned Schmidt, who presumably had very little voice in the proceedings himself, though one of the others may have been his representative. They were a bizarre trio: Sir Basil Zaharoff, the notorious arms agent; Sir Arthur Steel-Maitland, M P, then chairman of the Conservative Party and later Minister of Labour, and always a very respected and honourable politician; and Sir Leander Starr Jameson, Bt, who carried out the sensational 'Raid' over the Transvaal border in 1895 and had been Prime Minister of Cape Colony before he retired from South Africa in 1912 and came to live mostly in London – the famous 'Doctor Jim' whose rôle in this little affair of The Sunday Times may have escaped attention.

The same can be said of Zaharoff. Not even his biographer, Mr Donald McCormick, now foreign manager of The Sunday Times, knew that his quarry was in the deal. But then everything connected with Zaharoff is a mystery – his nationality, his age, his marriages, the precise details of his activities – for he had a habit of suppressing evidence and even altering public documents like birth certificates.

But Mr McCormick has established certain facts about the association of Zaharoff with Vickers, from whom he received enormous sums in commission-money and, more to the point, his habit in the years before the first world war of acquiring either direct ownership of French newspapers or a hidden interest in them. Such publications became the vehicles of his unobtrusive propaganda for, to take an elementary example, the superior virtues of the particular machine-gun or submarine which he was selling.

It is unthinkable that a man so notorious should have been allowed to maintain any financial interest in The Sunday Times after the Berrys bought it, but Camrose is believed to have kept up friendly correspondence with him. In 1929 a young man writing literary notes for The Daily Telegraph was told that Victor Gollancz, the publisher, had a book coming out about Zaharoff and that he was to try, without saying that Lord Camrose was interested, to bring back an advance copy of it. But Gollancz merely stared owlishly at the visitor, his hair like a wild halo round his head, and said that no advance copies of this particular book were available. Perhaps Zaharoff, who died in 1936, wanted to try to buy it up and suppress it.

And Sir Arthur Steel-Maitland? It is possible – he was a man of considerable fortune – that at some time he had taken a financial interest in the paper on his own account, as a Conservative watchdog. Up to the first world war rich men with political ambitions were always buying papers, running them at a loss for a few years, then selling them to the next aspirant down the line.

At any rate, the negotiations were concluded at last and the Berry brothers had their long-desired national paper. James White soon ceased to be a director of The Sunday Times. Newspapers were far from being his spiritual home.

III

They were lucky in the time of their purchase of the paper. Up to the first world war, as we have seen, Sunday journals were thought to be ungodly and were frowned on alike by the majority of the upper class, the middle class and the working class. Both The Daily Telegraph and The Daily Mail had enterprisingly started Sunday editions in the Boer War, but they had to abandon them after a few weeks because of the antagonism of Nonconformist ministers and the concern publicly expressed by Lord Rosebery, who was among other things an eminent figure on the turf. It is true that The News of the World was selling a million at the time of the Boer War, or very soon after it, but in the eyes of the many it epitomised the whole case against Sunday newspapers, with the emphasis it placed on crime and sexual squalor, which was the simple, enduring, and highly profitable formula it adopted after it was acquired by the Carr family in 1891.

In any case, secular reading of any kind on Sunday was not permitted in many homes, and the offence of the Sunday journals was the more grave because to the ungodliness of their contents was added the profanation of their being distributed and sold on the Lord's Day – the pearl of days as the Sabbatarians called it. They were thus, even the more respectable of them, such as The Sunday Times and The Observer, held to be the reading of unworthy citizens, and their circulations were tiny because everything they represented was rejected by honest folk who lived elsewhere than in cities and towns. Which was just as well, because it was highly difficult to get the Sunday papers to out-of-the-way places and almost as difficult to find anyone to sell them if you did.

By 1915, however, the old moral iciness was being thawed by the war and young readers were beginning to think less about the profanation of the pearl of days and more about being entertained and instructed on it. Sir Edward Hulton, who published The

Daily Sketch, sensed this changed attitude to Sabbatarianism in 1915 when he planned to launch the first illustrated Sunday paper (it duly appeared as The Illustrated Sunday Herald) and was beaten to it by a week or so by Lord Rothermere, of The Daily Mirror, who inevitably heard of what Hulton was up to and pipped him by brazenly scrambling together, with The Daily Mirror staff, the first issue of The Sunday Pictorial. This paper introduced its readers to the godly and patriotic exhortations of the editor of 'John Bull', Horatio Bottomley, and he became the favourite of a very large public, innocent of the fact that he was one of the biggest scoundrels of the time. In this and other ways the odium attaching to the Sunday paper began to disappear, particularly as the two new picture papers did not depend on crime or sex and could be introduced into the most righteous home.

War news and comment was helping all the existing Sunday papers too, particularly The Observer, the oldest of the London Sunday journals. Its editor and part-proprietor, J. L. Garvin, had become the oracle of the middle classes. By 1915 his paper had reached a circulation of 200,000, and his own contributions to it were approaching the length and punditry which made it the butt of humorists in the 1930s; even now they were spreading sometimes from the leader page to the main news page opposite. (News on the front page came much later.) Its only rival in what we now call the quality field was The Sunday Times, but The Sunday Times was trailing like an old hackney horse behind The Observer and was still essentially a provincial paper published in London. It had, however, picked up a few typographical and other tricks from its rival, and between 1912 and 1915, in which last year the Berrys took it over, it was beginning to bear some resemblance to what we should regard as a modern metropolitan paper.

The brothers paid at least £75,000 for it, which was a rather different story from the £5,000 put down for it by Hermann Schmidt in 1904. In the following year £5,000 was paid by Lord Northcliffe for The Observer; it had declined from its early nineteenth-century position and become of little importance, selling only a couple of thousand copies a week. Northcliffe persuaded J. L. Garvin to become editor in 1908, and like Barnes of The Times, Garvin asked for and obtained a share of the profits. But when he fell out with Northcliffe in 1911 on a political matter – he was a tariff reformer and in favour of taxes on food – this financial interest complicated the situation, and Northcliffe offered to sell the paper to him and gave him three weeks to find a buyer.

By coming up with one of the richest men in the world, William Waldorf Astor, who already owned The Pall Mall Gazette and who now bought The Observer for his son Waldorf, later the second Viscount Astor, Garvin is responsible for the confusion which existed in the public mind between The Observer Astors and (before Lord Thomson) The Times Astors. Northcliffe may have made one of his very few blunders when he let The Observer go, but he was essentially a newspaper and magazine creator and not a jobber in newspaper properties; and, anyway, Garvin *was* The Observer. (Garvin also edited Astor's Pall Mall Gazette, but that was a less happy story.)

Time has proved that the two Astors (The Observer was formally made over to the son in 1915) had a good buy, but the Berrys had an even better one. The respective circulations of The Observer and The Sunday Times in 1915, when William Berry installed himself as editor-in-chief, were 200,000 and 30,000 – which makes an observation by David Astor in 1969 that 'in 1956 we passed The Sunday Times circulation for the first time this century' rather mysterious.[1] Gradually this numerical superiority was reduced, and in 1933 The Sunday Times passed The Observer. Henceforth, except for a shaky moment in the mid-1950s, which will be related in its place, The Sunday Times was always ahead. The average figures for the first quarter of the year of writing, 1972, are The Sunday Times 1,450,000 and The Observer 803,000.

It could not have been circulation which the Berrys paid £75,000 for in 1915 – 30,000 copies a week was very poor and the paper was losing money. It must have been for potentiality and for a wartime boom in advertising which was just beginning to show. Not only was ordinary displayed advertising increasing, but Government advertising – recruiting appeals, patriotic messages, and so on – was making a spectacular show in The Sunday Times and The Observer, just as it was, in modified form, in the daily papers. It may have been intended as a covert subsidy for the press, a dole to save the weaker papers from going under. But whatever the reason The Sunday Times was showing signs of a paradoxical prosperity on June 1, 1915, when a four-line paragraph without a heading appeared at the bottom of a column in The Times: 'The controlling interest in The Sunday Times has been acquired by W. E. and

---

1. Smith's Trade News, February 1, 1969.

Opposite: William Ewert Berry, first Viscount Camrose.

J. Gomer Berry, of the firm of Ewart, Seymour & Co. (Limited), Windsor House, Kingsway, Publishers.'

On the following Sunday the same paragraph appeared, almost as obscurely, in The Sunday Times itself. Near it was a double-column advertisement which concluded: '*You* must join your King's Army and learn to sing "God Save the King" with a gun in your hands.'

I V

The name of the Berrys' firm suggests that the eldest brother, Seymour, had an interest in it, and he did. It was only a modest one, though, the £100 already mentioned, and this first Seymour (the second is the present Viscount Camrose) was never deflected from coal, iron, steel and shipping companies in South Wales. He had trained to become a schoolteacher but went instead into partnership with his father, and it was when he was extending the family estate agent and auctioneer's business that he attracted the attention of Lord Rhondda, Food Controller in the first war and a man of immense possessions in South Wales industries. Seymour was his protégé, and Seymour became, before being killed in 1926 while out riding, chairman of Guest, Keen & Nettlefolds, of John Lysaght, of Joseph Sankey, and the owner or chairman of many collieries and shipping concerns. He must have been a business genius, as Camrose was a newspaper genius.

There was deep brotherly affection between all three brothers, but Camrose was the architect of his own fortunes and the name 'Ewart' in the periodical publishing firm was his own, or very nearly so: he had been named by his staunch Liberal father after William Ewart Gladstone, but something went wrong with the spelling of the second name and he was christened 'Ewert'.

He was now nearly thirty-six. Tall, powerfully built, handsome, calm, optimistic, unimpulsive. He was always unimpulsive. When he bought The Daily Telegraph thirteen years later he addressed a meeting of the fearful staff, accustomed to the paternalism of its old chief, Lord Burnham, at the Memorial Hall in Farringdon Street, with the editor of the paper, Arthur Watson, in the chair. To add to the staff's alarm The Times had cattily remarked in a leading article that morning that Lord Camrose was getting al-together too powerful and omnipresent: already he owned the

James Gomer Berry, first Viscount Kemsley.

largest group in the country, Allied Newspapers, and it could happen that a journalist who left one of his papers through an honest disagreement might find it difficult to get another job. Undisturbed, Camrose promised his hearers gradualness, nothing violent. He was, in fact, so gradual with The Daily Telegraph that it took him five or six years to realise only the ground plan of the paper he wanted. With The Sunday Times, though the job was easier, he was if anything even more restrained, understandably: it was, after all, his first big paper.

In all this he was very different from Lord Kemsley, who could be the most impulsive man alive. Rather absurdly, The Times spent light-years in experiment before they put news on the front page. Kemsley decided on it one weekend early in 1941 and had it there the next. He changed the name of The Daily Sketch – it sounded altogether too sketchy, he said – back to its original Daily Graphic at a speed which struck panic into his circulation staff. There was something youthful and endearing about these shattering crescendos, particularly if they were observed from a suitable distance. It was different when, in 1959, he sold out everything to Roy Thomson with a fantastic lack of premeditation, for he repented of his action even more swiftly, and disappeared like a torpedoed battleship from the light of common day.

Cannily, Camrose did not want a Garvin or a Spender or somebody with a political mission as editor of The Sunday Times. As he has said himself, 'More than one newspaper has been ruined by the brilliant writer placed in the editor's chair.' Nor was he looking for a powerful personality of any kind – it is not a good idea in Fleet Street to have two lions in one cage. So Leonard Rees, who had been editor of The Sunday Special when it took over The Sunday Times in 1904, peppery but governable, was kept on, just as Arthur Watson, round-eyed behind his spectacles, taller even than Camrose himself, an impressively aloof figure as he stalked the corridors with his right fist always in his trouser pocket, remained at The Daily Telegraph as managing editor (for some reason he never had the superior title of editor), a good but not too brilliantly good head.

V

Money was tight at Windsor House, Kingsway. There was a girl called Grace Pugh, now Mrs Will Sandford, who went to Ewart, Seymour Ltd (another company was soon formed called The Sunday Times Ltd) straight from school in 1915, and sometimes she was sent out to the West End to collect a few pounds from newsagents on behalf of the paper. She remembers:

My first post was with Mr G. B. Hewett, secretary of the company, which was then a private one. Often when cash was rather short in the office he would ask me to go and collect accounts from various newsagents in the West End. Some of those shops around Leicester Square were rather frightening to a youngster like me, and I used to enter them rather fearfully – sometimes I would collect the cash but more often I got a rebuff.

I was very pleased when I was transferred to the editorial department. In those days there was the editor, news editor and manager of the office and two girls who covered all the work. There was no literary editor (this work being done by the editor) and only a part-time sports editor and City editor. I became the editor's secretary in 1920 and retained that position until I retired in 1959, there having been only three editors in all those forty years.

Miss Pugh saw something of Mr William Berry in these early days. It was only a small office, and he and Leonard Rees were in touch throughout the week about Sunday's paper.

It would not be true to say that a political line was being evolved, because the war had confused all that. When Lloyd George became Prime Minister in December 1916 The Sunday Times inevitably supported him. Unthinkable that William Berry could have opposed a man who had been given dictatorial powers to win the war and who was a Welshman besides. In any case, as time was to show, the Berrys were natural Conservatives and upholders of authority, even if they imagined at this time that they were Liberal in their political outlook. Lloyd George was a sacred symbol to them, but Gomer at least would have been deeply shocked if he had known then that the Prime Minister was called 'The Goat' privately at Westminster because of his womanising.

A year after Lloyd George succeeded Asquith as Prime Minister there occurred the incident of the Lansdowne Letter. It proposed a compromise peace, and it was a shock to the country because the writer of it, the fifth Marquess of Lansdowne, had been Governor-General of Canada, Viceroy of India, Foreign Secretary and, latterly, Minister without Portfolio. He sent it to The Times in November, 1917, at the darkest hour of the war so far, when Russia was defeated and useless and the Bolsheviks had seized power and come to terms with Germany. The Times refused to publish it and Lord Burnham's Daily Telegraph, smarting as always under the certainty of the eminent that The Times was the only place for their letters, cocked a bold snook at Printing House Square and used it.

The proposals of the letter, including a plea for the return to the *status quo ante bellum*, were unrealistic, but the uproar was immense, as it would have been if say Lord Halifax had called for a surrender to Hitler after the fall of France in 1940. It was The Sunday Times's first real test under its new owners, for mere conventional denunciation was not enough, and it came out of it with distinction. By now the headings of the articles on the leader page were set in the type known as Cheltenham, with the by-lines and cross-headings in a small size of the same fount. It was a style which persisted, with slight variations, throughout feature pages of the paper for a long time, and it had a peculiar effectiveness. It was used to display 'Two representative views' of the Letter, published in single-column on the leader page side by side, one a decent straight-forward attack on it by Lord Sydenham, a bigwig of the time, the other a rollickingly bitter savaging of Lord Lansdowne by G. K. Chesterton. The leading article itself, adjoining, was in that tone of exasperated charity culminating in a crushing finale which marks the outstanding operator. Berry and Rees, clearly, were doing nicely (though connoisseurs of press jealousy will be right in not expecting to find any reference to The Daily Telegraph). Clearly a new Sunday Times was beginning to emerge, the ghost of Hermann Schmidt was being exorcised at last.

But less than a year later everything nearly ended. The paper might have been sold to Lord Beaverbrook.

It is a curious story. In 1918 Lloyd George hoped to see The Daily Chronicle become the official organ of the Liberal Party. He mentioned this several times to its editor, Sir Robert Donald, and then there blew up the great Maurice controversy, which has an historic interest because it led to the factious fight with Lloyd George on one side and Asquith on the other which caused the suicide of the Liberal Party.

General Sir Frederick Maurice was Director of Military Operations at the War Office, and when he was dismissed, as a consequence of Lloyd George's fight with the generals, he risked prosecution by writing to The Times and accusing the Prime Minister of lying about our military strength. Savage passions were aroused in the House of Commons debate, and when, after Lloyd George had triumphed, Sir Robert Donald seemed to lend his support to Maurice, the Prime Minister thought it was time for his rich supporters, headed by Sir Henry Dalziel, to buy The Daily Chronicle in order that its 'loyalty' on future occasions might be beyond question. They discovered that its owner, Frank Lloyd, would sell if he could have the entire purchase price of nearly £1m in cash – he would not agree to a proportion of it in debentures. In their search for an additional large sum, Lloyd George's friends sounded out William and Gomer Berry, who said they were prepared to take a large holding in the new company provided, among other things, they were given full commercial control. There was some objection to this, but before it could be clearly formulated it became known to Lloyd George's representatives, disconcertingly, that before the Berrys could produce the money they had first to sell The Sunday Times for £200,000 to Lord Beaverbrook.

Beaverbrook, according to his biographer A. J. P. Taylor, was willing, but when it came to the crunch the Berrys backed out, alleging that F. E. Guest, the Coalition Liberal Chief Whip, had forbidden them to sell their paper to a Tory. It sounds a lame excuse, but if Taylor is correct the Berrys and others concerned had every reason to bolt from Beaverbrook just then, for he had a scheme for a Daily Chronicle–Sunday Times syndicate which could conceivably have led to his merging his then loss-making Daily Express with the prosperous Daily Chronicle and rounding everything off with a Sunday paper of great potentiality. Other rich men, such as the first Sir John Ellerman or Sir Arthur Steel-Maitland, might control newspapers through the purchase of shares, but they were working for the party and not for themselves, except for the hope, perhaps, of an honour for services rendered. Nobody believed that the Tory Beaverbrook was selflessly offering a covert subsidy to any party; and at the time of this affair F. E. Guest (and the Berrys) may, as Taylor puts it, 'well have recalled how Sir Max Aitken had gone into The Daily Express as agent for the Unionist party and then carried it off for himself.'

Anyway, the Berrys retreated, the Lloyd George group gave the

Max, Lord Beaverbrook.

cold shoulder to Beaverbrook and his little games, and Sir Henry Dalziel headed a company which bought The Daily Chronicle for Lloyd George, drawing £1m from the notorious Lloyd George political fund.

All that Lord Camrose says of this tangle in his book 'British Newspapers and Their Controllers' is: 'The Sunday Express saw the light of day in 1920,[1] after abortive negotiations between Lord Beaverbrook and myself, whereby The Sunday Times might have passed into his ownership and the Sunday edition of The Express never have been born.'

The sequel was a bitter one for Sir Robert Donald. On October 5, 1918, when the transfer of The Daily Chronicle took effect, Frank Lloyd informed Donald that the purchasers would be taking over the premises that same evening. Thus he went out at a moment's notice. His assistant was elevated to his job and gave Lloyd George every satisfaction.

---

1. This is a mistake. The first number appeared on December 29, 1918.

So for that matter did the £1,000,000 investment, for in 1926 the Lloyd George fund sold its share in The Daily Chronicle at a profit of £2,000,000. Four years later the final owner of the paper, William Harrison, merged it, at a few hours' notice, with The Daily News; and the resulting paper, The News Chronicle, suddenly died itself in 1960, amidst recriminations which still persist. Northcliffe's old enemies, the 'cocoa millionaires', were shutting up shop in Fleet Street.

VI

Nothing of the Berry–Beaverbrook negotiations were of course known to The Sunday Times staff in Windsor House, and it is possible that the whole story has never been pieced together before.[1] They were all quietly busy in Kingsway (telegraphic address: 'Feuilleton, London'), particularly A. E. Hake, John Murray, and (though he was only in an advisory capacity as yet) W. J. P. Clifton. All three were from the Berrys' Boxing stable, brought over to The Sunday Times for part of the week because, it was hoped, they would have a talismanic effect on its circulation – after all, the magazine, one of the few publications that the Berrys ever actually started, had caused even the Harmsworth chiefs to sit up and take notice. The editor of Boxing, Mr Murray, was therefore appointed leader writer of The Sunday Times; Mr Hake, publisher of the magazine, who used to haunt the sub-editors' room of The Sunday Times late on Saturday nights and croon over the 'thousands and thousands' of copies of Boxing he was selling because of Mr Murray's astounding skill, became publisher of The Sunday Times; and Mr Clifton, who was a compositor on the firm which printed Boxing, Love & Malcolmson, in Dane Street, Holborn, was being groomed to become manager of The Sunday Times. They all had a great admiration of each other and, as the darlings of Mr William, a slightly reserved attitude to the other inhabitants of Windsor House.

One of the first things the redoubtable Mr Hake did was to get the postal arrangements for the paper prominently displayed in The Sunday Times. They have a marked charm for all of us who

---

1. Written before the appearance of A. J. P. Taylor's 'Beaverbrook', Hamish Hamilton, 1972.

suffer from a postal system which is constantly being improved and constantly getting worse. (Mr Hake had also made special arrangements to send the paper to the Front – the Western Front. It arrived on Sunday evening!)

SUNDAY TIMES

———

Copies can be sent anywhere
at the following rates:

BY ORDINARY NEWSPAPER POST. –
Inland 1½d.; Foreign 2½d. per copy

BY RAIL. – To any Railway Station to which there are Sunday trains, by the first train from London, at an inclusive cost of 1½d. per copy. It is necessary for subscribers to send to the local station for the copy addressed to them.

BY INLAND LATE FEE POST. – To reach any part of the United Kingdom by first postal delivery on Monday morning at an inclusive cost of 2d. per copy.

BY FOREIGN LATE FEE POST. – To be delivered on the Continent by first postal delivery on Monday at an inclusive cost of 3½d. per copy.

Readers experiencing any difficulty in obtaining the paper will greatly oblige by communicating the fact to the Publisher, who will if possible arrange for delivery by an agent.

———

Head Offices:
WINDSOR HOUSE, KINGSWAY, W.C.
Telegraphic Address: 'Feuilleton, London'
Telephone Nos.: Regent 5426 and 5427.

Mr Hake was circulation manager as well as publisher, with a splendid girl named Gladys Latham to help him. (She had an equally splendid sister named Mona Latham, who joined the paper in 1915 and spent her whole working life with it in the advertising department, ending up as the devoted and indispensable secretary to the advertising director, then Michael Renshaw.) Mr Hake was soon reporting the most gratifying increases in circulation.

Of John Murray, a great shock-headed fellow who used to quarrel bitterly with Leonard Rees on Saturday night about the leading articles, the records and recollections are silent. He probably left the paper soon after the war, though he had a brother, Henry, who served as a kind of foreign news sub-editor on Saturdays and wrote book-reviews.

The third of the trio, Mr Clifton, was general manager for twenty-five years, and the Clifton legend is not entirely dead even yet.

He was not a manager such as they had on The Times, one who had the foreign correspondents under his command and was a figure of importance whose authority was exceeded only by that of the editor himself. Clifton had his importance, though, in that he had been instructed by Mr William to scrutinise every penny spent, and he took this as his excuse, perhaps legitimately, for interference in nearly every department of the office, though it was all on rather a humble level and his real economies were made at the printers. William Berry had met him when he was extending his knowledge of printing and production at Love & Malcolmson, printers of Boxing, where Clifton held a card from a trades union, the London Society of Compositors, and organised the firm's beanos. From their very first meeting Mr William seems to have mesmerised him, and henceforth Clifton had a mission in life: to be Mr William's man and see that nobody – particularly shifty printers and drink-sodden sub-editors – swindled Mr William in the matter of overtime or out-of-pocket expenses or stationery or even the odd pencil.

Clifton had no use for drinking or any form of office camaraderie – they would fit him the less for executing the business of Mr William. He did not hesitate to tread on everyone's corns – the staff and the whole alien world were probably up to something which was not to Mr William's good. Gliding about the office with cigarette burning down to nails bitten to the quick, bowed shoulders, darting, suspicious eyes, little black moustache, wisps of hair plastered across his head, he looked as gothic as a drawing by Phiz. Perhaps every office has to have its Mr Clifton: someone on whom a general dislike can centre. He wanted deliberately to preserve his isolation and so be free to exercise Mr William's mandate. He was an uneducated man except in the craft of printing, yet he was a very impressive personality in his single-minded devotion to the commanding young Welshman. With all this, dear old Clifton was an entirely different man outside the office. One day in the early 1930s someone on The Sunday Times had to see him on a Sunday at his home in a London suburb. He reported to the office on Tuesday that old Willie Clifton had been full of jokes and fun – not Silas Wegg but one of the Cheeryble brothers.

Mr Clifton was a nineteenth-century character strayed into the twentieth century. Over the years The Sunday Times printers had friction with him. It was in the works, operating independently of the irascible Leonard Rees, that he could really save money for the paper. One old printer, Richard Renaud, with 53 years in the composing room, bore him no grudge. Said Mr Renaud in 1968: 'Very keen chap. In his big days in the early twenties he must have saved Sir William a pretty penny. No extras and OT for us then – everybody had to be at it all the time. He had the what I call open sesame to Sir William and Sir William never forgot what he did for him.' He thought for a moment and resorted to mysterious craft talk: 'Right up to the time of a 38-page paper, on the Saturday night late-stop there was only one man performing with three pages go-back – that was Clifton's organising. He was never what you would call popular, though. Most people didn't like him at first sight, or second sight either. But you could rib him a bit and he wouldn't mind, and for all his funny ways he was a kind of tower of strength for a long time.'

On the editorial side, however, the Clifton mission was not quite so effective. There was no question of encroachment on Rees's territory – Clifton was too unlettered for that. His range above stairs was therefore restricted to running the office, superintending the delivery of household goods and effects to Sir William's home, bullying editorial helpers about late delivery of copy to the printers and explaining indignantly to them that corrections on proofs were charged at double-rates, keeping a ferocious eye on the office boy who sat gingerly on a bench in his room, and unwillingly doling out a guinea or two of expenses, signed for by Rees or the news editor, from an antique safe.

In this room lived another splendid girl who became as much an institution as Mr Clifton himself. She was his secretary, Irene Cameron, and like Grace Pugh and Mona Latham she joined in 1915. It was her rôle in life to pour balm into the bleeding hearts of the unhappy whom her boss had affronted. She was all mildness, helpfulness, and practical good sense. She was also in a way the first art editor of The Sunday Times. Today there are rooms full of art-department people – designers, picture researchers, graph-makers and goodness knows what. There was only Miss Cameron then. You took your print to her and when she had scaled it down she gave you a piece of copy paper cut to the size the block would be. With this and a sheaf of proofs you went down to the composing room and made up your page on the stone, giving the piece of paper to the stab-hand and indicating where the block was to go, and showing him the proofs of the articles you proposed to use, every so often scribbling out a heading on a scrap of paper which he would then take directly to the machine. No page make-up then from the design department, beautifully lettered and exact to the last line.

Sometimes Miss Cameron would scrutinise a print or a reproduction in a book (illustrations for the book pages were always taken direct from the book being reviewed, screen or no screen) and declare with a professional air that it wanted a bit of AW – art work. This meant that somebody in the process room might emphasise the outlines of the picture until it began to look like a half-tone reproduction of the 1890s – Augustus John once rang up The Sunday Times to suggest ironically, of a reproduction of one of his paintings, that the fee be given to the unknown artisan who had lovingly made it his own. But all this was in the late 1920s at the earliest. There were very few half-tone reproductions in the editorial columns at the period of the first war.

Altogether, Miss Cameron's room – it was never called Mr Clifton's room – was the kind of haven which doesn't exist nowadays in your great newspaper offices. It was the postage and packing department, somewhere where you could order coals for your private use or an electric lamp bulb for the kitchen, a ready source of messenger boys, taxis, typewriters, back numbers of the paper.

We shall hear more of Mr Clifton and his Miss Cameron. They are part of the history of The Sunday Times long before the office became its present sophisticated self.

VII

Mr Clifton distrusted everyone, and intellectuals in particular. 'A poet!' he would mutter disgustedly as some inoffensive reviewer, leaving Rees's room with a couple of books under his arm, passed him in the corridor. And he had a particular distrust of the dramatic critic of The Sunday Times, J. T. Grein, an arch-intellectual and the predecessor of Sydney W. Carroll and James Agate.

It was the spring of 1918 and for the British people a time of unexampled darkness: the worst and most disastrous period of an appalling war when the country and her allies seemed on the brink of defeat. Everything was short – ships, food, men, tempers. The Sunday Times stumbled on, but the strain of things was beginning to tell. (The horizon was a bit clearer when the brothers were thinking of The Daily Chronicle.) All this coincided with a certain domestic event at The Sunday Times which must have been a further strain for William and Gomer, who, it will be remembered, dreaded libel actions, and for Leonard Rees, whose exact rôle in this particular incident will probably never now be determined.

The centre of the event – unfortunately for him as it turned out – was the Dutch immigrant J. T. Grein. Of him, James Agate, a fascinating mixture of the intellectual and the philistine, wrote with the shrewdness and vivacity which have survived the years so well:

This little Dutchman was indeed an extraordinary personality, he was so tiny that one had the impression that when he sat in his stall his feet didn't touch the floor. He was always bubbling over with something or other, generally indignant at some misunderstanding of, or imagined affront put upon, his beloved Theatre. Vaguely one heard that he had some connection with the tea business, but I have always thought that the connection was not much closer than that of Mr Micawber with the coal and banking industries. It seemed impossible for Jack to have any existence outside the world of the playhouse. He was your true man of the theatre, and especially of the cosmopolitan and educated theatre; and this was perhaps why the little confidences with which he honoured one between the acts were invariably in French.

'Ce n'est pas ça, chér collègue, ce n'est pas ça,' he would say; and that clinched the matter. He could listen with equal facility to plays in the English, French, German, Dutch and Italian tongues, and did some thirty-five years of listening before, in 1897, he was appointed dramatic critic of The Sunday Times, which post he held for twenty-one years.

Agate doesn't mention the unfortunate circumstances in which Grein left the paper. But, then, Agate himself had been on the wrong side in a libel action or two, and perhaps he thought the whole unfortunate matter was best forgotten. Sydney Carroll was also involved in more than one libel case when he was on The Sunday Times, but the most unfortunate of all three was poor Jack Grein. He was grossly abused in what has been called the most sensational case of libel ever heard in a British court, suffered outrageously from the self-satisfied incompetence of the judge, Mr Justice Darling, was completely baffled, bullied, and beaten by his unscrupulous opponent, Noel Pemberton Billing, Independent MP for East Hertfordshire, endured an intolerable miscarriage of justice in having the verdict given against him, and had the mortification of hearing the inexplicable decision of the jury received by those in court with tumultuous cheering. In addition, there was another little trouble, as we shall see.

The case arose out of a production of Oscar Wilde's 'Salome'. Wilde wrote this play in French and it was translated into English by Lord Alfred Douglas. 'Salome' was played all over Europe in its theatrical version, though it must be added that when the opera that Richard Strauss based on it was sung at Covent Garden, in December, 1910, The Sunday Times music critic (not the great Newman, of course) condemned it as 'a wild study of perversity and bestial appetite'.

We go back to March 6, 1908, when the Canadian dancer, Maud Allan, appeared at the Palace Theatre. In her programme was a classical dance, 'The Vision of Salome'. It had no connection with Wilde's play, and she danced it in London many scores of times without official interference, although she was, for the time, very lightly dressed. Both Grein and King Edward VII greatly admired her, Grein declaring that 'Maud Allan brings youth and intuition and inimitable grace of manuflection. She is exquisite. Her long limbs are of a beautiful sinuous subtlety.'

The years passed. Then at the beginning of 1918 he gave Maud Allan practical proof of his admiration of her art by offering her the part of Salome in Wilde's play (it was banned in Britain) in private performances in a production for his Independent Theatre Society, an organisation of the highest repute and one which has its place in theatrical history. Mrs Grein, who in literature called herself Michael Orme, was to play Herodias.

It is here that the swashbuckling Pemberton Billing intervened. He was one of the earliest people in Britain to realise the importance of aircraft. He invented three aeroplanes himself, and one of them actually flew. He was a reckless speaker, impossible to disconcert, aggressively patriotic, an indefatigable liar, and altogether reminiscent of some half-mad eighteenth-century bravo. He did not care whom he ruined, or why. He controlled a gutter journal called the 'Vigilante' (just as his witness Lord Alfred Douglas published another little paper which libelled Winston Churchill by calling him a syphilitic), and on February 16, 1918, there appeared in it a scurrilous attack on the morals of Maud Allan and reflections on the Independent Theatre Society. Maud Allan and Grein thereupon sued Billing for libel.

The resulting trial was a scandalous exhibition, with Mr Justice Darling, who presided over it, much more interested in making the tiresome little jokes for which he was notorious than in keeping control. Billing defended himself, and he at least had a splendid time. He insulted the judge and defamed anyone who came into his head, including Mr Asquith and F. E. Smith, by now a friend of William Berry's. He challenged them to bring an action against him for libel but they were wiser than Grein and did nothing. Taking advantage of the wartime hysteria, the fear, and the dismay that were spreading over the country as the enemy still fought aggressively and apparently indestructibly, he said that there were 47,000 men and women whose sexual deviations were known to the Germans. These people, he said, were being blackmailed into not pursuing the war with sufficient vigour. Their names were contained in a Black Book compiled by German secret agents in Britain. This Black Book was in the possession of a certain German prince, but – and this was where Grein came in – many thousands of them were also on the membership roll of the Independent Theatre Society.

Against this torrent of irrelevant and completely unfounded abuse Grein was helpless. Billing blandly remarked that he had nothing to say against the private character of Miss Allan, and called the translator of the play, the wretched Lord Alfred Douglas, to testify that it was an immoral and wicked work. The trial then became an attack upon Wilde which appealed to the heart of every ignorant moralist in the country and the jury:

BILLING: Was he a sexual and moral pervert?

DOUGLAS: Yes: he admitted and never attempted to disguise it after his conviction. In my company he never disguised it. He always began by admitting it and glorying in it.

How old were you when you first met him?

Between 21 and 22. I was still an undergraduate at Oxford. I saw him in his house; I was brought to see him.

Do you regret having met him?

I do, exceedingly.

What do you think was his influence on most people?

I think he had a most diabolical influence. I think he was the greatest force for evil that has appeared in Europe for the last 350 years.

With this judgment the jury, and probably the nation, agreed.

Billing was found not guilty amidst thunderous applause.

The Sunday Times was outraged, chiefly on account of F. E. Smith and other public men. On the following Sunday it published a scathing attack on Mr Justice Darling:

> It cannot be said that the judge who tried last week's *cause célèbre* lived up to our expectations of the Bench; on the contrary, he permitted his position to be made ridiculous and English judicial procedure to become a travesty of itself. Through weakness which only the weak-minded can excuse, he let his court be turned into a bear-garden and a stream of mud be poured on many respected and honoured names. . . . The nation is too outraged in all its instincts for what is seemly to be satisfied to overlook such a scandal or to give Mr Justice Darling a chance of retrieving his deplorable error. An example should be made of a judge so injudicious. If this joker in ermine cannot be induced to see that it is his plain duty to resign a great office of the State on which he has brought discredit it is time he should be removed by formal petition of Parliament to the Crown.

This is fine, hard-hitting, manly stuff; and we should think even more highly of it if, whilst calling for the dismissal of Mr Justice Darling, The Sunday Times, for some mysterious and undiscoverable reason, had not itself simultaneously dismissed the blameless Grein, who went out into the world a shattered man.

He was succeeded as drama critic by Sydney W. Carroll, who had always been near in friendship and influence to the Berrys, particularly William. Everything he did was odd and picturesque, and as he is of great interest, if not of importance, in these early years of the Berry-owned Sunday Times, and as Lord Kemsley used him as an ideas-man in his own occupancy of the editor-in-chief's chair, with the result that suggestions which originated with Carroll occasionally popped up in the paper almost until the day of his death in 1958, we can ignore chronology for a moment while we take more than a passing glance at him.

He was a big man, with a harsh voice and attacking manner, as has already been said: but his readiness to give help when it was needed sometimes surprised those who were startled by his somewhat alarming appearance and manner – an appearance discounted by his boyishly humorous eyes. He wore his hair cropped short, and this gave him a Germanic air that sometimes led to misunderstanding. He was an Australian, and as we know his real name was George Frederick Carl Whiteman, but for family reasons – there had been a quarrel between his grandmother and grandfather – he called himself Frederick Carl in his early years in

Sydney W. Carroll.

England. He had a quick eye for acting talent in the young and it was he who, as a theatrical manager, gave Vivien Leigh her first chance upon the stage.

To the end of his life, when his giant frame had been prostrated in bed for a long time, he sent a weekly note to Lord K about the previous Sunday's issue, along with – this has been mentioned – an idea or two. Kemsley greatly valued these appreciations and suggestions from his old friend and loyal supporter. In a somewhat lordly and feudal way Lord K was a party-giver to his staff at his country house or in his London home, the great Adam house in Chandos Street called Chandos House. These were usually big parties at which he was a kind if condescending host, in the manner of say Arnold of Rugby dutifully inquiring about the progress of someone's stamp collection. When his people raised their glasses to drink his health, murmuring 'Lord Kemsley' in the usual embarrassed manner, a stentorian roar would subdue the mild, polite noises with a majestic 'VISCOUNT Kemsley'. And Sydney Carroll would stare around, at once smiling and pugnacious. You never knew whether he meant it or not.

When he became drama critic of The Sunday Times in 1918 he was forty-one years old and had led a very varied life. His father, John Whiteman, was known in Australia both as a poet and a politician, and his remarkable mother was 'Princess Midas': she it was who bought The Sunday Times at one of the darkest periods of its history in the nineteenth century as a present for her second husband.

Carroll himself was always lavish with money, he spent as hugely as he earned, and from his earliest days he knew wild vicissitudes of fortune. At nineteen he came to England and got a job as an actor. He took the stage name of Sydney Wentworth Carroll, and for some years played in the companies of Louis Calvert, Ben Greet, and Wilson Barratt.

It is evident that Carroll was not a pale and remote aesthete. On the contrary, he was a man of forthright, almost brusque, practicality. He left the make-believe world of acting, and as Frederick Carl became a periodical proprietor at the same time as the young William Berry, sharing a single room in some Fleet Street court with him. He had already worked on a few papers belonging to his mother, including 'Our Cats', and the first paper he started for himself was 'Cage Birds'. This he eventually sold to the Berrys in the late twenties, together with the very profitable 'Poultry World'. His Link House publications also issued a paper called 'Health and Strength' (acquired from the Berrys' company Ewart, Seymour) which was much patronised by office boys curious on the subject of male virility. During the first world war, as proprietor of 'Poultry World', he organised a national egg collection in order to get new-laid eggs rapidly from poultry-keepers to military hospitals in England and France. For this he was given the O B E.

His first review for The Sunday Times was published on June 9, 1918. In a style that was jerky, excited, emotional and brusque, Carroll soon began to put the whole force of his personality into his work. He would hit out at the favourite actors of the time. Of Ainley as Cromwell in John Drinkwater's play of that name he said that this adored player dominated 'the stage in the sense that he is always theatrically and emotionally impressive. . . . But the effect is not that of nature, but art. He is always picturesque, never actual.' He would offend the dignity of The Sunday Times's then haughty pages with slang; he cared nothing about good taste. He was always liable to burst out into excruciating sentimentality. Of a play by Dorothy Brandon – 'The Outsider' – he wrote: 'I am confronted with one of the most difficult problems of life – the problem of the cripple. I can hear the crippled children crying in their cots all over the world.'

And if his taste was sometimes uncertain, he was occasionally shaky about the words themselves. When he was film critic of The Sunday Times in the 1930s he went up to a confrere, the late Campbell Dixon, and gave him a reproachful look. 'Old boy, in your article on Monday you used the word 'nymphomaniac' as if you were referring to a woman!' It is true that the word has now become one that every schoolboy knows and that it was much less common then. He also rather shocked and at the same time thrilled another professional film critic, Canon Bernard Mortlock, by rumbling away, as they sat in the cinema together, that he had a simple physical test, a personal reaction, for determining the sex-appeal of a film actress.

He was by no means so wholly destructive a critic as he liked to think. He had his enthusiasms as well as his dislikes. In fact the very article which, on January 30, 1921, threw The Sunday Times office into disarray by bringing on yet another libel-suit (Gomer Berry, as the keeper of the coffers, must have demanded where all this madness of these critics would end) began with a compliment, not an insult – a compliment to Edith Evans. It was a review of Brieux's 'The Three Daughters of M. Dupont' at the Garrick, and it read:

Despite the alleged dearth of English actresses, every now and again I am amazed by an altogether unexpected and natural performance. I go to the Garrick expecting nothing but the magnificent propaganda of Brieux against marriages made by French parents, and some brilliantly wearisome fireworks from emotional Miss Ethel Irving, and I find a study of a live character by Miss Edith Evans that makes Brieux a reality, and outshines the pyrotechnical artist.

Under proper control Miss Irving is one of our finest comediennes. Latterly I have found her art sadly undisciplined. The actress saved up all her forces for the third act, and then devastated us. It was not a storm of passion. It was a tornado. Every shred of reserve was scattered to the flies; and the woman who wants children from a husband who refuses them became a raging, frothing epileptic, rolling on the floor, and biting her toenails. Now this is all very fine in its way, and the house deservedly responds, but it is not the true touch.

By contrast Miss Evans, who has been putting in some astonishingly good work of late in widely different character parts, was Nature herself opposed to Theatricality. Her Caroline, the quiet elder sister of the trio, made me cry like a child. Not for months have I been so deeply affected in a playhouse. The restraint, the conviction, the finish of the portrait of this yearning, self-sacrificing, ugly, ill-dressed spinster were almost perfect. Mr Leon M. Lion cleverly detailed with some over-elaboration and terrier-like emphasis the part of the old father. Mr Kenyon jumped backwards and forwards on the stage like a demented panther, but had moments of genuine pathos and realism. Nearly everybody else in the cast save Mrs A. B. Tapping had defective wigs or moustaches, over-acted, and seemed to think that because it was a French play they could shout and gesticulate in the accepted extravagant way of stage French-men. That was why, perhaps, Miss Evans, with her natural unforced mute sympathy, made such an appeal to me.

On reading this notice Miss Irving promptly brought an action for libel against Carroll and The Sunday Times, possibly as much outraged by Carroll's tactlessly phrased praise of Edith Evans as by anything which he had said in criticism of herself.

The case was tried before Mr Justice Darling, which was in itself a piece of bad luck, for he must have remembered what The Sunday Times had said about his conduct of the Pemberton Billing case. He could, however, afford to be magnanimous, since the paper's call for his dismissal had come to nothing. It was a very idiosyncratic trial all the same, including the customary outcrop of inferior judicial jokes.

Miss Irving objected in particular to the passage which spoke of her rolling on the floor and biting her toenails. She denied rolling, and this started Darling off at once. He said, quick as a flash, 'I have read somewhere – the poet's eye in a fine frenzy rolling.'

Not to be outshone, Patrick Hastings, defending Carroll and The Sunday Times, replied, 'Ah, my lord, but that was not on the floor.' There was laughter in court at this, and Darling, spurred to yet greater efforts, continued, 'It went on to say – "It glanced from heaven to earth",' and Hastings wisely acknowledged defeat with 'Perhaps your Lordship is right. Perhaps it was on the floor.'

Lillah McCarthy, Matheson Lang (who said rather cryptically that he did not know if Carroll had a high reputation, but that he himself thought highly of his criticisms) and Arthur Bourchier, who had been an early President of OUDS, gave evidence for Miss Irving. Bourchier showed himself a formidable witness, and easily scored off Patrick Hastings, who was a dramatist himself. He admitted that he had a great dislike for The Sunday Times, and Hastings, rashly as it turned out, took him up on this point.

HASTINGS: When you heard there was a chance of the libel action against The Sunday Times and Mr Carroll you said to yourself what would be the equivalent of 'What ho!', didn't you? (*Laughter*)

BOURCHIER: No, no. I remember that phrase appearing in one of your plays, Mr Hastings. (*Laughter*)

MR JUSTICE DARLING: In one of Mr Hastings's plays?

BOURCHIER: Mr Hastings sent me two plays by himself. (*Laughter*)

HASTINGS: Mr Bourchier, what a revenge!

MR JUSTICE DARLING: (*to witness*) What part did you play in them?

BOURCHIER: I did not accept them. (*Laughter*)

Patrick Hastings then brought up the subject of the review in The Sunday Times which had angered Mr Bourchier. It was a criticism of a production of 'Henry v' with which Bourchier had been involved. From then on the exchanges became heated. Hastings continued reading a letter that Bourchier had written about Carroll to The Sunday Times. It was quite as offensive as anything Carroll had said about Ethel Irving. It concluded: 'I have much pleasure in recommending him for the first class of the Ancient and Dishonourable Order of Ananias.' *(Laughter)*

HASTINGS: This unhappy critic is to be decorated as a first-class liar?

BOURCHIER: Yes, certainly, when he writes in that way.

The letter to the paper referred to poison gas and to Carroll's criticism of the pronunciation of the word Agincourt, suggesting that Carroll might be unaware that in each country the pronunciation and spelling of names had their vagaries. It continued: 'If not, let him take the names of Cholmondeley or Marjoribanks, whilst no doubt, when recently in Germany, he might not have been surprised to find his name pronounced Carl.'

HASTINGS: Did you not mean that the critic is not only a liar but a gentleman who issues poison gas and is a German?

BOURCHIER: No. I meant that he was a liar. I did not mean that he emanated poison gas; that was a simile. As to his being a German, I had no knowledge of that.

HASTINGS: You meant that he was a liar, a German liar, and that he wrote poison gas?

BOURCHIER: No. I meant he was a liar who had been writing so favourably of the German theatre that I did not think it advisable to employ the man to detract from British actors and actresses.

It all seemed to be getting a little remote from the affairs of Miss Irving, and Mr Justice Darling, for once at any rate in his judicial career, did a sensible thing. He suggested that the case should be brought to an end by both parties coming to an agreement. This idea was immediately accepted. An apology was made to Miss Irving and her costs were paid by the defence.

Carroll suffered no great damage. Luckier than Grein had been, he kept his job until he gave it up on his own decision. After that the Berrys came to his rescue financially over and over again. In the end, as we have seen, they took over two of his best papers and he sold the rest.

He turned up again later as film critic of The Sunday Times, and when he was still doing the job Michael Joseph, the publishers, announced that Sydney W. Carroll had written his memoirs, 'Shifts and Stages'. This was in the spring of 1939. The publishers agreed to pay him an advance of £150, with £50 down. The book was duly written and delivered, but it never appeared. It was said, in Michael Joseph's blurb, to be the story of a man 'who has known many of the greatest personalities in Fleet Street'. One of those personalities – rumour surmised Lord Kemsley – read it in manuscript and didn't at all approve. Rumour also surmised that it disclosed that in his earliest days Lord Kemsley had been a draper's assistant in his native Merthyr Tydfil.

Suddenly, in this same spring of 1939, Dilys Powell was offered the post of film critic of The Sunday Times. It seemed that Sydney Carroll was to be translated to higher things, to an editorship. It was true. He took charge immediately of Kemsley's Daily Sketch, where he invented, with his customary journalistic agility, a famous war-time feature called 'Inside Information'.

The memoirs are still unpublished, but at least the publisher had his money back – Carroll repaid it in two instalments of £25 in November, 1940.

VIII

But back to 1918 and the woes of war.

Horatio Bottomley, in his sanctimonious articles in The Sunday Pictorial (whose circulation in March of this year was 2,634,000, and who offered free air-raid and bombardment insurance) got the burgesses of England thoroughly mixed up about Armageddon. He was always talking about the coming of Armageddon. Some of his readers thought it meant a kind of armistice, others a super-dreadnought, H M S Armageddon, which would belch fire and somehow destroy Germany. Only a few clergymen and others nodded wisely and pronounced that it was all in the Book of Revelation, and that the present war would turn into the war of Armageddon, which would only be brought to an end by the Lord's personal return, the Second Coming.

But as the war progressed everyone forgot about Armageddon – the struggle with Germany became too dreadful a reality for fantasy. All the papers, including The Sunday Times, with its bold LATE WAR EDITION above the title-block on the front page and its twelve pages (price one penny until March, 1918, and thereafter 2d for ten pages) were dominated by the war even down to the advertisements. There was Fortnum & Mason: 'The War Catalogue contains a large assortment of suitable Goods and assorted Boxes, such as BOEF (sic) TEA (10/6d lb) and Champagne Jelly (1/9d bott.)' Or: 'The Stellite light-car: owing to the entire organisation and plant being devoted to the production of munitions of war, further deliveries of this cannot at present be made.' The National Service Office was always telling people, imperatively, in half double-column advertisements: 'More FOOD must be grown' or that something else must be done for the war effort. Only the stores advertising – Harrods (who sometimes took the whole of the front page), Peter Robinson, Barker's, Marshall & Snelgrove, Dickins & Jones, Whiteley's and Pontings – escaped the war blight, though not absolutely.

The editorial columns gave the impression of one gigantic war bulletin: all the new books seemed to be war books, all the new plays about the war. There were two columns of letters from readers, and 'Puzzled' and other pseudonymous characters were always dragging it in. The main news story would begin: 'Despite examples of their capacity for brazen effrontery given by Germans so many times during the war, yesterday . . .' and the leading articles would have headings like 'More Hun Tricks'.

There were two genteel gossip columns: 'Court and Society' and 'The Easy Chair: Topics of the Week', by Argus. There was a motoring column, a Paris letter, an auction bridge column, whole pages of official reports from the Western Front, and the inevitable and heartbreaking 'Roll of Honour: List of Officers Killed'. Leonard Rees was his own music critic and Frank Rutter, who was art critic until 1937, did 'The Galleries'. There was no cinema critic – he (or rather she) hadn't been born yet. There was a column by Harold Cox, who like Rutter went on till the mid-1930s. He was an economist and the hero of an office joke. At a lecture he asked the rhetorical question, 'What shall we do to keep down the population?' From a coarse member of the audience: 'Abolish Cox!'

The war ended, but by the spring of 1919 it was evident that peace had its problems. Influenza was ravaging the world and Britain herself, according to Maynard Keynes, was approaching the dead season of her fortunes. The Prime Minister had to return home from the Peace Conference, where he was attempting to reconcile the vindictiveness of Clemenceau with the idealism of Wilson, to deal with a threatened coal strike. Until it was known how the new map of Europe would be drawn, The Sunday Times complained, it was hopeless to expect settled government and the subsidence of political unrest in the enemy countries. (When the Versailles Treaty was concluded the paper was a supporter of Lloyd George, standing apart from the objections with which the left-wing surrounded it, condemning, as they did in particular, reparations, the occupation of the Rhineland, and the transfer of German territory to Poland.) So long as uncertainty continued, the paper insisted, Bolshevism would spread.

It deplored a 'Hands Off Russia' demonstration at the Albert Hall, and represented Russia herself at once as an international menace and a country internally impotent through creeping paralysis. From the 'pen of a cultured woman' came an anonymous description of life under the Red Terror. It was followed by a message from Copenhagen (nothing came from Russia herself) predicting an imminent stoppage of all railway traffic: whereas 'the Reds, two months ago, had at their disposal more than 20,000 locomotives, about half of which were in a fair state of repair, at the present time they have only 4,500 in a serviceable condition. At this rate by the middle of April Russia would be without means of communication.'

There were the Irish troubles too. A picturesque story of the escape of De Valera from Lincoln Prison was related to Reuter in Paris by Mr O'Kelly, the Sinn Fein delegate then in that city. According to him, De Valera was told how to break out of the gaol by other Irish prisoners working on a garden plot, who sang songs in Irish and so communicated with him in much the same way as Blondel communicated with Richard Coeur de Lion.

Germany was a worse problem than Ireland. British officers and men were to keep the Watch on the Rhine: the armies and air forces of occupation were 'the last argument of the Allies in enforcing just peace terms on the beaten foe'. They would continue to exist everywhere, in gradually diminishing strength, until the

THE WATCH ON THE RHINE

THE ARMIES OF OCCUPATION are the last argument of the Allies in enforcing just peace terms on the beaten foe. They will continue to exist, in gradually diminishing strength, until the Peace is settled finally.

Britain's share amounts to about 900,000 officers and men distributed over the —

Home Army.	Army of the Middle East.
Army of the Rhine.	Detachment of the Far North.
Garrisons of the Crown Colonies and India.	

In addition to these numbers for the Army, 81,500 officers and men of the Royal Air Force of Occupation are required to continue serving for the same purpose. Except for these numbers our great Army and Air Force are being demobilised as rapidly as possible.

THE ARMIES OF OCCUPATION are to be reduced in strength as circumstances permit.

Both are made up of—

(1) Men who joined the Colours before the war who have not completed their term of Colour service.

(2) Men who joined the Colours after 1st January, 1916, except those over 37 years of age, and those who have more than two wound stripes.

(3) Volunteers.

Every man who volunteers to remain replaces a man who wants to be released.

THINK IT OVER.

The Industry of the Country is *not yet* ready to work at full blast.

The man in the Armies or the Royal Air Force of Occupation has at least **one guinea** a week pay, plus separation allowance for wife and children or dependents, clothing, lodging and food, and plenty of recreation.

Leave is now given only to the Armies and the Air Force of Occupation.

Ask your Commanding Officer for full details and VOLUNTEER TO STAY.

March 2, 1919

Peace was finally settled. There was another advertisement directed at British soldiers everywhere: 'To the Army: Be patient'. There could be no general demobilisation yet – first in, first home must be the rule.

Obviously the army desired nothing so much, as is the way with the British, as to get back home and wash its hands of Europe, leaving France to pursue her dreams of glory there. Sir Herbert Morgan, who was to become ever more closely associated with the Berrys on the advertising and promotion sides, and was then one of their links with sophistication, contributed an indignant column on the scandalous lack of plans for officers who had already been lucky enough to exchange their uniform for mufti and were seeking civil employment.

And there was coal, the greatest British problem of all and one which particularly agitated the Berrys because their brother Seymour was by now a great coalmaster himself. Their leader writer said: 'The supreme interest of the country is to keep the coal industry, which is the main source of its economic vitality, prosperous and productive; and a miners' strike engineered for the purpose of imposing a higher minimum wage than the industry can afford to pay, or for the purpose of enforcing a scheme of "unification" as a stepping-stone to state ownership, would be destitute of all public sympathy.'

That, though, was only leader-writer's language and overlooked the dangerous emotional appeal of the miner, once the king of the artisans and now an intransigent and underpaid toiler in the dark. The humane everywhere, perhaps with a sinking feeling at the thought of class warfare and revolution, wanted him to be appeased.

The Sankey Commission, one of the most famous of all Royal Commissions, was created by Act of Parliament with the scarcely concealed intention on the Government's part (or so The Sunday Times said later) of preparing the way for the nationalisation of the mines. If that is so, Lloyd George must have had most decent citizens with him: they wanted to see an end to the unceasing friction between the miners and the mine-owners, the first led mainly by cloth-capped bullfrog exponents of the class war, the others by reactionary businessmen of the most hopeless kind. Birkenhead put the general feeling on a sixpence when he said he would call the miners' representatives the stupidest men in England if he had not previously had to deal with the owners.

The mines had been nationalised for the duration of the war and were still under Government control, as were so many other things, when the Sankey Commission was appointed in March, 1919. Three prominent Socialists – Sidney Webb, R. H. Tawney and Sir Leo Chiozza Money – were Government nominees for the men, and the fact that they had no particular knowledge of coal confirmed Tory suspicions that Lloyd George was bent on nationalisation. The mine-owners for their part were fighting nationalisation in an advertising campaign in The Sunday Times:

How Dare You Have Money! The men behind the agitation for the Nationalisation of the Coal Mines will follow the Marxian plan to the end. First they would nationalise Coal Mines, then they would nationalise Land, then Shipping, then Railways, and after that they would come after YOUR little savings. If the principle of Nationalisation were accepted your War Bonds, your War Loan Stock and your War Savings Certificates would be so much waste paper.

Passions didn't run so high in the editorial columns of The Sunday Times, but when the Sankey Commission was appointed it was quick off the mark in attacking the third of the Government nominees for the men:

ENCOURAGING THE ENEMY

In last week's issue of the Labour journal, The Herald, there is an article by Sir Leo Chiozza Money on 'The Coal Crisis'. The argument is based on figures which are obviously and ridiculously wrong, and shows an ignorance of the subject which one would not expect to be the position of a writer who has held Government office and written voluminously as an economist.

But Sir Leo Chiozza Money makes one statement which is worthy of note. He charges the Prime Minister with calling home the Guards from Germany as a weapon against the coal miners. The accusation is a lie on the face of it, and the man who makes it is doing his best to stir up the class hatred which Mr Smillie, Mr Thomas, and other leaders have condemned in the most positive fashion. To circulate such poison when both sides of the dispute are honestly trying to find a *modus vivendi* is a contemptible action from which any honest man would shrink.

The three Socialist nominees for the men on the Sankey Commission were set off by three nominees for the employers, and the six other members represented, in equal proportions, miners and mine-owners. The result was that it produced no fewer than four reports, but finally Sankey himself sided with the miners to recommend 'either nationalisation or a measure of unification by national purchase'. Because of a difference of opinion between Sankey and the miners on the way this was to be put into effect the Government chose to reject nationalisation. State control remained, the dogged miners, feeling they had been sold down the river, rejected various palliatives, and the trouble remained on the boil, the source of national confusion and despair.

This, however, was a period of prosperity for the coal industry; the export value of coal, home demand apart, was very high, though Britain was no longer supplying four-fifths of the world's export of it, as in 1913. But between December, 1920, and June, 1921, there was a sudden slump in the export trades – coal, textiles, iron and steel, shipbuilding – and unemployment, which was concentrated in them, passed the two-million mark (between the two wars it never receded to a lower figure than a million).

This completely altered the situation of coal from the financial point of view. The Government discovered that there was no longer any margin of profit on exports of it and that the whole industry was threatened with a deficit. It had been proposing to bring control to an end on August 31, but instead it advanced the date to March 31. It was an action which for once left miners and mine-owners in agreement. They argued that the Government was willing to control and fleece the industry when it was doing well but only too eager to abandon it and throw both sides back on their own resources when it was doing badly.

In all this the seeds of the General Strike of 1926 were sown.

And in any case there was a coal strike in that year, 1921. When the mine-owners were preparing to take over they showed that they had learned nothing and forgotten nothing. They proposed an agreement with the miners which not only cut wages but restored lower rates for pits with inferior coal. The miners asked for a 'national pool' to equalise wages throughout the industry and provide equal pay for equal work. Narrow-minded trades unionism and hard-faced capitalism went for each other bullheaded. The result was a lock-out on April 1.

The Triple Alliance, an understanding between trades unionists in the mines, railways and transport, now declared for a general strike beginning on Friday, April 15. But when the day came – the famous Black Friday – the miners were left to go it alone.

It was at this stage, or very soon after, that The Sunday Times made a farcical entry into the affair.

IX

Sir Walter Scott told his son-in-law and biographer, John Gibson Lockhart, that he would rather see him a dram-drinker than a journalist. There were two people on The Sunday Times at the time of this coal-strike to whom the news side of journalism was a form of dram-drinking. One of them was Hannen Swaffer, whose ostensible job was the provision of a weekly column called 'Plays and Players'; the other was F. W. Wilson, from The Times, who was news editor and deputy editor and who, like Lord Northcliffe in Max Beerbohm's cartoon, found the demons of sensationalism arising within him when he surveyed the news columns of the paper to which he had been newly appointed.

Swaffer was just over forty at this time and in his dress suggested a caricature of an out-of-work Victorian actor – it was his trademark. He had founded a page in The Daily Sketch called Mr Gossip, and he was currently writing for one of the other picture papers, the Berrys' Daily Graphic, as Mr London. He lunched at the Savoy Grill and picked up gossip in Shaftesbury Avenue and elsewhere and related all he had seen and heard with an egotism which suggested that he himself was a greater personality than any of the people he was writing about. He was the hero of taxi-drivers and waiters and the oracle of the West End to readers of the ha'penny papers. All of which meant, of course, that he was a very good popular journalist.

But at this time, in 1921, he still itched to demonstrate again the abilities which led to his becoming, years before, night editor of Northcliffe's Daily Mirror: to be once more a showman of news and a maker or inspirer of newsroom decisions.

The Berrys suspected nothing of this. They had just bought The Daily Graphic and hired him to write Mr London for it. From them he had one of those contracts to which they grew increasingly attached as their group of papers became larger, an arrangement under which certain of the contributors to The Sunday Times, such as Ernest Newman, also wrote weekly for one of their popular papers; or, as was the case with Swaffer, whose main job was on The Daily Graphic, a column for The Sunday Times. The Berrys merely knew that, with his eternally drooping fag, he was about the printers on Saturdays, correcting his proof or idling in the case-room or conferring with his crony Wilson.

To some men it is heady wine to be in charge of the sub-editors' room of a big newspaper, where decisions have to be taken on the wing and there is always the excitement of shaping the night's paper; and so it was with Wilson. He was an educated man who at Oxford in 1911 won the Gladstone Memorial prize for an essay on the English church in the reign of Queen Anne. He became a protégé of Northcliffe's and was given a job on The Daily Mail in

1913, and he was in Ireland for that newspaper during the Ulster crisis in 1914. In the war he was in the army and after it North-cliffe put him on The Times, which he soon abandoned to become news editor of The Sunday Times. With his dark and heavy good looks, his habitual silk hat and frock coat, and his bulldog pipe, he was impatient of the old men in journalism and eager to show what could be done with new methods.

Swaffer recognised those so-called new methods: he had grown up with them, and superior persons called them yellow journalism. But Swaffer wanted to join in for the fun of it and because he admired anyone who was willing to cross his proprietor; and in any case he was in the agreeable position of having Wilson look up to him as his mentor.

Both of them had no very great admiration of the Berrys. Swaffer's conception of a newspaper proprietor was a Northcliffe or a Beaverbrook, someone with a buccaneering spirit, a disdain of respectability, a strong sense of humour or impishness – all attitudes which he found lacking in the Berrys – and above all someone who would respond to his own jokes. He rarely smiled himself and his nose had a melancholy look which suggested that it had been pulled in some Grub Street quarrel. But he felt lost if he could not get a laugh from the chief.

With Sir William Berry he was out of his element. With Mr Gomer Berry he was possessed by a sense of deep unease. They were usually jovial with him, and their manner acknowledged his eminence as a Fleet Street card, but he sensed a lack of sympathy at bottom which told him that he would never be allowed to become on familiar terms. He was also persuaded that the Beri-Beri, which is what he called them privately to Wilson, were not truly appreciative of his 'Plays and Players', with its candid approach to actors and managements.

The more disgruntled he became the closer he drew to Wilson, and on Saturdays he haunted The Sunday Times, arriving early and staying late. He even had telegrams from a tipster sent to him there, and it was an understood thing that in his temporary absence someone or other in the sportsroom would place a bet for him with the office bookie, a linotype operator named Patsy Hart. One such telegram was not opened: it named two horses and both won. Swaffer went in search of the culprit, a gawky new sports sub-editor, hissed 'You unsophisticated bastard' at him, and went off in search of consolation from Wilson.

The sub-editors liked Wilson, for all his superiority complex. He would argue stoutly with Leonard Rees and try to obstruct him if he showed signs of trespassing on that part of the paper which began with the main news page on page seven of a twelve-page paper. It was the traditional place to start the news: not even The Daily Mail had news on the front then, and no one, not even Wilson, would have suggested putting it there instead of the rich-looking panels of restaurant and hotel advertising.

The sub-editors knew too that Freddie Wilson was a fine all-round journalist. He had recently sent some outstanding reports from Cologne, and he had made the controversial subject of black French troops in Occupied Germany one of his specialities. The sub-editors thought he would recover from his present attack of self-importance.

But there was something about being in sole charge on Saturday night, with Swaffer at hand, which was like dram-drinking to Wilson. At seven, when the first edition went to press, Rees would depart for the Savile Club, then in Piccadilly, for dinner and a little bridge, returning to stay until ten. Sir William would have left at six or so, and he would usually make a telephone call around ten. After that Wilson and Swaffer were alone and in a position to try a few experiments. Both knew that the heading types and lay-out in general were of Sir William's own design and therefore untouchable. But there were things to be done all the same. 'Giving the paper jip' was what Wilson called it.

These little experiments in sensationalism did not pass un-noticed. There were rows with Rees, who was conveying the uneasiness felt upstairs, and then, since that seemed to have no effect, confrontations with Sir William himself. At one of these, when taxed with inadequate treatment of some business story, Wilson was bold enough to attempt an airy joke. The brothers did not mind being called the 'Busy Bees' – they rather liked it. They were not pleased, however, when Wilson, appropriating from Swaffer, said he was a victim of Beri-Beri.

Then there arose the little affair of the coal strike.

Freddie Wilson put on his top hat one Saturday afternoon and with Swaffer rushed off to Downing Street to talk about the strike with Sir Robert Horne, the Chancellor of the Exchequer. Wilson had in his pocket an interview, done earlier in the week, with Robert Smillie, president of the Miners' Federation.

Wilson and Swaffer were out of the office for a long time.

The chief sub-editor saw the first edition to press, and in twos and threes the dozen sub-editors, including those in the sportsroom,

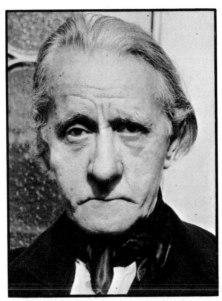

Hannen Swaffer

which was separated by a partition from the office Rees used on Saturday, strolled from the printers in Portugal Street, Kingsway, to the Mitre Hotel, Chancery Lane, where dinner and a pint of beer were on the firm. It was a pleasant stroll after the usual stress.

Sub-editors then, as now, are technicians of a peculiar breed. When G. H. Mair, who was famous on The Manchester Guardian between the wars, left his university, he applied to that paper for a job as sub-editor, assuming it to be, as many outsiders still do, some sort of assistant editorship. He did not understand that sub-editors work as a separate team, sitting round one big table, processing stories after their worth has been assessed by the chief sub-editor's right-hand man, the copy-taster. Reasonably satisfactory sub-editors can be made of men adroit enough to pick up the rules and tricks of the craft, but good sub-editors are born and have a certain creative power, particularly in the writing of headlines.

Some of these sub-editors on The Sunday Times were briefless barristers who had learned enough about the job to get by and had taken on the stint – two o'clock to eleven o'clock – as much for the fun of the thing as for the one-and-a-half or two guineas it brought them. Others were professionals from the daily papers, including two or three from The Times, men with families who were glad to earn extra money on their night off but who were also drawn in by the excitement surrounding the final process of the production of a big newspaper.

Their talk was usually shop talk; it would be related without malice that the new chief sub-editor had been entirely unintimidated when Sir William, in his shirtsleeves, had stalked into the room with page proofs in his hand and said 'There's a lot of corrections here.' The chief sub-editor had barely looked up. 'Right-o', he said, 'shove 'em in that tray and I'll see to 'em when I get time.' It had become known that Sir William, who sometimes wrote leaders on a Saturday afternoon, had approved this attitude as that of a keen man; he often had a word of praise for diligent servants of the firm, such as Mr Clifton or some crusty character in a lowly job in the accounts department who paid out the firm's money only after suspicious scrutiny.

There would also be talk of Leonard Rees, the 'old man', who would pop into the sportsroom to see how Notts were doing and show signs of petulance if things were going against them; his uncertainty of temper was an office legend. Most of the sub-editors were in awe of Sir William and a bit scared by Rees.

And there was Clifton, of whom they were not scared. Recently, in an excess of zeal, he had decreed that sub-editors must provide their own paper and pencils. It was ridiculous, and they had refused as a body; Clifton abandoned the idea instantly.

When he came to the Mitre that night at eight o'clock, to pay the bill for their dinner, they chaffed him as usual and he chaffed back. There was one sub-editor present, Roger Wilding, who was to have much to do with Clifton over the years. Leonard Rees liked Wilding and his driving energy and burst out one day that he was the most enthusiastic man in the place. He became chief sub-editor, then sports editor. In both of these jobs he worked part-time. The full-time editorial staff of The Sunday Times remained remarkably meagre until after the second world war and was only expanded to suitable proportions when Denis Hamilton took over the editorship.

It was time for the sub-editors to get back. They found Wilson and Swaffer impatiently awaiting them, and the sub-editor who customarily did the 'lead' story was told by them that the interviews with Sir Robert Horne and Bob Smillie had resulted in a great exclusive story. They must be run side by side with a long analytical 'standfirst' or introduction. In half an hour the expert returned to the side table at which Wilson and Swaffer were slumped. But the wretched man had failed to present the thing in a sufficiently serious light, and his headline made facetious play with 'The Two Bobs', a music-hall turn of the time. He returned to the big table crestfallen, leaving Wilson and Swaffer huddled over the copy.

Their deliberations produced a remarkable result. In the two interviews Wilson and Swaffer had seen points of agreement between the Government and the miners, and these they emphasised in the introduction: the sense of it all was that The Sunday Times had settled the coal strike.

Of course, it had done nothing of the kind, and there was a great row at the new offices at 186 Strand on Tuesday, when Swaffer's part in the coup emerged. But Freddie Wilson was unabashed and in the following weeks stumped on doggedly, with Swaffer at his elbow, as always, egging him on.

Both men were quite disinterested. Their sole aim was to give the paper a livelier look. But William Berry wanted his own kind of paper, a paper (like The Daily Telegraph later on) which you could trust, and he couldn't tolerate the idea of Wilson and Swaffer playing Northcliffe together when they were alone on Saturday nights. So (though the Berrys were always reluctant to give anyone the sack) they both had to go.

Swaffer attempted revenge some twenty-five years later when giving evidence before the Royal Commission on the Press. He had become something of a pretentious bore by then, and his evidence attacking the press lords, like that of some other Socialists appearing before a Socialist-appointed inquiry, was very fanciful. At one point he said:

> During the first war I was on terms of considerable friendship with James White, the financier. I knew him to be a very, very slick operator, but he fascinated me because of his grim humour and I used to go into his office after work. The Berrys had become associated with James White, who told me that he had loaned them £1,000,000 that week and they would be millionaires by the next January in consequence. Later on, Sir William Berry was associated with White over the cotton speculations of 1922, and at least part of the money which was the basis of the Berry fortunes came out of that kind of operation.

Replying to Swaffer before the Commission, Lord Camrose showed himself contemptuous of his credibility as a witness and categorically denied his evidence about James White. He said that he knew James White 'quite well – a most interesting character. But I never speculated in cotton, as Mr Swaffer stated, and he never lent me a penny-piece.'

And there was Wilson, whose weaknesses found him out. He teamed up again with his crony when Swaffer became editor of The People in 1924 and as political correspondent brought disaster with him: he wrote a sensational interview with Stanley Baldwin, who had recently resigned as Prime Minister, and had it repudiated by the Conservative Central Office. Neither of them lasted very long on The People, but its publishers, Odhams, went on loving Swaffer over the years and adoring his performance as the Ancient Pistol of Long Acre, until they canonised him by instituting the Hannen Swaffer awards for journalism, organised today by the International Publishing Corporation.

As for The Sunday Times, it was improving rapidly, both physically and in its content.

As we have seen, in Mrs Rachel Beer's time it was printed by St Clement's Press. It then went to the Argus Press, the other big job-bing house in London at that time and The Observer's printers for many years. This for some reason didn't work out and it was trans-ferred back to St Clement's Press, which itself owned (the first Sir John Ellerman, the shipping magnate, was involved somewhere) The Financial Times. A locally renowned citizen named Mr Con-nibiar was chief printer of The Financial Times, and for a few months he obligingly printed The Sunday Times with the staff of The Financial Times, paying them overtime and so on. But this was an offence in the eyes of the London Society of Compositors, who stepped in and ordered it to be done by a separate staff, which in turn disturbed Mr Clifton, who was delighted at the dual arrangement and considered a special shift for The Sunday Times alone to be a shameful waste of his employers' money. But the union won and a shift was engaged who did nothing but Sunday Times work. It started a small war between the London Society of Compositors and their member Willie Clifton.

It was reported to the Union that the manager of The Sunday Times was running about the composing room lifting matter and dropping it into pages as if he were a practising printer and not a member of the managerial caste: copy and galley proofs and page proofs were dead matter and could be handled by anyone; but type was 'live' matter and was sacrosanct to the brotherhood, no matter if Clifton did hold a union card and was originally a com-positor. He was warned off. In a huff he withdrew from member-ship of the society, and bad blood remained. The sequel was to come six or seven years later at the time of a national emergency.

There were great developments soon after this. With The

Sunday Times booming, William Berry began looking longingly
at The Financial Times. And attached to it – or it could be the
other way round, so glittering were both prizes – was the printing
works itself. He found the necessary money, bringing all his financial acumen and powerful personality to bear, and bought the
package. (Just after the second world war he sold The Financial
Times to Brendan Bracken and his associates of The Financial
News for £750,000.)

Things were going so well that new offices were needed for The
Sunday Times: Windsor House was outgrown. At 186 Strand,
nearly opposite St Clement's Church, there was a fine corner block
just vacated by W. H. Smith; it was ideal in every way. The Berrys
moved fast to get it but they found that Kelly's Directories had
moved even faster. So in their bold way the Berrys bought Kelly's
Directories and the offices with it, and The Sunday Times Limited
moved on to one spacious floor of the Kelly building.

It was the beginning of a happy and exceedingly prosperous
partnership with a very nice man, Sir Edward Iliffe, who owned
the directories and many trade and technical publications besides,
all part of the business founded by his father in Birmingham.
Until 1937 Lords Camrose, Kemsley and Iliffe were partners in
everything together, including The Daily Telegraph, and they had
perfect trust in each other and operated a joint account. In 1937,
with their children growing up, they separated, but with only
happy memories.

When William Berry and Iliffe did their first deal together over
Kelly's Directories, Iliffe was on the point of retiring from business
and going into politics. But Berry made a great impact on him, and
he had second thoughts when Berry proposed that he should acquire the Iliffe business and promote a big public issue of shares in
Associated Iliffe Press coupled with Kelly's Directories. It came
off and it was a big thing.

But it wasn't all. The Berrys were on the rampage. About this
time they bought, with fine indiscrimination, and with the intention, of course, of selling them back to the public in the shape of
shares, The Financier (amalgamated with The Financial Times),
the paper-pattern business of Welldon's (including a score of
papers for women), the periodical and book publishing and
printing business of Cassell's (another big deal which included
many magazines) and Graphic Publications, which brought them
a daily paper, The Daily Graphic, the first illustrated daily, and
two illustrated weeklies, The Graphic and The Bystander.

All this was concluded by June 1921, a period of extraordinary activity which culminated with a baronetcy for William Ewert Berry. Within a few weeks, at a celebratory dinner at the Savoy, the 42-year-old Welsh conqueror was bandying compliments with Northcliffe and Beaverbrook, Fleet Street's newest lion. In his speech he made one curiously mistaken prediction. He said that advertising rates were too high and needed to come down and that wages in the printing industry would have to follow. The advertising rates of The Sunday Times were certainly revised, but only upwards, time and time again. At first there had been no fixed rates – horse-trading was the rule. But about this time the printed 'card' was introduced and thereafter remained immutable.

But all this activity of the Berrys was only a beginning: their appetite for newspaper ownership remained insatiable. As we shall see, within two or three years they were to gather hundreds of other papers, big and small, into their imperial hands, until the Northcliffe possessions were dwarfed and they controlled the largest group in the country.

But before that happened the paper celebrated its centenary in October, 1922, and there were great rejoicings at a message from the King.

There was a message also from Lloyd George: 'My heartiest congratulations and good wishes to the great newspaper which is upholding the best traditions of British journalism.' Purely co-incidentally, one of the leading articles in the same issue had a congratulatory word to say about Mr Lloyd George: 'Throw into the scale every defect of personality that criticism may discover and every mistake of policy that may be imputed against him since the Armistice, Mr Lloyd George still remains of all living Britons the one to whom the country and the Empire are most indebted.'

Amidst all these lofty civilities Lord Leverhulme's tribute struck a note so homely that it might have been written by one of his own soap-boilers:

The very best of good wishes for completion of the one hundredth birthday of the *Sunday Times*, and I would like to give a greeting of a century old, the author of which, as far as I am aware, is unknown, but it seems to me to apply excellently to the *Sunday Times*:

> Come in the evening or come in the morning;
> Come when expected or come without warning;
> Thousands of welcome you'll find here before you,
> And the oftener you come the more we'll adore you.

The Editor of the *Sunday Times*.

The King congratulates the *Sunday Times* on the celebration of its hundredth anniversary, and His Majesty trusts that the newspaper of such varied interests may continue to enjoy many years of prosperity.

STAMFORDHAM.

At 186 Strand, little Leonard Rees was keeping shop happily while his employers roamed hungrily about the few square miles of jungle known figuratively as Fleet Street, basking before his contributors in reflected glory, amazing himself with the fertility and beauty of his ideas and, vigorously polishing his eyeglass with his handkerchief, interrupting his observations on the political situation with expressions of admiration for William and Gomer Berry or for his own prowess yesterday on the golf course – which he always called the links. In a few years he was to expand his social acquaintance by meeting Margot Asquith (a rare woman no matter what Dorothy Parker may have said in reviewing her autobiography) and of publishing these same reminiscences. They caused a great sensation, full as they were of indiscretions and careless artistry of phrase, and proved the truth of Denis Hamilton's dictum that the best serials of all are high-class gossip.

In the sanctity of his office Rees had one recurring homily for his leader writers – Gerald Barry (later Sir Gerald) was now one of them – and such of his contributors as were grand enough to be admitted to the presence. It was the importance of the team, of the team spirit, in the affairs of The Sunday Times. He as editor must care more for the paper than for any particular item in it; none of them must forget that they were members of a team, just as if they were playing for Notts, the cricket team for which he had a fanatic admiration. Everyone would nod agreement. But it must have been bleak doctrine for a captive audience who, being just as self-centred as writers always are, wanted praise for their own contribution above all else and wouldn't have minded if the rest of the eleven had come to some incapacitating harm or been arrested by the police for dangerous writing or wilful imposture of a writer. All, perhaps, except sleepy old Harold Cox, who damned Rees unfairly, while believing he was praising him, by saying in an obituary tribute that week after week he edited a paper which was entirely without arbitrary emphasis on particular subjects.

There was a vague belief in the office, though it was never closely examined by its best intelligences, that Rees was a great personality and a great editor. The first was certainly true. He was full of quirks and energy and enjoyment of life; as he rolled down the corridors at tremendous speed, the humble and lowly fell back before the rush of his personality. Yet in cultural matters he was an old diehard, and he had taken it upon himself to engage in a running battle with all manifestations of modernism. Alfred Noyes the traditionalist was his favourite modern poet, the young Sitwells were all charlatans. When he gave Dilys Powell, recently down from Oxford, a book by Herbert Read to review, he cheerfully instructed her to 'give him beans!' She didn't, but she wondered for a moment whether she was heading for trouble with her first editor and whether he would really expect her to do as she was bid. He didn't, she was allowed to say what she wanted to say. But Rees would always do the new young generation of artists and progressives a bad turn if he could, and he was, after all, his own literary and arts editor.

Strangely, however, he built up a team of arts writers so remarkable as to make his name an honoured one in the annals of The Sunday Times.

The first now makes his entrance: Sir Edmund Gosse.

For a good many years – from the 1920s to the early 1950s – the critics of the paper *were* The Sunday Times, just as Garvin in his heyday was The Observer. It had some very good things in it otherwise, and Camrose improved the news side until it left The Observer far behind, but it was never really a strong paper politically until the early 1960s.

When Gosse was appointed chief literary critic in 1919 he set a tone for the literary pages which was afterwards sustained by Desmond MacCarthy, Raymond Mortimer and Cyril Connolly. All three were sensitive men of the world with a strong aesthetic sense, attached to good society, serious without being too high-minded. The same may be said of Gosse. Ernest Newman, the music critic, and James Agate, the drama critic, were personalities of a different kind, but Leonard Rees brought in all three, and Dilys Powell as well.

Gosse was a tremendous figure to Rees. He had known many of the old Olympians, Swinburne, Browning, Robert Louis Stevenson, Rossetti, and he had written about them in a manner which wonderfully combined the artist and the journalist; in the time of his greatest success he had been, or was, the familiar of Thomas Hardy, Henry James, George Moore, Max Beerbohm, W. B. Yeats, Maurice Baring, even the young Siegfried Sassoon, whose mother was a friend of Gosse's wife Nellie.

All this and his social connections made Rees feel, rightly, that Gosse was the man to establish the book page of The Sunday Times, hitherto obscurely under the dominion of the industrious F. G. Bettany. But it was not Rees who introduced Gosse to literary journalism. As long ago as 1904 he had been the director of a weekly literary supplement which Northcliffe, touched by *folie de grandeur*, gave away with The Daily Mail. It had lasted for eighteen months and had brought him in £400 a year until it was stopped abruptly without warning.

At the end of the first war Gosse needed the money again and, though rather ashamed of putting his toe once more into the muddied waters of popular literary journalism, began to review for The Daily Chronicle. He was very aggrieved when this, too, ended abruptly: 'I have been dismissed by The Daily Chronicle without a day's warning. One day they were discussing the subject of my next article – the next day they bluntly informed me that no more articles would be required.'

This was early in March, 1919. A very eager Rees asked for an appointment with him. Gosse was always a temperamental man, and the benignness which he assumed in old age was easily cracked. Gleams of anger at often imaginary insults frequently flashed behind his gold-rimmed spectacles, when his thick crest of fair hair, hardly touched with grey even now, when he was 70, would fall distractedly across his forehead, his lips, half-hidden by a heavy moustache, would pout with uncontrollable anger; and it wasn't unknown for him to glide across the floor at some high-life

Sir Edmund Gosse by Sir William Goscombe John.

party and hiss at an unwitting offender, 'You have insulted me!'

It may therefore be supposed that Rees trod carefully. After suitable hesitations Gosse said that he would like to have a weekly platform but that he had learned a lesson from his dismissal by The Daily Chronicle. If he accepted Rees's offer he would have to bind The Sunday Times to put up with him for a year.

When it was all settled and in operation Rees became a worshipper of Gosse's; he counted the appointment as the biggest *coup* of his career and was stricken when the master died in 1928, still writing his weekly article, still seeing that The Sunday Times always had three of them in hand (even though this often put him behind his friend J. C. Squire of The Observer), the deity of an office into which he never ventured and whose hand-written copy was never touched by heathen hands.

Today Gosse has no reputation at all, unjustly. It was different when he acted as pall-bearer at the funeral in Westminster Abbey in 1928 of his friend Thomas Hardy, along with the Prime Minister, Stanley Baldwin, Ramsay MacDonald, Sir James Barrie, John Galsworthy, A. E. Housman, Rudyard Kipling, Bernard Shaw and others. As Gosse and Shaw left the Abbey together Shaw told him that he had just been 'staying at Cliveden with the Astors and, finding in my bedroom there a copy of 'Father and Son', had read it straight through. He said, "Had you not read it before?" I said, "Yes, of course: I read it when it first appeared; but this second time was the test; for I could not lay it down until I had been right through it again; and though I had always sworn by it I found it even better – more important – than I thought." "It is," I said, "one of the immortal pages of English literature." He stopped in the roadway and said, "Oh, my dear Shaw, you are the *only* one who ever encourages me."'

It was not true, for Gosse had a large circle of admirers. The trouble was that he had suffered for something like forty years from a persecution mania induced by an attack on him by a scholar named Churton Collins, who made himself the hammer of Victorian literary men. It had happened when things were going swimmingly for Gosse. From the religious darkness of his home and the clash of temperaments with his Plymouth Brethren father, so beautifully realised in 'Father and Son', he had escaped to London and a job as a clerk at the British Museum, but with no one to shove him along a little or humanise his life in lodgings at Tottenham. Nevertheless, he educated himself, married happily, made the acquaintance of all the leading literary figures of the day, acquired languages and a knowledge of the Scandinavian literatures, and was the first critic to write in English about Ibsen. He became a translator at the Board of Trade in 1875 and nine years later was awarded the Clark Professorship in English Literature at Cambridge. Two years after that came the experience which left him wounded for life.

He had published a book called 'From Shakespeare to Pope', and it had been reviewed and was on the way to honourable obscurity when it fell into the hands of Churton Collins, whom Gosse had counted a friend. Actuated probably by jealousy at Gosse's getting the Clark Professorship and by his own academic disappointments, Collins wrote to the editor of the 'Quarterly Review', in which he had scourged other living authors, and said that he proposed to make his pages 'bloody with the entrails of this miscreant.' The article ran to thirty pages, and with frequent reference to 'literary charlatans' and other abuse flayed Gosse alive for his mistakes in the book. Some of the mistakes were indeed whoppers, not (as Gosse said on a happier occasion) little harvest mice among the standing corn; and the daily and evening papers spread the news of the assault, and poor Gosse, who was always more of a creative artist than a painstaking scholar, was, as he told Hardy, 'felled, flayed, eviscerated, pulverised and blown to the winds,' and he hardly dared venture out lest somebody should point at him.

Being Gosse, the celebrity-collector, he had engaged himself to stay with Tennyson, the Poet Laureate, when the affair was in all the papers. He was greeted by his host with a growl. 'Would you like to know, Gosse, what I think of Churton Collins? I think he is a Louse in the Locks of Literature.'

Of course, Gosse never forgave 'Shirtn Collars', as he, his wife and his two daughters rather desperately called Churton Collins. He never forgave anyone. When he first met Oscar Wilde in 1881 Wilde bowed and said how glad he was to meet him. Gosse, who has latterly been revealed as a hidden homosexual, said that he, too, was glad – 'I was afraid you would be disappointed.' 'I am never disappointed in literary men,' said Wilde, 'I think they are perfectly charming. It is their works I find so disappointing.' Thereafter Wilde was the object of his scorn: 'What I principally hated about him, poor creature, was not at all his vices, but his unreality. He was like Punch on a stick, squeaking, and I don't like the squeak.'

His persecution-mania grew. 'You see that man opposite – he called me a vicious ape,' he said to somebody sitting next to him at a luncheon-party, sufficiently loud for Desmond MacCarthy, later to be his successor on The Sunday Times, to know that he was being referred to. MacCarthy blushed and concluded that Gosse had gone mad. MacCarthy was then literary editor of The New Statesman; and his investigation showed that one of his contributors had written a review which began by mentioning the hostile criticism through which all poets had to pass and comparing it to the crossing of a wilderness inhabited by monkeys, and had gone on to take up some remarks which Gosse had made much earlier on certain of Swinburne's poems. This was enough for Gosse. The reviewer, whose offence was not in any case very grave, had been expunged from his memory. It was the man opposite, the literary editor of The New Statesman, who had insulted him and called him a vicious ape.

Another of his feuds was with some backwoods peer with whom he had quarrelled when he was librarian of the House of Lords, a very grand librarian who gave lunches in his own domain and tea-parties for socially important Edwardian ladies. The peer blew out a light kept burning for heating sealing wax and the smoke drifted into the face of the librarian, who raised his head from his writing like a viper and demanded an apology. There was a quarrel which was taken by Gosse to the Clerk of the Parliaments, but he received no satisfaction. He was indeed compelled to retire, much to his dissatisfaction, when he reached the statutory age. Naturally, he never forgave the House of Lords.

With vicissitudes and tantrums like these behind him, and a few more still to come, Gosse in the spring of 1919 began delivering his Sunday Times articles.

In his time he had been something of a martyr to the misprint – his was a beautiful but gnomic hand. When Browning died Gosse closed a tribute with the words that to the end he was 'faint, yet pursuing'. The printer's reader queried it and an exasperated Gosse wrote 'Rats!' in the margin of the proof. When the eulogy appeared in print it said that Browning had died 'faint, yet pursuing rats'. Nothing like that happened on The Sunday Times. When he began he was the only contributor to whom a proof was sent.

On the whole his contributions were august and instructive rather than vivid and personal; he was too old to strike again his best vein. Yet not only Rees but the whole office was proud of its mandarin, and on Mr Bloxham, the head printer, Gosse's copy left an indelible mark; he would talk of its physical appearance, its neatness and regularity, thirty years afterwards.

Sometimes, under the influence of his adoring contact with the peerage, Gosse seemed to take a feudal view of readers of The Sunday Times. To judge from his message to them during the General Strike of 1926 he seems to have pictured them withdrawing to their castles and country houses and there abiding until the storm of the revolution blew itself out. As they huddled in their refuges remote from the terror, he exhorted them to calm their troubled nerves with good books.

What the elderly person for action all unfit was doing in The Emergeboy (*sic*) can interest very few readers. Nevertheless, for those few I will confess that I fell back upon the consolations of literature. 'Stone walls do not a prison make' . . . so long as my silent sentinels stood round the room in rows. If anyone cares to know it, I was deep in *Don Quixote* . . . Have we ever done full justice to *Tristram Shandy?* Now was the time for the *Canterbury Tales*. Depend upon it, in hours of suspense, the old books are the best books. Accordingly, I venture to advise all those who are good enough to look to the *Sunday Times* for counsel, if in troublous times they are not so fortunate as to be serving their country actively, to console themselves with the best authors.

It lacks life – there is too much about it of the ancient gentleman with the wing collar, the watch chain, and the black patch to hide the loss of an eye. But Rees had done something worth doing.

In 1944, sixteen years after his death, an abortive attempt was made by Miss Fannie Ratchford, curator of the Wrenn Collection in the library of the University of Texas at Austin, to involve Gosse in some share of the responsibility for Thomas J. Wise's now notorious production of fifty or sixty bogus 'first editions' of slender but popular works by a wide variety of nineteenth-century authors ranging from Wordsworth and Tennyson to William Morris and Rudyard Kipling. These pamphlet issues, allegedly privately printed in small numbers and dated to precede the regular published volumes in which their contents appeared, had been for many years cherished, often at high prices, by first edition collectors, especially in the United States. In 1934 they were exposed as forgeries by two young members of the London antiquarian book-trade, John Carter and Graham Pollard, in a book sedately entitled 'An Enquiry into the Nature of Certain Nineteenth-Century Pamphlets'.

The most celebrated (and expensive) of these little forged editions was Elizabeth Barrett Browning's 'Sonnets from the Portuguese'; a title half intended to conceal the fact that they were love poems written to her husband. They were first published (at Browning's insistence) in the second edition of her collected poems in 1850; but Wise with great ingenuity created a supposed edition privately printed for the author dated three years earlier. Produced in the early 1890s (Browning died in 1891) this quite plausible but in fact bogus edition needed some authentication before it could be marketed successfully, and Wise took advantage of the opportunity offered by his friend Gosse's preparation of an introduction to a new edition (1894) of 'Sonnets from the Portuguese' to feed him the story of the hitherto unrecorded private printing, which made a pretty bibliophile footnote to some pages of genuine reminiscence of the circumstances deriving from Browning himself. Unfortunately neither Wise nor Gosse knew, in 1894, that letters of Browning survived which established the date when his wife disclosed to him the very existence of the sonnets, viz. 1849 – two years after the date on the title-page of the fraudulent edition, whose ostensible *raison d'être* was thus exploded.

Embarrassing as this was to Gosse when the discrepancy was pointed out to him, those few who followed Miss Ratchford in regarding it as evidence of his complicity in the forgeries affair overlooked three crucial factors. Firstly, Gosse regarded Wise (as did many others) as bibliographically infallible and, with a copy of the '1847' edition in front of him, would have seen no reason to question the story which came with it from such a respected source. Second, Gosse was notoriously careless about dates. Thirdly, he was entirely implausible as a fellow-conspirator. Wise and his coadjutor Harry Buxton Forman (as we now know) in the production of the forgeries were tough, close men; professionals in the book-collecting game, not enthusiastic amateurs like Gosse; and Gosse, moving as he did amongst the rich, the titled and the famous, would never have dared to put these prized friendships at risk even if the forgers had ever thought of him as a colleague rather than, on this single occasion, a useful dupe.

Since then Edmund Gosse's reputation has been further clouded by a biography of his friend John Addington Symonds, written by a Canadian, Phyllis Grosskurth, from Symonds's unpublished autobiography. It seems that poor Gosse, who was such an eager correspondent of André Gide's, and had realised that Gide was a homosexual long before he read 'Corydon', an apologia for homosexuality, was, for all his calm detachment when writing about the book to Gide, one himself. 'I have had a very fortunate life,' he wrote to Symonds in 1890, 'but there has been this obstinate twist in it! I have reached a quieter time – some beginnings of that Sophoclean period when the wild beast dies. He is not dead, but tamer; I understand him and the tricks of his claws.' It seems that Symonds, ever a proselytiser, used to send the persuaded and the possibles photographs of naked boys. Gosse peeping at one of Symonds's photographs in Westminster Abbey on the occasion of Browning's funeral service sounds fantastic, but Miss Grosskurth records it as a fact. It would have made a great subject for Max Beerbohm. Except that Max Beerbohm himself was rent by the claws of the same wild beast.

Leonard Rees would have taken permanently to his bed had he known all this. Mr Bloxham would have been disillusioned beyond belief. Yet 'Father and Son' remains when all that is tiresome and hypocritical about Gosse has been thrown into the dustbin, and so in a minor way do some of his contributions to The Sunday Times.

XI

By March, 1922, the wartime boom was over and deflation was on the national doorstep. The Coalition Prime Minister was on the way out: Lloyd George was not the man for economical house-keeping. A lot of people were beginning to argue that it was time for the Conservative party to assert its independence of Lloyd George's Coalition and fight a general election.

Let us look at The Sunday Times for March 5, 1922, when the Conservative revolt was beginning to assume substance; and not only for that but because by then the paper had taken a shape, visually and in content, that was to continue in essence for some twenty years.

For these two decades it remained a paper conservative in its approach to things, a middle-class territory with enclaves of individualism in its pages on the polite arts.

There was a great attachment to reminiscential columns, some of them rather strange to modern eyes, like 'Men, Women and Memories', contributed successively by T. P. O'Connor MP, Sir Sydney Low, and (under the pseudonym of Atticus) John Buchan, not forgetting its little brother, 'The Town: Men and Intimacies', written in the office and signed Autolycus. There were two columns for women: Leonard Rees's second wife, a Canadian named Mary Macleod Moore, contributed a Wilhelmina Stitch kind of column in prose signed Pandora, and the other one,

'Court and Society', was full of crumbs from exalted tables, alternating with glimpses of the Countess's cabochon of diamonds or the hobbies of some retired governor-general. The other column was Frederick Grundy's weekly essay, 'From My Corner', which in the process of time and under another title was tenanted by the skilful E. V. Lucas and finally by the aged Hilaire Belloc, by which time it had come to permanent lodgment as the first column of the letters page.

This letters page, as has been said earlier, was always regarded as a most taxing task, and only the highest talent in the office, such as Rees himself or someone acting under his eye, was allowed to make it up. It always began with a very short, light letter, to get the reader hooked, and was followed by another just a little more substantial. Thus some rose (as Sydney Smith would have said) by their levity and others fell by their gravity. Practically every week a diligent inquirer, a lady who signed herself 'A Lover of Quotations', lowered everyone's pulse rate.

It was a large paper for the time: 24 pages at its heroic maximum; advertising was frequently available for even more, but the St Clement's Press machines couldn't manage it, and it had to be limited to 24 pages, price 2d, until the Berrys bought The Daily Telegraph in Fleet Street and began in 1933 to print The Sunday Times there.

Two things quickly strike the present-day reader about this issue of March 5, 1922. The first is that there are only a couple of pictures in the whole of the editorial matter. One of them is even more static than Northcliffe's 'Man looking at a turnip'. It is of St George's Chapel, Windsor, and shows with outstanding obscurity the Garter banners of the ex-Kaiser and other enemy Garter Knights before they were removed in May, 1915. It presumably has some reference, though the connection is unstated, to the recent award of the KG to Arthur Balfour. That is a half-tone. The other picture is a line block, a biggish cartoon supporting the Coalition government, and a very lively one, drawn by E. T. Reed, famous as a 'Punch' artist. (Four years previously there was only one block in the entire paper, advertisements apart: it was a facsimile of the signature of J. T. Grein at the foot of his article and its appearance was all the more mysterious because his name appeared also in type at its head.)

The second thing which strikes one about this particular issue, which is nevertheless a representative one also, is its astonishing mixture of the sophisticated and the unsophisticated. There is

Pandora on the wedding of Princess Mary, who became the Princess Royal and mother of Lord Harewood: 'If ever a bride went to her new life wrapped in the love of a people it is Princess Mary. The people who have watched her from a baby, who have read with tender pride and interest of her unselfishness, her kindness, her simplicity, wish her with all their hearts joy and gladness.' There is, in a less tender strain, the celebrated T. P. O'Connor, who must have been past his best, with an opening sentence to 'Men, Women and Memories' which can be counted the most insignificant eye-arrester ever devised: 'A correspondent writes to me to say that, in common with nearly every writer on the late Lord Harcourt, I mis-spelt his name by calling him "Lulu". What it should have been was "Loulou".'

They swim on, these favourites of the time, through a sea of mediocrity. Yet contributors such as Ernest Newman (the suave mingled with the savage in a denunciation of the pests who write to music critics), Edmund Gosse on modern essayists, and Frank Rutter on painting are there, too, all seemingly belonging to a different paper altogether.

But that Sunday morning the political news dominated the paper. 'The Political Crisis: Premier's Decision: Will Not Resign at Present: Probable Postponement of General Election' said two-column headlines over the leading news story on the 'splash' page or 'stunt' page as it was variously called in the office, and underneath the political correspondent complained, as journalists will, that he failed to understand what all the uproar had been about during the week, as he had predicted everything in his article of the previous Sunday, and no one should have been surprised by events.

There had, however, been one particular incident recently. Lord Birkenhead, the Lord Chancellor and a leading Tory in the Coalition government, had bitingly called Sir George Younger, the Conservative Party organiser, the cabin-boy who was trying to run the Conservative ship. Younger was much in disfavour with The Sunday Times. It called him a diehard and complained of his intrigues. But Younger, as the leader of a group of breakaway Tories, knew what he wanted: it was to free the party from the embraces of the Prime Minister, Mr Lloyd George, and to set it up in business again on its own, leaving the Welsh Wizard isolated in the political wilderness, for the Liberals were hopelessly divided and Lloyd George was a man without a party.

To this dumping of the Prime Minister The Sunday Times was

THE CABIN-BOY· IN COMMAND;
or, WE'LL HAVE A BIT O' DISCIPLINE ON THIS SHIP.

Cabin-boy (Younger): "Now, Chamberlain, put yourself in irons! Birkenhead shin up to the 'mast-head'—and stop there! (*I'll teach you something about* 'cabin boys'!!) Captain George, run and pick yourself out a nice *plank for the ceremony,* and look lively about it!"

bitterly opposed: it loved the Welsh Wizard, who 'always played cricket every time', and applauded the 'unanimous representation of his colleagues asking the Prime Minister not to resign at present'. All men of moderate views, indicated the leader writer and the political correspondent between them, must fall in behind the Prime Minister and his eminent and experienced Cabinet – Austen Chamberlain, Birkenhead, Balfour, Churchill, etc – lest

L.G.

the break-up of the Coalition resulted in a Labour government. And it seemed that the tactics of Sir George Younger were not only personally insulting to a great Prime Minister who had led the nation to victory but a serious embarrassment to his authority in the councils of the Allies.

This last reference was to the imminent Genoa conference, the 24th great international conference since the war and one which Lloyd George, who believed in democratic 'open' diplomacy and not the terrible old 'secret' diplomacy, had personally inspired.

Winston   *(see page 128)*

The Sunday Times even felt that the whole conference might be shipwrecked if talk of a general election persisted; and it was a conference which raised the highest hopes. It might conceivably give the knock-out blow, following that other immemorial knock-out blow to the enemy, to many of Europe's problems: it might happen that German reparations would be settled, Soviet Russia wooed back into the community of nations, and the war debt owed by the Allies to America written off.

Nothing of all this happened. The Genoa conference was a

fiasco, and the Prime Minister returned without a single trophy to dangle before a country that was growing restive and of a mind to see a new face, without that white, wild hair, at No. 10.

But the hopelessness of Genoa was as yet unknown. On this Sunday morning of March 5 a well-known voice spoke in the columns of The Sunday Times on the political crisis. They gave Winston Churchill, Colonial Secretary in the Coalition government and a Liberal, two columns for the speech he had delivered at Loughborough the day before.

> The Coalition is the best government I have ever seen. I stand for unity and the Coalition. Throughout the country in scores of constituencies, Liberals and Conservatives are to be found working together against the common opponent of Socialism. The only practical difference between a Socialist and a Communist is this: a Socialist will coax and wheedle you and argue you into ruin, and the Communist would ram ruin down your throat with a bayonet and a Russian flag. (*Laughter*).

It seems a highly-coloured pronouncement today, accustomed as we are to the domesticated manners of the Socialist Party, but in the context of those times it expressed an apprehension which was felt by many about the rising Labour movement, which had a revolutionary air about it and more than a passing regard for Russian Communism.

But for all Churchill's brave words and all the supporting exhortations, then and later, from The Sunday Times, the Coalition was doomed.

It wasn't until October 10 of this year, 1922, that the Cabinet grasped the nettle and elected for a general election on the Coalition ticket. It was no use. There was a revolt by Sir George Younger and his diehards, and nine days later there occurred the famous meeting of Conservative MPs in the Carlton Club, when by 185 votes to 88 they resolved to throw off the Coalition yoke and re-establish the independence of the party. Lloyd George resigned the same afternoon, never to hold office again, and the Conservatives won the general election in the following month.

And such is the resilience of newspapers and politicians and the mutability of human affairs that the Coalition Conservatives were with them in their victory and The Sunday Times behind them; and within two years even Churchill himself was back in the Conservative fold (having achieved the impossible in English politics and changed his party twice) and Chancellor of the Exchequer in the administration of the man who destroyed the best government Churchill had ever seen – Mr Stanley Baldwin.

But before that, in January, 1924, there arrived the first Labour government, and the out of office Tory ministers, as is the way with politicians when they go into opposition, began to write for the papers: they need both to keep themselves in the picture and restore lost incomes. The most spectacular and profitable noise of all was made by Lord Birkenhead, who wrote for The Sunday Times an eight-part series on 'Men of the Hour' – a notable series of portraits of Lloyd George, Asquith, Austen Chamberlain, Balfour and other politicians, including Ramsay MacDonald, the then Prime Minister. Birkenhead on his friend Churchill is more than just decent journalism:

He does not mean to be either reserved or rude, but he contrives to give the impression to those who know him little that he does not desire to know them more. Only his friends understand him well. And they know he has . . . in the intimacy of personal friendship a quality which is almost feminine in its caressing charm . . . Winston's education has been extremely partial, but he has attained by the force of sheer genius to a mental equipment more complete than most Senior Wranglers and most Heads of Colleges. It is reported of him, and I believe truly, that a friend once lent him Welldon's translation of Aristotle's 'Ethics' with a particular request that he should carefully study what that friend (rightly or wrongly) believed to be the greatest book in the world. Winston read it (or part of it) and is reported to have said that he thought it very good. 'But,' he added, 'it is extraordinary how much of it I had myself already thought out.'

Anyway, it has to be admitted that the paper as a whole for this Sunday in March, 1922, has enormous variety and readability and pleasing idiosyncrasy – particularly in its first half. Sydney Carroll on Sir Arthur Pinero's 'The Enchanted Cottage' and a revival of Galsworthy's 'The Pigeon'; Hannen Swaffer with his usual sharp column of theatre news; new fiction, unsigned but very well done, and a column of notes about forthcoming books. All these and the rest of the arts make an impressive show.

So, for that matter, do the sports pages. There are two columns of rugby football reports, the main one by the well-remembered D. R. Gent, three of soccer, and a column each to golf, racing and motoring. These are all at the end of the paper, as now, but the back page itself is given up entirely to illustrated property advertisements. 'Properties' were here for many years. It has been an important feature of the paper beyond living memory.

Northcliffe (who died in August of this year) had strong views about 'bludgeoning' advertisements which diminished the impact of editorial matter. The Berrys had no such objections. There is in this issue of March 5 a full-page advertisement from Hodder and Stoughton which blasts the reader out of his chair: it is a salvo for the twentieth edition of A. S. M. Hutchinson's novel 'If Winter Comes' and a succession of smaller explosions for a list of cheap editions.

At the other end of the scale the City advertising fills column after column in unrelieved minion, a type-size known today as 7-point. There are two company prospectuses: Hepworth Picture Plays are selling 150,000 Preference shares of £1 and 15,000 Ordinary shares of £1 at a premium of 5s, and Totalisators Ltd offer 490,000 Preferred shares at 10s each. (The tip by City editor R. J. Barrett that failed to come off by a million miles: 'The Russian revolutionary movement was apparently premature, but as the dictatorship of the proletariat is not likely to last for ever Russian bonds might be worth picking up at present "option money" prices to hold as a gamble for a long shot.') In an adjoining column, of modest size but bold display, there appears something which seems at first glance to combine the benefits of insurance with an even greater treasure: 'Insure your health under the best policy – CHASTITY. Free information and literature can be obtained (in strict confidence and in a plain cover) from the National Council for Combating Venereal Diseases.'

The Sunday Times Domestic Bureau displayed two columns of small advertisements – one for those looking for jobs, the other for employers seeking servants. This example, so evocative of vanished splendour, is not unrepresentative: 'Mrs Beaufort recommends her hall-boy (S. Frost) as second footman; can wait table; good plate cleaner etc. Disengaged.'

Columns and columns of advertising, displayed and classified, no matter if the war boom was busting. The Berry brothers were sitting on a reef of gold.

XII

Mr Gomer Berry (to go back a little) was holding one of his weekly conferences of the advertising staff. It was a special occasion. For the first time in its history The Sunday Times was to produce the

24-page paper, the long-desired 'size larger' which made everyone feel a size larger too. Mr Gomer explained that everything must be pushed forward. On no account must the editorial department be given the opportunity of saying that the advertisements were late and that production of the paper had thereby been delayed. Everyone listened in grave silence. The sense of occasion was marked.

It was not an informal meeting. Mr Gomer presided with the air of the chairman of a board of directors, handsome, stiff manner, tall collar, rich dark suiting, a slip of white waistcoat showing at the edge of his lapels, pearl tie-pin, small rose in buttonhole. The five other people present respected him, were struck silent by his grandeur, while understanding perfectly that he was the hottest advertisement director in Fleet Street.

'Mr Osler?'

The chairman of the conference was addressing the joint manager of his advertising department, a character locally celebrated for his devil-may-care attitude. In a crisis, such as the loss of advertisement copy or some delay in delivering blocks, he would pooh-pooh all fuss: 'Just let it wait till the morning – you'll find everything's quite all right.' He was bony-faced, shiny-eyed, hunched up round the shoulders, and when he was off to see advertisers and their agents he wore a soft curly hat which gave him a piratical air. This Bob Osler was a man of flair and a licensed eccentric. He was even accorded, in a strictly moral office, the right to exhibit occasional symptoms of mellowness after lunch; after all, everyone said sympathetically, his job demanded the giving and taking of a great deal of hospitality.

Now he grinned wolfishly at Mr Gomer and reported that bookings for display advertising were in a very healthy state. He gave no details – he did not believe in doing so.

'Mr Free?'

This was the other joint manager, conscientious, methodical, the exact opposite of Osler. He was the inside man, and his province was mainly the small advertisements. There were two Frees in the office, John Free and his son Reginald. The one retired in 1931, the other in 1963, after forty years in the advertisement department and becoming chief of the copy section. In those days John Free had no certified sales certificate to help him – it didn't come until later. Neither could he call on the volume of statistics poured out nowadays by the marketing division. Yet, curiously enough, those small ads were growing in volume every week under the conscientious eye of Mr Free, who now told Mr Gomer that his latest innovation, a special section for teachers of dancing, was doing very well. Mr Gomer seemed gratified – without exactly putting it like this – that the Jazz Age was getting under way.

'Mr Sandford?'

He was young, slightly nervous, dark, determined, and he became the link with the editorial department, shuffling the advertising around week after week, from page to page, and trying, and usually succeeding, in giving satisfaction to everyone. He was to marry Grace Pugh, the editor's secretary, thereby confirming the cosy, inter-related family traditions of the office, and to retire in the early 1960s, very much regretted by everyone. With some pride he told Mr Gomer that everything was well for the great 24-page issue.

'Mr Johnson?'

Theoretically Osler was in charge of City advertising, but Mr Johnson was the famed 'rep' for it. Today Business News has a small army of advertising representatives; then it was done practically by 'Johnny' alone, and not even as a full-time job, for he was with one of the City advertising agents. Grave and tall, and of a rectitude which is still remembered, he might have been, if appearance was any guide, the courteous but firm headmaster of a public school. Mr Gomer had a particular respect for Mr Johnson. He had even been known to smile at him. But he did not do so now.

Mr Gomer, in fact, exhibited signs of displeasure, and the wily Mr Osler had to break in breezily to congratulate himself and Mr Johnson on their triumph over the opposition last Sunday. There was a large company prospectus which The Sunday Times alone had collared. The Observer must have felt sick. He ventured to congratulate Mr Johnson once more. It was a scoop.

But Mr Gomer icily brushed the triumph aside. It was all very well but it was only what was expected of Mr Johnson. The Sunday Times was a great newspaper and advertisers naturally went to it first. What was worrying him was a two-inch advertisement – and he specified it – which inexplicably was in The Observer and absent from The Sunday Times.

Universal dismay, great rustling of copies of The Observer to track down the disgraceful defaulter. Hauteur and reproving utterances from Mr Gomer which extended the general gloom.

Then Mr George Cook broke in. He was the comic character of 186 Strand and a specialist in property advertising (which he called 'Estates'), with the maxim, 'Once I've called on 'em they never forget me.' Everyone knew that he had been on the stage as a young man in a dim way, and even now, after a good day, he would return to the office, light his pipe, and wave it around as he declaimed bits of Shakespeare. To relieve the tension in Mr Gomer's office Mr Cook, the irrepressible, was bold enough to recite a little joke – one told him, he explained, to appease the chief, by a big man in Harrods Estate Rooms.

It was successful. It made Mr Gomer smile faintly. He indicated that the meeting was over and they all stood up.

Then for the first time Mr Gomer relaxed his august demeanour and smiled warmly on the company.

'Thank you, gentlemen. You are doing very well. I am proud of you.'

They all felt a size larger.

XIII

In 1923 the Berry brothers went shopping again. They had heard that old Sir Edward Hulton was dying and wanted to sell his immense newspaper properties in London and Manchester, and they confidently marked them down as their next buy. After prolonged negotiations the parties arrived at what seemed a decisive point. The terms were all but settled, the contract tentatively drawn up, the capital found. 'Then,' as someone said at the time, 'at the fifty-ninth minute of the eleventh hour it was discovered that a comma was misplaced in the agreement, or some trifling omission was noticed, and the deal fell through.'

The truth was that Rothermere and Beaverbrook, alarmed by their younger rivals' progress, had drawn together and were now out to spoil the deal. Soon it was announced that they had bought the Hulton papers for something like £6,000,000 cash down – which was only about £100,000 more than the Berrys' offer.

A. J. P. Taylor[1] says that Beaverbrook beat the Berrys by offering Hulton ready money. Within a week he had raised the £6m and sold the properties, for the same sum, to Rothermere, keeping The Evening Standard as commission.

---

1. 'Beaverbrook', Hamish Hamilton, 1972.

The first Lord Rothermere, unlovable and difficult but always a remarkable manipulator of newspaper properties, had acquired his brother's shares in Associated Newspapers after Northcliffe died in 1922. These shares went into a public company which he called The Daily Mail Trust. The Hulton properties now went into it too. At the time the investing public was going crazy about newspapers. The Daily Mail Trust issue had asked for £8,000,000 and been offered £100,000,000.

The Berrys wanted some of the millions, too, and less than six months after the Trust issue they persuaded Rothermere to sell them, with the exception of The Daily Sketch, The Sunday Herald and, of course, The Evening Standard, the prize they had so narrowly lost, the Hulton papers, less also certain other valuable Hulton properties which Rothermere kept back. But by The Sunday Times Ltd in 1924 he was paid £4,000,000 in cash and £1,500,000 in debenture stock for the considerable residue.

The Sunday Times Ltd, which now became a new company, Allied Newspapers Ltd, sold The Sunday Times (valued moderately at £400,000 in the deal) and the Berrys' Hulton papers to investors for a total of £8,350,000, including £2,000,000 fully paid ordinary shares. These last were the perquisite of the Berrys and their friends, with a big slice for the brokers who bought the £4,750,000 8% cumulative preference shares. They were taken up by the public and within a year or two their market price had risen from £2,000,000 to £3,000,000.

Allied Newspapers was now a chain of considerable dimensions: two morning papers and one evening paper in Manchester, two Sunday papers in Manchester, about forty weekly and miscellaneous publications, the vast printing business at Withy Grove, Manchester, then the biggest· printing plant in the world, and, of course, The Sunday Times. Sir Edward Iliffe was in on the deal with the Berrys.

It did not end there. Later on, Rothermere yielded up The Daily Sketch and The Illustrated Sunday Herald to them, as well as The Sunday Mail of Glasgow: and a lot of other people wanted to sell provincial newspapers to them now. They took their pick and could boast that everyone rang them and they rang nobody. They bought properties in Sheffield, Newcastle, Middlesbrough, another in Glasgow, and elsewhere.

Two years later they made their biggest deal of all when they acquired from the executors of Northcliffe the fantastic complex of something like a hundred periodicals, goodness knows how

many encyclopaedias and other books of reference, printing
works, paper mills, and much else – the Amalgamated Press.

Harold Rothermere was eyeing them jealously all this time, and
he declared war when they bought The Daily Telegraph in 1928.
He raised public money to form a company called Northcliffe
Newspapers and tried to rout Allied Newspapers in the provinces.
A truce to the war was called in 1932, by which time it was
Rothermere who had been routed.

All these goings-on made the staff at The Sunday Times (before
it was linked with The Telegraph) look about in bewilderment.
They were now deriving benefits from belonging to a nation-wide
group, and now they had at their disposal the services of the old
Hulton London headquarters at 200 Gray's Inn Road (the home
of The Sunday Times today), with its impressive cuttings and
picture libraries. But all the same they yearned for their old splendid isolation, when, for example, it never occurred to anyone to do
something which is indispensable nowadays – to 'look at the cuttings'. There were no cuttings at 186 Strand. There was nothing
which bore even the most distant resemblance to a modern newspaper library. It may be that the indispensable Miss Pugh or Miss
Cameron kept a few odds and ends of newspaper clippings in a hat
box, but if this was so no one seems to have known about it.

There was one consolation. No matter how highly stacked his
newspapers now, The Sunday Times was still the cherished eldest
child of Sir William Berry. He was gathering an entourage about
him, close friends on whom he could rely: Edward Hunter, the
founder of Sun Engraving; Sir Herbert Morgan, another Welshman, who was going up in the world with him; the charming
Australian, J. Murray Allison, who was one of his advertising
experts; the stockbroker 'Mossy' Myers; his confidential secretary,
who looked like a farmer, W. T. Slatcher; and yet another Welshman, a young barrister named Cyril Lakin, who some people
thought was being groomed for the editorship of The Sunday
Times.

There were one or two trusties on the writing side too, among
them the mysteriously-favoured Dr J. M. Bulloch, a Scot with a
tiny body and a large square head whose prose style was based on
the more ineffective mannerisms of Carlyle, and Herbert Sidebotham, from The Manchester Guardian, who became Scrutator
of The Sunday Times and wrote also for The Daily Graphic as
Candidus: a gentle, shy, bespectacled scholar who walked crab-
wise along the corridors for many years and was the revered

arbiter of any Latin or Greek which went into the paper.

With a certain pride William Berry, Edward Hunter and others in the circle mostly of self-made men called themselves sometimes the 'Merchant Adventurers'. Eileen Hunter, the daughter of Edward Hunter, has given in a memoir of him[1] a brilliant little picture of two or three of them in domestic surroundings:

The first time I remember meeting William Berry was when, at the age of fourteen, I was taken to stay in his country house, Long Cross, Surrey, by my father and mother. He was a handsome man with a brisk commanding presence and a bold fearless eye; and Lady Berry was the soul of homely kindliness. William Berry's mother-in-law, Mrs Corns, was also there: an amiable old lady who made off to the sideboard at almost every meal, where she had to be restrained from cutting slice after slice of thin bread and butter, having once been told by her son-in-law that he was very partial to it.

Later on, I became aware that my mother was not making quite the impression my father had hoped and that her sprightly insistence on the superiority of the *Observer* to the *Sunday Times* brought a steely look to Sir William's eye even while he laughed. . . .

Gomer Berry was entirely different in appearance and character from William, being, I judged, of a more retiring nature but capable of sudden outbursts of gaiety and bonhomie which were startling by contrast with his habitual air of nervous diffidence. He lacked his brother's easy confidence, and when they split up their newspaper interests I thought the difference in their personalities became more marked. William always seemed to know exactly who he was and where he was going, whereas Gomer appeared, sometimes, to be confused by the welter of alternatives with which his wealth and power presented him.

In these years, and afterwards for that matter, Sir Gomer Berry had no use for hobbies, unless they were ones which might contribute to his social advancement. He was to try giving shooting parties, owning a yacht, and among other gentlemanly pursuits breeding cattle extensively and expensively, but he found them all grapes of thorns and figs of thistles. He used to relate that no sooner had he become a cattle-breeder than he was remarkably successful: for one day after work he went along to some important agricultural show and asked an attendant on the door whether anything interesting had been happening. The man said wonderingly that this Sir Gomer Berry, who'd never been heard of before, had swept the board. 'You must have been proud,' said

---

1. 'The Profound Attachment', André Deutsch, 1969.

someone at the office luncheon table to whom K told the tale. 'Oh, well, not really. I sold out soon afterwards – it never meant much to me.' He seemed to suggest that there was a wearisome lack of reality about this and all other hobbies, and that the flavour and colour of life were to be found only in his own office, with the perpetual conferences, the shower of messages, allegedly highly confidential, passed on by political and other correspondents, the conduits of shop talk, always tinged with printers' ink, which flowed ceaselessly throughout the day, the grandiose and conspiratorial plans in the small hours, and always the intoxicating sense of being the ruler of some grand duchy and the benevolent holder and dispenser of terrific if somehow undefined power.

There were other strongly-coloured characters around the offices in the Strand besides Gomer. One of them was the chief leader writer, a large, stately gentleman with grey moustache and comfortable belly and a courtesy of manner which made one think of the more agreeable Forsytes. He lived like a Forsyte too: fine tweed suits from Savile Row, Crofts 1908 port, the finest cigars, discreet lunches or dinners with lady-friends at Wilton's. James Agate called him in his diary 'one of the few remaining English gentlemen'. It was assumed vaguely in the office that he must be very comfortably off: you couldn't live like that out of being a part-time leader writer – most people were part-time in those days and came in only at the end of the week. With all this, he was a fine craftsman. Camrose thought the world of him, and though Rees was a little jealous in consequence, he was pleased with him too in his testy way. Unfortunately, however, there were occasional and inconvenient absences. Nobody knew quite why, and the general impression of the underlings was that his social life was such that he had to be off to Biarritz or Nice at intervals to preserve the circle of his cosmopolitan acquaintance.

He confessed the real reason, secretly, to someone in the office who became his confidant. He was both a hedonist and a stoic and he lived above his means as a matter of principle and even as a source of esoteric pleasure: 'A debt is a work of imagination no creditor can understand.' He carried on living richly until someone succeeded in a judgment summons against him, and then he would have to be off not to Biarritz or Nice but Brixton prison. He would give his friend in the office calm and ironical vignettes of prison life, 'Then, at eleven, there comes the curious ritual known as *exercise*.' He made friends on one of these occasions with some old lag whom he used to pay to make his bed, and being an extremely kind man, except towards his creditors, he used to send him a little money.

In the early days of the second war, when Kemsley restlessly wanted a change somewhere in the paper, he suddenly thought of this survivor of the heroic days of the Berrys and brought him back. He was then an old man, but he was still living off the pig's back and still a most accomplished political columnist.

Ernest Newman had met him somewhere. They had a great respect for each other. But it is almost certain that Newman did not come across him in The Sunday Times office, because Newman never went there. People about the place for a lifetime had seen him on one occasion only, and that was in 1944, when at a luncheon in the boardroom of Kemsley House he was presented with a gold watch. And not only was he invisible in the office but he was practically unapproachable on the telephone: his devoted second wife Vera was his barrier against the world, and she saw to it that he could work undisturbed in the great library in the garden of his house at Tadworth with only his cat for company. He was a god in a cloud.

If Gosse was the first old Olympian of The Sunday Times, Newman was the second. The printers knew that his copy, in his bold boy clerks' handwriting, was even more precious than Gosse's and that no printer's reader must so much as breathe on the article once it had been 'passed by author'. There was a calamity once, though. He always spelt 'choreography' without the 'e', and doubtless, being the scholar he was, for very good reason. When the impossible happened and it appeared one Sunday morning in the normal spelling, he wrote to the editor complaining that his copy had been badly 'pied' lately – a printing term for a disaster when lines of type fall to the floor or otherwise get in complete confusion. In matters of this kind he lost his usual sardonic humour.

Leonard Rees was musical himself – he had been, as we know, his own music critic until Newman's appearance. Whether it needed great perspicacity to discover Newman in 1920, when he was already famous, doesn't matter. Credit must go to Rees, who announced in The Sunday Times on February 29, 1920, that 'Mr Ernest Newman, the leading musical critic of the day, has joined the staff.' His writings, it was correctly claimed, 'have aroused the interest of the musical world by their brilliant insight and acumen and by their very fine literary quality.' Thirty-eight years later, when Newman retired at the age of ninety, the paper indulged in a little excusable self-congratulation by saying that the claim, 'fully justified then, is a thousand times more so now. In nearly two thousand articles Ernest Newman has aroused the interest of a far wider audience than the strictly musical world.' It heralded the ultimate accolade: in the same issue a column tribute signed 'K'.

It may be that Lord K, with his early interest in Boxing, was particularly drawn to his contributor on this irrelevant account, for the editor-in-chief's knowledge of music, as of all the other arts, was non-existent; and certainly one of the chief relaxations of Newman was professional boxing. He once invited a young worshipper of his on The Sunday Times to accompany him to the Albert Hall. Newman arrived by bus, his shining bald head covered by a flat cloth cap. He looked, indeed, with his battered features and bunged-up eyes, rather like an old pug himself, and throughout the contests he kept up, in a voice that still suggested his Liverpool origins, an ironical commentary which revealed his natural intolerance of the second-best even in boxing. 'They were just performing fleas,' he said disgustedly, preparing to slip away. He refused, with a rather startled air, as if the idea were too wickedly metropolitan to be entertained, the young man's invitation to come along and have supper at the Café Royal, but he began to quote sardonically: 'There in that exuberant vista of gilding and crimson velvet set amidst all those opposing mirrors and upholding caryatids, with fumes of tobacco ever rising to the painted and pagan ceiling. . . .' The young man didn't know at the time that he was quoting from Max Beerbohm on the Café Royal in 'Enoch Soames'.

Newman remained an old-fashioned puritan and freethinker all his life. The Sage of Tadworth believed in the gospel of work, and he probably needed above all else, after a few hours off, to get back to a cigar in the reassuring atmosphere of his workshop. No man ever more enjoyed a cigar. On another occasion he was smoking one in his library, ineffably happy, when his young friend from The Sunday Times asked him, as young men will, if there was one piece of music he loved above all others. He considered, blowing smoke towards the ceiling, and said that if all else had to go he would settle for Berlioz's Royal Hunt and Storm.

The public and private glee of Leonard Rees when he signed up Newman was no doubt sharpened by his having snatched him from The Observer, for whom he was working without a contract at the time. Perhaps, not unreasonably, Garvin considered him too old at 51 to begin a new full-scale career. Vera Newman, in her

The young Ernest Newman.

touching memoir[1] of Ernest, gives details of this episode:

In January, 1920, E.N. received a letter from the editor of the *Sunday Times*, offering him a five-year engagement as music critic of that paper at a salary of £850 a year, the engagement to begin in March. The contract required the exclusive use of his services with the exception that he was allowed to continue writing for the *Manchester Guardian*, or, if that should be discontinued, he would be allowed to write a weekly

---

1. 'Ernest Newman: A Memoir', Putnam.

Ernest Newman with Sir Thomas Beecham.

article on music for another provincial paper. He could, of course, write on non-musical topics in any paper. . . . His connection with the *Observer* was on a freelance basis because he wrote to Mr Garvin on February 1 : 'I am sorry to say that my connection with the *Observer* must end soon. A few days ago the *Graphic-Sunday Times* people offered me a more comprehensive engagement with their group of papers and it was sufficiently flattering to induce me to accept it.'

No one could have possibly foreseen at that date that he would continue to be music critic of The Sunday Times for the staggering period of 38 years. Possibly he himself felt he might be snatched away much earlier, for in the early days his mind ran much on the question of financial provision for his much younger wife. On April 12, 1920, he wrote to her when she was out of London:

The Grand Season at Covent Garden commences on May 12 and runs for twelve weeks – until July 31. That would set us free to go away in the first week of August: but – there's the question of money. We have spent over £400 since January 1; with my clothes and the remainder of this month's expenses it will be nearly £500. It doesn't look as if we shall be able to do the whole year on £840, does it? I *do* wish I could get free of that anxiety about our not saving anything. We must talk it all over when you come back, but I am chary of undertaking much expense over a holiday as things are just now. Perhaps a chair in Kensington Gardens each day will have to suffice.[2]

He had other problems to consider too, the sort of problem that occurs to critics in all the arts. This one he solved in the unbending way to be expected of a man from the north. 'By the way I have written to Lady Cunard explaining that it is better for me *not* to meet people like Clara Butt.'

Great men are apt to lose something of their outline behind wisps of legend. This is true of Newman. For one thing the range of his musical sympathies was far wider than the clerihew suggested:

> Mr Ernest Newman
> Said 'Next week Schumann.'
> But when next week came
> It was Wagner just the same.

For another thing, his attendance at concerts and opera was always more frequent than smart-alecks suggested. But he certainly did regard many London concerts as mere reviewers' work and not worth the attention of a serious critic.

Neville Cardus (who wrote about cricket in The Sunday Times in 1948–49) loved him, as all his intimates did, and as Rees did, and as Hadley did, and like them was under his spell over the years. It is a puzzle why a musicologist of his international stature was never in the honours list. Sir William Emrys Williams organised a powerful lobby with the object of getting Newman a C H on his 80th birthday, but nothing happened. Cardus has written:

In his younger years he was raven black of hair, walking with a poise that somehow expressed his quick, easy, intellectual responses. . . . He

---

2. *Ibid.*

was not an egghead. He revelled in the music-hall of his period, even as gustily as he revelled in the concert hall. As he approached his eightieth birthday, Hadley, editor of the *Sunday Times*, asked me to write Newman's obituary. On a foggy winter afternoon, and afflicted with a chill, I wrote it and posted it, then went forth on the way to hear an opera at Covent Garden. Out of the Charing Cross Tube Newman emerged, smoking a cigar, fog or no fog. 'Good heavens, Newman,' I said, 'what are you doing, out on an evening like this? Do you mean to tell me that at your time of life you are covering a concert?' 'Good God, no,' he replied, 'I am going to the Albert Hall to see a boxing fight.'[1]

If Ernest Newman at this stage of his life looked like a retired champion of the world, James Agate often suggested a racecourse tout: bowler hat, orange covert-coat, yellow gloves, cigar, the whiff of drink. He liked to give the impression that he was a Champagne Charlie: ' "Champagne's my wine", as the little shop-girl in Pinero's "Letty" used to say. I drink the stuff because I have to. Champagne exhilarates me, and brings forth such wit as I possess'; and after the second war he certainly had a bottle of Bollinger N V every night in the Café Royal after the theatre, when his appearance was conventionally distinguished (black tie, black soft hat, silk scarf etc), even if his companions sometimes reminded one of Wilde and his stable-boys at the Café. All the same, it was more likely to have been not champagne but whisky when he was slogging away during the day in his dressing-gown at the Villa Volpone, Swiss Cottage, or Grape Street Mansions, or Cranleigh, 107 Chalkwell Avenue, Westcliff-on-Sea, or some other of his always-changing addresses.

But even then, it wasn't really whisky or champagne which kept him going. It was his feverish love of a daily crisis, something to which he could surrender with abandon, bustling about, ringing people up, sitting up all night nursing his crisis – it often had to do with his Sunday Times article. If one met him a day or two afterwards, and inquired how it had all worked out, he would look at one blankly, and his great shining Rowlandson face, which sometimes looked like nothing so much as a bruised melon, would show his impatience. The old crisis was as dead as a door-nail. All he wanted to do now was to tell you about the new one.

You would come across him, after the theatre, in the grillroom of the Café Royal, furiously drafting a letter to Arthur Christiansen, editor of The Daily Express, on the back of a menu-card. But

---

1. The Guardian, November 30, 1968.

before you had time to thank heaven that it was his other paper which was in trouble you would find that The Sunday Times was involved.

'On Sunday, dear boy, I quoted an adaptation of a great line of French poetry in the paper: "*Dieu! Que le son du cor est triste au fond des bois.*" But for *cor* – horn – I deliberately substituted *cornemuse* – bagpipes. You read it?'

'Yes, Jimmie, very nice.'

'Very nice my arse! I got the gender of *cornemuse* wrong. It's really feminine, you know. I rang the Express library and they told me masculine. I'm writing to Chris to complain.'

'But why didn't you look it up yourself in your own French dictionary?'

'Well, you see . . .'

The explanation would go on, lucid, logical, lightheaded. He took immense pains to rid his proofs of mistakes, but a malign hobgoblin was always intervening. Sometimes this hobgoblin was crazily creative, as when he invented Johnson's Life of Boswell in the first of the Ego diaries.

Agate like everyone else venerated Max Beerbohm, and they had a common neuroticism in their fear of what the printer might do. Both resembled that old Italian poet who, on his way to present some verses to the Pope, went off his head with rage and chagrin in the coach when he discovered a tiny error in the printing. You would get a rare book review from Max, and it would be accompanied by a letter, in the most polite and elegant terms, explaining that though his style of expression was ever discursive he was in reality a painfully careful writer who could never put down one sentence that could be omitted without ill-effect. The review must therefore appear without excision of a monosyllable! That was perfectly all right, and it was reasonable of him, too, to ask one to endorse his appeal to 'Printers and Proof-Readers' and tell them that the typescript must be followed with *minute fidelity*. There would be a PS and a PPS about the desirability or otherwise of including the book's sub-title or something like that, and then a good deal of work on the typescript itself with blue ink and red crayon.

The ink was applied in big blobs to make it impossible for some eccentric printer to set matter already crossed out by the 'X' of the typewriter, the red crayon employed to draw balloons in the margins of the script. Inside these balloons would be desperate little notes in his own hand:

To Printers and Proof-Readers
Please follow my punctuation
exactly throughout. (Also my

division of paragraphs; quotation-marks;
italics; capital letters – and everything!)
                                    M.B.

To Printer
Please place the type here in such a
way that neither of these two words
shall be hyphenated from the end of
one line into the next line.
                                    M.B.

To Printer
The word is of course disparate,
not desperate.
                                    M.B.

To Printer
Colon, not
semicolon, after Adonis.
                                    M.B.

Sorry, I have thrown away
the "jacket" and can't
remember price of book.
Please insert price.
                                    M.B.

Unfortunately, you would then find that in this busy exercise in
perfectionism he had himself made some elementary error, like
spelling Harrap, the publisher of the book, 'Harrup'.

Agate didn't dare go to such lengths with The Sunday Times
printers, and in any case he knew that they weren't very fond of
him. He had a peremptory way of demanding a match to light his
cigar which irritated them, though even they were perfectly aware
that in all his wild industry The Sunday Times article was his personal devil – he wrestled with it up to the last moment. But he
realised only too well that he was an extemporiser; he was always
having to ham it up, work it over, inject little shots of vivacity.[1]

---

1. Or as he said himself in 'Ego', 1935 (Hamish Hamilton): 'By hopping about
from one bit of gusto to another like a kangaroo I give the illusion of good
writing. But that's only because it doesn't bore you. Of what really makes
writing – the bone and the muscles under the skin of the prose – I know nothing
whatever, no more than I did twenty years ago.'

Nevertheless, in his Sunday Times articles he gave some wonderful performances.

Of course, being a born romancer, he loved in his diaries to impose artistic order on the chaos of the everyday and round off some fragment of autobiography with Balzacian detail. Unlikely as it sounds, however, he did start off as a successful calico salesman in his family's Lancashire cotton mill. From 1907 onwards he wrote drama criticism, first for The Daily Dispatch of Manchester and then for his great love, The Manchester Guardian. It is said – but not by Agate, and anyway it is probably untrue – that he had to leave The Daily Dispatch hurriedly when old Hulton asked what this chap who was always hanging about the office in the small hours, waiting to see a proof, was paid for the theatre notices. 'Five shillings,' they told him. 'Too much – sack him!' In these years Agate lived and worked through the great days of Miss Horniman and the Manchester school of dramatists, and had a poor opinion of both. Intellectual drama and lounge suits were, for him, sure means of killing the theatre.

The war took him to France but not to the front: he spent two years in Provence buying hay for army horses. He married a Frenchwoman there, but it was all a mistake and there was a friendly divorce. Of his marriage he never talked to ordinary friends, but one little superficial detail had left a mark on his mind. It was a rubbish-chute in the house of his wife's parents. He used to say, with amazed eyes, and lisping excitedly, that it went right down into the bowels of the place and hadn't been cleared for twenty years.

Then he made the classic assault on London, with £2,000 as his realised share in the cotton mill. That he kept a small general stores in Lambeth is improbable but true, and it is also true that he persuaded Filson Young, the admirable editor of The Saturday Review, to take him on as drama critic. For twelve months, for £4 a week, he contributed a weekly article over which he spent three days, re-writing it as many as six or seven times.

Then one day he got a letter from Leonard Rees. Time has shown that he was Rees's third great trophy.

But Agate, like Rees himself, was a man who provoked strong reactions, and after a happy honeymoon poor Agate was offered not veneration but mutilation. The young Dilys Powell, a wondering observer of the strangeness of life in a newspaper office, was rather startled by the high-jinks between the editor and the drama critic, and she found herself entirely on Agate's side. She

The young James Agate.

says all these years afterwards: 'Leonard Rees was a dear good man, and I loved him, and I owe a lot to him. But I can't help thinking that he treated Jimmie shamefully. He would grab a pen, peer down at the proof, and make great z-marks haphazardly as he ran his eye down it – whole paragraphs out, heedless of what went before or came after.'

Of his wrestle with Rees he wrote this true, funny, and poignant record:[1]

The next big thing that happened to me was in June, 1923, when I received a letter from Leonard Rees, editor of the *Sunday Times*, asking me to call. This is the most important letter I ever received in my life, for as a result of it I entered into what I must call my life-work. I am conscious of no absurdity in saying this; the point is not the size of the work but how much a man puts into it. If a man is no more than an inventor of mouse-traps and gives a hundred percent of himself to inventing them he is doing his life's work, and a Napoleon cannot do more. When I told Filson Young that I was leaving the *Saturday Review* and joining the *Sunday Times* he said, 'These Sunday papers will cut your stuff to hell! The only thing to do is to send them yards and yards of it and not care a damn what happens.'

Never did anybody utter a truer prophecy. For a time all went well, and indeed for three or four years I got on capitally with Rees. He was approaching seventy then and it is important to remember two things about him. First, he had been twenty years making the *Sunday Times*, and he had made it, coming to complete success very late in life. Second, he had an inferiority complex, the result of knowing that he was not the intellectual equal of members of his staff like Gosse and Newman. He was very short, so that I, who am not tall, towered over him. Now it is extremely difficult to dominate people to whom you have to look up. This explains why all small men have a tendency to take after the bantam – strut and become dictatorial. I am a little given that way myself and when two bantam cocks meet the feathers have to fly. I am perfectly certain that Rees was well disposed towards me, and after all it was to him that I owed my position. He had eyes for other men's work and chose mine.

We played golf together, at which game I would give him two strokes a hole or eighteen bisques. He was tremendously keen and I always paid him the compliment of winning if I could. Once I thought he was going to win, for he stood on the last tee at Dulwich with five bisques in hand. The hole is a spoon shot and, as I could play a bit in those days, my ball stopped about three yards from the pin. Rees, when he arrived on the green, had played seven and he proceeded to take at least four putts. It was a Monday and on the previous day my stuff had appeared with the words 'light woman' altered to 'a woman unstable by nature'. Having missed his tee shot for the sixth or seventh time at the sixth, Rees turned to me and said, 'I wish you would tell me what's the matter with my driving.' I said, 'I'm afraid, Sir, it's unstable by nature.' He put his eyeglass in his eye, looked me steadily in the face, and said, 'I thought you were very good yesterday.'

---

1. 'Ego'.

And then a certain *cacoethes* overtook the old gentleman – the itch for whatever is the Latin for cutting. Now I have never minded my stuff being cut, provided I am allowed to do it myself or it is done intelligently. For five years I gave up every Saturday morning, which meant sacrificing golf and week-ends, to attending at St Clement's Press to cut my stuff to the required length. This done and the article finally approved, I would leave about four o'clock and then hang about till the first edition of the paper came out, when I would find an almost unrecognisable residuum. Again, I did not mind that, provided that whoever did the cutting had arranged for the residuum to make sense. Now Rees's habit was to cut as he read, and leave in the untouched part references to things which he had deleted. For example, he would cross out a reference to Henry Irving and in the next paragraph leave some such sentence as: 'This was never the old man's way.' The reader who thinks that I am making a great deal of fuss about nothing has never put his heart and soul into any work and then seen it destroyed. I tried protests, first the plaintive sort and then the angry. I consulted lawyers. I wrote paragraphs beginning, 'Notwithstanding the foregoing,' to ensure that the foregoing was kept in, and worried lest one Sunday morning I should wake up to find a whole article beginning that way! I used to sit late into the night arranging my stuff so that if all the odd sentences were deleted it would still make sense. Then I would try with all the even sentences deleted. But nothing availed or could avail with Rees who, one day, in reply to my protest that he could not cut an article, said, 'Damn it, man, I could cut the Lord's Prayer!' Had there been any other available platform I should, while the old man was editor, have resigned a score of times. But one does not give up one's life-work so easily and it is not in my nature to bluff. Instead, in 1928, I had a nervous breakdown. I still have on my desk the wicker tray marked 'Rows with Rees'. For years this was never empty.

In the middle of these blazing excitements the old man would send me a letter like the following:

> 31, Bullingham Mansions,
> Kensington, W.
> 4:xi:1928

My dear Agate,

A line to congratulate you on today's article, which I think tip-top – thoughtful, sound, sympathetic, and with style. I couldn't have cut a word, and you finish with your flavour unexhausted.

> Yours sincerely,
> LEONARD REES.

On one occasion he sent for me and presented me with his entire theatrical library. I was intensely sorry when the old man died, for in a way I was fond of him. I had always hoped that for my sake he would retire, and for his own spend another twenty-five years sunning himself on the front at Brighton.

James Agate by Bernard Venables

Perhaps Rees was just coming the Great Editor over Agate. Perhaps he just couldn't stand him. But there is another possible explanation: Rees's prudishness. It is curious that Agate doesn't make any particular fuss about Rees's altering 'a light woman' – a perfectly acceptable euphemism at the time – to the absurd and inexact 'a woman unstable by nature'. Rather, he takes it for granted and makes an elaborate if wry little joke about it. This suggests that Rees had done the same thing before and was excessively prone, even in the context of the time, to moral shock; and it could have been that after the first three or four years he was told by someone that Agate was another Oscar Wilde, and that his response was in the nature of a moral lesson to his dramatic critic.

After all, the news was a long time getting round to Lord Kemsley; when he heard it some twenty years later he yearned to take stern action and get rid of his drama critic. Perhaps he was particularly aggrieved because in the 1930s Agate had been the guest of himself and Lady Kemsley on a yachting trip to the Mediterranean. The Kaiser used to say that King Edward VII went boating with his grocer, Sir Thomas Lipton. Lord Kemsley in his later grandeur may well have thought it a social indiscretion to have gone boating with his dramatic critic, particularly one who afterwards published a rollickingly ironic account of it in one of his 'Ego' books. But he would have thought it more than a social indiscretion for him to have entertained, day after day, a man notorious for homosexuality.

In the 1930s Agate became, with his contributions to The Daily Express, his many books and his broadcasting, one of the great factory-workers of writing. But it was all only a way of paying for his expensive hackney ponies. The important thing was The Sunday Times.

In his early days on the paper, writing about J. B. Fagan's production of 'The Cherry Orchard', which had been brought from Oxford to the Lyric Theatre, Hammersmith, he went overboard: 'I am always being asked which is the best play in London. This is. For the highbrow? Yes, and for butcher, baker and candlestick-maker as well. I suggest that "The Cherry Orchard" is one of the great plays of the world.' It would require little perception or bravery to write these words in the 1960s or 1970s. But that may be because Agate wrote them in the 1920s. It is not too much to say that his notice of 'The Cherry Orchard' revolutionised taste and temper in the theatre.

At the time when the honeymoon between Rees and Agate was coming to an end, Rees recruited Dilys Powell as book reviewer, editorial assistant, and writer of light leaders. She was the first woman to join the general editorial staff full-time, and it happened in the haphazard way which characterises things in newspaper offices, where improvisation and not planning, muddle and not logic, govern day-to-day affairs.

She was a raven-haired girl with a fair complexion; she was modest and coloured easily but was sufficiently determined; and she had started, like Agate, by making the classic assault on London, though in a more humble and desperate way. Her much-loved father, a retired bank manager who lived in Bournemouth, had wanted her to be a schoolteacher, but she wished to become a journalist. So he gave her £50 and it was understood between them that if she couldn't keep herself by the time it was exhausted she would have to come back home and serve as a waitress at Beale's or something.

She was just down from Oxford, and to her own annoyance and the bewilderment of her loyal family she had been in a scrape there. It had all got into The Daily Mail. She had a young man, an immensely tall undergraduate at Christ Church named Humfry Payne, whom she later married and who became, before his untimely death, a great classical archaeologist. The Mail revealed, correctly, that she had been caught climbing in over the wall of Somerville at night, when she should have been safe in college and not out dancing with an undergraduate, and that in consequence she was to be rusticated for two terms. The principal of Somerville wrote to her mother sinisterly saying she had been guilty of 'clandestine meetings with a male undergraduate'.

All this medievalism enraged another undergraduate of left-wing tendencies, and one whom she didn't know. He got up a pink pamphlet about the affair, deriding such things as Somerville's permitting undergraduates to have tea with women undergraduates in the west wing only if there were present two men and three women – the women had to outnumber the men. Twenty years later, when she was a witness in a libel action, she met her champion, Gerald Gardiner K C, who was on the way to becoming Lord Chancellor. 'You got me sent down from Oxford,' he said expressionlessly, as he turned over his papers.

Anyway, she got her First and put all the Somerville nonsense behind her. From a boarding-house in Earls Court, where she paid £2 12s 6d a week, she set out to get a job.

Fleet Street, like practically everything else, was a male preserve in those days, but there were a few women around, writing fashion and social notes. The most eminent of these was Miss Billington of The Daily Telegraph, a haughty lady with a distant resemblance to an undernourished version of the Ugly Duchess, who sat bolt upright at a little round table in The Telegraph library, near one of the big coal fires at each end of the vast club-like room, writing her yards of copy about Queen Mary or the January sales. She had an introduction to Miss Billington, but Miss Billington wasn't hopeful. It seemed that if she hadn't been madly ambitious herself and of exceptional talent she would never have made her present exalted position. The prospects were dark for less superior aspirants.

So she turned to her next introduction, which was to the London editor of The Manchester Guardian, James Bone, and explained to him that though she was without experience of professional journalism she had written for the 'Isis' when she was at Oxford. 'If I were you I should keep quiet about Oxford,' said Mr Bone sourly. He added that Rachel Montague, whom she had known there, and who was the daughter of C. E. Montague of The Manchester Guardian, was just down from Oxford too, but she was a brilliant girl of whom much would be heard.

She went out into Fleet Street gritting her teeth.

She tried The Daily Chronicle with a little news story told to her by a friend, and Valentine Heywood, later of The Sunday Times, came out to see her and said he liked it. But that same afternoon she had to go back and withdraw it because her friend's father, all conscience about the origin of the trifle, said he feared it would be a breach of confidence if it appeared in a newspaper.

It went on hopelessly like this, and still she hadn't earned a penny. Then one day she walked along Fleet Street to the beginning of the Strand, went up to the first floor of Number 186, and filled in a form to say that she wanted to see the editor – literary editors were unheard of in those days – about reviewing. After a long delay the news editor and deputy editor, one Brodie Fraser, came out to see her with a suffering look. (Before the war there were always long delays in seeing callers at The Sunday Times office. She herself would sometimes be rustled up to do it, and on one of these occasions she met a young man called Graham Greene – inevitably, he wanted to do reviewing.) It was true that Brodie Fraser eyed her with the suspicious glance of a man who is not sure of himself with women, but at least he asked her to come back and see the editor himself.

It was different with Leonard Rees, who was charming and gallant and did a lot of business with his eye-glass. He told someone long afterwards that he was drawn to her because she reminded him of his dead daughter. He gave her a book to review, sliding it towards her down a long table. To her unexpressed horror it was volume seven of some interminable history of France, and she thought, dismally, that it would need Mr Bodley himself to make an impression with that. Still.

The next Sunday – she had handed in the review the following day – she was to meet her brother Lloyd Powell, the pianist, for a walk in Kensington Gardens. He came hurrying towards her, waving The Sunday Times. 'It's in!' he cried, and would have seized her hand if such demonstrations of family affection had been permissible at their age. She had, unaccountably, overlooked it that morning. It was the great moment, the banal great moment, of every young writer and journalist, hackneyed by universal experience but never forgotten. And it was worth £1 11s 6d.

She went to see Leonard Rees again and he disturbed her by having views on Herbert Read. On her third visit he inquired, 'Are you a whale on poetry?' Thenceforth she was the office expert on modern poetry.

Things began to happen after that. Camrose wanted a little

The young Dilys Powell by Robin Guthrie.

light leader every week, a Times fourth-leader kind of thing, and he stipulated, regrettably, that each must contain a scrap of Latin: scholarship must not be submerged in the struggle for circulation. On one occasion he liked it and said, 'We must do something for that girl.' She never saw Camrose in her life, not even in the lift or the corridors: he was somewhere upstairs, the mighty one. But he still holds, along with Rees, a special place in her affections.

Dilys Powell today by Otto Karminski.

She was put on the staff at nine guineas a week. On Fridays she wrote the last little leader, always called the comic strip, as well, sometimes, as the one above it, which was more of the 'It is high time that' variety. On Saturdays she went to St Clement's Press at nine in the morning, occupying a dusty little ante-room used by The Financial Times people in the week and still untidy with their reference books, and read the proofs, with interruptions for lunch and dinner, until nine-thirty in the evening. Of the rest of the editorial staff she saw nothing. Rees came over from 186 Strand after lunch and shut himself away in his office nearby, unapproachable by all. She was solitary, working in a void, happily disturbed only by the occasional appearance of Mr Bloxham, the head printer, who was scared of Rees, like everyone else, and would beg her to take a page proof into 'his majesty'. No one told her what to do, not even Mr Clifton. At first if she had to cut a proof, or alter some turn of phrase, or take out something which was incorrect or silly, she left whole paragraphs for the printers to reset instead of filling out individual lines or making the famous 'straight cuts'. It was left to Mr Bloxham to give her a few unobtrusive hints: the printers in her experience were always the most humane of men.

Then, after dinner, there was the first half of the paper itself to read, the printed first edition. For many years this first edition was thrown together; there was too much to do for the tiny staff, and editorial and typographical errors abounded. James Agate used to collect the little references to 'two young ladies will sin' or 'Mrs So-and-so is a good speaker and leads a vigorous pubic life', or 'six years ago he lost his life and has never recovered from the shock'.

She was never formally introduced to Agate. There was a shadow in the doorway one day and she was conscious of someone sitting down behind her. He turned to her suddenly, and she thought from his appearance that he must be the racing correspondent. He was curt: 'Do you read my proofs on Saturday?' 'I'm afraid I do.' 'Well, last week, you know, you changed "paros", meaning Parian marble, to "paroi" meaning stomach-lining. Very unfortunate!' She was crushed. But they became great friends.

When she left St Clement's Press at half-past nine her eyes were so tired that she could hardly see, and next day she could hardly read at all. But she was a journalist.

It went on, entrancingly, until she married her young man and departed to live in Greece. He died. She returned to the paper after five years, to the office that was her second home, and was to remain so, and still is.

XVI

Trouble was boiling up in Britain at the beginning of March 1926: the report of yet another Royal Commission on coal was imminent. Yet the advertisement columns of the paper suggest a prosperous, unworried community before whom is spread a wealth of expensive merchandise. It begins on the front page with the restaurant and hotel announcements. There is a dinner-dance that night at the Hotel Cecil, in the Strand, with Jack Payne's band, tickets 12s 6d inclusive. At the Empress Rooms, Royal Palace Hotel, Kensington, there is, at the same price, a demonstration of the Charleston by the world's tango champions, with Frakson, the man with the hundred cigarettes, as one of the entertainers. On Tuesday the third edition of the Midnight Follies, 'the first and foremost of all London's suppertime entertainments', opens at the Hotel Metropole.

One turns the pages. A big advertisement for Bluthner grand pianofortes, the 'Stradivarius of pianos' and the 'only instruments fitted with the Aliquot Scaling', is followed by another, just as big, for the genuine 'Pianola' piano from the Aeolian Company of the Aeolian Hall, 131 New Bond Street. Here a distinguished-looking old gentleman is telling his prospective son-in-law, as they smoke an after-dinner cigar and watch his daughter at the Pianola, that he enjoys 'all the delights of this wonderful instrument without the slightest financial risk or strain' – he is buying it, in fact, on the never-never. The Cosmos radiophone, it seemed, has an enviable reputation – if you heard it you would understand why it was called the Musicians' Set. (Incidentally, Sir Harry Lauder, who had sung the night before on 2LO, was opposed to the Government's taking over the British Broadcasting company, which was kept going by a group of manufacturers. He explained that with national ownership you would have stagnation and people 'grouching up' about the fees paid to artists.)

With the properties, Mr Cook is going strong – more than ten columns of advertising, anything from landed estates in Scotland to £3,000 houses, with three acres, in South Norwood. For their Easter fashions Harrods take a full page. There are six or seven big advertisements to support the motoring column. Singer seem

JANUARY 11, 1925.

A "SUNDAY TIMES" PUZZLE.

CROSS-WORD VOGUE.

The SUNDAY TIMES, which has always made a feature of such popular pastimes and skilled games as Acrostics, Chess, and Auction Bridge, has fallen a victim to the universal craze of Cross-Word Puzzles. A feature of the SUNDAY TIMES Puzzles will be their instructive nature, and it is hoped to give tests in different languages.

Prizes of three novels, to be selected from the publishers' advertisements in the SUNDAY TIMES, will be given to each of the five competitors whose correct solutions are first opened.

When you have completed the square, paste it down on a piece of white paper, add your name and address in *block letters*, and post to "The Editor, The SUNDAY TIMES, 186, Strand, W.C.2," with the words "Cross-Word No. 1" marked plainly on the top left-hand corner of the envelope. Solutions must reach the SUNDAY TIMES by first post on Thursday. All competitors must accept the Editor's decisions as final and legally binding. It is no use sending incomplete solutions.

CROSS-WORD PUZZLE.—NO. 1.

	26	27	28	29		2	30	31	32	33
3						4				
5				6	34			7		
	8						9			
10	44			11		35		12	36	
			13							
14		37		15			16		38	
	17					18				
19	39			20		40		21	41	
22			42			23	43			
24						25				

THE CLUES.

ACROSS.
1. Bottle.
2. Product of a cane.
3. Hurry.
4. Imitative.
5. Quadruped.
6. Toy.
7. Greek letter.
8. Adverb.
9. Exists.
10. Type of No. 4.
11. Goddess of Discord.
12. Small English river.
13. Jewish festival.
14. Casket for coins.
15. Relatives.
16. Character in Dickens.
17. Pronoun.
18. Conjunction.
19. Name of a fly.
20. Greek letter
21. King of Judah.
22. Continuous attempt to gain possession.
23. What Horatio was, more than a Dane.
24. Insect.
25. Perform.

DOWN.
1. Genus of herbs.
14. Commonplace discourse.
26. Possesses.
39. Border.
27. Offspring.
37. Woody tissue.
28. Preposition.
42. Metallic symbol.
29. Hindrance.
11. Sea-bird.
30. Favorite.
34. Bird.
2. Undermine.
35. German one.
40. Anger.
30. Adverb.
43. Forward.
31. Name of a moth.
15. Stage play.
32. Quadruped.
36. Owner of a salt.
41. North American Indian.
33. Oof.
38. Act as carrier (*dialectical*).
44. Look closely.

In its present form the crossword puzzle seems to have been invented by a Liverpool man named Arthur Wynne. He had emigrated to America, and The New York World began running his puzzles in *1913*. By *1920* they were a national craze. It wasn't until *1924*, however, that they reached Britain, when on November 2 The Sunday Express printed one of Wynne's crosswords. Above is the first which appeared in The Sunday Times – on January 11, 1925. The solution (below) appeared a week later.

No. 1 PRIZE-WINNERS.

The following are the five competitors whose correct solutions to Puzzle No. 1 were the first to be opened:—

Miss E. G. RANSLEY, 30, Goodmayes Lane, Goodmayes, Essex.
E. NORTON, The Cottage, Warlingham, Surrey.
PAUL H. MANGIN, 10, Priory Road, Kew, Surrey.
LEONORA JOHN, 14, Cwrt-y-vil Road, Penarth.
S. F. PASCALL, 267, Holmesdale Road, South Norwood, London, S.E.25.

SOLUTION OF CROSS-WORD PUZZLE No. 1.

ACROSS.—1, Phial; 2, Sugar; 3, Haste; 4, Apish; 5, Ass; 6, Top; 7, Psi; 8, Up; 9, Is; 10, Ape; 11. Ate; 12, Yeo; 13, Purim; 14, Pyx; 15, Kin; 16, Dot; 17, Ye; 18, Or; 19, Orl; 20, Phi; 21, Asa; 22, Siege; 23, Roman; 24, Emmet; 25, Enact.

DOWN.—1, Phaca; 14, Prose; 26, Has; 39 Rim; 27, Issue; 37, Xylem; 28, At; 42, Ge; 29, Let; 11, Auk; 20, Pet; 34, Ostrich; 2, Sap; 35, Ein; 40 Ire; 30, Up; 13, On; 31, Gipsy; 16, Drama; 32, Ass; 36, Eno; 41, Sac; 33, Rhino; 38, Trant; 44, Pry.

proud of the 10/26 horse-power limousine saloon, four cylinders, four doors, four seats, £280. American cars are in evidence. There are the Essex Coach, from Shaw and Kilburn, and the Willy's Knight Six with sleeve-valve engine: 'When the finest of poppet-valve engines are worn out the everlasting engine of your Willy's Knight sleeve-valve automobile is just coming into the full manhood of its power' – roadster or touring car, £520, saloon £695. There are the usual advertisements for petrol and car accessories: 'Captain Malcolm Campbell holds both mile and kilometre world's records, won with his 350 hp Sunbeam at Pendine Sands on July 21, 1925, where his average speed was over 150 mph. He used Lodge plugs.'

In all this, the trams are not giving up without a struggle. There is a charmingly designed advertisement for the London County Council tramways which tells you that at the foot of the Waterloo Bridge stairs 400 trams for South London pass in an hour and that you can get, for example, to Clapham Junction (for sixpence return) in twenty-seven minutes. The London General Omnibus Company announces that it is to put fifty more covered-top buses on the streets in the next fortnight. The Ministry of Transport is worried about the too free use of white lines. 'Over-lavish use of "white lines" in one locality may tend to give drivers an unwarranted sense of security in adjoining districts where highway authorities may not have used them to any extent.'

The air age is really just beginning. 'A new record for a pas-senger flight from London to Paris was created yesterday by a new model Handley-Page 16-seater machine, which flew from Croydon to Le Bourget in 1 hour 37 minutes at an average speed of 143 miles an hour. The average speed for the Croydon–Le Bourget flight is two and a half hours.'

On the other hand, E. V. Lucas, who has started to contribute his famous column 'A Wanderer's Notebook' to the paper, wasn't over-excited by the first flight of his life. He was a publisher, a gourmet, an altogether delightful man whose guidebooks were immensely popular in their day and are by no means forgotten yet.

Six years after this he was made a Companion of Honour, and an envious James Agate reflected that after all the CH would have been no use to him; he wanted to be Sir James Agate or nothing, if only to prove to the people back home in Manchester that he was a success, and he would be willing to assure the King that he would not use the title south of the Trent. He toyed with the idea

E. V. Lucas

that three Sunday Times writers would one day be honoured – Sir Ernest Newman, Sir Desmond MacCarthy and himself.

Meanwhile, like everyone else, he was well aware that Rees had done a good thing in getting hold of Lucas, whose 'Wanderer's Notebook' was one of the pleasures of the paper until its author died in 1938.[1] This is the Wanderer on that first flight:

> You have to leave Paris at eleven in the morning, which is a bad hour in a country where the importance of breakfast is misunderstood; Le Bourget is five or six squalid miles away, and, when you arrive there, a routine sets in very different from the simple process of taking your seat in a train. Your passport is disquietingly removed from you; you are asked to sign a book, stating not only your name and address, but your occupation; your luggage is twice paraded, and you are each time bidden by name to stand beside it; you are very hungry but can buy only an unappetising box of food at twenty-five francs, which is little enough

---

1. W. W. Hadley held Lucas in the greatest respect. He wrote years afterwards: 'There are works of art on which no rude hands should be laid. For years I read every week the copy of a column essay written for the *Sunday Times* by E. V. Lucas. I do not remember ever altering it; but he was the perfect contributor. The article was always on my desk on Tuesday morning. He received his proof on Wednesday morning and on Thursday it was back, shortened if it were too long, lengthened if it were too short, though usually it exactly filled the column.'

to us, but must strike the French as iniquitous. [*The franc was then at 130 to the pound.*] You may have been over-solicitously pressed to take out an insurance policy, so that, by the time the last minute comes, you are, if not actually shivering with fear, nervous and exhausted – particularly as the whole world is pulsating with the explosive throbs and shattering whirr of propellers in the act of being tested. The Croydon procedure – at any rate, when one arrives – is more humane, less exacting; but, of course, it is a drawback to be so far from London. The actual flight takes less than three hours, but the terminal ceremonies bring it to over five. All the same, I shall do it again.

(When E. V. Lucas died Hadley offered his column to Max Beerbohm, who declined but suggested Hilaire Belloc. Belloc took it on without ever quite bringing it off, though he was a brilliant success here compared with his failure as a military commentator in the early days of the second war. He and Hadley, both old men, had hoped to repeat in The Sunday Times the success Belloc had enjoyed in a similar rôle in 'Land and Water' in the first war.) In this issue Agate writes on the opening of the Plaza Cinema in the Haymarket. The paper had no film critic as yet, and Agate, who was the first critic in England to give serious attention to Charles Chaplin, in The Saturday Review of 1921, occasionally popped a piece about a new film into his 'Dramatic World'. The opening of the Plaza found him in highly critical mood:

No, I will not call these places theatres. They may, and do, steal the drama's thunder, but that is no reason why we should give them the temple's name. 'Pictures' inhabit 'palaces', an abode which they have in common with archbishops, monarchs and gin. . . .

Everybody had come to see the pictures, and pictures were the one thing which the management seemed reluctant to show. When, after inspecting the house, one concentrated upon the stage it was to find Mr Max Darewski luminously bathed in pink and violet lights toying with a grand piano to the accompaniment of a full orchestra. He was joined presently by a solo dancer and a ballet. Next a kind of lift came up from the cellar bearing with it the keyboard of the organ. . . . After which we were entertained by a ballet of the inevitable Edward German Dances. All of which may have been magnificent, but was not, I submit, 'the pictures'.

At last *Nell Gwyn* came and the film enshrining her turned out to be of the description-beggaring order. Thousands of dull feet were succeeded by thousands yet duller, unredeemed by any notable feature. The orange girl is portrayed by Miss Dorothy Gish. . . . Legend has it that the ex-orange girl filled a room with her mere presence, whereas her present portrayer's quality of pinched *gaminerie* empties the scene of significance.

Hilaire Belloc

(see page 161)

In a near-by column Frank Rutter has some doubts about modern French painting:

The much-experienced observer is apt nowadays to find impressionist paintings almost too literal in their rendering of facts, but persons brought up on the pictures of Leighton and Millais still find these works bewildering. Monet, Pissarro, and Sisley invented a new language of colour which we must certainly learn and understand before we can begin to appreciate the beauty of their work.

These things being so, how unreasonable it appears to condemn a large number of people because they are unable to see any beauty or development! With good will a person with some knowledge of impressionist painting can perceive the brilliant luminosity and intense feeling in Van Gogh's fieldscape of Arles (18), but without some sympathetic understanding of the painter's cerebral condition any observer may be pardoned for failing to be moved by the pathetic intensity of his Femme sur fond bleu (19). Indeed, when we realise the emotional and intellectual complexity which has characterised so much of modern French painting, even the most hardened investigator perceives how much can be said in favour of a return to simplicity. A certain relief, then, will be felt both by the expert and the layman in noting that the most recent painting shown by M. Picasso is also his simplest and most clearly intelligible. His femme assise (34), painted in 1923, shows even this indefatigable inventor of new things in paint wearying of geometrical complexity and returning to an eminently normal and scrupulously economic presentation of the essentials of the things seen.

The book page was rather nondescript that Sunday. Radclyffe Hall's novel 'Adam's Breed' was unworthily singled out as the best piece of fiction for several years, and Edmund Gosse was dull. At an earlier date, reviewing one of the most notable of all books of the 1920s, Geoffrey Scott's 'Portrait of Zelide', he had concluded by trying to resist the Zeitgeist: 'I have been sorely tempted to leave this book unnoticed, excellent as it is. Before publication the publishers have been announcing it in these terms, "This book is a masterpiece". It is not for them to puff their goods beforehand in this presumptuous fashion. The practice is becoming much too prevalent. The business of publishers is to produce books, and leave readers to decide the value of their merchandise.' Margaret Kennedy's 'The Constant Nymph' was the current fiction best-seller.

There was a serial too. Not very long before there had been the memoirs of Sir Johnston Forbes-Robertson, the actor. Now it was Sir Felix Semon, the distinguished German-born laryngologist.

Still turning the pages of the front half of the paper one finds the leader writer niggling at the Chancellor of the Exchequer, Mr Winston Churchill, in the name of economy – which was everyone's theme at this stage of the 1920s: 'He was saying on Tuesday that large savings could only be made if the fighting forces were reduced to impotence, or if the social life of the people were suddenly and notably lowered. If the Chancellor means that the "social reform" legislation of the past twenty years, the insurance schemes, and the dole and the Labour Exchanges and so on, are to be immune from enquiry, then the cause of economy is all but hopeless. It is precisely in these directions that we have been spending most lavishly beyond our means.'

And elsewhere in the paper the Liberal Sir Donald Maclean, father of the wretched Donald Maclean of our own day, takes a more particular line in a week-end speech (Maclean was an intense campaigner against Churchill and an almost fanatic preacher of economy): 'For the first time since 1919 the annual reduction of debt has been arrested. It was useless for the Chancellor of the Exchequer to try to sidetrack the consequence of the coal subsidy and its effect on this year's Budget.'

The chief trouble was indeed coal, as we shall see in a moment. Meanwhile on the Saturday of March 6, 1926, there had been a grave *contretemps* in foreign affairs.

The Prime Minister was Stanley Baldwin, and as if in reaction to the adventurism of Lloyd George, nationally and internationally, he wanted tranquillity, brotherhood, a minimum of party strife. This was 'Baldwinism', a worthy ideal. But Baldwin was not pressingly interested in foreign politics, and at this time they were largely the creation of his Foreign Secretary, Sir Austen Chamberlain, who at Locarno on Lake Maggiore in the previous autumn had through his eyeglass seignorially surveyed the Prime Minister of France, Aristide Briand, and Gustav Stresemann of Germany and concerted the lofty Locarno Pact with them, with picturesque ceremonies at the Palais de Justice and triumphal excursions on the lake in the twilight. Henceforth France – whom Sir Austen loved like a mistress – was to be kinder to Germany, and Germany was to be admitted, as a reward for being amenable, to the council of the League of Nations. For Locarno was conceived as the first great step in the reconciliation of Europe; and for inaugurating this new era of international cooperation Sir Austen was given the Garter and a half-share in the Nobel Peace prize for 1925.

But there was mist on the lake by the following spring – or, as the wicked Lloyd George put it, 'the wine of Locarno was already badly corked.' The trouble was that Briand had charmed Chamberlain into thinking that Poland might be allowed to join the League of Nations too: ever realistic, France wanted to have a friend of hers in the club in case Germany made a nuisance of herself again. There was great perturbation in London about this, and the Government found it necessary, though ever so gently, to disavow Sir Austen, even if in the House of Commons the Foreign Secretary had taken refuge in a dim religious light, leaving some people rather uncertain as to what precisely was afoot. The leader-writer, nevertheless, spoke forthrightly for the British people: this hedging of bets was, he said, although in not quite these words, an unsporting action – Germany's admission was on the agenda and was acceptable, but there must be no return to the old balance-of-power systems by allowing Poland, one of France's allies, to join.

On the morning of Saturday, March 6, as the paper chronicled it, the Foreign Secretary (his glory a little tarnished) was on the platform at Victoria Station, surrounded by his entourage, and in the act of leaving to meet Briand at Geneva, there to gather the first-fruits of Locarno (and strictly the agreed first-fruits only) when a messenger brought the news that the Prime Minister of France had just been defeated in the Chamber and had immediately resigned. 'It could not have come at a more awkward juncture,' said the leader-writer thoughtfully but not despairingly; and he concluded, almost with a tinge of relief, that the meeting at the League of Nations might be hung up *sine die*.

It is possible that neither Mr Baldwin, nor the British people, nor even their stern spokesman, the leader-writer himself, were desperately attached to the idealistic Locarno Pact. It might be necessary to pay the deepest respect to it and deplore a return to the wicked old system of European alliances. But it is more likely, to judge from the temper of the time, that the British people (or such of them as understood it) looked upon this treaty of non-aggression between France, Germany and Belgium, under the guarantee of Britain and Italy, as all part of a European miasma or shiversome never-never land. Whereas the problem of coal – British coal – was a rocklike reality and one whose intractability was bedevilling everything.

Harold Cox certainly thought this. In that Sunday's paper his article prepared his readers for despairing news from the new Royal Commission on Coal, whose chairman was Sir Herbert Samuel, and looked at the insoluble with the outraged indignation of an orthodox *laisser-faire* economist:

The number of persons employed in the mining industry of the United Kingdom has increased by over a quarter of a million, whereas the output of coal remains practically the same as it was twenty years ago. Meanwhile, the wages cost of producing this coal has risen from £67,000,000 to over £143,000,000.

We have to sell our coal in world markets in competition with other countries. We have also to sell coal in competition with oil. The miners' leaders, like most Socialists, seem to imagine, or pretend to believe, that it is possible to regulate industry on the basis of what is called 'a living wage' for the man who produces it. Buyers of coal, like buyers of everything else, try to buy as cheaply as they can. . . .

The cumulative effect of these different factors was to destroy in the earlier portion of last year all possibility of profit throughout a large portion of the coal industry of the UK. The directors of that industry consequently found it necessary to state that they must either reduce the cost of production or shut down the pits. The miners responded by threatening a universal strike, and by organising sympathetic support from other advanced trade unions. The Government took fright. On July 30 in the afternoon they said that they would never consent to a subsidy; before the evening was over they had consented. At first the subsidy was only used to maintain rates of wages which experience had proved to be uneconomic, and the owners in many districts continued to bear throughout August and September very heavy losses. In the succeeding months the State contribution was increased so that owners' losses were diminished, and some collieries once again began to make 'profits' – profits derived, not from the coal industry itself, but from the blackmail levied on the other industries of the nation.

'Where,' he concluded, 'is this madness to stop?' The answer was in the 'universal strike' which the miners had threatened on July 30, 1925, and which became a reality some two months after Harold Cox wrote.

The report of the Samuel Commission was a document in some ways unusually creative, but in the miners' eyes its proposals for the future were diminished to vanishing point by its recommending an immediate reduction in wages; and for their part the owners wanted not only lower wages but longer hours. Said the miners, 'Not a penny off the pay, not a minute on the day.'

They were locked out on May 1, and the General Council of the TUC, who had been trying to find a solution, approved plans for a general strike two days later, while still continuing to negotiate with the government. To Baldwin and the members of his cabinet the whole thing seemed an exercise in revolution.

Then late on the evening of Sunday, May 2, when a formula was on the point, more hopefully than realistically, of being set down, Baldwin received a telephone message. He called the TUC officials into the cabinet room and gave them a memorandum which stated that as 'overt acts' had already taken place the government could not resume negotiations until they 'had been repudiated and instructions for a general strike immediately and unconditionally withdrawn.'

What had happened was that compositors on The Daily Mail, acting on their own initiative, had refused to set an anti-strike leading article. The Government made the mistake of leaving the TUC no route for retreat, and the general strike (which was not quite literally general) started at midnight on the Monday. It lasted for nine days, but the wretched miners stayed out doggedly until December, capitulating finally on the owners' terms. It was an extraordinary episode heaped high with confusion, and it left a mark of long-term intransigence on the trades union movement. But, paradoxically, its immediate result was a more conciliatory leadership.

Perhaps the correct answer to Harold Cox's question, then, is that the madness stopped on January 1, 1947, when the industry was transferred to national ownership. But national ownership didn't prevent a national strike and another national disaster early in 1972.

XVII

The Sunday Times minced no words about the general strike in the hotly patriotic four-page edition which it managed to produce at the Newcastle office of Allied Newspapers for May 9 (with 'This England never did nor never shall lie at the proud foot of a conqueror' in one of the ear-pieces by the title-block) :

> What is now at stake goes far beyond the fortunes of any single industry, however important. It concerns the very spirit and structure of the State. It is a struggle in which the nation can only yield by surrendering everything that has made Britain what she is. Once permit a junta of trade union officials to overrule Parliament by bringing the business of the country to a stop, and all that has been most deeply cherished in the British system goes by the board. We cease from that moment to be a self-governing people. We become the victims of a rapacious tyranny.

Its editorial policy remained implacably stern, even vindictive, when the strike had collapsed. The industrial challenge to the government reminded the leader writer of all that had been most evil in recent history :

> The great thing about the strike was that it failed. If it had gone on longer its collapse would have been even more complete. Faced with an attempted hold-up of Great Britain that was on all fours with Germany's

hold-up of Europe twelve years ago, the nation grappled with the domestic crisis as it had grappled with the foreign. In spite of the plainest evidence of their eyes and ears, there were people who would not believe that Germany intended war. Similarly there were those who for long were wilfully blind to the fact that there existed in the governing councils of British Labour a group that reproduced, in the sphere of industry, the same spirit and tactics, and were bent on very much the same programme as the Prussian military clique of the pre-war days.

A second leader, however, was more conciliatory. It tended to regard the strike less as an assault upon the citadel of British freedom than as a matter of congratulation for all concerned. 'There have been many features of the strike,' it said, 'which, if we were a people given to boasting, might well make us proud of ourselves.' Especially admirable, it seems, had been the police and the strikers themselves. 'They might have made things very ugly; they did, as a matter of fact, make them tolerable, if not wholly easy. The greatest of strikes in British history was also the best-tempered and the most orderly.' And the Prime Minister was naturally not left out of the universal sunshine: 'The man who has come out best is Mr Baldwin ... Mr Baldwin's restraint sometimes amounts almost to a sort of ostentation like the pride that apes humility, but when he does expand it, it is to reveal both strength and beauty of mind.'

Amidst complacency of this sort only Lord Darling struck a sombre note with his poem 'The Victim, May 3, 1926' (the same Mr Justice Darling who had been earlier denounced by the paper). Its opening line suggested a caption to some Victorian painting:

Doctor, you tell me I shall die tonight –
And I am glad that my down-weighted eyes
Shall ope no more; although the sun must rise
To flood again the weary world with light.
When every lawn and lifted hill show bright,
That makes not England. Slaves share fairer skies.
Let me not linger on where freedom dies,
And honour fades un-honoured from the sight.
Lost are the English, should they ere accept,
In place of ordered Liberty, the chain
Of mob-made tyrants, or the lawless crowd
For every art of government inept,
Who see in ruined States their certain gain.

Opposite : This four-page general strike edition was produced at Newcastle by William Redpath and distributed by air. Most national newspapers had a mimeographed sheet.

THE STRIKE: ITS SIGNIFICANCE.

SECOND EDITION.

e at the earliest
resumption of
bring peace and
to our coalfields,
cial weapon which
inadvisably drawn
sheathed."—Lord
squith.

Sunday Times

Established 1822. AY SPECIAL. 103rd Year of issue.

No. 5378. SUNDAY, MAY 9, 1926. PRICE TWOPENCE.

"THIS ENGLAND NEVER DID NOR NEVER SHALL LIE AT THE PROUD FOOT OF A CONQUERER."

RNMENT AIMS IN USTRIAL CONFLICT.

REITERATES THAT DOOR PEACE IS STILL OPEN.

ERS' FEARS ALLAYED.

ATTLE TO LOWER STANDARD OF LIVING.

ay of the national strike, promoted by the General Council nion Congress, finds the country cheerful and unperturbed, siderable inconvenience and economic loss.

news of negotiations between the Government and the . The Prime Minister, backed by the Cabinet, Parliament ion, declines to enter into official communications until led off.

end of the country to the other, essential services are being d, thanks to the voluntary assistance rendered by all community. As the strike continues, these will nprove.

in addressed a striking wireles message to the nation text of which is given below.

day Times " appears to-day in a totally unfamiliar and d form. Our readers will, however, understand the acute h we, in common with almost the entire British Press, g.

the London Station of ight, Mr. Baldwin gave sage dealing with the

rike has now been in ly a week and I think as Prime Minister, I ation once more what e lamentable struggle

istinct issues—the stop- ndustry and the general

n the coal industry has months' inquiry and

at to secure agreement of the Commission's the time comes, as I , to discuss the terms coal industry is to be ll continue my efforts y settlement justice is miners and the owners.

MENT IS FIGHTING.

the issue for which is fighting? It is fight- hile negotiations were the T.U.C. ordered a presumably to try to and the community to

ject, the T.U.C. has railways shall not run, hall not move, that the s shall stop, and that ach the public. f electricity and the f the food supplies of been interrupted. declares that this is trial dispute, but their ing the miners is to unity. Could there be attack upon the com- t a body not elected by country, without con- ple, without consulting unionists, and in order ions never yet defined, he life of the nation and into submission? king the standard of ple? Is it the Govern- only sought to bring ible settlement in the r the T.U.C., who have which, if continued, increase unemployment, n of rates and taxes and e whole standard of life

make it as clear as I he Government is not lower the standard of miners or of any other the workers. That is being spread about, e.

OF MINERS.

lieve that any honest t that my whole desire the standard of living , and that I am ready mployers to make any s end, consistent with dustry itself in working

many people who say with the general strike, deal of sympathy with do I. But after Parlia- twenty-three millions in g industry, and had re- rt of an exceptionally , what else could it do about a settlement on at that Commission de- ly condition upon which n be kept in existence? eat, therefore, that the prepared now, as it has accept the Report, and rt, if the other parties

I have said, and I repeat it now, that the Government will take whatever steps are practicable to carry out the re-organisation proposals in the report.

The Government remain convinced that these steps are an essential factor in getting the industry on to an economic basis, so that the country may be preserved from a repetition of the serious disputes in the coal trade.

CONDITIONS FOR NEGOTIATIONS.

We are prepared, as soon as circumstances permit, to consult with the owners and the miners to see in what way effect can best be given to this policy, and the country may rest assured that when the time comes the Government will be ready with proposals.

We are being asked: Is the Government taking the position that it will not negotiate? The answer to this question was given in the statement made on behalf of the Government in the House of Commons on Monday last as follows:—

"Anyone can approach the Government who has authority, and can parley with them, and it is our duty to parley with them; but the T.U.C. have only to cancel the general strike and withdraw the challenge they have issued, and we shall immediately begin, with the utmost care and patience, with them, again, the long, laborious task which has been pursued for these many weeks to endeavour to rebuild on economic foundations the prosperity of the coal trade."

This is our position. No door is closed. But, on the other hand, while the situation remains what it is, we have no alternative whatever but to go forward unflinchingly and do our duty.

Meanwhile, notwithstanding the dislocation of transport and of fuel supplies, I hope employers will do all in their power to keep their works running in order to mitigate those hardships which must necessarily fall upon the people in an emergency such as this.

A MAN OF PEACE.

This is the Government's position. The general strike must be called off absolutely and without reserve. The mining industry dispute can then be settled.

This is a fair arrangement, and it would be a thousand times better to accept it than to continue the struggle, which can only increase misery and disaster the longer it lasts.

The solution is within the grasp of the nation the instant that the trades union leaders are willing to abandon the general strike.

I am a man of peace. I am longing and working and praying for peace, but I will not surrender the safety and security of the British Constitution. You placed me in power 18 months ago by the largest majority accorded to any party for many many years.

Have I done anything to forfeit that confidence? Cannot you trust me to ensure a square deal for the parties, to secure even justice between man and man?

CUP CONTEST.

PARIS, Saturday. ederation de Baume has ues Worth and M. du nt France in the inter- tennis competition for p, which is to take place ay 10 at Prince's Club. Special.

r and Company, chemical have been obliged to ir Middlesbrough works throwing out of employ- men.

has been created through l. The men had not ctions from their union the general strike.

WARNING TO MINE?

Ammanford and district, which was the storm centre of the anthracite strike last year, is peaceful, and the strikers are enjoying cricket and football matches daily. The railwaymen at Ammanford have warned the miners that disturbances or night demonstrations will lead to reconsideration of their position, and they have protested against the admission of Communists into the local Trade and Labour Councils.

The windows of five shops in Middlesbrough were smashed by young hooligans late on Friday night.

Several steamers, loaded and ready to sail, are detained at Antwerp because their crews refuse to leave until they have received instructions from London.

MORE RAILMEN GO BACK TO WORK.

TRANSPORT IMPROVING DAILY.

THE TRAMS POSITION.

Further improvements in the nation's railway services and transport generally were reported yesterday. More railwaymen returned to work.

The Southern Railway announced that 12,614 men of all grades have remained loyal or have returned to work in spite of their unions instructions

Fifty-six per cent. of the Southern's supervisory and clerical staff are at work.

Practically all the railway staffs at Chelford, Alderley, Handforth and Cheadle Hulme returned to work yesterday.

The improvement in the Birmingham train services was maintained. Several services of Corporation 'buses, manned by volunteers, were re-started.

The London General Omnibus Company is now operating over 300 'buses.

Over 80 per cent. of Liverpool tramwaymen are now at work.

Railway clerks at Cardiff are appealing to be reinstated. The Great Western clerks at Pontypool have already returned.

Cardiff tramwaymen are re-starting in considerable numbers.

L.N.E.R. ARRANGEMENTS.

The L.N.E.R. announces that there will be no passenger train service to-day.

The only trains to be run in the Newcastle district will be the foodstuffs train, 8 a.m. Newcastle to Carlisle, and the 12.32 p.m. Carlisle to Newcastle.

A new emergency time sheet will be exhibited at all stations to-morrow, embodying additional services which it has been possible to arrange. A new emergency time book will be available at the booking offices on application.

FOOD HELD UP.

Hull Dockers' Refusal to Unload Trawlers.

A serious extension of the general strike, and one against the promise of the Trade Union Congress, occurred at Hull yesterday

Six steam trawlers with heavy cargoes of fresh fish reached St. Andrew's Dock, four from Iceland and two from the North Sea The men who discharge the fish on to the quayside held a meeting, at which it was agreed to strike.

None of these large cargoes of perishable fish could be discharged yesterday. The authorities hope to discharge them by volunteer labour under naval, military and police protection, and to remove the fish by train and motor transport to inland towns to help maintain the food supplies.

RAID ON FOWL HOUSE.

Charitable Police Provide Thieves With Food.

A remarkable instance of police charity was related at Ashby-de-la-Zouch Police Court yesterday, when two married miners and a pipe-yard hand were charged with stealing five hens, valued at £2, from a fowl-house. When arrested by the police they admitted their guilt.

A police superintendent said: they found no food in the house, and the children were wanting a meal. The police made a collection among themselves, and food was procured.

Remanding the accused to the petty sessions, the chairman of the Bench advised the defendants to remain steady and to assist in preserving order. He would be pleased to add a subscription to the fund kindly subscribed by the police.

The accused, who were remanded in their own recognisances, expressed gratitude to the police for providing them with a Sunday's dinner.

BALLOT OF SEAMEN.

Mr. Havelock Wilson Sends a Message to Ships' Crews.

The following message from Mr. Havelock Wilson, general president of the Seamen's Union, to the masters of all ships of the British Mercantile Marine.

"Please read the following message to your crew:—"Unauthorised persons are calling seamen out on strike—they say on instructions from the Trade Union Congress. They have no authority to do so. The council of your union is the only body who have power to do so, and then only if members of the union have balloted. It is the right of seamen to decide such questions as strikes for themselves. The ballot has not yet been completed because of the difficulties of the postal services. I hope to have the ballot completed by Thursday of Friday of next week.

"If the ballot is declared in favour of a strike it is my duty to inform you that in the course of the law no strike money can be paid from the union funds for sympathetic strikes. It would be helpful if you would cable whether the crew of your ship endorses my view of ballot before strike."

PLEDGE OF PREMIER.

Case of Trade Unionists Who Remain at Work.

The following additional guarantee from Mr. Baldwin was broadcast yesterday afternoon:—

"Every man who does his duty by the country and remains at work, or returns to work, during the present crisis, will be protected by the State from loss of trade union benefits, superannuation allowances, or pensions.

"His Majesty's Government will take whatever steps are necessary in Parliament or otherwise for this purpose. — STANLEY BALDWIN."

CALL TO LEGIONAIRES.

In a message issued yesterday, the British Legion states that in the present state of emergency it is the duty of all loyal citizens and men of good intent actively to support the cause of law and order, and do everything in their power to uphold the Constitution.

All ex-service men should offer their services to the authorities.

CABINET MEETS.

A fully attended Cabinet meeting was held at 10, Downing Street last evening when further emergency measures were considered.

About the time the Cabinet was assembling the Earl of Balfour and Lord Londonderry called at No. 10. The former remained, while the Cabinet was in session. Lord Londonderry remained only a few minutes.

LONDON'S STRIKE GARB.

POLICE GUARDS ON THE 'BUSES.

SENTRIES IN KHAKI.

"SPECIALS" PATROL THE WEST END.

London, basking in warm sunshine, presented a customary "Saturday afternoon" atmosphere of desertion in its central districts yesterday.

'Buses were running in frequent succession, and even queuing up at the principal stopping points. Beside each volunteer driver, however, was a constable, while with the conductor was a special

Most of the volunteers were of the university student class, and boarded windows on some of the 'buses gave indications of possible attacks.

For the first time since the strike began, special constables in civilian clothes, with their gauntlets, appeared on patrol duty in the West End, walking in couples.

A group of these stood about the "Morning Post" office in Aldwych, at which men in "plus fours" were unloading huge rolls of newsprint for the "British Gazette."

TIN-HATTED SOLDIERS.

Occasionally a lorry with a few tin-hatted soldiers on board drove by, bound for the docks, which is the only district in London which has been put under military patrol.

In Hyde Park the number of lorries had greatly increased, owing to the difficulty of garaging them in their own sheds. The line of cars extended from the Marble Arch all the way to Knightsbridge.

Theatres continued to do business. Many gave matinees, and a few played to full houses.

Perhaps the most noticeable features in the streets in the morning was the appearance of daily papers again. Nearly every paper brought out editions.

ACTIVITY IN WHITEHALL.

Whitehall, particularly in the neighbourhood of New Scotland Yard, was the scene of considerable activity. Contingents of special constables were for a period continually emerging from the police headquarters and marching westwards, attracting much public attention.

The famous Horse Guards sentries were replaced by dismounted men of the Life Guards in Service dress, bearing rifles.

A similar change was made at Buckingham Palace and the various Royal residences where the Guards post sentries. All were in service khaki.

The Horse Guards Parade was one vast park of motor cars and motor cycles. Volunteers were in readiness to proceed at a moments notice on errands of national importance.

UNFAMILIAR SIGHT.

Lorry Loads of Troops Moved About Capital.

During yesterday a number of troops were moved about London. Lorry loads of men in full fighting kit passed down Southampton Row about midday, and dismounted near the entrance to the underground tramway which runs under Kingsway to the Embankment.

It was rumoured that it was intended to reopen the tramways, and that the soldiers were there to guard the tunnel, but after a while the men re-entered the lorries and were driven away towards the East End.

At midday a motor transport column about a mile in length arrived in London. The majority of the lorries appeared to be empty, but at intervals there were lorries carrying armed men in full Service dress. They were not molested, as they passed, in any way by the hundreds of men who were standing about on the pavements in the East End.

KILLED WHILE ON STRIKE.

Thomas Kinder, aged 46, of Claycross, a miner on strike, fell down a disused quarry in the darkness, near Bakewell, and was killed. At the inquest yesterday a verdict of "Accidental death through a fall down an old quarry" was returned

BAN ON IRISH SHIPMENTS.

It was announced at the headquarters of the Irish Labour Party, in Dublin, yesterday that the General Council of the British Trade Union Congress had intimated to the Irish trade unions that shipments from Ireland to British ports should cease.

Printed in Great Britain and distributed by air.

SPACE FOR LATE NEWS.

REPLY TO SIR JOHN SIMON.

T.U.C. AND AIMS OF THE STRIKE.

LEGAL RIGHT CLAIMED.

It was stated at the press conference held last night at the headquarters of the Trade Union Congress that, in regard to the general situation, reports which covered the greater portion of the country went to show that solidarity was maintained, and if possible increased. The second line of defence men were coming out steadily.

"In his speech in the House of Commons," proceeded the statement, "Sir John Simon appears to have attempted to prove that the general strike differs essentially from a stoppage in a single industry, and he concluded by saying that the attack on the community had deprived the miners of a great deal of sympathy they thoroughly deserved.

"We are bound to repudiate afresh the allegation that the Congress is engaged in an attack on the community. It appears to us that strenuous attempts are being made to turn the public mind into a channel that we are engaged in a fight against the Constitution, and that this is, purely a political struggle, camouflaged in an industrial dispute.

"NOT FIGHTING THE PUBLIC."

"We are not fighting the public, nor are we attempting to overthrow constitutional government.

"The trade unions have exercised a legal and long-established right of withholding their labour. This is not only a legal but a moral right, and it has been done to protect a section—namely, the miners—against the degradation of their standard of life.

"It is inevitable in a general stoppage that contracts should in certain instances have been broken, but neither Sir John nor anybody else can take that fact to signify that the movement as a whole is engaged in a sinister conspiracy to wreck the community.

"We began the struggle, and it is being carried on by the Council, purely as an industrial struggle. In our judgment, the argument of Sir John Simon and Cabinet Ministers that we are engaged in an attempt to overthrow the Constitution and undermine Parliamentary institutions is a wilful and deliberate attempt to confuse the issue.

MONEY FROM MOSCOW RETURNED.

"An attempt is being made to confuse and prejudice the position of the trade union movement by an allegation that we have received money from Moscow. This morning a cheque arrived from the All-Russian Central Council of Trade Unions, Palace of Labour, Moscow. It ran into some thousands.

"We fully considered the matter, and decided to send a courteous reply, expressing our appreciation, but our inability to accept the cheque, and it has been returned.

"The statement has been made that the National Free Church Council had placed the whole of their organisation at the disposal of the Government. We have the authority of the Rev. T. Nightingale, secretary of the Free Church Council, that this statement is not in accordance with the facts. The matter has not been considered by the Executive Committee.

LONDON TRAIN SERVICE.

"We have had interviews with the pickets in the London district regarding the reports that hundreds of trains are running. Our information is that 90 per cent. of the goods coming into London are coming by road, and not by rail. In an hour's test at Waterloo there were about four trains in the hour. At King's Cross they are practising with empty trains, presumably containing volunteers, and there was only one train in two hours. At Paddington a number of lorries went in to pick up food. Seven went in and came out empty.

LEVY ON WORKERS.

"The Council have decided to instruct that all men in work shall be called upon to pay five per cent. of their wages as a levy for the strike funds. The Council are appealing to trades unions and sympathisers abroad for financial contributions.

"There is to be a meeting on May 11 of the Labour and Social International and the International Federation of Trade Unions at Amsterdam to discuss the dispute internationally."

[Sir John Simon's speech is reported in full on Page Four.]

BLOW AT FLOUR MILLS.

The transport workers have ordered out all men engaged in the flour-milling industry at Liverpool, Birkenhead, Seacombe and Ellesmere Port. The delivery question is to be dealt with by union area officers.

There are large stocks at the Seacombe mills, but motor lorries arriving there yesterday were sent away empty. An official announcement has been made that steps will be taken to keep the flour mills open.

MILK PRICES IN TOWNS.

The Civil Commissioners have announced that the statement, as already broadcast, of an increase of twopence per quart for milk applies only to the London district. The statement appears to have been misunderstood in some Midland districts, and an advance has been made in price. This should not have been done, and has no justification.

PAPERS SENT BY AIR TO LONDON.

Enterprise of North Country Journalism.

Among the most conspicuous feats of journalistic enterprise exhibited during the week of crisis was that of the "North Mail and Newcastle Daily Chronicle," which is being produced day by day by a small emergency staff.

On Friday an edition of this paper, four pages in size, admirably printed and illustrated, was sent by aeroplane from Newcastle to London, where it was very rapidly sold out.

Both the Prime Minister and Mr. Winston Churchill had copies, which they examined with great interest and approval.

A record has been established at the "Newcastle Chronicle" offices, in that morning and evening papers have been regularly produced under strike conditions, and the Sunday publication, the "Sunday Sun," is also on sale to-day.

"ENGLAND WINS."

(From the Home Secretary to the Editor of the "Sunday Times.")

I am delighted you are going to publish to-morrow. Sunday without its "Sunday Times" would be a sad day.

Please tell the loyal people of our contry to keep a good heart and a stiff upper lip.

The news to-day is good. The first convoy from the London Docks came out this morning, and was received with cheers; while the guards who marched down yesterday afternoon to dockland had a perfect ovation. One of the battalions, by the way, was the one which the lying bulletins stated had mutinied.

Tell your readers to believe no news that is not official. England wins to a certainty.

May 8, 1926. W. JOYNSON-HICKS.

IF VIOLENCE IS USED.

Minister and Employment of Armed Forces.

In a letter to the Canterbury Conservative Association, Mr. Ronald McNiel, Financial Secretary to the Treasury, says:—If the condition of affairs means that this country is nearer to actual civil war than it has been for centuries, it is incumbent upon every loyal man and woman in the country, whatever their ordinary political opinion may be to rally to the support of the Government to enable them to avert an unspeakable disaster.

If the public realise the magnitude of the issue, and submit to privation and inconvenience with as much cheerfulness as they can command, the Government which in this matter represents the whole nation, must prevail in the end.

"The difference between the colliery owners and the miners was an industrial dispute," said Mr McNeill, "although no doubt one of the first magnitude, but the general strike which has now been called is quite different.

"Its avowed aim is to coerce the nation as a whole, and to produce such a general paralysis as would force the Government to surrender at discretion to a combination of committees without a vestige of constitutional authority. If the Government were to be forced to make such a surrender it would be the end of constitutional Government in this country.

"All revolutionary elements in the country are, of course, doing their utmost to exploit the situation to their own advantage, and every day that the conflict lasts must increase the danger of an outbreak of violence which would have to be met by employment of the armed forces of the Crown, the consequence of which it is utterly impossible to foresee.

"There is no use disguising the fact that this is a very real danger, and it is for this reason that it is so necessary for the public everywhere to remain calm and to place at the disposal of the Government all the resources they have to enable the administration to be carried out."

'ABSOLUTELY NO CHANGE'

Mr. A. J. Cook on Week-End Outlook.

The Executive of the Miners Federation held a short meeting in London, yesterday, and received reports on the situation.

Mr. Herbert Smith and Mr. A. J. Cook were in consultation with the T.U.C. General Council all the morning. Mr. Ramsay MacDonald being also present at the conference.

Mr. Cook stated afterwards that there had been "absolutely no change" in the situation, and that there were no signs at present of any peace moves.

The position had been "considerably strengthened" from the trade union and the miners' point of view, he added. He did not anticipate any developments over the week-end, and there was not likely to be any new phase in the general situation earlier than to-morrow.

SCENES IN SUBURBIA.

Traffic Normal and No Food Shortage.

The suburbs of London presented a comparatively normal appearance yesterday afternoon. There was practically no road traffic out of the ordinary.

The Southern Railway, which by the aid of volunteers had maintained a wonderful service of electric trains during the past week, slackened down somewhat yesterday afternoon after the midday exodus, and trains reached Victoria and Waterloo at intervals of an hour or so, instead of every twenty minutes as formerly.

As far as could be ascertained, there was no shortage of foodstuffs in the outlying suburbs, and for the most part shopkeepers loyally refrained from exploiting their customers on account of the strike.

Regular services were being maintained in London on the Underground Railways.

LOYAL RAILWAY CLERKS.

WHY THEY DECLINE TO STRIKE.

HONOURING BOND.

SOME HOME TRUTHS FOR UNION.

The loyal clerical staff at a large goods station in the North-eastern area of the London and North Eastern Railway has issued a series of replies to the demand by the Railway Clerks' Association that they should strike. The demand was supported by the following reasons:—

(a) To give direct assistance to the miners' cause.

(b) Because if this case is lost we ourselves shall be the next to be "attacked."

(c) Because the R.C.A. has asked us to do so.

The answers to these three reasons are:—

"(a) It does not matter one iota to the miners' cause whether we strike or not; our assistance is a negligible quantity. We sympathise with the miners, and realise that theirs is a hard and dangerous calling. We believe they are entitled to expect the best possible pay and conditions the industry can afford. But further than that we cannot go, and we must leave them and the owners to work out their own salvation. They have never rendered the railway clerks one ha'porth of assistance, nor do we suppose they have the slightest interest in our affairs.

"(b) There is not a shred of evidence to support this theory, and we are quite in the wrong to strike in anticipation of something which may never happen. We cannot strike against imaginary grievances.

"(c) After the able and masterful way in which Mr. Walkden put forward our case in the recent proceedings before the Wages Tribunal we deeply regret to decline to follow his instructions now. We can only submit that he has been badly misled by his advisers if he ever assumed that the staff would wholeheartedly support a strike of this kind. The reason why we make this submission is that the R.C.A. in many centres is governed by a small coterie of extremists, high-minded and autocratic, who pander to socialistic ideals which are not by any means the ideals of the majority of the staff."

ON SIDE OF LAW AND ORDER.

The statement adds:

"We are not sure that this is not more of a political or class war, or even a war upon the staple industries of the country, and in the absence of any serious official contradiction we are bound to place ourselves on the side of law and order, and constitutional methods.

"Can you explain why the railways, struggling desperately at the present time to make ends meet, should be victimised by having their men called out whilst their rivals on the roads are allowed to step in and seize the traffic.

"To strike against the railways now and leave their competitors free is to aim a cowardly blow at the industry which provides us with a livelihood. And it will recoil on our own heads, for our prosperity is closely bound up with that of our employers. The more traffic goes to road, the worse for us.

"Have the railwaymen and miners given any thought to the most serious distress which their action will cause to those less fortunate than themselves? Have they considered the unemployed, the labourers, the casual workers who have to struggle at the best of times to earn a precarious living?

POINT OF HONOUR.

"Why has our agreement, reached after years and years of constant struggling, been so ruthlessly broken at a moment's notice? Let us honour our bond, and do not give the company the chance to say we have dishonoured it.

"We think very strongly that before arriving at a decision on the question of alliance with other unions, the R.C.A. might at least have consulted its own members individually, so that they might have had an opportunity of expressing their views on the subject.

"If the R.C.A. cannot run our affairs without dragging us so hopelessly into the squabbles of other unions, they must stand down and make way for someone who can."

COUNTRY VICTIMISED.

Railway Chief on "Blackest Spot in Labour's History."

Sir Felix Pole, the General Manager of the Great Western Railway, in a message on victimisation, says:

"Victimisation is usually imported at the end of a strike, the trade unions invariably asking that there should be no victimisation.

"At the present time the country as a whole is being victimised by a strike which is the blackest spot in the history of labour in this country.

"That thousands of men with no grievance against their employers should have been instructed to leave work, and that so many of them should have done so, passes all comprehension.

"It can only be explained on the ground that there was a deep conspiracy against the State. Thank God, such a conspiracy cannot succeed, and can only result in the discrediting of its promoters and the disillusionment of those who have been used as pawns in the game."

BISHOP AND STRIKERS.

A service of intercession held in St. Albans Cathedral, yesterday, was attended by 1,[illegible] people thrown idle through the strike.

The Bishop of St. Albans discussed the situation with a group of strikers outside the Cathedral.

JOBS IN JEOPARDY.

Messrs. J. Lyons and Company state that employes who struck were given until midday yesterday to report for duty or lose their jobs permanently. A new permanent staff of transport and dispatch workers is being assembled.

Sir William Berry was a very resolute man but not an over-imaginative one, and the main leading articles at this time show in exaggerated form the political tone which his paper henceforth adopted: a forthright and unalleviated Toryism.

He had, however, one bitter regret about the general strike. It originated not at The Daily Mail but at The Sunday Times, and he was robbed of the chance of making a decisive gesture against Labour because of the weakness displayed in an emergency by the manager of the paper, Mr Clifton, and the news editor, Brodie Fraser.

Around this time members of one of the paper's printing unions, their feelings sharpened possibly by some disagreement with Clifton, had been showing a peculiar intransigence. The sports editor, for example, was astonished one Saturday night to be approached by a little deputation of men who complained of one of his headings, 'Lancashire's Day in the Cup'. Their pathetic point was that it was a controversial statement for a London paper and that the sports editor, as a north-countryman, was seeing things out of perspective. When he pointed out that The Sunday Times was a national paper and not a parochial weekly they agreed not to press the matter, but only grudgingly, and they remained angry at the Lancashire clubs having swept the board. So much for the supposition that bad sportsmanship is a development of recent times.

The attitudes and actions of the men were more serious in the early hours of Sunday morning, May 2. The 'overt act' in the composing room of The Daily Mail was anticipated by nearly 24 hours in the composing room of The Sunday Times.

In the paper for that day there was an $8\frac{1}{2}$-inch double-column advertisement issued by an unofficial body (the name of which was the Organisation for the Maintenance of Supplies) and calling for volunteers to help break the strike, giving addresses in London, the home counties, and the provinces to which volunteers should go. Throughout the Saturday evening there had been tenseness in the composing room about the advertisement, but nothing happened until the paper was finally put to press. Then a deputation of foundrymen and machine-room men approached Clifton and Fraser and told them that production of the edition would not be proceeded with unless the advertisement was battered at its head and its purpose obscured.

As it happened, the Berrys and Leonard Rees were unavailable. Clifton, probably rightly, declined to make a decision, and the

O. M. S.

LONDON.

Headquarters: 70. St. Stephen's House. Westminster, S.W.1.

Battersea: 26, Kyrle Road, S.W.11.
Chelsea: 69a, King's Road, S.W.3.
Fulham: 6, Harwood Road, S.W.6.
Greenwich: Kidbrooke Parish Room, Kidbrooke Park Road, Blackheath, S.W.3.
Hammersmith: Bridgeway House, Hammersmith, W.6.
Hampstead: Hon. Sec. O.M.S. Committee, Town Hall, Hampstead, N.W.3.
Islington: 270, Upper Street, Islington, N.1.

Kensington: 5, Hillsleigh Road, Campden Hill, W.8.
Lambeth: 60, Stockwell Park Crescent, S.W.9.
Lewisham: 139, Burnt Ash Hill, Lee, S.W.12.
Paddington: The Town Hall, Paddington, W.2.
St. Marylebone: 49, Beaumont Street, W.1.
St. Pancras: 19, Park Street, Camden Town, N.W.
Stoke Newington: 35, Stamford Hill, N.16.
Woolwich: 45, Thomas Street, S.E.

HOME COUNTIES.

Bexhill: Crantock, De la Warr Road, Bexhill.
Bishop Stortford: Kahote, Hadam Road, Bishop Stortford.
Brighton: 36, Grand Parade, Brighton.
Broadstairs: N. Foreland Golf Club, Broadstairs.
Bromley: 32, Widmore Road, Bromley, Kent.
Chelmsford: 4, Duke Street, Chelmsford.
Cheshunt: 140, Crossbrook Street, Waltham Cross.
Clacton: Dunkirk, Edith Road, Clacton.
Colchester: Monks Horton, Colchester.
Deal and Walmer: Brook Cottage, The Beach, Walmer.
Ealing: 15, The Mall, Ealing, W.5.
Eastbourne: Burntwood, Bedfordwell Road, Eastbourne.
Gravesend: 4, The Grove, Gravesend.
Harlow: The Old Ford, Harlow, Essex.
Hoddesdon: St. Cross, Hoddesdon, Herts.
Horsham: Alec Chasemore, Horsham, Sussex.

Hounslow: Waverley, Spring Grove Road, Isleworth.
Hytha: Templence, Earlsfield Road, Hythe.
Leyton: 35, Lyndhurst Drive, Leyton, E.10.
Maldon: Heybridge, Maldon, Essex.
Margate: Surrey Hall, Cliftonville, Margate.
Newport: The Orchard Cottage, Newport, Essex.
Rickmansworth: Mayfield, Rickmansworth, Herts.
Robertsbridge: George Hotel, Robertsbridge, Sussex.
Sidcup: Park Side, Elm Road, Sidcup, Kent.
Southend: 505, London Road, Southend.
St. Albans: Birtles, Battlefield Road, St. Albans.
Surrey: 3, Station Approach, Purley.
Tonbridge: 91, High Street, Tonbridge.
Tunbridge Wells: 5, Calverley Parade, Tunbridge Wells.
Watford: Town Hall, Oxhey, Watford.
Westgate: Sussex Mansions, Westgate.
Witham: Collingwood Road, Witham, Essex.

PROVINCES.

Alresford: North Court, Bishop's Sutton, Alresford, Hants.
Alton: 65, High Street, Alton, Hants.
Axminster: Weycroft Manor, Axminster.
Barnsley: 29, Church Street.
Basingstoke: 27, Winchester Street, Basingstoke.
Bath: 4, Argyle Street, Bath.
Bideford: Mayfield, Bideford, Devon.
Birmingham: 75, New Street, Birmingham.
Blackburn: J. Campbell, County Bank Chambers.
Blackpool: 1, St. Ive's Avenue, Blackpool.
Bolton: 188, Chorley New Road.
Bournemouth and New Forest: Danestream, Milford, Lymington, Hants.
Bradford: 17, Piccadilly.
Bromyard: Birchyfield, Bromyard.

Leominster: Shrublands, Kingsland, Herefordshire.
Lichfield: 12, Market Street, Lichfield.
Lincoln: F. Chambers, Cornhill, Lincoln.
Llandudno: Ribbleton, Llandudno.
Market Bosworth: Estate Office, Coleorton, near Leicester (A. E. Caldicott).
Melton Mowbray: Burrough Hall, nr. Leicester.
Monmouth Co.: 35, Commercial Street, Newport.
Northants City and County: Higham Ferrers, Northants.
Northumberland: 21, Lovaine Place, Newcastle.
Norwich: 32, Prince of Wales Road, Norwich.
Notts County: Cuckney House, Mansfield.
Okehampton: Cawsandslide, Southzeal, Okehampton.
Oswestry: Savings Bank, Oswestry.
Plymouth: Messrs. Viner and Carew, Prudential

This advertisement, an unofficial one which called for volunteers to help break the general strike, was censored by Sunday Times printers, who battered out the explanation at its head.

responsibility fell on Brodie Fraser. He had come from The Daily News to succeed Rees's son, 'Lal', who had taken over as news editor when F. W. Wilson had been sacked; and he was notoriously of such a nervous temperament that he was apt to tremble uncontrollably when sent for by Sir William Berry.

Someone who was present remembers still the agony of the poor man. Either the paper went to press on the men's condition or it would not appear at all; and if delivery times were to be met, there could be no delay now. With sweat streaming down his face, Fraser gave in. The men went away and battered the explanation at the head of the advertisement.

The Berrys were understandably angry that their paper, with its strong views, should have bowed completely to intimidation,[1] and they formally noted their regret in a leader note on May 23:

> The protest was made at a time when the authorities responsible for the conduct of this journal could not be communicated with, and when the many and varied issues raised by this unprecedented action could not be determined off-hand. It is satisfactory to know that no such attempt at a censorship is ever again likely to be repeated, and that the right of the British Press to print and publish such appeals, advertisements, news, and editorial comment as it thinks fit is henceforward placed beyond challenge or dispute.

Beyond challenge, that is, until 1970 and 1971, when censorship of a related nature occurred.

Brodie Fraser was a broken man, and after a decent interval Ernest Munton was appointed news editor. Considering the size and range of the paper, however, the full-time editorial staff remained astonishingly small. Apart from Dilys Powell the only acquisition had been Maitland Davidson, who was now writing the Hannen Swaffer column, 'Plays and Players', and doing various editorial jobs. He left the paper eventually to become executive editor of Gilbert Frankau's new magazine, 'Britannia', but it was a flop and he never recovered his once-promising position in Fleet Street.

In 1928 there was another change. When Sir Edmund Gosse died Rees filled the vacancy with another inspired selection. It was 'Affable Hawk' of The New Statesman – Gosse's old imagined enemy, Desmond MacCarthy.

XVIII

The editor of the paper had his little ways. He kept an account book in the drawer of his desk at the office, and every morning, as soon as he arrived, he would enter his winnings or losses at bridge for the evening before; if he made a profit at the end of the year

---

1. There was trouble also at The Sunday Express. A. J. P. Taylor tells us that Beaverbrook was called to the office about the advertisement. On the telephone Birkenhead advised him to compromise, but Churchill said, 'Close down; you can afford it.' In the end the fathers of the chapel were satisfied when Beaverbrook removed a few words from the advertisement. This was on the Saturday.

1936]   'AFFABLE HAWK' APPEARS

no one could escape his rejoicings. He was by no means as imperturbable as W. W. Hadley, who succeeded him, but all the same he never allowed himself to be unduly disturbed by the business of getting out a more and more ambitious newspaper. He did not, in fact, make the mistake of confusing incessant activity with creative efficiency. Saturdays were always the busiest day of the week, yet it was always on Saturday that a barber would arrive at 186 Strand at 12.30 pm to shave him and trim his hair. He would sit in his chair with a towel around his shoulders, shut away from the discreet hum of the office, while Miss Pugh guarded the door against intruders.

There was another ritual in which Leonard Rees liked to indulge, and that was the Tuesday morning distribution to reviewers. Miss Pugh would set out the new books in two rows, one fiction the other non-fiction. The critics would congregate and peer at them – Ralph Straus, who contributed the novel reviews for many years, Henry Murray, the little Scot Dr J. M. Bulloch, Dilys Powell and one or two others. Before Rees rolled in there would be uneasy talk in lowered voices, and when he did appear great and perfectly sincere respect would be paid to him. He would agree or disagree with the critics' choices, say some crushing words about any upstart young moderns he saw on the horizon, and presently depart for lunch and bridge at the Savile Club, or to meet the gentlemanly politician, Philip Morrell (husband of Lady Ottoline and a scion of the Oxfordshire brewing family of the same name), tall, aquiline, rubicund, a pundit out of an early novel by Aldous Huxley and an occasional reviewer for Rees.

These Tuesday morning gatherings were not attended by the chief literary critic. The provision of a book for Sir Edmund Gosse, and now for Desmond MacCarthy, was a matter on a higher level. Gosse did his consultation by letter, like a good Victorian; MacCarthy would ring up, or call, or meet Rees at his club. But whereas Gosse could do no wrong, MacCarthy, in the three years which remained before Rees departed to a place where there are no newspapers, could do little right. He was heard to complain, with a rueful smile, that Rees's attitude to him was like that of a man who had lost his first wife and married again: 'Rees looks at Gosse's picture on the wall, then looks hard at me, and says, "How different from my dear Jemima."'

The atmosphere at The New Statesman, whence Desmond had come, had been more casual, the intellectual attitude of his editor there, the brilliant but ill-fated Clifford Sharp, more understanding. It was not that Rees conducted a running battle with him, as he did with James Agate; it was nothing to do with his work. But whereas MacCarthy considered himself, a little optimistically perhaps, a highly practical man, Rees found in him something feckless and was disturbed by his dilatoriness, by his finishing his articles at the last minute in the printer's office, by his not saying good-bye on the telephone (a Bloomsbury habit still indulged in by Raymond Mortimer and Cyril Connolly), and by his forgetting appointments altogether or arriving late for them. (When Desmond was reading manuscripts for Heinemann he was always losing them in taxis or buses.) There was also his spelling. 'He is the only man in the world,' said Rees, 'who doesn't know how to spell Jane Austen.' MacCarthy was a Liberal and close to the Asquiths, a friend of Winston Churchill, and a week-end guest at the great houses; his charm and his brilliant conversation made him the pet of hostesses. It is possible that Rees was a little nettled by all this social success. There was trouble, too, when MacCarthy, as the passionate champion of Asquith, attempted a full-dress attack on Lloyd George in the course of some book review. Lloyd George was still a name venerated by the Berrys, and in any case Rees took the view, and Hadley felt it even more strongly, that politics was a walled domain in which only the initiated like themselves could wander – literary men such as Desmond would do better to keep to purely literary subjects. MacCarthy usually took this sort of scolding with good grace, but beneath his charm there was a proper steeliness of conviction: it would emerge occasionally, and there would be a row. On his first night at Eton, reacting instinctively, he had given a black eye to a boy who had threatened to throw his hairbrushes out of the window; he was very apologetic afterwards, but he knew that he had been right. In his tiffs with Rees and Hadley he relied on this same instinct, and if his fighting spirit flashed out they knew he would not easily give way. With Hadley he was never really at ease. 'Like most timid men he is apt to seize suddenly on some tiny occasion for a display of obstinate authority. Never encourage him.'

One of his greatest trials was the prudishness of Rees and Hadley about what was or was not fit for their readers – Podsnap (as Agate said) still ruled the island. Dilys Powell, vexed by the same censorship, laid a trap for Rees one day and managed to carry her point. She quoted in some notice of a book of poetry a

Opposite: Sir Desmond MacCarthy by Douglas Glass.

line by Henry Vaughan: 'How brave a prospect is a bright back-side!' It was removed from the review, but she restored it in proof, producing a dictionary, with a display of indignation, to show that in Vaughan's usage the word meant merely a retrospect. Rees gave way, but it caused a sensation in the printers, and finally, on Saturday afternoon, Mr Bloxham formally presented the page to Mr Rees and asked for express permission to go to press.

Desmond MacCarthy made his protests too. One Friday after-noon, desperately dashing down the last page of his copy in Mr Bloxham's tiny office, with Mr Bloxham himself hovering around like a bald-headed bishop of the sweetest disposition, and saying every now and then, anxiously, 'Only waiting for you, sir,' he put down something like this: 'Mr Thing preserves on most occasions a grave sacerdotal air in his examination of church ritual, yet there is some trace of wildness in his outlook and one is always trembling lest at some moment he should seize the chalice and piss in it.'

He didn't expect it to appear. Nor did it. But he couldn't resist the combination of joke, protest, and putting everyone, including the printer's reader, into a panic.

From Cambridge onwards, where he was an Apostle,[1] MacCarthy had kept the highest intellectual company, starting with G. E. Moore, the philosopher, and growing up with members of the Bloomsbury group – Virginia and Leonard Woolf, Roger Fry, Lytton Strachey – before they had become legendary figures. Bloomsbury certainly did its best to bring out Desmond's talents. It wanted him, when he was young, to write a novel, to be the new Henry James, and to this end founded a Play-Reading and Novel Club. Desmond was supposed to bring along chapters of his novel and read them aloud to the members – which included Clive and Vanessa Bell, E. M. Forster, Roger Fry, Duncan Grant, Maynard Keynes, the Woolfs, and Desmond and his wife Molly. The club collapsed when it was found that Desmond was speaking extem-pore from blank sheets of paper.

But Desmond was not exclusively attached to the coterie – they for their part deplored his catholicity of taste – and was on inti-mate terms with older figures such as Asquith, Wilfrid Scawen

---

1. He had the distinction of being one of only six undergraduate members of 'The Apostles', a university intellectual society founded in the 1820s.

Blunt, Maurice Baring and Hilaire Belloc. No one had a wider group of friends of genius or near-genius and this for all its benefits may have had a discouraging effect on him, making him lose the name of action. When he joined The Sunday Times he saw an affinity between himself and Hartley Coleridge, the son of the poet, as one who had great gifts and attracted affection but was destined never to exert himself sufficiently to win the prize. As a young man he began to write for literary journals, both as dramatic critic and literary critic, because he found it the easiest way to make a living. He wanted to go on from there but didn't. Then and later – throughout the whole of his life – he was haunted by the books he ought to have written. A mixture of *dolce far niente* and the love of life (he was, as he said of Dr Johnson, incorrigibly devoted to human nature), of observing and talking, kept him from working on them.

Instead his fate was to be shut away in a printing office the size of a matchbox hastily composing his article, while like Goldsmith in his garret or Johnson composing one of his best Rambler essays in Sir Joshua Reynolds's parlour, he was harassed by the knowledge that the printer was hovering round anxiously waiting to carry it to press. Sometimes he wrote it at home, but even then disaster often attended: he forgot to put it in his attaché-case or gave it to someone to deliver who proved unreliable.

Just as he had so large and varied a circle of acquaintances, so he had an extraordinarily wide range of literary sympathies. He couldn't (like Hazlitt, only rather differently) keep Coleridge out of it, and he struggled to penetrate the mind of the magus on many occasions; and from him he could pass without condescension to a homely humorist like Nathaniel Gubbins of The Sunday Express. For years he carried about the confession of Samuel Herbert Dougal, the Moat Farm murderer, published by The Sun newspaper after Dougal was executed in 1903. He killed a Miss Holland for her money and buried her body in a ditch, and Desmond used to relate, with the little gurgles of laughter he reserved for occasions when human folly or oddity was more than usually evident, that when Dougal was awaiting trial he was very worried about the assassination of the Queen of Serbia. 'What a dreadful piece of business!' he wrote.

Desmond in the end became almost as revered a figure as Gosse in The Sunday Times office, and it was undeniable that his reputation was in large part founded on his writings for the paper. Yet even then, in his last years, still haunted, he was talking

The young Raymond Mortimer, disciple of Desmond MacCarthy and his successor on The Sunday Times.

excitedly of writing a book of memoirs arranged in alphabetical order – A for Asquith and so on.

He would dash off notes to the then literary editor, Leonard Russell, writing always in pencil, about books he did or did not want to review:

Raymond Mortimer today by Janet Stone.

I'm doubtful if I want to write about *The Typewriter* (Cocteau). I have
something to say about Cocteau but it is not clamouring for expression.
He seems to me a genius without roots – like Picasso: wonderfully clever
at composing first in one style, then in another and another, to the gaping
admiration of contemporaries. But really important artists have never
developed like that: their experiments and periods have grown one out

179

The young Cyril Connolly by Augustus John.

of the other, whereas Picasso and Cocteau every 5 or 10 years have
chucked up and started afresh – followed by the docile young – along the
road of some new method which had *no relation* to the preceding one.

Think of P's different *styles* or stages. (1) The blue consumptives,
acrobats, pictures drenched in morbid sensibility and lovely in a fashion,
followed by (2) the grey-brown cubistic period (3) *patterns* made out of

Cyril Connolly today by James Reeves.

things, scraps of wood, leather, newspaper cuttings (4) bloated 'balloon' statuesque figures (5) his last geometric interpretation of humanity, with its implication of total *indifference*. These phases have no connection with each other.

So it is with Cocteau's phases: aesthetic Whistlerian epigrammatist; *poète maudit*; Dadaism, *Le boeuf sur le Toit* etc; Fairy-tale symbolism plus circus conventions, *Orphée* etc; Greek method, Oedipean tragedy plus a little psycho-analysis ... ; *The Double-Headed Eagle* – back to 17th-century shake-scene drama. ...

No *development*, only *experiment* – try this, try that; cleverness for gaping goslings its only persistent characteristic. I suppose *The Typewriter* belongs to his pre-1914 psychological realism à la Hervieu, Capus etc etc *Les Parents Terribles*. I'll have a look at it.

He was sympathetic to the young and was always keeping an eye open for new young writers. In all the 25 years he wrote for The Sunday Times he was deeply outraged by new movements only once: by the doctrine from Cambridge which called among other things for the 'dismantling of Milton' and whose Dr Leavis in turn showed amusing contempt for the 'Sunday paper' writers – Raymond Mortimer more than Desmond perhaps. But in his heart MacCarthy must have known that such clashes of critical opinion are inevitable and right. 'Otherwise,' as somebody said to a grumbling Rees, quoting a forgotten wit, 'we should all be champing acorns.'

Raymond Mortimer says of Desmond:

When literary editor of the *New Statesman*, Desmond MacCarthy gave me my first regular job as a reviewer; he would go through my typescripts, suggesting improvements in the choice and placing of words, as if he were giving an undergraduate a tutorial. Eventually I succeeded him, first as literary editor of what had become the *New Statesman and Nation*, then as reviewer in the *Sunday Times*. While differing from him in some of my tastes and interests, I still regard myself as his disciple. Cyril Connolly, who also started reviewing under his aegis on the *N.S. & N.*, shares my admiring affection for him; and Desmond Shawe-Taylor comes from the same stable, because I guided his apprenticeship on the lines I learnt from Desmond MacCarthy who had chosen as his pseudonym 'Affable Hawk'.

This indicates the virtues he exemplified as a critic and required as an editor – an open mind and a courteous manner combined with a sharp eye for silliness and inaccuracy as well as for quality. He emphasised also the reviewer's need for consulting the work of more learned critics, and for continual recourse to the London Library. (Obedient to his instructions I often read three books and look at several others to brief myself for a review.) A tireless polisher of his own articles, he expected from us a similar concern with the shaping of a sentence, a similar distaste for the slipshod. Whereas the teacher-critic can demand the attention of his pupils, the reviewer has to catch and to retain the interest of the general reader.

Then in 1928, the year in which Desmond MacCarthy joined the

staff, a new phase began for The Sunday Times when Lord Camrose bought The Daily Telegraph. This was history repeating
itself, for we have seen that in 1855 the proprietor of The Daily
Telegraph, a printer in a fairly important way named Joseph
Moses Levy, had become chief proprietor of The Sunday Times;
and his son Edward was a newspaper genius who, according to
Lord Camrose, was the 'originator of morning journalism as we
know it today'. Edward Levy received his training on The Sunday
Times and left it to become editor of The Telegraph. He assumed
the surname of Lawson, became Sir Edward Levy-Lawson in 1892
and Lord Burnham in 1903.

The beginning of a decline set in when, with Edward's death in
1916, the control of the paper passed to his son, the second Lord
Burnham, Harry Lawson, who was more interested in public life
than in newspapers. Under him the sales of The Daily Telegraph
continued to run down, until in 1927, at the price of twopence,
they were not much above 80,000.

At this point Lord Burnham, who had agreed to go to India
with the Simon Commission, put out a feeler to Lord Camrose,
who says:[1]

I was at that time editor-in-chief of the *Sunday Times*. Burnham wrote
me a letter saying that he had noticed the progress of that paper and
wondered whether I would be interested in trying my hand with a daily
newspaper, of the same character. After, I think, two interviews, terms
were arranged and my brother, Lord Kemsley, and I, in conjunction
with Lord Iliffe, became the proprietors, on January 1, 1928. No over-
tures were made in any other direction.

Lord Burnham's nephew, Colonel Fred Lawson, who became
the fourth Lord Burnham, was general manager of the paper
under his uncle, and he stayed on, to the entire and expanding
satisfaction of the new proprietors. Says Lord Camrose:

He had been on the paper for a number of years and knew everything
there was to be known about the *Telegraph*. Incidentally it used to be said
that he was one of the few people who really knew their way about the
old extensive but mystifying building and that when his uncle attempted
to show visitors round he always lost his way![2]

Some bizarre characters inhabited corners of those old buildings, men in green baize aprons who wandered about with no

---

1. 'British Newspapers and their Controllers', Cassell, 1947.
2. *Ibid.*

apparent duties, wizened creatures in cloth caps who would creep up from the bowels and disappear again as if they feared the light of day, seemingly pensioners who had no other home. It was axiomatic that you never got sacked (it still is); equally, if there was a vacancy in a department which required someone presentable, such as the circulation department, it was automatically filled by an officer of the Royal Bucks Hussars, of which Lord Burnham, who lived in great state at Hall Barn, Beaconsfield, was honorary colonel.

The main building of the paper, which embodied Peterborough Court, had a magnificent frontage on Fleet Street, and there were uncharted regions behind it and at the side of it. It was put up in 1882, and with its stone face it had the air of having escaped from the terrace of great clubs in Pall Mall. Its pillar-hall was one of the sights of London, and here in the early 1920s, while the paper went on decaying, groups of visitors gathered night after night to be shown the grandeurs by Lord Burnham, a tubby little man with a very loud voice and a self-important manner, or a guide specially employed for the purpose.

On the first floor, among busts of Gladstone and Disraeli, and paintings of ruined temples by Panini and Spy caricatures of George Augustus Sala and Sir Edwin Arnold, the traditions of the place were guarded by a number of tottering old gentlemen which included the editor, Sir John Merry le Sage, who had never used a telephone in his life, and a soft-footed general manager with a grey beard – an Imperial – and glittering gold-rimmed spectacles, J. Hall Richardson, who had rescued Sala from penury in Paris when the old lion was sick and before he joined The Sunday Times in the 1890s.

Above this powerhouse was the vast library running the length of the building, and here at five every evening the night editor and the five assistant night editors took their places, to read the proofs in a silence and an atmosphere appropriate to a club library, even down to horsehair sofas and chairs. Shielded by a curtain, Miss Billington, the woman's editor, sat here, occasionally remarking in a piercingly patrician voice to the night editor that the Queen had given her a special smile at some ceremony; but she went in the early evening and the undisturbed silence would continue for a long time, except for cries for a copy boy or stifled giggles from one of the assistant night editors who tended to behave rather strangely after dinner.

Above this magnificent room, with the gentleman's library

which was rarely consulted by anyone, was a mahogany gallery, with one end of it partitioned-off into a long narrow room. Here, in the late afternoon and early evening, special writers in frock-coats turned out a column or two, pen travelling with fatal calmness over paper – they all wrote shorthand and practically no one in the whole office used a typewriter. Usually they would be joined at six by three brisk young men in lounge suits; no one quite knew what they were up to – it was something to do with the Stock Exchange prices. When the three young men disappeared again, with an air of pride, and the special writers drifted off, the room was left to the oldest survivor of an older day, a hunchback who sat at a little table shoved against the window looking on to Fleet Street. When he was finally alone he would stoke up the big fire in the room and dry his handkerchief before it. Like Mr Nadgett in 'Martin Chuzzlewit' he was always drying his handkerchief; and when he wasn't doing that he was carrying the monstrous burden on his back, with a swinging motion, off to some secret recess to make a pot of tea, which he drank out of an old enamel mug. Tea, snuff, and dried handkerchiefs were the sweeteners of his existence.

This old man with the blotched red face was named Harry Gellatley and was the librarian of The Daily Telegraph. He cut out and gummed-up selected items from the paper and buried them away eternally. No one ever seemed to ask him for them. The paper of today has a fine cuttings library, but it was started from scratch by Sidney Macer-Wright when Camrose rebuilt the offices.

In the gallery adjoining this long narrow room sat a youth with red hair who has been on The Sunday Times for nearly forty years, Leonard Russell. He had no duties worth the name then. The review books came to him, and he entered details of them in a ledger. Once a week the distinguished literary editor of The Daily Telegraph and editor of The Fortnightly Review, W. L. Courtney, would pay him a visit. Dr Courtney was very old, like so many others about the place, and wore mittens, and was very frail, and very tall, and very bowed, and very charming. He would instruct Russell to send a book or two to Arthur Waugh, Evelyn Waugh's father and chairman of Chapman & Hall, publishers of The Fortnightly Review, who with Courtney himself wrote a weekly article for the book columns. There was nothing else for Russell to do. So he educated himself by reading the review books; and occasionally, to relieve the tedium of the long evenings, he talked to the old librarian, who was of a crusty nature and had to be in the talking mood.

He had revelations for Russell, though. He had known Willie Wilde, the brother of Oscar Wilde. Willie Wilde had been a leader-writer on The Telegraph, but he had cut the files of the paper – fancy that, thought Russell, looking blandly at the paper's intelligence officer and his system – and been kicked out. And, of course, there was George Augustus Sala.

Though Sala had died some thirty years before, his memory dominated the place. Matthew Arnold had talked about 'the young lions of Peterborough Court'. They were forgotten in the place now, at any rate among the rank and file, except Sala and his drunkenness, his fancy waistcoats decorated with bugle beads, which he bought from a theatrical costumier, his walking sticks, his trips to Russia 'to study Muscovy and the Muscovites', his books on London and cookery, his emergence, as he put it himself, 'from the low estate of a scene-painter in a theatre, of a hack engraver, of a draughtsman on wood', to the glory of being one of Dickens's young men on 'Household Words' and, by the time he was twenty-nine, 'the most picturesque essayist of the day'. He claims that he was paid 'an ambassador's salary' by The Telegraph for writing a daily leader, 'from the price of beef to a coronation', and for being its special correspondent when something important was happening abroad, such as the Franco–Prussian war. It all brought him about £20 a week from The Telegraph – he had no contract and sent in a weekly bill. But from the many books he compiled from his articles and from his other work in Fleet Street he must have made almost as much again. For The Illustrated London News he wrote for forty years a causerie called 'Echoes of the Week', and in the last years of his life he transferred it to The Sunday Times, the editor of which was then Arthur à Beckett, whom we have already met. Sala carried on the feature until the summer of 1895. He died a year later.

This, or bits of it, was living history to the librarian, whose attitude to Sala was nevertheless ambiguous. For to him he was at once a wonderful character and a deplorable drunken Bohemian, with some vice so sinister that it could never be mentioned. Russell would try to get him going:

'You actually knew him?'

'I should think so! He'd storm into Sir Edward's room and say, "You bladdy Jew, give me some money!" And when he got it – he'd be drunk already when he went on like this – he'd disappear for days. The East End, I think. Sometimes Brighton too.'

'A stupor?'

'Worse than that – he was what they call a pervert.'

'You mean like Oscar Wilde?'

'No – not that. He was married twice.' A pause. 'I remember he wrote a book – a novel – called "The Baddington Peerage". They called it "The Paddington Beerage".'

'But what was his vice then?'

'Never you mind, young fellow. And now I must get on with my work.' And he would gulp his tea from the enamel mug and make a preparatory clicking noise with his scissors.

Russell never did discover from the old boy the secret vice of the man who, according to his biographer, Ralph Straus, of The Sunday Times, boasted more mileage than any other writer. But Straus, for all his detailed investigation of Sala's life, never dared in his book to get round to the vice either. Russell much later discovered that it was flagellation; or, at any rate, that in 1881 Sala wrote a privately printed book – by 'Etonensis' – called 'The Mysteries of Verbena House, or Miss Bellasis Birched for Thieving'; goings-on at a Brighton seminary for young ladies which earned the commendation of the great Victorian connoisseur of dirty books, H. S. Ashbee, otherwise 'Pisanus Fraxi', a character even more strange than Sala himself.

As Russell was free in the day he got a job as a reporter on a soap paper – two guineas a week from The Telegraph and the same from the other. He was just about thinking of getting out altogether, because even to him, with all his inexperience, the place seemed to be dying, when Lord Camrose took over.

Soon after this a good-looking Welshman of thirty paid a call on him. Somehow Russell knew that he came from 'upstairs', that he was one of Lord Camrose's entourage, had been called to the Bar, and had learnt a little journalism on The Western Mail of Cardiff, in which the Berrys and their brother, Lord Buckland, had a controlling interest. His name was Cyril Lakin, and he had come to borrow some crime stories, to read, not to review.

Russell explained the impossibility of the request. He was under strict instructions from the soft-footed manager with gold-rimmed spectacles – who had since retired, leaving Russell even more remotely placed than before – that no one was to be lent any books, and that, anyway, they had all to be returned by the reviewers, including (in his time) Arthur Waugh. Lakin listened curiously. What happened to them then? They were all sold to

Foyle's. Lakin looked amused, said something about its all being rather different now, and disappeared to Camrose's offices on the fifth floor with half a dozen novels by J. S. Fletcher, Edgar Wallace, Sydney Horler and so on, promising nevertheless to return them in a fortnight. He never did. Regularly he came for more, and when Russell asked him what he was to do about the ledger, he just smiled.

Then in 1929 Camrose made his protégé literary editor and assistant editor of The Daily Telegraph, and Lakin in due time paid another call on Russell. He was looking for an assistant – would Russell like to join him?

So it came about that when the Berrys pulled down the old building, and re-erected another, the present one, with a deck of fast lifts and blue *rubber floors*, which were sensational in their day, Russell found himself spending his time in Cyril Lakin's office, next to the editor's on the first floor. They were two babes in the wood. Lakin had only a tiny experience of practical journalism, Russell none at all. But Camrose had picked Cyril Lakin to take charge of The Telegraph's leader page and book pages – twice a week, Tuesdays and Fridays – because he believed, rightly, that he had flair, though not as a writer, and that he knew the way that he, Camrose, wanted things done; and the general belief was that once all the old gentlemen in all the odd corners had been humanely retired, and The Telegraph had responded to Camrose's unspectacular but certain touch, Lakin would be the editor after Arthur Watson. Which was very satisfactory for Russell, who made all the usual mistakes but learnt quickly about inside-the-office journalism.

At this moment in its history practically no one on the editorial staff of The Daily Telegraph knew the names of heading types or of display types in general or of body types. Point-sizes were not yet in use in newspaper offices, and if the article was an important one you marked the first paragraph LP (long primer) the next one bgs. (bourgeois) and the rest of the article brev. (brevier). As for the headings to leader-page articles or book reviews, you wrote them on a sheet of paper and left it to the printer – and he then exercised a strictly utilitarian routine.

This was not good enough for Lakin: he wanted magazine make-up for the leader page articles, just like The Daily Mail. He consulted Russell and they agreed that they must learn about types. Just at that moment, as a development of the new Daily Telegraph, R. D. Blumenfeld's son Dave (R.D.B. was famous as the editor of The Daily Express) was compiling a type-book for The Telegraph, for the use of the advertisers. So Lakin and Russell took home the brand-new type book, and in the course of a couple of weekends learnt to identify type and type sizes, immediately applying their new knowledge to the leader page and book pages.

They left The Telegraph together to go entirely to The Sunday Times in 1937, and there too no one on the editorial side of the paper could identify even a famous type like Caslon. There was nobody to design the pages, of course; you did it yourself. It was not until the late 1950s that The Sunday Times was systematically designed, though before that Robert Harling worked on individual features.

In the early 1930s Lakin, full of enterprise, was very much the crown prince, but he left the grind of the job to his assistant, who loved it and him. For Lakin had winning ways, and was handsome, like a milder version of Basil Rathbone as Sherlock Holmes, and was always emptying his ashtray into the waste-paper basket (everyone smoked cigarettes then) and wore expensive square-shouldered suits with enormously wide lapels and double-breasted waistcoats, and had a charming rich wife and a young daughter called Tuppence. He was ambitious, but not in a way which precluded his having a life of his own, and he danced about on the balls of his feet like a middle-weight boxer. He liked to play golf, in orange plus-fours, at Holtye, near East Grinstead, and potter about in his weekend cottage close handy, and have drinks before dinner from a silver cocktail shaker, and an occasional bottle of Lanson champagne, and *foie gras* on toast, and an occasional trip to Paris with his wife, but he wouldn't for a moment have thought of giving up his cherished family life for a great social success or for dining out night after night with important but boring contacts. But his journalistic ambitions remained, and he was pursued by people who thought him the unspoken editor-elect of The Telegraph. Yet he managed to reconcile everything, including his habitual disdain of donkey-work, which he left to his assistant.

Rebecca West was one of Lakin's successes. Lakin brought her to The Telegraph to review books, and Cyril Connolly to do the detective stories and Cecil Day-Lewis to review ordinary fiction, and Camrose was impressed and doubtless more than ever convinced, without finally making up his mind, that the young man whom he had promoted from his private office was going places, either at The Telegraph or (more likely) The Sunday Times.

Lakin thought so too. Russell was coming into the office one afternoon, walking up the marble stairs of the new building, when Lakin came clattering down, struggling his arm into his overcoat as he ran.

'Rees is dead!' he called as he went by, and it seemed to Russell that he had, like Hamlet, one auspicious and one drooping eye. Russell knew of course that The Sunday Times was now on the fourth floor; he knew – just about – that Leonard Rees had been editor, and that an old boy named W. W. Hadley from The Daily Chronicle was helping him; and he concluded, from something in Lakin's manner, that Lakin was to be the next editor of The Sunday Times. Obviously, Hadley wasn't quite up to it; he had been a political correspondent, not a desk man, and Lakin was twenty-five years younger and had Lord Camrose's confidence.

Leonard Rees died suddenly on January 19, 1932. Lord Camrose wrote in The Sunday Times that the editor of that newspaper for thirty-one years had 'passed to the Great Beyond' at the age of seventy-five:

He died in harness, as he would have wished. Last Saturday morning he attended the funeral of one of his contributors, Sir Sidney Low, very nearly of his own age. Sir Sidney Low died while he was engaged in writing his weekly contribution to the *Sunday Times*, and, in conversation with members of his staff on Friday, Rees described Low's passing as the happiest he could imagine. He expressed the hope that his own would come in a similar way while he was still in active work on the paper which he loved. To describe Leonard Rees as 'a great editor' in the old manner would not be correct – he was too human and too fond of the daily intercourse with his fellows. . . .

No immediate decision was taken about Rees's successor. In fact, William Waite Hadley, who was sixty-six when Rees died, always said, with a wry and quiet smile, that no decision was ever taken at all. He was a tiny man, shorter even than Rees, and apparently much less robust. With his high, old-fashioned trilby hat, his spectacles, his little grey clipped moustache, his umbrella, his slightly tottering walk, he might have passed for some official in local government. He was a reserved, unruffled man who never raised his voice or lost his temper; but the cast of his mind was quietly ironic, and his heroes included Labouchere, who was MP for Hadley's own Northampton and who delighted him for his wit and impudence. He was a student of British politics, and he had spent his life watching Asquith, whom he admired, and Lloyd

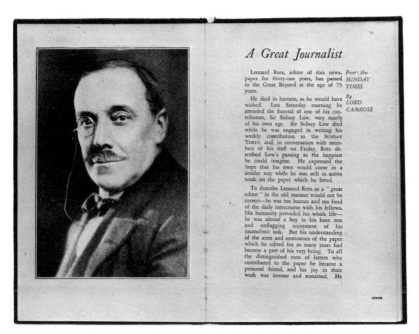

Leonard Rees: the title-page of a little book of reprinted tributes.

George, whom he admired but distrusted. He was also a rather distrustful observer of Winston Churchill, at this time at any rate, and he would describe how he had seen him pacing up and down like a caged lion awaiting the result of the Dundee election of 1922, in which he lost by 10,000 votes to an absurd candidate with fanatic views about prohibition. Hadley was also fond of imitating Asquith coming into his office and hanging up his hat and saying, 'And what is the state of Sir John Simon's guts this morning?'

The state of Hadley's guts was always sound, and this, combined with his kindness, endeared him to his small staff, who regarded themselves as belonging to an exclusive little club, with Hadley as chairman. No one left his presence feeling ten-foot tall, but no one left him without his confidence having been quietly increased. He had, too, an endearing way of hinting a doubt if he disliked something in your copy, reminding one of the famous Lord Halifax when Pope was reading aloud to him his translation of the 'Iliad': 'I beg your pardon, Mr Pope, but there is something in that passage that does not quite please me. Be so good as to mark the place and consider it a little at your leisure. I am sure you can give it a little turn.'

He was the son of a Northamptonshire gardener and one of ten children. Until he was fifty-eight he had worked on unimportant provincial papers, and then he decided to the surprise of his friends to come to London as political correspondent of The Daily Chronicle. When that paper collapsed in 1930 William Berry remembered him and asked him to come to The Sunday Times, and just before Rees died he was appointed assistant editor. Nothing significant was said to him on the death of Rees, and he was not the man to make a fuss or ask questions. He quietly did Rees's work until he was told to stop. He never was told to stop, and as he said to Harold Hobson many years later, by 1940 he began to think that he might with reasonable safety call himself editor. Iain Lang, then in the sub-editors' room, used to say, cynically but affectionately, that Hadley's early association with William Berry should be a lesson to everyone. 'We should all go round patting all little boys' heads. On the law of averages it must pay off in the end.'

Hadley was not a brilliant or spectacular editor and his range of interests was very limited. For a journalist, and particularly an editor, he had a curiously incurious mind. A newspaper is nearly all trees and no wood, and the trees which really interested him were few. With British politics he was completely at home, and his knowledge of its nineteenth-century by-ways, including the literature of the subject, was exceptional – he was in this field a very well-read man. But the increasing international chaos of the 1930s left him a little bewildered. Quietly, and with humour, he would relate Palmerston's ruses in dealing with all these difficult foreigners.

Neville Chamberlain became his hero, and when Chamberlain was Prime Minister Hadley saw him once a week. By the time of the Munich crisis Hadley had gained confidence in himself and he emerged, with Lord K leading, as one of the most determined apostles of appeasement. He published a book to defend his position, though all the time he may have had a nagging feeling, as an old Liberal, that he was in slightly doubtful company. But he was essentially a dove, not a hawk, and in the great and eternally unsolvable Munich riddle a man's position was determined, perhaps, by this simple classification.

For all his mildness, however, Hadley was never hustled by anyone into doing or saying anything against his will. He had stronger powers of resistance than many who were superficially tougher. Since he was always calm inside, what nervous energy

W. W. Hadley by Douglas Glass.

he had was expended only slowly, and thus it went a very long way; and his delicate little ironic refusals were sometimes as pleasing as other men's acceptances. There was James Agate, for instance, who after his experience with Rees thought it diplomatic to take the new editor out to lunch. George Bishop, who was now writing 'Plays and Players', was there too, and they tried to get Hadley to provide more space for the theatre in crowded weeks. He was far less eminent than his drama critic, and the handsome and immensely tall George Bishop, with his entreprenurial bald head, was a forceful as well as agreeable personality. (Bishop was succeeded when he moved over solely to The Telegraph in 1937 by Richard Clowes, who disappeared from the staff of his own volition when the second war came, still marvellously funny in private conversation and still referring to the paper, as he does to this day, as The Kemsley Scorcher.) But Hadley was not in the least intimidated and made one of his little essays in irony. 'It's a terrible thing,' he said, 'to forego reading what Agate thinks of a little new play at Kew. It's a more terrible thing to forego a £100 advertisement.'

This was the kind of language which Agate understood. He made no demur. 'A most sympathetic editor,' he said, and must have breathed a sigh of relief that here was a man with whom he would be able to get on, as he did.

Except for Desmond MacCarthy, whom he hectored a little, adopting Rees's traditional attitude (he made a great fuss when Desmond reviewed the first number of Cyril Connolly's 'Horizon', on the ground that it was a magazine and not a book), everyone got on with Hadley: Herbert Sidebotham, the brilliantly fair-haired Gerald Barry, who had not yet given up writing leading articles to start The Week-end Review, Eiluned Lewis, the tall charming red-haired Welsh girl who wrote a best-seller called 'Dew on the Grass', R. C. K. Ensor, leader writer and Side-botham's successor as Scrutator, and Ernest Munton, the news editor. But Munton died suddenly (his sister Mary was to join the staff as a general reporter) and Hadley brought in to replace him an old friend of his, Valentine Heywood, the managing editor of The Sunday News, one of whose special duties, once he had settled in, was to deal with Hanslip Fletcher, the artist, a deaf eccentric whose drawings of London were a popular feature of the paper.

This was in 1933. There were other changes in that year. Cyril Lakin with Russell came in to run the book pages; so Lakin was now assistant editor and literary editor of both The Daily Telegraph and The Sunday Times. It is not known whether Lakin put up the idea of his editing The Sunday Times books pages to Camrose, or whether it was done because Camrose was thinking of him as Hadley's successor. But there was no doubt that the book reviews in The Sunday Times had been allowed to run down by Rees and Hadley: MacCarthy was there splendidly every week, but otherwise it was mostly a rag-bag, with some of the writers dating from before the first war and some, like Henry Murray, vaguely on the staff and doing reviews to fill up their working day. With his Telegraph success behind him, Lakin was the obvious man to rejuvenate the pages, and this he quickly did. The difficult J. C. Squire was now a Sunday Times reviewer: he had left The

Observer after being its chief book critic for many years and found refuge with Rees, who used him obscurely under the rather humiliating heading, 'J. C. Squire's Corner'. He never became a great light of The Sunday Times, but Lakin, among his many changes of critics and design, used him prominently.

In the printing arrangements there was a momentous change. After many years Lord Camrose's St Clement's Press was given up and Mr Bloxham, his successor Gus Wingrove, who as a boy used to take proofs to Mrs Beer, the owner of The Sunday Times when its offices were over a stamp shop opposite the Tivoli in the Strand, and the rest of a fine 'ship' moved from the vicinity of Lincoln's Inn Fields to Fleet Street. The offices of The Sunday Times were now on the fourth floor of the new building of The Telegraph and the paper itself had the use of all The Telegraph's services – at last, for instance, it could call on a proper team of foreign correspondents. It all marked a great new day in the paper's history.

Still under Camrose's watchful eye, it was to become, while retaining its individuality, the seventh-day paper of The Telegraph. Now more than ever it had the resources to assert itself over Garvin's Observer.

Garvin regarded himself as a genius – as a seer, as a Merlin of Fleet Street. At this time his voice seemed sibylline to the point of parody. He was, in any case, losing his way now, for the great liberal prophet was inclining to Mussolini. In 1933 his journal fell below The Sunday Times in circulation. Privately, Camrose rejoiced in this success with his entourage, particularly Sir Herbert Morgan, who had various promotional schemes up his sleeve, including The Sunday Times book exhibitions, in which Michael Renshaw was to play so large a part; and the staff rejoiced too, though discreetly. Discreetly because, in a newspaper office, there is never time to stand off and wholeheartedly congratulate or condemn oneself – the immediate tasks and uncertainties are too pressing. All the same, the debacle on the Saturday night when The Sunday Times was printed at The Telegraph for the first time was so complete that it was talked about for weeks after. The printers couldn't find out where things were – their rules, their formes, all their everyday paraphernalia. Mr Clifton, Mr Bloxham, the news editor, Valentine Heywood, the chief sub-editor, Lewis Broad, all went raving mad with shame as the evening wore on. In the middle of everything the amiable D. R. Gent came in with his rugger copy, handed it over, and hastily retreated. But he did have time to notice that the only calm person around was the 'old man' – W. W. Hadley.

Agate was around too, and he wrote this note about the shambles:

Last night (Oct. 15, 1933) the *Sunday Times* was printed for the first time in the *Daily Telegraph* office, and on the D.T. machines. Eiluned Lewis said that on the previous Saturday St Clement's Press, where the S.T. was printed for many years, was full of the ghost of old Rees. I must always remember about that old man that after all it was he who spotted my work in the *Saturday Review* and offered me the job on the S.T.

Everything went wrong at the change-over. Every train to every part of the country was missed, including the Paris trains. The paper did, however, get to Paris, being rushed down to Folkestone by special motor-cars and then across the Channel by a fishing-smack hired for the occasion! To be quite accurate, we don't know yet whether the paper reached Paris. We do know it left Folkestone.

Later: Hadley told me that any other newspaper after last week's debacle would have held an inquest and sacked three or four people. Lord Camrose merely telephoned to Hadley saying: 'It's a wonder you got the paper out at all – I think you did very well!'[1]

In so many a crisis Hadley preserved an amused calm that one may be pardoned for recalling the only occasion on which he is known to have displayed agitation.

On a night when Russell was working in the small hours in The Sunday Times office a male cleaner in the traditional green baize apron showed him a copy of a Fascist newspaper called Action, published by Action Press Ltd. It was dated April 2, 1936, and it implied that Lord Camrose was a Jewish international financier with no loyalty to the Crown and no sense of patriotism, and that in his conduct of The Daily Telegraph he allowed his duty to the public to be subordinated by his own financial interests. The article was written by John Beckett, a former M P, of Sanctuary Buildings, Great Smith Street, s w, who had gained some celebrity by imitating Oliver Cromwell and walking away with the mace, and was now editor of the paper Action.

Lord Camrose had known nothing of the article. But as soon as he read it he began an action for libel against Action, Argus Press Ltd, the printers, and John Beckett.

Action Press Ltd was defended by Gerald Gardiner, K C, who maintained that it was 'utterly extravagant to say that the

---

1. 'Ego.'

ordinary person who read this article would think that it imputed that no decent Englishman ought to read The Daily Telegraph.' But when Beckett was put into the witness-box he adopted a line bordering on the sensational. He came to the verge of quarrelling with his own side's counsel. Such as his principles were, he stuck to them. 'I do not desire,' he said, 'to go into the witness-box to attempt to justify this article along the lines that it has been defended by Mr Gardiner. I am not in agreement with that line of defence at all.' He then proceeded to make some very dark allusions to the way in which the article had come to be written:

When I wrote that article I wrote it because I honestly believed it to be true; because I had the information in it given me by people on whom, rightly or wrongly, I placed great reliance. I did not mean it to be the weak, cooing, inoffensive article that Mr Gardiner has suggested.

If those facts were true which were given me I meant that article to say exactly what it said. Unfortunately I have discovered that these facts are not true. A very great number of them can be substantiated; some can be partly substantiated; but the two cardinal facts that matter above all were entirely wrong, and to my mind they were two of the deadliest insults that could be offered. To me, to tell a man that he is a Jew and that his financial interests are far greater outside this country than in it are two of the greatest insults that can possibly be offered to any man.

When I discovered that, so far from the information my titled friend gave me about Lord Camrose being a Jew being true, he was a Welshman – if I may say so, he is an obvious Welshman – I did not want to go into the box to justify that.

John Beckett then said that an interesting point made by Mr Gardiner was that he, Beckett, was to blame because Sir Oswald Mosley had influenza when the article was written. 'The proofs were read, the article instructed and approved by a certain individual,' Beckett declared. 'It is quite true that was not Mr Gardiner's clients, Action Press. I did not even know who the directors were.'

Later he observed: 'I think I one day went out into the street and saw a fight to open the door of Sir Oswald Mosley's motor car, and was told it was the directors of Action Press. I must say,' Mr Beckett added, 'that I envied Mr Watson – editor of The Daily Telegraph – when he was in the witness box. His chief, at any rate, was man enough to say he was the chief, and did not get behind a £100 company, in one instance, and send his typist into the witness box, in another, to say that he had influenza.'

The result of the trial was that Lord Camrose was awarded damages of £12,500 and The Daily Telegraph £7,500. These were very large sums, and they were given in spite of the fact that the plaintiffs' counsel, Roland Oliver, KC, had said that 'it is obvious that Action Press Ltd, is not worth a farthing.' That, however, he added, was no reason for small damages. 'Who are they?' he asked. 'They are only a shell. At No. 1, Sanctuary Buildings, is located a sort of nest of companies, and there also is situated the British Union of Fascists and Sir Oswald Mosley directing things.'

Some echo of Roland Oliver's words must have remained in Hadley's mind, because when he wrote a leading article for The Sunday Times on the trial he declared that the damages would never be paid, the defendants being men of straw.

That Saturday night, in the big night editor's room in The Daily Telegraph building on the first floor, overlooking Fleet Street, Russell, Richard Keane, the diplomatic correspondent, and Dilys Powell sat round the long table with Hadley at the head of it to proof-read the first edition of The Sunday Times. Lakin had gone off to his country cottage. It was a chilly October evening, but the younger trio were in high spirits, having dined well and uproariously at Simpson's in the Strand, as was their custom. But Russell read the leading article with some alarm. 'But suppose they do pay?' he said to Hadley. 'Suppose they deliberately raise the money and sue *us* for libel, just for the hell of it and to make us look silly?'

There was no lawyer in attendance. There never was a resident legal staff until Denis Hamilton became editor of The Sunday Times and recruited the invaluable James Evans. Hadley turned pale, walked agitatedly up and down the room, argued, dismissed the idea, took it up again. If the article were cut for the later editions it was still on record in the first edition. He picked up the telephone, replaced it, went off indecisively to the printers.

Then his normal calm reasserted itself, and they all turned to their different areas of the paper. But Hadley did not forget the incident. He told Russell the following Tuesday that for the first time in his life he had not been able to sleep for worry.

XX

It was nearly seven o'clock. Lakin was again struggling his arm into his overcoat when Russell went into the room. His manner expressed excitement.

As he made for the door he said, 'They're going to make me editor of The Sunday Times. Right away.'

Russell asked: 'How do you know?' fully expecting that Lakin had just seen Camrose. But the news wasn't as hard as that.

'Rebecca West rang and told me.' It seemed that she had met Gomer Berry at some dinner-party, and he had told her.

Russell knew Rebecca West, and liked her very much, just as Lakin did, and was sure that she had reported reliably. But he didn't know Sir Gomer Berry, except as a kind of junior partner in the brothers' alliance. Somehow he felt a qualm.

But Lakin was very excited. 'Let's have dinner tonight.' They went to the Trocadero. Lakin said that in the new dispensation Russell would have to give up the book pages and become assistant editor. Russell didn't particularly want to pass them on to someone else. He found the publishing world of the mid-1930s an exciting place. There were cocktail parties for authors every night, and huge advertisements on Sundays from Gollancz and Walter Hutchinson, and everyone was fighting it out in a gentle-manly way, including of course The Observer and The Sunday Times. J. L. Garvin's daughter, Viola, was literary editor of The Observer, and was always around with Humbert Wolfe, the poet. Her chief fiction reviewer was Gerald Gould, who was also Gollancz's reader, and there was a lot of feeling because he was given to reviewing Gollancz's novels. The Sunday Times was more discreet. Ralph Straus, an unintellectual reviewer if ever there were one, had his eye on the lending library public, and if he liked a novel he could easily sell out the first edition. The crime stories were reviewed by the creator of Lord Peter Wimsey, Dorothy L. Sayers – she insisted on the L – who wore a pork-pie hat, a blue mannish-looking suit and flat shoes, and who became, with her passion for correct grammar, the terror of poor slaphappy writers of crime stories.

Besides, there were The Sunday Times book exhibitions. Rubicund old Sir Herbert Morgan, who liked giving little

Cyril Lakin – elected to join Lord Kemsley (see page 203).

dinner-parties for some ancient royal lady, combining this with a dashing attachment to dining-out with musical comedy actresses, and a habit of wandering into one's room and out again without ever coming to the point, had really got them going. (We all owe a debt to Sir Herbert Morgan. Forty years ago he told the great James Braid at Walton Heath that The Sunday Times was looking for a golfing correspondent. Braid said he did not know anyone suitable but made some mention of a young fellow who had been captain of the Cambridge University golfing team and was now working on a little golfing magazine. His name was Henry Longhurst and he duly joined The Sunday Times at six guineas a week.)

Lakin abandoned detail and drew happy pictures of the future, seeing himself as a brilliant, unorthodox young editor, consorting with the distinguished and escaping the boring everyday routine. They broke up early. Perhaps Lakin felt that Camrose or Sir Gomer might ring him up after dinner. If the call came, he must be there.

Next day and for the next few days he sat in his office, smoking all the time and continually emptying the ashtray into the waste-paper basket, and hardly able to pick up the house telephone when it rang.

XXI

The call did not come. It never came. Lakin, looking dreadfully dejected and quoting from some source which Russell couldn't identify, muttered despairingly that it was 'a six-barred, barbed-wired, spike-topped mess-up.' He had one small resemblance to Wordsworth in that he had an almost insurmountable aversion to letter-writing – from the first Russell was amazed at the nonchalance with which he stuffed the drawers of his desk with unanswered letters. Now the pair of wire trays on either side of his blotting-pad were piled high too for all to see. He felt that he was in his prime and would soon be over the edge, no matter if old Hadley was somehow managing to keep going. He gave up saying, as he did when he had pulled off a good stroke, 'Well, if I'd done nothing else, I'd have earned my money this week.' Totally frustrated, he began to think about becoming an MP. And then, at the end of 1936, the great imperial division took place, and Lords Camrose, Kemsley and Iliffe divided their possessions, partners no longer.

About this time there was another Imperial affair: the Commonwealth wouldn't hear of King Edward VIII marrying Mrs Simpson. In newspaper offices, including The Sunday Times, everyone knew about the attachment, but such was the respect in which 'the Palace' was held in those days that no one thought seriously of breaking the news. Until, that is, the Bishop of Bradford, knowing nothing at all about the affair of the King with Mrs Simpson, said that the King was in need of God's grace. Certain provincial papers read significance into the words, and news of a constitutional crisis then followed on the front pages of the national newspapers. Predictably, The Sunday Times opposed

Lord Iliffe: one of the triumvirate

the idea of a King's Party when Rothermere and Beaverbrook, in their newspapers, supported the King's compromise of some form of morganatic marriage. Churchill was also for the King, and pleaded for more time for everyone.

Amidst all the gloom, the excitement, the indignation, Camrose and Kemsley, in entire harmony as always, completed their arrangements. William had four sons and Gomer six; Iliffe also had two sons. For the sake of their children, because of the difficulties of inheritance, they had decided to part. Rarely can an empire with three heads have been more harmoniously governed. When the brokers drafted their first separation plan The Sunday Times was retained by Lord Camrose. However, the new Lady

Kemsley (he had been made a baron in this same year of 1936 and married her in 1931 after his first wife's death) saw that Allied Newspapers without The Daily Telegraph *or* The Sunday Times would be insignificant as a political force, and she forced a change.

So Camrose took The Daily Telegraph as his own property and retained control of The Financial Times and the Amalgamated Press, while Kemsley bought his brother's shares in Allied Newspapers and became chairman of the company and editor-in-chief of The Sunday Times. (Iliffe took over Kelly's Directories.) A later and outward and visible sign of this separation, so plain that every wayfaring man could observe it, was that in 1943 Lord K changed the name of Allied Newspapers to Kemsley Newspapers, and that of its London and provincial offices to Kemsley House. From 1945, under the title block of each newspaper in the chain, the words appeared 'A Kemsley Newspaper'. In a way it was an answer to the complaint of John Beckett and others that no one quite knew who was responsible, financially and otherwise, for any given newspaper. (Kemsley added to the group, and just after the war it consisted of twenty-three London and provincial papers, with a circulation figure of 26½ million copies a week – the largest of all chains.)

Cyril Lakin was Lord Camrose's man, but Lord K, who had considerable respect and affection for him, hoped that he would leave The Daily Telegraph completely and join him at Kemsley House, in his present rôle of assistant editor and literary editor of The Sunday Times, with the generous salary (even if it doesn't seem so nowadays) of £2,000 a year and £500 expenses. No promise was made of the reversion of the editorship. Nothing, indeed, was said about the editorship at all. But Lakin, swallowing his disappointment on this score and grimly reflecting that Hadley was nearing seventy-five, accepted Lord K's terms. And along to Kemsley House went Russell too.

So on January 1, 1937, the rainbow was in the sky for Lord K, even if, on the international horizon, there were ominous clouds.

'A Kemsley Newspaper,' May 20, 1945

PART 3

The Kemsley Era

1937–1959

PART 3

The Kemsley Era

I

Now that he had acquired complete and undivided control of The Sunday Times Lord Kemsley wanted to make a stir in the world.

He had come into this authority at a very difficult time. The Treaty of Versailles was bringing in its revenges, and Hitler, aided by the impudent improvisations of Mussolini, was becoming more and more audacious. Lord K believed that some sort of understanding could be established with Hitler, and therefore the policy of The Sunday Times was one of appeasement. He was a devout follower of the Prime Minister, Neville Chamberlain; and Hadley, as has been noted, had weekly access to Chamberlain.

These Chamberlain–Hadley encounters were regarded in The Sunday Times office with a certain cynicism by younger members of the staff, such as Richard Keane, the talented and handsome young diplomatic correspondent, who was passionately opposed to appeasement and a supporter of Anthony Eden before Eden resigned as Foreign Secretary, sick and tired of Chamberlain's interference. Raised voices were unknown in The Sunday Times office. But now, such were the passions of the times, young Keane or Alexander Werth, over from Paris, could be heard booming at his editor, who it must be said preserved his habitual equanimity. But Keane (whose father Sir John Keane was a director of the Bank of Ireland and Dublin correspondent of the paper for many years) scored at least one little triumph.

On February 11 and 12, 1938, the daily papers had been full of a quarrel, one which might have the most serious consequences, between the Prime Minister and the Foreign Secretary. On Saturday afternoon, February 12, Keane came in with the same story, fully authenticated by his contacts at the Foreign Office (he was contemptuous of a rival official foreign news service organised by Sir Horace Wilson at No. 10 which was saying that everything was normal). Hadley had seen Chamberlain the day before and been told there was no rift between the Prime Minister and Eden, but Keane stood his ground – he said that Chamberlain wasn't

Shooting party given by Sir Gomer and Lady Berry at Lord Burnham's Hall Barn, Beaconsfield, 1932. Front row (left to right) : Mrs du Plessis, Mrs Neville Chamberlain, Mme. Flandin, Lady Berry, the Countess of Cavan, and Mme. Van der Heyden à Hauzeur. Back row (left to right) : The Earl of Cromer, Mr Lionel Berry, the Earl of Cavan, Mr du Plessis, M. Flandin, Sir Gomer Berry, Mr Louis Van der Heyden à Hauzeur, Mr Neville Chamberlain, and Mr R. A. Walter.

telling the truth. Just before dinner that Saturday evening a perturbed Hadley sent a handwritten note round to the Prime Minister at No. 10 – the messenger was Leonard Russell and he was to wait for an answer. It came in written form, and next day, February 13, The Sunday Times published a *démenti*, written on the 'highest authority' by its political correspondent, Hadley, of any differences between the Prime Minister and the Foreign Secretary:[1]

A POLITICAL CANARD
Premier and Mr Eden
IN COMPLETE AGREEMENT
By OUR POLITICAL CORRESPONDENT

There is no truth in the stories published yesterday of acute differences between the Prime Minister and the Foreign Secretary and of a consequent Ministerial crisis.

Though the reports vary in scope and detail, they agree in representing Mr Chamberlain as the adventurous spirit in foreign policy and Mr Eden as the advocate of more cautious and slower action.

By night there was 'a political crisis of the first magnitude'; unless there was a compromise, it was said, resignations from the Cabinet were inevitable.

I have the highest authority for saying that there is not a word of truth in all this. The Prime Minister and Mr Eden are in complete agreement.

A few days later Anthony Eden resigned, plunging Churchill (as emerged later in his war memoirs) into the deepest despair and giving him the unique experience, even taking into account the crisis of 1940, of a sleepless night as he contemplated the consequences of this newest success for the dictators. As for The Sunday Times, it had been humiliated.

Somehow, Kemsley and Hadley were usually unfortunate in their political adventures. Even in this matter of appeasement they never led the field. The decisive and disastrous keynotes of appeasement were sounded by Kingsley Martin and The New Statesman and Geoffrey Dawson and The Times, the latter sug-

---

1. 'The PM himself put the notice in yesterday's *Sunday Times* denying rumours of differences between himself and Anthony.' 'The Diaries of Sir Alexander Cadogan, 1938–1945', Permanent Under-Secretary at the Foreign Office. Cassell, 1971. Chamberlain purblindly wrote to his sister: 'I saw Anthony on Friday morning and we were in complete agreement, more complete perhaps than we have sometimes been in the past.'

gesting in its notorious leader of September 7, 1938, that if the Sudeten areas were allowed to go to Germany the rest of Czechoslovakia might be safer and more united. As a supporter of appeasement Kemsley was outbid on the Socialist side as on the Conservative. The Cliveden weekends of the Observer Astors and Lady Astor's luncheons at their London house at 4 St James's Square, were, despite left-wing exaggerations, one of the moral supports of the policy, famous or rather notorious to a degree which Hadley's private conferences with the Prime Minister could naturally never rival.

Possibly Lord K himself had a very simple private reasoning or intuition behind it all. Communism was the great and real enemy, and we must turn Hitler, by hook or by crook, on to the Russians; for Conservatives to come to terms with Communists was an impossibility – a view which was shared by Chamberlain and the cabinet in the long negotiations with Russia which blew up when Ribbentrop went to Moscow and on August 23, 1939, signed the Nazi–Soviet pact with Molotov. Before that Kemsley and a lot of other people believed we could buy Hitler's friendship and encourage him to contain Communism.

But there is this to be said for Lord K and Hadley. The Sunday Times may have been a 'committed' paper as regards appeasement, yet it allowed Alexander Werth, its Paris correspondent, regularly to put the case for the other side. It did not plead 'editorial policy' and exclude him, as The New Statesman excluded George Orwell when, after a visit to Spain in the Spanish Civil War, he attacked the Spanish Government. The New Statesman may have claimed that it was 'committed' politically, but to Orwell it was simply exhibiting 'the mentality of a whore'.

In these anxious years frustrated Cyril Lakin, who became a Tory MP in the war, took his first tentative steps towards the political arena, although he was not really a political animal. With Kemsley's agreement he established connections with a group known as the Tory Reformers (as did Henry Longhurst, who also became an MP in the war); and its leader, Sir Frederick Hooper, later head of Schweppes, was recruited as an occasional political leader writer for the paper; and he was a very competent one.

Encouraged, Lakin introduced Lord Vansittart, who became an unofficial political adviser to Kemsley after resigning from the Foreign Office and wrote for the paper early in the war a series of epigrammatic articles about the seven principles of foreign policy which revealed his increasing hysteria about Germany – the hysteria that took almost pathological form in his notorious book 'Black Record'. Vansittart, who had every gift except sound judgment, had alienated his old colleagues at the Foreign Office, where he had been permanent under-secretary ('he is all façade and nothing else' said his jealous successor, Sir Alexander Cadogan) until Chamberlain, determined to have no sabotage of appeasement, pushed him upstairs to a dead-end advisory post – chief diplomatic adviser. He had as a young man pitched his tent on Parnassus, and he returned to poetry in his attack on German barbarism in a dreadful poem in the paper:

> But heaven was overcast
> The clouds grew black and low,
> For in the heart of Europe
> Lived the Men of Prey.

This legendary figure with a rich and beautiful and devoted wife, one of the few diplomats, possibly the only one, to have refused the British Embassy in Paris, was on the way down when Kemsley took him up: Kemsley's judgment of men was notoriously erratic, and left to himself he could have been an outstanding collector of men on the way down. Happily, after the war, which was a sterile interregnum for newspapers because of censorship and paper rationing, he was influenced by young men on the way up and by the level-headedness of his son Lionel, another wartime M P, and he picked more winning ideas than losing ones – for The Sunday Times but not for his group as a whole.

But meanwhile, on the eve of the war, he involved himself in another political failure, urged on by Hadley, who in turn, it was said in the office, was urged on by Neville Chamberlain.

It began on May 21, 1939, when The Sunday Times reported:

There will be much eagerness to know the result of a very interesting proposal made on Friday by Lord Kemsley to Dr Dietrich,[1] the official director of the German press. Yesterday week the *Volkischer Beobachter* and other newspapers in Germany published an article by Dr Dietrich in which he referred to an offer he had made to the head of one of the most important newspaper groups in the United States. This offer, the article said, was 'to put the entire German press at the disposal of his

---

1. Otto Dietrich, who worked under Goebbels, was tried as a war criminal at Nuremberg in 1948. He was sent to the war crimes prison at Landsberg, Germany, and released in 1950. He died two years later.

best American writer' on condition that an informative article about Germany was put in the group of American papers.

The offer was rejected and, says Dr Dietrich, the American replied that 'he feared being reproached by his competitors with being under German influence'.

On this Dr Dietrich commented: 'Nothing could have illuminated to me the destructive attitude of mind in a not inconsiderable part of the international newspaper world more than this characteristic answer.'

When Lord Kemsley saw the German article he sent a telegram to Dr Dietrich in which he stated: 'On behalf of the *Daily Sketch* and my important group of London and provincial morning and evening newspapers I shall be glad to accept this offer for publication on the same terms. Full liberty of comment to be reserved on both sides.'

If Lord Kemsley's offer is accepted by Dr Dietrich it is understood that 'Candidus' [Herbert Sidebotham], whose brilliant work in the *Daily Sketch* is so well known, will state the material facts and arguments of the British case in an article for the German press.

This was in any circumstances a naïve offer to make. No one knew what American papers had rejected Dr Dietrich's advances. No one even knew whether such advances had really been made or whether the whole story was not merely a propagandist invention. In any event Kemsley laid himself open to the risk of a public snub.

However, on May 26 The Daily Sketch reported: 'In answer to many hundreds of inquiries as to whether there was any reply from Germany to the offer made to Dr Dietrich by Lord Kemsley on May 19 last, we are in a position to inform our readers that yesterday an answer was received by Lord Kemsley from Dr Dietrich, which necessitates an exchange of views upon the suggestion made. It is not possible to say more at this juncture.'

After this nothing was publicly heard either of Kemsley's offer or of Dietrich's reply, but later in the summer both Lord and Lady Kemsley went to Germany. Kemsley's own papers reported this visit only briefly, and The Times noted merely on July 28: 'Lord and Lady Kemsley, who are at present visiting Germany on the invitation of Dr Dietrich, the Reich Press Chief, were received yesterday by Herr Hitler at Bayreuth.' The News Chronicle was slightly more explicit: 'Lord Kemsley, the newspaper owner, had an interview lasting an hour with Herr Hitler today in the Villa Wahnfried, where the Fuehrer is living during his visit to the Wagner Festival. While Lord Kemsley would make no comment on the meeting, he intimated that it was no more than a "courtesy visit". He came here to talk to Dr Dietrich, Nazi Press Chief, about an exchange, if possible, of English political and German

political Press articles. It is presumed that this was discussed by
Lord Kemsley and Herr Hitler.'
    Whatever may have been discussed, Cyril Lakin, who accom-
panied the Kemsleys, returned to England a scared man. Of what
had happened he would say nothing. His sole private comment
was: 'I think war is going to break out in a matter of weeks.'
He was right. It came some four weeks later.
    In March, 1940, Lord Kemsley explained in his papers exactly
what had taken place between him and Dr Dietrich. On May 19,
1939, Kemsley had made his offer to put his various publications
at the disposal of Dietrich if a corresponding English article were
given equal publicity in Germany. Six days after that Dietrich
replied, 'expressing misgivings as to whether the proposal would
really serve the cause of peace, and asking for certain assurances,
mainly of a character protective of German interests, and the
definiteness of the exchange to be made.'
    This coyness on the part of Dr Dietrich should have opened
Kemsley's eyes to the fact that the whole thing was really a bit of
Nazi propaganda. But Kemsley and Hadley would not call it off.
'Six days afterwards, on May 31st,' says Kemsley, 'I wrote once
more to Dr Dietrich agreeing unequivocally to all the points he
had raised. . . . On July 23rd, on the personal and urgent invitation of Dr Dietrich I went to Germany to discuss all the points
with him, and on July 27th I arrived at Bayreuth, where I had an
interview with him, with Herr Hitler, and important German
officials.'
    At this meeting with Dr Dietrich, Lord Kemsley, as he ought
to have foreseen, found the Nazi press chief in a difficult humour.
He obviously had no desire to carry out the proposed exchange of
newspaper articles. Kemsley, in his naïve way, asked for naïve
action, whilst Dietrich was concerned only to procrastinate. He
said uncomfortably that the moment was not ripe for publication
of the articles and that a later date, when the international
atmosphere was better, would be more appropriate. This, of
course, made nonsense of the entire purpose of the proposed
articles. But Kemsley persisted, and he secured from the reluctant
and embarrassed Dietrich a more or less favourable reception of
his expressed hope that the German article would be ready fairly
soon.
    Nearly a month passed by, and then there happened the sort of
ill luck which dogged Kemsley's ventures into greatness; it was
known in the office as the 'Kemsley banana skin', and it included

such misadventures as buying at the Festival of Britain an exhibition car so large that without reversing it couldn't get round the corner from Langham Place into Chandos Street. On August 18 Dietrich posted in Munich the so much desired draft (in German) of the Nazi article. It was addressed to Lord Kemsley at Chandos House, Chandos Street; and Kemsley, who had been moving heaven and earth to get it, was not there when it arrived. On August 20, when the letter reached Chandos House, he was at Deauville with his wife and some of his entourage. The letter was forwarded to him; it appears to have reached him on August 21, and he immediately ordered a general return to London. On that day it was announced from Berlin that a Soviet–German pact had been successfully negotiated.

This event moved Lord K to utter one of his great political judgments. He wrote: 'As this document established and finally decided a complete reorientation of Germany's traditional anti-Communist policy, and foreshadowed the coming of an aggressive alliance between Germany and Russia against the Allies, it made any hope of agreement by discussion very improbable. This was my view at the time, and I was supported in that view by some of the highest political authorities in the country.'

Yet the Nazis had not quite finished with Lord K. On the afternoon of August 22 (the day before the Nazi–Soviet pact was actually signed) Dr Hesse, the German press attaché in London, having been ordered to do so by Dr Dietrich, called on Lord Kemsley at Chandos House. He wanted to know if the article had been safely received. Hearing that it had, he gave the indignant viscount 'a personal message from Dr Dietrich to say that the article representing Germany's case should be published in Britain before the one stating the British case was published by the German papers.' Lord Kemsley was astounded at the impudence of the proposal but kept control of his temper. He merely said that this 'ingenious suggestion' was unacceptable.

It would be instructive to know what took place between the Fuehrer and Lord Kemsley. No detailed record of their conversation seems to have been kept by Kemsley, but in a letter to Dr Dietrich written on August 1, 1939, he gives some idea of the general lines of the interview. This letter concludes with the hopeful tactic believed in by Sir Alexander Cadogan, Barrington-Ward of The Times and other apostles of appeasement, that of asking Germany 'to state her terms' – no one in the Kemsley party, by the way, could speak German.

Chandos House, London, W.1

Dear Dr Dietrich,

I have been thinking over the conversation that I was privileged to have with the Fuehrer at Bayreuth on July 27th. You will remember that in that conversation, as well as in my talks with you, Herr Rosenberg, Baron Weizsacker, and others, I laid emphasis upon the wholehearted support which is being given in this country to the Prime Minister's policy. Everybody here recognises that, while on the one hand our Government look forward wholeheartedly to the time when confidence has been sufficiently restored to make it possible to begin the constructive work of building peace, they have no alternative, on the other hand, but to take the steps that have been taken to consolidate the strength of the country. Those steps – which resulted from a conviction that they must resist further attempts to impose by force unilateral changes – have received the complete support of every section of public opinion.

I am not sure how far I succeeded in conveying to the Fuehrer that British opinion, although it would like to arrive at an understanding with Germany, has had its confidence so shaken that discussions with that object in view do not seem to be feasible in present circumstances. It is very important, and indeed essential, that the facts should be known by the Fuehrer and there is no question whatever as to the fact that confidence here does not exist.

As a means to establish this confidence Kemsley went on:

Do you think it would be possible for you in confidence to obtain the Fuehrer's views and to secure his authority to send me a statement showing with some precision what he has in his mind –
(*a*) As to the matters which, for his part, he would propose should be discussed, and
(*b*) What proposals he could authorise me to put forward for the purpose of establishing that confidence which must necessarily be a preliminary to any settlement acceptable to public opinion here and elsewhere.

Dr Dietrich's reply was polite but did not carry the matter much further. He wrote: 'It . . . seems to me that I can best respond to your friendly suggestion by setting myself to express to your wide circle of readers my own frank and sincere opinions,' by which he was supposedly referring to the unpublished article.

It was the end of Lord Kemsley's pathetic little mission.

II

But Lord K was in some ways an exceptional man and in all an undauntable one, titter as one may at his little mishaps; his big nose grew more obstinate as he advanced in years. He fell back now from his unhappy incursion into international affairs with a renewed determination to express himself in every byway and corner of The Sunday Times and thereby make it into a newspaper which ranked with the world's best.

The coming of the war was not, of course, an auspicious time for the realisation of his ambitions. His sons went into the army (one of them was killed in action), enterprise had to be sacrificed to the war effort, staffs throughout the whole of his group were depleted, newsprint was in short supply. His beloved Sunday Times was reduced to a size no bigger than it had achieved a hundred years before, all its usual features were miserably diminished in length, and its critics complained (like some character in Congreve) that they had become mere epitomisers of words and speakers of shorthand.

Meanwhile the production of the paper in London was carried on by a minimal staff. The news editor and deputy editor was charming Valentine Heywood. 'Hang Valentine Heywood,' said James Agate (adapting a remark made to him once by Arnold Bennett of Eddie Marsh), 'he's one of those miserable men who enjoy everything.' 'Everything' was hyperbole; Heywood's enjoyments were restricted to the novels of Dornford Yates, history, genealogy and the pleasures of living in Chalfont St Giles – all else was a desert, particularly theatres, art galleries and so on: he was a happy man without all that. Happy but nervous; the slightest upset in the office would drive him into one of his states. He would rush around, his pale face contorted with anxiety, his wiry white hair on end. The steadier nerves of Hadley, however, usually calmed him down, and he was much liked in the sub-editors' room for his fairness and – crises apart – sweet temper.

He was fascinated by the minutiae of British titles, and his knowledge of the aristocracy (so far as it could be gained from books) was phenomenal. His political judgment might be unreliable, his outlook provincial, but on the proper modes of address attaching to everyone in the peerage he was infallible – his book on the subject is a standard one. If there had been no such thing as an English peerage, one would have had to be invented in order to keep him amused. He was to remain on the staff for a good many years yet, always holding a very exalted position, but it is probably true to say that, competent newspaperman though he was, he operated always above his ceiling; his mind was so innocent of subtlety that he could never see the implications and complications of things. But much has to be forgiven him for his goodness of heart and game struggle with a duodenal ulcer. His deep affection for English tradition was understandably outraged when in the mid-1930s Kemsley changed the name of his then country house from Farnham Chase to Farnham Park. He never forgot it and years later would instance it as an action worthy of Sir Gorgius Midas, whose disastrous social gaffes du Maurier chronicled in last century's Punch. 'To abandon a wonderful historical term like chase!' he would lament.

One of the chief difficulties Heywood had directly to contend with was the shortage of newsprint. Soon after the war started there were fears of a paper famine, and it was expected that a lack of newsprint would drive some of the weaker papers out of existence. The situation became critical in 1940, when the sham war ceased and Hitler invaded Norway and France. Scandinavia had been the greatest source of newsprint supply, and the failure of the British move to dislodge Hitler produced gloom amounting almost to panic in newspaper circles.

At this point the Lords Beaverbrook and Kemsley had a conversation which produced beneficent results. Some papers had contracts with Canadian mills; they generously agreed to put this paper into a common pool. It was agreed to form a co-operative company, non-profit-making, and to invite the leading newspapers outside London to participate as well. An arrangement was made that all newsprint in Britain should be rationed to newspapers by a Newsprint Supply Company. Thus all papers shrank in size, but they did so proportionately to their bulk before the war, and none had reason to complain either that it was peculiarly unlucky or that it was being unfairly treated in comparison with its rivals. Short of outright defeat of the country in war, it was thus guaranteed that all papers could continue their existence on a relatively stable basis. In fact, for the weaker papers the war was a positive business benefit. They could not be outclassed in size by their richer or cleverer rivals, and the amount of advertisements being limited by the number of pages in each issue, which was constant for a given period, they were spared the financial and nervous strain of clawing in revenue.

But though the elements of competition were absent, it was still possible during the war for a successful newspaper to increase its circulation. During it The Sunday Times nearly hit the half-million and the Observer 361,367. As the years went by, as will be related, the historic competition between the two papers became keener and keener. In the 1950s it became something of an obsession; even contributors like Henry Longhurst, who came into the office rarely, doing their work on the telephone or posting in their copy, were tinglingly alive to the battle. In 1961 the intervention of The Sunday Telegraph was chiefly resented, in Grays Inn Road at any rate, for no more serious reason than that it was getting in the way of the time-honoured tussle with Tudor Street.

The first hope of The Sunday Times after 1940 was that its repute would be increased by the achievement of its war correspondents. They were never less than conscientious and competent, but it became more and more clear as the war went on that none of them was a Moorehead, an Alex Clifford, or a Christopher Buckley.

There was, though, Alexander Werth, a great cross between a special correspondent and a war correspondent who made his name with his despatches to The Sunday Times on the fall of France in 1940. He was in London on and off throughout the war, a lanky figure in a Hitler raincoat and brown beret or tin hat: if it was a period when air-raids were on he wore his tin hat persistently and quite unselfconsciously. His rubber lips were always smiling, his pop eyes sparkling with amused intelligence, while all the time there would flow from him mordancies about anything from our conduct of the war to the quality of the coffee in the canteen. Brilliantly eccentric, not at all modest, he combined being born in St Petersburg (in 1901) with a degree at Glasgow University. Constitutionally he was excessively nervous, particularly when bombs were falling on London; yet he nerved himself to become a brave lion and exposed himself, cursing and criticising, to many hazards.

Just before he died in 1969 in Paris he wrote the following about his connection with The Sunday Times:

Despite my dramatic and truly absurd resignation from the *Sunday Times* in October 1946 (a step I often regretted), I have nothing but the happiest memories of my association with the paper. I think the real

highlights were: the Munich period; as you know, Kemsley was violently
pro-Munich and kept in personal touch with Neville Chamberlain; I
was equally violently anti. But it is only fair to say that, apart from a little
toning down, they let me say pretty much what I wanted to say – i.e.
state the anti-Munich case. Then I shall always remember the blitz
winter in London, when I used to see a great deal of K., Hadley, Leonard
Russell and Cyril Lakin; we'd have supper at the top of the *Telegraph*
building and wait for the sirens. The next thing was my going to Russia
almost immediately after the German invasion – fantastic way of going
by flying-boat in one hop from the Shetlands to Archangel; then the
dreadful first months of the war in Russia. I returned in November and
then went back to Russia by convoy (always for the ST!), which was
dive-bombed by the Germans for six days – the most dramatic of all my
wartime experiences. I had the unique experience of going for the ST to
Leningrad during the blockade in 1943 (the Germans were still a couple
of miles outside the city, and were shelling it good and hard). The
Soviet censorship was very reasonable during the war, compared with
what it became during the Cold War. I might mention other highlights
during the war – Stalingrad, where I went twice, just before and just after
the German capitulation; and many other trips to the Front, either solo
or in a group of correspondents. Finally, Poland and Berlin.

Now I must mention a piece of my own psycho-analysis. I first returned to London in October 1945, and was still completely starry-eyed
about the Russian war effort, and then, at a big dinner which Kemsley
gave, one of the guests, Sir Andrew Duncan, suddenly said: 'The only
solution is to drop the atom bomb on Moscow.' I was quite incredibly
shocked, and this is the *real* reason why I resigned from the ST a year
later – though it wasn't at all Kemsley's fault that some of his friends
cherished such monstrous ideas. But it rankled with me for a year. The
trivial reason I gave for resigning was, in fact, neither here nor there. It
was an altogether irrational gesture, since I was just then in the highest
favour with Kemsley, having just had my famous Stalin interview!
People can be very odd, don't you think?

Oh, of course, I was also with the ST during the French collapse in
1940!

Kemsley and Hadley on the one hand, Alex Werth, so foreign
in his manner and emphases, on the other, were men poles apart;
yet they were drawn together by the feeling of mutual trust and
friendliness apparent throughout the whole office. Richard
Vickers, copy-taster for years, expressed the feelings of everyone
when he said, on going into semi-retirement in 1970, that on
The Sunday Times you could be sure that no one would ever
stick a knife in your back. This confidence – tiffs and tantrums
excepted – has characterised the office for at least the last thirty

years. It has been as strong under Lord Thomson, C. D. Hamilton, and Harold Evans as it was under Kemsley, Hadley, and H. V. Hodson.

The consideration consistently exercised by editor or proprietor was demonstrated in the early days of the war in connection with someone who was later to join the critics, Harold Hobson.

In 1938, just before the Munich crisis, Hobson rang up the Board of Education and asked what places the schoolchildren of London would be evacuated to in case of war, and how the evacuation would be arranged. Somewhat to his surprise he was told the complete plans. They could have been found out by any journalist with a telephone, but apparently no one had thought to ask. Hobson took his story to The Sunday Times and was interviewed by Iain Lang, who had already recruited Henry Brandon to the staff. Lang was Heywood's deputy as news editor, a Scot of philosophic bent of mind, sardonic speech, deep culture, and wide artistic interests – after the war he contributed a regular column on jazz. He was with all this a brilliant all-round journalist and chief sub-editor. (Nobody, as Dilys Powell had found, ever tells you anything in a newspaper office. Lang had little tips for Hobson later on: for example, *more than* a thousand and not *over*; never begin two consecutive sentences with *the*; in paragraphing, an occasional very short paragraph leavens the lump.) He took Hobson's story as a scoop and displayed it prominently in the next issue. A week later Hobson took a second news story to Kemsley House. Lang being out, Heywood read it instead. He turned pale when he found that it contained the name of Tennyson, a literary man, though a lord. He promptly rejected it, and Hobson realised that news stories of literary interest would get accepted only on the days when Lang was in authority.

The next time he saw Lang he asked to be introduced to the literary editor, hoping to get some books to review. 'The man who matters on the book pages,' said Lang, 'isn't Lakin, but Leonard Russell, his assistant.' The introduction to Russell (a turning-point in Hobson's life) was duly made, and thereafter a constant stream of books came his way.

Soon after this happy contact had been made Hobson suffered a serious financial disappointment. His worried wife told Russell that he was anxious about money, and Russell told Hadley, and Hadley asked Hobson to go and see him. 'How much money a year do you need?' was Hadley's first question. '£600,' said Hobson, somewhat surprised at his own boldness, for £600 in 1942 was still quite a sum, and he was doing another regular job. (Agate got no more than £1,500 a year at the end of his career, when his salary was at its height.) '£600?' echoed Hadley. 'It isn't enough. We'll give you £900.' Hobson asked what he was expected to do for this at that time quite princely sum, and all Hadley would say was, 'Oh, hang around till the war's over. We shall need lots of people then.'

Thereafter every Friday Hobson came to The Sunday Times office about half past twelve, crossed the road with Russell to lunch off sandwiches and coffee, and corrected proofs till five or six o'clock. The same process was repeated on Saturdays, except that lunch was taken in The Telegraph building, with Hadley, Heywood, R. C. K. Ensor, the City editor, Norman Crump, and of course the ubiquitous Russell. Cyril Lakin, the literary editor, was sickening for a serious illness.

One afternoon, a Friday, in the hot and crowded atmosphere of The Telegraph composing-room, Russell and Hobson received a fright. On Friday afternoons Desmond MacCarthy would be found tightly wedged into Russell's cubby-hole, desperately trying to finish the article the printers had already begun to set up in type; if the V-1 raids were on he would have with him a squiffy little attaché-case in which was a bottle of port. On this particular Friday Desmond collapsed spectacularly with what he and everyone else thought was a heart attack. But the doctor who appeared with magical speed pronounced it merely severe indigestion.

All the same, the incident made Russell think. He began to ask himself what would happen if Desmond disappeared from the paper. (The alarm was premature and Desmond went on writing the principal book review for years.) After the war Russell was to bring in Desmond's disciples, Raymond Mortimer and Cyril Connolly, choices which were very successful. Now, after an interval, his eye lit on Charles Morgan.

There was some doubt whether Morgan would accept a regular assignment on a newspaper, for he had resigned from The Times as drama critic at the beginning of the war in order to devote himself to work of more permanent value than theatre reviewing. But he had been writing a series of articles for The Times Literary Supplement, and this encouraged Russell to suggest that he contribute regularly to The Sunday Times. Morgan accepted the offer speedily but with well-bred calm and kicked off with a general statement of his attitude to literature. It was as cold as an iceberg, and everybody in The Sunday Times office except Russell (who sensed that he had made one of those dreadful mistakes) was delighted with it. When Hobson told Morgan of its success he said swiftly, 'But did it please the important people, the people at the top?'

Week by week – or was it fortnightly? – Morgan's articles came in. They were always early and never remarkable. They were easy but empty. Russell grew more and more dissatisfied, particularly as Lord K became Morgan's patron and encouraged him to write diehard Tory articles for the leader-page.

There came a time when Russell felt positive that he could use that Morgan money in some better fashion; on C. P. Snow and Michael Sadleir, for example, as fiction reviewers. He got his way, and Snow was a genuine discovery.

He first met Snow at the Savile Club soon after the war when Snow was almost unknown as a novelist. Russell would see him about the place, an impressive, bulky figure sometimes in a cream tussore suit and large black hat: great domed naked head, fore-head creased with concentration, gimlet eyes behind thick round spectacles. One night Russell asked a man sitting next to him at dinner if he knew the name of this member. 'I'm afraid I don't,' was the cool reply. 'I privately call him Dr Frankenstein-Brain-storm – he's a Cambridge scientist, I think.' And Snow did indeed look like everyone's idea of a wizard scientist, a distinguished Superman.

When they got to know each other they would retire to the horsehair benches of the snooker-room after dinner, where Russell discovered that Snow was a brilliant and high-spirited conversationalist much given to sudden shouts of laughter and saying 'mmm' repeatedly and interrogatively after making some remark. He also discovered that Snow was interested above all things in the art of fiction and, with the example of Roger Martin du Gard before him, was planning a whole saga of novels. They would talk endlessly about novelists past and present, and Russell discovered that Snow was a campaigner against what he called the 'moment-by-moment' story-telling of Virginia Woolf and of esotericism in general. Russell was not entirely sympathetic to this thesis but he was impressed by Snow's passionate approach to the practice of fiction. Then one night in the snooker-room Snow pressed a typewritten document into his hand. He went home and read it and that same evening sent Snow a wire offering him a job as a fiction reviewer for The Sunday Times.

Lord Snow says now – 1972 – to Russell about this characteristic document, 'I think you are the only person who has ever read
it.' It was called 'Credo', and he has given permission for it to
appear here:

1. The great books of the world have dealt with human beings, in their
flesh and feeling: set in the surroundings of their time: living the major
experiences of their lives.

This credo is concerned with novels, but (1) is true of the entire
literature of human truth, from Homer, Petronius and the Latin
novelists, the sagas, Lady Murasaki, Chaucer down to the great nineteenth-century novelists. Dostoievski, Tolstoi, Dickens, Balzac: the
succession is clear down to the present day in the fine, though minor,
stream of French novelists, Martin du Gard and Mauriac.

The great books are stories about human beings, stories about human
beings in exactly the same sense as tea-time gossip: differing from tea-
time gossip in depth, range, technique and truth, but not in primary
intention: differing less from tea-time gossip than either does from
Finnegans Wake or similar specialised writing.

2. This century has seen the first serious attempt to *specialise and narrow
the scope of prose-fiction*. Thus *Finnegans Wake* narrows the scope from the
major experiences of life to the semi-conscious verbal wanderings on the
threshold of sleep: Virginia Woolf narrows it to a visual impressionism.

(Proust, a great writer in the sense of (1), both told stories about
human beings and specialised in his presentation of time and memory.
Similarly Henry James: and it is the *specialised function* which is the subject
of admiration in the present Henry James vogue.)

3. The experiments of (2), in this extreme form are:

(*a*) Unreadable. Nearly as unreadable to us, trained literary persons,
as to the ordinary Times Book Club subscriber. *Finnegans Wake* is
literally unreadable.

(*b*) Sterile. They have produced no successors, and even very little
pastiche.

(*c*) Attractive to persons with no human taste or appetite, but with a
similar specialised sensibility. For various reasons, social, psychological,
and accidental, these persons, small in number, dominated the *New
Statesman* and its environs from 1930 to the present time.

4. The effects of (3) are to *produce a gap*, unknown before in prose fiction,
between the esoteric 'literary' value and that of the ordinary cultivated
reader. This has had grave effects.

(*a*) Told that *Finnegans Wake* is literature and that e.g. *The Old Wives
Tale* is not, the ordinary cultivated person has said 'so much the worse
for literature'. And the standing of both literature and the literary profession is far lower now than in the nineteenth century. Then, Trollope,
George Eliot, Thackeray, were venerated figures: it is hard to imagine

anyone venerating most of the contemporary practitioners. It is probable that the standard of aspirants trying to make a career of letters is getting lower.

(*b*) The fractionation of literary *genres* has proceeded very fast. Finding these esoteric values meaningless to him, the ordinary cultivated person has taken refuge in detective stories – where he finds some of the attractions that he expects and understands: i.e. the narrative, human beings, readability. In the same way, the bewildered young writer has often taken to hopeless and talentless reportage, usually about environments that he does not instinctively comprehend: see *New Writing*: this movement appears to be already dead. The serious development of technical skill along the chain of (1) has in this country been frustrated for a generation.

(*c*) The gravest evil is, however, the sheer existence of a gap between esoteric critics and the cultivated reading public. For an art to consist of a popular entertainment side and an esoteric prestige side is in the long run death. See what has happened to films.

5. But prose fiction is not dead. To condemn it, because the experiments of (2) have run up a blind alley, is nonsense. If we think of (1), it becomes obvious nonsense. Some of the most fundamental experiences of life have not yet been treated profoundly in fiction. Off-hand, one can think of: enduring marriage (Tolstoi ought to have done it but did not). Old age (ditto Goethe). Of experiences less universal but still vital: *odi et amo* (ditto Dostoievski). These examples are the first that come to mind: there are many more. The number of characters and types of character not yet attempted is very large. The number of situations and stories is infinite, particularly in a world of violent change, which produces its creative difficulties but throws out a creative challenge and provides overwhelming creative opportunity.

6. What is to be done?

(*a*) Popular taste is often nearer to the right line than esoteric taste. *********** is more nearly a major writer than Virginia Woolf: he happens to falsify the truth, and so is not serious. But it is necessary for us to find serious writers with his virtues: remember that he is read for his virtues at least as much as for his falsifications: those virtues are power of emotion, narrative, and humanity. It is not impossible to combine these virtues with a passion for the truth. That is the case with the great writers of (1). We must get back to the main stream.

(*b*) But with, of course, some evolution. The experiments of (2) have been sterile. They have explored, however, regions of sensibility by which all later writers will be enriched – and will use, to the extent that they do not obscure the major intentions of stories about human beings. If Trollope were living today, for instance, his visual scenes would be sharper – simply because visual presentation has been so greatly studied between 1900–1940.

(c) Books are meant to be read. No novelist of the highest class (with the solitary exception of Stendhal) has failed to win a large public in his lifetime. The novelist of human truth (6a and b) must study technical problems which, owing to the experiments of (2), have been neglected for twenty years. The depiction of character (without which analysis is useless): the relation of narrative to scene and of both to commentary: and so on.

A warning. There has been a great progress in the stream-lined technique of non-serious narrative. The pace of Nigel Balchin is three times George Eliot's: but there are mutual contradictions in all arts, and if you secure that pace in the novel, you lose heart, gravity and power. The pace of a great novel should be the fastest consistent with telling the *full* story of human beings – or the slowest at which the reader will comfortably persevere. This pace is a good deal slower than the slick American one, but it must be held there.

7. No new literary movement is worth twopence unless it is full of faith. In our case, faith that it is a good and valuable thing to tell the stories of human beings as deeply and as vividly as we can. Passion, human curiosity and compassion, the wish to live in the odour of man, are more important than anything else. It is this passion which the esoteric literature has completely lacked.

Unless we have it, novels are not worth writing. And the novel as a great art form will inevitably die.

Snow believed that left-wing doctrines in art were allied to the opposite tendency in politics, and that 'realism' in art was one of the signs of a progressive society.

Another Cambridge figure who reviewed for the paper at this time was C. K. Ogden, the originator of Basic English, the widespread use of which, said Churchill in 1943, 'would be a gain to us far more durable and fruitful than the annexation of great provinces'. In 1946 Ogden assigned the copyright to the Crown for £23,000. Russell used to give Ogden dinner at the Ritz or dine with him at the Coq d'Or in Stratton Street, but he was without Snow's charm and conversation and their meetings were glum and silent. Ogden, who was responsible for a wonderful record of James Joyce reading from 'Anna Livia', had two related interests: orthology, which is the science of correct speaking, and what he called the 'debabelisation' of the world. Somewhere in this programme was inserted the study of sounds, and one night, in desperation perhaps, he took Russell to his home in Gordon Square. He had an institute there, and the place was crammed with mechanical figures, music-boxes, fair-ground organs and so on. All performed actions and made sounds, ranging from twirping to a roaring. Ogden set a couple of dozen of them going simultaneously, and the effect of noise and action was so eerie, so like a moment with music from some mad old film like 'Dr Mabuse', that Russell was glad when he was out on the silent pavements of Bloomsbury again.

III

The war did not prevent certain departures from usual practice in The Sunday Times. On January 21, 1940, for example, in the very middle of the long pause that inaugurated the second world war, advertisements were for the first time removed from the front page and news substituted for them. It was something which Lord K decided upon almost overnight. It was rather naïvely explained that this was done in order to conform with the practice of newspapers all over the world. It is not often that The Sunday Times thus formally disclaims originality; it was conceivably the first quality paper in the country to do it.

It was on the whole a bold and striking front page (in an 18-page paper). Its principal war stories were almost gay and buoyant. Brave headlines on the right-hand side proclaimed 'Ministers' Faith in Victory. Factors that Will Prove Decisive Are On Our Side'. Churchill declared that things had never gone better in naval war – 'The first U-boat campaign was utterly broken, the mine menace was in good control, our shipping was virtually undiminished, and the oceans of the world had been freed of surface raiders.' But the front page also had attention to spare for other things besides war. It was noted that it was one of the coldest winters on record, the temperature at Davos in Switzerland being 60 degrees below freezing. A diplomatic correspondent (unnamed) stated that Italy would not tolerate Russian intervention in the Balkans, and Sir John Reith, newly-appointed Minister of Information, said he would sit in Parliament as National Member for Southampton.

The circulation of the paper, after a momentary drop at the declaration of war, was beginning to climb again. In September, 1939, it had been 327,800; in October, 324,174; in November, 348,880; and in December, 349,461.

These figures gave Lord Kemsley great satisfaction. On the leader page of this issue of January 21, 1940, he expressed this in straightforward terms. In the centre of his article was a reproduc-

tion of the first page of the first issue, October 20, 1822. He declared that the aim of the paper was to be of the highest quality
and that nothing would be allowed to interfere with this. He
noted that, as long as seven years before, the circulation of the
paper was at least equal to that of any other Sunday paper of
comparable class. Since then the sales had steadily risen. They
were now running at 140,000 a week more than in 1933. The
actual yearly figures were:

1933	210,225	1937	270,072
1934	216,641	1938	292,075
1935	231,822	1939	330,135
1936	254,134		

Moreover, the circulation had risen in quality as well as in
numbers. Kemsley added, rather characteristically, 'It includes
an extraordinarily high proportion of the wealthy and educated
classes, and indeed of leaders of all classes.' When he turned his
attention from what had already happened to what was going to
happen, he showed himself full of confidence, in an old-fashioned
diction which bore the stamp of Hadley:

Of the future this may be said . . . the *Sunday Times* will maintain its
character as a newspaper of the highest quality. Its comprehensive and
balanced news services will be as accurate as the utmost care can secure.
Public affairs will be discussed spaciously and with a sense of responsibility. On the cultural side, literature, the drama, music and the arts
will as now be dealt with by specialists of the highest authority. And that
rule will be applied also to the sports and games that are so important a
part of the life of this country.

On the whole Lord Kemsley's promise was kept, and the consequence was that by December, 1945, the circulation had risen
to half a million. This was an achievement of which Lord K had
every reason to be proud, even if allowance is made for the favourable circumstances provided by the war, paradoxical as that may
sound. Yet for Kemsley, as for other newspaper proprietors, the
war brought primarily a terrible sense of frustration. He and they
knew that you could never run a real newspaper in war-time – you
were tied with so many restrictions.

On the cultural side his confidence was particularly well
founded. With Dilys Powell writing about films The Sunday
Times no longer had need to worry about C. A. Lejeune in The
Observer; and with Agate on drama, Ernest Newman, peren-

Luncheon at Kemsley House, 1944. Back row: Leonard Russell, Eric Newton, Norman Crump, W. T. Bliss, D. R. Gent, Hanslip Fletcher, Cyril Lakin, Brigadier Anstey, Dilys Powell, G. R. Osler, R. C. K. Ensor, Valentine Heywood, Charles Gayton, Douglas Woodruff, Desmond MacCarthy. Front row: Lionel Berry, W. W. Hadley, Lord and Lady Kemsley, Ernest Newman, James Agate.

nially young, on music, and Eric Newton on art, the paper need fear no competition from any quarter. On books MacCarthy, in his easy but sharp-eyed way, was incomparable. The latent threat to him from Charles Morgan did not seem to trouble him at all, and it was becoming increasingly evident that there was no reason why it should, though as late as December, 1945, Morgan was still being given more space than he was. Their respective articles were used at the extreme left and right of the page – the two pillars of Solomon's Temple, Desmond used to call them, Jachin and Boaz. Said he one day at this time: 'This week – as I was pleased to hear you say over the telephone – your old friend Jachin is distinctly readable, but Boaz is poxed to the bone.'

Other stars were rising in specialist fields. Peter Masefield was becoming an exceptionally knowledgeable aviation correspondent. Commander Russell Grenfell and Brigadier Anstey were powerful naval and military commentators. Most popular of all was George Schwartz.

George was and still is mystified as to why he came to be offered a job by the paper. Vaguely, he is inclined to think that the original idea came from Kenneth Pickthorn, the right-wing Tory MP for (later) Cambridge University. The political ambitions of Cyril Lakin may have brought him into touch with Pickthorn, and supposedly the MP pressed the idea on him, but George knew neither Pickthorn nor Lakin and is still unclear about their precise rôles. All he is certain of is that one day Norman Crump, the city editor, came along with a proposal. George said in 1972:

I was flabbergasted. I'd done no writing except a very occasional article for reviews like the *Nineteenth Century*. It couldn't have been anything to do with my work at the London School of Economics or anything like that. Well, it was the end of the war, and I was 53, and I thought it was time I made a change in life, so I accepted Norman Crump's offer. There were grandiose schemes at the time for setting up a Kemsley News World Service, with tentative ideas of an international economic and financial survey. An appointment for that purpose fell down.

Looking back, what impressed me and still impresses me was the discipline imposed by the newsprint shortage which went on for a long time after the war. To write only 800 words and then be told by Valentine Heywood, 'George, you're two inches over, and if you don't cut it I shall' was exasperating and in the event salutary. Would that the *New York Times* had the same spell of discipline.

We were a cheerful little crowd then, with a family atmosphere, and we kept the show going on a handful of oatmeal, as Sydney Smith once put it. I can't forgive the way Kemsley walked out on us over the weekend.

I miss the life but felt it time to give place.

In his own words on another occasion, he had spent twenty years teaching students at the London School of Economics the virtues of mobility of labour and felt it was time to set them a good example. His column attacking economic nonsenses, so homely in its illustrations and deadly in its argument, became internationally famous. Before he retired on his 80th birthday (it was George Schwartz who in 1960 recommended William Rees-Mogg as City editor of The Sunday Times) he had written just over a million words for the paper, despite the brevity of his early columns, and his admirers were legion. They included Rebecca West, who herself regularly contributed splendidly to The Sunday Times, but unfortunately withdrew through misunderstandings and incompatibilities, to the mortification of Russell, to whom she had been a fabled creature since his and her Telegraph days. The misunderstandings and incompatibilities were certainly not with him.

The situation on both the editorial and news sides of the paper towards the end of the war was not satisfactory. Though Hadley had been bred a Liberal he accepted Kemsley's unintelligent brand of Conservatism with a certain complacency. The extravagant leading article of December 2, 1945, after Churchill's defeat at the 'Gestapo' election, was typical of this insensitive attitude:

Mr Churchill stated the dramatic truth when he declared on Wednesday that the vote at the General Election was one of the greatest disasters that has smitten us in our long and chequered history. His emphatic words are fully justified. This vote was obtained by presenting a picture of a brave new world in which smaller effort would command a greater reward. No responsible politician believed that picture to be true. All knew that on the contrary only the most intense effort could preserve our standards of living. Yet not only did the Socialist Party, with an irresponsibility unequalled in our political history, secure support by promises no Government could fulfil, but it committed itself in advance to the Socialist method for their fulfilment. Now, intoxicated by an unexpected majority, the Socialist Party insists on treading the primrose path, to the dismay of all those who set the national well-being above party scores.

Nor was this monolithic political outlook offset by comprehensiveness or brilliance of news-gathering. This latter, unlike the former, was a defect that the management set about rectifying as soon as the war was over, but, as we shall see, with only partial success.

Something must be said of the difficulties and frustrations of bringing out a paper in war-time. Richard Vickers here speaks modestly and phlegmatically for the sub-editors and technicians of all kinds who carried on in the blitz:

The big news was still breaking on Saturdays, as it had done in Hitler's heyday before the war, but now we had the censor, lack of space and, later, air raids to contend with.

We had a good many raids, of course, but never once was production stopped completely. When things got too bad the editorial staff moved to the basement of the *Telegraph* building (where on Saturdays the paper was edited and printed), which was fully equipped with news and other services.

There were even sleeping quarters in the basement – bunks with sheets and blankets in an airless room, and a sort of valet who made the beds and brought you tea in the morning. Some members of the *Telegraph* staff almost lived there.

The make-up man was the hardest hit by the air-raid regulations. If a raid was on the printing was done only on machines in the deepest depths, and he worked right next to the thunder of the presses. Answering the 'phone from the night editor in those circumstances was difficult.

After duty we did our roof-spotting (to deal with incendiary bombs if they fell) either on the roof of the main building or at the garage in Salisbury Court. There were several near misses with HE bombs, including one which destroyed part of the *Telegraph* building in Peterborough Court and a fire bomb which set another part alight. The narrowest escape for Fleet Street was when a parachute bomb descended and was caught on the wires of the street lights outside the *Daily Express*. One story is that when it was carefully lowered for removal and defusing, a passing dog cocked its leg at it to help.

The V-1 bombs, and the rockets later, were a more trying experience because by then we were working upstairs again. When the well-known buzz was heard there was a tendency to dive under the desks, but most of us played a sort of 'chicken' game.

Even in these dangerous days the *Sunday Times* was changing and improving as far as newsprint restrictions would allow. Lest the London plant got knocked out it was decided to do a duplicate print at the Withy Grove works at Manchester, and this Manchester print added considerably to our problems. It was a northern edition in name only because in every respect as far as content went it was supposed to be identical down to the last comma. So everything had to be duplicated in some way or other. Some of the matter went up in proof form, some in flongs and much by wire. The sub-editor had to send his copy either 'Manchester and printer', which meant it was put on the wire first to the north, or put a black in wherever possible. Staff copy was duplicated and subbed twice. Headlines and make-ups were transmitted mostly by phone, and two men were on duty all of Saturday for this purpose alone.

All this meant a considerable expansion of the effort. The wire-room had to be fully manned seven days a week, more telephonists had to be engaged. Willie Wilson, imperturbable with his pipe, who was in charge of the London end of the operation, had to keep his eyes and ears alert for the sudden change and warn his opposite number at Manchester. And there were plenty of queries from Manchester, too, with which we tried to deal patiently, but tempers were sometimes strained.

At this time Irene Cameron, nominally assistant to W. J. P. Clifton, the general manager for many years, was a tower of strength to all. (After Clifton retired his post was never filled – the paper has gone on happily all these years without any real counterpart.) During the week she kept track of all the copy that Manchester should have, sent dozens of advertisement and other blocks (all carefully wrapped and identified), made lists of everything and bullied even the most august of contributors for their copy. She left the paper in the late 1950s and went to live in Australia with her sister.

In Manchester the scratch staff made it all work out – it was a once-a-week miracle.

In 1943 I was deputy chief sub-editor on the *Telegraph* and general filler-in, working late hours, doing my roof-spotting, but still enjoying my Saturday stint for the *Sunday Times* as a 'casual'. It was not until some years that it was found necessary to have a full-time chief sub-editor, and I then moved over completely.

On Saturdays, before the *Sunday Times* started to print on its own plant in Thomson House, we started at the gentleman's hour of 11 a.m. first at Kemsley House and then transporting as many of the *Sunday Times* staff as my car would hold to Fleet Street, along with the casuals' wages and any copy lying around.

As the paper was released, very slowly, from the emergency restrictions its size began to expand again, but for some years we had no full-time reporting staff. Soon after the war Cyril Ray was the chief and only reporter on the home side. Henry Brandon was the up-and-coming Washington correspondent. It was usually my first and most important job on Saturday morning to deal with his message. This often meant typing out a cable garbled in transmission and trying to make sense of what had been said.

I think, finally, of the subs who bore the heat and burden of the day in my early days and later – Alec Spoor, Rowan, Shattower, Willie Wilson; only a handful, but we got through an immense amount of work, spurred on before the war by the dynamic chief-sub Lewis Broad, who rarely saw eye to eye with Hadley or Heywood.

Those are Mr Vickers's notes on some of the unsung heroes of the paper. The following is by another of them, Norman Bridge of Manchester:

For 24 years the *Sunday Times* was printed in Manchester as well as in London. Starting on the first day of September, 1940, when the Battle of Britain was at its height, the northern print provided an insurance against disruption in London and also shortened the then difficult lines of communication with a large number of readers, who thereafter got a much later printed paper.

The operation was performed at the Kemsley plant at Withy Grove, Manchester. It was carried out at very short notice, but the then biggest printing establishment in the world, with an output of newspapers approaching 5,000,000 each Saturday night, coped easily with the extra 100,000 needed to cover the *Sunday Times*'s northern circulation at that time.

Not quite so easy was the editorial work involved. In mid-week Mr N. H. Booth, the director and managing editor of all the company's publications in Manchester, was told from London – 'We want you to print the northern editions of the *Sunday Times* in Manchester starting this Saturday.' Natty Booth put his deputy, Laurence Carley, in charge of the *Sunday Times* operation, and together they scraped up an editorial staff from the war-depleted sub-editors' tables of other papers in the building. Although Withy Grove once employed more than 200 journalists, this task was not easy then, for the other papers were mainly competitive in their requirements and the three Sunday papers had already mopped up the journalists who were not being absorbed by the war effort. However, the men were eventually recruited – mostly from the *Daily Dispatch*, the company's northern morning paper, which was to merge with the *News Chronicle* in 1955 and later to become absorbed again in the *Daily Mail*.

The hurriedly gathered staff received a few instructions and no style-sheets beyond a copy of the previous Sunday's paper, which the sub-editors were told to 'follow as closely as possible'. For the first issue a few proofs of early-set articles came by train from London, together with pictures, matts and advertisement blocks; other material came during the day by teleprinter; but for the most part the Press Association and the other agencies provided the raw material from which the paper was put together, and one often faulty telephone link with London gave Manchester its sketchy instructions as the day progressed.

With so little preparation, such an unfamiliar staff, and such primitive liaison with London, it seemed incredible that a paper of the quality of the *Sunday Times* could be printed simultaneously in two centres with any degree of similarity between the two issues. But in each succeeding week techniques improved, until eventually it became almost impossible to discover which was the London print and which the Manchester – except from the very careful editionising of material that took place. In broad appearance – and in all essential content – both London and Manchester papers seemed identical.

It took time, of course, and much devoted effort by a loyal and almost fanatically keen staff, who became so expert that it often seemed that they could read the minds of their London colleagues – who in turn also developed reciprocal faculties. They also received increasingly sophisticated technical help, but even after the maximum assistance had been extracted from the many telephone, teleprinter, telephone and human links that were gradually established, it was always the human element that made the final interpretation, and the small group of journalists who worked on the Manchester print became a band of brothers in their dedication to the task, some of them staying with the paper for the whole of its 24 years in Manchester.

Laurence Carley had to go very soon, however. His managerial duties in Withy Grove made his journalistic work on the paper impossible, and after a week or two the northern editorship was taken over by Alexander Nicol in addition to his duties as editor of the *Daily Dispatch*. His *Dispatch* news editor, Eric Yeadon, became the Manchester *Sunday Times* chief sub-editor on Saturdays, and both he and another *Dispatch* man, myself, who was then No. 3 on the *Sunday Times*, eventually succeeded Nicol as northern editor, Yeadon on Nicol's retirement in the early fifties and myself as the final one in 1957.

The big peacetime story all recall was the Bolton football ground tragedy of March 1946, when 33 people died, mostly from suffocation in the mud, when they fell under the pressure of the surging crowd of spectators – most of whom were unaware of the tragedy at the time. That Saturday Manchester made its own *Sunday Times* 'lead' story, a large part of which was provided by Ken Compston, until recently the paper's sports editor in Gray's Inn Road, but then a reporter on the *Evening Chronicle*.

The starting circulation of 100,000 for the Manchester print of the *Sunday Times* was roughly one-third of the paper's national total, and this proportion was maintained over the years until the northern circulation had quadrupled to about 400,000 by 1963. By then Manchester was catering for the whole of Ireland and Scotland, and all of Northern England and Wales above a line drawn approximately from Lincoln to Aberystwyth. This was done in seven main editions, covering separately Ireland, Scotland, the North-East, Yorkshire, North Wales and West Lancashire (including Merseyside), and Greater Manchester, which was then receiving a paper printed as late as any other national newspaper produced in either London or the North. There were also slip editions for other areas and other purposes. And, of course, the size of the paper had increased fantastically, quite apart from the new colour magazine.

It was this inexorable increase in size, together with other pressures on the resources of Withy Grove – which was by this time printing also nearly four million copies of the *Sunday Mirror* and the *News of the World* each Saturday night – which made changes inevitable. By 1963 too the London production of the *Sunday Times* was well established on marvellous new plant in Gray's Inn Road, and concentration of the entire print thus became possible at the paper's headquarters.

So, in October, 1963, the production of the north-east edition left Withy Grove for London, followed by the Irish edition in November and the Welsh and Yorkshire runs the following March. This still left a circulation of 240,000 covered by Manchester, but in August 1964 this print too went back to London, leaving Withy Grove to cope with its other voracious customers. The plant achieved the distinction of being first with 'back-setting' for the *Sunday Times*. This is an ingenious manipulation of the rollers and folders of the giant presses in such a way as to permit the paper to be printed with separately folded sections but all finally delivered together as one complete newspaper.

It seemed a big break-through when first accomplished in the autumn of 1959, at Withy Grove, several weeks before back-setting was first introduced into London's print. But Withy Grove – which is now not very far from its centenary – had always prided itself on its achievements, right from its start as a newspaper office on May 23, 1876, when the then owner, Edward Hulton, produced the *Sporting Chronicle and Prophetic Bell* at 2 Mark Lane, Withy Grove. This 'tissue', as it was popularly known, had been started in other premises by Hulton, a one-time printer's apprentice on the *Manchester Guardian*, and was to form the basis of his fame and fortune as by far the biggest newspaper proprietor outside London. (He died in 1904 leaving £557,000.) There followed Hulton's *Sunday Chronicle*, 1885, and in 1897, largely under Hulton's second and only surviving son Edward, the *Evening Chronicle*, which eventually attained the largest evening circulation in the country; Eric Cheadle, who was a notable general manager of Kemsley Newspapers in the 1940s and 1950s, operating from Gray's Inn Road, was originally a sub-editor on the paper. The *Daily Dispatch* followed in 1900; this was edited finally, until its merger with the *News Chronicle*, by A. T. P. Murphy, who was sports editor of the *Sunday Times* before his editorship and managing editor afterwards.

So, on August 23, 1964, when the last page of the final edition of the *Sunday Times* to be printed in Manchester was going to press, the printer asked me, as northern editor, to give it the final honours by 'planing it in' – hammering a flat block of hardwood across the surface of the type to make sure no line stood higher than the rest. And then, as the page was slid gently under the 'mangle' – the press that moulds the matrix used for casting the semi-circular plates from which the paper is printed – a compositor who was also a musician played the 'Last Post' on his silver trumpet.

Over the years many papers have left Withy Grove as others have joined it, but none had such a moving farewell as that given to the *Sunday Times*.

Nobody hears about the Norman Bridges or the Richard Vickerses of journalism, about the experts in the process-room or any of the many other technical departments. Their names are never in their paper unless they are eminent enough in their own line to rank a paragraph when they die; such are all honourably enrolled in the army of people which produces The Sunday Times – on Saturdays nowadays there are many more than a thousand people working on the printing, production, and distribution sides.

Before the war and just after it there were some enchanting characters belowstairs – nearly all gone long since. Joe Tanner, the head reader, for example, always punctiliously called Mr Tanner. Under him the columns of the paper devoted to the polite arts were fabulously well 'read', for he and some of his boys, ill-educated though they may have been, had the intuitions and the dedication of scholars. Wheezy, stout Mr Tanner, with his enormous shoulders and his pinches of snuff, performed prodigies of checking from his little collection of out-of-date reference books. For the verification of Latin quotations he would scrabble, unasked, through the 'Aeneid' or any other suitable works on his dusty shelf, and usually find them. With French he was likewise in unknown territory. One day the 's' on 'Je viens' seemed to worry him frightfully. 'I'd sooner see it with an 'x' meself,' he muttered.

The phrase was for years a household word in the literary department.

IV

The war was over. A new excitement was in the air at 200 Gray's Inn Road. At the Dorchester Hotel on November 29, 1945, the new Viscount and Viscountess Kemsley were giving a dinner to some 120 top executives of Kemsley Newspapers.

This legion of honour came from every outpost of the Kemsley empire as well as from the London headquarters: legendary proconsuls like William Veitch of The Aberdeen Press and Journal, Sir Robert Webber of The Western Mail, the diminutive and imperious 'Natty' Booth of Manchester. There were H. N.

Heywood, editorial director, J. W. Drawbell, editor of The Sunday Chronicle, Grafton Green, editor of The Sunday Empire News ('Lady Kemsley,' says an advertisement of 1949, 'has personally inspired and guided the policy of The Sunday Empire News'), Norman Hamilton, who had succeeded Sydney Carroll as editor of The Daily Sketch, the omnipresent F. Scully, who daily drew up a bulletin of inside information, called 'Scully's List', primarily for Lord K's eyes, and Edward Shanks, the poet and novelist, who wrote leaders for The Daily Sketch and book reviews for The Sunday Times and who was trying to interest Kemsley in the private press publishing of limited editions which led eventually to the expensive venture with the Dropmore Press (named after Lord K's house near Taplow) and the Queen Anne Press, which was eventually superintended by Ian Fleming. (Shanks the sensitive poet, and the most engaging of men when you really knew him, was a little embarrassed about his connection with The Daily Sketch and adapted an old story. 'My wife,' he said one night at the bar of the Falstaff in Fleet Street, after another large gin and tonic, 'thinks I earn my living playing the piano in a brothel whereas I really write leaders for The Daily Sketch!')

Of course, there was a detachment from The Sunday Times at the dinner: Hadley, who was by now a director of the company, Heywood, Charles Gayton, the political correspondent, W. T. Bliss, the news editor, Norman Crump, George Schwartz, Crump's deputy as City editor, the disheartened Cyril Lakin (completely out of the running by now as Hadley's successor, a victim of ill health and a disillusioned politician who had failed to hold his seat against Labour at Llandaff and Barry in the 1945 election), Leonard Russell, the new literary editor, and G. R. Osler, the piratical advertisement manager, who went back, it will be remembered, to the Berrys' earliest days with the paper and who before long was to give way to Michael Renshaw, still away with the Welsh Guards (he commanded the Provost Company of the Guards Armoured Division in Normandy) but soon to be restored to the office to lend it style and elegance with his exquisite manners and clothes; he was one of the few members of the staff who were in society. Sir Herbert Morgan, his pre-war boss, had left by now. But there was at the dinner the man who had taken Morgan's place as Lord K's chief courtier and adviser, the Canadian Sir Beverley Baxter, who had written Atticus for The Sunday Times. Witty, sardonic, a brilliant public speaker, an MP, Baxter must have looked with amazement on the earnest Kemsley 'style' after his close association as editor of The Daily Express with Lord Beaverbrook, who worked mighty mischief and didn't give a damn. (A typical Baxter crack – he said he served in France in the first war 'with no decorations, because I was neither sufficiently forward nor far enough back'.)

So the London men mingled awkwardly before dinner with the men from the midlands and the north. Some were old co-workers and friends, some knew others by name only, and some were unacquainted: everyone had to wear, in the American style, an identifying badge in his buttonhole.

But there were four people present who were virtually unknown to the guests: all handsome, assured men of the world who in the most civil way possible seemed deeply uninterested in what was happening at some doubtless horrible branch office and who showed only a trifling interest in the food set before them, which the more unsophisticated invaders from the north seemed to regard as a rich metropolitan extravagance, *la crêpe Newburg* and *la volaille du Surrey rôtie à la broche*. The first of these exotica bore on his badge the name 'I. L. Fleming', and that evening he looked (he was never a good mixer) like the bust of a slightly embarrassed and disenchanted Roman emperor of a very good epoch. It was rumoured around the big room that he alone of the company had not drawn his place at dinner democratically from a hat, as had been done even by the Hon. Lionel Berry, the Hon. Neville Berry, the Hon. Denis Berry, and the Hon. Oswald Berry, the handsome sons of the house and all directors (with Lady Kemsley) of the company. No, this I. L. Fleming's place beside Lady Kemsley, whom he was reported to call Edith, had been engineered by the chairman himself; obviously Fleming had a pull with the family and was likely to become a privileged pet. Somehow from that moment the old Kemsley pros never had much affection – the dislike was reciprocated – for Ian Fleming. The word went round that he was joining The Sunday Times, to become its foreign manager: a specially-created post.

There was, secondly, Robert Harling, a dandy in dress, a youthful Mephistopheles in looks. He had served in convoys in the Atlantic, worked with his friend Fleming in Naval Intelligence at the Admiralty, and was now in an advertising agency. He, too, was to join The Sunday Times – as typographical adviser.

Opposite: Lord and Lady Kemsley, 1954.

He was also to work with Norman Hamilton on the faltering Daily Sketch, the rejuvenation of which loomed large in Lord K's expectations. It was to be renamed The Daily Graphic and devoted to a policy – and it all sounded very blameless and depressing – of 'decency in journalism'.

There was, next, H. V. Hodson, a Fellow of All Souls between the wars, tall and strikingly handsome, an academic with great charm of manner and a particularly endearing boyish grin. He was Norman Crump's brother-in-law and had chucked the civil service to go to The Sunday Times as assistant editor.

In the next twenty years these three were to play a not inconsiderable part in the paper's fortunes. And so – though to a lesser degree – was the fourth man, William Mabane, later Sir William and finally Lord Mabane. He had been National Liberal M P for Huddersfield for years and Minister of State in Churchill's 'caretaker' government before the general election of 1945. Now, a loser at the election, he was one of Kemsley's courtiers, an adviser whose counsel varied between the very good and the very bad, but altogether a most sympathetic character and a good influence on his new master where the affairs of The Sunday Times were concerned. He had an endearing belief or dream that he had invented the phrase, 'Politics is the art of the possible'.

To say that he was unknown to all the company at the Dorchester Hotel that November evening is obviously incorrect. There were half a dozen political correspondents present, and Bill Mabane had been a reasonably prominent politician for years. But he was just as unknown as a journalist as Fleming, or Hodson, or Harling (though Ian had had a stirring time at Reuters in the early 1930s).

Speeches at the dinner, of course. One was from Lionel Berry, who had been head of the Manchester office for six years before the war and was deeply intimate with all the complexities of the vast business, with its publishing centres in London, Cardiff, Manchester, Sheffield, Macclesfield, Stockport, Blackburn, York, Middlesbrough, Newcastle, Glasgow, and Aberdeen, from all of which, at this time, six Sunday papers, eight dailies, nine evenings and ten weeklies were produced. He was his characteristic calm self, demonstrating the self-effacing resource which always made him so admirable a counsellor to his more impulsive father. His brother Neville, still in the Army, spoke rousingly for the younger generation and foresaw the day when The Daily Sketch would be the greatest picture paper in the world, a triumph of clean journalism. It was left to Mabane, the orator, to lift the proceedings to a poetical level and symbolically see the rising sun glinting on the windows of every Kemsley lodgement in the land. Then people began popping up all over the room with little speeches and boredom set in.

All the same, it was an inspiring occasion. Everyone present knew that there were big problems ahead for the group, some of which, alas, were to prove intractable while Lord K was its head, though nobody could have foreseen that certain restrictions imposed in the war were to extend, stiflingly, long into peacetime and that, worst of all, newsprint would fail to become free of all controls until late in the 1950s and would rise year after year to a staggering price.

No matter, everyone left the Dorchester dinner with a conviction that a brave new breeze was sweeping through Kemsley House. Some of the younger Sunday Times people, it is true, were depressed by Lord K's uncompromising political attitude, officially stated by Ian Fleming (a diehard and a radical combined) a little later as foreign manager: 'Kemsley newspapers support the Conservative view and concentrate particularly on the championship of free enterprise as opposed to nationalisation and controls.' But the paper came first with them, and at any rate it was clear that Lord K was busily recruiting young lions in these first heady months of peace.

V

Another clutch of bright young men came along. Desmond Shawe-Taylor was appointed radio correspondent (no post-war TV yet), was unhappy with the medium, left, and returned to become chief music critic in November, 1958. Felix Aprahamian had already begun a long connection with the paper's music side.

From the 15th Scottish Division came the burly Pat Murphy, for a short time assistant sports editor of the London Evening Standard. As sports editor of The Sunday Times he snatched the Australian Jack Fingleton, a great cricket correspondent, from The Observer, and helped Henry Longhurst, by presentation and precept, and by letting him go to see golf in America, where no other correspondent had ventured regularly yet, to become a star. At the front of the week Murphy was also editor of the letters page, a responsibility which showed Hadley's confidence in him, for the letters page was still considered, no matter what certain young office heretics felt about it, one of the main supporting columns of the whole edifice. Murphy, a Roman Catholic, went far on the paper, becoming in the course of years, and after an interval as editor of Kemsley's Daily Dispatch, a vigorous deputy editor and managing editor, an untiring stalwart who took practically the entire Sunday Times office under his wing. (He was editorial director of Thomson Regional Newspapers when he retired in 1970.)

Another newcomer left a dashing career in the navy, the debonair J. W. Lambert, the present literary and arts editor. With Godfrey Smith, now editor of the magazine, and even in his youngest days at Kemsley House a Holbein sketch for Henry VIII without the beard, Donald Stephenson, who regrettably left to join Shell, and Gerald Pawle, he was being groomed on Lord Kemsley's sacred third floor. Cyril Lakin was there too, now, and Jack Lambert was his assistant before going downstairs to help Russell in the literary and features department. This department was busy. About now Russell negotiated a series of agreements for retainers with some distinguished writers – about a dozen in all. They were 'tied' to the paper but not strictly on the staff. Of them all, his greatest admiration went (and still goes) to Hugh Trevor-Roper, whose contributions to The Sunday Times over nearly 25 years – articles as well as book reviews – have reached an extraordinary level of excellence. John Russell, one of Ian Fleming's protégés, became art critic, succeeding to a post which had been held from before the war by the unfortunate Eric Newton, with his starved intense face and muddy complexion and sudden angelic smile.

The truth was that poor Newton was virtually fired in circumstances which reflected great discredit on the paper and Lord K personally. It was one of the very few occasions of importance when the editor-in-chief could not be prevailed on to give way in a matter in which he had no knowledge or particular interest. He had been naïve enough to believe, in this particular instance, something told him by a diehard RA next to whom he had sat at the Royal Academy dinner, namely, that Eric Newton was too madly advanced in his views to be considered a suitable art critic for a great and sensible journal like The Sunday Times, and that, moreover, he consistently treated the Royal Academy's annual exhibition with contempt. Overcome at this revelation and determined to demonstrate his authority, Lord K worked himself into a rage, a rather splendid rage, about Newton's treatment of such a great and holy institution as the Royal Academy – the man must go, there could be no argument about it. But as there was argument about it Kemsley, still bristling, privily instructed Heywood, as deputy editor, to do something. So the unhappy Heywood tried to wrap it all up in silver paper by telling Newton the little yarn that as The Sunday Times at the time was so small in size – a mere eight pages – it had been decided to suspend art criticism until newsprint supplies improved. Not suspecting the real reason, Newton told Sir Kenneth Clark and others that The Sunday Times, incredibly, was abandoning art criticism. There was a great to-do, and Kenneth Clark among many other distinguished people asked for appointments with Lord Kemsley to persuade him of his error in dropping art criticism, to the great chagrin of his lordship, who couldn't very well say that he intended to do nothing of the kind. The affair went rumbling on for weeks, and in the course of it Lord K discovered that the art critic of whom he had rid himself so cavalierly was possibly the best in the country. There had been nothing like it since Hazlitt was sacked from Perry's Morning Chronicle because he criticised the painting of Sir Thomas Lawrence at a time when Perry was having his portrait painted by Lawrence. It was all a salutary experience for Lord K. Only once again in the field of the arts did he attempt such drastic interference.

Anyway, Newton's regrettable expulsion left the way open for John Russell who, be it said, knew nothing of the facts of the imbroglio; nor did Newton himself know the true story until a few months before his death in 1965, when it was told him by a still penitent Sunday Times man. John Russell quickly established an even higher reputation and treated the Royal Academy with, if anything, greater disrespect than his predecessor.

VI

We have seen that Ian Fleming, Robert Harling and Leonard Russell were at the Dorchester dinner. But the man with whom, over the years, they and many more on the paper were to work so closely and who was to stand also in a special, animating relationship to Godfrey Smith, J. W. Lambert, and others of the younger recruits, was not present. His name was C. D. Hamilton. He had not yet surfaced at Gray's Inn Road and when he did so in 1946 he had a modest-sounding title: personal editorial assistant to Lord Kemsley. All the same, it was known to be a post with potentialities; for had not Hamilton's predecessor, C. B. Livingstone, left it to become a director of the company in the very important centre of Glasgow?

Hamilton is pre-eminently among the key-figures in this book. He and his early achievement can be looked at in a little detail now, no matter if chronology becomes disturbed.

In 1944 Tyneside people learned from The Newcastle Chronicle that a local soldier named Charles Denis Hamilton, who had joined the Durham Light Infantry as a Territorial Army officer early in 1939, had distinguished himself in the fighting in France. Understandably, the newspaper took particular pride in his progress – particularly when he won the DSO at Nijmegen after he had been promoted to lieutenant-colonel in the battle of Normandy – as Hamilton had been a reporter on its evening paper and had started in journalism in Middlesbrough. All this became a source of local pride, and the young man – he was 27 when he was demobilised in 1946 – got the glamour treatment usually reserved for fighter pilots.

The Newcastle Chronicle and Evening Chronicle were Kemsley newspapers and the management saw to it that the chairman of the group was kept informed of the war record of the former reporter. Lord K had a powerful sense of being the inspirer of all 'Kemsley men', and it seemed to him fitting that if any of them particularly distinguished themselves they should receive his personal congratulations. When Lord and Lady Kemsley visited Newcastle in 1945 as part of a personal tour of the whole newspaper organisation they heard more about Hamilton, and it was Lady Kemsley who remembered him in mid-1946 when a vacancy with her husband occurred.

Hamilton had been invited to stay on in the Army by Montgomery himself, but felt he was not cut out for peace-time soldiering. (He nevertheless maintained his contact with the Field-Marshal, and it developed into a very close friendship.) He therefore returned, to the surprise of the staff, to the Newcastle reporters' room at £8 a week, though he wondered how soon he could reach an income sufficient to keep his wife and four young sons. As it turned out he had only been back a month when he received a telephone call from Lord Kemsley, whom he had never met – would he travel to London overnight for an interview.

The position of Lord Kemsley's personal assistant had become vacant. The interview at Kemsley House was pleasant and brief: the appointment was offered and rapidly accepted by the young ex-soldier, who was slightly dazed at Lord Kemsley's saying that he would not dream of paying him anything less than he had been receiving as a colonel.

By the beginning of the next week Hamilton was working in Gray's Inn Road, installed next to Lord K on the third floor. The attractive Olive Hamilton and their young sons followed him to London (Hamilton is very much a family man), and he felt justified, now that his salary was much in excess of £8 a week, in renting an expensive house in The Bishops Avenue, N2. Now he lives even more grandly at Stag Place, at the backside of Buckingham Palace – as the estate agent Roy Brooks was *not* allowed to say in The Sunday Times.

Settling down in Kemsley House was made easier for him by the fact that, a week or two after he arrived, Lord and Lady Kemsley went off to South America for a long and quasi-ambassadorial tour. Hamilton felt that his first duty was to get to know The Sunday Times people. He made an immediate hit with them by providing the front-page lead story on two successive weeks – both of them about plans for the peacetime army. For years he acted as an extra military correspondent of The Sunday Times, and it was in this capacity that he wrote a leader page article about Eisenhower's book 'Crusade in Europe' which caused a stir. In those days it was unusual to criticise Ike or question his generalship, but Hamilton was unwilling to allow the Americans more than their fair share of credit for Operation Overlord.

Within two years he became the *éminence grise* of 200 Gray's Inn Road. There was plenty to do. Lord Kemsley and his directors (six of the eighteen were members of his own family) were trying to rationalise and expand an empire which had acquired a distinctly ramshackle air. If it owned The Sunday Times and the great regional papers, it was also responsible for some obscure and rather shabby publications emerging from Withy Grove. It was also losing money on The Daily Graphic, The Sunday Graphic and The Sunday Empire News. Kemsley realised that to maintain the position of The Sunday Times *vis à vis* the rapidly growing Observer and to improve various ailing properties he had to recruit good young men – university graduates, for preference – both for the editorial and management sides. It was Hamilton who organised this recruitment of journalists and put into execution a related plan very dear to his master's heart – the Kemsley Journalists training scheme. It was one of Lord K's great services to journalism. He set out to attract the young to the profession, but was sufficiently disinterested not to repine when some of those who undertook the Kemsley editorial plan went on to work for other organisations. In 1950, after three years' experience of the plan, Hamilton edited the 'Kemsley Manual of Journalism', one of the standard books on practice and principles. He also organised the Kemsley Empire Journalists scheme, which brought promising young editorial men from the Commonwealth to London for a year, and the Kemsley Flying Trust.

In all these early years at Kemsley House he was in the thick of managerial and editorial affairs, not to mention tragic domestic occasions. Everyone on The Sunday Times was shocked when Cyril Lakin was killed in a motoring accident in France; and everyone somehow assumed that to Hamilton could be left the rescue and consolation of the distraught widow.

He drove himself so hard that his health, impaired by his war services, nearly broke down. But he was sustained and encouraged by a few editorial executives who were trying to let some air into the ugly and only part-completed building in Gray's Inn Road. They went to Hamilton with their problems – he himself was younger than any of them – and he would usually manage to persuade Lord K, often against his elderly inclinations, to try some new experiment.

Gradually Lord K's attention came to focus on The Sunday Times almost entirely; and to reassure himself about the health of an empire which, as it was then constituted, was really un-manageable, Kemsley made Hamilton a director of the company and editorial director of the group, with powerful if undefined responsibilities for The Sunday Times. This was in 1950.

Too much was wrong. Far from expanding, the group began to shrink, and there were closures big and small. The continuation of newsprint rationing, with the resulting lack of growth in advertising revenue, the eternal labour troubles, the rising costs – all the cards were stacked against Lord K, who maintained his native buoyancy nevertheless. Time and change were laying their stealthy fingers on his kingdom. The best brains in the place, editorial and managerial, were increasingly concentrated on

The Sunday Times, with the redoubtable Eric Cheadle in charge of promotion, and this collective effort managed to keep its circulation ahead of The Observer's. In this tussle Denis Hamilton played a decisive rôle by virtue of something which was known in the office as the big read.

There was nothing new in serialising books: The Sunday Times, we know, was doing it more than a hundred years earlier; and throughout the years, down to the second world war, it had continued to do so. But it had usually used articles of only about a thousand words. Hamilton's fresh idea was for it to be done on a grander scale. So in a six- or eight-page paper a whole page of editorial space would be given to the serial, with sometimes a proportionate rise as papers grew larger. The big read was an innovation, and a daring one in its context. Almost the entire office was against it, with everyone from news editor, departmental heads, and special writers complaining in the corridors that they were being robbed of valuable space. Yet in the battle with The Observer it was really only an expediency. The Sunday Times wasn't good enough to hold The Observer without it.

For the truth is that there was something wrong with The Sunday Times in the first two decades after the war. Not with its critics, its sport, its political direction or leading articles, given that it was very positively a Conservative paper. H. V. Hodson, who succeeded W. W. Hadley as editor in 1950, had writing ability, a humane outlook, and a force of personality strong enough to triumph sometimes over the obscurantism of his editor-in-chief. Where then was the weakness? Why did it look a little jaded when put beside the brilliant Observer, which at that time had not paid overmuch attention to the siren-call of the merely fashionable?

Some men at the top thought they knew: the parts were better than the whole, and the whole was not somehow right because of Lord K, who was outdated and impossibly autocratic and shut off from everything which was of significance in post-war Britain. He was the inescapable cross they had to bear.

It was by no means the whole answer. For one thing, the editorial executive talent wasn't extensive enough for a paper the size of The Sunday Times. For another, the editor temperamentally disliked delegating, and communication between him and the various departments was constricted. Worst of all, there was no full-time general reporting staff. This absence of full-time hard-news men meant, to take a simple example, that no investigatory work could be done during the week if some big running story happened – some City scandal or Whitehall sensation. When the abdication crisis occurred Cecil King was horrified to find that The Daily Mirror had no contacts with people who would know what was going on. In the same way The Sunday Times had neither contacts nor reporters to add something on Sunday morning to a story which had been running all the week. The Observer was beginning to see the point of what we would now call an Insight story, whereas The Sunday Times seemed to feel that the dailies had exhausted the interest of it. The editor could not be blamed: he was deprived of full-time hard-news reporters in the name of economy; and it all went on in the same unenterprising way until Denis Hamilton took over the editorship and discovered, when the Profumo affair was beginning to develop, that The Sunday Times had no investigatory stories about it or appropriate contacts. He quickly realised that the reporters' room must no longer be the pauper of the office.

The Kemsley régime was marked by a further weakness: the system of trying to settle too many things in conference. Since 1937 Lord K had held a Sunday Times conference every Tuesday morning; it was an institution of which he was deeply proud, and with his talented little post-war team around him he beamed sometimes with deep satisfaction, the Prime Minister of Gray's Inn Road. At these conferences, he told the Royal Commission on the Press in May, 1948, the policy of the paper was gone into very thoroughly. Sir David Ross, the chairman, seemed impressed and asked for the minutes of the meetings for a year – a request which Lord K had anticipated, for he had brought them along with him. But the commission was plainly disillusioned, even bewildered, by the documents. 'They seem to relate to the contents of the next number or criticism of the last number. There is apparently no discussion of policy such as we had presented to us in similar minutes of the Westminster and Beaverbrook groups.'

No wonder Sir David Ross was unhappy. Policy in his sense was formed mysteriously in the mind of Lord K or formulated for his approval by his editors. The matters discussed at the Tuesday conferences were usually short-term and tactical. Most of those attending would come along with a little crop of ideas for the next issue, and there would be much shooting down and ganging up; there would also be lengthy post-mortems on the current paper, and an absurd scrutiny of trifles such as 'Do You Know?', a two-inch quiz feature which operated for years under a weekly barrage of complaints from William Mabane.

It is possible to realise now that these conferences were really very muddled. Good ideas were talked out or blown to pieces in the cross-fire; and the post-mortems, critical for the most part, depressed the rest of the staff when they were passed down the line. The paper was never more than eight pages for a very long time; it was easy to know every word of it and trifle away a Tuesday morning by picking it to pieces, particularly if, like some of those present, including members of the Kemsley family, you had no direct responsibility for any part of it.

Sometimes Kemsley would declare himself outraged by a particular feature; and this usually signified that he thought the offending article should have been discussed with him before it went into the paper, no matter how high the authority of the writer. Raymond Mortimer, for example, who had by now succeeded Desmond MacCarthy as chief literary critic, fell briefly into the deepest disgrace when he criticised Kipling in a book review; everyone surmised that it was not the editor-in-chief's unaided opinion but that some ancient guest at Dropmore at lunch on Sunday had protested to Lord K about a desecration of a national idol. These were antics which seriously sapped the paper's spirit.

Yet, for all this, in some strange way Lord K transcended his domestic critics. You couldn't brush aside such an overpowering personality and his occasional good ideas, and those of his executives who imagined that without him they could have produced a smashing paper were probably indulging their own vanity. He kept everyone in a state of competitive tension, and when he was away on holiday the temperature of the office and its effectiveness dropped dramatically in the absence of the ever-watchful eye of Jove.

For that matter, Lord K did very well when, supported ably by Lionel and briefed by Mabane and Hamilton, who produced all the written evidence, he gave evidence before the Press Commission. The whole inquiry was rather a fatuous exercise, even if it redeemed itself by suggesting a Press Council – an idea which Lord K opposed in his evidence. The argument for Attlee's setting up the commission depended substantially on what was always being described as increasing public concern at the growth of monopolistic tendencies in the control of the press. This meant that Lord K, the chairman of Britain's largest group of newspapers, was the prime target. He and Lord Camrose had no difficulty in showing that while it all sounded rousing stuff from Labour's point of view it was really innocent of the facts of life.

There was one trifling moment when Lord K found himself farcically questioned by a member of the Royal Commission who was on his own staff, R. C. K. Ensor, a scholarly ex-Fabian without a trace of humour, and his idea of what constituted intrusion into personal privacy staggered even the correct Lord Kemsley (who always called him 'Enser' and made him sound like the touring theatrical companies who entertained the Services in the war).

ENSOR: There was a picture of either Mr Ernest Bevin or Herbert Morrison arriving at Northolt and being greeted by his wife, and a close-up of his wife kissing him, taken from a distance of about two feet. That seems to be a perfect outrage. Do you agree?

KEMSLEY: No, I am sorry to say I do not. After all, it is his wife; it is an indication that they are on the most friendly terms, as husband and wife should be.

ENSOR: Yes, quite; but from some points of view that makes it all the worse. It's an intrusion on privacy.

KEMSLEY: I do not really think there is any harm in it myself.

ENSOR: It shocked me profoundly.

The don Sir Robert Ensor, who had for a long time written leaders for the paper and then, in 1941, had become its justly admired political writer Scrutator, was utterly out of touch with ordinary life. He was tiny in stature, like Rees and Hadley, and he walked with bent head, blinking all the time like a gnome who had just come in out of the dark. Hadley had met him when they were both on The Daily Chronicle, where Ensor was chief leader writer and had a formidable reputation as a sage of Liberalism. Earlier he had been on The Manchester Guardian, and Hadley or Rees always felt safe and reassured with men who had been on that paper – among them Herbert Sidebotham, Ernest Newman, James Agate, Eric Newton, Neville Cardus, Alexander Werth, Cyril Ray. As Scrutator, Ensor lacked the humanity of his predecessor, Sidebotham, but he showed himself a political commentator with a wide range of knowledge which he evinced on a grander scale in that classic contribution to the Oxford History of England, 'England 1870–1914'. It is axiomatic that all sincere men wish to convert their personal impressions into universal laws. Ensor was more sincere than most men and also more obstinate; he would never give way, and he remained to the end a prim intellectual divorced from flesh and blood aspirations.

In a different way Lord K too was divorced from ordinary aspirations. He moved between his two great houses and his office by Rolls and hadn't been on a bus for fifty years. All the same, there was ardour in his loins, and somewhere within that enormous frame a Northcliffian spirit of adventure was always trying to get out. That it was repressed too frequently by his devotion to respectability and formality was one of the causes of the malaise of The Sunday Times for twenty years, and it led to something which can only be described as a personal tragedy for him.

VII

Of Lord K's weekly conferences Ian Fleming left a lively, precisely defined, and only slightly dramatised account, written in 1962 when he was at the height of his success with James Bond and recalling a series of articles on the Seven Deadly Sins which he had suggested for the paper – one of his many stunning ideas. Kemsley had gone by now and his family with him, and Mabane and Heywood too, and this thinned down the attendance on Tuesday mornings. But the spirit of the meetings is preserved:

I invented the idea of this series when, a couple of years ago, I was still a member of the Editorial Board of the London *Sunday Times*. This Board meets every Tuesday to comment on the issue of the previous Sunday, discuss the plans for the next issue and put forward longer-term projects.
It is quite a small Board of seven or eight heads of departments – I was foreign manager at the time – together with the editor and the proprietor, Mr Roy Thomson, and we are all good friends, though at the weekly meetings, beneath the surface of our friendliness, lurk all the deadly sins with the exception of gluttony and lust. Each one of us has pride in our department of the paper; many of us are covetous of the editorial chair; most are envious of the bright ideas put forward by others; anger comes to the surface at what we regard as unmerited criticism, and sloth, certainly in my case, lurks in the wings.
The same pattern is probably followed at all executive meetings in all branches of business. When someone else puts up a bright idea, however useful or profitable it may be to the business concerned, traces at least of Envy, Anger, and Covetousness will be roused in his colleagues. Yet, on the occasion when I put forward this particular 'bright' idea for the future, I seem to remember nothing but approbation and a genial nodding of heads.
The project was outside my own sphere of action on the paper and I heard nothing more of it until I had left the *Sunday Times* to concentrate on writing thrillers centred round a member of the British Secret Service

called James Bond. So I cannot describe what troubles the Literary Editor ran into in his endeavours to marry the Seven Deadly Sins to seven appropriate authors. So far as I can recall, the marriages I myself had suggested were closely followed, except that I had suggested Mr Malcolm Muggeridge to write on the theme of Anger on the grounds that he is such an extremely angry man. In the event, as you will see, Mr W. H. Auden was the brilliant choice.

Harry Hodson, just after he had resigned the editorship of the paper, took serious exception to use of the term editorial board, on the ground that no such body existed and the suggestion therefore diminished the authority he had held when he was editor. He was right; the editorial board was one of Ian's little fictions, possibly used in the above quotation expressly to annoy Hodson, with whom he had had disagreements. (Ian, who carried a soft black hat but rarely wore it, said that somehow he could never manage to feel a soul-mate of anyone who wore a bowler hat and carried an umbrella.) But then, Fleming had disagreements with quite a few people during his fifteen years on the paper, particularly on the conception, construction, and execution of his enormously ambitious project, the grandly-titled Foreign and Imperial News Service of Kemsley Newspapers, known in the office and to the cable companies as Mercury. We shall come to that in a moment.

As a boy Fleming had been the difficult member of his rich hunting and shooting Edwardian family, and in an elusive way he remained the difficult one at Kemsley House. Not that he was bad-tempered or in any way offensive: he had an irresistible laugh, was charmingly hail-fellow-well-met, and couldn't be bothered to quarrel with people he disliked. But there seemed to be some thin sheet of glass between himself and most of The Sunday Times people. Of his talent as a writer and an offbeat executive no one had any doubt, yet to many who came into regular contact with him he seemed neither a working journalist nor a purely decorative appendage round the place (most offices know the charming friend of the owning family who disappears as mysteriously as he came after six months). He was never seen in the John Street club, which was the executive canteen, or at an office party. He was certainly not a snob, but he gave the impression of drawing back from the ordinary traffic of the place. With characteristic contrariness he had no love for Eton, which was his school, and he resigned from White's club because he couldn't stand the shits at its bar. This was all part of being the difficult one, as was his faint disdain of 200 Gray's Inn Road – the 'prison', he called it.

In private life he could be an enchanting companion if he were with someone like his close friend Robert Harling. But in Kemsley House he was a loner who would only drop his mask when some inefficiency was revealed. At such times he would burn up with rage for a minute or two, before shrugging it all off with a little exasperated laugh. Or he would complain to his patron – nobody of lesser rank would do – Lord Kemsley.

Ian had met Lord K in the war at the Dorchester Hotel, which in the blitz winter of 1940–1 was the home of the best people. The Kemsleys lived there, and they were impressed by the social circle in which the dashing lieutenant-commander from the Admiralty moved – he seemed to know everyone at the Dorchester, including the then Lady Rothermere, whom Fleming married later. Kemsley himself, with his natural reverence for bankers, was interested to discover that Fleming belonged to the merchant banking family of that name and had been a foreign correspondent for Reuter's in Russia before leaving journalism and uninterestedly drawing an income again from stockbroking. He knew too – and it surrounded the tall, extremely good-looking officer with special glamour – that Ian's job at the Admiralty was a hush-hush one.

Fleming was a newspaper proprietor *manqué*; he loved, then and later, all the big talk about circulations, advertisement rates, developments in this or that group. Ideas would flow from him for starting new papers or transforming old ones, most of them crazy, some of them brilliant, all of them unconventional.

To someone like Lord K, who was itching to become as well-known as Beaverbrook once the war was over, Ian seemed to have immense potentialities. They drew closer together, and they evolved a plan, or rather Fleming evolved it: a great foreign news service for Kemsley Newspapers, which was to become the best chain in the country, if not in the world, this news service to be started from scratch by I. L. Fleming, who would become foreign manager of The Sunday Times in addition; the whole thing to be inaugurated as soon as the war was over.

It is not bending the truth, unlikely as it may sound, to say that in his early years at Kemsley House Ian Fleming came to regard himself as a spiritual son of Lord K. A cynic and a realist he may have been, but he was always looking round for support from an older man – his own valiant father had been killed in the first war. This is not to say he was starry-eyed about Lord K, or that Lord K had no hesitations about him, but they nevertheless enjoyed a special relationship in which admiration and reservation were

The young Ian Fleming by Augustus John.

fused. After Fleming had been working in the office for a year or two Kemsley came to perceive that his foreign manager was not really an utterly dedicated slave in the Gray's Inn Road galleys:

Opposite: Ian Fleming at the height of his success.

he was not always as busy 'throwing a fly' – a favourite expression of Ian's – over someone as his vehemence at the conference might suggest. Yet Kemsley went on admiring him and backing him, though not to the extent of making him a director of the company, which was a secret sorrow to Fleming: a small hurt to his pride, as if he had been blackballed for the Turf; and Ian on his side, though he had a deadly eye for Lord K's weaknesses, would defend the old man from scoffers like Randolph Churchill, encourage him when he was disappointed, and automatically be on his side at the conference if, as sometimes happened, The Sunday Times editorial people showed a disposition to cross their editor-in-chief on some particular point.

VIII

Not unnaturally Ian Fleming brought with him to Kemsley House and its foreign service something of the jargon and a great deal of the organisation technique of the wartime Admiralty, where he had been assistant to the Director of Naval Intelligence: a briefing message was a 'signal' and a rebuke to a correspondent a 'Mark I bottle'. His temperament underneath everything was essentially romantic, and terms like these stimulated his imagination: they made him feel that running a newspaper department had something of the same excitement as conducting a branch of the war, and that it called for the same kind of zest. He has frequently been portrayed as an ideas man of Kemsley's outfit, which he was, but not enough credit has been given to his powers of organisation and his solid, if sometimes unconventional, gifts as an administrator.

Mercury, when it started late in 1945, was extremely well planned, and it was evolving all the time; Fleming was responsible for this in his own right. His influence extended from the selection of personnel to the authorship of the detailed and constructive foreign correspondents' guide-book which was issued for the education of his staff – it was unknown generally in the office – under the curt title 'Reference Book'. Bibliophiles are not aware of the fact, but this was Ian Fleming's first book, years before 'Casino Royale', and it is a little masterpiece of its kind.

'It was,' says Donald McCormick, then a correspondent in North-West Africa, and now himself foreign manager of The

Sunday Times, 'worth a little fortune to any stringer,[1] for it pointed the scope for a wide variety of stories and features, and any correspondent who couldn't earn a living from it deserved to be sacked.' It is out of date and unknown now, but curiously fascinating all the same.

The nucleus of the team which Mercury put in the field included the war correspondents who had served The Sunday Times and the other papers in the Kemsley group. Ablest among these were David Divine, who became the paper's defence correspondent, and the late Arthur Morley Richards, who had been correspondent in the Pacific theatre of the war.

But Fleming yearned for fashionable sophistication and soon the professionals were outnumbered by correspondents of a very different sort, the gifted amateurs who could at times write splendidly impressionistic passages but who not infrequently slipped up on really big stories, fumbling because of lack of experience and journalistic know-how. The truth was that immediately after the war British journalism suffered from a dearth of young talent, and this resulted, especially in the foreign field, in the emergence of correspondents who had the qualities of social style, the right public school background, and facility in languages, but were not really newspaper men. The efficient but unpicturesque professionals alongside whom they worked both despised and envied them.

During this period Fleming himself was partly to blame for some of the failures of the Mercury team. His marked preference for what he called 'sophisticated men of the world' went hand in hand with his distrust of the Kemsley House old hand or, equally, any boring old bishop or played out politician. Two living writers he admired were his friends Evelyn Waugh and Cyril Connolly, both the scourge of the conventional. (He was always talking at the conference about 'throwing a fly' over Waugh, but some of their private references to the editor-in-chief were hilariously disrespectful.) But after a few years' experience of some quixotic characters Fleming was ruefully content to abandon his visions

---

1. 'Non-staff reporter who is paid on the basis of what is published, plus, perhaps, a small retaining fee. Term most generally used for overseas reporters, freelance being the commonest term for domestic non-staff contributor. The term comes from the old accountancy habit of saving the outside man's newspaper clippings on a string, or pasting them together as a continuous ribbon. The verb, to string, means to work as a stringer.' Harold Evans: 'Editing and Design, Book Three, News Headlines', London, Heinemann, 1972.

and settle for a certain pedestrian tenacity. Slowly the authors of brilliant books who had drifted into the Mercury camp gave place to journalists who understood the meaning of news.

Within three years the number of foreign correspondents serving Mercury totalled eighty-eight, and by the end of 1949 the emphasis on professionalism had changed the composition of the team to such an extent that thirty-three per cent of it had been full-time journalists associated with Kemsley newspapers before taking up assignments overseas. The foreign department at this time conducted an analysis of their personnel: ninety-eight per cent were of British nationality at birth; sixty-three per cent had had a university education; their average age was thirty-eight; seven out of the eighty-eight were women, and on an average each correspondent knew three foreign languages. The most outstanding of all the correspondents was Henry Brandon, British but born a Czech.

In 1946 the total wordage of Mercury correspondents published in Kemsley Newspapers was about two and a half million. Three years later it had risen to nearly four million. But the catch was that only a very small percentage of this wordage appeared in The Sunday Times. This was all the more galling because it was in this period that David Astor began to build up The Observer's own foreign service and the widely syndicated Observer foreign news service.

The Fleming experiment was imaginative, if expensive, but it was a case of launching the right idea at the wrong moment. Between 1945 and 1949 British newspapers were still not very much larger than in wartime. Thus the only way in which Mercury's outflow of copy could be effectively used was by spreading it around the group, in The Stockport Express just as much as in The Sunday Times or Sunday Graphic. In total wordage the results were effective, but a closer examination should have revealed far earlier that the enormous cost of the Mercury service – this 'fantastically expensive toy', as one managerial man, never an admirer of Fleming, put it – could not be justified by what was printed in the provincial dailies and evenings and in the already dying 'populars', such as The Sunday Graphic and Sunday Empire News. It was the stringers who scored heavily in the 'populars' and provincials, and the man who concentrated on The Sunday Times made less money than they did, though he acquired more repute.

The correspondent who complained that he never seemed able

to get a story into The Sunday Times was apt to be reminded that
it is 'The Empire News and The Daily Graphic that earn our
bread and butter, not The Sunday Times'. And indeed whereas a
first-class story in one of the 'populars' would earn twelve or
fifteen guineas in those days, even a page-one story in The Sunday
Times rarely rated as much as five guineas, thriftily 'marked up',
except on special occasions, at the usually depressed rates
by Jerry Sefton, who looked after contributors' accounts (as
Ronald Meakins does so ably today) and was father of the present
circulation director, Jack Sefton. The result was that stringers
especially began to neglect The Sunday Times, while many
staffers became content to seek by-lines in the 'populars' rather
than aim for prestige in The Sunday Times.

Before Mercury came along by-lines had been used sparingly in
The Sunday Times and regarded as vulgar in its news pages.
With the support of K, who loved to see his own name or anyone
else's in the paper, provided he were 'safe', Fleming personalised
and publicised his foreign team, insisting that all Mercury stories
should carry the correspondent's by-line and even persuading The
Sunday Times to adopt his policy. Sometimes he ordered a correspondent to change his name if he didn't like the sound of it – he
even crankily complained at a Tuesday conference of a book review
in The Sunday Times, not for its content but because he didn't
like the name of the reviewer – Sir Arthur Grimble, who happened
to be a beautiful writer. So Mario Modiano of Athens became
Michael Manning and Geoffrey Bocca in New York received a
peremptory cable: 'Allez Bocca, ave Barker.'

When Anthony Berry, Lord Kemsley's youngest son, was
editing The Sunday Chronicle a story dealing with security at
Gibraltar came in from the correspondent there with a request
that his by-line should not be used. 'We must have some by-line,'
said Tony, always as amiable as he was shrewd. 'Why not James
Bond?' Fleming must have gritted his teeth, no matter if he forced
a smile. He was just breaking through with his novels, and he took
them more seriously than his friends did. In any case they were his
fantasy escape from the 'prison' in Gray's Inn Road, and he
wanted no mingling of the two. But the name James Bond duly
went on to the story.

Not all the blame for the meagre space which The Sunday
Times gave to foreign news in those days, compared with The
Observer, could be attributed to lack of newsprint. The Observer
deliberately concentrated on foreign news and began publishing

long despatches from its overseas correspondents. Amazingly, The
Sunday Times did not even have a foreign editor before 1949, an
omission which reflected the complacent insularity of Hadley and
Heywood. (Hadley always spent his holidays at Droitwich,
Heywood was attached to Felixstowe, though he did become a
convert to Banyuls, not very far from Perpignan, in his later years;
otherwise they hardly ever left Gray's Inn Road.)

Fleming was never foreign editor. He was manager of the
foreign department, special writer for The Sunday Times, and
deeply involved in the paper's progress. There were colourful and
distinguished characters in Fleming's early Mercury team, such
as the artist and traveller Dick Wyndham, killed by a sniper's
bullet in the Arab–Israeli conflict in the Middle East. But in the
late forties and in some cases afterwards the key men as far as The
Sunday Times was concerned were Henry Brandon in Washington,
Frank McDermot and Stephen Coulter in Paris, and Frank Oliver
in New York (W. T. Foster, Cal McCrystal, Arnold Field, Evelyn
Irons, who was at Somerville with Dilys Powell and who made her
reputation on The Evening Standard, were in New York after
him). McDermot was an Irish Francophil with a flair for unravelling the complexities of French political life under the fourth
republic; he had been soldier, banker, barrister, politician and
journalist in turn and he lived with great elegance. Coulter, now a
successful novelist himself, helped Ian Fleming greatly with some
background details for 'Casino Royale'. Oliver was a former old
China hand with Reuters. Brandon had made a name for himself
when, during the war, he had secured a world scoop with his exclusive report of de Gaulle's refusal to meet President Roosevelt in
Algiers. Early in 1948 he had the unusual distinction of being
asked to go to Geneva as expert consultant to the United Nations
for the conference on freedom of information, and Kemsley
Newspapers agreed to lend his services temporarily to the UN for
this purpose.

Serving, as it did, daily, evening, Sunday and weekly newspapers, Mercury in London maintained a round-the-clock seven-
day week. Two of its staff have since distinguished themselves –
Aubrey Jones, chairman of the now dissolved Prices and Income
Board, and Peter Kirk, a junior minister in Mr Heath's administration.

All in all, Mercury was magnificently impressive. But it was
economically unsound.

By the autumn of 1949 the devaluation of the pound brought

the first rumblings of discontent with the Fleming régime, and economy was urged by a committee set up to examine Mercury's finances. Fleming, who disdained to quarrel seriously with his critics and was usually charmingly *dégagé* instead, had incurred the hostility of a few and the jealousy of many because of his closeness to Lord K.

The criticism, much of it justified, was threefold. It was argued that the cost of the foreign department was far too heavy and that devaluation must be followed by some pruning. He was attacked for maintaining too large an administrative staff in London. He was severely criticised for the quality and duplicatory tendencies of his news service: too often Mercury tried inefficiently and belatedly to compete with the major agencies.

He made a minor counter-attack by bringing from the editorship of The Sunday Graphic a new deputy foreign manager and at the same time persuading Lord Kemsley to confirm this same man as foreign editor of The Sunday Times. It was Iain Lang, formerly of The Sunday Times, with his tortured face and dandy's dress. Lang, though he had once been Mr Gossip of The Daily Sketch, had never been happy editing a popular picture paper, and he found The Sunday Times, when he rejoined it, a civilised haven once more.

In one sense the move was admirable. Lang, who had injured a hip when parachuting in the Far East as a war correspondent, had a sharp and analytical mind and a sound knowledge of foreign affairs. However, the relationship between Lang and Fleming became uneasy. Fleming treated politics with amused boredom, and a puritanical streak in Lang caused his left-wing conscience to become irritated by Fleming's levity. Lang also became increasingly critical of Mercury.

What should have happened at this stage was a complete re-organisation of Mercury and the concentration on a smaller but powerful team of correspondents who were all Sunday Times material. Instead Mercury continued to service all the Kemsley papers, and both staff men and stringers continued to find it easier and more profitable to concentrate on the group rather than on The Sunday Times.

On the other hand Ian Fleming made a valiant effort to get something going from Russia when Cyril Ray was appointed to Moscow for The Sunday Times. But again this proved to be the right idea at the wrong moment. The mercurial Ray, enthusiastically on the left and eager for adventure, found it all dust and ashes. Under the Stalin régime Ray was restricted in movement and prevented by the Russian censorship from writing anything but descriptive and diminutive essays on Moscow life. An elaborate fiction was maintained that there *was* no censorship. Correspondents were graciously accorded 'literary guidance'. He sometimes asked to see the censor, to argue a point. 'But there *is* no censor, Mr Ray.'

Ray was a scintillating writer from The Manchester Guardian who had made a reputation for himself for his 'notebook' reporting in The Sunday Times. He now became very frustrated, as did the paper, for the expense of keeping him in Moscow ran to £12,000 a year: 'not,' he says now, 'because I was recklessly extravagant but because of the quite arbitrary rate of exchange, deliberately flattering to the rouble. (I cannot remember precise examples now, but I think even breakfast cost a couple of pounds or so.)' There was a Retreat from Moscow.

By 1956 Mercury's activities were drastically reduced and its London staff, apart from Fleming, reduced to two: William Todd, a wartime associate of Fleming's, who looked after the department's travel arrangements, and Donald McCormick, who first brought himself to Fleming's notice in 1942 by producing out of a nocturnal adventure in Algiers a detailed street map of the still enemy-infested Kasbah. Between the mid-1950s and 1960 the outflow of Mercury stories was not even a twelfth of what it had been; finally the service to the group papers ended.

Only once in this prolonged twilight of the foreign department did a gleam of real brightness light up the gloom on the second floor. Richard Hughes, The Sunday Times Far-Eastern correspondent, returning from London, after his biennial leave, to the Far East, with new headquarters in Hong Kong, was assigned by Fleming to visit Moscow and secure nothing less than the first exclusive press interview with Khrushchev. 'So', says Hughes, 'I was lucky enough to land the Moscow assignment – which failed miserably in its primary objective of netting Khrushchev, but fortuitously flushed out the two missing diplomats, Burgess and Maclean.'[1] Thus a Sunday Times man was on the spot when the Russians decided to announce the traitors' presence in the Russian camp. The rugged Hughes, a splendid journalist and personality, dined out for years on the story.

Any candid assessment of Ian Fleming as foreign manager

1. 'Foreign Devil', André Deutsch, 1972.

should give some final indication of his limitations and virtues. He did little homework on international affairs, and his views seemed to be based on club and dinner-party gossip. He read The New Yorker, Life and Paris-Match, but not The New York Times or Le Monde. He warmly approved Iain Lang's attending meetings at Chatham House but wouldn't have dreamed of exposing himself to that sort of boredom. He put in a lot of work – in and out of office hours – on the Dropmore Press and the Queen Anne Press and his bibliophile magazine, The Book Collector, and read avidly anything about fast cars, golf, canasta and bridge. (He published some notable books at one or other of these private presses, including Cyril Connolly's masterly 'The Missing Diplomats'.)

But in spite of all this he was a very effective foreign manager: he had that magnetism which made people work for him with far more than routine conscientiousness. He was quickly receptive to useful ideas, from whatever source within the department they came. He had complete confidence in Lang and Ian Munro: the latter was in charge of syndication. Inevitably there were some duds among the many people who came in and went out of the service, but when these had to be liquidated Ian did the gruesome job as considerately as possible. All his staff unenviously admired his enormous zest for living, his debonair charm, his generosity – when anyone connected with Mercury became involved in personal difficulties his reactions and actions were always generous. They have the pleasantest memories of drinks – very long strong highballs – in Montagu Place and Cheyne Walk (his home in Victoria Square came after his marriage) and luncheon at Boodle's or the Etoile in Charlotte Street.

At the end of 1959 he left the foreign managership. Characteristically, his final thoughts were for the tiny team he left behind: he secured for them a reprieve which might not otherwise have been granted, and sent each a personal farewell note in his own hand.

He was by now a world-famous author. But though his pride was bruised by Mercury's failure, he was forming, in his romantic way, a deep attachment to the ugly old 'prison', no matter how sardonically he had rejected 200 Gray's Inn Road in the past; and right until his untimely death he found it impossible to sever himself completely from The Sunday Times.

IX

But this picture of the failure of a worthily ambitious idea, of Ian Fleming walking the dirty yellow corridors of Kemsley House with managerial assegais planted in his back, is not entirely relevant to The Sunday Times. It is related at some length to make the point that he was of much greater use to the paper as a writer than as foreign manager.

For as Mercury began to crack up he left the detail of the foreign service to Lang and opened a new career as special writer for The Sunday Times. Between early in 1953, when he passed the proofs of 'Casino Royale', and 1959 he showed himself a master of what may be called sardonic adventure writing, with series on Jacques Cousteau's underwater search for a Graeco–Roman galley off Marseilles harbour, 'The Diamond Smugglers', 'Thrilling Cities' and others. 'Although,' says John Pearson in his 'Life of Ian Fleming', 'he had been working regularly as a journalist on The Sunday Times since 1946 'The Diamond Smugglers' was his first major success as a reporter and it seemed to offer him a new reputation almost overnight: the role of reporter could complement his rôle as the best-selling author of James Bond.'

Earlier on, he was Atticus for a term. 'Atticus,' says Pearson, who worked with Fleming on the column, had become 'an insufferable old bore, a pseudonymous weekly column for peddling the stale left-overs of smoking-room gossip and high-table reminiscence. But it *was* an honour of a sort for Fleming to be offered it. In its day it had been written by genuine writers like John Buchan, and inside the office – and out of it for that matter – it still trailed wisps and tatters of prestige.'

Hadley was very proud of John Buchan's Atticus, but it was, *pace* Mr Pearson, stiff, correct and devoted almost exclusively to the formalities of Westminster and Whitehall. Sacheverell Sitwell, a Hodson appointment, had given the column a unique style, though not a popular one.

As Fleming had highly individual notions about the kind of column it should be (and they were almost a revenge on the John Buchan style), he would not accept the job, which had recently been vacated by Sir Robert Bruce-Lockhart, unless certain conditions were met. Mr Pearson continues:

From the beginning of his association with the *Sunday Times* he had insisted, very properly, on anything he wrote for it being immune from editing or interference; it was a matter on which he had strong feelings and which brought him for once, somewhat to his discomfort, into agreement with Randolph Churchill, who occasionally dined [at Fleming's home] in Victoria Square and with whom he sometimes had a bellowing match there. Allied to this was his advocacy of more candour in the paper, more controversy, more vigorous praise or blame – and he usually wanted blame – of public figures. Since those days the *Sunday Times* has gone far and soared high, as Fleming acknowledged to Denis Hamilton before he died. But in the early 1950s the pall of genteel discretion which hung over certain areas of it, allied to the invincible predictability and 'soundness' of its political opinions gave Fleming exquisite discomfort. He therefore stipulated for freedom in the Atticus column, even to the extent of being allowed to mention Mr Cecil King of the *Daily Mirror* or any other person about whom Lord Kemsley, as editor-in-chief, happened to be less than enthusiastic. And, as vehement and obstinate as ever in conveying his views to the old autocrat, he won his point.

He took trouble with Atticus, turned it into a wonderfully offbeat entertainment, but one far from the slashing West-End column which gossip-writers have always unavailingly dreamed of since the days of Thackeray's 'Pendennis', and left a legacy of freedom to his successors – Godfrey Smith, Robert Robinson, Nicholas Tomalin, Hunter Davies, Philip Oakes, Michael Bateman. When Kemsley fired him from Atticus by telegram – he was in Jamaica, enjoying the annual two months' leave which he had stipulated for when he first joined Lord K in 1945, and writing another novel – he shrugged it off, probably with his usual exasperated little laugh. He was getting bored with the weekly stint anyway, and he suspected – rightly – that Denis Hamilton wanted to get him out of London in search of the bizarre and the exotic, writing valuable three- or four-part features for the paper. He never lost his passion for spies and treasure-hunts, and was always abstracting dodges from the annals of both, especially the CIA-inspired tunnel from the US zone into East Berlin, for possible use in his own fictions.

Now that all the fuss about Mercury was over he was growing deeply attached, as has just been mentioned, to The Sunday Times, attending the conference and still talking about throwing a fly over Evelyn Waugh or Augustus John, another of his admirations, even when he gave up going to the office daily and had his own headquarters in a Fleet Street court, where the efficient Beryl Griffie-Williams presided over his business affairs, now grown enormous because of his success.

No longer the debonair crown prince of Gray's Inn Road, as Cyril Lakin had been before him, he was nevertheless the loyal liege of Lord K even when the old man sold out so stealthily in 1959.

Fleming had known at least three press lords intimately, but the new man Thomson was utterly unlike any of them. At first he was rather puzzled by him, then appreciative, and finally devoted, reckoning him the best of the bunch. It was in Thomson's office at Gray's Inn Road, now without the precious desk and chair taken away by Kemsley and the bronze bust of him by Reid Dick, that Fleming had his first heart attack, sitting opposite a portrait by Raeburn from the collection of Thomson's son Kenneth. He was mortified that the pain made him incapable of joining in the discussion, which he said afterwards was obviously going to be of enormous importance to the paper. It was Thomson's proposal for The Sunday Times colour magazine.

X

The shortage of newsprint not only during the war but for so long after it was one of the hardest and most frustrating problems the newspaper industry has ever had to face. It is easy to forget that rationing was in force in some form for seventeen years – from early 1940 until 1957, twelve years after the end of the war.

The first real discord over the rationing scheme came in March, 1947, when The Times and Daily Telegraph made strong protests. At this time The Sunday Times, instead of alternating between eight and ten pages, was confined to eight only. The Observer had to drop its one-in-four weeks' ten-page issue.

More restrictions were to follow as the dollar crisis continued: 'food or newsprint' explained Fleming sternly to his foreign correspondents. In July of the same year there was a further cut, and the price of the paper was raised from 2d to 3d – the cost of newsprint had gone up and copies were restricted. It was at this time that the slogan 'Pass your Copy to Your Friend' was introduced. The circulation had reached 586,346 – which was 49,149 up on the previous year – but the choice now was either a cut in size or in circulation.

It was circulation which suffered, although the demand for the paper was increasing steadily. In October, 1948, Lord K was able to claim that since December, 1947, The Sunday Times had been the only full-size national Sunday to publish eight pages every week. The majority, choosing circulation, published eight and six on alternate weeks.

In July 1950, the newsprint crisis flared yet again, and the following February a further five per cent cut in supplies brought stocks to the lowest since 1940. But this seems to have been the turning-point. A year later extra newsprint was available, and in May, 1952, a ten per cent rise was permitted in consumption because of improved supplies.

In August of that year newspapers were given an increase in size and sales, but since newsprint was then costing £53 a ton, compared with less than £10 pre-war, life was not easy everywhere in Fleet Street.

Indeed, some of the weaker papers, as Randolph Churchill pointed out, were very happy with the rationing. 'To some extent they are dependent on the "over-flow" from the stronger papers. If newsprint were freely available they might lose to their stronger rivals some of the advertising they have got at the moment.'

However, freedom from controls gradually returned, although the Government did not abandon all restrictions until the end of 1956, and even then the industry itself continued a form of control. For the next twelve weeks the big newspapers had a trial period of freedom from page limitation. They were then obtaining all the newsprint they needed. But it was not until August, 1959, that the Newsprint Supply Company was wound up and the newspapers felt they were their own masters again.

It is remarkable that in spite of the high cost of newsprint and the falling value of money the price of The Sunday Times remained at 2d throughout the whole of the second world war. It was increased, as has been noted, from 2d to 3d on July 27, 1947, and from 3d to 4d on May 13, 1951. On April 4, 1954, it was actually *reduced* – from 4d to 3½d. It went back to 4d on October 23, 1955.

The reduction from 4d to 3½d, far from being an act of altruism on the part of Lord K, covertly acknowledged that over-confidence and over-impulsiveness had led him into error. Eric Cheadle came to an agreement with The Observer that both papers would go up from 3d to 3½d, but Lord K wasn't having it. At the last moment he said to Cheadle, 'Let's get the money in. Let's make it 4d.' It was too late – or perhaps too shaming – to notify The Observer, who duly went up to 3½d. But as a result of the ½d difference between the two, The Sunday Times lost circulation steadily to The Observer, and in the end had to go back to 3½d.

In the middle of all the general frustration Lord and Lady Kemsley went out one afternoon and bought up an international travel magazine called 'Go'. It was not that the editor-in-chief felt desperate to get an extra paper ration of any kind. He had watched with pride the progress of Elizabeth Nicholas's travel department in the paper (strange as it sounds, Mrs Nicholas was the first of all travel correspondents), and like Lord Thomson after him he felt there were potentialities in the travel business. Overnight practically, Leonard Russell and Mrs Nicholas became editors of 'Go'. They had neither staff nor office but they were old comrades, for the travel column had been his idea and Mrs Nicholas his choice for it; together they had produced three highly successful Sunday Times travel guides, fat books packed with hard-won information. Even today Elizabeth David's six-weeks' trip from Marseilles to Menton, in which she ferreted out dozens of decent hotels, is jolly reading.

Leaving Jack Lambert to look after the book reviews in The Sunday Times, but maintaining his other work, Russell set up 'Go''s office in his own office in Kemsley House and produced the first issue under its new ownership with the help of Jack Andrews, who was the art editor and designer, or visualiser as was then the fashionable term. Soon they were joined by Maurice Wiggin, who has turned his hand to many things in his time, always with verve and exceptional brilliance. In all his years on the paper he has remained the most delightful companion and a humane, funny and sharp commentator and critic, whether it has been radio, fishing, gardening, the countryside or television.

Others came along to join in with 'Go', among them Lady Kemsley's daughter, Mrs Ghislaine Alexander, as she was then, a fledgling, amused, amateur fashion editor as good as any professional in Fleet Street, Mrs Kaye Webb, now with Puffin Books, Anthony Curtis, Joyce Emerson, and Stella Frank, still with Russell after twenty-one years. Four or five issues were produced and the circulation steadied at about 50,000, which at the time was much better than bad for a 3s 6d glossy, particularly as The Sunday Times advertisement people – it was published 'in association with The Sunday Times' – were bringing in plenty of expensive advertising.

One little editorial idea was to publish anonymously a short

story by Bertrand Russell and offer a prize for its identification –
Lord Russell was amused by the plan. But when the coloured cover
of the issue, with its announcement of the stunt, had already gone
to press, he rang up Leonard Russell one lunch time and told him
that he wished to withdraw the story: he seemed to see a new
reputation opening before him as a writer of fiction and wanted to
include this particular story for the first time in a collection. When
he was told it was too late his usually precise speech lost definition
in a scream of barrack-room language, which included the parting
shot, 'You always were a bloody band of robbers'. This seemed
excessive to Leonard Russell. He did not know then that the
venerable and patrician philosopher had a habit of calculatedly
abusing the peasants if he were crossed and turning away unruffled when he had gained his point. Nor did he know until 1972
that the first prize in the competition was won by Cyril Connolly,
who sent in his entry in the name of his wife's charwoman.

A sequel, if you can call it that, came ten years later. Sir Stanley
Unwin, who had published Bertrand Russell's books with remarkable success, offered the great man's autobiography for serializa-
tion in The Sunday Times – Unwin had never before negotiated in
person with the paper. Quite wrongly, Leonard Russell, who was
still resentful of his lordship's manners, was made vaguely uneasy
by the thought that the autobiography might cover ground
already explored in 'Portraits from Memory' and other books. He
therefore pressed Unwin for an assurance that the autobiography
was an original book and not noticeably a re-jig. In the end, after
increasingly acid exchanges with Unwin, who asked a very large
price, the serial was lost to The Observer, and on the whole
Leonard Russell wasn't sorry to see it end that way.

But he remained guiltily conscious that this intrusion of personal
feeling was a mistake, telling himself that in similar circumstances
Denis Hamilton, calmly and patiently, would have nursed the
prickly Unwin into a sympathetic frame of mind and finally
landed the book, as he had done so frequently in the past. A serial
which really sells the paper is what every editor worth the name is
looking for, while realising perfectly that its proper long-term
effect can only be achieved if the paper is good enough for the new
reader to continue to take it. For Sunday papers the serial stakes
are particularly high, for as recently as 1967, as will be related,
a serial brought in more than 150,000 new readers to The
Sunday Times; with the prospect of a prize like this there is no ·
room at all for small resentments in negotiation. Fortunately, The

Observer used Lord Russell's autobiography in their magazine, and its potentialities seemed obscured by a wealth of pictorial illustration. At the time The Sunday Times flattered itself that it could have made the autobiography a national sensation, presenting it on the front of the Weekly Review, giving a lot of it, and promoting it with the punch acquired from many years' experience. It lost the chance by its own error, but through no fault of Denis Hamilton or Harold Evans – in this kind of situation Evans has learnt fast and proved an apt pupil of Hamilton.

'Go' continued to show a moderate loss, which rather puzzled its senior editor as everything was on a shoe-string, and when Lord K showed signs of wanting to institute yet another series of conferences, this time about the magazine, with still more members of his family present, he pleaded that his place was with the paper. So the magazine was quickly sold and everyone in the firm agreed that it was sensible for Kemsley Newspapers to stick to what it knew about, which was selling newspapers, diplomatically ignoring the kiss of death which had fastened, or was about to fasten, on quite a few Kemsley newspaper properties.

When it was all over, Russell, out of curiosity, had the printing and production of the magazine costed by an expert. It had been entirely produced at Kemsley printing centres, even down to the colour pages; and he found that everything had been charged at double rates – overtime rates – because the plants were fully occupied with their routine work. When the magazine was sold it was, in fact, given normal production costs, making a comfortable little profit.

Russell was too ring-worn to care.

There was a tiff with another Cambridge author of international distinction. E. M. Forster had published his collection of reprinted pieces, 'Two Cheers for Democracy', at a time when space for book reviews was still very meagre because of newsprint rationing. Raymond Mortimer had recently written a full-dress appraisal of him, and someone else had contributed a birthday tribute: he was the master and reverentially acknowledged as such. It was thought, naïvely as it turned out, that someone of his humanity would understand if his new book were given a mere three inches of space, instead of going to one or other of the main critics for an 800-word review, and the room thus saved given up to books by unknown writers. This notion was conveyed to him, but there was no answer. However, after the appearance of the brief but warm notice the paper wanted to get a picture of him for Douglas Glass's Portrait

Gallery – it may have been because of his libretto for Britten's 'Billy Budd' or something else out of the strict literary path. But Forster refused, on the ground that if The Sunday Times couldn't give a proper review of his book it shouldn't be interested in a photograph of him.

He was a nice man, though, and all little disagreements had been forgotten by the time he came to the office for a luncheon for his friend Raymond Mortimer, on the occasion of Mortimer's seventieth birthday.

XI

James Agate had died and his deputy Harold Hobson taken his place: everyone liked Hobson, including Lord K, who had a joking relationship with him (as he had with Robert Harling) when they met at parties; there was something about Hobson's ironic pleasantries which tickled his fancy. From the beginning Hobson was extremely brilliant, and he soon became the most influential drama critic in the country.

At this time the younger Sunday Times set went out to restaurants a lot, though some of them were really loners, particularly Fleming, Harling, Hobson and Russell. Hobson almost lived at the Ivy and later the Caprice. Fleming and Harling went, often together, to the Etoile or Scotts. In the war Russell had practically edited his annual *Saturday Books* in the grillroom of the Ritz, and he remained faithful to it. Sometimes they would all find themselves at the same restaurant, perhaps with Michael Renshaw or Jack Lambert, and there would be laughter and shop talk and as it were ironic hand-kissings and hiccups in the direction of the sternly progressive Observer. All the same, they knew that the paper had simply got to be modernised and improved.

Hadley was on the point of retiring, and there began a shadow-boxing contest for his job. Valentine Heywood, the acting editor, was a dear good fellow whom no one wanted to hurt, particularly Lord K, whose heavily paternal and indulgently sceptical attitude towards him was accompanied by private generosities. These gestures and one thing and another made Heywood feel that he was in the running, but he had had no real encouragement. The truth was that though he was experienced on the news side he was ill-equipped beyond it; his health had been uncertain for years.

Nevertheless, he conceived that there was to be a contest. 'Fighting for my life,' he would gasp, inaccurately, as he rushed lobbying about the corridors. (You never got the sack: the patriarch didn't like disturbances in the family.) It must have been a difficult moment for the aged Hadley, who had known Heywood for a long time and brought him on to the paper, but the veteran, though he had considerable affection for his deputy, knew his limitations as well as anyone. Yet Heywood had done good work with a little band of contributors who were also his friends, the best of them being Sir Miles (now Lord) Thomas, motoring correspondent for many years.

Five years before, Henry Vincent Hodson had become assistant editor, and he rapidly showed that, politically and socially, he was the finest acquisition The Sunday Times had ever made. Before him the men at the top had usually been journalists risen from the ranks, and doubtless many of them were better craftsmen than Hodson was or ever became; but from the start he had an air of distinction and education, and in this he was the superior of the late Cyril Lakin or anyone else in living memory. At Balliol he had won many academic successes, and he had been a Fellow of All Souls. He had edited the influential foreign affairs publication, the Round Table, in the 1930s. He had been reforms commissioner in the Government of India and head of the non-Munitions Division in the Ministry of Production. He was of a striking presence, tall, slim, with a keen intellectual face and poetically disarranged hair which early turned to silver. He looked, and perhaps was, essentially, the brilliant young sophisticated don.

On all this the homely and ingenuous Heywood gazed with admiration mingled with despair. It was indicated to him at one stage that if he hoped to keep ahead of the brilliant young man he must at the very least get himself elected to a reputable West End club. Great efforts were made on his behalf, for everyone liked him, and eventually he got into the Garrick. But it was not enough, it did not show up particularly well against Hodson's membership of the Athenaeum and of Brooks's.

It is in one sense a trivial fact that while Heywood lived remote from London life amidst the lesser business magnates in Chalfont St Giles, Hodson and his attractive wife Margaret and their three sons had lived in one or two distinguished London houses. In another sense, in the personal fortunes of Valentine Heywood, the fact is not trivial. Had Heywood been a robust democrat, caring nothing for the high social life, Hodson could have lived in Blenheim itself and it would not have mattered. But Heywood was not a man of this kind. He was the admirer from a great distance of lords and lordlings. He wore spats long after everyone else had given them up and an eyeglass which he never used. One night Hodson gave a great party – was it in Sargent's house in Tite Street? Lord K was invited, and Heywood, too, but Heywood sat in a corner, sad. The next morning he said with a wry face to his colleagues: 'Everybody was there, everybody.' He was too disheartened to tell one of his Stock Exchange stories – he belonged to a generation the members of which actually told funny stories to each other in the train – or to rush about hiding his innate simplicity and sensibility beneath the exterior of the suburban good fellow.

So there was really no contest for the editorship when Hadley retired in 1950. Hodson was inevitably made his successor; Heywood was given the consolation prize of the new post of managing editor; and Russell and Murphy became assistant editors, to be brought into the general direction of the paper while retaining their control over the literary and sports pages. Hodson later said, truthfully, that Heywood 'in these relationships, which could have been difficult . . . was unstinting in his help and guidance and unfailing in loyalty and friendship'. He also said that The Sunday Times was always a 'happy ship' largely because of Heywood's modest and warmhearted personality.

There was a *contretemps* on the day Lord K offered the post to Hodson, who asked for time to consider it. That evening Denis Hamilton was having dinner in the House of Commons, and it was there that he was fetched to the telephone to speak to a furious Lord Kemsley – Hamilton it will be remembered was editorial director of the whole group. 'Today,' said Lord Kemsley, 'I offered, as you know, the editorship of The Sunday Times to Hodson. It is now nine p.m. and I still haven't heard from him. When I offer a man one of the greatest jobs in the world I do not expect to be kept waiting. Will you kindly ring him up and tell him that if I do not hear from him tonight the offer will be withdrawn?' Hamilton passed on the message in a suitably serious manner. Hodson accepted with suitable celerity. You had to be careful with Lord K about smaller things than this. Hamish Hamilton, the publisher, to whom he had done a service, offended his dignity by sending a note of thanks which, though warm and handwritten, was, said Lord K with a snort, 'absurdly short'. An outsider was

H. V. Hodson.

wise if (like the rather mad stranger who mistook the identity of G. K. Chesterton's grandfather, a house agent) he adopted the simple posture that he was addressing a Monument and a Landmark.

Ian Fleming had no use for people who had, as he put it, 'sold out' to Lord Kemsley. He abstained from doing so himself, despite the intimacy of their association, and Hodson abstained too. He made an impact such as his high abilities foreshadowed, but whether he was a heaven-sent editor of a paper under pressure, as The Sunday Times was from The Observer, is another matter. It is instinct, not intellect, which makes great editors. Nor could he look to Heywood for a quota of original ideas or even capable, all-round support; the outlook there was too tinged with provincialism.

The new young men were breaking out now to make the office a livelier place. There was J. W. Lambert, educated at Tonbridge (his university, as he remarked, was the same as Gorki's) and risen in the war from ordinary seaman in the RNVR to commander. He had been decorated for bravery, and his ship, during one of the darkest days of the war, had fished out of the Atlantic in which she was drifting the celebrated Greek actress, Katina Paxinou. From his earliest youth he had been fascinated by the theatre, of which his judgment is as sound as his knowledge is prodigious, and by music, especially singing. He had had two ambitions: to make a useful mark as a drama critic and as a literary editor, and he has achieved both, immensely assisted in all things by his beautiful wife, Catherine.

In this he illustrated a striking feature of life at The Sunday Times in the 1950s – and onwards for that matter. There can be few organisations in which the family life of the top layer has been so considerable a factor in professional achievement. Heywood had been, as Hodson said, 'utterly devoted' to his Jennie, and when she died two years before him he was a 'heart-broken man'. Hadley had noted the domestic happiness of some within his immediate range – Lakin, Hodson, Hobson, Murphy, Russell (who had married Dilys Powell in the war).

The same can be said of many others: of Godfrey Smith, for example, but Godfrey's finest hour belongs to another part of this book. It can also be said of Kenneth Pearson and his wife Patricia Connor, who has written much for the paper. Pearson joined it not long after Lambert, and like Lambert was passionately interested in the theatre. In the 1950s he invented and

began to organise the series of National Union of Students/
Sunday Times drama festivals, carried them on into the 1960s, and
met Pat Connor at one of them. Besides the theatre they had
another common enthusiasm: archaeological excavation, which
led them to discoveries as far away from home as Turkey and as
near as Fishbourne, near Chichester, the Roman palace which
was made a centre of interest by the inspiration of Denis Hamilton
and the enthusiasm of Kenneth Pearson.

Lord K himself was also the happiest of men in his married life,
and he evolved a philosophy from it: all true Kemsley men should
be married with children. It is evidence of his stern uprightness
and narrowness of vision that when he unexpectedly learned in
1945 that James Agate was a homosexual he was deeply shocked.
As was said earlier, he wanted to sack him at once and put Harold
Hobson in his place. 'Hobson,' said Kemsley, 'is a married man;
moreover he has a daughter.' But this was altogether too much for
dear old Hadley. Flushing slightly, and abandoning his habitual
mildness, he objected that Agate's sexual idiosyncrasies had
nothing whatever to do with his capacities as a critic. The un-
regenerate Agate, who about this time had to flee a male brothel
off Gray's Inn Road without his trousers, retained his job until his
death in 1947. When Kemsley read the world-wide obituary
tributes to him he mused over them for a long time, and with a
species of wonder. All the writers of them must have known that
Agate was homosexual, yet here they were treating him like a
great man. This was one of the very uncomfortable facts which
Lord K never incorporated into his vision of things.

Very occasionally, in conversation, Agate would indicate that
he was not ashamed to be a homosexual; the only thing that made
him feel ashamed was the spectacle of a homosexual pretending
to be otherwise; he never forgave one famous author for writing in
an article in a popular Sunday paper of Hitler's having brought
'painted men' out on to the streets of Berlin in 1933 in order to
gain public favour by arresting them. On one occasion Agate was
injudicious enough to go overboard on the subject in a veiled way
in his Sunday Times article. It had been a week when an officer
and his batman had been sentenced for gross indecency, and on
the Friday afternoon, when he had delivered his copy, it was
found that he had completely abandoned dramatic criticism and
made instead a bitter attack on British hypocrisy, at the same
time withholding from the reader the reason for the outburst. 'I
see Agate has no play this week,' was all innocent old Hadley

mildly remarked when he read the proof, but when Agate's little lapse was spelled out to him he was uniquely angry. A notice in the paper that Sunday announced that Mr Agate was on holiday.

Later on homosexuality became something of an obsession at Chandos House. At a party given there for one of The Sunday Times book exhibitions a member of Kemsley's family heard Cyril Connolly mimicking Brian Howard – whom he had known and detested and parodied in 'Where Engels Fears to Tread' – to Stephen Spender and others. Not having the faintest notion what it was all about, she reported the incident to Lord Kemsley, and he jumped to the erroneous conclusion that Connolly was another of them.

There was an immediate sequel. At the next weekly conference the editor-in-chief said he felt that Connolly wasn't writing as well as had been hoped – was not, in fact, in the same class as Raymond Mortimer, the chief critic (it was not so long before that Lord K had yearned wistfully for Desmond MacCarthy, now dead). He therefore felt that when Mortimer went on holiday Connolly's article should not occupy his position; a special guest critic must be brought in instead. At this Ian Fleming, despite himself, un-expectedly threw back his head and roared with laughter, ridiculing Lord K as a judge of literary form and wondering what on earth it was all about. Russell, the literary editor, red in the face, embarked on an indignant harangue of the room on Con-nolly's unique qualities. Everyone looked extremely uncomfort-able, and Lord K lost something of his monolithic majesty. The literary editor knew his Dr Johnson and felt that they should not be teased with such unnecessary scruples while they all had to live together in a world bursting with sin and sorrow. There was another scene later on when his lordship expressed shock at Connolly's having been permitted to review a Penguin, he apparently believing that insignificance of price denoted in-significance of content.

Why did the senior staff accept Lord K's unenlightened dictatorship? Though most if not all of them could have got better jobs elsewhere, not one left the paper between 1945 and the year of Kemsley's disappearance. The answer is that despite everything Lord K was a leader, an inspirer, and had the bulk and presence of one. Sometimes, when one expected him to be at his most pre-judiced and narrow-minded, he could show charm and under-standing, and his little letters of appreciation were much desired. He was a kind man fundamentally and many people about the place, and particularly Raymond Mortimer, would wish to bear testimony to the amiability and hospitality of him and his wife. Above all, as was said earlier, he created a Sunday Times mystique. His top editorial and managerial men fought like fanatics to maintain and extend the quality and circulation of the paper. The Observer, under its unconventional young editor, David Astor, might be breezing along close up to The Sunday Times, but it had become a point of honour to keep ahead. Naturally, people had fugitive grievances and withdrawal symptoms, but Denis Hamilton, who throughout the fifties was growing steadily in authority, watched everyone closely, the staff in those days being small enough for such a thing to be possible. Small enough, too, for the club-like atmosphere noted earlier to persist and for the brighter sparks to enjoy each other's company outside the office as well as in it.

Lord K was a hard taskmaster, but he drove himself as hard as anyone. He could be amusingly mischievous. It was with glee that he ordered special stickers for The Sunday Times posters which used to be on the hoardings all over London advertising Montgomery's memoirs or some other serial. He had been told by Eric Cheadle that some people seemed to imagine that The Sunday Times was connected with The Times – was, in fact, its Sunday edition. If this was so, Kemsley retorted, it was bad for business and must be corrected – The Times in those days was too unadventurous to attract young readers. Hence the stickers: 'No connection with any daily paper of the same name.'

Harry Hodson has asserted that as editor he was always given, and always exercised, full and untrammelled authority. This sounds overstated: for one thing the Kemsley conference system meant that heads of departments attending the conference had the green light for their plans on Tuesday morning from the patriarch himself. Again, whatever 'untrammelled authority' may mean in this connection, we know that Hodson could never have run his campaign for a greater understanding of homosexuals without the assent – it was a very reluctant assent – of Kemsley, who made a regal and dynastic declaration to Hodson when he appointed him editor in April, 1950: 'It is, of course, to be understood that I will retain my active control of the paper as editor-in-chief, and that final authority in all matters of policy will reside in me. In my absence the deputy chairman [Lionel Berry] will exercise my authority, and, furthermore, it is my intention that a member of my family should always occupy this position.'

It is very different now, in 1972. The editor of The Sunday Times has real authority, and Harold Evans can make up his own mind about any of the great social or political questions. The editor-in-chief, Denis Hamilton, can warn or counsel. If he were to command, and the editor refused to accept it, breaking-point would be reached, and the dispute would have to go to the board of Times Newspapers Ltd.

This is what full and untrammelled authority for an editor means. Geoffrey Dawson had it on The Times and Rees-Mogg has it too. It bears no relation to the position of an editor under Lord Kemsley, who exacted maximum meaning from the term editor-in-chief.

However, it was when Hadley was editor that Lord K's direct influence on the paper was greatest. Hadley laid no claim to be an independent, policy-forming editor. He was, as we have seen, at first a Liberal, but he easily adopted Kemsley's Conservatism. He felt no betrayal of principle in this – Arthur Christiansen, a great editor of The Daily Express, played the same role *vis à vis* Beaverbrook. Hadley was an executant rather than a creative editor, and he put a lot of his energy into writing. He was his own political correspondent, he wrote some leaders, and he signed a great many articles and book reviews – as W. W. Hadley, of course, not as editor.

The only occasion on which he departed from this practice was both ludicrous and disastrous. It was his attack, on the front page, on Norman Mailer's best novel 'The Naked and the Dead'. Both Hamilton and Russell pleaded against anything so silly, and thought they had made their point, but that was on Tuesday morning. Later in the week Lord K privately incited Hadley to denounce the book, and at lunch-time on Saturday Hadley wrote a little story and sent it down to the printer after the protesters had left for the weekend. All else apart, it contained an unfortunate phrase, which was seized on by Peter Fleming in The Spectator, about not letting the book lie about for fear that our womenfolk should read it. Hadley said afterwards that what he really meant was that the book was an insult to women – it degraded them.

At any rate, with an air of moral satisfaction, in the middle of page one, Hadley declared that Mailer's book was too objectionable for review in The Sunday Times. The proof of the story when it came up from the printer at 2.30 p.m. read startlingly: 'AN OBSCENE BOOK. By the Editor.' Someone at least attended to that *gaffe*.

The article had the result which might have been foreseen had Hadley and Kemsley been men of the world. 'The Naked and the Dead' was published by the firm of Alan Wingate, of which André Deutsch was then the boss. It was in May, 1949, and Deutsch, on the Sunday morning, was at work early in his office when a friend rang him up and asked if he had seen The Sunday Times. He hadn't but when he did he naturally became extremely disturbed. Deutsch had met Desmond MacCarthy some time before and he drove out immediately to Garricks Villa, Hampton Court, to see him. He found MacCarthy suffering from an attack of asthma. Nevertheless, he had already written to Russell and other members of The Sunday Times staff protesting against Hadley's story. He comforted Deutsch, who found, on the Monday morning, that he could hardly get into his office for the pile of orders.

The most interesting point of all was that Kemsley and Hadley were staggered and chastened by the anger and protest which the article aroused. More than three hundred protesting letters arrived at the office, and the press censure was considerable. But although Hadley and Kemsley learned a lesson, the liberal arts policy pursued for nearly twenty years by The Sunday Times was damaged. The Tuesday conference was an unhappy one.

For Deutsch the next few weeks were a period of both pleasure and distress – pleasure at the mounting orders and alarm at the possibility of prosecution. An officer from Scotland Yard came to his office, sat in it, carried out no search, but just watched. In the end Tom Driberg raised the matter in the House of Commons, and the Attorney-General, Sir Hartley Shawcross, scolded the book but decided against prosecution. When the annual Sunday Times book exhibition was held at Grosvenor House Deutsch remembers filling his stand with copies of the attacked novel.

These book exhibitions, which Russell ran with Michael Renshaw after the war, were a feature of London literary life. At the last of them André Deutsch, now publishing on his own, displayed a book called 'Memorable Balls', published by Verschoyle, a firm he had recently acquired. When it was learned that Queen Mary was going to tour the exhibition with Lord Kemsley he told Tom Maschler, then with him, to withdraw all copies of 'Memorable Balls' and plaster the stand instead with the text of 'The Boy Friend'. But one copy of 'Memorable Balls' somehow got overlooked, and Queen Mary pounced on it, said 'What an intriguing title!' and handed it to Russell to go with the other books she had chosen at the exhibition, amidst a mild commotion on the stand.

Russell was touched when asked by Queen Mary to give her what she called 'a shove up behind' when she came to a slope in the exhibition hall which was trying for her aged limbs. He found her sweet, knowledgeable, and very shy: not at all the dragon insisted on by the smart boys eager to believe anything unfavourable of royalty. He had heard the stories of her being a ruthless collector, one whose methods were summarised, as late as 1971, in The New Statesman by Paul Johnson, reliably or unreliably one cannot say: 'Wealthy hosts paled at her "You have Our permission to present Us with . . ." and antique dealers put up their shutters when they saw her ancient Daimler nosing round the corner.' At any rate she took away something like a hundred books from the exhibition, and next morning a cheque arrived for the full amount from the Master of her Household.

It was at one of these exhibitions that The Sunday Times people were amazed at a photograph in the paper which had as it slogan 'Decency in journalism', Kemsley's Daily Graphic. Queen Elizabeth the Queen Mother, after touring the show, sat for a picture, with Lord Kemsley on her right and the president of the Publishers' Association, co-sponsors of the exhibitions, standing behind their two chairs. Next morning the photograph appeared in The Graphic with a bookcase painted in where the publisher had stood – he had been blotted right out, leaving Lord K alone in his majesty with the Queen Mother.

The presentation of the annual Sunday Times £1,000 literary prize, an award which made a disappointing impact, except for the prestige and sales it brought to Richard Church for 'Over the Bridge' (John Hayward, who was retained by the paper, was an irrepressible member of the selection committee), took place on one occasion at the book exhibition. The winner was Winston Churchill, and Lord K had to present him with the cheque before a large audience. Churchill was a close friend of Camrose's but had brushed Kemsley off on some encounter in the war, complaining to a third party that he was 'too familiar'. It may have been this which made Kemsley nervous at the presentation, but in any case he was a bad public speaker. Everyone had to draft speeches for him – the best literary talent in the office was tapped. He rejected them all, and was heard to say self-consciously as he turned to Churchill with the cheque, 'The winner of this year's prize needs no introduction'. There was a derisive little titter from the audience and a quote in 'Sayings of the Week' in The Observer.

Winston's son Randolph made regular attacks on Kemsley in

The Spectator, and despised Kemsley for forbearing to reply. (But the patriarch was not always so meek; when Sir Hartley Shawcross, Attorney-General in Mr Attlee's administration, accused him of running a 'gutter press' he threatened a libel action, and the accusation was withdrawn.) The story of Randolph and Lord Kemsley and the other press lords has a more than ordinary interest in the annals of Fleet Street.

Randolph's one-man press council, conducted in the columns of The Spectator, The Recorder, and elsewhere, with occasional sallies on BBC television and at public luncheons, got going in the early 1950s. It had a greater effect in Fleet Street than might have appeared and caused particular perturbation in Gray's Inn Road. His target here was not The Sunday Times but The Empire News and The Sunday Graphic. He accused Kemsley and Rothermere of being purveyors of pornography – which of course they weren't; but he was on surer ground in his denunciation of the popular papers for intrusion into personal privacy. One of his key remarks in his battle with the proprietors was that 'they can criticise anybody but they get awfully sensitive and upset if anyone criticises them'. It certainly upset Lord Kemsley to have his name associated with pornography.

Randolph made this new reputation for himself when his political ambitions had foundered. He had started out as a golden boy, wonderfully handsome, in the certainty that politics was his vocation and that, like the younger Pitt (he read great significance into the fact that they had the same birthday) he couldn't fail to be Prime Minister by the time he was twenty-five. But the bad fairy as well as the good had visited him in his cradle. He had an uncontrollable temper, he drank too much, he had a cold and cruel heart, he charged around insulting people, he upset the Conservative Central Office; and though he was devoted to his father and, as he said, went along with him all the way, he 'suffered from living under the shadow of the great oak tree – the small sapling, so close to the parent tree, doesn't perhaps receive enough sunshine. . . . I became sort of bloody-minded, I suppose.' Said Noël Coward, 'I'm so fond of Randolph, he's so unspoiled by his great failure.'

But he boxed on, as he used to say. It was when he was wrecked as a politician and reduced to turning out what were once called pot-boilers that he had the brilliant idea of setting up as the scourge

Opposite: Lord Kemsley with Queen Mary at a Sunday Times book exhibition, 1949.

of the press lords, combining this with political journalism. He knew them all, and even more than Ian Fleming he was a press lord *manqué*. He had been at Eton with Michael Berry and David Astor, but he was after gamier game – Rothermere, Kemsley, Beaverbrook, the last of whom tried to tame him but never succeeded. They had a curious love-hate relationship, and both uncharacteristically claimed the same rather modest rôle. 'I remember,' Randolph said in a conversation with Clive Irving which appeared in The Sunday Times, 'Beaverbrook once saying to me: "Well, of course, at heart I am just an old concierge. I like to know what's going on." Well, I think I am a sort of middle-aged concierge. I have a great desire to know what's going on.' When the old concierge threatened the middle-aged one with a libel action Randolph took counsel of Lord Camrose, for whom he had a high degree of admiration. 'Treat it as a joke,' Camrose advised him. 'Beaverbrook would never admit that he can't see a joke.' He was perfectly right.

Anyway, Randolph invented the job of press-critic and brought to it an extraordinary mixture of knowledge, verve, the needle, inaccuracy, indiscretion, and childishness. No one else has been half as good. He did not boringly analyse newspapers' contents week after week, he got news about newspapers; and he got it from the top. That dreaded voice on the telephone from East Bergholt, usually quarrelling with the operator as he was being put through, wrested secrets from everyone and betrayed everyone's confidence. He had first news of Thomson's acquiring The Times from Thomson and political intelligence from Harold Macmillan. One of his more pleasing qualities was his rollicking humour. Here he is speaking at a Foyle's literary luncheon on September 10, 1953:

One suggestion I have heard was that it would have been appropriate in Coronation Year to have appointed a Pornographer Royal and Criminologist Extraordinary. The project even went so far that a short list of suitable candidates for this new appointment was drawn up. I do not wish to appear discourteous to Mr Hugh Cudlipp, and I am sure he can take his medicine like a man, but I am sorry to say that I don't think he even got on to the short list.

By far and away the strongest candidate for the new office, indeed the People's Choice, was, in the early spring, Lord Rothermere's editor of the *Sunday Dispatch*, Mr Charles Eade [who serialised the novel *Forever Amber*]. If the new post had been filled in the spring then I think the choice must have fallen unanimously on him. But since then Lord Rothermere has gone into business with the *News of the World*, has acquired the *Daily Graphic* from Lord Kemsley and has changed its name to the *Daily Sketch*.

It's a sort of 'ringer' like Francascal [a notorious racing substitution of the time]. It is now a paper which wallows in crime to a degree which is fast becoming the envy and despair of other purveyors of sensation. Even the most experienced pornographers are alarmed.

A month later, in another speech, he returned to Lord Kemsley's sale of The Daily Graphic:

Lord Kemsley, lacking the ability to make the *Daily Graphic* saleable without crime, sex and other vulgarities and being too honourable to take the easy way out, found that he could no longer maintain this paper, with its dwindling circulation and advertising revenue. Eight editors in nearly as many years had failed to achieve even a fifth of the sale of its rival the *Daily Mirror*, and so poor Lord Kemsley had to sell this paper, which was the only daily London mouthpiece for his not very original views, to Lord Rothermere, who does not suffer from the same honourable inhibitions.

He deeply regretted the disappearance of Lord Kemsley, in August, 1959: he felt cheated of one of his favourite victims – and perhaps that disappearance had more to do with Randolph himself than Randolph realised. But when he came to know his successor, Roy Thomson, Randolph the cynic had a great, a lasting, and a delightful shock. Here at last was a newspaper proprietor who had nothing to hide – 'I think,' he said in 1964, 'that he is one of the most honest men I have ever met.'

But all that comes later.

XII

In the early 1950s The Sunday Times was engaged in two actions which in their different ways made legal history.

The first, in June, 1951, clarified the legal position on the ownership of pen-names, and it has remained the leading case on the point ever since.

The action arose when Mrs Muriel Forbes, who had been woman's editor, sued because The Sunday Times had continued, after she had left the paper, to publish articles under a pen-name that she had used. The name in question was 'Mary Delane' and it had been personally selected by Lord Kemsley. The argument was simply about who owned the name. It had been chosen when Mrs Forbes first joined The Sunday Times in 1946, and she had used it until she left at the end of 1950.

The judge, Mr Justice Wynn-Parry, decided that it all depended on what agreement was made between Mrs Forbes and The Sunday Times. The paper agreed that nothing had been specifically agreed about the ownership of the name but argued that it was to be implied into the contract with her that the name was to belong to The Sunday Times.

The judge ruled against The Sunday Times and said that there was no ground on which it could be said that when Mrs Forbes left its employment she had to leave her pen-name behind. The judge ruled that she was entitled to use the name 'Mary Delane' in the future and granted an injunction against The Sunday Times from publishing any article which was not written by her as being 'by Mary Delane'. He also ordered an inquiry as to damages.

Since then, newspapers who wish to retain the rights to a pen-name, even when the original user of the name leaves the staff, have written an express term covering the point into their contract.

In the other case, in April, 1954, The Sunday Times was involved in one of the oddest libel actions of all time. It was unique in that the words complained of were in an apology which The Sunday Times had published. The plaintiff was Miss Honor Tracy, the novelist, who lived in Ireland and had been engaged by the paper to write a series of regular articles.

In 1950 she had written a piece called 'Great Days in the Village' which related how the inhabitants of a small village in Ireland were agog about a fine new house which had been built for the local priest. Although the priest was not mentioned by name, he instituted a libel action against The Sunday Times in the High Court in Dublin, and The Sunday Times, having taken the advice of Irish lawyers, decided to arrange a settlement with the priest. They paid £750 to the St Vincent de Paul society and published an apology for Miss Tracy's article in the paper.

Miss Tracy, however, was not a party to the settlement and did not agree to the publication of the apology, and she then instituted a libel action against The Sunday Times in England. Her claim was that the terms of the apology were such as to suggest that she was a reckless and irresponsible journalist. In short, the English litigation was really one libel action inside another, because the result of the English action depended very much on whether the

English jury thought Miss Tracy's original article was a libel on the priest.

Whatever view the jury formed about this, they certainly decided that the apology of The Sunday Times for her own article had libelled her and they awarded her £2,500 damages, plus a further £500 for a letter written on behalf of The Sunday Times in the course of settling the Irish action. She was also awarded costs.

The case has proved an historic one in the law of libel and has meant that newspapers now, as a matter of course, get the express agreement of any journalist concerned before they publish any correction, apology or disclaimer about anything he has written. If they do not they are in danger of what libel lawyers now always refer to as 'doing an Honor Tracy'.

XIII

The year was 1956, the year of Suez, up to which event David Astor had had eight years of uninterrupted success as editor of The Observer, no longer the 'sleepy old Observer' of the late nineteenth century. Now, in the summer of 1956, he was breathing right down the neck of The Sunday Times and Lord K was becoming increasingly irritated.

His paper was much better than it had been under Hadley, but somehow it still wasn't quite right, hard as Hodson and everyone else had tried to improve it in every hole and corner. Perhaps that was part of the trouble; too much nagging attention to detail and no full-time reporting staff to gather or analyse news, too much worrying at the conference about whether V. Sackville-West, The Observer's gardening correspondent, was or was not superior to The Sunday Times contributor, too many little exhibitions (and big inhibitions) of one kind or another, too much diversionary energy on tiny circulation-raising gimmicks, such as the broadsheets on a variety of arts subjects, designed to be reprinted as they stood from the paper and sold at half-a-crown, though one of them, Edwin Smith and Olive Cook's 'The English House' went over the 100,000 mark. All the really creative work on any paper is always done by a very few people, however large the staff, and here the staff was absurdly small: if these superior talents spread themselves too thinly and spend too much effort on the accidence, not the essence, things go wrong. There was painstaking effort but no real strength, nothing exceptional in political authority, such as William Rees-Mogg introduced later, nothing to compare with the fresh assessments of things such as were attracting the post-war young to The Observer. If it hadn't been for the serials, which had sometimes chalked up an extra 20,000 or even 50,000 copies a week when they had been most needed, The Observer would have been level or even ahead by now.

So Lord Kemsley was worried. It was perfectly understood in Gray's Inn Road that he would feel personally disgraced if his paper had to take second place to the inspired amateurs of Tudor Street. There were stricken faces at the conference, rather as if, should the worst happen, the dishonoured editor-in-chief might elect to fall on his sword one Tuesday morning before his assembled vassals.

It was a bitter drink to set before Lord Kemsley. He and his brother had eclipsed The Observer before the war and seen it withering away during it. Now, unbelievably, it had bounced back. The son of the Astor who had ejected the great Garvin after his more than thirty years in the chair had taken it up and regenerated it.

Lord K had had mixed feelings about the disappearance of Garvin in 1942. True, the Great Editor was running the paper down, thereby making life easier for The Sunday Times, but then he was a monument of Fleet Street and a national institution, and Kemsley had a natural veneration for national institutions. He had heard rumours in 1942 of a bitter dispute between the second Viscount Astor and his editor, and it was said that Astor wanted to appoint a joint-editor: he would put up no longer with Garvin's habit of editing the paper by telephone from his home at Beaconsfield. The connected story seems to run like this.

Contrary to common belief, Garvin was odd man out in the Cliveden set and cordially disliked Geoffrey Dawson. When the war came, and his closest friend in the group, Lord Lothian, died, Garvin felt isolated and embarrassed by Cliveden's dislike of Churchill and Beaverbrook: the antipathy between Churchill and Nancy Astor had long been notorious. Breaking-point came early in February, 1942, with the Cliveden set believing that the Prime Minister should give up being his own Minister of Defence and that Beaverbrook, who had just resigned as Minister of Supply, should not be allowed to return to political office. Lord Astor wrote an anti-Churchill letter to The Times, but his views had the whole-hearted disapproval of Garvin, who opposed them

J. L. Garvin   LOW

in the paper on the following Sunday. Understandably furious, Astor claimed that an agreement about the direction of The Observer's policy had been broken by Garvin, and referred the difference to a small tribunal which existed to give a ruling in such disputes. Its uncompromising verdict was that Garvin must go. He left immediately, accompanied by his daughter Viola, the literary editor. 'They wanted to change the thing (The Observer) into The Cliveden Gazette,' he told his stepson Oliver Woods, of The Times, when he, Garvin, had gone straight to Beaverbrook's Sunday Express. 'Cliveden wanted the thing to be its own . . . and wanted me ceasing to be editor, to write under the direction of the committee. It was a horrible fight . . . when one thought of the paper one had created out of nothing and the over 30 years' devotion of a man's whole being one had given to it.'

All the same, 'The Chief', as Garvin had always been known in The Observer office, was in his late seventies and only a shadow of the figure he had been before and during the first world war. Said that irascible judge of men, Sir Alexander Cadogan, who was in charge of the Foreign Office when he met Garvin and Lothian at Lady Astor's in February, 1938, 'Garvin talks as he writes – very emphatic bilge'. As a boy David Astor had been fascinated by this legendary character because he had such a 'terrific opinion of himself', and with the passing of the years Garvin had indeed become almost a caricature of the Great Editor. He was deeply read, widely cultivated, a mill-race of intellectual energy, and he had the gift (like Lord Kemsley) of inspiring those who worked for him; but for years he had been concentrating all his energies on 'the article', his message to the nation, which would be rushed to The Observer office by Rolls and train on Saturday afternoon, it having absorbed his attention all the week. Somebody who was near to him says that he was unconsciously jealous of other contributors to The Observer; in his eyes the paper should be bought for 'the article' alone. He was above being interested in such developments as news on the front page – unless, that is, his own article could somehow be accommodated there.

In his overwhelming portrayal of the last of the great writing editors, alternating between quoting Wordsworth at you and knocking you out with accounts of his earlier political intimacies, he seems to some journalists of today a faintly repugnant figure. He may have been, as Lord Francis-Williams said, the founder of serious Sunday journalism, but they prefer the Christiansens or the Harold Evanses; not the dominating writing editor loftily removed from the daily struggle, but someone who knows every technical trick and can make up the front page if the occasion demands it. It is true that Garvin thought himself an all-round professional, but judging from the appearance and the headings (which he wrote himself) of 'the article' he was living in the street of illusion.

He had many qualities, but David Astor says that he went on too long, and Mr Astor should know. For it was he who rescued The Observer (after a short caretaker editorship by Ivor Brown) from what could easily have been extinction if Garvin had persisted in continuing, and in doing this Mr Astor himself became one of the notable editors of our day.

Gray's Inn Road was gloomily suspecting this unwelcome truth, and statistical proof at least came in September, 1956, when for that month The Observer passed The Sunday Times by about a thousand copies – the figure for The Sunday Times was 624,557. It is commonly believed even today around 200 Gray's Inn Road, among old hands on the fringe of things, that the disaster was successfully kept hidden from Lord Kemsley, and that the circulation losses The Observer suffered by opposing Suez righted the situation without his ever having been aware of it. But it is not true.

When he was informed that The Observer almost certainly had its nose ahead he called a special conference on a Monday afternoon to mark his displeasure. Departmental heads who would normally have been enjoying a holiday on that day were warned of the unprecedented event by his secretary on the Sunday evening.

It opened as a very icy conference, and The Sunday Times people (as distinct from the Kemsley clan and members of the entourage like Sir William Mabane) were annoyed to find that Ian Fleming, looking a little unctuous, had lined himself up stiffly with the editor-in-chief. Lord K and his sons appeared excessively grave,

> But hardly had he said a Word
> When Murmurs of Dissent were heard.

The iciness gave way to recriminatory warmth on both sides as it emerged that some of the executives felt that the paper had fallen behind because at its highest level the direction was faded at the edges: a criticism, of course, of Kemsley and not of Hodson, who was in the box along with the others. The frustrations of many years were touched upon, even down to such a homely subject as infant bed-wetting. Somebody had wanted to have it written about in the women's pages, but Lord K had trodden heavily on such an unwholesome idea. . . .

It was an historic conference. It shook Lord Kemsley. Things were never so difficult after that. Everyone could give a rest now to those safe sociological series about prison reform and the new towns, which always seemed to be under discussion in some form or other, and assume greater daring and enterprise.

And then, about a month later, came Suez.

XIV

The Sunday Times had had information that Anthony Eden was to marry Clarissa Churchill, Sir Winston's niece; it was what Cyril Lakin used to call one of those real, old-fashioned, twin-screw, double-funnelled, copper-bottomed exclusives, rarely seen at this time in the paper because the pressure to find them ceased when Camrose withdrew. From its source Lord K himself knew perfectly that it was unchallengeable, but he nevertheless felt that he himself should check with Eden, putting the business on a kind of high political level, as if the inquiry came from the cabinet in Gray's Inn Road, where Ministers were always coming to lunch and having their photographs taken to be put on the walls, and was directed to the only slightly superior cabinet in Downing Street. But it all fell flat on its face. The story was denied, The Sunday Times politely spiked it, and Eden duly married the girl in August, 1952.

Nobody about the office who knew of the incident seemed much put out, except a few heretics who held that Eden should have shown more finesse in his denial and that Beaverbrook or Camrose wouldn't so easily have sacrificed such a big exclusive. (Camrose watched news extremely closely and had a Telegraph man come in at 5 a.m. daily to prepare for 9.30 a.m. a ten-page digest of it in all the morning papers, down to the smallest paragraph.)

This was before the Suez affair, which was another occasion when Eden is thought to have shown a certain lack of finesse. But not by Lord K, then or afterwards; for he was the great hawk himself on Suez, and when Pat Murphy, now promoted managing editor, went to see him on October 30, 1956, the day after Israel attacked Egypt, and hinted that the paper might take a mildly anti-Suez attitude, he had such a vial of wrath emptied over his head that he still paled days later when recounting it to Russell, who had been in the United States at the time.

The editor, H. V. Hodson, was in the United States too when the Israelis attacked; he had been travelling here and there, as the paper put it, 'studying the Presidential election'. From Washington for the crucial issue of November 4 he sent an article for the leader page called, truly, 'The Anglo–US Alliance will Survive', though no one knew that Eden and Macmillan had so trifled with the alliance as to make no formal or informal disclosures about the use of force to America, believing that Eisenhower and Dulles understood their intentions perfectly well and viewed them with secret satisfaction. Even to this day Macmillan remains ironically staggered by the US government's reaction.

To a minority on The Sunday Times staff it all seemed, even putting aside the moral issue, an exercise in madness, a giant impracticality, as it did to the British Embassy in Cairo, whose advice was never sought, who were kept utterly in the dark, and who at the time wrung their hands at the impossibility of getting rid of Nasser in this way. But those in the office who held such views were not those who sat on the political bench of the paper.

Yet for all this, the leading article on November 4 did not flinch from a sensible and realistic appreciation of the consequences of the great hazard:

If we have embarked on a gamble, the fervent prayer of millions all over the world must be that history will show that the gamble has come off. If it does, success will bring an entirely new possibility of peace to the Middle East; it will also be applauded in the United States, restore international confidence in Britain's sagacity and power, and go far to lift the prestige of the West from the moral palsy into which it had seemed to have fallen.

These are high stakes indeed, and it must be recognised that, if the present Anglo–French operations do not come within a measurable distance of achieving their aims in, say, the next fortnight, reactions will be equally profound. Not only the future of the present Government, but the character of the Western Alliance, the destiny of the Commonwealth, the flow of oil and the stability of the whole Middle East will be profoundly affected.

In these circumstances, criticism from the side-lines cannot be disguised as responsible action. The need is far more positive. As a nation we are in this together and a minimum of national unity is vital if we are to see the crisis through.

On the front page of this same Suez-dominated issue (20 pages), in which many of the usual features had to be pushed out, Antony Terry was reporting from Budapest on the Russian intervention in Hungary (a shameful story of 'peaceful co-existence' which Sir David Kelly, who had been British ambassador in Moscow and was around this time the paper's Kremlinologist, examined on the leader page), Henry Brandon from Washington on the reactions to Eden's proposal for an international police force for the Egyptian-nationalised Suez canal, Terence Lyons from Tel Aviv –

'Israel today has complete mastery of the Sinai Peninsula, an area five times that of Israel itself' – and, perhaps most poignant and pathetic of all, there was a report of Sir Anthony Eden's speech on television on the Saturday evening.

After referring, very disingenuously, to 'the forest fire we had to put out' the Prime Minister, looking so ravaged and ill, moved many a viewer when he touched on his personal burden – a lifelong man of peace in a situation like this.

On the Sunday of that talk's appearance in print the fiasco grew really frightening. In the morning, says Lord Butler,[1] the sitting Cabinet received a message, before our troops had even landed, that 'the victorious Israelis were about to cease fire'. The forest fire was out, then, and there was no justification for invasion. Faced with this proposition from R. A. Butler and Lord Salisbury, Anthony Eden said that he might have to give up unless he had united support, and retired upstairs to consider his position. 'When Eden returned,' says Butler, dead-pan, 'a message came through from the Israeli Foreign Minister, Mrs Meir, that there would be no cease fire.'

Eden's crack-up – called 'severe overstrain' by his doctor a week later – followed quickly, and by the 23rd he was flying to Jamaica for three weeks' rest. It was a convalescence which was arranged secretly and injudiciously by the Colonial Secretary, Alan Lennox-Boyd, now Viscount Boyd, but when the sanctuary for the invalid was announced a faint breath of glory struck the cheeks of The Sunday Times. Amazingly, to anyone who had been there, such as Hamilton or Renshaw, it was Ian Fleming's bungalow Goldeneye, at Oracabessa, on the north shore.

There were two further and separate fiascos here. First, the doctor had talked, as doctors will, about his patient Sir Anthony needing relaxation. 'It did,' says Lord Butler, 'sound the most extraordinarily remote suggestion in the middle of such unprecedented troubles'; and it caused Harold Macmillan to fly off the handle and tell the doctor that 'the Prime Minister could not possibly be withdrawn to that extent, leaving our troops in an uncertain predicament'.

Eden was withdrawn, though, and off he and his wife went to the other fiasco – Goldeneye.

Just after the war Fleming had paid £2,000 for the land, which was on the old donkey race-track at Oracabessa, and another

---

1. 'The Art of the Possible,' Hamish Hamilton, 1971.

£2,000 for the building of the white cottage itself. It was rather spartan and not very large, but he had talked romantically to his friends about it, and a myth had formed round it, and now here it was, the centre of the nation's interest and a retreat for Suez's walking wounded. 'Not the least difficult thing,' says the wondering Lord Butler, 'was that major decisions had to be checked with Anthony in Jamaica, and the only method of communication was by telegraph to the Governor, who then had to send a messenger on poor roads all the long distance to Ian Fleming's home.' John Pearson fills in the details:

> As he sat at his large desk in his large office behind Westminster Abbey making his discreet preparations, the Colonial Secretary overlooked only one small fact. It was that neither he nor the Edens nor the Governor of Jamaica, Sir Hugh Foot, had ever been to Goldeneye. He knew nothing about the iron bedsteads or the cold water in the shower or the absence of a bathroom or the bush rats in the roof or Violet the cook's curried goat or the fact that the nearest telephone was nearly a mile up the road. Graham Greene could have told him, or Noël Coward, or even Truman Capote. But the Colonial Secretary never asked them. Instead he asked Ian Fleming, and consequently the reality of Goldeneye eluded him.

XV

If Suez was a watershed in our national history it was also the event which determined the struggle for circulation between The Sunday Times and The Observer. It was a struggle, be it said, in which neither side sacrificed quality nor trimmed its views in order to sell more copies.

The Sunday Times was sincerely pro-Suez, The Observer was sincerely anti-Suez, along with The Guardian (still The Manchester Guardian then). In its opinion columns The Observer dealt so severely with the Prime Minister that one was reminded at the time of that prince of pamphleteers, John Wilkes.

If it doesn't sound so devastating now, that must be because there is more robust talk in British newspapers today. The leading article began like this:

EDEN

We wish to make an apology. Five weeks ago we remarked that, although we knew our Government would not make a military attack in

defiance of its solemn international obligations, people abroad might
think otherwise. The events of the last week have proved us completely
wrong; if we misled anyone, at home or abroad, we apologise un-
reservedly. We had not realised that our Government was capable of
such folly and such crookedness.

Whatever the Government now does, it cannot undo its air attacks on
Egypt, made after Egypt had been invaded by Israel. It cannot undo the
deliberate employment of haste so that our nearest allies had no opportunity to express disagreement. It can never live down the dishonest
nature of its ultimatum, so framed that it was certain to be rejected by
Egypt.

Never since 1783 has Great Britain made herself so universally disliked. That was the year in which the Government of Lord North, faced
with the antagonism of almost the whole civilised world, was compelled
to recognise the independence of the American Colonies. Sir Anthony
Eden has the unenviable distinction of leading the first Administration
since the days of George III to reach such an isolated moral position.
His eighteenth-century predecessors succeeded in losing us an empire,
Sir Anthony and his colleagues have already succeeded in losing us in-
calculable political assets.

So long as his Government represents this country, we cannot expect to
have a good standing in the councils of the nations. It has attempted to
prove those councils futile by rendering them futile. This it has done by,
first frustrating the Security Council of the United Nations through
the use of the veto, and then by defying an overwhelming vote in the
General Assembly. The Eden Government has become internationally
discredited.

In an adjoining unsigned editorial article there was reference to
a subject mysteriously absent from The Sunday Times: 'Only
historians with access to the files of diplomatic secrets will be able
to prove conclusively whether or not there was collusion between
Britain, France, and Israel in the attack on Egypt . . .' On this
same page there was another telling article and a full column of
letters of protest, with one from the Bishop of Chichester, who
insisted on the moral issue, at its head. The total attack was as
well-marshalled as it was destructive. It was what old Barnes of
The Times would have called firing ten-pounders.

But The Observer lost readers immediately, probably 30,000
or so in a week, just as The Guardian lost 30,000 or 40,000 in a few
days (the editor of The Guardian has said so on television at any
rate, but Mr Cecil King seems to think that that paper had a rise
in circulation because of Suez). The reason could be that many
people, while disapproving in their hearts of what Eden had done,

were incensed with the objectors for not accepting, as The Sunday Times had put it, that 'as a nation we are in this together'.

These were honourable wounds for The Observer, incurred in a controversy of the highest importance. Yet as a result of them it dropped away behind The Sunday Times in circulation.

Somebody who was of importance in The Observer office at the time, Hugh Massingham, made this comment just before his death: 'It was a traumatic experience for David Astor. Before he became editor, when Ivor Brown was in the chair, he had organised the paper's foreign news with great success. He took over and had a dazzling period when everything went right for him. Then came Suez, with its loss of circulation, and it sapped his confidence.'

(That may be true or it may be exaggerated, but it is certain that Astor had regained his confidence sufficiently within a few years to recognise that The Observer might go out of business altogether if it didn't follow The Sunday Times and start a colour magazine.)

Anyway, Lord K and his staff faced the new year of 1957 with restored confidence. He understood now that his paper must be liberalised to some degree, and Hodson and the rest went to work with zest. The serialisation of Peter Fleming's book 'Invasion 1940' had already been a success and put on some thousands of copies.

A year later, Hamilton, who was still overlord of the serial policy, the development of which will be described later on, revealed to the conference that he had something big cooking – the memoirs of Field-Marshal Lord Montgomery. He had organised the deal single-handed and in secrecy, not even telling Lord Kemsley of the financial terms, and now he disclosed that it would be ready for publication in the autumn. The conference was discussing the best way of presenting it when there was a spontaneous combustion of ideas in which three or four people, without premeditation, found themselves suggesting a magazine section. Nowadays, when it is a commonplace, it seems a very simple idea, but it was revolutionary then. For with the inauguration of its magazine section in September, 1958, The Sunday Times became the first national newspaper in the history of British journalism to be published regularly in sectional form. This departure, says a publicity handout, with the usual lack of modesty –

was instantly acclaimed by readers, and its merits have since been confirmed by imitation. The magazine section is designed to be easily re-moved from the rest of the paper, conveniently handled, and kept for leisure reading. It contains serialisations of books of outstanding interest, series on important contemporary topics specially written for the *Sunday Times*, reviews of new books, criticism of the arts, the woman's page, and Mainly for Children. 'Like most inspired ideas,' wrote one of the many readers to applaud the innovation, 'it triumphs by virtue of its very simplicity.'

At the conference that Tuesday nobody bothered to go into the problem of 'back-setting' (see page 235), but in the end it was Withy Grove which got it right before London, where the paper was still being printed on The Daily Telegraph presses. It was called the magazine section until the colour magazine was started, and then, because confusion was arising with advertisement bookings, blocks, etc, it was renamed the Weekly Review.

XVI

The magazine section began as a pull-out on September 28, 1958, and the following week it launched Montgomery's memoirs, which ran for fourteen weeks. It was unprecedented in both length and span – the serials usually ran for three or four weeks, with a maximum of seven or eight for such successes as 'The Traitors', by Alan Moorehead, which began his long connection with the paper, or 'Invasion 1940'.

Montgomery put on 100,000 new readers, and all but a tiny fraction of them became permanent ones. It is the greatest serial success the paper has ever had, with the exception of William Manchester's 'Death of a President' in 1967.

From the early 1950s onwards The Sunday Times has never lost a serial it desperately wanted with the exception of Svetlana's 'Letters to a Friend', which became an immensely confused inter-national deal and went in the end to The Observer, where it was rumoured to have been a great circulation disappointment con-sidering the money paid for it – maybe £100,000.

Victor Louis, a Russian who combines acting as a correspondent in Moscow for various Western papers with being a literary agent for the Soviet, came along to The Sunday Times well before The Observer began publication, peddling a rival translation of the book and hoping that The Sunday Times would queer its rival's pitch by publishing in advance. Like Nebuchadnezzar, the Russians in their rage at Stalin's daughter seemed to want to be revenged on the whole earth. To get rid of him he was told that a legal point called 'confidence' was involved – there was no copyright impediment as the translation he was offering had been done by one of his own people and the manuscript was in Russian. Obstinate and suspicious, he regarded 'confidence' as a legal fiction until he was correctly told that the Prince Consort had once brought an action under it. He was then convinced and even mildly impressed. (He was concerned later in the hawking around of a synopsis of the Philby memoirs, but dropped out when Philby himself took over negotiations and asked The Sunday Times to send an executive to Moscow from London: the paper decided not to publish his memoirs.)

Otherwise the big books came, and continue to come, to The Sunday Times first. In twenty years it has serialised a remarkable library, from books of the highest literary quality, such as Lord David Cecil's 'Lord M' or James Pope-Hennessy's 'Life of Queen Mary', to the simple document such as that of the brave prisoner-of-war, Anthony Deane-Drummond, who spent thirteen days in a cupboard and described his ordeal in 'Return Ticket'.

The big successes, and here one is speaking of circulation successes and not necessarily of literary merit, were expensively promoted; and in case it is thought by anyone that the big battalions of The Sunday Times spent a lot of money on promotion and The Observer very little, it should be emphasised that in this, as in all things, The Observer gave not an inch.

Organised by the master hand of Eric Cheadle, who was assisted, as usual, by his trusted Jim Lee, John Rodger, and the late Bob Simpson, then circulation manager, the promotion for Montgomery was appropriately run with the thoroughness of a military campaign. It is fashionable now to put the money into TV advertising; then it was a direct mail shot to 8th Army men, luncheons for newsagents with a 'Monty menu', a reprint of the first instalment as an advertisement in all Kemsley papers, posters, press advertising (though not in The Daily Express, who wouldn't take advertising for it) – Monty himself entered into the thing with gusto and addressed newsagents at a party at one of the big London hotels, bringing it off superbly with his usual incisiveness and humour. Many of them got a toby jug with his head on it.

In the paper itself he was called F-M Viscount Montgomery, but Cheadle plumped for Monty, and to get round this difference of opinion with Hamilton he told John Rodger to have two sets of posters printed, a formal one for areas where they were likely to be seen by Hamilton and Montgomery and another, much more widely distributed, where the hoardings shouted that 'Monty tells all'.

This whole promotion cost more than £100,000: a commonplace now but unique then. It was a great bargain. In those days newspapers thought themselves exceedingly lucky to get new readers at a pound a head. Here The Sunday Times got a fantastic 100,000 for £100,000, apart from the purchase of the memoirs themselves.

XVII

Newsprint was unrestricted now and The Sunday Times was rushing ahead.

From The Sunday Graphic came James Dow, a beloved figure on the paper for a dozen years – 'the general favourite as the general friend' – and latterly one of the managing editors. He was promoted to the new post of assistant editor (production), and his skill in headline writing and easy adaptation to the paper's requirements of the techniques he had learned in popular journalism brought great benefits. His deputy was Oscar Turnill, a most unusual combination of the 'hard news' and the literary journalist: one who can with equal ease lend a hand in the sub-editors' room, look after the front page of the Weekly Review, or deputise as TV critic. He was a promotion from Lord K's Newcastle Evening Chronicle. Pat Murphy liked him because he had played rugger at school and Hodson because he had done Latin. He was in, no matter if these weren't terribly relevant reasons, any more than it was relevant of The Financial Times to have offered William Rees-Mogg a job when they heard that there was an undergraduate at Oxford who read that paper in bed over breakfast every morning.

These new faces, and a few others, were encouraged generally by H. V. Hodson and specifically by Pat Murphy, who was opening up the news side of the expanding paper with marked effect. One of his most useful lieutenants was H. J. Deverson, the picture editor, who had been on Picture Post; he soon put an end to front-page photographs of the Heywood type – 'Sweeping up autumn leaves in Blackburn's Corporation park'. Indeed the gentle Dev achieved many changes of importance, aided by his bright-eyed researcher Gabby Karminski, wife of Otto Karminski, the photographer, and Cliff Parker and Derek Alder – Derek still does a lot of drawing for the paper.

Robert Harling continued as typographical adviser, and for ten years and more had been improving the look of features and news; but he wasn't available at all times throughout the week as his main job was with a leading advertising agency. Deverson began as the picture editor; but gradually this and that department began to take him whole pages to design, and he showed himself a good typographer and designer, if without Harling's purer taste and scholarship. In a few months the whole impact of the paper changed; pictures were bigger, type displays bolder, the total effect more sophisticated.

At this point Harling came up with a slogan: 'I remember saying at one of those lunches that K gave in the board-room that the then ST slogan, claiming to be the greatest something or other, was too brash: we ought to be more assured, and I suggested the more modestly arrogant, 'One of the world's great newspapers.' He made a note on that appalling little notebook he kept by his cheese-knife. That seemed to be that. Within three weeks I was astonished – though I shouldn't have been surprised, knowing his tenacity – to see the new slogan on all the ST vans.'

With typographical display generally Lord Kemsley was much less authoritarian than Lord Camrose, but even so he had certain old-fashioned reticences and still occasionally hankered after a statuesque seven-column page for the news pages. To the astonishment of the old hands Dev's innovations went unprotested on the third floor; though at the same time they were innocent innovations, for Deverson didn't know the form and wasn't aware that he was doing anything out of the ordinary. But Murphy knew and was there to protect him if tantrums occurred.

That they didn't must be ascribed to Kemsley's resilience; the patriarch had learned a lot from his scare about The Observer – which remarked darkly that he was going all out for quick expansion. In Gray's Inn Road there was faint surprise at the statement; odd that the eclipsed rival should so openly reveal its unhappiness. But perhaps it was not so odd. Perhaps, remembering what was to happen in 1959, David Astor knew something after all.

Several considerations may have been ghosting about in Lord K's mind. First, the Kemsley family and their friends only just

A. T. P. Murphy by Maurice Wiggin.

controlled the company with thirty-five per cent of the shares, and this was a time when stealthy take-over bids were fashionable; secondly, now that newsprint was unrestricted and advertising more buoyant, this might be the most favourable time to take the cash and have done for ever with the trials of owning newspapers, particularly the never-ending troubles with the trade unions; and, thirdly, the value of the group apart from The Sunday Times might seriously waste away, even if the chief loss-making properties were being shut down.

Denis Hamilton suspected nothing so devastating as the sale of the group. Now as always he wanted still more sales for The Sunday Times with still higher quality. Here is a memorandum he circulated in 1958 implying that too much reliance was being placed on out-of-date methods of conducting the now rocketing Sunday Times:

> In my view an extra senior man would be an asset to the paper, if one who would fit in could be found immediately. Both the editor and Mr Murphy have been under severe strain this summer and Mr Hodson has not had an adequate holiday. Any emergency affecting either of them in the coming year for any length of time would be serious for the paper, and an even greater burden would be placed on the other.
>
> Part of the trouble is that *too* much detailed control is invested in Mr Hodson and Mr Murphy. They hardly seem to have time to delegate. The traffic in and out of their rooms is never ending, and I would suggest they are accessible too easily to all on matters of pure routine. Now their command is growing they must reorganise themselves.
>
> Could the paper not be more split up, with precise 'departments' under the Assistant Editors? It would have the additional merit of improving their long-term efficiency by giving them more responsibility now.
>
> If we cannot get a third man then attention should be switched to giving more responsibility to Messrs James Dow, Godfrey Smith, J. W. Lambert and John Gay Davies, who are all excellent people but who should be given more scope, and perhaps a clearer idea of their function.
>
> Mr Hodson and Mr Murphy would then be freed of much detail and could plan ahead a little bit more than they can do now.
>
> I suggest that Mr Russell is given complete charge of all administration and presentation of major features, and that Mr Lambert is given the week-to-week responsibility for the book pages, under Mr Russell's long-term direction. These major features are a vital part of the campaign to increase the *Sunday Times* sale, and demand one person concentrating on them. Responsibility is too diffused now.

Though he wasn't aware of it, Hamilton was foreshadowing his own style of editorship: sweeping delegation to departmental heads, with the commander-in-chief giving his attention to more important things than the nuts and bolts.

XVIII

The Sunday papers have always run serials, including fiction: apart from Harrison Ainsworth's 'Old St. Paul's' and Lady Blessington, there is reproduced on page 41 of this book a handbill of 1843 announcing the 'exclusive serialisation' in The Sunday Times of James Sheridan Knowles's novel 'Fortescue'. After the end of the second world war there had begun a confused and haphazard bidding for likely-looking books. Nobody quite knew what they wanted or how much to pay.

Of the general disorder and the attempts by literary agents to form a pecking order and some kind of price-list Hamilton was a close observer. In 1949 he nearly entered the big time himself by trying to buy the serial rights in one of the best of all the war-adventure stories, Eric Williams's 'The Wooden Horse', for The Sunday Graphic. But Lord K wasn't enthusiastic (it must have been the price), unlike Russell, who got Sir John Slessor to write about it for The Sunday Times. The reception of this piece – it was only a long leader page article – made Hamilton and Russell raise their eyebrows. It was so much talked about that Hamilton went looking for other adventure serials, which were given about the same space in The Sunday Times – say a thousand words an instalment – as had been devoted before the war to extracts from books like John Buchan's 'Cromwell'. Hamilton began to argue that if you were paying as much as £5,000 for a book you must get your money's worth, and when in the face of a lot of competition he acquired Moorehead's 'The Traitors', about the atomic spies Fuchs, Pontecorvo and Nunn May, the paper gave a full page each to seven instalments – in a six- or eight-page paper. The policy of the big read was evolving, despite the objections of most people at the conference, who clamoured for more news in the paper, even if it wasn't used very successfully when extra space was found for it.

Hamilton, however, gradually got his way, and he let it be known to agents and authors that the paper wanted the best and was prepared to pay for it, even if it meant financially underwriting some particular book several years before it was published, as happened with James Pope-Hennessy's official biography of Queen Mary.

Hamilton summarised it all to Phillip Knightley in 1972:

When newsprint became unrestricted the industrial expansion at the time resulted in a great increase in advertising. TV advertising was not yet a competitor. It may be Hard Times now but it was Great Expectations then. The massive increase in advertising meant that we had more editorial space. How were we to play the newspaper? How were we to use the extra space?

As the paper had certain weaknesses on the news side I felt the best thing we could do, until we got them right, was to develop our features aggressively. I was therefore strongly for developing the magazine section. The hierarchy hankered after more news, and I lost the first round. I came back six months later with strong backing from Ian Fleming and Leonard Russell: with Leonard I had formed a partnership dating back a long time. For more than thirty years he has done the serial versions of nearly every book – certainly every important book – we have ever published, even down to writing the headings. He has a genius for it.

It was a very rich period when in effect we launched the Review front with Monty. We captured and dominated the serial market, and the paper shot away in circulation from its competitors. It was nothing then for serials to run seven or eight weeks. Monty ran for fourteen. We became famous – some would say notorious – for our war serials, but there was no particular policy about that. Things like Deane-Drummond's 'Return Ticket' we used because they were thrilling adventure stories. Monty, Bill Slim, Alanbrooke, Alex and so on were another matter – they were contributions to contemporary history.

It is no secret that Monty put on something like 100,000 copies. I initiated the whole thing before he had put pen to paper. I studied the tax laws relating to memoirs, considering the problems of people who were not authors by profession – I wanted to find some way of alleviating the tax that a large payment would attract. Monty, for example, gets an annual amount for the rest of his life, and since he is still going strong he has done very well out of it. In fact, the total sum involved was so large that I did the deal with him without telling anyone in the office. I was that scared! If I had said 'Look, this is what I have got to pay Monty for his story', they would not have allowed me to do it. Once it was a success it was all right.

At first, after the war, there was no real planning among editors for serials. Most of them would say at the beginning of the week, 'What can we have in the paper this Sunday?', and then they would ring a few agents and publishers to see what was going. I believed that we should cultivate authors, agents and publishers. By understanding the tax laws I was able to offer authors a way – I mean the setting up of trusts etc – of easing their financial burden.

Alexander of Tunis – you know, Alex – had never thought about writing anything. I went to see him in 1960. The *Sunday Telegraph* was coming along, and I needed a programme for the coming year: I suggested that the *Sunday Telegraph* would try to buy everything in sight, and it was so. We sat on the patio of his house at Windsor. I made him an attractive proposal. He said, 'My God, I'll be able to get a first-class motor-mower and a boy to come in for a couple of days a week to help me with the garden.' I found it touching – he was not a rich man. A great commander deserved a bit of luck.

Leonard, too, had his own connections with publishers and agents, and they were very valuable. Ian Fleming had one great serial *coup*. He went to his friend Somerset Maugham and got a series on the ten best novels in the world. We bought it blind – I remember Ian saying that he had told Maugham that we would publish anything he sent, absolutely without alteration, unless it happened to offend Lord K by embodying lengthy extracts from *Fanny Hill*. In the middle of our serialisation Maugham was made a CH, and that helped too. It ran, believe it or not, for fifteen weeks – one more even than Monty. For the first time in the history of the paper the back-dates department ran out of copies even when the serial was still on. The point is, though, that all this was back in 1954, and we gave two pages to it in a paper of only fourteen pages. That is what we meant by the big read.

But our biggest success of all was with William Manchester's *Death of a President*, which I bought when I was editor of the paper and we used just before we joined up with *The Times*. The serial rights were owned by the magazine *Look*, whose top brass I had cultivated for years, and a copy of the manuscript was brought over by an emissary. Leonard had to go along to the Dorchester, or perhaps it was the Hilton, and read it in a locked room. He came back and said to me, 'It's going to be a landslide'. I was electrified – he was usually pessimistic.

There was a great deal of competition, but we got it in the end. I'm not sure of the exact figure it put on, but it must have been something like 150,000 a week. It was a bigger bargain even than Monty.

By now the reminiscences of Presidents and Prime Ministers have become big business; great sums are involved, particularly in the United States. Mr Roy Jenkins,[1] talking of what he calls 'a great new wave of political memoirs', thinks that nowadays on both sides of the Atlantic 'the desire to describe and justify appears to have grown enormously, independently of any question of financial need or incentive'. He may be right, but one doesn't

---

1. The Times, September 11, 1971.

have to be a cynic to believe that a former President or Prime Minister, however disinterested or wealthy, could be mightily stimulated to describing and justifying by the knowledge that he and his family could be raking in say $1,000,000 or a fortune in sterling for all rights in his work. In Britain the big money for serials notably began to flow with Anthony Eden's memoirs – Churchill was *sui generis* and Lloyd George, before the war, not all that expensive. One day in 1959 Brendan Bracken rang up Lord Kemsley: on behalf of Eden he offered The Sunday Times all rights in the Eden memoirs, the first volume of which was nearly finished, for £100,000. Kemsley, alarmed at the price, said 'no' very decisively, against the advice of Hamilton, but The Times had no such scruples and paid up. They repented of their bargain when they found that the work proved too discreet (in the appropriate volume Eden was evasive – like Macmillan in turn – about Suez) to make any notable impact on their circulation and tried to sell the last of the three volumes to The Sunday Times. There was no deal, however – Eden insisted that it had been bought by The Times and must appear there.

Nobody should imagine that large sums are uniformly paid by the Sunday papers for serials: the higher prices asked by literary agents or publishers are arrived at in the comfortable knowledge that for some particular book the newspapers or magazines will be in fierce competition. The price for a quite average serial in The Sunday Times, say in three parts, is something over £1,000, and it can go lower than that, depending on stock in hand, an over-run budget, or the hunch that some particular book may not in the end work out as a serial and that it would be safer to make only a modest investment in it. The Sunday Times magazine has a standard rate for other than exceptional serials – £50 a thousand words. But here the pictures are important, and it usually researches its own.

It was a very rich period, said Hamilton, referring to the Montgomery serialisation and its aftermath. Some of the serials and special series of that time still float happily in the memory.

In 1959 there were Christopher Sykes's 'Orde Wingate' and Sir Arthur Bryant's 'Triumph in the West', the completion of the war diaries of Field-Marshal Lord Alanbrooke, begun with 'The Turn of the Tide'. These diaries were of great importance to the paper, and Bryant's insistence on 'balance' in the serial version and Russell's on every last detail of the more sensational quarrels and criticisms led to some indignant telephone calls between them and the shuttling of versions backwards and forwards across Hyde Park – Bryant, an old and valued contributor, lived in Rutland Gate, and he would walk across the park, with his beloved mongrel dog, Jimmy, to leave a proof at Albion Street on Russell, who in turn would walk across to Bryant, accompanied by *his* beloved dog, with provocative emendations. But it all worked out in the end, and the diaries were a notable circulation-raiser.

The next year there were things as various as John Betjeman's long autobiographical poem, 'Summoned by Bells', Alan Moorehead's 'The White Nile', and Sir Ralph Richardson's 'It All Began with Growcott', a little classic of autobiography specially written for the paper. There followed (or maybe preceded, it doesn't matter) Augustus John's reminiscences of Dylan Thomas, another instalment of Lady Diana Cooper's memoirs, J. B. Priestley's 'Margin Released' and, among single articles which survive in the memory, Henry Moore on Epstein and Sir Isaiah Berlin's 'Philosophy's Goal'.

It could be expected that some of these eminent authors would have ideas of their own about the serial versions of their books. Russell remembers that they nearly all approached the idea nervously but were won over by the time the proof stage was reached. The only person he ever quarrelled with, through some misunderstanding, was Emlyn Williams, who did his own serial version of his wonderful autobiography, and wasn't happy when Russell didn't like it. Later on, Charles Chaplin, always the captain and the cat, threw away Russell's treatment of his autobiography and did his own, to the great satisfaction of everyone.

There is no standard technique of extracting a serial from a book. Some of the big American magazines are apt to try to reduce the original to a lilliputian version – a kind of shrunken head. The bare facts, they seem to say, are the important thing, and they rewrite the material, usually in words of one syllable, to cram them all in. The result of this is that any originality in the author's own handwriting inevitably disappears; for his own style there is substituted the characterless industry of some anonymous scribe. The Sunday Times rarely practises this method. It prefers to leave the author's words and characteristics of style as undisturbed as possible. At the same time, it has a prejudice against italicised explanatory paragraphs: it tries to keep these down to a minimum and frequently does without them entirely. Of course, enormous areas of the original work have to be sacrificed. But with sharp-eyed selection and skilful compression things can be done to please the newspaper reader without disgusting the author.

It is only very rarely that a complete 'rewrite' job is found necessary, usually because of some author's literary inexperience, but this is never undertaken without the permission of the author or his passing the proofs. Very occasionally an author, usually an eminent one, will try to make it a condition that some particular episode in his book does not appear in the serialisation, fearing the glare of newspaper publicity. This is never acceptable to The Sunday Times, and serials for it are bought on the traditional understanding that the paper has a free hand in its choice of material.

There was a time, as has been remarked, when the critics *were* The Sunday Times. At this later period it was the serials which kept the paper in front in the circulation-race. We now approach the years when all the elements of news and views and entertainment were properly integrated and The Sunday Times really became what it had claimed to be in its slogan of the 1930s – a newspaper, a magazine, a review.

> Ever since the first news was published of my negotiations to acquire control of the Kemsley group of newspapers I have emphasised my admiration for THE SUNDAY TIMES. For years I have followed its remarkable progress, achieved with an ever-increasing enhancement of the high standards which have made it truly, as its slogan says, "One of the World's Great Newspapers."

August 23, 1959

PART 4

The Thomson Takeover

1959–1961

PART 4

The Thomson Takeover

I

Roy Thomson from Toronto (not yet a British citizen), who now lived modestly in Edinburgh and was hauling in something like £1 million a year with his newly-formed Scottish Television Ltd, and continuing to watch every penny spent on his paper The Scotsman, was trying to organise a lunch with Lord Kemsley.

They had met once or twice, and Lord K was amused by him. But his deeply conservative instincts must have been shocked by the Canadian's disrespect for, or rather unawareness of, many of the things held sacred in the upper and middle layers of British life. Whether you were at the top on The Times or The Sunday Times, whether you were a social rebel like Northcliffe or a conformist like Kemsley, and whether your name was Geoffrey Dawson, Denis Hamilton, H. V. Hodson or Cyril Lakin, there were certain things you believed in and aspired to. You believed in the good public school and Oxford and Cambridge (at any rate for your sons if you hadn't been to either yourself), in the intellectual supremacy of All Souls, in the satisfaction to be found at the right London dinner-parties, in the certainty that a tiny area of London contained all the really civilised amenities of existence and that beyond London – though you might have been born elsewhere yourself – all was a social desert; you believed in a good club, a good tailor, a good shirtmaker; and if, miraculously, you made it in a really big way you would buy a grand house and a Rolls (and perhaps a butler) to go with it and enjoy days of unostentatious magnificence. You would hope to get a title one day but you never said a word to anyone about that. You aspired, in sum, to a traditional style of English life, and though your aspirations might be entirely unfulfilled the ideal was always before you.

Of this ideal Roy Thomson knew nothing – in which he resembled some of the young men from the north, the new wave, in Fleet Street today. He didn't necessarily scorn it, and he certainly didn't wish to dynamite it because he had strong conservative instincts himself. He just didn't know about it and to this day, probably, doesn't understand the attraction of any of its details, save that of getting a title – which, characteristically, he talked about all the time even when he was still in Edinburgh.

It wasn't that he was anti-social either. Indeed, he showed an inexhaustible appetite for parties and other social occasions. But in Edinburgh and for a long time afterwards there was no discrimination in his acceptances. If it wasn't Holyrood House it was a local police dance – all was one to him. He didn't drink or smoke, and the only thing he ever wanted to talk about was newspapers or business; no wonder, therefore, he attended social functions not for pleasure but out of a dogged conviction that it was good for business for the boss to be seen around. His happiest moments were in his home in Braid Avenue, Edinburgh, studying balance sheets, just as, when he came south, he settled into a £15,000 stockbroker-type house at Gerrards Cross, Buckinghamshire, and restricted his joyless social life to London.

He had no use for a Dropmore; at first, when he came to London, he shunned the Rollses left over from the Kemsley régime, travelling to and from Uxbridge by Underground – it was quicker, he said. He has a Rolls now – RHT 1; but when one sees him myopically entering it, from beneath a kind of metal marquee outside copper-tinted Thomson House, with his square expressionless face and his black hat shoved well back from his forehead, the splendour of the car seems to embody some marketing man's dream and to have little gratification for the barber's son from Toronto; and anyway he only takes it in the evening just down the road to King's Cross station – it's still quicker by Underground.

It wasn't that he was too old to change his ways when he came to Britain. He may have been just on sixty when he left behind his little Canadian newspapers and radio stations to become proprietor of The Scotsman, but in his outlook he was far from elderly, and physically he was vigorous. He was simply an original.

In Edinburgh and London everyone liked him, except snobs or fools, everyone was charmed by the warmth of his personality, yet everyone thought him crazy. In the beginning they couldn't understand just what pleasure anyone could get out of owning an ever-expanding group of tiny Canadian papers, The Moose Jaw Gazette and things like that, although it was true that The Scotsman made more sense. Then they thought him dangerously crazy because he began to urge everyone he met to come in with him and make a fortune out of commercial television in Scotland at a time when all the clever boys were certain, such were governmental restrictions and exactions, that independent television would be a financial disaster anywhere – the highly expensive advertising would never come in. Lord K could have had the prime London licence, but he backed out. Beaverbrook told Thomson that newspapermen should stick to newspapers. Not many people put money into Scottish Television Ltd; among them were two local music-hall comedians who fell for Thomson and ventured £1,000 each. It was a £400,000 company, with £240,000 lent by the National and Commercial Bank of Scotland. When the loan, in the form of debentures, had been quickly redeemed Thomson owned 32,000 out of the 40,000 £1 shares. The company went on the air in August, 1957. Within two years to the month its shares were so valuable that Thomson was able to take over Lord Kemsley's entire newspaper chain.

No wonder he made the famous, exultant remark, one of his innumerable verbal indiscretions, that it was 'just like having a licence to print your own money'. The Socialists and the Liberals and The Times who had fought independent television so hysterically, predicting a collapse of moral standards if BBC Television (which at that time used to show little films of breaking waves and potters' wheels in the middle of the evening) was allowed a rival, were outraged by the remark. Thomson was philosophical about the storm. He just didn't know that you didn't say that kind of thing, and in any case, as he explained in The Sunday Times office later on, back in Canada it was only a catch-phrase, like 'don't take any wooden nickels'.

Anyway Scotland was Thomson's kingdom now; and to get his commercial image right, and to surround Scottish Television Ltd and The Scotsman with the right atmosphere, he applied to the Lord Lyon King of Arms in Edinburgh for a Thomson tartan and a Thomson coat of arms. He also began to yearn for more territory, like some ancient Scottish chieftain, and he cast covetous eyes simultaneously on two newspaper properties – The Glasgow Herald, of which he was foiled, and The Press and Journal of Aberdeen, which was owned by Lord Kemsley.

The lunch with Kemsley which Thomson had angled for in the spring of 1959 came off in the boardroom at 200 Gray's Inn Road, the walls of which, as has been said, displayed a formidable gallery of photographs of politicians who had come to lunch in the last twenty years. The kitchen adjoined the boardroom, and the usual lugubrious waiter, whose face was seamed by his high responsibilities, was in attendance.

The food was not good, perhaps a shade better than the office canteen's, but Lord Kemsley always ate heartily. Over the clear soup he twinkled at his guest and said, knowing that Thomson, with his newspaper-collecting mania, could have nothing else on his mind: 'I know why you're here. You want my Aberdeen newspaper.'

'Is it for sale then, Gomer?'

Kemsley somehow didn't mind Thomson using his christian name, but normally you had to know him for a long time to get away with it. He found it difficult to call his visitor 'Roy'.

'All my papers are for sale.'

'Glad to hear it, Gomer.'

'Yes – at a price.'

'And what is the price of the Aberdeen Press, Gomer?'

'To you, as a favour, £2,500,000.'

Rich chuckles from Lord K at the joke. Thomson brought his thick spectacles, as he does when eating, to within a couple of inches of the soup plate.

'Jeez, Gomer, I thought we were talking seriously. That paper only earns £100,000 a year.'

'Perfectly true,' said Lord K, looking even more enormous than usual, enjoying himself hugely but entirely without malice as he looked down at Thomson. He loved doing newspaper deals, even if they were only imaginary ones. He loved to think that people might be saying 'And what's Kemsley up to now'. And he loved to dress like a Victorian Governor of the Bank of England, with his dominating nose, silver hair, black coat and striped trousers, symbolical stiff collar, black silk tie, pearl tie-pin: an impressive but anachronistic-looking figure whose voice occasionally had the suspicion of a Welsh intonation.

It has been fashionable lately to say that this or that public man hates himself; Lord K wouldn't have known what was meant – for thirty years his self-love had been as serene as it was deep. He was 76 now; his energy was prodigious, his health magnificent, his hearing good, and his sense of smell as keen as ever, especially when it came to sniffing-up the incense offered by his entourage. He had given up smoking cigarettes, but sometimes he would have a cigar after lunch (and with a curiously reluctant air for so generous a man sometimes throw another across to some executive who was known to be a cigar-smoker). Thomson didn't smoke, and he drank water. With his cigar Kemsley had a modest brandy.

All in all he made Thomson a little angry. Thomson knew he wasn't being baited, but all this fooling around was a waste of time. He twitched his neck slightly as if his collar was too tight – one of his little tics – and looked like a sick panda.

There was to be no mystical experience. Not yet.

But soon: the greatest ecstasy in the life of the world's most single-minded newspaper-collector (an ecstasy greater even than when he acquired The Times) occurred as the result of a telephone call from Lord Kemsley a couple of months later.

It was July 1, 1959. Kemsley wanted Thomson to come to London from Edinburgh immediately. Characteristically impatient, whether he was selling his newspaper empire or buying one of his black silk ties, he couldn't wait a moment. Thomson must catch the sleeper that same evening – it was something serious.

So Thomson bustled off to London accompanied by the managing director of The Scotsman and Scottish Television, James Coltart, who had formerly been in charge of a Beaverbrook newspaper in Glasgow: a man to whom he owes a great deal and one who in his wizardry with figures, his equable temper and his native shrewdness bears many temperamental resemblances to Thomson himself. They speculated endlessly on what Kemsley could have meant by 'serious', and they continued to speculate over breakfast at a lorry-drivers' café in Covent Garden, to which the thrifty Thomson led his astonished managing director. After all, they had booked in at the Savoy and breakfast there after the train journey would have been the natural thing, but it seemed that the good pull-up for carmen was one of Thomson's usual haunts in London, and he wouldn't be separated from it.

In the end all they decided was that Kemsley must want to sell something, and that by now he knew Thomson well enough to realise that there was nothing doing unless he talked realistically. But what? The Aberdeen paper?

Thomson had a hunch that it was a great deal more than that, and at half-past ten a.m. on the third floor of Kemsley House, in the panelled room which had a view over the wastes and back lots of Clerkenwell and was spotted in the foreground with a red rash of Royal Mail vans from Mount Pleasant, the room which had de Laszlo's portrait of Lady Kemsley above the mantelpiece and on the Chippendale desk a brass figure of a barefoot boy selling newspapers, a miniature version of a garden statue at Dropmore, he learned that he was right. It was everything, The Sunday Times included. For £6 a share: in effect £16 million.

Twitching away nervously with neck and chin, Thomson said with his usual honesty that he hadn't got that kind of money and he couldn't borrow it. Kemsley was soothing and massively charming. All that, he said, was a matter for their financial advisers. He would talk immediately to Lionel Fraser of Helbert Wagg (Thomson was to learn later that Fraser's father had been butler to Gordon Selfridge). And who, Lord K beamed, would be acting for Thomson?

'Warburg's – Henry Grunfeld'. Thomson didn't know it yet but Grunfeld was a genius.

'Very well, then,' boomed Lord K, with a mixture of condescension and disinclination to continue the conversation which Thomson found offensive. He was out again on the pavement in Coley Street in twenty minutes flat, having been saluted by three commissionaires at various stages of his descent in the old-fashioned little lift and left forlorn on the door-step of Kemsley's shabby private entrance, looking vaguely at a row of parked cars which included his lordship's black Rolls-Royce and Ian Fleming's Thunderbird.

The negotiations lasted for more than four weeks, and complete secrecy was preserved. In the middle of it all Lord Kemsley called a special Sunday Times conference, with a larger attendance than usual. Both the old hands and the younger men were required to come along to discuss ideas for the paper for 1960 – The Sunday Times was going to surpass itself in the coming year. It wasn't exactly stated but everyone assumed that there was going to be a fantastic drive to reach the million – the circulation then, in July 1959, was 886,000. It was an unprecedented conference: never before had there been such long-term planning. Everyone went to the editor-in-chief's room determined to shine, and there was a confused and lengthy orgy of putting-up and shooting-down, with a beaming Lord K allowing much more than the usual licence and making vague but persistently encouraging noises. It was very puzzling to everyone: no one quite knew whether his ideas had been accepted or not, and there was something a little disquieting, eerie even, in the chairman's air of absent-minded benevolence. He seemed to be thinking of something else, as indeed he was. As the negotiations with Thomson were at a crucial stage there was always the danger of a leak and a consequent stock-market stampede. With elephantine subtlety Lord K had called this long-term planning conference in an attempt to throw dust into the eyes of Rumour, should she enter painted with many tongues.

II

It was a very complicated deal, and for it Henry Grunfeld invented something which made history in the City of London. It was the reverse take-over bid, in which the larger company, Kemsley Newspapers, swallowed the lesser company and the lesser company, after a series of most delicate regurgitatory exercises had been performed by the larger company, somehow ended with the other in its belly.

At the end everyone seemed satisfied, not excluding the public holders of Kemsley ordinary shares, who had the choice of selling them at 90s each or of going along with Thomson. The Kemsley family seemed content to end up with £5 million (the figure of £16 million mentioned by his lordship to Thomson on July 1 was apparently a mere airy starter), and the contentment of Roy Thomson was – understandably, as we shall see – as deep as a well. Peering into the thickets of figures and losing oneself in the labyrinth which Grunfeld had conjured up, to the admiration of both sides, one emerges with the impression that in the end all Thomson had to find in hard cash was £3 million. It is not a bagatelle. But still.

He got it, in his usual confident way, from the bank, and while the ends were being tied up he went down to Kemsley House to meet the directors of the company other than the Kemsleys. None of them had a contract, all were resentful that the deal, up to this last stage, had been kept secret from them. It didn't matter though. All of them clicked immediately with Thomson, all stayed on, all were soon plunged into the details of his rapidly-produced plans for expansion and diversification – or *progg*-ress, as he called it. (They had one difficulty though: for years in talk he was always getting confused between pounds and dollars.)

All but one of the senior editorial staff were without contracts too – they had either run out or never been given. The exception was H. V. Hodson. He had in fact just negotiated a new one. Although his old one had still some time to run, he had approached Lord K in June about the terms of its renewal, because at age 53, with over nine years of editorship behind him, he felt that if ever he was to make a change it should be soon, and he wanted to see the ground ahead before deciding. Lord K offered a new contract, on more favourable terms, with immediate effect. Whether the sale of the paper was then in his mind must be a matter for speculation: Hodson firmly believes it was not, but there are those who think that the meeting with Roy Thomson in the spring of 1959 had given Lord K ideas. The contract included a clause excusing Hodson from attending the office on Saturdays except as might be necessary in relation to matters of editorial policy or features with which he was specially concerned. Of this clause – which was wrongly believed in the office, when its existence leaked, to say that the editor need never attend on Saturdays, whereas its intention was only to spare him the obligation to work late on Saturdays week after week – Hodson very rarely took advantage, but it stuck in Roy Thomson's throat when he learned of it, and he made it an issue when he decided, two years later, that he wanted a new editor. Indeed, he resented the whole contract, made as it was on the eve of the sale of the paper, and thus tying his hands.

When the deal was completed, however, Lord K had sent for Hodson and said, 'On my side I gave you my word, and the contract stands if you want it, but you made it believing I would be chairman, and if you now want to get out of it I will tear it up.' Hodson had already decided to stay, at least to see the paper over a transitional period, so the contract stood. Office rumour had it that just before selling up Lord Kemsley had been to see the Prime Minister with this contract in his hand and had explained to Mr Macmillan that he had engineered it to ensure that there would be continuity of editorship and that the paper would continue to support the Conservative interest. It is true that it was Mr Macmillan who made Roy Thomson a baron. Perhaps Viscount Kemsley thought that as a result of his subtlety, however heavy-footed and ineffective it might seem to others, and because of his fanatic support for Suez, Mr Macmillan might be in the mood to see that he was rewarded with a leg-up in the peerage – the earldom for which he yearned and beside which the GBE – Knight Grand Cross of the Order of the British Empire – awarded him in the New Year's honours of 1959, with its gorgeous sash, was but an immoment toy. He had never stopped indulging himself in dreams of power and glory and was now apt to mistake the illusion for the reality and expect the reward due to accomplishment and wisdom.

Opposite: Lord Thomson by Snowdon.

Like so many others, Denis Hamilton, who had been working in the closest intimacy with Lord K for more than twelve years, had no piece of paper to sell if Thomson elected to get rid of him. Nothing was said to him, but on Lord Kemsley's farewell appearance he was summoned to say goodbye, and there were copious thanks and a warm handshake. As he was turning to leave Lord K suddenly thrust a package across the desk – 'a souvenir', he said. It was not a cheque – but what was it? Nothing more valuable than a photograph of a cheque for £3.5 million which the Rt Hon. the Viscount Kemsley had received from S. G. Warburg and Company Limited.

'Not even the first edition,' says Hamilton wryly.

It was the insensitivity of Kemsley, the sacred monster, at its shattering worst. Yet the strange thing is that no one now alive who was close to him from 1945 onwards, in those frenzied years, dislikes him or has a harsh word to say of him. At the time of his selling out it was inevitable that there should be bitterness. It has gone now. The memories of him which remain, generally speaking, are respectful and even affectionate (though sometimes touched with sardonic humour). The same may be said of the three sons who were quartered in Kemsley House – the sterling Lionel, the present Viscount Kemsley; Neville, so lively-spirited and energetic; and Anthony, whose charm and ability were patent when he was in charge of the letters page of The Sunday Times.

They had all with their father seen the beginning of a transformation of Fleet Street. It had led to the failure of some of their properties and death-bed throes for others. None of them believed in public brawls with heretics like Randolph Churchill – their habit of secrecy was too deep-seated for that. Besides, they had a new generation of Berry children to consider. Neville Berry is said to have been the first to press the idea of selling-out: no reason why he shouldn't. As it turned out it was a good notion for everyone except perhaps the old autocrat himself, with his long record of pride and prejudice. When it happened Othello's occupation had gone. That was his tragedy.

Like a good Victorian – and a rich one – Lord K died, at the age of 84, at Monte Carlo, to the grief of his devoted Edith; he was retired absolutely from public life and enshrouded in an obscurity even deeper than that which hid Lord Baldwin in his later years. He told Robert Harling, who had lunch with him from time to time, that selling The Sunday Times was the greatest mistake of his life. He was obviously a miserable man.

When he took over the paper its circulation was 263,000 and when he sold it it was 885,000. 'The causes of this success,' H. V. Hodson has written, 'were manifold. Some lay in the national background of rising education and taste. But it is impossible to leave out the impact of the man at the top.'

Most certainly true.

III

In 1972 Cyril Connolly looked back over his lengthy association with the paper, particularly during the Kemsley era. This is what he says:

I have been a regular contributor to the *Sunday Times* for twenty years, at first once a fortnight, now once a week. When I joined the paper it was a family business, now it is an organisation. The organisation is huge, efficient and benign, the family business was paternal and sometimes interfering. You had to watch it. I once wrote of an imaginary restaurant which would serve only the knowledgeable or the attractive and where the 'rich were sent empty away'. 'Rich' was altered to 'others'.

I never knew the Kemsleys well, though I had met them on and off for years. I once said to Ian Fleming that I liked to imagine Lord Kemsley as a fine judge of prose, saving my article till last and rolling the sentences round his tongue. 'Well, you're not altogether wrong,' he replied, and very occasionally I would receive a personal letter of congratulation from him which made me deliriously happy, for I admired him and his family, tall dark folk with long legs and easy manners, and wanted to be approved by them.

This was not always reciprocated. There were several about the office in various rôles and there were older members of the staff as well who could be critical. When my name cropped up at their weekly meetings I was always defended by Ian Fleming, who had got me my job and who could do no wrong in their eyes, and very little in mine, and by my old friend Leonard Russell.

When I joined the paper Desmond MacCarthy was still the chief literary critic. People remember his charm; they have forgotten his authority. He belonged to a larger age and he then had a larger column which spread over most of the page, he had read everything and he was wise, just and kind, with a talent for epigram. I had known him well, worked for him and loved him; he published my first writing. Curiously enough he and Raymond Mortimer had both been my literary editors on the *New Statesman* and we possessed an even stronger link in the friendship of Logan Pearsall Smith, who had nothing to do with the *Sunday*

Times but who adored Desmond, enjoyed Raymond and also helped to foster the rising talents of Jack Lambert, John Russell and Hugh Trevor-Roper. I had once been his secretary.

I suppose the *Sunday Times* of Lord Kemsley was a very conservative paper; there was a gentlemanly charm about it; one of the editors was an expert on heraldry; William Rees-Mogg was a bibliophile, like Ian Fleming and Robert Harling. 'Leading articles in the *Sunday Times* are written from a firm background of Christian morality.' There was also a good deal of inconspicuous waste, including a resident travel agent who had made a study of the plagues of Egypt. I expect there was a doctor somewhere in the building and a treatment room for persecution mania.

I suppose what every journalist asks for is appreciation and security, and newspapers which provide both can be counted on the fingers of one toe. 'In our profession,' Desmond once said to me, 'we go on till we drop or till we are dropped,' and I am confident that my funeral, should it fall on a Tuesday, will be remarkable for a hand holding an article thrusting itself out of my coffin.

An office is an extraordinary place to grow old in, yet people do. Leonard Russell, Jack Lambert, Raymond Mortimer, John Russell, Desmond Shawe-Taylor, la serenissima Stella Frank, we have all been here a long time; fearful changes and catastrophes may have taken place in our private lives, death's make-up man pencil more wrinkles on our brow or sprinkle our heads with dusting powder, wives leave us, friends forsake us, children come and go but the rooms on the fifth floor still bulge with new books, resound with jokes and greetings. (I have never interrupted a conversation of the literary editor's that wasn't about the theatre.) It is like swimming under water in a mistral. Outside, on the surface, it may be ice-cold, the waves buffet and clatter round one's head; submerge a foot or two and we enter an immense radiant tranquillity. I have said that writers need appreciation and security, the editors supply the first which takes the form of expertise. I have never written a piece for twenty years that one of them has not gone through carefully, checking it for mistakes and even for what Logan used to call 'little awkwardnesses'.

This taking of trouble is what editors contribute and what they can provide only if they in turn are appreciated at the top of the pyramid. Lord Kemsley gargling prose ('doubtless God could have made a better Berry but doubtless he never did'), Lord Thomson with his Pickwickian glow, indispensable elegant Denis Hamilton – they must appreciate the appreciators, encourage the encouragers – and then there are the young assistant editors and secretaries, who come and go and seem far more expendable than their elders, for they always leave to better themselves. Each time it seems one will never manage without them.

How difficult to write about one's livelihood without self-congratulation. There are very few jobs like mine: I wish there were more – it keeps me still learning; it forces me to be just (so much harder than being merciful), it keeps me humble, for there is nothing I write that might not be used to light a fire a few hours later; when better writers are neglected I am groomed and cosseted; I love books, I am paid to read them; when people commiserate with me on my weekly grind I thank them but I know that without it the duns would long have been picking my bones. But what more can I say? My life on the *Sunday Times* has rushed by in a happy blur – a golden shower of books and proofs and telephone calls – endless trouble, infinite patience, occasional spats but in all these twenty years of close collaboration with Leonard Russell, Jack Lambert and later Michael Ratcliffe and John Whitley never a disagreement still less a quarrel.

Not generally considered a happy man, here I have found happiness. 'You can say anything you like of your old friend,' Desmond once wrote to me, 'except that he is dishonest or that he does not love literature.' To love literature is to want to make other people love it, the difficulty of writing once a week is how not to put them off. One hopes for the best, tries to avoid pedantry and nagging or the cult of personality, to check references, vary treatment and subject matter, but it's no good, there by the grace of Thomson House one will be next week, even (d.v.) the week after.

One can say in extenuation that the enthusiasm and vigilance that goes into the arts pages of the *Sunday Times* must have affected public taste over the years more than any other medium: authors have been encouraged, publishers refreshed – a good book by a new writer has more chance of recognition here than anywhere else. Take away our literary pages and the world of letters would be the poorer, for neither television, radio, nor the 'I can tell a book from a Bath Bun' type of critic can replace the magic and dignity of the written word, the printed word, the properly edited and presented word.

When Mr Connolly first wrote for the paper the London office was still a tightly-knit little group, with everyone knowing everyone else. It has grown larger, more sophisticated, more departmentalised, and acquired the same links with The Times as it once had with The Daily Telegraph, but the same sense of family nevertheless remains, and to some like the present writer occasionally brings confusions with it. He is apt to forget that he is now a grandfather in this large and ever-expanding household and that some younger members of it with whom he once worked, say William Rees-Mogg, never knew Cyril Lakin or Desmond MacCarthy or other figures of the not so distant past. Again, someone like Michael Ratcliffe, formerly of The Sunday Times and now literary editor of The Times, is to him still one of The Sunday Times's promising boys who, rather unaccountably, isn't seen any more in Gray's Inn Road. Never mind, the staff join him in detecting and cherishing this strong family affection, and in thinking, even, that what it knits-up is the first family in Fleet Street.

Printers and the other technicians who have been through many a storm and crisis alongside the editorial people feel that way too: no one more than the present head printer, George Darker, always rock-steady and four-square, or his deputy, Frank Davy, almost as swift and mercurial as he was when he first worked (and George too) with the present writer in the case-room of The Sunday Times at the Daily Telegraph nearly forty years ago. Arthur Bloxham, who died at the age of 85, was head printer then. Gus Wingrove (who, as we know, went back to the days of Mrs Rachel Beer and died in March, 1972, aged 84) succeeded him in 1946, to be succeeded in turn by Mr Darker in 1960. No one now remains at work of the famous 'ship' which left St Clement's Press in 1933 (one of them, Alexander 'Tommy' Atkins, started in Portugal Street in 1903 and didn't retire until 1957) and transferred to Fleet Street to print The Sunday Times; the last of them was Albert Playfair, who retired in 1971 after sixty-five years – sixty of them as a compositor. Remarkable men all and most of them remarkably long lived.

H. V. Hodson, who knew all of them, sends this note about life upstairs:

> The *Sunday Times* always was, and still is, a friendly, happy place to work. We had pessimists but hardly a grumbler; men of ambition but no empire-builders; disagreements but no feuds. Praise and thanks are due not only to the skill but also to the co-operation and comradeship of all who served with me during my twelve years in the editorial chair, particularly to those two stalwarts Valentine Heywood and Pat Murphy, who as deputy or managing editor took heavy burdens and worked intimately with me from hour to hour; and to Leonard Russell, under whose literary editorship, with the lightest of editorial reins, The *Sunday Times* became the most respected critical organ in the country.
>
> Val Heywood was heartbrokenly disappointed when I was made editor over his head on Hadley's retirement: he would have given his right hand to end his journalistic career as editor of the *Sunday Times* 'even for a month', as he once said to me. Yet any jealousy he may have felt was soon drowned in his generous character, and his loyalty was unblemished. It takes solid men like that as well as 'fliers' to run a good newspaper.
>
> In a way, Lord Kemsley was the bogey of our office lives. He took his rôle as editor-in-chief very seriously, not only on questions of editorial opinion, and one never knew on what detail he would not intervene.

This enforced one's own attention to detail – excellent discipline, and not personally out of character, but unconducive to delegation of authority. K's most disagreeable habit, from the editor's point of view, was to telephone around 10 o'clock on a Saturday night, after seeing the first edition and no doubt showing it to his family and his guests. Often he would sharply criticise some small point – a minor headline, the caption to a picture – and would brook no defence. 'It's bad journalism,' he would say. When one had already worked round the clock, and knew that Lord K, for all his great newspaper experience and flair, could have been seen off by a junior sub-editor as a practising journalist, this was hard to take.

Nevertheless, there was no senior member of the staff who did not look up to K with admiration and affection. He was a strong man, with the strength to change his mind; often obstinate, but ready to see another point of view (except sometimes on details). He was generous and more than just, as quick to forgive as to help a man out of some financial difficulty.

If he clung too long to a few who were better replaced, it was because he cherished loyalty and shrank from dismissing anyone. So indeed did I, and at least two members of the *Sunday Times* staff whom he did not like kept their posts because I refused to fire them without orders, and he could not bring himself to wield the axe. Likewise his clinging to tradition had something staunch and admirable about it, like a stout piece of Victorian mahogany, though it was sometimes absurd, as when he insisted that on the Sunday after every Lord Mayor's Day we should carry a leader praising the outgoing Lord Mayor of London and congratulating the new one.

His political formula was simple: the *Sunday Times* was conservative and anti-socialist, from which it followed that at election times it gave all its weight to backing the Conservative Party; but within that specification particular issues were open to argument, and the new Toryism was free of the *Sunday Times*. On such matters as race relations one could keep up a steady pressure for liberal attitudes against the prejudice he found elsewhere. Editorial freedom grew steadily like a plant, bedded in mutual experience. The polarity of proprietor and editor can make a constructive contribution to a newspaper's vigour. But it was a relief to enjoy the full liberty which Roy Thomson rightly boasts he gives his editors. In the two years that I served under his chairmanship he only once spoke directly to me about the contents of a leader, telephoning me from London Airport one Saturday morning with a thought that had occurred to him – 'Just a suggestion, Harry; it's for you to decide.'

K's conservatism extended to the make-up and appearance of the paper itself. I shared his preference for typographical modesty, and under Robert Harling's brilliant guidance we produced as handsome a format as the *Sunday Times* has ever had. But basic reform of the page-order, which was vitally needed as the number of pages grew and different interests developed, was thwarted by his fiat that the 'City page' had always been page 2 and must stay there; this arrested both the natural expansion of the news in the front of the paper and the development of the business coverage. Within a few weeks of Thomson's arrival I was able to change the page-order without argument.

When I became editor in 1950 the *Sunday Times* had 10 pages; when I left in 1961 (newsprint control having ended in 1956) it regularly had 48 pages. The circulation in my time more than doubled, from around half a million to more than a million.

In this connection stress has rightly been laid on the pulling power of our 'serials' – the 'big read'. These gained many new readers, sometimes in large gulps; but if the new reader who buys the paper for Monty's memoirs or Ian Fleming's 'Wicked Cities' is to remain a reader he must like what he finds. Circulation boosts are futile if they do not stick. Our new readers liked what they found in the rest of the paper. With the relief from newsprint control we embarked on policies to gain and hold a wider social group and a new generation – remembering that between a fifth and a quarter of our readers would disappear anyway in the course of nature every decade. Sport, music, women's interests and business comment were expanded; books came back into their own; jazz and motor-racing were added to regular features; a general liberalisation set in.

News was always a problem. A Sunday paper is deprived of many of the normal sources of daily news – Parliament, official publications, the Stock Exchange, the High Court and most minor courts. In compensation it has the big day of sport. So it has largely to create its own home news. (If 'news' is something that happened in the past 24 hours, or inherently could not have been reported a day earlier, there is no more 'news' today in a 72-page *Sunday Times* than there was in a 36-pager.) Apart from the political and diplomatic correspondents, whose business it is to find fresh news stories, our news-creating apparatus was thin – virtually non-existent under Bill Bliss, scanty under Michael Cudlipp. Its great expansion has been an outstanding achievement of the *Sunday Times* in the past decade. But by 1961 we were on our way.

All this meant new method and new men. My appointments wore well – William Rees-Mogg (now editor of *The Times*) as City Editor, Frank Giles as Foreign Editor (now also deputy editor), Ernestine Carter as women's page editor, James Margach as political correspondent, James Dow as production editor – a new post and the key organisational reform – and many others still there, either on the staff or as regular contributors.

I come back to where I began this reminiscence – the making of a newspaper is team-work, and the achievements of those great and happy years were the work of one of the ablest groups of men and women ever teamed together in Fleet Street, who were my colleagues and are my friends.

But we have got away from the Thomson takeover.

IV

Overnight Kemsley House was renamed Thomson House; and it became known that the never-completed part, facing Gray's Inn Road, was to be reconstructed as a modern office block. Meanwhile everyone continued to work in the dingy old building, and along the dun-coloured corridors of The Sunday Times and the lavatory-tiled passages of the hinterland, legacy of the old Hulton days, where obscure toilers worked for the provincial papers, or merely stored envelopes, a persistent rumour engaged attention. It was expressed in the single word 'budget'.

Thomson was said to be a scientific newspaper owner whose whole success was based on tight budgeting. No one knew anything at first-hand about his Canadian papers, although that didn't stop people saying that the purchase of an extra ball of string was an impossibility under their system, but it was confidently held by the knowledgeable that The Scotsman, edited from 1956 to the spring of 1972 by Alastair Dunnett, formerly a notable Scottish correspondent of The Sunday Times (and considered as a candidate for the editorship when Hodson was leaving), had a budget so tight that even the economically-minded locals paled before its stringencies.

But in a few weeks, on The Sunday Times at any rate, nobody was heard to mention budgets again (well, not for years), nor did anyone continue to speculate darkly on Thomson's alleged intention of running the paper on a shoe-string. The reverse, indeed, happened. Money was spent freely on big and little improvements, and new faces began to appear in practically every department. There was a general feeling that the paper was really beginning to boom, and everyone felt relaxed now without Lord Kemsley's tight grip and magisterial presence.

A distinction was noticed between Roy Thomson and Lord K. Thomson was a philistine utterly indifferent to all forms of art but with a sharp knowledge of world affairs; whereas Kemsley was a philistine with a respect for the arts but no knowledge of them and only the sketchiest idea of world affairs. A modern Prime Minister is said to have confused Malaya with Malaysia and an older one Silesia with Cilicia. Lord K would have been magisterially foggy about the lot without impairment of his habitual air of statesmanlike gravity and discretion. (Thomson had no discretion. With the ink not dry on the agreement he went off to Canada and told the press that some of the Kemsley group papers 'have been badly run'. Threatened by Kemsley with a libel action, he had to explain that he had been misreported.) Kemsley had certainly been bad at picking staff, putting too much faith in the externals – the smiles, the deference, the family-man-with-children ideal. No matter, The Sunday Times was all right now with Thomson.

Wonderful new machinery was installed at 200 Gray's Inn Road by Thomson, who probably knows more about plant and how it works than any other proprietor in Fleet Street, past or present. It had to be put into Gray's Inn Road at great speed when a coolness arose between him and Michael Berry. The Telegraph had printed The Sunday Times in Fleet Street since 1933; and one day Thomson, mad about expansion, went along to see Berry to ask him if it would be possible for The Telegraph presses to print a forty-eight page Sunday Times. Berry said it wouldn't. Thomson then asked him, partly serious, partly kidding, as was his way whenever he met a newspaper proprietor, however important or insignificant, whether he would sell him The Daily Telegraph. The answer was a curt no.

Soon after this Thomson received from Berry, who was planning The Sunday Telegraph, six months' notice to end the printing contract. This term of six months, as Thomson fortunately noted, was a strange mistake – it should have been a year. But, even so, and allowing for some extra time which Thomson legitimately gained before correcting the mistake, it was a desperate business to get the new plant installed in time. It was achieved with literally three days to spare. The contract expired on Wednesday, January 25, 1961. If the presses at Thomson House hadn't been ready by the following Sunday there would have been a major disaster. They were run-in from the Wednesday. Eric Cheadle recalls: 'It was a colossal challenge, but by using the five old Sunday Graphic presses (converting tabloid to text), installing a new Goss machine, diverting to Gray's Inn Road a 5-unit Crabtree Viscount intended for the Cardiff office, and by working round the clock in a great team effort, we were ready in time. It also meant demolishing lift shafts and staircases, reinforcing foundations, reorganising the composing room, and automating the despatch room. Among the men who helped beat the clock were H. M. Stephen (now managing director of The Daily Telegraph), Sydney Kirton and

John Kavanagh on the works side, with Willie McMunagle loaned from Edinburgh and Dennis Whitney from Middlesbrough.' Two months before this The Sunday Graphic, a notable money-loser for years, had been shut down. There was no room for it now. As Russell Braddon, Lord Thomson's biographer, remarks, Thomson in one brilliant stroke 'simultaneously abandoned a losing paper and a troublesome printing contract'.

The Sunday Times which was being produced at this period was Hodson's paper at its strongest. There were two new men at the conference, William Rees-Mogg, who had replaced Norman Crump as City editor, and who came from The Financial Times, and Frank Giles, from The Times, who was the new foreign editor, with Iain Lang as his associate. (Lang was succeeded as deputy foreign editor by Nicholas Carroll, who retained the job of diplomatic correspondent.) Otherwise the conference, first under Roy Thomson and then Denis Hamilton, assembled the familiar faces of H. V. Hodson, Patrick Murphy, managing editor, Leonard Russell, literary editor (whose health was beginning to crack), J. W. Lambert, his deputy, Iain Lang and Ian Fleming.

About the office now the emphasis was on youth. Michael Cudlipp the news editor (now a deputy editor of The Times) was only twenty-four, and youthful, too, were at least two of his staff, Susan Cooper and Gavin Lyall. Peter Wilsher, a City correspondent, Brian Glanville, soccer and other sports, Robert Robinson, radio, Siriol Hugh-Jones, an occasional essayist who died young, and Joyce Emerson, who helped on the book pages, were none of them veterans.

In the list of foreign correspondents there were the names of Henry Brandon, Antony Terry, and Richard Hughes. One of the most prominent at that time has gone: Tom Stacey, who was based in London with the whole of Africa as his territory, has forsaken journalism to become a publisher. Trevor Philpott, who was senior reporter, has since distinguished himself on BBC Television. Douglas Glass, the photographer, is remembered for a most successful run with his Portrait Gallery.

As early as 1955 the paper had won its first Annual Award for Newspaper design, and Robert Harling was still playing an important rôle: he had made it in its type design an unobtrusive tribute to Eric Gill, that sculptor and letter-cutter of genius, drawing on him for both the text type – Jubilee – and the heading types of the feature pages – Perpetua bold and italic. The heading types of the news pages were set in the series known as Century, in

Harling's opinion the most successful newspaper display types of modern times. For years Harling fought a battle, strongly supported by Ian Fleming, against 'earpiece' advertisements on either side of the front-page title-block; his point was that for the sake of a pittance in advertising revenue some of the paper's dignity was being lost. Lord K was not to be moved, but they were abolished when Hamilton became editor. They remain on either side of the Weekly Review title-block.

In the 1950s Harling made various other typographical innovations or removed certain obsolete practices. He was the enemy of initial letters, those 'dropped caps' which had been used for a generation, if only because they were such a waste of the printers' time. He was also opposed to what Henry Luce called 'cookies' – the making of half-tone blocks in irregular shapes. And it was he who abolished the 'overrunning' of blocks – i.e. placing half-measure type down one side or both of a picture. The time and money spent on 'overrunning' from the 1930s onwards must, apart from aesthetic considerations, have been prodigious.

Harling used to write regularly on architecture and design, and was an inspiration to the brighter sparks around the office. Now he combines the editorship of Condé-Nast's House and Garden with weekly typographical design for the paper's leader page and main news pages.

Other names must be mentioned. There was George Schwartz, deputy City editor to William Rees-Mogg but indispensable for his weekly column; Elizabeth Nicholas, a travel editor unmatched in her time; Brian Nicholson, the advertisement manager, who went to the top post at Beaverbrook Newspapers, leaving Michael Renshaw, the advertisement director, to give a chance to Donald Howard Barrett; Gus Wingrove, the head printer, had retired and been succeeded by the admirable George Darker; and Donald Robinson, the circulation manager, much liked in every department as 'Robbie', who died tragically and mysteriously. In his last years he bore the title of general manager, but neither he nor anyone else quite seemed to know what it meant, for he had nothing to do with the day-to-day affairs of the office. He remained always the shrewd but apparently languid charmer with the RAF moustache.

So though there had been a revolutionary change at the top, no loss of continuity resulted: the spirit of the paper went on.

Still, it was quickly realised that revolution, if only a strictly peaceful one, was on the way. Even at his first conference, when

Roy Thomson was merely feeling around, the mandarin style vanished. Whereas under Lord K the atmosphere had been formal and circumspect, now it was easy and wise-cracking, friendly yet urgent. Large speculations began to fill the air, excitement and long-term schemes replaced the too curious consideration of every trivial feature.

As one of his first innovations Thomson made it clear that he believed in the unfettered freedom of the editors of his papers, but this resolution was received with a notable lack of frankness and generosity by his rivals. It had been urged against Kemsley – and coolly admitted by Beaverbrook before the Press Commission – that he used his newspapers for the propagation of his own views and prejudices. When Thomson disclaimed any such desire for himself it might have been expected – ah well, perhaps not in this wicked world – that he would be praised for his impartiality. Soon Mr Cecil King set himself up sourly as his critic-in-chief, explaining indignantly that this Canadian was interested in nothing but making money (of the other Canadian press lord Mr King expressed the extravagant opinion that Beaverbrook 'always seemed to me the only authentically *evil* man I have known'). This was at the time when Mr King, buttressed by the importance of the International Publishing Corporation and with a victory over Thomson in the battle for Odhams–Newnes, was to all appearances a strong man; it has looked otherwise since his sudden *congé*, delivered one morning when he was shaving, for he now seems to be a strangely naïve and forlorn character who retains, however, his old belief that he has proved something by the mere assertion of it. This ingenuousness was the making of his hair-raisingly frank book of memoirs, 'Strictly Personal', serialised with success in The Sunday Times.

Thomson, in fact, has had the last laugh (not that he has ever actually laughed at Cecil King's misfortunes). There was that occasion when IPC's own journal, the Statist, with Mr King still in charge of IPC, had a little piece about the two men:

> I asked Lord Thomson, who doesn't have a competing daily, what he thought of the *Sun*'s chances.[1] He answered immediately: 'It hasn't a hope.' He may remember that Cecil King was equally forthright in expressing his doubts about the *Sunday Times* colour supplement. Perhaps next time it will be Thomson's turn to eat his words.

---

1. This was when The Sun had newly appeared and before it was sold to Mr Rupert Murdoch.

Tuesday morning conference after the Thomson takeover. Left to right: Ian Fleming, Iain Lang, Godfrey Smith, J. W. Lambert, Leonard Russell, A. T. P. Murphy, H. V. Hodson, Roy Thomson, C. D. Hamilton. Thomson soon thought it proper to be succeeded in the conference chairmanship by Hamilton.

The late Lord Francis-Williams, as Harold Evans has noted, was one of the few commentators on the press honest and intelligent enough to have seen that Thomson has made a genuine contribution to the development of a free press. Evans also remarked that Francis Williams 'was the only commentator who had a good word to say when Roy Thomson and Denis Hamilton launched a Sunday Times colour magazine to hoots of derision from the trendy cynics.'

When politicians or others approach Thomson seeking editorial attention he tells them that they should speak to his editors; unlike the then publisher of The New York Times who said 'My God, you can't do that!' when his nephew told him he was going to China for the paper – the publisher had promised Mr Foster Dulles that no one would be sent without Dulles's consent.

In the earliest days of his ownership of The Sunday Times Thomson said at the conference that the paper must become 'a kind of public utility' and open to the widest variety of views. In the more liberal climate of today, to which Thomson has contributed much, this seems a modest ideal, but it wasn't so modest in the heyday of the autocratic press lords, of whom Kemsley and Beaverbrook were really the final survivors. Two quotations from Randolph Churchill may be cited:

> One of the greatest blessings of a free press is that it allows the millionaire proprietors entire liberty to exercise their prejudices without any accountability, even to their shareholders. There is no quest for truth; simply a desire to smother it when it is inconvenient to a press lord. This maxim does not apply to the latest press lord, Mr Roy Thomson.[1]

And Churchill emphasises what is really the 'public utility' attitude in an interview with Clive Irving which first appeared in The Sunday Times:

IRVING: Are you prepared sometimes to admit that the editor must have final responsibility for what appears?
CHURCHILL: Not a signed article.
IRVING: You've battled for a long time over this problem of having your stuff censored.
CHURCHILL: They've got the editorial columns to express their opinions in, and if I've entered into a contract with them to write stuff under my own name it's got to be my stuff, not their stuff. I don't care whether they tear one of my articles to pieces in the editorial columns, say

---

1. Spectator, January 17, 1964.

they disagree with what I've said. I don't join a paper because I agree with its political opinions, it's only because I have an opportunity of expressing my own opinions.[1]

Randolph had a long record of going against the grain. His father 'had hated most of his schooldays' and

was most concerned about how I would get on. He said to me: 'There is a boy at Sandroyd called Max Aitken. He is the son of a very great friend of mine, Lord Beaverbrook. I am sure you will get on with him very well. Lord Beaverbrook has told his son to keep an eye on you.' I settled down quite happily at Sandroyd but it seemed that a week after I got there I wrote to my father and said, 'You will be sorry to hear that the boy I hate most in the whole school is Max Aitken.'[2]

So we see that from his earliest years the unmanageable Randolph was (like Dr Johnson) actuated by a spirit of contradiction. However, there was no real trouble when he contributed to The Sunday Times. Best remembered is a serial by him, drawn from an account of his first twenty-one years, which began, memorably, 'I was born in London on 28 May, 1911, at 33 Eccleston Square, of poor but honest parents.' (Randolph had literary pretensions and was given to laying down the law about words, but no one could take very seriously in this rôle someone who made so many elementary mistakes such as writing 'titivate' when he meant 'titillate'.)

He had a lucky break with this book, inasmuch as it was only a fragment of a full-length autobiography which he knew he would never complete, and the unrevised manuscript was lying unregarded on his shelves at his beautiful house Stour, at East Bergholt, when Russell went to stay with him one week-end. On the Saturday at midnight he rang his young secretary, Barbara Twigg, who lived in a cottage near by and was one of the very few people who were unawed by him, to dictate a letter, after which he settled down to a monologue and a fair amount of whisky. At two o'clock he shuffled over to a shelf to consult the manuscript of the book on some point, started to read it aloud, found it fascinating, and was still at it at 4 a.m., with Russell half asleep and the three or four pugs whom Randolph adored snoring in all the other armchairs. But Russell had comprehended enough of it to know

1. 'Twenty-One Years', by Randolph Churchill. Weidenfeld & Nicolson, 1964.
2. *Ibid.*

that it would make a very good serial (it wasn't his business to judge it in its entirety as a book), and he took the manuscript away with him, fatigued with too much whisky and good food and talk and rather appalled by Randolph's frivolous Sunday-morning attitude to Mr Heath, brought over for a walk round the garden of Stour by Lord Blakenham, a neighbour of Randolph's.

There was one passage in the manuscript which was difficult then (1963) but probably wouldn't be considered so today (1972). It couldn't be omitted from the serial because in its sequel it involved Randolph's father in a remarkable light:

> I suffered one disagreeable experience at Sandroyd when I was about ten years old. There was a young assistant master who made some pretext for me to go and see him in his room. When I got there he made me sit down beside him on the bed. He undid his trousers and caused me to manipulate his organ. I was much surprised but stood in awe of him and cannot pretend that I found it particularly disgusting, or even that I had any sense of guilt until the housemaid came in without knocking to deliver his laundry. He went scarlet in the face and jumped to his feet, rearranging his dress as quickly as he could. I realised then that there was something wrong and took my leave of him as soon as possible.[1]

In the summer holidays he told his sister Diana about this strange experience. (Someone who was at Sandroyd at the time remembers to this day that the miscreant master also 'stole Terry Rattigan's penknife'.) The nanny overheard, and the story got to Winston Churchill, who took by no means the tolerant attitude which Randolph's friend Evelyn Waugh ('the little man never writes a dull page,' said Randolph) showed in his autobiography to similar behaviour on the part of the original Captain Grimes:

> I remember very well how my father sent for me one morning when he was still lying in bed and having his breakfast and asked me about the truth of the matter. I told him the truth as I have always done. I don't think I had ever seen him so angry before or since. He leapt out of bed, ordered his car and drove all across country – the round trip must have been well over two hundred miles. He returned late that night. He had seen the headmaster who told him that the young assistant master had already been dismissed on other grounds. My father said to me, 'Never let anyone do that to you again'. This was the only homosexual experience I ever encountered.[1]

The Sunday Times bought the book, and Hamilton, who had ambitious plans for Randolph, and wanted to get him in an

---

1. *Ibid.*

agreeable mood, paid a very good but not excessive price by the scale of those days – £10,000.

A delighted Randolph quickly found a publisher for the book through Curtis Brown, his literary agents. He also sought out Roy Thomson: one original liked to have an occasional chat with the other original – it may have been the Sunday when he flew by helicopter from Stour and landed on the lawn, which had been painstakingly marked out with white lines, of Thomson's home at Gerrards Cross. What Randolph chiefly wanted to say to a press lord who was always sensitive about the huge fees commanded by some writers, and actuated by his usual spirit of contradiction, was that The Sunday Times had paid him twice what the serial was worth. He probably made an impression on Thomson. He may have planted a seed of mistrust. But that was Randolph Churchill: courageous, honest, caddish, a busybody who would gash even himself with knives to make a striking story, and an incorrigible hand at stirring-up trouble. No wonder some of the young men who supplied him with inside information about the press used to invoke an old gag: you didn't need enemies if you had Randolph for a friend.

Anyway, the serial was a nice one, even if the head printer of The Sunday Times was coolly certain that the difficult passage would never get into print. Judging the situation from his experiences under the Kemsley régime, and trying to avoid the frustrating business of 'bringing the page back', George Darker held it from its usual time of 'going away', 11 a.m. on the Friday morning, to 3 p.m. Then, as one of his predecessors, Mr Bloxham, had done on a like occasion, he formally requested permission to go to press with it. Hamilton (editor then) stood firm and it went.

In the event nobody seemed very shocked, with the predictable exception of Randolph's old sparring-partner and supreme sensitive plant of our generation, Mr John Gordon of Beaverbrook's Sunday Express.

Earlier Russell had surmised that Randolph nursed a secret desire to be recognised as a gardener or rather as a planner of gardens, one whose eye for massed colour and design would evoke murmurs of admiration all over the county; for the moment, until he could get going on this larger ambition, he confined his gardening experiments to ritual visits to cut a rose for a guest or to picking the heads off a couple of dead flowers on Sunday mornings. He and Russell talked about Randolph's tulip-tree at Stour, of which he was greatly proud, and it was agreed that Randolph was to do an article for Mark Boxer in the magazine on tulip-trees, with photographs in colour. Anxious to further his reputation in this new sphere, Randolph attempted nothing less than a census of tulip-trees in Great Britain, advertising in The Times for owners of them, supplying printed forms to be filled in, getting his Miss Twigg to set up an elaborate filing system, and summoning Edwin Smith, an outstanding and under-recognised photographer, and ordering him to take hundreds of colour photographs – Edwin travelled all over the country and ended up with a selection of fifty. Eventually, justly, Mark Boxer reduced the vast enterprise to a single page in the magazine – not even a spread.

Randolph wasn't offended, though; the great tulip-tree hunt itself meant more to his restless spirit than the article, and in the course of it he conducted an unwontedly dignified correspondence with a large number of the landed gentry. One of these was his old friend Evelyn Waugh, the wartime comrade from whom he had been estranged for a long period. Waugh now wrote from Combe Florey to say that, though he wasn't to be quoted in the article, 'a man about the place' had told him something or other – it doesn't matter what it was – about tulip-trees. This suggestion that Waugh owned a park, with anonymous servitors in odd corners, was too much for Randolph's gravity. He had the sharpest eye for social niceties, and despite the egalitarianism of White's bar he broke down into tremendous bouts of wheezy laughter at the nerve of his admired friend in presenting himself to *him* in the character of a landed gentleman. 'A man about the place!' he kept repeating brokenly, his blue eyes bulging with enjoyment. Anyway, he found the tulip-tree hunt a refreshing change from writing for Beaverbrook – or was it The News of the World at that point?

By now Beaverbrook himself was jealous of Thomson: the fellow Canadian whom he had encouraged and patronised at first had become a tall poppy – and, as Lloyd George said, it was Beaverbrook's habit, while not bothering about the stunted flowers, to cut off the heads of the tall poppies. But Thomson can take baiting attacks with astonishing *sang froid*. He could afford to now: The Sunday Times had reached a circulation of one million copies a week in October, 1960.

V

The year is 1961, H. V. Hodson is still editor, and Thomson House, with that marvellous new printing plant in the basement, is buzzing with activity. With it there could now be a seventy-two or eighty-page Sunday Times: it was a gleam on the horizon, part of Thomson's bold plans, something which the new Sunday Telegraph (or The Observer for that matter) couldn't encompass. The colour magazine – called originally the Colour Section – was coming early next year, Business News was contemplated if not talked about. Whole new departments were springing up on the advertising and business sides, including the very expensive marketing division – absolutely necessary, it seemed, for getting the magazine across to advertisers. In one way and another Roy Thomson was putting a great deal of money at risk, and the whole pyramid rested on the £5 million new plant in the basement. There had to be bigger papers with more advertising or a lot of it was money squandered. (The Guardian was now printing on the plant, but that wasn't a big deal.) There also had to be better papers – there were now two rivals in the field.

But what were better papers? Nobody knew, nobody ever does. With the disappearance of Lord K some driving force might have been lost, but the advantages easily outweighed the drawbacks and Hodson was turning out a very fine paper by the standards of the old régime. Was it enough, though? And could Hodson, who had had nearly twelve gruelling years as editor, find the energy and ideas to conduct, or at any rate overlord, the three-in-one paper that was coming?

Nobody knew in the board-room, including Denis Hamilton, the editorial director. But there was a feeling that Hodson's style of editorship was too constricted for the big changes at hand. He was a writing editor, a brilliant and scholarly Chatham House figure, with a consuming interest in Anglo–American relations and Commonwealth problems. There was also a feeling in the board-room that the political tone of the paper, despite its increasing liberalisation on social questions, was still too robustly Conservative to attract younger readers and that the Toryism of someone like the 33-year-old Rees-Mogg, soon to become political editor, might provide a more progressive political direction.

Mark Boxer by Marc.

It all ended when Hodson and Thomson agreed, in the course of a discussion about Hodson's contract in which Hodson felt that Thomson was trying to worsen its terms, that he would soon cease to be editor. There was no quarrel, no bad blood, least of all with Roy Thomson, who got on very well with Hodson. It was made easier because Hodson, who of course was compensated when the contract was terminated, knew by this time where he wanted to go – a job close to his own heart. His connection with The Sunday Times was not entirely severed, for he continued to be retained as a leader-writer and editorial consultant.

The staff, as distinct from the management, first guessed there was something in the wind when James Margach, who was always coming along with secret information, reported that there had been some approach to Geoffrey Cox of Independent Television News. There was silence until the end of October. Then Hamilton called in Russell, who had been away ill for most of the year, told him there were to be changes, and asked him to write an announcement for Sunday.

Russell, who knew something but not everything, took down the details. They came to the two most important appointments of all. 'And C. D. Hamilton?' he asked at last. 'Editor-in-chief, of course?'

'I think I'd like you to put me down as editor,' said Hamilton slowly and uncomfortably.

The announcement (see page 345), on October 29, 1961, ran:

Thomson Newspapers Limited announces that Mr C. D. Hamilton who, as Editorial Director of the organisation, and latterly also as Chairman of The Sunday Times Editorial Board[1], has been closely associated with the direction of the paper for many years is, in addition to his existing responsibilities, assuming the Editorship of the *Sunday Times* following the appointment of Mr H. V. Hodson to be Provost of Ditchley [created to provide an educational centre for Anglo–American studies and conferences at Ditchley Park, near Oxford. Mr Hodson was its first Provost].

Mr A. T. P. Murphy continues as Managing Editor and Mr Leonard Russell as Associate Editor and Chief Literary Editor.

The City Editor, Mr William Rees-Mogg (33), is promoted to Political and Economic Editor.

Mr Mark Boxer (30) has resigned from *The Queen* magazine, where he was Art Director, to become Editor of The Sunday Times Colour Magazine, which is to appear in the New Year.

1. This was incorrect. Hamilton was chairman of The Sunday Times conference (see page 252).

Mr Roy Thomson, Chairman, said last night: 'I and all Mr Hodson's colleagues join in wishing him every success in his new and most important assignment. He has been with the paper for 16 years, 12 of them as Editor, during its unprecedented increase in sales and stature. I thank him for all he has accomplished for the paper. I hope that his long, happy and highly successful association with the *Sunday Times* will not be entirely severed.'

This was the beginning of something. Hamilton had found a young political editor whom time has shown to be a figure and an influence in the class of J. A. Spender and H. W. Massingham. For the Colour Magazine he had discovered, with Harling's help, someone who had never worked in the hackney-stables of Fleet Street and whose approach to his new job was unconventional enough to alarm some of the old hands about the office. 'We see the colour section,' said Mark Boxer in the paper a month or so before it appeared, 'as being concerned primarily with surprise, with young ideas and with an open-minded approach to affairs over a wide range. It will entertain, inform, occasionally even shock.' He meant it, and within a couple of months, to the consternation of the old Kemsley hands, was publishing colour pictures of hippies giving themselves fixes in the public lavatory at Piccadilly Circus. The magazine was firmly planned for the younger reader: it was not to be a mere extension of the paper itself with pictures added.

Change was needed, too, in the paper proper. The English newspaper was read originally mainly in coffee-houses and clubs, and fundamentally Northcliffe's halfpenny Daily Mail would have been perfectly understood there, despite what the Olympian Lord Salisbury said about its being written by office boys for office boys. In the same way The Sunday Times at the end of the 1950s was still mainly a superlative coffee-house journal, a compendium of varied but on the whole undisturbing information and political opinion. It was too elderly. It was afraid to risk looking callow. It was fearful that if it edged any nearer towards the popular it might lose some of its A and B readers.[1]

All this made Hamilton uneasy. He might by temperament be a coffee-house man himself, but he was certain that the paper should have links, by way of new and young executives and

---

1. Definition by National Readership Survey of social groups: A, upper middle class; B, middle class; C1, lower middle class; C2, skilled working class; D, working class; E, those at lowest levels of subsistence.

reporters, with the larger and ruder world. Like everyone else, he had been astonished in the autumn of 1960 when the Public Prosecutor's case against D. H. Lawrence's 'Lady Chatterley's Lover' had failed before a jury. It was a portent: there were obviously going to be sexual and social changes in the 1960s. There couldn't have been a more interesting time for a man to take up the editorship of a paper like The Sunday Times.

The Sunday Times
Important New Appointments

THOMSON Newspapers Limited announces that Mr. C. D. Hamilton, who, as Editorial Director of the organisation, and latterly also as Chairman of THE SUNDAY TIMES Editorial Board, has been closely associated with the direction of the paper for many years is, in addition to his existing responsibilities, assuming the Editorship of THE SUNDAY TIMES following the appointment of Mr. H. V. Hodson to be Provost of Ditchley (as reported on Page 3).

Mr. A. T. P. Murphy continues as Managing Editor and Mr. Leonard Russell as Associate Editor and Chief Literary Editor. The City Editor, Mr. William Rees-Mogg (33), is promoted to Political and Economic Editor.

Mr. Mark Boxer (30) has resigned from "The Queen" magazine, where he was Art Director, to become Editor of THE SUNDAY TIMES Colour Magazine, which is to appear in the New Year.

Mr. Roy Thomson, Chairman, said last night: "I and all Mr. Hodson's colleagues join in wishing him every success in his new and most important assignment. He has been with the paper for 16 years, twelve of them as Editor, during its unprecedented increase in sales and stature. I thank him for all he has accomplished for the paper. I hope that his long, happy and highly successful association with THE SUNDAY TIMES will not be entirely severed."

October 29, 1961.

PART 5

Hamilton the Innovator
1961–1966

PART 5

Hamilton the Innovator

I

The launch of The Sunday Telegraph in February, 1961, caused considerable reaction in the serious Sunday newspaper world. The Observer, which had dropped behind The Sunday Times, had already been upset by Roy Thomson's expansionist plans. The launch of a third quality Sunday paper now presented another threat. The Observer, obviously suffering under the strain, took the opportunity for a swipe at its old rival:

> . . . the first number of the *Sunday Telegraph* brought one unqualified pleasure – it did not look like the *Observer*. For years, the *Sunday Times* has copied almost every new idea or feature that we have introduced. True, it grouped its cultural features in a 'magazine section' before we grouped ours in a 'weekend review', but this division of the paper was a functional necessity of growing size. And we tried to make our division look as different as possible.
>
> In contrast the worthy *Sunday Times* deliberately imitates the paper, right down to typographical details. No doubt we should be flattered; but it becomes farcical. Last week it announced a new feature on Leisure (two weeks after the *Observer* had started its Leisure page) with the splendid words, 'Suddenly another revolution is upon us.' Well, well, well.

It was only poetic justice, then, that the decision of The Sunday Times to launch a colour magazine should further worry The Observer – not to mention The Sunday Express. Indeed, hostility to the idea became almost universal. A colour magazine would not last three months; there was no 'known demand' for a colour supplement in Britain, it was filling 'a purely commercial purpose'; technical and union problems would defeat it before it even started, and even if it did start no advertiser would support it. Thomson was able to accept several bets of 100 to 1 against the magazine surviving a year.

The magazine not only survived; it changed the course of journalism in this country to an extent not yet fully appreciated and became such a financial success that two of its critics, The

Observer and The Daily Telegraph, were forced to copy it. A third, The Sunday Express, got as far as preparing a dummy for a colour magazine of its own and The Mirror group lost a fortune on one.

But, as we said earlier in this book, it was not easy. After a shaky start advertising support failed to materialise and the situation became desperate. Criticism of the editorial content of the first issue was widespread. To the rest of the newspaper world nothing the magazine did was right. There was a campaign to frighten newsagents, unions and advertisers out of having anything to do with it. The engagement of Lord Snowdon as artistic adviser caused an uproar that in retrospect appears almost unbelievable. (Even Izvestia took sides.) And when the magazine was finally established it was then attacked for being a success. In fact, the one factor that has remained constant throughout the magazine's ten-year history has been that professional reaction to it has remained almost totally adverse.

II

Roy Thomson, with his knowledge of North American newspaper practice, first began to talk of a colour supplement early in 1961. His original idea was to produce one for his regional newspapers. Collectively, these could have offered an assured circulation of more than a million – at first sight an attractive proposition for advertisers. But the longer various working parties looked at the idea the clearer it became that a colour supplement for the regional newspapers would not make any money. The main reason was to do with the economic classes of regional readership; the higher advertising rates a colour supplement required to make it viable could only be assured if the supplement was put into The Sunday Times, where circulation was concentrated upon the most worthwhile (from a marketing point of view) segment of the population. All thinking on the colour supplement now switched to this idea.

Negotiations for an editor had already started before two Thomson executives, Donald Barrett and Peter Mooney, went to New York to study the us supplements. John Anstey, then with Go, the erstwhile Kemsley holiday and travel magazine, who had done several dummies of a Saturday supplement for The News

Chronicle before its death in October, 1960, had been approached
by the then Sunday Times editor Hodson in May, 1961. After one
discussion about supplements in general Hodson offered Anstey,
at their second meeting, the job of editor of the projected supplement. Anstey accepted but before starting work went off to Nassau
to finish an article he had been writing for his magazine. There he
had received a cable from Hodson asking him to join the Thomson
team in New York and look at the editorial side of American
supplements. On his return to London he found the whole project
in some confusion. Hodson (who by this time was giving up the
editorship anyway) had gone on a tour of Kenya and Australia,
and Anstey arrived at Thomson House with only a few people
knowing what he was there for and with strict instructions not to
tell anyone what he was doing. This did not make for happy working relations, and trouble developed, mainly over what sort of
magazine it should be and what power the editor should have. In
the end Anstey left. He went on to work on a magazine idea of his
own, Europe Observed, had a spell with a financial group in the
city, and in 1963 became first editor of The Daily Telegraph
magazine – a job he holds at the time of writing.

Mark Boxer, who took over from Anstey, had had a brilliantly
varied career in journalism. At Cambridge he had been a highly
controversial editor of Granta, the university's oldest magazine.
His professional career began in 1954 with Ambassador, a glossy
magazine concerned with textiles; it is now part of the Thomson
group. He had sold art criticism to Punch and drawings to The
Daily Express; he had been men's fashion editor of the magazine
Lilliput, working with Jocelyn Stevens, the nephew of Sir Edward
Hulton, and photographer Antony Armstrong-Jones. When
Stevens had taken over Queen in February, 1957, he had engaged
Boxer as art director and the two of them had given the magazine
the face-lift which had made it so successful. In November, 1961,
Boxer was a guest of David Hicks and Lady Pamela Mountbatten
at lunch at their house at Britwell Salome, Oxfordshire. Another
guest was Robert Harling. Harling told Boxer he thought Boxer
had gone as far as he could at Queen and that it was time he tried
something new. Boxer also felt that Stevens was not prepared to
advance him further. He took the cue. 'I'd like to try something
new,' he said. 'In fact, I'm sorry I was not asked to do The Sunday
Times magazine.' (It was to appear in the following February.)
Harling said he would arrange for Boxer to see Hamilton, who was
editor by now.

The appointment was fixed in two days. Boxer was impressed with Hamilton and surprised to find him so young, and Hamilton on his side found that the more he talked with Boxer the more he was certain that he had discovered the right man.

I was looking for someone who was going to produce a lively magazine full of surprises, something to appeal to the bright young man who had previously walked across the heath on Sundays aggressively carrying the *Observer*. I wanted him to head a team of young men in their late twenties and early thirties, a group more rebellious than the rest of the staff. I wanted this team to tilt at a lot of windmills and I would protect them while they did so. In short, I wanted a magazine that would have little interest for anyone over forty. I had watched the build-up of brilliant new graphic design – the outpourings of art schools in the late forties and fifties. No newspaper was storming away in this field and I wanted the magazine to do so.

Terms were quickly agreed. Boxer was to get £5,000 a year and a year's contract. Officially he was to be special personal assistant to Hamilton but secretly he was to be editor of the colour magazine. Boxer wrote to Stevens, who was in Scotland, resigning from Queen. Both agree that Stevens took it badly at the time. 'I don't feel bitter,' Stevens, now managing director of the London Evening Standard said later. 'That's the law of Fleet Street – every man for himself. But the way in which it was done was unfortunate. I think one should be able to face people and tell them things.'

At any rate, Boxer took over at a difficult time. He inherited nothing from Anstey except some of the early staff: Ivor Lewis, Kenneth Pearson, Joyce Emerson, John Pearson, Graham Turner, and art editor Gordon Moore. (Ernestine Carter had signed Robert Carrier to do the cooking section.) Boxer's first appointment was a production manager, Stan Daw, then Susan Raven and Duncan Gardiner. When Gordon Moore resigned after the tenth number (to look ahead a bit), Boxer engaged Michael Rand, consultant graphic designer on The Daily Express. 'He was doing very clean, direct stuff and was excellent at diagrams, which was important for what we wanted to do. I felt I was good on the design ideas front but I needed someone to put my ideas into action. Within five minutes of Moore's resigning I was on the telephone to Rand to offer him the job.'

Mike Rand, a product of Goldsmiths' College School of Art, had been freelancing before he joined The Express in 1955. He immediately accepted Boxer's offer:

It was obvious even in those early days that the colour magazine was going to change publishing in Britain and I wanted to be a part of it. Mark said he wanted to make the magazine more journalistic than a glossy and needed someone used to working under pressure. I told him about my first experience with Harold Keeble on the *Express*. I had called on him one afternoon as a freelance and had shown him some samples. 'Fine,' Keeble said. 'Here, do this layout for a features page.' 'When do you want it? Will next week be all right?' 'Hell no,' Keeble said. 'Five o'clock this afternoon.' So my experience was what Mark wanted and the job suited me from the beginning.

As we shall see, Rand was to become a decisive influence in the moulding of the magazine.

Boxer's other main appointment was Clive Irving from The Observer, as deputy editor at £4,000 a year; he came in at about the fifth number, and was a skilled typographer. Boxer felt it was essential to have a deputy because he had found that his immediate job was not only to get the editorial side of the magazine under way but to help sell to the advertising agencies what was a revolutionary idea in the British magazine world.

The men who were tackling this task had run into trouble, mainly because advertising agencies are by tradition conservative when it comes to trying new media. The team was led by Michael Renshaw, advertisement director for the Thomson Organisation, Brian Nicholson, advertisement manager of The Sunday Times, and Donald Barrett, advertisement manager for the magazine, but these three brought in everyone they could think of who might be able to help them sell space, from Roy Thomson to Mark Boxer. The first dummies were mailed to agencies in September, 1961. The date for the first number of the magazine was February, 1962. Now, anxious to reach as many agencies as possible before the Christmas slow-down, the advertising department had a presentation box prepared with a 35-mm back projector, and early in October Roy Thomson, Harry Henry the marketing director, Donald Barrett, and Mark Boxer appeared before the board of Crawfords.

The Crawfords men were interested but wary. Thomson told them why he thought Britain should have a colour magazine, Barrett showed them the film on what the magazine would look like, and Boxer told them the editorial policy he envisaged – the wonders of the world, the youthful social revolution which had taken place, the whole new concept of young people making joint buying decisions. The Sunday Times team was enthusiastic and,

they thought, convincing. But it was hard going. Crawfords, like
the other agencies that followed them in those busy days before
Christmas, failed fully to grasp what the publication would be
about, its attitude, its tone. The questions indicated the difficulties:
'Are you going to do things like Princess Margaret's wedding?'
and 'Why don't you make it hard and topical?' Boxer explained
that it was not going to be another magazine devoted to colour
photographs of Royalty week after week, Barrett made clear that
it could not be hard and topical because, although it planned to
undercut all copy schedules which then existed – usually three to
four months – it would still take from five to six weeks to produce
each issue.

Then Roy Thomson gave a series of luncheons in the board-
room as a way of selling the basic idea. He sat at the head of the
table, carefully remembering everyone's name, eating sparingly
of a cold ham salad, his bottle of sweetening tablets by his side,
while well-wined and well-fed advertising men threw objections
at him. Clive Irving says the most important thing he remembers
about this period at the magazine was 'the stoicism of Roy
Thomson at those lunches, when he was confronted by whizz-kids
with slide-rules who marshalled statistical arguments allegedly
proving that this new medium was not required.'

There were bitter disappointments. At one stage Campbell's
Soups, a major colour advertiser world-wide, looked almost
certain to take a series booking provided it could have its traditional position – the first right-hand page after the major editorial
feature, and provided it liked the look of the magazine. While
Boxer worried about the restrictions this would place on his
layouts Campbell's changed its mind and decided to stay out. But
slowly other advertisers came round, and by January the first
issue was treble-booked and could comfortably have carried sixty
pages of advertisements. There was only one difficulty: many
were one-off insertions. The advertisers were prepared to give the
magazine a trial; if the first issue failed to create the impression
The Sunday Times team insisted it would, then they had not lost
too much. It was a dangerous situation for the magazine and, in
the event, nearly killed it in its infancy.

Meanwhile, on the circulation side there had been startling
developments. Distributing the magazine was a major challenge,
for no one had tried before to print part of a newspaper at a place
different from the main plant, distribute it at a different time, and
marry the two so as to reach the reader on Sunday morning.

The first intention was to distribute the magazine by road, but then Eric Cheadle, the deputy managing director of the Thomson Organisation, found that British Rail had a lot of sheds at Watford Junction, not far from the printers, that were not in use. The magazines could be stored there while awaiting distribution. As well, using the railway was only right, British Rail said, because newspaper distribution was traditionally done this way.

Cheadle and Donald Robinson, the chief circulation manager, agreed that Jack Sefton, the southern circulation manager, was the man to work out a plan to get the magazine from Sun printers on the Monday and have it distributed throughout the country at the latest by the following Saturday. Although Sefton devised a scheme that seemed foolproof in theory, there was no time for a dry run, so as Sefton remembers, 'We checked and rechecked and then prepared to wear out a lot of prayer mats.' (In the event the first issue achieved a 99 per cent success rate and the other colour magazines which have appeared since have copied The Sunday Times distribution system.)

With the unions and the newsagents matters were not going so smoothly. Cheadle had started talks with them as soon as the magazine had been announced but had run into heavy opposition. The printing unions argued that the magazine would take advertising away from the newspaper, that the newspaper would thus grow smaller and soon men would be out of work. After a lot of negotiation Cheadle satisfied them with an assurance that there was no intention of taking advertisements away from the newspaper.

The newsagents were a tougher proposition. With the Beaverbrook organisation, IPC, and The Financial Times stirring matters, the newsagents wanted nothing to do with the magazine. Sunday Express officials, they said, had convinced them that if The Sunday Times was successful in launching a colour magazine then all the other Sunday newspapers would follow and the newsagents could find themselves stuffing millions of magazines into millions of newspapers each week. Cheadle tried to show them that no other Sunday newspaper planned to follow The Sunday Times, but the newsagents' officials went off to Fleet Street and came out of the Express building with a dummy of a Sunday Express colour magazine.

IPC for its part tried to persuade the newsagents that giving away a 'free' magazine with The Sunday Times each week would hit the sale of ordinary magazines, one of the newsagents' main sources of income. As a result of all this the newsagents began to talk of wanting at least fourpence a copy to handle The Sunday Times magazine, and only a month before Christmas the National Federation of Retail Newsagents announced that they would not handle it at all. Cheadle replied by sending a leaflet to every newsagent in the country. Its main point was that the magazine was to be an extra section of the paper, not a new publication: 'The Sunday Times will remain one newspaper with one editor. We are not opening a new business next door. We are enlarging the shop'. He offered an increase in the profit margin for the newsagent from 25 to 33⅓ per cent for the extra work.

Finally, with time running dangerously short and after nights of talks, Cheadle reached agreement with the newsagents on January 22. Their margin was increased by ¾d a copy and – the factor which finally won the day – they were authorised to charge their customers an extra ¾d a copy for delivery. It was more than Roy Thomson wanted to pay. 'He thought we were mad to give way at the figure we did,' Jack Sefton, the present circulation director, recalls. 'But we had no choice. If we hadn't then the magazine would never have come out.'

Cheadle made two concessions. The first was that the magazine would carry on its title page a note saying that the ¾d delivery charge was an authorised one. And such was the resistance of the newsagents to the idea of a 'free' *magazine*, that Cheadle had to agree to its being called instead a 'section'. (It remained a section until 1964, when with the whole affair almost forgotten history it officially changed its title to magazine.)

III

On January 5, Fleet Street's interest in the magazine, already strong and not very objective, suddenly flared when it was announced that the Earl of Snowdon, the freelance photographer who had married Princess Margaret the previous year, would be joining The Sunday Times as artistic adviser. Since the appointment caused a reaction unusual even for such an emotional place as Fleet Street, it is worth pausing to set down how it came about, what it involved, and how it worked out.

Antony Armstrong-Jones, as he was before the Queen made him an Earl in October, 1961, had been a highly successful photographer. He had studied architecture at Cambridge, taken photographs for Varsity and, after working with Baron, mainly in theatre photography, had branched out on his own in 1950, operating from a former ironmonger's shop in Pimlico. He had been an immediate success, specialising in theatre photography but also doing reportage, mostly for Harold Keeble at The Daily Express. His work appeared often in Vogue, Harpers, Queen and Lilliput. He had had a successful exhibition at Kodak's in 1958 and had done a book on London, designed by Mark Boxer. His own estimate of his gross income in the late 1950s was about £20,000 a year.

Then with his marriage to Princess Margaret his career appeared to end overnight. John Gordon in The Sunday Express showed concern that Lord Snowdon was 'living in a fairytale world . . . of almost complete . . . idleness', and there was a general undercurrent of criticism that Snowdon appeared to show no desire to get back to work. Actually he *was* working. He had agreed to design a new aviary for the London Zoo, but he saw no reason – 'since I was not being supported by the State' – why he should defend himself by revealing this. He had no intention of giving up photography and was interested in expanding his career further into film-making and design. (He had joined the Council of Industrial Design as unpaid adviser.) But he could see the problems which would have arisen if he had gone back to being a freelance photographer.

At this difficult moment in his career he was approached by Mark Boxer. 'I'd known Tony for some years. He had been good on Queen – a bright idea a week at least. I could see the problems he had. I mean he couldn't go back to working for social magazines again, yet what was he going to do? I got Hamilton's okay to make an approach and then I rang Tony up and we had lunch.'

There is no doubt in Snowdon's mind why The Sunday Times wanted him. 'I'm conceited enough to think that Mark asked me because he liked my work that he had bought and used over the last ten years. Anyway, I'm not going to defend why I was asked. Why were you asked to do the history of The Sunday Times?'

The discussion with Boxer over lunch went well. Snowdon was interested but wanted time to consider. A week later he and Boxer had lunch again and Snowdon said he would like the job provided certain safeguards could be agreed. Boxer took Snowdon to meet Hamilton, who then rang Roy Thomson in Canada to put him in the picture. The contract was sorted out between Snowdon and Hamilton. Its details have been secret, but because of exaggerations about his salary and position Snowdon now feels it important that they should be known. He was to get £5,000 a year to include all his services, i.e. there would be no extra payment for photographs used (but he would retain the copyright). He would not work for any other newspaper or magazine in Britain. His name would not be used in any way to advertise The Sunday Times, it would not be used for publicity purposes, and it would not appear on the cover of the magazine. His by-line would be in the same size and type as that of the writer of any article and would appear after the writer. He would accept only those assignments which would have been available to any other Sunday Times photographer and his name would not be used as a possible aid to arranging an interview or a sitting.

Snowdon now says that if the contract appears over-protective it was because opinion was very different a decade ago.

At that particular moment in time my working for a newspaper was thought to be wrong. It was thought that I would be involved in policy-making on the paper, involved in political decisions. The contract was to protect me from being exploited because of my marriage, and it worked out very well. Anything I have done for the *Sunday Times* could have been done by any other photographer. Once this was realised things changed. In the early days of my marriage there used to be photographs of me taking photographs. Now no one would buy such a picture – no news in it. On assignments now I get on with taking photographs and afterwards, often, no one can remember who the photographer was. Looking back now it's amazing to see how controversial it all was at the time.

It is amazing. Following Hamilton's announcement on January 5, in which he made it clear that Snowdon would be expected to do 'a real job of work', first reaction was favourable. The Daily Mail welcomed Snowdon back into the ranks of working journalists and welcomed also 'the way members of the Royal Family are being allowed to move deeper into the life of the nation'; and Cyril Ray, a former Sunday Times reporter, whose ideas of the paper were out of date, quickly warned Snowdon he would find the office snobby, the pace sedate, and respect for his rank fairly marked. (All of which, Snowdon says, turned out to be wrong: the paper was fairly egalitarian, the pace was fast, and respect for his rank did not prevent writer Peter Dunn getting into a nasty argument with him, at the magazine's Christmas party!)

John Gordon, in an item out of tune with his paper's later attitude, said it was an 'excellent decision which will have wide public appeal and remove a cause of much recent criticism' –

including his own! The Observer reported the announcement in its issue of January 7, in 17 words without comment. But during the week its fury must have grown steadily, because on Sunday the 14th, it opened a two-pronged attack. In its news pages it demanded: 'How did Lord Snowdon's strange appointment to the Thomson Organisation come about? Did no one warn the Queen of the possible consequences of his involvement in the highly competitive battle for advertising and circulation in which Fleet Street is engaged, including the possible political consequences to the Royal Family? Apparently not.' It said the Palace's first anxiety was that Snowdon should have more of a job, and that after taking safeguards that was all there was to it. 'But, of course, that is not all there is to it. The Thomson management are believed to consider that Lord Snowdon's appointment will help them to put on 200,000 readers – and that is worth to them several hundred thousand pounds.'

In the same issue The Observer continued the attack in its leader columns under the heading SELLING SNOWDON:

Everyone, including the *Observer*, has said that a royal marriage should not preclude Lord Snowdon from doing work. But we believe he has chosen the wrong kind of job. The Queen's brother-in-law has already proved to be a major commercial asset to Roy Thomson in announcing his coming magazine. His special value will not be as a photographer and lay-out man. It will be as an attraction to potential advertisers in the vastly-expensive new colour-printed supplement which Mr Thomson plans to finance by advertisements alone. To do business Thomson space-sellers need only remind hesitant space-buyers of Snowdon's unique curiosity value, especially to women. It will inevitably seem unfair to rival newspapers and magazines that the Queen's close relative is used for the enlargement and enrichment of the Thomson empire.

The Observer's campaign set Fleet Street off and the matter rapidly grew out of hand. On the Monday The Times reproduced every word of The Observer's comments, and in later editions of The Daily Mail there was the rather surprising sight of The Daily Mail quoting large chunks of The Times quoting The Observer. Other newspapers, as well as television and radio, rushed to join the row. The Daily Mirror said those hostile to the appointment were a bunch of fusspots and hypocrites. Varsity claimed – incorrectly – it had once sacked Snowdon 'because he couldn't take decent photographs'. The News of the World said, 'Give Tony a Break', and Randolph Churchill in his column in that paper was splendidly Randolphian: 'When Lord Snowdon obtains a job for which he is particularly qualified, there is a great deal of disingenuous raising of eyebrows because, of course, this gives everyone an opportunity to natter about the Royal Family – which is the easiest way for stupid Editors to sell their newspapers.' The Sunday Express, despite Gordon's earlier approval of the appointment, supported The Observer. The late Robert Pitman, writing under the pseudonym of Percy Howard, said The Observer had acted in the interests of the Royal Family, and he made a sour attempt to discomfort Snowdon: 'The present proposal that he should join the Thomson group is unsatisfactory and harmful on every count. It would involve the Royal Family in politics and in competition between rival newspapers. It brings disrepute to the Throne without even giving Lord Snowdon the satisfaction of knowing that he was being employed primarily for his own undeniable gifts.'

The Daily Mail carried a cartoon showing Thomson pasting up a poster alongside one which showed a man in a bowler hat and bore the slogan, 'Top people read The Times'. Thomson's poster showed Lord Snowdon in a coronet: 'Top people R U N the Sunday Times.' The Times at first refused to comment or to print any of the letters it received. Then on January 22 it ran two carefully chosen letters, one pro, one contra.

The debate continued on Independent Television's 'What the Papers Say' (with Michael Foot taking a neutral rôle but adding that he would be delighted to give Snowdon a job on Tribune), on the BBC's 'Any Questions' (where one of the audience made the comment Snowdon remembers best of all: 'Why shouldn't Tony be allowed to take his snaps if he wants to?'); and on 'Panorama', where The Observer's editor, David Astor, defended his paper's stand to William Connor (Cassandra of The Daily Mirror). Connor had written trenchantly in favour of the appointment:

Tony Armstrong-Jones is a Royal Dicky Bird . . . who has flown from Kensington Palace to the jungle that is Fleet Street. . . . The Tony bird has been caught by a handful of corn and raisins with fish-hooks inserted in them by that most wily old feathercraft, Roy Thomson, of the Sunday Times. In a trice the macaws, the parrots, and other screaming birds in the inky undergrowth have set up a-screeching and a-yelling that splits the eardrums. . . . I would like to say at once that as an old jungle man, I welcome man mountain Snowdon.

It went on. Society photographer Marc Henrie tried to take

legal action to prevent Snowdon from taking up his job, the Liberal Party leader, Jo Grimond, attacked the appointment, and on January 30 the Labour MP, Mr Eric Fletcher, failed in the House of Commons to get the Prime Minister, Mr Macmillan, to extend the terms of reference of the Royal Commission on the Press to enable it to express an opinion on Snowdon and The Sunday Times. French, German and Russian newspapers reported the controversy (Izvestia said Snowdon was 'a victim in the play of the beasts-of-prey in the capitalist jungle') and The Daily Worker announced that if it had a vacancy for a photographer then it would offer Snowdon the job at £10,000 a year – if it had £10,000.

Some of the comment was hardly objective. Mr Jocelyn Stevens, obviously still annoyed at the loss of Mark Boxer to The Sunday Times, suggested Machiavellian goings-on – non-existent in fact – in an interview in The Sunday Express: 'I think that Mr Boxer was employed by the Thomson group partly for his undoubted ability and partly for the fact that The Sunday Times thought he might be capable of obtaining Lord Snowdon's services to their staff. . . . Look at it this way: If Lord Snowdon was not Princess Margaret's husband would he have been offered The Sunday Times job?'

The answer to this question was provided by Roy Thomson, interviewed on his return from Canada. He was frank and blunt: 'We want him for his ability,' he said. 'If his name helps, well that is all right. But he will have a job to do. Don't make any mistake about that.' Did Snowdon's name have anything to do with his getting the job? 'It was a factor probably, but he is a man of great ability and we want him for that ability.'

Perhaps the most pertinent comment of all was that of columnist Dee Wells in The Daily Herald. 'Let Lord Beaverbrook howl, let David Astor be cross,' Miss Wells wrote. 'But both of them would have been delighted to hire Tony if they could have got him.'

Snowdon started work on February 1, 1962. His first assignment – to photograph the French artist Georges Braque – fell through when Braque refused to see him on the ground that he never allowed anyone to take photographs of him at work. His next job, to photograph Fonteyn and Nureyev at rehearsal at the Covent Garden ballet school – where he often worked before his marriage – brought cries of protest from other newspapers. Snowdon was allowed to take photographs on his own, before, as The Daily Mirror put it, 'other (non-titled) Press photographers were allowed in'. The Observer also found this strange. 'While the Earl of Snowdon (by very special arrangement) was snapping away,' it wrote, '. . . non-titled photographers were collecting for a later on-stage run-through.'

The explanation, as Covent Garden pointed out in a statement a few days later, was simple. 'The Sunday Times took the initiative and approached the Royal Opera House in the first place for permission to take photographs of Nureyev in rehearsal at the Ballet School. In view of the widespread interest in Nureyev's debut at Covent Garden photographers from other newspapers were invited to take photographs in the Royal Opera House itself.'

The incident gave Snowdon his first experience of the difficulties under which he would have to work. There were others. On the set of the film 'Billy Liar' and later during the shooting of 'The Victors' he was accused by fellow photographers of using his title to obtain special privileges, and an unsuccessful complaint was made to the National Union of Journalists.

Snowdon was rapidly getting fed-up. The Evening Standard had recorded the number of days in one week that he appeared at The Sunday Times office, The Daily Mail photographed him taking photographs, and The Daily Sketch ran a story saying he was about to resign. However, as it became clear that he intended to stay despite the difficulties and that The Sunday Times was not unfairly exploiting his name, interest faded and he was allowed to get on with his series of portraits of artists at work which eventually became the book 'Private View', with John Russell and Bryan Robertson.

In the magazine office Snowdon's presence created no great stir. He got on well with the rest of the staff, and if he minded Dunn's lecturing him at the Christmas party on how Dunn thought he should behave he did not show it: in fact he specifically asked if Dunn could go on a Far East assignment with him. His photographs were treated strictly on merit. On occasions Boxer would say, 'It's simply not good enough, Tony – go away and do it again'; and Snowdon admits that some of his assignments ended in the waste-paper basket.

There are varying opinions as to which story constituted his breakthrough. Hamilton considers it was the issue on India which he did with writer David Holden in April, 1966. Snowdon says: 'Hamilton suggested I go. At that time everyone was doing poverty in India. I said I would go only if I could do a pro-India piece.

I feel photography is a way of informing people visually. I don't take photographs for other photographers. I felt that anything I did that concentrated on the social gap in India would have been photographs for other photographers rather than comprehensive visual information. On the other hand we didn't ignore the poverty. We made the point without hammering at it.' The result was a comprehensive examination of 'the huge and dusty face of modern India' from the Punjab to Kerala not concentrating – as Indians complain so much Western reportage does – on what still remained to be done, but on what had already been achieved.

Snowdon himself is the first to admit there are some jobs he cannot undertake because of his position. There was a project for him to go to Russia. The Foreign Office let it be known that it was not keen on the idea and Snowdon agreed he was not the man for the job. 'I wanted to go, but anything I did would have had to have been too sycophantic and P R O-ish so as not to be politically controversial. In a case like that it was better to send another photographer.'

Michael Rand and assistant editor Francis Wyndham, through whom Snowdon works, realised that he produced better black-and-white photographs than he did colour ones and that he was obviously happier working on stories with some social significance. Snowdon says:

I liked the piece I did on Venice with Francis. We looked at the social problems and the city's future as well as the usual things. The social problem features – old age, cruelty to children, loneliness and mental sickness – have meant more to me than any others. They were challenging and very difficult and I became emotionally involved. I took two or three months on each of them. I didn't want to do them just in London – newspapers tend to concentrate a bit too much on the south-east and to think that Birmingham is in Africa. And they were difficult because you musn't take photographs at the expense of people. With features like old age and mental sickness, particularly mental sickness, it's a hairline of taste whether you are doing it at their expense or helping other people to understand. It's a strange thing. I do a nice head of Sophia Loren and people notice it and say complimentary things. On the mental sickness piece I didn't get a single reaction of any kind. People just don't want to know.

Snowdon's contract has latterly been altered to allow him to go back to working for the English Vogue, and he does occasional advertising and promotional photographs for organisations like I C I and Shell. He has increased the time he spends on his docu-

mentaries for TV and has, in consequence, been doing less for The
Sunday Times. Working with him is not easy. All the writers who
have been on assignments with Snowdon say he drives himself so
hard and develops such nervous tension that he is exhausting to
work with. (Wyndham recalls that Snowdon took an hour getting
ready to photograph Dame Edith Evans. He had arrived at her
flat early but he wanted to calm his nerves before he started.)
There has also been the problem of what to tell the subject.
Wyndham says: 'Before we go on a job Tony always says, "Don't
tell them it's me."' But Wyndham usually uses his own judgment.

Two occasions when subjects were not told have provided the
magazine staff with their favourite Snowdon stories. On the first
he was photographing theatrical landladies. After watching him
at work for several hours one tough landlady pressed a £1 note
into his hand as he was leaving. 'You've worked bloody hard,
lad,' she said. 'I know they don't pay you boys much. Go out and
get yourself a good dinner.' Snowdon says it was one of the nicest
things that have happened to him. On the other occasion (when
Wyndham was away) he and a reporter were to call on a well-
known left-wing writer. The reporter rang to arrange a time and
was promptly invited to lunch. She accepted and added, 'Oh, I'll
have a photographer with me.' 'That's all right,' said the writer.
'There's a nice pub across the road. He can eat there.' The
reporter kept quiet, arrived at the writer's house, introduced
Snowdon as the photographer and then watched the rather
frantic rush to set an extra place.

IV

While Snowdon was weathering in silence the controversy over
his appointment to the magazine, Boxer was putting the finishing
touches to the first issue. It was forty pages and featured 'a sharp
glance at the mood of Britain', with a feature on the city of
Lincoln, an article by Tom Stacey, a piece on the new generation
of pilots, John Russell on the pioneer of pop art, Peter Blake,
Ernestine Carter appraising Mary Quant, and a James Bond
short story. Although fifteen of the forty pages were in colour, all
but two of the editorial features were in black and white, a fact
which was to figure in the torrent of criticism the first issue was to
receive.

The first printing was launched with a party at the Sun printing works at Watford on the afternoon of January 29, 1962. After tea in the directors' dining-room Roy Thomson pressed the button which started the print and made a brief speech: 'What we are doing today is something that many newspapers have wanted to do for a long time – but everyone said it was impossible. Now we have proved that it *is* possible and we are doing it; I and all of us here know it will be a great success.' The machines started running and the first copies came off the presses. Thomson picked one up, peered at it, turned to Hamilton and said, 'My God! This is going to be a disaster.'

Hamilton did not agree. 'The first issue wasn't outstanding, true. But I could see what it was going to do. Only one outside person had the foresight to see what was happening and to see what we were aiming for: Francis Williams. He said the magazine didn't interest him but he was sure that it would go over well with his daughter. In six months it had changed the face of journalism.'

They were a desperate six months. The first issue brought twelve hundred letters of protest – mostly about the magazine's 'too modern' appearance. Hamilton answered all the letters personally. 'I explained that I was a family man with four lively children and that I believed passionately that we had to open our minds to the changing world. I got back the most extraordinary letters, often enclosing photographs of the writer's own children. This sort of personal touch is very important. I consider that an editor at his peril neglects paying attention to a reader with a grievance.'

Thomson, for his part, immediately admitted his disappointment in his usual blunt terms: 'We were fooling around with something we didn't really understand and we botched it the first time. But the next issue will be better and the one after that better still.' Boxer agreed with the criticism. 'Frankly the magazine was a disaster to begin with. I'm sure that they had thoughts of replacing me.'

Losses were soon running at around £20,000 a week, and there was a certain amount of gloating and 'I told you so' in Fleet Street. The Financial Times said that colour was bound to bring heartbreak except to those who owned the colour printers – 'colour ads are conspicuously lacking, for example, in a most conspicuous place, The Sunday Times colour section' – and Beaverbrook started a joke at Thomson's expense. 'Roy Thomson has taught us something new in journalism: how we may have colour without advertisements or, alternatively, advertisements without colour.'

But in all this gloom there was one bright fact – botched or not, the first issue of the magazine had increased sales of The Sunday Times by 150,000 copies a week. Clearly reader demand was there – but could it be sustained?

There were further staff changes. George Perry arrived and Tom Margerison, science correspondent of The Sunday Times, moved to the magazine to tighten up the administration. 'Mark couldn't handle both the editorial and the administration sides and then C.D. said to me, "I want you to do the colour mag, Tom. It's going to come to a stop unless something is done. Can you go in today?" He was not entirely clear what the job was to be and I went in thinking that I was taking over from Mark as the new editor. But Mark stayed on. Well, I thought, we are going to be co-editors, but it finally became clear to me that I was the deputy. The combination worked well. Mark was concerned mainly with visual effect, I think at the expense of words. One of his catch-phrases was, "Well, this is a nice layout. Now, where are we going to put the wordies?" On the other hand I was interested in words, so everything went smoothly.'

Slowly the editorial deficiencies were made good. But the poor start had so depressed the advertising prospects that improvement had to be fought for, column inch by column inch. Hamilton went on television to be cross-examined by Woodrow Wyatt. He vigorously defended the decision to start the magazine – 'at one stroke it has put on fifteen per cent additional sales. It is quite unique in British newspapers to have done this so quickly' – and forecast that it certainly would be 'an irresistible success as the months go on'. Roy Thomson – either showing his confidence that the magazine would succeed or pulling off a brilliant bluff – announced on July 2, only five months after the first issue, that he had signed a five-year contract with Sun Printers so that they could 'make plans for the expansion of the colour section'.

Although Thomson and Hamilton were right it was not every-one in Thomson House who agreed with them at the time. The advertising department had had to fight off a suggestion from some of the directors, alarmed at the magazine's losses, that it should be turned into a sponsored magazine. Boxer – 'I was almost hysterical at the idea' – joined forces with Donald Barrett to defeat the suggestion. Next the advertisers had to be persuaded to stop standing on the sidelines and watching to see whether the magazine would survive.

Roy Thomson began his lunches again. 'They had the rate

cards out before we had finished the main course,' remembers one of the guests, Alan Eden-Green, then of Wedgwoods. 'It was blunt talk on both sides.' Brian Nicholson says that the blunter the talk became, the harder Roy Thomson sold. 'He had the ability to convince people of his faith in the eventual success of the idea. No one left those luncheons other than fully convinced that Roy meant business and that the magazine would go on.'

Yet two months after the launch the magazine was down to four pages of advertisements and staggering dismally into the summer period. The sceptics who had bet Thomson 100 to 1 that the magazine would not last a year got ready to collect. But in June came an unexpected boost. Three months had been allowed to elapse before any reader research was undertaken, and the results of the first test were startling. Circulation of The Sunday Times was at nearly 1,100,000 and holding steady – an increase since the launch of the magazine of 127,000 copies. Nothing which had been added to the paper except the colour magazine could have caused The Sunday Times to have pulled so strongly away from The Observer. Elated, Barrett sent the figures to the advertising agencies and followed up a few days later with further figures to show that the new readers were, as far as advertisers were concerned, the right sort of readers.

The lunches in the boardroom now increased in frequency and intensity. 'We would get, say, the managing director of J. Walter Thompson, Tom Sutton, to bring along eight or ten of his top executives,' Barrett recalls, 'and eight or ten of our boys would give them the hard sell. They were very much "gloves off" affairs. But the agencies' innate caution could not be overcome – everyone was still standing back waiting to see who would lead the way.' Barrett realised how serious a problem this 'waiting for a leader' syndrome had become when he saw a letter Thomson had written to the important agency of Mather and Crowther. Addressed to the chairman, it sought further support from the agency. The chairman had passed it to the manager for a decision. In the margin the problem was set out. Mather and Crowther had bought £50,000-worth of space in the magazine in its early days. Should they now buy more? Someone had written at the bottom of the letter: 'Let's wait and see who else goes in.'

Michael Renshaw, the advertisement director, Brian Nicholson, and Barrett had a talk. They decided on a desperate gamble to break this 'waiting for each other' attitude which was threatening the magazine and which had threatened Picture Post when it was founded in 1938. First Barrett set his sights on advertisers who were so big that if they came in others would have to follow, and to get these key advertisers he broke all the rules about discounts. The Ford Motor company, for example, was allotted 12 pages at a discount of 40 per cent. The Central Office of Information was offered a double page RAF advertisement in colour for the black-and-white rate in return for revealing what the response was. (This proved a breakthrough. The COI, which had always been against colour on the grounds that the increased cost was not justified by an extra response, was astounded at colour's pulling power. The colour advertisement brought four times the number of replies drawn by similar black-and-white advertisements in the magazine; the edict against colour advertising was lifted and colour became a regular COI medium.)

Once the bookings from large advertisers were enough to look respectable, Barrett – with Renshaw's full approval – wrote in long-hand to sixty of his agency contacts, tipping them off to the state of the magazine's forward bookings and enclosing a list of actual space reservations for the period January–June 1963. He fully realised how risky this was, especially as he did not dare ask permission from the advertisers who had booked space in case it was refused, but he felt that the risk was justified.

The scheme worked. Bookings increased, and as Harry Henry and Peter Mooney of the marketing department poured out promotion material and badgered the agencies with the results of their research, they increased again. A jubilant Roy Thomson, while agreeing that the losses had reached 'terrifying figures', announced on October 26, 1962, that the magazine had passed break-even point – 'just as I was considering suicide'. When they were able to tell him in January, 1963, that bookings for the year ahead already amounted to nearly £1 million, he decided that a celebration of its first birthday was in order. Some of Henry's men under Ghriam Grant were given the job of working out what form the celebrations should take. At Tony Martin's suggestion they decided on a week-end in Moscow, practically the only place in the world where you could take 138 top business-men and know they had not been there already.

In three weeks Thomson and his executives managed to arrange the whole affair. This included persuading the Russians to lay on for free a TU 114 turboprop aircraft, then the largest passenger plane flying, checking that Moss Bros. had enough fur coats and, biggest coup of all, getting the Russians to agree to waive individual visas, a precedent in Anglo-Russian relations. The guests were given a reception by the Foreign Trade Ministry, a lunch with the Union of Soviet Journalists, tours of the Kremlin and the Pravda newspaper plant, and finally an audience with Khrushchev himself at which the Russian leader and Thomson traded political wisecracks.

It was a birthday party no one could ignore, especially when Whitney Straight, deputy chairman of Rolls-Royce, went off and looked up his old Cambridge friend Guy Burgess. Yet the immediate rivals of The Sunday Times, The Observer, The Sunday Telegraph and The Sunday Express, reported the trip as flatly as possible, identifying Thomson merely as 'the Canadian newspaper proprietor'. 'Intermural jealousy,' Time magazine commented, 'kept Thomson's competitors from reporting a good story.' There were to be other Thomson trips to Russia, but the first took the limelight.

V

By the summer of 1963, when technical improvements allowed the printing of back-to-back colour, previously impossible, it was clear beyond all doubt that the magazine was an outstanding success. The cost had not been negligible. In its first year of operation it lost nearly £900,000, but once established it never looked back. Advertising expanded steadily, reaching its peak in 1968–9; in the autumn of 1969 there were eight 96-page issues in a row.

As advertising improved, so did the editorial content. Stronger use of editorial colour forced the advertisers to improve the impact of their advertisements. In some issues the advertisements now threatened the editorial matter. Margerison remembers an advertisement from the Jamaica Tourist Board: 'It was a real stunner, but it gave us the problem of how to stop it overshadowing the editorial.'

Boxer was convinced that the answer was better features:

I deliberately went outside the newspaper to get writers: people like David Sylvester, Francis Wyndham – a great mixture of intellectual and pop journalist – and Dick West, who was bound to get us into controversy, but I thought that we should welcome this.

The newspaper wasn't too happy about writers coming from outside, but my whole idea was not to have in the magazine more of what was in the newspaper. I used to say at conferences, 'That's the kind of thing the newspaper would do. Let's not do it.'

With its policy taking shape and its staff settling down the magazine began to produce some good issues, and by mid-1964 it was clear that the idea was working so well that the other quality Sunday papers would have to compete to survive. On July 24, Time magazine, in a piece headed 'Imitating the Imitator', wrote, with some degree of misinformation in its drama:

They scoffed in 1962 when Thomson tacked a New World gimmick, the four-colour magazine supplement, on to the anaemic corpus of one of his new London properties, the *Sunday Times*. They gloated when Thomson's Folly, as the Times supplement soon was dubbed, lost $2,250,000 in its first 18 months. But by last week, with Thomson's Folly an established success and its creator ennobled with the title Lord Thomson of Fleet, they were imitating the imitator all over London. At the *Sunday Observer*, a quality paper that has steadily yielded ground to Thomson's renascent *Sunday Times*, Editor-Owner David Astor rushed plans to add a competitive colour supplement of his own this fall. The *Sunday Telegraph*, which has also slipped in the quality Sunday standing, informed its readers that they would shortly get a Sunday-type supplement on Friday. . . . Max Aitken, Beaverbrook's son and heir, is fabricating a Thomson-like appendage for the *Sunday Express*.

The Observer's magazine began on September 6, 1964, despite Astor's comment made to his staff at the time of The Sunday Times magazine's launch, 'It's not the sort of thing The Observer would go in for.' The Telegraph magazine began on January 12, 1964. The Sunday Express did not go past the dummy stage. It was a satisfying moment for Thomson and The Sunday Times team, and Boxer says with some understatement: 'We realised that we had made it into quite a respectable magazine. We had made it work when everyone said it couldn't be done.'

Then, surprisingly, he decided to leave. On May 4, 1965, Illustrated Newspapers, a member of the Thomson Organisation, announced a new magazine, London Life, which would incorporate the old Tatler. It was to be under the direction of Mark Boxer, who now says: 'I was looking around for a fresh challenge. When the chance to do London Life came up I decided to take it.'

It turned out to be a mistake. London Life failed and Boxer's spell as editor lasted only six weeks. He returned to The Sunday Times, had a spell on the newspaper, is now an associate editor of the magazine, and draws cartoons as 'Marc' for The Times. (London Life, after several changes of name and editors, finally folded in 1968.) The man who succeeded Boxer on the magazine was Godfrey Smith.

VI

Smith's earlier career on the paper has been mentioned in an earlier part of this book. He joined The Sunday Times in 1951 after coming down from Oxford, where he had been president of the Union. He became Lord Kemsley's personal assistant, then news editor of the paper, then Atticus. He left Gray's Inn Road in 1961 and spent eighteen months with The Daily Express; by October, 1962, he was back at The Sunday Times working with Boxer on the magazine. He contributed ideas, wrote profiles, processed copy, edited material and for fifteen months helped generally to produce the magazine. Then he moved to head a special projects unit, an idea of Hamilton's which concentrated on long-term propositions and included some good young journalists like Margaret Laing, Pauline Peters, Stephen Fay and David Leitch. Smith says: 'In March, 1964, Mark told me he was leaving the magazine and asked whether I would like to take over. I said I'd like to think about it, went off to the South of France for Easter and when I came back said yes, I'd be delighted to do it.' There was an overlap period and Smith officially became editor on June 28, 1965.

His first problem was the assistant editor, Derek Jewell, who had originally joined the paper in 1962 as personal assistant to Hamilton. Hamilton had moved Jewell to the magazine in 1963: 'to push the harder kind of news story', Jewell says, 'and to provide a balance of personalities – I think. I like to believe that I am a fair catalyst.' Smith's first move was to take Jewell to lunch. 'I said, "Look here, I've got this job and I don't know if I can do it. I'm going to need your help. Let's work together." He agreed and we did very happily for five years.' (Jewell then left to become publishing director of Times Newspapers Ltd.)

Smith agrees that he took over a magazine already functioning well, and he therefore decided against any drastic changes. 'The only brief I had from Hamilton was that the magazine should have variety and surprise. I started ideas meetings about every two or three weeks. We'd have some cold food and a few bottles of wine and formulate things. I didn't sit down and write any policy. I suppose I just tried to produce a magazine my friends would like. Anyway, it was soon running like a cabinet with collective decisions and ideas.'

Competition from its two rivals had not proved worrying. Figures for 1964 showed that the magazine had carried an average of 22 pages of advertising in a 48-page issue, and in spite of a 10 per cent increase in advertising rates and the share of the market taken by the Observer and Telegraph magazines the demand for space continued to increase. By 1969 it reached 1,757 pages and in 1971, 1,851. In 1969 the magazine won the Gold Medal of Design and Art Direction for Don McCullin's photographic coverage of the Vietnam war, and in 1970 it won it again for its serial 'The Thousand Makers of the Twentieth Century'.

Smith says: 'We go for all the middle-class preoccupations – the car, houses, the cinema, antiques, health. Our technique, when we decide to do a big project, is to get the best young expert we can find and instruct him: "You tell us about it in your own way and then we'll turn it into visuals and text." We throw at him every kind of question we can imagine. Take the issue we devoted to the Pill (April 28, 1968). We got the experts to provide the nitty gritty and then it was up to us to make it digestible – lots of photographs and devices to make it an easier read. But – and this is important – no matter how frivolous the illustrations might appear, the text is impeccable. The Pill issue became the most up to date and authoritative work on the subject and went on to become a book.'

For his part Jewell found his No. 2 position on the magazine ideal. 'I would have had doubts about being editor because I wouldn't have had a chance to write. Looking after production, writing, and organising big issues suited me perfectly.' Jewell organised the first Automania issue in October, 1965. Advertised heavily on television it added a remarkable 70,000 copies to the newspaper's circulation that week. It also launched on a success-ful career in design the then unknown Alan Aldridge, who painted the psychedelic mini on the magazine's cover – very startling stuff for that time. Another of Jewell's major issues was in 1967 when he, Michael Rand, and Donald McCullin spent a bizarre ten days with F-M Lord Montgomery in the Western Desert.

As art director, Michael Rand has proved one of the magazine's most important influences, especially as Smith, less of a design

man than Boxer, left the design side in Rand's hands and production to Nick Mason. Rand had been joined in 1965 by David King,
who had designed the Briefing pages for The Observer. King was
appointed art editor and with Rand's encouragement began
producing unusual and stimulating layouts. Rand's aims for the
magazine were precise. 'We are one of the few magazines that are
still basically visual. We can use pictures and drawings and diagrams at their best. If we want to give large coverage to something,
we can. We gave Donald McCullin six spreads on Ireland. They
can't do that even in Life or Paris Match.'

Other continuing influences on the magazine are Francis
Wyndham, perhaps the writer with its widest intellectual grasp,
who went with Boxer to London Life and then returned; and
Peter Crookston, the magazine's deputy editor. Crookston, who
arrived from The Observer in February, 1964, left to edit Nova in
1969, and returned to The Sunday Times a year later. (This led
associate editor of the paper, Leonard Russell, to remark, 'They all
come back' and to recite a long list which included Murphy,
Boxer, Smith, Irving, Tomalin, Wyndham and Crookston.)

Under Smith, Jewell, Rand, and Crookston, the magazine's
emphasis has been more on social reporting – with, for example,
Peter Dunn on the way of life in the provinces and Philip Norman
on aspects of the United States; on long-term investigations by
reporters James Fox and Peter Gillman; and on articles of consumer and educational interest, usually put together by Robert
Lacey. And although it still covers fashion, its fashion editor,
Meriel McCooey, presents it in a refreshing and irreverent way.
On the visual side, photographers like Donald McCullin, Snowdon, Ray Green, and Philip Jones-Griffiths, all more interested in
socially-significant photography than in trend-setting, have contributed their share to the magazine's change.

Perhaps the most successful project the magazine has so far
undertaken is 'The Thousand Makers of the Twentieth Century'.
The idea was Smith's.

I got it in the bath. I have a great friend in the circulation department:
Bob Sloman. We were in the RAF together. We have lots of conferences
about circulation. Sloman was always telling me that we pushed too hard
in the spring and autumn – which are peak circulation periods anyway.
He wanted us to find a way of straightening out the slump in the summer.
I was sitting in the bath thinking of how we might do this. Would a series
work? Traditionally, no one ever runs a series in the summer. The
universities are down, the schools are closed and a lot of our readers are

away on holiday. Would a different type of series work? Something to collect, something to cut out?

Then suddenly I thought of the thousand names. I got out of the bath and rang Harry Evans [by now editor of the *Sunday Times*] and he said straightaway 'go ahead'. The aim was to put into the thousand names every person who had coloured the imagination of the twentieth century. Each would have a bibliography: if anyone reads every book we recommended it would take him ten years.

It was a risky business to devote the whole energy of the magazine staff to such an untried project, and we had all sorts of early troubles. For example our prototype binder. We had a meeting in Hamilton's room to discuss it. Derek Jewell had just done a business course. He looked at the binder and said 'Will it stand up to the wear and tear it's likely to get around the house? The only way to find out is to test it.' He flung it on the floor and the whole damned thing fell to pieces.

In the event, the project was a great success. It didn't cost the paper a penny because we did it out of our ordinary page-rate budget. The advertising people said we should sell a thousand of the expensive binders (at 17s 6d each) and ten thousand of the others (at 4s). In fact we sold 60,000 and pulled in an extra 60,000 circulation for thirteen weeks. The only thing on the debit side was that we devoted so much of the magazine to the One Thousand Names that there wasn't much room for anything else.

Smith is confident of the magazine's future. He stresses that it has, apart from 1962–3, made a profit every year and that it now has 42–44 per cent of the total pool of colour magazine advertising – a pool which, largely due to the launch of The Sunday Times magazine, has grown to £11 million a year. The most recent National Readership Survey figures show that at 4,286,000 the magazine has 268,000 more readers than the newspaper itself. It has a compact staff – eighteen full-time (average age about thirty) and a number of freelances and people on retainers – compared with more than 100 on the newspaper itself. The magazine has broken a lot of new ground in techniques, brought a number of changes to British photography, and since it publishes about a million words a year has offered enormous scope for freelance writers.

All the same, as has been said, commentators' reaction to it has remained almost totally adverse, down to a woman don's view expressed in a BBC radio discussion: 'One ought to recognise quite plainly that there is an evil there.' The evil, she said, was the stimulation of the craving for pleasure and possessions; the supplements justified and glorified this craving.

Karl Miller, editor of The Listener, continued this criticism in an article for The Sunday Times magazine. The case against the magazines, he wrote, was that advertising contracts corrupted, that the context depraved, and that 'it is insulting to set down photographs of starving children amid photographs of matchstick models. Pictures of Getaway people do not go with pictures of ghetto people; pictures of Martini people or After-Eight people do not go with Richard Avedon's or Lord Snowdon's pictures of mad people.' Miller tended to agree with the case against the magazine, its sharp contrasts, its staple subject matter. He saw the typical magazine subject as 'a very gifted avant-garde artist, under thirty, who consigns his costly masterpieces to a vault in a region of Venezuela accessible only to the Mafia and the CIA.' He believed that colour journalism, in responding to the appeals generated by its advertisements, had created an ethos 'of spending, of owner-ship, of opportunity and expansion, an ethos in which the respect for affluence that radiates from the advertisements is tempered by sharp feelings of guilt and social responsibility.'

Smith sees nothing wrong in this – 'that's what life is about for the middle class: eating their soufflés and discussing Biafra over the dinner-table'; and Miller agrees that there are examples of the magazine's contributing to argument and criticism on important subjects. He cites its championship of Biafra – 'they (were) alive to the progress of the war as few other British newspapers... and they held out against Foreign Office orthodoxy to which the parent paper at times proved receptive' – and the analysis by Richard Wollheim of the aims of protesting art students. 'The magazine can claim to have assisted the expansion and experiments associated with the art of the Sixties.' One might add Norman Lewis's exposé of the condition of the Amazon Indians, Bruce Page's piece on corruption in Ghana, Richard West's profile of Jomo Kenyatta, the three issues on the United States, Donald McCullin's disturbing work on Vietnam, to mention but a few; while entire issues devoted to The Mind and the Body, the Human Face, the Camera, the Cinema, Old Age, Loneliness, and The First Year of a Child's Life were outstanding.

There are valid criticisms of the magazine. It has occasionally pushed a good idea too far. After a 20-man saturation coverage – known to the staff as 'reporting in width' – on a day in the life of Cambridge, it went on to do a day in the life of London Airport, and then, with less success, a day in the life of a Jugoslav town. But it is not afraid to experiment, and it is prepared to try ideas which would daunt the rest of Fleet Street. So one cannot escape the feeling that a lot of the criticism of the magazine, particularly in its earlier days, arose because the idea and the changes it implied were unwelcome in what is after all a basically conservative industry, and because the men devoted to making a success of the magazine were regarded as too brash, too bright, too confident, and too young. Perhaps, as Smith says, it will not be until the history of journalism is written at the end of this century that the real impact made by The Sunday Times magazine will be properly assessed.

VII

Denis Hamilton's accession to the editor's chair in October, 1961, had been made on his own clearly defined terms. As editorial director of Kemsley Newspapers he had lacked the independent editorial control necessary to make the radical changes he felt The Sunday Times needed if it was to maintain its lead in the increasingly competitive field of quality newspapers. Now he demanded and got from Thomson a free hand to expand the paper along lines he had been considering for some time:

I had this strong feeling that there was an immense amount of sale lying around in the middle classes waiting to be tapped. I felt that they did not want to read a rehash of the week's news, and in those days little seemed to happen on a Saturday. I was impressed by the great post-war success of *Time* and *Newsweek*, especially the popularity of their back-page features, the non-hard news pieces on health, business, housing, the Press – the sort of thing which at that time was not getting into British Sunday papers at all. I also wanted to get a long read into the news-pages, something on the lines of a *Time* cover story, a way of covering contemporary things in greater detail. Pat Murphy and I had discussed this many times and we agreed that when we could find the right sort of reporters to do it we would go ahead.

The idea of what was to become Insight, one of the landmarks in the development of The Sunday Times, was, it can be seen from this, clearly in Hamilton's mind. Yet there are members of the staff prepared to swear that it was Pat Murphy's. Murphy himself has an explanation. 'One of the secrets of Hamilton's success is that he has a way of making people believe that they originated an idea

Opposite: Denis Hamilton by Snowdon.

themselves. It was only later when you thought back on it that you realised that Hamilton had planted the idea with you and that he was really behind it. Practically every innovation the paper made during this period of expansion came originally from Hamilton.'

After the initial enthusiasm about news-magazine journalism nothing seemed to happen. Murphy put the idea down in a memorandum and two dummies were worked up, but there was no possibility of starting the project without recruiting new staff. Hamilton did not want the average casual reporters but 'first-class men, at home in any field, able to write well and produce copy under pressure, and not worried about undertaking schemes that could go on for months.'

He went off to the United States (where he had two interviews with President Kennedy) and the idea got pushed to the back of the shelf. Then late in 1962 two events occurred which brought up the project again.

The first was that Godfrey Smith, who had gone to The Daily Express, mentioned to his erstwhile mentor, Murphy, that he would like to come back. Murphy suggested to Hamilton that Smith could put the background-to-the-news scheme into operation. In the event, as we have seen, Smith went to The Sunday Times magazine to help Boxer and later headed the special projects department. But Murphy's suggestion about placing Smith revived Hamilton's interest in the news-background idea (he also recollected and was spurred on by Roy Jenkins's splendid inside story of the ICI–Courtauld fight which appeared in The Observer in 1961) just at the time that the second event occurred. In December the news magazine Topic folded.

Topic, a gallant attempt to create a British equivalent of Time or Newsweek, had brought together a number of bright people, some of whom have since gone to the top. Those relevant to the story of The Sunday Times include Clive Irving, now consultant to Newsday, Long Island; Ron Hall, now a managing editor of the paper; Jeremy Wallington, now executive producer, Granada Television; Michael Parkinson, TV star and occasional Sunday Times sports columnist; Alan Brien, its present TV critic; and Nicholas Tomalin, one of the paper's best special correspondents.

Hamilton saw Topic's collapse as a chance to recruit some highly-suitable talent for his news-background scheme. He contacted Irving and offered him the job. Irving, who had been editor of Topic for only ten weeks, also had offers from Michael Berry, who wanted a news-analysis operation for The Sunday

Telegraph, and Geoffrey Cox, who thought the technique could be translated to television for IT N. Irving naturally listened to what each of the three had to offer. 'Berry seemed to get easily put-off when we talked about departmental autonomy. Cox was worried about chain-of-command and such. Hamilton said simply "Do it".'

Irving was hired at £4,000 a year and Ron Hall and Jeremy Wallington, both unknown to Irving before Topic, were engaged with him on his recommendation (at £2,000 a year each). Hamilton met Hall and Wallington briefly – 'Just to make sure we didn't each have two heads' – and the whole operation was marked down to begin on January 1, 1963. Before we see how these three ex-Topic men created what became Insight, we need to look at Hamilton's approach to being editor, because this played a vital part in the subsequent success of the scheme.

The first thing to understand about Hamilton is that it is difficult to separate Colonel C. D. Hamilton, DSO, from Denis Hamilton, editor. One made the other.

My university was the British Army. I wasn't a fightin', shootin', huntin', regular officer but a Territorial. My friends who had been a little older than me had gone to Spain for the Civil War. It was clear how things were going, so I joined up at the time of Munich. The war taught me one very important thing: you can do anything if you have the right sort of people. You don't have to have a lot of time for training – just the right sort of people welded into the right sort of organisation. I became. convinced that the so-called art of leadership is in selecting the people to work with you.

A wartime experience clearly helped confirm this view.

I commanded a battalion that was ordered to go to Normandy. I went to a fellow battalion that wasn't going and I raided its best officers. I took a night train to London and I bludgeoned the War Office into agreeing to let me have them. As an editor I have tended to behave in a similar manner. I look over the battlefield and then go hunting for talent.

There are several examples to confirm Hamilton's skill at this hunting out of talent; the one concerning the present editor of Insight, John Barry, is characteristic. Barry was doing a course in journalism at the Regent Street Polytechnic in 1961. He was seventeen-and-a-half. One night Hamilton delivered the lecture. Barry questioned him closely on how The Sunday Times worked. Hamilton asked Barry to call to see him at the office, where it was arranged that Barry should go to work for The Sheffield Telegraph and Star. When he had been there two-and-a-half years Thomson got rid of the Sheffield papers. Barry thought he went with the deal but Hamilton remembered him and sent for him and he was hired for The Sunday Times, where he started in the newsroom a few days after his twentieth birthday.

Allowing the theory that an editor's first task is to recruit the right sort of talent as lieutenants and then allow the lieutenants to recruit in their own right, Hamilton's choice of Irving made eminent sense. To anyone else there would have appeared many drawbacks. Irving was not an uncritical admirer of The Sunday Times and had been sniping at it in Topic, but this had probably helped rather than hindered his selection. 'Hamilton doesn't like criticism any more than anyone else but he feels that someone smart enough to make valid points should be working for *him*.' As well, Irving was, in conservative Fleet Street circles, considered something of a 'wild boy', undoubtedly talented, but bound to overstep himself sooner or later.

'I knew all this,' Hamilton says. 'I knew some people would say that I was taking a risk with Irving. But I prefer to cope with people I have to pull back than with those who stay still. I can handle people who get me into trouble whereas I don't know what to do with people who do not move at all. I knew I was creating difficulties in hiring Irving and his Young Turks. We were all set for a collision course at once and the whole thing could have fallen apart.'

In the event it very nearly did. Irving, Hall, and Wallington arrived at Thomson House on New Year's Day, 1963, in the middle of a snowstorm. Irving was there first because in those days he had a habit of keeping his watch twenty minutes fast. Pat Murphy installed them in a corner-room on the fifth-floor. Murphy was an editor of the old school, painstaking, meticulous and very professional. He had come up through the ranks – in the library at The Daily Telegraph, sports editor of The South London Press, assistant sports editor of The Evening Standard – and his influence was dominant in most departments of the paper. Every Friday night he would collect a bundle of page proofs from The Sunday Times printer and take them to Crockfords, where he would dine and play bridge. At about midnight he would move to the East India club, where he had a room, and sitting up in bed he would read the pages, finishing at about 3 am. At 8.30 am he was at the house of the production editor, James Dow, for coffee and by 9.15 the pages were back with the printer.

After H. V. Hodson left in 1962 Murphy might well have hoped to be the next editor. When Hamilton, never a newspaper technician, became editor himself, Murphy devoted his solid technical talents to getting out the paper, running it like a military operation. Facts were sacred, corrections shaming, vulgar words unheard of, and every page went to press on time or someone suffered. 'I belonged to an older generation of journalists. Insight represented a different generation. Irving and his team wanted a free hand. My job was to control them.' Since Irving was determined to establish his team's separate identity even to the extent of subbing its copy and seeing it into the paper himself – usually late – clashes were inevitable.

Irving realised this and deliberately began quietly. First, he, Hall and Wallington had a series of discussions over what the section should be called. Irving suggested 'Scrutiny', but the others said, tortuously, that it sounded a little obscene. He then tried 'Insight', but Hall and Wallington at first rejected that too. 'Pretentious . . . not what it's about.' As the group got down to producing dummies it became clear that Irving already had visions of Insight beyond Hamilton's original brief and that these visions could only cause more tension. He says:

My first idea was to try to work along with the *Time* brief that Pat Murphy had prepared, of translating the 'heavy' specialists for general readership. But this would have meant that we would have become a desk of rewrite men, dependent on the specialists and without our own reporters. I decided to try for much greater responsibility for idea-initiation than had been foreseen. In other words I wanted to make reporters of the specialists rather than just take their regular offerings.

So Irving sent out a memorandum notifying the specialists of Insight's arrival and asking them to a meeting to discuss its future. The memorandum does not seem to have survived, but many an indignant specialist can still remember why it upset him. 'It was full of phrases like "we will be extending the frontiers of journalism" and "we plan to present the news in a completely new dimension",' one of them recalls. 'Then it went on to remind us that there were "not only scoops of fact but scoops of interpretation".' Maurice Wiggin, then TV critic and now a columnist, is blunt about it. 'The whole thing aroused great animosity – nausea almost. After all, most of us had been at the journalistic game twenty years or so. News is quite definable and we all knew what it was without Insight having to explain it to us. And we found Irving and his team so rude, so insensibly rude.'

Other specialists turned up at the meeting in a mood of some caution to hear what Irving had to say. To appreciate the atmosphere it must be remembered that Irving was only thirty. He had been at The Sunday Times earlier as deputy editor of the magazine and had then left to join Topic. Now he had returned with two other young men, neither of whom could be said to fit the traditional Sunday Times image. 'Good God,' one of the older members of the staff said soon after Irving's arrival as Irving, Hall and Wallington roared away from the front of Thomson House in an open vintage car, 'we're being taken over by a bunch of Teddy boys.' If Irving had any hesitation confronting the assembled specialists at the meeting to explain to them how they could help extend the frontiers of journalism he did not show it. He was his usual confident self, but he was received, Hall remembers, with a mixture of 'scepticism, ridicule and even hostility'.

The first issue came out on February 17, 1963, to a mixed reception. It occupied two pages, had thirteen stories, and was introduced with a modest 'INSIGHT: the news in a new dimension'. Topics ranged from religion and insurance to shipping and sociology, and each was given the 'soft news' approach. A piece on education began, for example, 'The greatest aid to education is a child's imagination'; and one on unions started, 'What is a troublemaker?' The layout was striking. The page had been divided into squares and rectangles and each story was self-contained in its area, guarded by heavy rules.

The first reaction came from Leonard Russell, who sent a telegram early on Saturday morning: WELL DONE FIRST INSIGHT EXCELLENT. Most adverse comment concerned appearance. 'You have to remember that in those days stories usually wrapped around each other in the page,' Hall says. 'It was quite revolutionary to divide the page into squares. It was also virtually unknown to use a designer, as we did. On the writing side the idea of delaying the news-point to the second paragraph was unheard-of and contrary to all training. But we had to do it in order to get over ideas that had previously been considered too complicated for the lay press.' Irving was disappointed. 'It was readable, but it wasn't important.'

For the next two months there was little improvement on that first issue. Kenneth Pearson, who had been on the magazine, joined the group, but it was still understaffed. Irving began to go outside the paper for writers. His budget was too small to pay standard rates, and for three or four days' work a freelance found that he could get as little as £5. But, amazingly, there were no complaints: 'We'd started something new and people were willing to do it just to be part of the development.' (Russell says that Irving had great glamour for the young reporters around the office, particularly for the talented young like Hunter Davies.) Even so, Insight would probably have been stuck with its initial concept had not a number of factors in the spring of 1963 combined to make its next leap possible.

The economy in early 1963 was in a 'go' period and advertising was expanding rapidly. In turn this had pushed up the size of the paper – The Sunday Times was in the process of bursting away from 42 to 72 pages. This meant that there was space to allow journalists to write at length, while Hamilton's policy of hiring the best men he could find and allowing them to get on with their projects without interference meant that there was no shortage of writers with the ability and the initiative to use this extra space. If nothing else, Insight had proved Irving's thesis that a group of good journalists used to working together could get away from the '24-hours fashion' of treating news and by looking at it more deeply could give it deeper interest. All that was needed was news of sufficient importance on which to employ this potential. It came at exactly the right moment.

Late in 1962, before Insight had started, and while Fleet Street was preoccupied with the Vassall spy case, word began to get around that another scandal was brewing which would make the Vassall affair very tame. Early in 1963 the name of the Secretary of State for War, John Profumo, was introduced in these rumours. In brief, the story being circulated was that Profumo had been involved with a model, Christine Keeler, who had also been friendly with Captain Eugene Ivanov, assistant naval attaché at the Russian Embassy. Other names mentioned were Dr Stephen Ward, a Marylebone osteopath and society artist, who was Christine Keeler's sponsor, and the third Viscount Astor, at whose Buckinghamshire estate, Cliveden, Miss Keeler and Profumo were said to have met. Colonel George Wigg, then the Opposition authority on defence, began to make his own enquiries and became convinced that there were security implications.

On Thursday, March 14, 1963, John Arthur Edgecombe, a friend of Miss Keeler's, appeared at the Old Bailey charged with possessing a fire-arm with intent to endanger life. The prosecution said that Edgecombe had fired shots at Dr Ward's Wimpole Mews flat where Miss Keeler was visiting. What had promised to be no more than a routine case took an unusual turn when the prosecutor announced that Miss Keeler, who was due to be called as a witness, had disappeared.

Some of the newspapers then began to develop a kind of code – nonsense to the majority of their readers but meaningful to those on the grapevine. The Daily Express tried an old trick of juxta-posing seemingly unrelated items: the morning after the an-nouncement of Miss Keeler's disappearance the main story, headed WAR MINISTER SHOCK, said that Mr Profumo had offered his resignation to the Prime Minister, Mr Macmillan, 'for personal reasons'. Directly under the headline, and only one column away from the text of the main story, was a three-column picture of Christine Keeler and the story of her disappearance. On March 20 The Daily Mail tried a similar ploy in order to link Miss Keeler's name with Mr Profumo. But again all this probably did was to increase the ordinary readers' bewilderment.

The next day Colonel Wigg raised the matter in the House of Commons and the next morning Profumo made a personal statement to the House saying that he had been on 'friendly terms' with Miss Keeler but that there was 'no impropriety what-ever'. He denied that he had anything to do with her disappear-ance from the Old Bailey trial and added, 'I shall not hesitate to issue writs for libel and slander if scandalous allegations are made or repeated outside this House.' (This was no bluff. In the High Court on April 11, Profumo was awarded £50 agreed damages against the English distributors of an Italian magazine which had suggested that Profumo might have been having an improper relationship with Miss Keeler.) Miss Keeler, who had been abroad, returned and said much the same as the Italian magazine, but newspapers were warned by their legal advisers that Miss Keeler's unsubstantiated word could not stand up against Mr Profumo's, and publication could not be risked.

There the matter appeared to rest. A puzzled public read little about the affair during April but on May 21 Dr Ward asked for an interview at Admiralty House, where the Prime Minister was then living, and there made a statement to his principal private secretary. On May 29, the leader of the Opposition, Mr Harold Wilson, approached the Prime Minister direct, taking a file of information contributed by Labour M Ps who had been interested in the case.

Parliament broke up for Whitsun, but on June 4 Mr Profumo saw the Government Chief Whip and confessed that he had lied to the House when he had denied an improper association with Miss Keeler. His confession was translated into a letter of resignation to the Prime Minister which Mr Macmillan accepted, saying, 'This is a great tragedy for you, your family and your friends.' The Prime Minister's office issued a statement about the resignation late on June 5, and the story was a national sensation the following day, a Thursday.

The news was out but the public was still confused. The story had appeared piece-by-piece over several months and, as journalists have since realised, day-by-day coverage of a running story can actually *obscure* what has really happened. Many of the vital moves leading to the exposure of Profumo had still not been made public. The Daily Express, for instance, could only write, 'Since then (April 24) confidential moves that made Profumo's resignation inevitable have been under way.' So at Thursday morning's Insight conference Irving suggested, 'Let's tell everything, right from the beginning.' He had long been an admirer of The New Yorker style of narrative reconstruction, where the reader is taken carefully, stage by stage, through the story. This was a chance to apply the technique to the Profumo affair.

Two days' digging – mostly by Irving, Hall and Wallington ('We had, but didn't know it, been waiting for a story on which *we* could be the reporters and not have to rely on others') – produced the facts to fill the gaps in the daily newspaper stories, and on Sunday, June 9, Insight left the multiple subject format, known to the team as 'the ologies', and for the first time devoted itself to a single topic.

In a story which ran to 6,000 words, an exceptionally long read in those days, the Insight piece took the reader step-by-step through the four phases of the affair. By today's standards there is little in the piece to excite attention. In 1963 it was remarkable. Apart from the narrative presentation, which made it compulsive reading, there was that close attention to detail which was to become an identifying feature of Insight: 'When, just before midnight on March 14, other newspapers got copies of The Express, they sent reporters to find Mr Profumo. At 1.5 am on March 15 he arrived at his home at Regent's Park with his wife. He had been at the House of Commons. Asked about The Express report, he said, "There is no truth in this story at all – I have not seen the Prime Minister."' But above all the Insight story was the first to tell the

Profumo affair from start to finish, and the lesson was that what had worked with Profumo would work equally well with other big stories.

VIII

These now came thick and fast. Journalists looking back on 1963 refer to it as a vintage year for news. On The Sunday Times, as we have seen, not only were all the factors present for extensive news coverage – money, space and manpower – but now, week after week, culminating in the assassination of the President of the United States, story after story broke.

First came the Rachman exposure, an account of the rise of a Polish immigrant whose name has now entered the language to mean a grasping, unscrupulous, slum landlord. During the trial of Dr Stephen Ward (he was charged with having lived on the earnings of prostitution) which followed Profumo's resignation, the name of Peter Rachman cropped up as the wealthy benefactor of Mandy Rice-Davies, a friend of Christine Keeler's. In the emotion-charged atmosphere of the Ward trial any name mentioned was automatically grabbed at by the newspapers and investigated. Rachman's name had produced little interest because it turned out that he had died of a heart attack on November 29 of the previous year.

A stocky, balding businessman who had lived in a large house in Winnington Road, on the north side of Hampstead Heath, he had been apparently a devoted family man who had made his money in the property boom of the 1950s. In the London Polish community he had been respected as a witty, intelligent and courteous man – 'a doctor or a professional type.'

But Ron Hall had a friend in the property business who painted a different picture of Rachman, one sufficiently sinister to persuade Hall and the other members of the Insight team that it would be worth while trying to uncover the real Rachman. Hall quickly had enough to write the first of a three-part series on Rachman, and on July 7 this was the lead story in Insight. Headed 'The Life and Times of Peter Rachman' it told how Rachman had used a simple technique for exploiting racial tensions to increase the value of some of his slum property by as much as five-fold. The technique was to 'put in the schwartzes and de-stat it'. Insight explained:

'Schwartzes is Anglicised Yiddish for coloured people; the "stats" are statutory tenants, whose rent and tenure of homes were controlled by law; to "de-stat" means to persuade the controlled tenants to leave.'

Insight showed how Rachman managed to avoid prosecution, despite the interest of the police, the Paddington Borough Council, the Public Health authorities, and the Paddington and West London rent tribunals. With his properties the right to collect rents appeared to belong to one person, the responsibility for repairs to another. Ownership was regularly shuffled or assigned to various nominees who were in fact merely holding it 'on trust' for Rachman, or who had given promissory notes for part of the income still to go to him. The idea was so to obscure ownership under a cloud of transactions that nothing short of a full-scale legal investigation would have arrived at the facts, which the over-worked Public Health authorities and rent tribunals had little prospect of unravelling.

The significance of the Insight exposure of Rachman went beyond its immediate impact. (There were debates in the Commons, a police investigation, and a special section on Rachman in the Milner Holland report on London housing.) In the first place it launched The Sunday Times into a new field. Until then exposure journalism had been the province of newspapers like The People and The News of the World; for a serious newspaper to tackle the Rachman story was unheard of. In the second place, it achieved an internal breakthrough at The Sunday Times. Pat Murphy had supported the Insight investigation and was pleased with the story: 'Very interesting. Run it.' But the legal problems could have been daunting. The staff had, until then, considered legal advisers in general as barriers to getting good stories published. 'It was unusual to come across a lawyer who would *help* you get your piece published,' Hall recalls. But the recently-retained Sunday Times lawyer, James Evans, later to have his own office in Thomson House, did just that and developed in the process a new approach to difficult stories which was to make Insight's further development possible.

In October, Irving decided to expand the Insight technique into an area which had long intrigued him – politics. The basic idea was that James Margach, the political correspondent, who had become very helpful, would provide the equivalent to Time 'files'. The Insight team would feed into his material information from other sources, and would carry out some of the crucial interviews themselves. Put together the result would, they hoped, provide an extended narrative that would reveal to the reader a coherent, chronological account of how an important political event had occurred. In the second week of October the ideal opportunity to test the scheme unexpectedly occurred. On Tuesday, October 8, four days before the Prime Minister, Mr Macmillan, was due to address the Conservative Party conference at Blackpool, he fell ill. As the first wave of sympathy receded everyone realised that the Premier's political position was hopeless and that the manoeuvring to find a new leader would have to begin. Margach was in Blackpool. Irving contacted him and said, 'Instead of just sending a story send *everything* you know.' Margach did just that. He put 10,000 words on the telex to London. With this, and with 'files' from Wallington and Hall, Irving put together for the front of the Review section on Sunday, October 13, a story headed, 'Backstage at Blackpool: hour by hour in the fight for power'. The story took the reader through what had happened within the Tory party from the moment Macmillan had asked his staff to call a doctor at 4 am on Tuesday morning to Lord Hailsham's emotional speech to the Conservative Political Centre at 10 pm on Thursday. 'It was a first-class piece of journalism,' James Margach recalls. 'And it was important for The Sunday Times for two reasons; it was a breakthrough in revelatory political journalism, and it was Insight's first big pull-together job – where Clive took all the material from all the sources he could muster and pulled it together into a narrative.'

Inspired by the comment the story caused, the Insight team returned the following Sunday to the selection of the Prime Minister, this time to spell out how the peculiar workings of the Conservative 'magic circle', with its 'soundings of opinion at all levels of the party', had confounded the two most likely candidates, Mr Butler and Mr Maudling, and had instead produced as leader by compromise the former Foreign Secretary, Lord Home.

In all the two pieces were the best exposition of the Insight narrative approach produced until then, and 1963 could have quietly faded out with most people at The Sunday Times content with the paper's progress. But on November 22, and as a climax to a year so crowded with news, President John F. Kennedy was assassinated. News of the shooting came over the agency teleprinters at The Sunday Times at about 6.30 pm on Friday, just as many of the staff were preparing to go home. Hamilton was not there and Murphy was in charge. He immediately called a conference which had just started when an agency flash announced Kennedy's death. Twenty-eight pages of the paper had already gone to Manchester, where the northern edition was produced. These would all have to be cancelled and the paper torn to pieces and remade if The Sunday Times was to give the event the coverage it felt it deserved. Murphy, who set about organising it, says, 'It was a fine example of team work. Within hours, Leonard Russell, by telephoning to Boston, had bought the serial rights in a forthcoming book to which Kennedy had contributed. Mark Boxer produced some Kennedy family photographs he had been saving for the magazine and we used one right across the Weekly Review. We had the news coverage – Henry Brandon had been with the presidential cavalcade – the feature coverage, the photographs. We only needed a piece for the "Focus" page and Denis Hamilton came in and wrote this himself, basing it on his two meetings with Kennedy a year earlier.' ('I came away an English New Frontiersman, determined to try to create in Britain some of the spirit Kennedy had inspired in America.')

Murphy saw the issue right through, perhaps his best effort in his long career with the paper. 'Pat was at his peak,' Hamilton says. 'It was a fine professional job. We changed twenty-one pages and in my opinion produced a better coverage of the event than The New York Times.' Rees-Mogg, who wrote a memorable leading article, adds to this tribute to Murphy. 'It was an astonishing example of Pat's organising virtuosity and I would say the best single piece of editing I have seen in my career.'

For Insight its significance was that it showed that three or four Insight men, used to working together, could do a 'crash job' on important news stories better than a large news staff used to working independently.

Hamilton, Murphy and Rees-Mogg now decided that the correct move was to spread what had been learnt by Insight around the rest of the paper – a plan which, incidentally, had been discussed when Insight had first started. There was also another reason. 'Clive Irving tended to create so much personal loyalty as distinct from loyalty to the paper,' Rees-Mogg says. 'At times Insight had been virtually fighting the rest of the paper for stories. We felt it would be better to have people go into Insight for a spell and then come out of it rather than become tied too much to its editor.'

Accordingly, Irving became managing editor (news) and Wallington assistant editor (co-ordination). Hall became editor of

Insight and Bruce Page, who had been working on Fielding's Diary on The Daily Herald, was brought in as Hall's assistant. Insight's first phase was over. It had lasted less than a year but its effect on The Sunday Times – and on journalism in general – was immense.

IX

The year 1963 saw the beginning of a steady move of the paper's political line to the centre of Conservatism and, later, to the left of centre. Hamilton handled long-term development, relations with the Thomson board of directors, strategy, and the recruitment of the talent he felt the paper needed if it was to progress. As he was both chairman of the board of a new company called The Sunday Times Ltd (a title used by the Berrys for a time nearly fifty years earlier) *and* editor his power was considerable and he was able to make the changes he wanted 'without getting involved in management by committee'. Rees-Mogg looked after the leading articles and the political side generally; Murphy handled production; and Russell was mainly concerned with serials and special features for the Weekly Review.

Hamilton and Rees-Mogg naturally saw a lot of each other but were usually so occupied with the problems of the moment that they seldom had time to sit down and discuss the whole horizon of The Sunday Times. Nevertheless they soon reached agreement on the political line the paper should take. Firstly, they felt that The Sunday Times, in so far as it had a *party* political view, should remain Conservative rather than move to Labour. Next, it should move more the way its younger Conservative readers were thinking – to the centre. Thirdly, it should, however, take a more independent line, while preserving the paper's 'essential sense of responsibility'; that it should become, in Rees-Mogg's words, 'the great independent paper of the centre.' Thus it was sympathetic to Gaitskell and attacked Macmillan; sympathetic to Wilson when he was in Opposition, less so when he became Prime Minister. Fourthly, Hamilton and Rees-Mogg wanted the Conservative Party to transform itself, to make itself into a younger, more radical party. As Rees-Mogg puts it: 'To get away from the feeling of dead weight which existed in the Conservatives under Macmillan.' Both editor and political editor had been heavily influenced by the Kennedy administration – 'He was the one authentic hero of the postwar world' (Rees-Mogg) – and had become excited by the possibility of changing the mood of a country as Kennedy had done in the United States, 'of getting away from the Old-Guard politics that dominated Britain at that time.' (This excitement later changed to exasperation with British politicians when such a change did not come about.) Both were Europeans, disappointed when Britain failed to gain entry to the Common Market, and determined that the paper's policy would be to press for further efforts. (Later, Frank Giles, foreign editor, continued this pressure both in the leader columns and over his own name, and in 1967 the paper appointed John Lambert as resident Common Market correspondent in Brussels.)

There were soon signs in the paper of this new thinking. The political correspondent James Margach felt the impact. 'I suddenly had a new dimension of freedom in what I wrote – not only in my comment but in hard political news as well. It encouraged me to be more critical of both parties instead of going softly on the Tories. There was a completely different mood on the paper.'

Another sign was the attitude of The Sunday Times to the Profumo affair. After Profumo had confessed to lying to the House of Commons and had resigned, Rees-Mogg wrote an article in The Sunday Times of June 16, 1963, called 'A Time for Justice.' He argued that the Profumo affair was not a moral issue and that 'in the end even a scandal has to be brought back into proportion: the life of Britain does not really pass through the loins of one red-headed girl.' Looking back he is even more convinced that this was the correct attitude. 'We didn't think it was right to throw mud at Profumo when he was down. The other papers were hysterical. We didn't join in the riding down of the victim and we were more sympathetic to Ward than the rest of the press. The press killed Ward but we had no part in it. We were most unsympathetic to Haley's leader in The Times that this was a moral issue.'

When the Conservative party rejected Butler for leader and chose instead Sir Alec Douglas-Home, The Sunday Times was bitterly critical – Rees-Mogg had fully expected Butler to win. When he had learnt that Macmillan was relinquishing the leadership he had been to see each member of the Cabinet and had asked him his preference: 'I found that they would not have Hogg, who had been strongly tipped, and that most wanted Butler.' But Sir Alec became Prime Minister. In a leader-page article headed 'Turning Aside from Progress' Rees-Mogg said:

It has been sad to see an administration formed by an honourable man who has little knowledge of modern social and economic subjects and whose succession was opposed by so many of his chief colleagues. . . . The rejection of Mr Butler, the most loyal Conservative there ever was, has created a dissociation not just between Mr Butler and his party but between those who shared his ideas and his party. I now know of no convincing arguments which I could put to a young scientist or university teacher to persuade him that the Conservative Party was both the best way of fulfilling his political ideas and a party in which he would be at home, an equal in his own natural environment. That is a new situation, a very sad situation, and I believe an extremely perilous one.

Almost immediately The Sunday Times began to warn the Government that an economic crisis was developing, and by the October, 1964, election it had repeated the warning twenty-seven times. The Government constantly denied that this was the case. Sir Alec himself, appearing on BBC television in February when Rees-Mogg's warnings were becoming intense, said that the economy had seldom been stronger. Unfortunately for Sir Alec less than twenty-four hours after the broadcast the import-export figures for January were released, showing a highly adverse situation. Pressed by Rees-Mogg later in the Independent Television programme 'This Week' about his optimistic statement Sir Alec replied, 'I suppose if any measures are necessary to take the pressure off the economy then of course the Chancellor of the Exchequer will take them. . . . But this particular drop in exports has, I think, defeated the experts.' This whole affair served further to convince Rees-Mogg that Home was not the man to lead the Conservative Party, and in the general election in October Hamilton and Rees-Mogg felt strongly inclined to support Labour.

James Margach had introduced both of them to Wilson and they had been seeing a lot of him. Rees-Mogg knew the chairman of Elliott Automation, Leon Bagrit, and although Bagrit was not a Socialist Rees-Mogg thought it would be worth while to bring him and Wilson together. So he arranged a luncheon and invited Wilson, Bagrit and Hamilton. The three men spent the meal trying to convince Wilson how important the right approach to technological development would be. So when it appeared that they had succeeded and Wilson made technology a plank of his statement of policy at Swansea in January, 1964, Rees-Mogg expressed his whole-hearted approval: 'I have written a tiresomely repetitious series of articles urging on the Government the need for much more active policies of economic expansion . . . this advice can now be paralleled, sentence by sentence, in Mr Harold Wilson's Swansea statement of policy.' Was Labour now the party for 'the young scientist or university teacher'?

A lot of discussion went on at the fifth floor of Thomson House. The Sunday Times carried a series of leading articles putting the case for each party and then one long article summing up. In the end it gave its support, albeit in a lukewarm manner, to the Conservatives. 'But for Europe it would have been very difficult to choose,' Rees-Mogg says. 'But we thought that we could not ask our readers to support an anti-European party. I was probably more convinced than Denis Hamilton that this was important and that Labour's attitude to Europe was too negative. But when Labour did get in we agreed that it should be given every chance to succeed and we did our best to reassure the City, which was getting very panicky.'

Rees-Mogg also felt it important to suggest what had gone wrong with the Conservative Party: it had lost the progressive middle-class voter because people of the centre had come to believe that the Conservatives were 'too much under the influence of what might be termed the fuddy-duddy right'. The party would have to adapt to the needs of the new Britain, Rees-Mogg wrote. 'If the Conservative Party had been able to align itself with the new society in 1964 it would have won the election; if it fails in the next year to align itself with the new society it will very probably lose the election by an increased majority.' Rees-Mogg left no doubt as to what he considered should be one of the first steps: 'I would prefer that [Sir Alec Douglas-Home] use the common sense, the wisdom of the countryman . . . and recognise that he is not now the right man to revive a defeated party.'

Rees-Mogg hammered this view the following year in an article which, it is generally agreed, brought Sir Alec's term as Conservative leader to an end. It appeared in The Sunday Times on July 18, 1965, and was headed 'The Right Moment to Change'. Sir Alec had not been as bad a leader as had been feared, Rees-Mogg wrote, but the time had come for him to go. 'It is clear that Sir Alec cannot tell the nation what it might have to do at a very dark and critical moment. Others may not have the right answer. He does not have an answer at all. A man cannot lead a party successfully who does not in his heart of hearts feel absolutely convinced that he knows what ought to be done. It is hard to resist the very widespread view that the Conservatives, unless after

a national disaster, will not now win a general election while Sir
Alec remains their leader.' Four days later Sir Alec resigned and
was replaced by Mr Heath.

That The Sunday Times should have reached a point where its
criticism of the Conservative Party had brought down a leader and
where, at one stage, it had considered supporting Labour in a
general election marked a major swing in what had been its
traditional political attitude. This swing was to continue under its
next editor, Harold Evans, until some readers have come to
regard The Sunday Times on certain issues as farther to the left,
and certainly more radical, than The Observer. In general, the
paper's stance is one of independence from any party label.

X

As well as fundamentally pulling the paper's policy away from
the old Tory line of the Kemsley period, Hamilton and Rees-Mogg
were principally responsible for another important development
of this period: Business News. The paper's production capacity
had increased steadily and the flow of advertising meant that more
pages were available for another section. But what should it be?
Thomson had seen the success of business sections in North
America and was firmly in favour of launching one here. The
advertising department on the other hand began to put pressure
on Hamilton to start a classified advertising section. Their
arguments were persuasive: it had been done by a lot of American
newspapers. It was an easy idea to sell. It could be highly profitable. If The Sunday Times did not do it, another paper would.
Hamilton held out:

Firstly, I felt it was the wrong thing for a quality Sunday newspaper,
and, second, I felt the real growth would be in business advertising. We
were coming out of a long period when British management had been out
in the cold, when Britain was being passed in development because her
business leaders lacked training. As this ended all sorts of new jobs in
administration were occurring – financial controllers, cash flow experts,
and all the skills associated with computers. Unit trusts had started and
were looking for an advertising medium suited to their message. Also, I
had been very impressed by the growth of the *Financial Times* and rather
amazed that *The Times* and the *Daily Telegraph* had allowed Brendan
Bracken and his brilliant team to get away with it. This made me

worried that if we didn't get in first and start a business news section the *Financial Times* might feel confident enough to launch a Sunday edition, a *Sunday Financial Times*, which would give us stiff competition indeed.

Accordingly, Harry Henry, marketing director, undertook the job of surveying the prospects for a business news section. His report set out the arguments for the new section in some detail. They were most persuasive. Over the previous three years The Sunday Times had pulled in some 300,000 new readers. Over 100,000 of these had come from the launch of the colour magazine two years earlier. What were these new readers interested in? What should the newspaper be carrying to keep them as readers? Henry's report, compiled from surveys admittedly taken with Business News in mind, was nevertheless highly encouraging.

The new reader of The Sunday Times was most likely in business, concerned at some level with running a company. He was young, ambitious, and interested in making money. He was *not* interested in the Stock Exchange, he was *not* particularly interested in reading about the general state of the economy, of the Gross National Product or generalisations about industry. He *was* interested in other young men running companies, their successes, their problems, and their failures. But above all he was interested in money – 'anything to do with £sd.' The new section could, therefore, be sold to advertisers as a weekly business paper with a starting circulation of over 1,200,000 – larger than any other business newspaper in the world – and with readers of the right purchasing power.

Armed with such a favourable report and backed by Thomson's enthusiasm – some say obstinacy – Hamilton made the decision to go ahead, despite misgivings among other executives, and on April 12, 1964, the new section was announced for September. 'The Sunday Times will once again pioneer a new concept in British journalism by launching The Sunday Times Business News Section. . . . The Business News will include special features researched in depth on modern developments in industry, and international and scientific business news.'

The name 'Business News' had been carefully chosen by Rees-Mogg after long discussion. He wanted to make it clear that the new section would be very different in character from the financial pages of the daily newspapers – that it would be about *business* in its widest sense rather than about finance. The word 'News' was also deliberate. There had been some division during the early stages of the scheme as to whether or not there could be such a thing as a *Sunday* business news section. Murphy had argued against devoting an entire section to business on the ground that if there were a slump, and the paper had to be reduced in size, any *separate* section would dominate the smaller paper and destroy its balance. And, Murphy said, how could stories about business still be *news* by Sunday? If they were the daily newspapers were not doing their job. Murphy had been voted down.

Rees-Mogg convinced Hamilton that Business News could have a substantial news content. 'I considered that it should not only provide features – which, of course, would always be a large part of its content – but major news stories and Insight-style coverage in depth of important issues in the business and industrial world. I foresaw a team effort between Business News reporters and Insight reporters on those stories which might combine both a business element and a crime element. There the ability to master the business intricacies plus Insight's investigative experience and techniques of presentation would make an excellent combination.' (The case of the Fire, Auto and Marine Insurance company collapse was an example of what Rees-Mogg had in mind.)

There was a lot to do between the decision to go ahead, made in April, and September, when the first issue was due. On the advertising side Thomson used the same tactics as he had with the colour magazine. There were a series of luncheons in The Sunday Times board-room to which prospective advertisers and advertising agency men were invited, and Thomson and his senior executives toured the country speaking to businessmen and industrialists; at the luncheons Hamilton or Rees-Mogg would speak, setting out the thinking behind the new section.

Others who were present recall that the advertising men tended to listen stony-faced, but when Thomson spoke, at first persuasively, and then in his usual blunt manner – 'We're going to start this new section and it's going to be great and we know you'll want to be in it with us right from the beginning' – they were nonplussed. Against the weight of all opinion Thomson had rammed through his colour magazine and it had proved an outstanding success. Could he also be proved right about this new business section? Obviously no one could afford to bet against it, and the first bookings began to flow in. By the launch the first issue could have been booked four times over, and Business News remains a new section started by The Sunday Times that began ahead of its advertising target and has consistently remained so. (Its revenue went from £197,000 in the last quarter of

1964 – its first three months of existence – to £308,000 a year later.)

While the advertising side was proceeding satisfactorily, the editorial side was lagging. The new section as envisaged by Rees-Mogg – with its emphasis on a substantial news content – was clearly going to require first-class executives and reporters. Where were they to come from? Two were already with the paper. Rees-Mogg had brought in as City editor Anthony Vice, who had been deputy City editor of The Daily Telegraph for five years. Before that Vice had been with The Times, but Rees-Mogg had known him from The Financial Times, where he had been features editor during Rees-Mogg's period as leader writer. The two were used to working together and Rees-Mogg was confident Vice would produce a Business News section that was both lively and readable. Accordingly, Vice was appointed the first editor of the new section.

His deputy was Peter Wilsher, who was also on The Sunday Times city staff, after a varied career in popular journalism which had included a spell as a gossip columnist on Kemsley's Sunday Graphic. Vice was given authority to hire two industrial reporters and two financial reporters; after some hunting around he engaged Keith Richardson, a bright young industrial reporter who had been on The Financial Times and The Statist, Charles Raw, who had covered the discount market for The Times (declining to wear the traditional top hat), and Roger Nuttall, from The Mining Journal and The Evening Standard. After the launch he added Stephen Aris, a newsroom reporter formerly of The Times and New Society, who had been producing Business Insight, an offshoot of the main Insight operation.

There was considerable pressure on Vice and Wilsher to produce some dummy issues so that everyone could see how the new section was going to look. But reporting the mounting economic crisis for the old-style financial pages of the paper kept them so busy that they managed only two. They were terrible. Somehow the original Insight idea of a background-to-the-news feature had filtered through to Business News, and all the early ideas consisted of pages filled with the chemicals column, the insurance column, the investments column, etc. 'But, frankly, we never intended to follow them,' Wilsher says. 'What we wanted was basically an expansion of The Sunday Times City page to cover industry plus long Fortune magazine-style profiles on companies.'

So a very experienced writer was commissioned to do the first long profile, on ICI, for the first issue and it was decided to refer to this in the promotion campaign for the launch. Because of the impending general election and because of the earlier division of opinion at the paper over the new section, Hamilton had plumped for a low-key promotion with little advertising. But this concentrated heavily on the ICI profile. So it was with steadily sinking hearts that Vice and Wilsher read the copy: it was accurate and well-presented but it was long and just not right. There were murmurs from the news side of the paper that the article 'puffed' big business, and someone said it should be scrapped. 'It's too late,' Rees-Mogg said. 'It's mentioned in the promotion, it's been advertised. We'll just have to run it.' So two pages in the first issue, which appeared on September 27, 1964, were devoted to the first part of the ICI profile. 'It taught us a lesson,' Wilsher says. 'It was obvious that the Fortune-style profile was not for us and we would have to be much more discriminating about the "long read".'

Luckily the first issue – planned well in advance – was given a last-minute boost by its front-page lead story. Written by Peter Wilsher, it was about Duo-Matic Ltd, a huge direct sales washing machine company, and it stated flatly that the company was in danger of liquidation. (It collapsed, in fact, the very next day.) The piece fulfilled everything that Vice wanted for Business News: 'It was a major story, it was news, and it was exclusive. Every consumer durable man would have had to read it.'

The new section was a success from the beginning. True, the path had been opened by The Financial Times, and to a lesser extent by Nigel Lawson, first City editor of The Sunday Telegraph. The Financial Times had pioneered the reporting of business and financial matters in simple, easily-understood language devoid of technicalities or jargon. But it had featured industry in general rather than individual companies, management rather than managers. Lawson had shown that business could still be news even on Sundays.

The Sunday Times Business News now took this basis and developed it by adding drama and personalities to the mix. And urged on by Vice, the reporters went all out for news stories. It was an exciting period, for they rapidly discovered that the field was wide open, and the news stories which emerged were, if anything, too many for the small staff to handle. As George Schwartz, The Sunday Times veteran City columnist wrote at the end of the first year:

It's all enough and more to fill a business newspaper. 'Home loans decision upsets some societies'. Yes, and the 'Assam war threatens Britain's tea stake'. Interest rates are coming down on page 1 and going up on page 2. A big campaign is being launched for a new hair-wash, but there is a shortage of electricians. Dublin Corporation has vacancies in town-planning, Australia needs actuaries in Canberra, Swindon offers 6 per cent for loans. Thus Business News has perforce to omit the football results while keeping an eye on the pools and the bingo-halls in case they prejudice the next issue of national savings certificates.

Advertising continued way ahead of target. The original plan had been for 8 to 12 pages. Now, stimulated by the boom in unit trust and appointments advertising, 24-page issues became common and there were occasions when the advertising department reluctantly had to turn away bookings. 'Some weeks the Business News section could have been the biggest of the three,' Hamilton says, 'and to keep balance we had to limit its size.'

Staff increased, new features were added, and in 1969 Campaign, the weekly magazine for the advertising world, paid Business News the following compliment on its fifth birthday: 'The march of the business supplements continues. Hard on the heels of the new Times Saturday supplement especially geared to personal investment and finance comes The Observer's pull-out business section. So, belatedly, The Observer catches up with its great rival, The Sunday Times, which pioneered the business supplement some years ago.' Campaign quoted research figures to show just how successful Business News had been: 80 per cent of stockbrokers read The Sunday Times Business News against only 46 per cent reading The Observer. Among class A businessmen (a choice target for advertisers) 58 per cent read The Sunday Times business section and 60 per cent The Sunday Times as a whole, compared with only 23 per cent who read either the news or review section of The Observer.

It had been an eventful five years. Business News had chronicled ten budgets and quasi-budgets, four major sterling crises, a host of minor eruptions and one devaluation. It had obtained a copy of the notorious National Plan several weeks before publication, but George Brown had persuaded Hamilton to hold it out 'in the national interest'. It had recorded the arrival on the British commercial scene of North Sea gas, totally unheard of in 1964; mini-skirts, boutiques, Carnaby Street, and the leather look. It had noted the growth of package holidays, microcircuits, Barclay cards, and the cashless society. It had plotted money coming and going: £2 million apiece to Bob Tanner and Peter Whitfield out of selling their Clubman's Club group to Mecca; £7 million lost to the unfortunate seekers of high interest rates who trusted their cash to the now defunct Pinnock Finance.

A number of stories had been notable 'firsts'. It was Business News in 1965 which first revealed de Gaulle's strategy for converting his dollar balances into gold and which in turn triggered off the whole international currency helter-skelter. It was Business News which wrote a cautionary article about the whole car insurance business – the week before Fire Auto and Marine went spectacularly bust. And it was Business News which was first publicly critical – and privately sceptical – of Bernie Cornfeld's 10s (of which more later).

It was probably during those first five years that Business News reached its first peak – at a point where its novelty had worn off but the sheer strength of its reporting put it on top of The Sunday Telegraph, and well ahead of The Observer; when it was clear that The Financial Times had been deterred from launching a Sunday edition and when the research figures showed that at a critical moment in the history of the three serious Sunday newspapers the new section had pulled to The Sunday Times a large slice of business advertising.

Vice left in January, 1967, to become editor of The Times business section (he has since gone to Rothschild's), and his deputy, Wilsher, took over. Everyone agrees that Vice and Wilsher had been a formidable combination, 'a happy balance,' says Rees-Mogg, 'between Vice's City news interests and Wilsher's interest in business and industrial feature articles.' Now under Wilsher the section's emphasis changed.

As we have seen, Vice was principally a City man and his emphasis on hard news stories had got the new section away to a confident start. But a feeling later developed that the section was too much about money and not enough about people: 'unless the story involved at least £1 million, Vice felt it was not really worth using', and the staff took to rating each week's efforts by adding up the figures in the headlines: 'This Sunday is a forty-million-pound issue.' Vice denies it. 'No sensible person would choose a financial story solely or mainly on the grounds of size. I certainly did not. I would accept that I did push Business News towards hard news stories – rather than opinion or colour pieces or in-depth analysis for its own sake.'

By now Harold Evans, who had read economics, had become

editor of The Sunday Times. While still chief assistant to Hamilton, and then managing editor, he had been a source of ideas for the section. Now Evans and Wilsher had lunch and thrashed out a new policy. Evans felt that the news approach for the front page of Business News had become 'too bitty'. Wilsher agreed, set out his ideas for changing it, and went away with Evans's authority to go ahead.

I wanted to make the front page more flexible than in Vice's day by interspersing hard news with feature pieces, or with an opinion piece based on a news item. You get more impact if instead of running just two or three facts you write in an opinion as to how those facts come to occur. I tried to expand our audience and write not just for managers and executives but for the mass of people whose lives are affected by economics. I tried to find new, striking, and amusing ways of presenting what otherwise might be rather arid and boring stuff to a mass audience. We succeeded in some areas and failed in others. The international currency crisis has been one of our main failures. Everyone from my barber to people I met at parties used to say, 'What's it all about?' We've tried everything from diagrams to comic strips but people still don't understand.

Wilsher introduced new features to broaden the appeal of Business News. City and Investment affairs were concentrated into a compact three-page section, and a new column, Prufrock, started with the aim of keeping 'a sharp eye on people and events who make up the business kaleidoscope'. Evans had suggested to Wilsher that he should have a column of some sort on the front page. He had also advised, as a matter of policy, that the consumer angle should always be mentioned, on the ground that at the end of all business stories there is a consumer somewhere. Wilsher now combined the two ideas into a consumer column which he called 'Shop': 'to give up-to-date news on products, prices, promotion, quality improvements, and the value of the pound in your purse.' Edited, at the time of writing, by Brenda Jones, this feature has proved one of the most popular in the section.

A new agriculture writer, Graham Rose, was engaged to write about the personalities in farming as well as the products, and Stephen Aris and Richard Milner undertook long investigations – sometimes with colleagues from the news or feature departments – which became a sort of Business News Insight operation. (Aris's report on Cyril Lord, the ex-carpet king, was so good that Harold Evans grabbed it from Business News and used it in three parts on the front of the Weekly Review in May, 1969 – much to the alarm of Leonard Russell. 'I thought there was bound to be fireworks. I've never admired Evans's courage more. Left to myself I wouldn't have dared.')

One of the key decisions Wilsher made, and one which perhaps typifies his approach, concerns the head of GEC, Sir Arnold Weinstock. The relationship between Business News and Weinstock started in 1966 when Vice was editor. Intrigued by stories of Weinstock's ruthless sacking of senior executives who had not produced what he had demanded of them, Business News reporters Stephen Aris and Oliver Marriott spent several weeks compiling a list of top GEC executives (and those of its subsidiaries) who had 'left suddenly'. They had interviewed many of them to get details of their falling out with Weinstock and when the dossier was complete Vice arranged a meeting so that they could confront Weinstock with it. Weinstock had been stunned. At that period it was unknown for two business reporters to devote so much time to investigating the hiring-and-firing policy of a large company and unheard of for them then to confront the chief executive of that company to demand an explanation. Weinstock to his credit handled the situation brilliantly. He went straight to the attack. 'Before we begin, gentlemen,' he said, 'there are two things I want to say. The first is that I deeply resent The Sunday Times going behind my back and listening to a lot of tittle-tattle. The second is that this person sitting beside me is my legal director. Now what is it you want to ask me?' The two-hour interview which followed was, Aris says, 'one of the hairiest I have ever had.' But at the end of it Weinstock, convinced of The Sunday Times's determination to be fair, and apparently impressed by the accuracy of the reporters' research, had set out frankly and clearly whom he had sacked and why.

Aris and Marriott had then written a 2,500-word feature – 'GEC – Profits and The Man' – from which Weinstock had emerged as a bright but ruthless manager. It was a tough but fair article and it concluded: 'To many Weinstock's methods seem unduly harsh. And undoubtedly the image of the company has suffered. But does it really matter? Weinstock would rightly argue that a company should be judged not by its image but by its results – and these by any standards have been magnificent . . . Life in GEC may now be tough, but for many it is also rewarding.'

The affair had increased Wilsher's interest in Weinstock – 'He recognised us as hard but fair. We came to regard him as an outstanding man and devoted a lot of time to him.' So in 1967, when GEC began its mammoth battle to take over Associated Electrical Industries, Wilsher took a far-reaching decision: Business News would not simply report the take-over battle, it would take sides. 'We decided that Weinstock would win and deserved to win and we put the entire weight of Business News behind GEC.' In an article called 'The Weinstock bid for Power', which appeared on October 1, 1967, Wilsher wrote: 'The GEC's bid for AEI is the biggest, and in many ways the most hopeful, move we have seen since Mr Wilson started talking about restructuring the economy. It will need very strong and serious argument to justify its failure.'

It was not new in financial journalism for a newspaper to take sides in a take-over battle, but to do so in an article of such length and in such a strong manner, and in a battle which had political undertones – the Government's Industrial Reorganisation Corporation was making its first entry on the national scene in supporting GEC – *was* a departure. Wilsher was gratified, therefore, to see in an Economist Intelligence Unit survey, conducted after GEC had been successful in its bid, that The Sunday Times had clearly been the most important of the Sunday newspapers in influencing the result.

Under Wilsher's guidance Business News was, by 1968–9, producing issue after issue of twenty-four pages. Its staff had grown to eighteen with surprisingly few changes at higher levels: Keith Richardson left to go to industry but returned after two years to become industrial editor; Charles Raw left to become City editor of The Guardian; Nicholas Faith came from The Economist to be deputy editor. On a good week advertising revenue from the section would reach £80,000. In this buoyant atmosphere there was no need to look too closely at the logic of its success. Affluence was adding something like a quarter of a million new shareholders to the pool of prospective readers – and advertisers – each year. Unit trusts were spreading shareholding into households that had once regarded bank deposit accounts with suspicion. Industry needed more and more executive manpower, which meant that appointments advertising continued to soar. The future of Business News was thus very rosy – just so long as the boom continued.

XI

While the rest of the paper was progressing, Insight was going through something of a crisis. The original team had broken up and early 1964 saw Hall and his new assistant, Bruce Page, uncertain as to where Insight should now go. It continued rather unhappily with the 'ologies' while Hall tried to decide whether the Rachman articles had vindicated the insistence of James Evans that every defamatory statement should be provable by *legally-admissible* evidence. The difficulty was that although Hall could have proven his case against Rachman down to the most minor of details, he was not called upon to do so because Rachman was dead when The Sunday Times published the Insight exposure. Dead men cannot be libelled, so the crux of Evans's theory would remain unproved and the possibilities of investigative reporting in depth unexplored until a suitable story emerged. Fortunately this occurred much sooner than anyone expected.

In July, 1964, Hall and Page prepared a story showing that a small but highly-effective group of adventure-seeking Britons was fighting as a mercenary force for the Royalists in the Yemen civil war. A former army officer, peripherally involved in the affair, at that time engaged on a project for the Thomson Organisation, learnt of the story and immediately telephoned Hamilton to ask him to drop it. Publication, the former officer suggested, would be 'damaging to British interests'. Hamilton told him that he would not interfere with Insight's story – 'a highly important decision,' says Page. 'If Hamilton had kept the story out of the paper then morale on Insight would have been so shattered that there would never have been another investigation.' In fact the knowledge that, no matter where its probing led, appeals to Hamilton or any other high-ranking Sunday Times executive would not bring any strictures has been a vital factor in Insight's success. At the time of writing all Insight editors agree that they have never been asked, ordered, or had hinted to them, that they should drop an investigation, or – other than for legal reasons – that they should tone down their conclusions provided that the facts justified them.

Yemen was important in more than one aspect. 'Page had been unsure of himself until the Yemen story,' Hall says. 'Now he became a valuable irritant by his sheer determination to make new ideas work.' Insight now swung heavily in favour of investigations, and conscious of James Evans's demands for convincing proof for every important story, entered its brief 'electronic period', when its office had such things as miniature tape recorders, and miles of recording tape. The main reason for most of this was the arrival of one of Insight's most colourful contributors, Colin Simpson. Simpson had been combining freelance journalism with antique dealing and had done a story for The Sunday Times on the activities of oil companies in the Middle East. 'I then told Page about an antique dealers' ring that I had taken part in. I told him I had all the evidence necessary to prove the ring existed and to show how it worked. I had actually charted the salesroom history of a Chippendale commode sold at auction two years earlier. I said I had tried to interest other papers in the story but they had turned it down.'

Page was very interested but felt that the story needed updating. As Irving and Hall were on holiday he accepted the responsibility himself and told Simpson to go ahead and prove the story again.

Page was taking what could have been an expensive risk. The ring's system was that members would refrain from bidding against each other for the choicer items at good sales. After the sale the ring would meet in a private room of a convenient public house and re-auction the items among themselves. Since the items would have been bought at the auction at prices well below their real value (because of the lack of competitive bidding) and would now be re-auctioned among ring members at a price approaching the real value, the difference could be distributed among ring members who were not successful at the ring's own auction.

The only event which could upset this highly illegal operation would be the regular attendance of a non-member of the ring whose bidding could force prices at the auction too high to make the ring's activities profitable. The ring usually took care of such a dealer by bidding him to completely uneconomic levels in the hope of keeping him away. But if this failed then the only other tactic open to the ring was to invite the troublesome dealer to join.

This is what Page and Simpson were counting on; Simpson was to do the rounds of the country auctions where he knew the ring would be operating, and with spirited bidding make himself a nuisance. If he was invited to join the ring then he would be in a position to collect the proof Page would need to convince The

Sunday Times to run the story. But if anything went wrong then The Sunday Times would find itself the owner of a number of expensive antiques.

As it happened the plan worked well. At a sale at Tunbridge Wells Simpson cost the ring so much money by forcing them to bid more highly than they needed that, after the auction, he was approached and invited to join the ring at a sale of the effects of the late Captain E. G. Spencer-Churchill, at Northwick Park, Blockley, Gloucestershire, the following week, September 28, 1964. Page and reporter Lewis Chester decided the only real way to prove what went on at the ring's private auction was to record its proceedings – no easy task in 1964 when electronic techniques were not as advanced as they are today.

Insight could find no tape recorder small enough to conceal about the person, so a system was worked out whereby Chester secreted in his clothing a tiny microphone. The microphone would pick up the proceedings at the ring's private auction and they would be relayed to a nearby van where reporter John Barry and an electronics engineer with a receiver and a tape recorder would record them.

As it turned out, the results were hard to decipher (a fact in Insight's decision to abandon all forms of electronic bugging) but there were sufficient names and other information on the tape for reporters to have someone to confront. As is usual, so as to prevent consultation, all the major dealers involved were seen simultaneously, the extra staff this needed being seconded from the newsroom. The story appeared on Sunday, November 8, 1964, headed, 'The Curious Case of the Chippendale Commode'. It was written by Chester and then edited by Kenneth Pearson and Ron Hall. It began by charting the history of a Chippendale commode sold on November 22, 1962, in a saleroom at Leamington Spa.

The commode was sold to a Worcestershire antique dealer for a mere £750. Insight established that on the same evening, at the ring's private auction, it was knocked down to another dealer for no less than £4,350. The difference between the public auction price and the private ring auction price, some £3,600, was distributed among those dealers who had held back from bidding for the commode at the public auction. There were six and each took £600 as his reward.

The commode was then sold to a reputable Mayfair firm for about £5,200, and it subsequently became a star exhibit in the Antique Dealers' Fair with a value in the region of £10,000.

The article then went on to detail the experiences of Simpson and Chester at the ring's private auction after the Spencer-Churchill sale. Reaction was immediate. Two former presidents and nine other members of the thirty-two-man council of the British Antique Dealers Association (BADA) resigned. The BADA soon after made it a condition of membership that the applicant sign a declaration that he would not be a party to or participate in any ring or 'knock out' agreement. Scotland Yard began enquiries and the Board of Trade looked into the situation.

The success of this investigation not only firmly decided the line Insight's development would take but began the newspaper's continuing interest in the antiques business. One other story of the many which The Sunday Times has published in this field is worth mentioning here. It was a special antiques issue of the magazine, written by Nicholas Tomalin, David Leitch and Colin Simpson, devoted to an Insight analysis of the whole business. Published on August 14, 1966, it included an Insight-inspired hoax, the repercussions of which are still rattling around the trade. Briefly, Colin Simpson went to a small studio in Horner Street, Marylebone, w1 and commissioned its owners, Vilmo Gibello, a master framer with legendary knowledge of the colours and techniques used by early craftsmen, and Eduardo Pirotta, a gifted Maltese carver, to 'create' two '18th-century Venetian' blackamoor figures. A baulk of seasoned pine, which had formerly been a telegraph post at Ascot racecourse, was bought for £12 and in eight days Pirotta had carved two Nubians, a male and a female.

Gibello then spent a month decorating and 'ageing' them, building in abrasions, repairs and a 200-year-old patina. In February, 1966, Insight floated the fake figures off into the antiques trade. In March they turned up in Knight Frank and Rutley's auction rooms in Hanover Square catalogued as 18th-century Venetian 'in the manner of Viani'. Simon Fleet, saleroom correspondent of The Observer, wrote a paragraph about them on March 20: 'The splendid 18th-century pair on the right, to be auctioned by Knight Frank and Rutley on Friday, sport colourful loincloths and stand 6 ft 4 in high on octagonal pedestals.'

They were withdrawn from the sale at Simpson's request, but not before one leading dealer had submitted a written offer to the vendor, through the auctioneers, of £650. Eventually exported to Paris as modern reproduction ornaments, the blackamoors have appeared at the Paris Antique Dealers' Fair and at the time of writing are on sale in a Paris dealer's shop priced at £6,000.

XII

In the 1950s the paper's newsroom, always understaffed and undermanned, seemed to be slipping into extinction. Then in October, 1958, Michael Cudlipp arrived from The Evening Chronicle, Manchester, to take over from Godfrey Smith, who was becoming Atticus. Smith had had a lot of writing talent about him – Susan Cooper, John Pearson, Gavin Lyall, Brian Gardiner – but it went into news features and not into hard news. Cudlipp wanted to change this. He began to fight for better recognition of the news department. It was a fight against some odds. 'The news-gathering side of the paper was not only understaffed but geared to producing rather soft, gentlemanly news. It had practically no money to spend and too many part-time specialists.' It was a long job to change this. When Cudlipp had first arrived, aged twenty-four, and admittedly rather fresh-faced, one senior executive had said to a colleague, 'I see they're hiring children now.' The news editor's office did not even rate a carpet, and the one Cudlipp found in his office when he took over was speedily removed by Mrs Godfrey Smith. 'I had bought it for Godfrey for his birthday. I wanted to brighten up his office – it was so awful and incredibly depressing. When he moved I said "Damn it all, The Sunday Times can afford a carpet for its news editor", so I went and took Godfrey's one away.'

Cudlipp had two early victories. He managed to have the news desk manned continuously on Saturdays right through to the final edition; and since he felt that two staff writers – Susan Cooper and John Pearson – was a ridiculous number to run any kind of hard news operation, he got an increase authorised. First the number went up to four by the addition of Euan Bowater and William Foster, and then by the recruitment of Michael Hamlyn (later to succeed Cudlipp as news editor when Cudlipp became an assistant editor), Lewis Chester and John Barry (both later editors of Insight), Anthony Cowdy and Michael Moynihan.

The news department now began a period of expansion that was to make it by 1964–6 one of the best in the newspaper business and that was to attract to it some of The Sunday Times's best journalists. The climate that led to this growth was important. It started with a series of awards for the paper. In February, 1964,

Henry Brandon, one of the three associate editors of the paper and its distinguished Washington correspondent, was named best news reporter of 1963 in the Hannen Swaffer Awards for Journalism, sponsored by Odhams Press, now IPC. The award was given to Brandon for his long and revealing special report on the Skybolt missile (December 8, 1963). Ron Hall received special mention for his Rachman stories and Granada television's 'What the Papers Say' named Insight as 'the year's most valuable contribution to journalism'. Morale at Thomson House was high.

'It was a period of unalloyed success,' Rees-Mogg remembers. 'It is impossible to think of a period on a quality newspaper when things went so consistently right.' With profits beginning to climb and the outlook bright, Hamilton had no difficulty in persuading the board to plough back money into buying more talent. 'I was determined to get the best men I could even if there was no space in the paper at the time to use them. The only one we wanted and didn't get was Michael Frayn. He wanted to come but by this time we were drawing so far away from The Observer that he felt it was his duty to help it. I admired him for it.'

So as The Sunday Times rocketed upwards to 64 pages, it recruited the cream of the journalistic talent from London, the provinces and overseas, until there seemed to be so many reporters on the paper that one wondered what they all did. Actually, a group of them, the Special Projects Unit – Hamilton's original scheme for a department that would produce articles for both the paper and the magazine – was working on long-term projects. Margaret Laing produced profiles on John Bloom, the washing machine magnate, George Brown, MP, and Robert Maxwell, of Pergamon Press. Pauline Peters wrote about Dulwich village, and the affluent Midlands. David Leitch compiled a long piece on European business executives. Stephen Fay examined the awarding of defence department contracts, and Godfrey Smith, the head of the unit, wrote a profile of Harold Wilson, a long article on West End Central police, a three-part study of the Duke of Norfolk, an article on psychiatrists, and another on the Negro aristocracy of the United States. (When Smith went to the magazine, the unit broke up, and its gap came to be filled by what is now called the features department.)

During these early days of expansion the doors of The Sunday Times were open to anyone with talent, and in many cases the formalities of recruitment went out the window. True, many future stars of the paper were hired in the established manner, but

Hall, Page, Cudlipp and Hamlyn were ready to see anyone at any time who had an idea for a story.

Two examples will serve to illustrate this. The present writer, Phillip Knightley, walked into The Sunday Times on June 30, 1964, with an account of a loophole in Ministry of Agriculture regulations that enabled tinned corned beef to be imported into Britain from uninspected foreign abattoirs by routing the meat through a Commonwealth country – in this case, Gibraltar. Knightley was interviewed by Cudlipp, who said, 'I don't know you so I can't take your story unchecked. I'll get one of my men to check it and write it but I'll pay you as if the story was yours.'

The following week Knightley appeared with another story, about a visit to London of Sheik Mohamed Babu, a minister in the Tanzanian government who had once been a Post Office clerk at Acton. The next week Cudlipp offered Knightley a story to do. In three months he was working three days a week for the newspaper, and at the end of a year he was full-time.

The Sunday Times, like other Sunday papers, adds to its staff on Saturdays. After he had been at the paper six months Knightley recommended to Cudlipp for Saturday casual work an Australian compatriot called Murray Sayle, who had just been sacked from the subs' table at Reuters for poor time-keeping. On his first Saturday Sayle wrote the church notices, a piece which, although certain to get into the paper, offered him little scope for his many talents. The second Saturday he was not rostered for duty at all. On the third Saturday he outpaced the opposition following Goldie, the eagle which had escaped from London Zoo, by using his bicycle to ride around Regent's Park. The fourth week Sayle noticed something which began his highly successful career for The Sunday Times: that if a reporter – even a freelance one – sat around the newsroom from Tuesday morning onwards, at some stage during the week the news editor or the Insight editor, temporarily short of men, would give him a job. Sayle found what appeared to be a vacant desk and moved in. Within a month he had a regular slot in Insight and various casual arrangements with the newsroom. Within a year he was a member of the Insight team which cracked the Fire, Auto and Marine insurance fraud and the reporter who covered Sir Francis Chichester's single-handed voyage around the world. (We shall return to both of these stories later.)

In 1969 Sayle was named International Reporter of the Year in the IPC awards and in 1970 Reporter of the Year by Granada's

'What the Papers Say'. He covered the Six-Day War in 1968, the invasion of Czechoslovakia the same year, the civil war in Jordan in 1969, the International Everest Expedition in 1971 (reporting for The Sunday Times and the BBC for thirty-four days from a camp at 23,000 feet) and has filed a distinguished correspondence on many occasions – from Vietnam, Cambodia, Laos, Pakistan and Ulster. He reported The Observer trans-Atlantic yacht race in 1968 and was a competitor himself in the Round-Britain yacht race in 1970.

Apart from Sayle's natural ability, a rise such as this – from church notices to award-winning foreign correspondent in five years – says a lot for the flexible approach of The Sunday Times during this period and its recognition that there should always be room in a newspaper for the recruitment and encouragement of unorthodox talent. (Sayle is still not technically on The Sunday Times staff, preferring, as do several other correspondents, to come to his own personal freelance arrangements with the management.)

The news department soon showed the results of the encouragement which Hamilton's editorship provided. There was, for example, the Aberdeen typhoid outbreak of May, 1964, a fine piece of team reporting by Stephen Fay, Anthony Cowdy, Arnold Field, Michael Moynihan and the late Dr Alfred Byrne. Morale remained high as the ordinary reporter in the newsroom was given a chance to shine. Michael Hamlyn had a fresh look at a series of sex attacks which had occurred on Jersey. These had started in 1958 and despite intensive investigations by local police and Scotland Yard, the person responsible had still not been detected by 1964. (He was not caught, and then largely by accident, until 1971.) Hamlyn, in quite a daring article for that time, stated openly what other newspapers had not printed: 'The only clue to the identity of the attacker is that he is thought to be a homosexual, by the nature of his assaults on boys and by the fact that he also attempts to use the little girls as boys.'

Arnold Field broke the story in the general press of the split in the British Jewish community over the case of Dr Louis Jacobs, who had been appointed rabbi at London's New West End synagogue. Dr Jacobs had rebelled against the religious establishment by suggesting that the Bible should be investigated in the light of modern scientific and archaeological advances. The then Chief Rabbi (now Sir) Israel Brodie, vetoed the re-appointment of Dr Jacobs. Jacobs was deposed by the United Synagogue, the parent organisation which governs the majority of synagogues in London, and became spiritual head of the New London Synagogue founded by the rebels who supported him. The controversy split the lay and religious sections of British Jewry and in the three months that it lasted attracted attention throughout the world. The Chief Rabbi refused to make any statement until a very late stage in the fight. Field, however, had a contact who kept him fully informed of every move. His stories were front-page on The Sunday Times week after week and were picked up and quoted extensively in news-starved Jewish newspapers world wide. As Cudlipp says, 'It showed Fleet Street that no politics are more fascinating than religious politics.'

But perhaps the most important news development in this period was in the field of campaigning crime reporting. It really began with a story written by Cal McCrystal on November 22, 1964. McCrystal, a gentle, soft-spoken reporter, had arrived on the news staff the previous January, recruited by Cudlipp from The Belfast Telegraph.

Cudlipp had heard of an upsurge in protection rackets in London strip clubs, gambling casinos, and betting shops. He assigned McCrystal to look into it. 'I picked McCrystal because he *wasn't* a crime reporter. In the old days a lot of crime reporters tended to be middle-aged men who fiddled their expenses just like middle-aged policemen fiddled theirs. They got on well with policemen but had never met a criminal in their lives. I wanted someone who didn't know any policemen, who was prepared to get to know criminals, and young enough to work all hours at the job. In return I would promise him that the appointment would be only for a limited period.'

McCrystal accepted, went to work, and uncovered more than Cudlipp had hoped. He revealed the activities of a gang led by Charles Richardson in South London, and of an East End gang controlled by the Kray brothers, Ronald and Reginald. In the battle to squeeze out smaller gangs, betting shops had been attacked, night-clubs had been smashed, and rival gang members beaten up. It was explosive material, and far from traditional Sunday Times journalism.

McCrystal wrote it in a low key, avoiding emotive adjectives and describing gang terror tactics in a flat, almost courtroom style: 'Some of the East End gangs' front men . . . are being frightened away from their usual haunts, but it is generally accepted that their leaders, who also employ vicious methods (one victim was nailed through his knees to a floor; another had his kneecaps shot off), will mount massive reprisals against the trespassers.' McCrystal wrote of 'a South London combination of five gangs . . . drawn from an area embracing Southwark, Camberwell, Balham and Tooting', and 'personal hostility' between two groups [the Richardsons and the Krays] 'who form the hard cores of the South London and East End gangs'. No one in the underworld was in any doubt as to whom the story referred, which makes the gang leaders' later reactions all the more amazing.

The first thing to happen when the story appeared was that the then deputy Commissioner of Police, Sir Joseph Simpson, rang Cudlipp to complain that it cast the police in a poor light. Cudlipp invited Sir Joseph to lunch in a private room at Brown's Hotel and there, the following Wednesday, they discussed the article. Cudlipp found Sir Joseph apparently baffled as to why The Sunday Times had carried the story and was alarmed to hear him state flatly that 'there are no criminal gangs in London'.

Cudlipp and McCrystal were still puzzling over this remark when, early in the new year (1965), Thomas Albert Marks, a thirty-seven-year-old small-time haulage operator, known to his friends as 'Ginger', disappeared from Bethnal Green in strange circumstances. Marks was walking past a public-house called The Carpenter's Arms when there was a series of shots. Police called to the scene found blood, Marks's horn-rimmed spectacles, a ·22 cartridge case, a bullet mark on the wall and nothing else. The week following the incident the daily newspapers speculated as to what had happened to Marks. The general feeling was that he would eventually turn up, a belief the police shared.

On Sunday, January 10, McCrystal, who had by now built up a number of excellent sources of information about underworld goings-on, wrote that Marks had been shot dead because he talked too much about his gangland friends. The following week McCrystal interviewed a friend of Marks's who feared he would 'go the same way as Ginger' and the third week wrote that Marks's body 'lies weighted at the bottom of the Thames at Chertsey, Surrey'.

The Sunday Times passed this information to the police and suggested that they would no doubt want to search the area where the body was said to be. The police declined to do this unless McCrystal revealed the source of his information, which he said he could not ethically do. 'So we decided if the police were not going to send frogmen down then we would,' McCrystal, now Sunday Times news editor, recalls. 'We hired three frogmen and set them to work. Unfortunately the stretch of river at that point was about two miles, and the frogmen said to search it properly would take weeks. After a day or so, their enthusiasm waned. We could not afford the cost of such an operation – and we had another theory about Marks having been "cremated" in an East End bakery – so we called it off.'

Marks, at the time of writing, has never been found and although legally presumed dead there has been no trace of his body or any clue as to who shot him.

Cal McCrystal's most important crime story began in 1966. On March 8, in a gun-fight at 'Mr Smith's Club' in Catford, a man died and two others – Edward Richardson and Frankie Fraser – were wounded. (Fraser was later found not guilty of murder but he and Richardson were each sentenced to five years' imprisonment on conviction of causing an affray at the club.) The day after the affray an acquaintance of the Richardsons called George Cornell was shot through the head in the Blind Beggar public house at Stepney. Clearly there was more to these shootings than had been reported, and on March 13 in The Sunday Times, under the heading 'Crime syndicates hired gun-men to carry out gang killings', McCrystal reviewed the state of the London underworld. Despite Sir Joseph Simpson's assurance to Cudlipp the previous year, McCrystal now gave details of 'two organisations with links in many parts of the world'.

These were new types of gangs. 'Their leaders have offices in the City, large investments in Africa, and dozens of carefully chosen men looking after less ambitious schemes (including protection) at home. . . . In London alone there are as many as forty-five lawyers whose practices are devoted almost entirely to advising and looking after the interests of the big gang leaders and their henchmen.'

Two months later McCrystal had an opportunity to carry his story further. In a Johannesburg court Mrs Corris Waldeck, widow of a murdered mining prospector, told the judge that Charles W. Richardson, a South London scrap metal merchant, and brother of Edward Richardson mentioned above, was 'at the top of the pile of ruthless London hoodlums'. The court heard many other allegations about Charles Richardson, including testimony by the man convicted of Waldeck's murder, Lawrence Bradbury, that Richardson was the leader of a vicious South

London gang.

McCrystal arranged an interview with Richardson through an intermediary and at Richardson's house in Camberwell, and later at his office in Park Lane, put a series of questions to him. The result was a highly unusual story. It began with Richardson agreeing that he was a wealthy man: he or his family owned a South African mining company, a property company, a plant and machinery concern, a scrap metal business, a share in sandpits at Romford, four wholesale and retail fancy goods shops, and some warehouses. The flavour of the rest of the interview is best caught by one of the question and answer exchanges in which it was written.

Q. Bradbury claims that a gang of which he alleges you are the leader cut him up with a razor and slashed the tendons between his forefinger and thumb with a broken bottle because he would not obey orders. Is there any foundation for him stating that?

A. It's so ridiculous, my friends are laughing. A man must be mentally deranged who would think up the idea that I nailed a man to the floor through his knees.

(The article was even more remarkable than was appreciated at the time because it was for acts similar to these that Richardson was sentenced to twenty-five years' imprisonment after his trial at the Old Bailey the following year.)

There were other 'spin-offs' from the South African trial. Lawrence Bradbury provided Cal McCrystal through an intermediary with a list of eight London policemen whom he alleged took bribes from London gangs. On July 10 the paper published the fact that it had the names, gave details of why and how the bribes were paid, and described how the gangs organised fraudulent companies. It said that the names and such other details as might assist Scotland Yard in its enquiries would be given to the police.

On July 30 the police acted and arrested Richardson in a dawn swoop on his home. His reputation died hard. At first the underworld did not believe he could be arrested. It was thought he could buy the whole police force. Then it was believed no one would give evidence against him; then that the jury could easily be influenced. (The Sunday Times considered that it had evidence at one stage during the trial that the jury, despite a guard involving eighty-two special police officers, had been threatened, and accordingly it attempted to interview various members of the jury to try to confirm this evidence. The paper was warned off by a court officer at the Old Bailey on contempt grounds.) Finally, incredibly, the underworld said that Richardson could buy any judge. When Richardson was convicted – after Mr Justice Lawton had described the torture offences as a 'disgrace to civilisation' – and sentenced to twenty-five years' imprisonment, McCrystal wrote, 'More corks were drawn by villains on Thursday night than anyone can remember. One reign of terror was over.'

The other reign of terror was that of the notorious East End twins, Ronald and Reggie Kray, and their frequent mention in the news columns of The Sunday Times, until they were convicted of murder and sentenced to life, was another spin-off from McCrystal's interview with Charles Richardson.

The Krays were amazed that a serious newspaper should devote so much space to a crime story and annoyed that it should choose a rival gang leader as the principal character. Accordingly, they got in touch with McCrystal and arranged a meeting at which they volunteered their views on the state of the London underworld, the police, and relations between the two. This was the beginning of a period when hardly a week went by without one or other of the Krays calling McCrystal. They invited him and a fellow Sunday Times reporter, Lewis Chester, to Reggie's wedding. They sent him Christmas telegrams, birthday greetings and invitations to parties. Nothing of importance occurred in the criminal world without the Krays telling McCrystal about it.

The present writer, who once occupied a desk alongside McCrystal, took a telephone call for him late one Friday night. It was Ronald Kray. He and his brother had just been released after having been detained by the police 'to help with enquiries' and were about to hold a press conference to express their indignation at having been taken to the police station on their mother's birthday. The newspaper reporters were all gathered in a Bethnal Green public house ready for the conference, but the Krays would not start until McCrystal arrived.

It was a strange relationship because McCrystal wrote about the Krays as he would have of any other underworld protection racketeer, emphasising, tongue-in-cheek, those facets of their existence most likely to interest Sunday Times readers – their part in fund-raising and charitable activities and their taste for being photographed with celebrities ranging from civic leaders and boxing champions to show-business personalities and the occasional aristocrat.

For those who knew, the articles often contained neat *double entendres*, such as in the Insight piece written by McCrystal's colleague, Lewis Chester – 'The charitable life of the Brothers Kray.' This was a straight account of the Krays' career interspersed with details of their fund-raising activities and ending, dead-pan, 'As philanthropic fund-raisers their background may not be entirely conventional, *but no one can deny their remarkable persuasive powers.*'

The Krays remained delighted with everything McCrystal and Chester wrote, almost as if they believed that mention in a 'respectable' newspaper conferred respectability – which may be why they cultivated at least one MP and were delighted to have visits to their East End club of well-known personalities.

It all came to an end at 6 am on May 8, 1969, when Superintendent Leonard Reed and a few discreetly armed policemen broke down the door of the Kray twins' flat and arrested them. At the same time crime squads throughout the Metropolitan police area were arresting twenty other men. Legal processes dragged on until October, when the twins were refused leave to appeal to the Lords, but their reign had effectively been broken by their arrest.

With their eclipse ended a vintage period of Sunday Times crime reporting. Michael Cudlipp, who was news editor and assistant editor (news) throughout the Richardson and the Kray affairs, claims for The Sunday Times a measure of the credit for the police success in breaking up the two gangs:

After Sir Joseph Simpson had told us that there were no gangs in London, when we knew that there were, we made an editorial decision to try to push the police into doing something about them.[1] It was the beginning of gang-busting stories in quality newspapers, and although we were new to this sort of reporting I like to think that what we wrote about the Richardsons and the Krays and the London underworld was quite startling for its time.

Cudlipp adds: 'It was a frightening business for McCrystal and his wife Stella – we seriously considered evacuating his family at one stage – and when it was all over we kept our promise, relieved him of crime reporting, and assigned him elsewhere.' (McCrystal was appointed chief reporter and sent on foreign assignments. He then became Sunday Times correspondent in New York for three years and returned to London in 1970 as news editor.)

---

1. When Cudlipp went to The Times (where he is now deputy-editor) in 1967 and allegations of police corruption came his way he decided – because of this earlier experience – to publish first and tell Scotland Yard later. The Times won an IPC award for its efforts.

The Krays–Richardson period has a flavour about it that has fortunately not occurred since. Its importance here is that it was the press, with The Sunday Times to the fore, which crucially helped to get the gangs broken up and the leaders prosecuted: campaigning journalism in the best of newspaper tradition.

XIII

The close of 1964 found The Sunday Times buoyant. It had been an excellent year all round; how excellent was not fully realised until the early months of the new year. Although, with modest understatement, Lord Thomson described the year's trading as 'satisfactory', the Organisation had, in fact, achieved a record consolidated trading profit of more than £6½ million.

In February Denis Hamilton was named Journalist of the Year in the Hannen Swaffer awards 'for his distinguished work in making The Sunday Times one of the great newspapers of the world'. (Bruce Page and Lewis Chester were commended for their work in uncovering the antique dealers' ring.) With the coffers flush and prestige high, Lord Thomson felt justified in throwing 'a little dinner party' in Hamilton's honour, and on March 16 he took over the Abraham Lincoln room at the Savoy for 150 guests, including the entire editorial staff of the newspaper, distinguished contributors, and executives of other departments who had helped the paper's expansion. The outsiders included Hamilton's friends Harold Macmillan and General Sir Brian Horrocks; John Freeman, formerly New Statesman editor and then about to become British High Commissioner to India; and Sir Linton Andrews, formerly editor of The Yorkshire Post and one of the Swaffer awards judges.

Apart from its social interest the dinner was important for what emerged from the two main speeches of the night – those of Lord Thomson and of Denis Hamilton. Thomson spelt out in hard accountant's terms what the editorial success of The Sunday Times had meant. In 1959, when Kemsley Newspapers had become Thomson Newspapers, The Sunday Times had had a circulation of 885,000. 'Today, under Denis Hamilton's inspired leadership,' Thomson said, 'it is 1,275,000. From 28 pages an issue it has grown to 56. From 200 tons of newsprint consumed an issue we now use 1,000 tons.'

Hamilton spoke of his relationship with Thomson. There were, he said, three types of editor-proprietor relationship: total domination; a proprietor who left the editor free for a week and then changed everything he had decided; and mutual respect but with the editor exercising his own judgment in a climate of freedom. Hamilton said that he and Thomson enjoyed the third type of relationship, and that: 'I look forward to every talk – and we talk every day – with this remarkable man, uncorrupted by his success, trustful of his subordinates, his enthusiasm greater with the passing days, his willingness to risk millions without ringing up every five minutes to see what's happening.' The message of the two speeches was clear: success inspires further confidence.

Yet at this moment important editorial changes were taking place. Two of Hamilton's young Turks, Clive Irving and Jeremy Wallington, left – Irving to become a director of IPC publications and Wallington to be assistant editor of The Daily Mail. Irving later regretted the move. He says, 'When I left there was already much back-stairs talk about Thomson taking over The Times, but it didn't seem very likely to me. I realised that if it did happen there would suddenly be a lot of scope for promotion and I was tempted to hang around for that. But when Hugh Cudlipp came along and offered me a lot of money, a private bathroom and bar, and an Alfa-Romeo, avarice got the better of my judgment. But none of the high-style living at the Mirror compensated for my abject misery of working in that paralysed dinosaur. It was a mistake to leave The Sunday Times then, but hindsight supersedes insight.'

Before Irving left, Hamilton had taken up with him a point that had been concerning him for some time. 'I had a phobia that Whitehall was under-reported. Certainly most papers had diplomatic correspondents, defence correspondents, education correspondents and industrial correspondents. And the Treasury was looked at in an obsequious way by the City editors. But I wanted The Sunday Times to move to a position, as in America, where each Ministry has a watchdog – actually The New York Times has more than one man watching each department. I felt British civil servants were not being challenged enough by facts, and I thought that we should have a man, not a lobby man, who could watch Whitehall day by day.'

The man they had chosen was Anthony Howard, co-author with Richard West of 'The Making of the Prime Minister', an account of Wilson's success in the 1964 General Election. Howard, then thirty, had been president of the Oxford Union and had read for the Bar before entering journalism. He had good contacts in both the Government and the Civil Service, and he was enthusiastic about the job. But his attempt to bring a critical eye to the workings of Whitehall did not work out, and Howard was involved in a brief but bitter episode which included the intervention of the Prime Minister, Harold Wilson. The full story of what went wrong has not been set down before, and it highlights the problems which, despite recent improvements, still plague relations between Whitehall and the press.

Howard was introduced to Sunday Times readers on January 17, 1965, in a low key so as not to offer the Government an excuse for an immediate confrontation. His first article was presented as being by 'Anthony Howard, who has joined The Sunday Times as Whitehall correspondent'. Any hope that this modest statement of Howard's duties might pass unnoticed was shattered by what Howard wrote and, contrary to accepted versions, it was this article which infuriated Wilson. Headed 'Ministry of No Resources', it set out the problems facing the Ministry of Land and Natural Resources which, Howard said, 'Mr Wilson almost casually created one Monday afternoon in October – and which ever since has seemed to be in grave danger of dying of neglect'. Howard said that the Ministry had been set up to produce and pilot one of Labour's most complicated legislative proposals – the Bill setting up the Land Commission and introducing the entirely fresh concept of Crown-hold into the British law of property. 'But in Whitehall it is already possible to detect the odd shudder of apprehension over whether Mr Wilson has really found the right instrument for his purpose.'

It was, of course, all right for newspapers to attack Ministers: as political heads of departments they are considered fair game. But to attack a Ministry as an entity – civil servants and all – was opening new ground in the view of Mr Wilson.

On Friday, February 19, Wilson had been invited to lunch at The Sunday Times. At the Cabinet meeting the day before he had raised the question of Howard and, assured of Cabinet backing for his attitude, he went to Thomson House in an aggressive mood. He had been invited fifteen minutes before the other guests, and Hamilton took him to a private room for a drink with Lord Thomson. The Prime Minister went straight to the attack. 'I'm not going to have Howard writing about my civil servants,' he told an astonished Lord Thomson. 'They can't answer for themselves. I'm the only one who can defend them and I'm going to discharge that responsibility.' Thomson, who had not heard of Howard until then, was momentarily nonplussed. 'Who's this guy Howard?' he said. 'Have I bought myself a headache?' He deflected Wilson's assault to Hamilton, who resented both its manner and its timing. The lunch, a lengthy but frosty affair, was attended by Howard himself, who had broken off in the middle of his piece for the following Sunday – an examination of the power struggle between the Department of Economic Affairs and the Treasury. Howard knew nothing of what had gone before. 'Wilson gave me a beady stare and I could tell he was angry about something.'

After the lunch Hamilton and Rees-Mogg discussed what should be done. It was clear that if Wilson meant what he had said and used his power as Prime Minister to enforce it, Howard's career as Whitehall correspondent was already over. Every door in Whitehall would be closed to him. Nevertheless, Hamilton was upset about Wilson's attitude and decided it should not pass without some reply. Accordingly Rees-Mogg wrote a leading article, 'Power and the Press', which with Howard's piece on the Treasury–DEA battle, 'A Clash Has Been Arranged', are generally considered to have been responsible for Wilson's decision not to allow the 'Whitehall correspondent' experiment to continue. (Whereas in reality, as we have seen, Wilson had clearly decided this *before* Rees-Mogg's leader and Howard's second article.)

If Wilson had in fact had any glimmer of doubt about his decision it was dispelled by the reaction in Whitehall when The Sunday Times appeared. Rees-Mogg set out the case for covering Whitehall: 'The job of a newspaper is to bring into public information the acts and processes of power. National security alone excepted, it is the job of newspapers to publish the secret matters of politics whether the secrets are the secrets of the Cabinet, of Parliament, or of the Civil Service.' Rees-Mogg pointed to Howard's article as an example of what he meant. 'It discusses the attitudes of civil servants with the same freedom that it discusses the attitude of politicians, and treats the Ministries as open to normal reporting methods.' Since Rees-Mogg was already aware of Wilson's attitude he could not pretend that he was certain Howard would succeed. 'Right or wrong, this is a major departure, and one which, if it is successful, will change British newspaper practice in an important way.'

Howard's article was brisk, hard-hitting, and very readable. It began by suggesting that the reports of conflict between DEA and the Treasury were wrong in presenting the clash as one between the two Ministers: George Brown and Jim Callaghan. 'It would, indeed, be more accurate to describe the present dispute not so much as a Ministerial row as a genuine conflict of economic view between two highly able professional civil servants – Sir "Otto" Clarke and Mr Douglas Allen.' Howard described Clarke as 'the last Gladstonian fiscal apostle remaining in the British Civil Service . . . reputed to be the sole senior Treasury official to have personally supported the Suez operation of 1956,' and Allen as 'an unusual figure for a senior Treasury official in being neither a public schoolboy nor an Oxbridge graduate . . . in formal title he is merely a deputy secretary in Mr Brown's department; but over the past few weeks he has emerged progressively as the real Whitehall force within the Ministry.'

The reaction in Whitehall was immediate. Sunday morning saw Clarke knocking at the door of No. 11 Downing Street to ask Callaghan's permission to begin legal action against The Sunday Times and Howard, or at least to be allowed the right of public reply. In the event this extreme step was not necessary. Wilson handled the affair personally. He contacted the permanent head of the Civil Service and on Monday a memorandum went out instructing civil servants that under no circumstances were they to talk to Anthony Howard.

Two further steps consolidated this move. Mr George Younger, Conservative member for Ayr, raised the matter in the House of Commons, asking Wilson: 'A leading Sunday newspaper announced last month its expressed intention to probe the private and political opinions of senior civil servants. Does he not agree that this would undermine the principle of ministerial responsibility and would put these civil servants in an intolerable position?' The Prime Minister replied: 'I entirely agree . . . This new departure is being met quite firmly as far as we are concerned, and anyone appointed to do this job will have no more facilities than any other journalist.' And there were rumours, no doubt deliberately started, that a Labour peer might have to put down a motion in the House of Lords drawing attention to the unconstitutional conduct of one of Lord Thomson's newspapers.

It all worked. Within days it became clear that Howard was going to get nowhere in Whitehall. He suggested to Rees-Mogg that he should write an account of what had occurred but Rees-

Mogg said no. 'At that point I still hoped that we would be able to wheedle our way in, if not with Howard then perhaps with someone else. Some quite high civil servants were in favour of the idea and I did not want to slam the door for ever.'

Howard then asked to see Wilson, and in the Cabinet room at 10 Downing Street heard Wilson's attitude bluntly explained. 'He was courteous but firm. He said he understood I was only trying to do my job but he had a job to do, too, and his was more important than mine. He made it very plain that all conventional sources of information would remain shut until I was willing to return to the cosy but essentially sham game of being a political correspondent.'

Howard lingered on the paper until August and then accepted an offer to become The Observer's Washington correspondent (he was appointed editor of The New Statesman in April, 1972).

Could The Sunday Times have given him more support, and if it had done so would it have made any difference? Colin Seymour-Ure, of the University of Kent and author of 'The Press, Politics and the Public' (Methuen, London, 1968) believes so: 'The failure of the "Whitehall correspondent" idea was caused primarily by the strength of the Government's commitment against it and by the weakness of the commitment to it by The Sunday Times.' Rees-Mogg denies that The Sunday Times commitment could have been stronger. 'The idea failed because discipline in Whitehall at the time was too effective. It was also felt in some quarters that Howard's approach was too personal.'

But the idea did not disappear with Howard, and other ways of working towards the same aim have been employed. The Insight approach, which ensures anonymity for the final article, has protected civil servants and reporters alike from the reaction Howard suffered. More correspondents covering individual departments have been introduced, not only on The Sunday Times but on most national newspapers. And the original scheme, the Whitehall correspondent looking at the Civil Service overall, which Howard pioneered, has not been abandoned, only postponed.

XIV

For the latter part of 1965 and early 1966 Insight concentrated largely on the kind of short feature stories which it had dealt with originally. They were bright, engaging journalism, but it was looking for something bigger. It came in 1966.

On Saturday, July 2, of that year the 400,000 motorists insured with the Fire, Auto and Marine Insurance company were alarmed to read in the morning newspapers that they should immediately seek cover from other insurers; FAM was unable to pay its debts and was applying for immediate winding up. Although the whole field of motor insurance had looked shaky for some time (Charles Raw had, in fact, prepared an article for Business News for that Sunday, setting out what was wrong with this section of the insurance business) the collapse of FAM was a decided shock. Formed only three years earlier it had rapidly expanded, mainly as a result of its imaginative approach to what had become a complacent and uncompetitive field.

FAM specialised in private cars, assessing the risk by computer. It paid brokers a commission running as high as 20 per cent and, most important of all, it undercut established motor insurance rates by as much as half. As a result the money had poured in – FAM's premium income was to reach £3½ million a year before the end.

The firm moved to its own brand-new building on the North Circular Road, where the office of its flamboyant founder, Emil Savundra, featured an £11,000 electronic mural. Savundra (full name Savundranayagan) a Cingalese, had crowned an adventurous career as an international businessman with his venture into car insurance. He was an affable, genial host, an enthusiastic if mercurial driver of expensive power-boats, a radio amateur (his call sign was 007), a lover of fast cars (he ran two Aston Martin DB5s, a Rolls, and a 3.8 Jaguar) and the mysterious 'Indian doctor' mentioned in the Christine Keeler affair. In conversation he appeared highly knowledgeable about insurance and international finance, a man of intelligence and integrity.

It is understandable, therefore, that the first newspaper reports of FAM's collapse suggested only that the company might have over extended itself. The Daily Express quoted a director of the company as saying, 'We are owed about £1 million from brokers. If we had been paid all we are owed we would not have had to go into liquidation.' When the editorial conference at The Sunday Times met on the Tuesday morning all the story appeared to offer was a further Business News piece suggesting more stringent Board of Trade safeguards for car insurance firms.

Hall was on holiday, and after the conference Page and Harold Evans, then chief assistant to the editor, talked about finding some other way to build a story on car insurance, using the FAM collapse as a peg. Evans remembered that an MP friend of his, Norman Atkinson, had once discussed an idea for a government-run car insurance scheme, so he and Page went to see Atkinson at his flat. In the course of talking about his idea Atkinson casually said, 'It's interesting, isn't it, about this Pakistani who's got away with all this money?' Evans and Page looked at each other and tried to draw Atkinson. But apart from saying that he had learnt about the 'Pakistani' from someone at the Board of Trade Atkinson could add nothing more.

It was soon clear that the 'Pakistani' was actually Savundra, but where to go from there? Evans and Page consulted Business News editor, Peter Wilsher, who said that his reporters had been un-impressed by an earlier look at FAM and would not be at all sur-prised 'if Savundra turns out to be a crook'. Before making the final decision to commit Insight's resources to the story, Evans telephoned a Cingalese friend, Tarzie Vittachi. 'What do you know about a man called Emil Savundra?' he asked. 'Watch him,' Vittachi said, 'he was done for fraud once before.'

By that evening the Insight team had decided its approach to the story. A contact in the Board of Trade had felt able to say only, 'Look in Zurich,' so Lewis Chester got on a plane to Switzerland that night to be on the spot if this lead developed any further. Jordan and Sons Limited, which specialises in searches at Companies House, had been engaged to dig out everything it could on FAM and its directors. Cables had been sent to Sunday Times correspondents in Colombo for information on Savundra's background and then, as this began to come in, others went to Accra, Liechtenstein, New York and Paris, to trace Savundra's complicated business deals.

Murray Sayle, posing as a businessman with connections in international finance and based in Geneva – a rôle he was well qualified to play because at an earlier period he had actually worked for such a concern – went off to meet the FAM directors 'to make them an offer for the company: provided, of course, I could have a look at the books'. Sayle did not get very far and Chester, in Zurich, suffered a serious set-back. Trying to interview a certain Dr Paul Hagenbach, whose name appeared on various F A M documents, he was arrested for 'tapage nocturne' (making a noise at night). Hagenbach had objected to Chester's ringing his doorbell at 10.30 pm and had called the police. In itself *tapage nocturne* was not serious – Chester was fined only 15 francs – but he was officially warned not to repeat the offence. Clearly, confronting Hagenbach was not on; and when Chester called at the nursing-home where Savundra was said to be having treatment for a heart condition he was told that the patient had checked out.

Back in London the Insight team were convinced that they were on to a big story. But by Thursday they were still no closer to cracking it. Throughout the day they pored over the F A M returns, copies of which had come from Companies House, and listed all the important unanswered questions. F A M's reserves were shown as amounting to nearly £900,000. These reserves were listed as comprising shares in 'blue chip' companies, but the returns did not state what these holdings actually were; and a search through earlier returns had failed to show when the shares had been purchased.

Here was an area well worth further investigation, and Page sent Colin Simpson to look into it. Simpson took the name of the F A M auditors from the most recent return and went to see them. Simpson asked whether, during the audit, the numbers of the share certificates which comprised F A M's reserves had been listed. The auditor to whom Simpson had been speaking called in a junior member of the firm, who had actually been working at F A M's headquarters, and repeated the question. 'As a matter of fact, I did,' the junior said, 'and it's strange you should ask me that. The Board of Trade inspector asked me the same thing half an hour ago!'

He produced his list, but the senior auditor flatly refused to let Simpson see it. Simpson was at his eloquent best. He spoke of public duty, the necessity of bringing the whole affair into the open, of justice, of protection of sources, and of the two sorts of publicity – good publicity and bad publicity. The telephone rang. The senior auditor answered it and said, 'Excuse me, I've got to go out for five minutes.' When the auditor left the room he also left the list of share certificates on his desk. Simpson frankly admits that he copied it.

It was now late Friday afternoon, and Evans and the whole Insight team still in London gathered for the next obvious step – to check whether the share certificates listed as FAM's reserves, nearly £900,000 worth, actually existed. The only way to do this was to telephone the chairman or secretary of every company concerned and to ask him if share certificate number so-and-so existed and was it registered as belonging to FAM. It was realised that this would need to be a high-level approach, so Evans undertook it himself. His first call was to the chairman of Burmah Oil, and his response was typical of most of the other puzzled executives Evans telephoned throughout Friday night. 'He was marvellous,' Evans says, 'he caught on immediately what we were up to. He also caught the spirit of the chase and he couldn't have been more helpful.' His answer, as other company chiefs hopped into Rolls-Royces all over the Home Counties stockbroker belt and headed for their offices and their records, was also to be typical: no certificate of the serial number said to be held by FAM in fact existed. (Only one company, Beaverbrook Newspapers, after high level consideration, declined to answer.) The conclusion was obvious: FAM's share certificates were bogus and the company's assets therefore non-existent.

Once this crucial heart of the story had been established, the rest was easier. A dossier on Savundra's earlier career had been built up from correspondents' cabled reports and old newspaper records. It made interesting reading. In 1950 Savundra had been involved in an 'oil for China' deal in which a million dollars had disappeared; in 1964 a 'rice from Goa' deal ended with $865,000 missing; in 1958 the 'Camp Bird Company' scandal in West Africa had ended with Savundra's deportation; and in 1959 he had been mentioned in the 'coffee bean' swindle on the Costa Rican Government. The Goan rice deal had resulted in Savundra serving fifteen months of a five-years' jail sentence which a Belgian court had imposed for fraud.

FAM directors, flabbergasted at events, had spoken freely and frankly about the last days of FAM and of their relations with Savundra and Stuart de Quincey Walker, the man who had taken over as FAM chief when Savundra had resigned on June 22. With their statements, Savundra's background, the share certificate information, and odds and ends from the diggings of the other reporters, Sayle, Mark Ottaway and Chester, Page wrote throughout Friday night and Saturday morning, and Harold Evans edited, 'The Master Mind of Dr Emil Savundra', which appeared on July 10. Evans wanted it to be a page one lead, but lost. The story was sensational enough, with a page one pointer headed, 'Fire Auto had almost £1 million in bogus assets'. Evans brought in a leading company law specialist on the Saturday morning, and James Evans, The Sunday Times legal adviser, vetted the story. He was helped considerably by the fact that Colin Simpson persuaded other directors of FAM to come to The Sunday Times offices on the Saturday to sign the page proofs of the article and agree that they were a true record of the events at FAM which had concerned them.

The story was followed up heavily during all the week as the daily newspapers attempted to catch up on the lead The Sunday Times had established. There remained one major aspect of the story which had not been solved: given that a huge amount had 'disappeared' out of the accounts of FAM, where had it gone? And if it had gone to Emil Savundra, how had he worked it?

It was The Daily Mail team working under one of the original Insight reporters, Jeremy Wallington, which spelt out in its issue on Saturday, July 16, where the money had gone. The key was a Liechtenstein investment company, Merchants Finance Trust, controlled by Savundra and Walker. Money from FAM was 'invested' in MFT and MFT in turn lent £600,000 to its controllers, Savundra and Walker – £387,534 to Savundra and £216,762 to Walker. The loans were over twenty years at the ridiculously low interest rate of $\frac{1}{4}$ per cent a month.

The FAM saga dragged on for a further two years. Savundra returned to Britain from Ceylon, was arrested and, with Walker, charged with various offences involving FAM's collapse. On March 7, 1968, at the Old Bailey Savundra was sentenced to eight years' imprisonment and fined £50,000; Walker received five years and a fine of £30,000.

The affair exercised three important influences on the development of The Sunday Times. First, it was Harold Evans's first big story on the paper and it gave both him and Insight a further taste of the satisfaction provided by investigatory journalism. Secondly, the story represented the first exposition in Insight of the mass-reader approach to a complicated business matter, the presentation of financial affairs in clear, lucid terms devoid of jargon and technicalities. Its success led to the in-depth Leasco–Pergamon Press affair in 1969 and reached full fruition in 1970–1 with the massive international inquiry into the affairs of Investors Overseas Services, the Geneva-based mutual funds empire of

Bernard Cornfield. Finally, it raised, indirectly, a most important legal matter involving newspapers and their relations with the courts.

After Savundra returned to Britain but before his arrest and trial he agreed to appear on David Frost's television show and be interviewed by Frost. Frost's researchers asked Insight to provide a briefing as a basis for Frost's questions, and this was done. The interview went out on Friday, February 3, 1967, and became one of the most bitterly disputed confrontations in the history of current affairs television, the main accusation being that it was 'trial by television'. Since the programme had been so controversial, and because Savundra had raised a number of points The Sunday Times was in a position to answer, Harold Evans, by then editor, decided to run a transcript of the interview the following Sunday. The piece was headed 'Savundra's bluff' and was introduced with 'this [the interview] was such an important occasion – for what it revealed of Dr Savundra's attitudes and of absurdities in the law – that The Sunday Times has made special arrangements to put on record today the detailed exchanges – with Insight comment [in italics] on the facts.' Evans ran the comments because he was shocked that after all The Sunday Times had exposed, Savundra had still not been charged. It was, it turned out, a very risky thing to do because although Savundra had not been charged, a judge was later to rule that it was contempt of court to publish such material when a prosecution was 'imminent'.

After the Old Bailey trial Savundra and Walker both appealed against their convictions, one of Savundra's grounds being, as his counsel expressed it, that 'he did not have a chance because the air had been so poisoned by publicity before the trial that it was inevitably prejudiced'. The appeals were dismissed, but Lord Justice Salmon singled out the Frost television interview and its reproduction in The Sunday Times for criticism. A free press had a right and a duty to comment on the failure of an insurance company, Lord Justice Salmon said; it was in the public interest that that should be done and it was sometimes as a result of facts disclosed by the press that a crime was brought to light; and an individual was covered by the law of libel if the defamation complained of were untrue. But the television interview with Savundra was deplorable. He was faced with a skilled interviewer whose clear object was to establish his guilt before an audience of millions. None of the safeguards that existed in a court of law was observed and, surprisingly, the whole interview had been reproduced in a Sunday paper.

Lord Justice Salmon then issued the warning which has since given many an editor a sleepless night: 'No one should imagine that he is safe from committing contempt of court if knowing, or having good reason to believe, that criminal proceedings are imminent, he chooses to publish matters calculated to prejudice a fair trial.' Every editor understood the risk he was running if he published a story about a man against whom criminal proceedings had already begun. Most understood that the risk could remain if they *knew* that criminal proceedings were imminent. But until Lord Justice Salmon's warning none knew that the risk still remained '*if having good reason to believe*' that criminal proceedings were imminent, they went ahead and published.

It is the thought of how courts might interpret 'having good reason to believe' that has seriously concerned editors since the Savundra affair, and – despite pressure for reform of the law of contempt – at the time of writing this major legal problem for all newspapers remains unresolved.

XV

It is tempting but not possible here to re-tell the whole of the famous bogus Burgundy story which appeared on the front of the Weekly Review on November 27, 1966, written by Nicholas Tomalin and Insight. But since in many respects this was the perfect Sunday Times exposure story some of its previously un-revealed highlights deserve mention. The idea itself was not new. Official figures showed that Britain drank four times more 'Burgundy' than France sent us, so obviously a lot of the wine was fake. Other newspapers had attempted from time to time to show this, usually by arranging for experts to taste wine sold in Britain as 'Burgundy'. But the results were not legally-verifiable proof, and the reader was left with the possibility that the expert could be mistaken. The first effort by The Sunday Times – scientific tests of fifteen bottles of Burgundy bought in London by Nicholas Tomalin – was equally unsuccessful. The real opportunity came, as so often happens in journalism, by chance.

Colin Simpson, house-hunting in the Ipswich area, met the manager of a French wine company which ran a bottling plant near by. The manager mentioned to Simpson that this plant sold cheap, blended wine to a number of British firms and that this wine appeared with a label which often bore no resemblance to the contents of the bottle. Simpson passed this information to Ron Hall and Hall assigned Tomalin to investigate. Tomalin paid two visits to the Ipswich plant, taking photographer Bryan Wharton on one. Bruce Page went to confirm Tomalin's information. What they saw there, and photographs which Wharton took of the plant's blending book, proved beyond doubt that the cheap blended wines from various parts of France were bottled and sold to British shippers who labelled the wine 'Châteauneuf du Pape', 'Nuits St Georges', 'Beaujolais', and even 'Vin de l'année 1963, Château de Corcelles, Beaujolais Cuvée speciale au Château de Corcelle . . . Mis en bouteille dans nos caves'.

On the Friday night before publication, surrounded by bottles of wine, Page wrote the first page of 'The Art of Cooking Bogus Burgundy' and Tomalin wrote the second. Somehow during the long hours one of the three bottles needed for legal reasons was mysteriously emptied, causing Hall some concern: 'We're buried under bloody wine and someone's had to pick the evidence to drink.' Hamilton asked for a few qualifying sentences so as not to make it appear that the whole wine trade had been guilty of selling bogus Burgundy, and with minor modifications James Evans passed the article as legally safe for publication. It would normally have appeared under the by-line 'By Insight', but Tomalin made the point that he was not an Insight reporter. Later he changed his mind and asked Hall to leave his name off altogether. Hall did not hear and when the page proofs appeared with Tomalin's name Tomalin frankly admits, 'I wasn't quite strong enough to insist that it should come off.' It was a wise decision. There was a Board of Trade enquiry, questions in the Commons, a row in the trade, and finally, the following year, a new code of practice from the Wine and Spirit Association. And for Tomalin the article remains to this day one of his best-known by-lines – 'In a way I've been looking for a bogus Burgundy story ever since.'

The importance of the story in the context of The Sunday Times was that it gave a vivid and legally-verifiable account of an abuse that everyone knew was taking place but which no one had been able to prove. It convinced the Insight team that given the time, the resources, and a reasonable amount of luck, there was no plot that it could not eventually crack – a theory put to the test a year later with the Philby affair. But this meant either moving

Insight away from the small background feature stories which had launched it or splitting it in two – one section to handle the 'ologies', the other to be a long-term, informal team putting into practice the investigation techniques that had proved so success-ful. The decision was to be not Hamilton's but that of the new editor, Harold Evans.

January 15, 1967

PART 6

Evans: Vive la différence
1967 . . . .

PART 6

Evans: Vive la différence

I

To Fleet Street the announcement in the paper on January 15, 1967, that the new editor of The Sunday Times was to be Harold Evans must have come as somewhat of a surprise. To begin with, Evans was not in the tradition of Sunday Times editors. The son of a railway driver, he had started as a reporter on a Lancashire weekly at the age of sixteen, had done his National Service in the RAF and had interrupted his career in journalism to graduate at Durham University. Although his rise to the editorship of The Northern Echo (via a job on The Manchester Evening News) had been rapid, and his campaign for a posthumous pardon for Timothy Evans had won him many admirers, he was better known in the provinces than in London, and he certainly seemed no match for the distinguished candidates which the editorship of The Sunday Times had attracted. How then had a northern working-class meritocrat who had actually learned shorthand and typing arrived at being – at only 38 – editor of one of the world's great newspapers?

After Clive Irving's departure Hamilton took a hard look at the staffing of The Sunday Times. He saw a newspaper strong on the cultural and critical side, strong on the political side, 'but short of the highly-professional executive journalists of the Pat Murphy and James Dow type'. There was a need for people to administer, control, and direct the energies of the restless young men who had been attracted by the renaissance of The Sunday Times, a need for lieutenants to tackle the presentation of the paper. It was a period of good profitability, so Hamilton could afford to invest in men at the top, and he began to look around.

He had a clear idea of the type of man he wanted. At this stage he had already had discussions with Lord Astor about The Times. 'I had said that in my opinion The Times would fall apart unless it managed to get the cover of a big organisation. Nothing came of our talks at that time, but I had a feeling that I should keep The Sunday Times topped up with first-class executives.'

The leading candidate for the main job – then unidentified – which Hamilton had to offer was, within the Thomson Organisation, David Hopkinson, one of Hamilton's protégés, then editor of The Sheffield Telegraph and now editor of The Birmingham Post. To line up candidates outside the organisation, Hamilton began to ask every senior journalist he met: 'Who's the leading editor in the provinces?' Nearly everyone named Evans.

Hamilton checked further. 'I found that Evans was at a point in his life when he would have to decide whether to sign a new contract with the Westminster Group, who owned The Northern Echo, or move to Fleet Street. I liked the work he had been doing for the International Press Institute, particularly in the East. I was impressed by his handling of the Timothy Evans affair. I decided I was not quite ready to bring Hopkinson to London and I asked Harold Evans to come to see me.'

Evans came with some slight trepidation. He had met Hamilton at an IPI meeting in Paris and at several sessions of the National Council for the Training of Journalists, but his brief contacts with The Sunday Times had not all been smooth. Evans had on one occasion written to complain about a book review which had contained a slighting reference to the town of Darlington and Hamilton had obligingly telephoned to mollify him. Then, after Evans had criticised The Sunday Times in the independent television programme 'What the Papers Say', Hall had written him a rude post-card. In London Evans was surprised when Hamilton, after chatting for a while about The Northern Echo, said, 'Do you want to be groomed for managing editor here?' Evans asked for time to think about the offer. He was excited about Hamilton's broad, detached view of journalism but he was reluctant to leave the North. He came back to London twice, the first time to meet Pat Murphy and the second to meet William Rees-Mogg, and then decided to accept Hamilton's offer. Hamilton wrote to him on May 28, 1965, suggesting that he should join as 'Chief Assistant to C. D. Hamilton as Editorial Director of the Thomson Organisation and as Editor of The Sunday Times'. 'This,' Hamilton said, 'would give you the authority to take a major part in the operation of the Group from the moment you arrive as my special "trouble shooter", yet having certain specific tasks on The Sunday Times.'

Evans gave The Northern Echo as much notice as he could, and so did not start at Thomson House until January the following year, 1966. One of his first jobs had been mentioned in Hamilton's letter of appointment: 'to give a fresh slant to the sports pages.'

Now Hamilton expanded on this. 'He called me in and said that he was concerned that no one seemed particularly interested in the sports pages and that my first assignment would be to re-jig them.' Evans, who had come on ahead of his family and was staying at the National Liberal Club ('up on the top floor with the cleaning ladies and the pigeons'), would have preferred news to sport but was nevertheless pleased to get to work.

It was a testing first assignment. The sports editor, Ken Compston, had been in charge of the department for seventeen years. He had first worked for The Sunday Times when the paper's northern edition was printed in Manchester and Compston was crime reporter on The Evening Chronicle. He later came to London for The Chronicle, continued to do Saturday casual work for The Sunday Times, and when the sports editor, Gerald Pawle,[1] left, Compston took his place.

He inherited the theory of sports reporting propounded by Pat Murphy – 'a blanket coverage'. The idea was to cram into the paper as many reports of as many sports as possible, and when there was no room for a report then at least you printed the result – in $5\frac{1}{2}$ point if necessary. So The Sunday Times not only covered association football, rugby, cricket, hockey, athletics, etc, but lacrosse and croquet as well. There is a lot to be said for the blanket coverage method, but it was not what Hamilton wanted for the new-image Sunday Times. But how to change it? And what should the new theory be?

Evans's first move was to prepare a detailed analysis of what the sports section contained. Then he went to all sports enthusiasts he knew and asked them what they thought of The Sunday Times, what did they want to read that was not there and, in general, how they believed a sports section of a Sunday newspaper should function. He put down all his conclusions in a memorandum to Hamilton which began: 'The ideal is obvious – full authoritative reports on all fixtures in all sports. But we have space problems so we have to make choices. They are hard ones, but unless we make them and stick to them we will not have a clear sports policy. We shall confuse the reader and frustrate ourselves.'

The answer, Evans suggested, was to hit upon an attractive mix

---

1. Pawle had originally been one of Lord Kemsley's young men after the war. He was an outstanding writer, a good games-player, and a highly attractive personality. He withdrew from regular journalism and went to live in Cornwall when he married the widow of Kemsley's son Oswald.

of live sport and features: each week should have a Henry Longhurst column, a live topical feature with a picture, and they should bring in Michael Parkinson to write a piece of nostalgia. The rest of the space would go to live sport. Since this space would obviously not be sufficient to report as many games as before, the answer would be to report fewer games more fully. 'The thousands who come each year new to a sport are eager for the depth reporting, the insightful discussion of techniques, strategy and personalities.'

Evans got one of the young colour magazine designers, David Hillman, to design new pages for sport, with emphasis on grouping together in clear rectangles, to give the section a fresh appearance as well as a fresh policy. All this took about a month, during which time no small part of Evans's energy was devoted to persuading Compston to accept the idea. Compston, whose own style had been rather cramped by his having to work under the eye of ex-sports editor Murphy, but who was nevertheless a tough but fair man, agreed only when he realised that Evans was not all theory and was quite capable of putting his ideas into practice.

After the sports pages Evans turned his attention to news and features, and at Rees-Mogg's invitation wrote occasional editorials. He persuaded Hamilton to begin a campaign for a better national programme of cervical cancer detection. He arranged the first major national newspaper report on Ulster, calling it in a headline 'John Bull's Political Slum'. (This provoked outraged complaints from Belfast for suggesting that Stormont could not be trusted to get on with political reforms and Hamilton had to cope with a flood of protests.) He argued for a continuing campaign on environment – then not such a fashionable word – and, as we have seen, as managing editor he led the investigation into Emil Savundra and Fire Auto and Marine. He took charge of the extensive coverage of the Aberfan tip disaster and it was his idea that the paper should try an historical reconstruction of the Zinoviev letter affair, which led to a series in the paper and, eventually, to a book by Hugo Young, Stephen Fay and Lewis Chester. Evans was hard-working – 'a bloody whirlwind', one of the reporters said – and in August, after being on the paper for only seven months, he was made managing editor.

It was clear, therefore, that when Thomson bought The Times and Hamilton became editor-in-chief Evans was an obvious candidate for one or other of the jobs which the merger produced: editor of The Times and editor of The Sunday Times. There were three other men under active consideration: William Rees-Mogg, Frank Giles, and Charles Wintour (then as now editor of The Evening Standard). There was also a candidate in the wings: Pat Murphy, by now editorial director of the Thomson regional papers.

Rees-Mogg seemed favourite for The Times and Giles for The Sunday Times but the issue was not that simple. Randolph Churchill had been lobbying for Wintour to be editor of The Times even before the change-over, and if he had been offered the job then Wintour would have taken it. Hamilton considered all the possibilities for both jobs. He chose Rees-Mogg for The Times. 'The Times needs an editor with political experience and with very sure political judgment. William seemed to me ideally suited for the job.' He decided against moving Murphy. 'Pat no doubt felt a slight sense of disappointment that I didn't recall him, but he was not in the best of health and the regionals, still the backbone of the organisation, needed a strong editorial voice.' That left Wintour, Giles and Evans. Hamilton felt firstly that Wintour was perhaps too closely identified with an anti-Common Market stance. But in the end his decision was a subjective one: 'I couldn't face going outside the paper when we had such a splendid team here. At the end of the day I decided it was more appropriate to keep the position in the family.' This meant either Giles or Evans. Giles was clearly more in the tradition of Sunday Times editors. He had been to Wellington College and Oxford. He had served in the war and had been attached to the Foreign Office in 1945–6. On joining The Times he had become successively assistant correspondent in Paris, chief correspondent in Rome, then chief correspondent in Paris. At one stage he was Hamilton's first choice and to many it seemed certain that he would get the job. In fact Mark Boxer, meeting Evans in the corridor during this period, told him, 'You'd be a candidate for editor, you know, but you're considered too left wing' – a remark which moved Evans to 'going around trying to look as true blue as I could'. But Hamilton's final decision had nothing to do with tradition or politics. 'Newspapers go through cycles. Each cycle cannot be allowed to last too long. An editor must not stay for ever. I had already considered how I would stage myself out. As a matter of commercial judgment a newspaper like The Sunday Times needs people in day-to-day editorial charge who are close to the coming generation. A new cycle was starting for The Sunday Times in 1967 and I wanted an editor who would take the paper a stage further than I had done, someone who would be innovative and who would take chances, someone I might occasionally have to restrain, and someone the young men around the office would be prepared to follow.'

At the first meeting of the new board of Times Newspapers Hamilton told his fellow directors that he would be happy if they would approve the appointment of William Rees-Mogg as editor of The Times and Harold Evans as editor of The Sunday Times.

The Friday before this board meeting Hamilton gave Evans the first hint of what might be in store for him. 'I'm considering appointing you editor of The Sunday Times,' he said. 'Over the week-end let me have a memo on how you think the paper should be developed.' Evans presented the memo on Monday and the next day went up to the 6th floor at Hamilton's request to meet Sir William Haley: 'We had common interests. We had both worked for The Manchester Evening News and we were both mad about table tennis. So we had a relaxed hour's chat.'

The full board now met Evans and questioned him. 'How independent will you be as editor of The Sunday Times?' Evans: 'I'm certain that the judgment of the Monopolies Commission was correct. I shall be completely independent. Unless I was certain of this I would not be prepared to accept the job.' 'What is your attitude to Thomson's commercial interests?' Evans: 'The same as my attitude to any other commercial interests. If there is any news in them, then we will print it.' It was a rather nerve-racking experience for Evans, considering that his future might well depend on his replies, and he came away unhappy at his performance. 'I'm sure my answers were not very good. If it had been a BBC board I probably wouldn't have got the job.'

With the board's approval Hamilton announced Evans's appointment on Friday evening January 13 to a gathering in his office of the senior and junior executives. Giles, who had been called to the board-room earlier in the afternoon to be told of his appointment as deputy editor and foreign editor, was among the first to congratulate Evans. In fact Hamilton believes that the Evans–Giles combination has worked out better than expected. 'There are some executives on The Sunday Times whose judgment tends to get carried away by their emotions. I don't believe in emotional journalism but I didn't want the paper to lose the fire-works these men are capable of producing. Frank Giles with his

Opposite: Harold Evans by Snowdon.

438

unemotional approach and loyalty to Harry Evans has proved an ideal moderating influence. He is a great asset to the paper, with his outstanding knowledge of foreign affairs, his deep interest in the arts, and his capacity to administer well. His judgment is excellent – and judgment is the prime requirement of men at the top in journalism.'

Evans's first year was a vital one. For the staff it showed that the new editor was as different in his own way as Hamilton had been from Hodson. For Evans it gave an indication of how tough a task he had undertaken. It took only a week for the first major difference between Hamilton and Evans to emerge. Evans, wiry, lively, and intensely curious about everything and everyone on The Sunday Times, had got to know all the staff while still managing editor. He called them by their Christian names and they called him Harry. Hardly anyone had referred to Hamilton as Denis – it was either 'Mr Hamilton' or 'CD' – and when Evans became editor it was clear that the switch from Harry to Mr Evans, or even H. E., was not going to be easy. Evans allowed no one to attempt it. He remained Harry to his face and Harry behind his back (except to Hamilton, who usually calls him Harold). Hamilton had run The Sunday Times from his office, concerning himself with the broad outlines of the paper, its overall strategy, a leader who believed in delegating the details to his capable lieutenants. Evans, it soon emerged, planned to attend to everything himself. He began to run the paper as much from the reporters' room, the chief sub's desk, and the stone as he did from his own office. As Queen magazine said, 'Everyone sees more of him . . . some think they see too much. Many found their provinces invaded by their shirt-sleeve editor, who would rewrite their headlines, sub copy on the stone, and plan the re-make of the pages before the managing editor's pencil had stopped on the first edition.'

Two examples illustrate the different style of editing. It was unusual to see Hamilton's desk cluttered with proofs. Evans's desk is seldom free from them. It was unusual to see Hamilton write a story. Evans frequently does. (The present writer, struggling with a legal problem on a Rent Act story, watched Evans puzzle over a proof for some minutes while he listened to argument from Ron Hall, and then whirl around to the battered portable typewriter he keeps on his desk and pound out a legally-acceptable revision. Many have had similar experiences.)

On the personal side, Hamilton maintained friendly but detached relations with his staff. Evans plays squash with them, attends their weddings, and listens to their domestic problems – a far cry from the day in the early 1950s when art critic John Russell offered Hodson his resignation because he was about to be divorced and he did not think that The Sunday Times was the sort of paper that would want to employ a divorced man. Hamilton was approachable, but some complained that he was hard to talk with, given to long periods of silence. Evans was also approachable but in this case the complaint was that he had trouble in listening because he was talking so much himself.

Maurice Wiggin, who has worked under both editors, wrote of Hamilton,[1] 'He takes very seriously activities which I regard as a complete waste of time, such as administration and organisation, he is a great family man and a devoted, ceaseless worker, and the honorable values he stands for are to my mind completely unquestionable.' Of Evans he wrote[2]:

I like to see him whizzing through the office like a flame; literally at the double, in his shirt sleeves. He is the complete working newspaperman, and when I see him bringing his galvanic perfectionism to bear on every detail of the paper, I am irresistibly reminded of those far-off days when I, too, really loved the craft of newspaper production better than almost anything else. Harold Evans is infinitely tougher than I ever was, and he has that genuine feeling about news and public affairs and all that tosh whereas I was only really and truly concerned with the drama of the layout and headlines: nevertheless . . . I do see a likeness. It does me good to see the old enthusiasm permeating every cranny of the paper, the restless perfection, the personal touch, the insatiable inquisitiveness and above all the zest and contagion of his zeal. I think he has come at the right moment. The old world is dying and the old *Sunday Times*, the one I joined, is changing to meet the demands of the new.

This change, and Evans's part in it, made heavy demands on his energy and Hamilton became worried that Evans would set the pace too fast. He tried to ease the burden. 'I had stolen some of his executives for The Times – Cudlipp and Vice and later Hamlyn – so I took responsibility myself then for the magazine. Harold also had a good boost, just after he started, with the Manchester book, 'The Death of a President', which had come to us as a result of my long nurtured contacts in the United States and which took The Sunday Times over the one and a half million mark.' (The new

1. 'The Memoirs of a Maverick', Nelson, London, 1968.
2. *Ibid.*

editor and his team managed to keep it there for the remainder of the year.)

For the rest, 1967 brought Evans a taste of the volatile existence that being editor involved. In that one year the original Insight split into two new departments; the Chichester story, Evans's project from the beginning, reached its climax off Cape Horn; the Six-Day war broke out in the Middle East; the Philby spy saga, again his project from the beginning, got Evans into a public row with the Government and took away half his staff; and just before Christmas he narrowly missed being sent to prison for contempt of court.

II

We shall start Evans's period as editor with the Chichester story both because he had nurtured it since his first months with the paper and because it marked the beginning of The Sunday Times success in adventure journalism, a field it has come to dominate in recent years.

The paper's interest in Chichester began almost by accident. Evans, working on the sports pages, received in April, 1966, a detailed drawing of *Gipsy Moth* IV with an accompanying letter from the editor of Yachting. This was the boat, the letter said, in which Francis Chichester would shortly be setting out to sail single-handed to Australia, aiming to equal the time of the famous clipper ships. Was The Sunday Times interested in publishing the diagram? Evans bought the drawing and used it on the sports pages.

The following week Peter Crookston, deputy editor of the magazine, suggested Chichester's adventure would be a ready-made series for the paper and that The Sunday Times should buy it. Hamilton was not enthusiastic and opinion among other executives was largely against the idea (with the exception of Michael Cudlipp, the assistant editor). Finally Hamilton told Evans that if the price was not too high he was to go ahead and make Chichester an offer.

Evans had a meeting with Chichester's agent, George Greenfield, of John Farquharson Ltd. It was not encouraging. Hamilton had in mind £1,000 as a fair fee for world rights to Chichester's running story of the voyage. Evans was alarmed to learn that

Greenfield was thinking of £10,000. Evans went away and did some sums, estimating what return there would be from North American and Australian syndication rights and what the chances would be of involving schools in some sort of map exercise. Evans, who has a way of getting what he wants while keeping everyone happy, recommended the scheme to Hamilton as 'a potentially refreshing contribution for the autumn'.

Hamilton was still considering this when he met Alastair Hetherington, editor of The Guardian, and told him about it. Hetherington thought that The Guardian could well share some of the cost in return for a weekly message from Chichester but he, also, was less interested after speaking to Greenfield and learning the amount Greenfield had in mind.

Chichester himself broke the deadlock. He rang Evans and after a brief chat they decided to discuss the project over lunch. Evans, Mark Boxer, then features editor and whose aunt, Mrs Miles Smeeton, had sailed round Cape Horn, met Chichester at the Forum. The Sunday Times men were happy to find that Chichester was more interested in getting the scheme underway than in bargaining over money, and a deal was quickly arranged. In brief, The Sunday Times would pay £2,000 and The Guardian £1,500 for first British serial rights for the story of Chichester's 'clipper trip' to Australia, and would have an option on the return journey.

Chichester sailed from Plymouth on August 27 of this year – 1966. Sixty-two days out he was hit by violent gales and on day 80 Gipsy Moth's self-steering gear was broken beyond repair. It was now obvious that Chichester could not reach Sydney in his target time of 100 days, but interest – especially in Australia – remained high. At this stage of the venture The Sunday Times had no plans to send anyone to Sydney to meet Chichester. Rachel Moodie, news desk assistant, had handled arrangements for Chichester's weekly radio messages with quiet efficiency and no need was felt for any special arrangements in Australia. But two factors caused a sudden change in plans. Chichester made a firm decision to continue his voyage home by way of Cape Horn, and in discussions about whether or not to take up the option for the return voyage Rachel Moodie and Michael Cudlipp suggested to the marketing department that an exhibition of Gipsy Moth at the end of the voyage could be both a commercially viable proposition and a good promotional project for The Sunday Times to undertake. So Evans decided to take up the option for the second part of the voyage and to send someone to seek Chichester's approval for the exhibition. This decision coincided with an editorial problem. The paper wanted stories about the problems of the outward trip, the repairs and modifications which *Gipsy Moth* would need, and Chichester's plans for the homeward voyage. Who was to write this copy?

Evans and Cudlipp, assistant editor (news), decided to send Murray Sayle, the freelance reporter who had joined The Sunday Times two years earlier. But with everything apparently neatly arranged the whole project suffered a setback when The Guardian announced that it did not propose to take up its share of the option on the return voyage. This left a new contract to be negotiated, in which The Sunday Times either put up the whole £3,500 or else found a partner to replace The Guardian.

Fortunately such a partner was to hand. Thomson had bought The Times only a month earlier and Hamilton, the new editor-in-chief, agreed to The Times taking over the Guardian's share of the project. The negotiation was the last job Cudlipp did before moving to The Times. 'I had got to know the Chichester family quite well during the outward voyage and, with Rachel Moodie, liaised between them, The Guardian, the International Wool Board, George Greenfield, Denis Hamilton and Harry Evans. For us The Guardian dropping out when it did – they wanted to put up only £250 – was a stroke of luck which on The Times we turned to our advantage.'

Within a week of the new contract the first stirrings appeared of the controversy which soon made it apparent that The Guardian had been too hasty in its decision: Alan Villiers, one of the last sailing-ship masters, who had sailed a replica of the *Mayflower* from Plymouth, England, to Plymouth, Massachusetts, in 1957, wrote to The Guardian urging Chichester to abandon the idea of returning single-handed and to take on a crew. Other newspapers followed up with interviews with Villiers. 'I beg Chichester not to attempt it,' Villiers said in The Daily Mail. 'The outward trip he has made is simple compared with this one. I don't know what drives this man to go on tempting the might of the seas. God has been very good to him and very patient. But to handicap yourself with such a monstrously small yacht in those seas at the age of 65 and after a serious operation seems to me to be asking a little too much of God.' Cassandra took up the plea in The Daily Mirror. 'What more does this mariner need?' Although Chichester scoffed at the warnings the British public now realised for the first time the extent and danger of the homeward voyage.

As Chichester's chances became a matter of concern Evans realised that the arrangements originally made to cover the attempt to round the Horn were inadequate. True, The Times correspondents in Sydney and Wellington, NZ, and Robert Lindley, who covered South America out of Buenos Aires, had been briefed to forward any messages picked up by local radio stations; the Argentine and Chilean navies were listening, the British Antarctic Survey Base and HMS *Protector* had been alerted, and Marconi had requested all ships in the area to try to make contact. But newspaper rivals were also listening – a Chilean radio amateur picked up a message from Chichester and it eventually found its way to agency tapes.

As well, there were worrying rumours reaching The Sunday Times of the extent of the coverage planned by other national and foreign newspapers and magazines. Paris Match, The Daily Express and BBC radio and television were said to be organising expensive expeditions to the Horn itself. The Newspaper Publishers' Association had reached an arrangement with the Admiralty for HMS *Protector* to carry a number of journalists and photographers – chosen on a rota basis – to try to rendezvous with Chichester off the Horn.

The Sunday Times felt it had to move to protect its interests. Warning telegrams were sent to newspapers on the question of copyright in messages from Chichester to The Sunday Times picked up by other radio stations, and James Evans wrote to the Newspaper Publishers' Association: 'Times Newspapers would regard any attempt by others to interview Sir Francis Chichester or to obtain quotes from him (whether by radio, loud hailer or otherwise) as inviting him to depart from his contract with this company.' Yet it was obvious that The Sunday Times would have to have a man of its own on the spot, both to get the story and to remind Chichester not to talk to other newspapers.

The logical choice was Sayle, the reporter who had been with Chichester in Australia. Sayle had stopped off in Vietnam on his way back from Sydney (the first of many tours of duty he was to make there) but was now available for the Horn assignment. Evans considered sending a photographer as well, but as The Times was selected for the NPA rota on HMS *Protector* he decided to depend on Sayle either to take any pictures himself or to engage a freelance photographer in South America.

Sayle left on February 26 with £500 in dollars, a Leica camera, a list of radio frequencies on which Chichester would be broadcasting, and Evans's assurance that the Chilean Air Force would do all it could to help. In the week before his departure Sayle had been doing a lot of thinking about his assignment. He had reasoned that with dozens of newspapermen in the area there was going to be nothing remarkable about a story which began, 'Sir Francis Chichester rounded the Horn to-day' and that the real scoop would be the first *photograph* which showed *Gipsy Moth* off the Horn. So he broke his flight in Geneva and invested some of his dollars in a 500 mm telephoto lens for his Leica.

In Buenos Aires he wasted two weeks trying to persuade the Argentine Air Force to fly him south of the Horn and in trying to make radio contact with Chichester. The Air Force wanted nothing to do with the scheme and the radio station there managed to raise Chichester only once.

Time was slipping away, so leaving The Times representative, Robert Lindley, to listen for Chichester, Sayle flew on to Santiago in Chile to take up the Chilean Air Force's offer to help. He was disappointed. There had been some misunderstanding, the Air Force said. It had not imagined that anyone would be so foolhardy as to want to fly over Cape Horn. 'We've never been there, and we're not going.'

Low in spirits Sayle took the next flight to Punta Arenas, just above Cape Horn. Santiago to Punta Arenas is probably the roughest air route in the world, and it was a very shaken Sayle who stepped off the plane and began to check his chances of hiring a private aircraft. To his alarm he found that rival newspapermen had been there for weeks and that every available aircraft had already been chartered. He was even more alarmed to read in the local newspaper under the heading, 'The Battle of the Pressmen', how extensive his opposition was going to be. There were thirty other reporters, photographers, television cameramen, commentators, broadcasters and technicians waiting for Chichester. Paris Match had chartered a DC3. The Daily Express had a Cessna Skymaster, two photographers, and a portable wire-photo machine to transmit its photographs to London – a huge advantage because the only other machine was in Santiago, 3,000 miles away.

Next morning Sayle wandered out to the airport. 'It was like a scene from the second world war. One by one the press planes took off and then they circled, watching each other. Suddenly one broke away and immediately all the others followed him. They thought he had the dope on where Chichester was.'

The Sunday Times had arranged with the BBC for Sayle to have a seat on an aircraft which had been chartered for a BBC television news team by reporter Clifford Luton, working with cameraman Peter Beggin. It was an arrangement which turned out well. Sayle was expecting an accurate fix on Chichester's position from Lindley, in Buenos Aires, while Luton, himself a yachtsman and a navigator, had set up a radio watch in Santiago which was giving him *Gipsy Moth*'s position each time Chichester made a broadcast.

Next day they all went down to the airport to meet the aircraft Luton had ordered. Instead of the Skymaster they would have liked to have seen, in flew a battered ten-year-old Piper Apache piloted by a laconic Chilean called Rodolfo Fuenzalida. Certainly Fuenzalida was to prove a brilliant pilot, but at first sight neither he nor his plane inspired much confidence. Fuenzalida, who expressed an admiration for the Red Baron, made his living as a fish-spotter. Endurance is a vital factor in successful fish-spotting, and Fuenzalida's reputation was that of being able to stay in the air longer than most. But even he had under-estimated the fuel needed to get back to base on three occasions, and had crash-landed each time – hence the dents and repair marks on the Apache.

It was impossible to change planes, so Luton and Beggin began a preliminary search for Chichester, making three fruitless trips, including one on which they were forced down by bad weather.

Back in Punta Arenas a telephone call Sayle had been waiting for finally came through. The powerful radio station in Buenos Aires had been listening for Chichester and it was possible that Robert Lindley now knew *Gipsy Moth*'s position. Sayle had booked a call to Lindley, but three days had passed without the Punta Arenas exchange being able to get through. Then at midnight on Sunday Sayle got Lindley on the line. The connection was faint and intermittent. 'Chichester's position,' Lindley shouted, 'is fifty-six zero one south and . . .' Then the line went dead and repeated attempts to restore the connection failed. Sayle, Luton, and the pilot conferred. Lindley's position showed Chichester very close to where Luton estimated him to be. All three agreed that dawn that day would be their only chance of seeing Chichester rounding the Horn. So with four lifejackets borrowed from Lan Chile (the Chilean airline), a rubber boat bought from a toy store in Punta Arenas, and wills deposited with a Chilean Navy sergeant, the Piper Apache, with Fuenzalida flying, Luton navigating, Beggin in the right-hand pilot's seat, and Sayle behind,

447

took off from Puerto Williams heavily loaded with extra fuel.

Fuenzalida told them, as they weaved their way through clefts in the 12,000-ft mountains of Navarino Island, that he was emptying the wing tanks first. If they lost an engine and had to crash-land these would keep the aircraft afloat, he hoped, long enough for them to scramble into the rubber boat. If the aircraft sank before they could do this then, with the water temperature only a degree or so above freezing, they would not last five minutes.

As they flew over Cape Horn island the weather deteriorated. They could see HMS *Protector* battling against heavy seas, and Fuenzalida tried to raise her on the plane's radio but failed (they later learnt that the Apache's aerial had been blown away). Then, about 15 miles south of *Protector*, Luton's work in plotting Chichester's positions over the previous three weeks paid off. There below them was Chichester, running under bare poles with only a tiny storm jib. The sea was breaking over his deck and he was huddled under the storm cover on the cockpit. He waved. (Chichester wrote later: 'A tiny yellow plane came flying through the storm practically skipping over the top of the breaking waves.') Fuenzalida and Beggin had switched seats on the way out so that Beggin would be able to film through the small navigation flap in the window of the left-hand front seat. Sayle, sitting behind, began to hand over cameras, and with icy professional calm Beggin shot 100 feet in black-and-white film, a roll of black-and-white stills, then a roll of colour stills, and finally 100 feet of colour film.

After the sixth pass, with the weather now at full-gale strength, Luton decided that they had better leave. As they turned for home the aircraft began to break up – or that was what it felt like to Sayle. 'The wings began to shake and the plane creaked and groaned under the strain. I braced myself for the end and then I realised what was happening. It was "Red Baron" Fuenzalida waggling his wings to salute Chichester.'

The danger was not yet over. The aircraft was crossing the Strait of Magellan when the oil pressure in the right engine dropped to zero. Fuenzalida shut it off and on the local radio (which was still working) called a full alert at Punta Arenas, but they made the airport on one engine without incident. Everything now worked in their favour. No other plane had taken off that morning because the weather was so bad, and there was great glee among the opposition press and television corps who, ignorant of

BBC–The Sunday Times team's success, knew Fuenzalida would
not be able to take off again. So in Sayle's camera was the only
picture of Chichester rounding the Horn (and in Beggin's the only
television film). But how to get them back to London?

Fortunately the team had booked two seats on every flight to
Santiago (where there was a wire photo machine), and that day's
flight was on the runway ready to leave in thirty minutes. In that
time Sayle filed a back-up story to London and in his excitement
opened his camera before winding the film back into the cassette,
thus possibly ruining it. He sweated out this likelihood on the
five-hour flight to Santiago, 'the longest five hours I have ever
experienced'. The Cable and Wireless representative in Santiago,
alerted by a telephone call from Luton at Punta Arenas, had
arranged for the Santiago newspaper, El Mercurio, to process
Sayle's film – in return for which Sayle agreed to allow the paper
to help itself to prints. Sayle waited outside the darkroom. 'After
what seemed ages a man came out and said that only nine were
fogged. The rest were fine.' Sayle raced the prints around to the
wire photo machine, where they were soon humming away to
London – to The Times because it was a week-day and The
Sunday Times readily agreed to pass its scoop to its sister paper.
Then from The Times Michael Cudlipp came on the line: HAVE
PIX. WHERE STORY? So Sayle sat down and tapped out his
account direct to London. Then he returned to El Mercurio offices,
where he was handed a six-page special insert of the Chichester
photographs which the paper was running as part of that morning's issue. The atmosphere was one of jubilation. 'Everyone was
wondering how to celebrate when the editor came out into the
newsroom with a case of pisco, the local drink, and we all got
royally piscoed.'

In London the photograph arrived in The Times office at
2.20 am when Cudlipp was putting the paper to bed. 'I splashed it
across the front page with the headline "The First Picture: Sir
Francis turns for home". We ran on with an extra print and had
the circulation reps out changing up copies all over Central
London. For us it was a fantastic world scoop, thanks to Murray.'

Sayle, still unaware of just how successful he had been, and not
feeling too well after the celebrations at El Mercurio offices, flew
back to Punta Arenas next day. The plane carried copies of El
Mercurio's special edition with the photographs of Chichester off
the Horn, and by the time Sayle reached the Cabo di Hornas bar,
favoured by the press contingent, these were already being mourn-

fully passed from hand to hand. Reaction from London was now pouring in. One British newspaper team received a cable which read 'YOU BEATEN. COME HOME. PARTY OVER.' Evans cabled Sayle: 'CONGRATS BRILLIANT SERIES OF EXPLOITS STOP AM CREDITING YOU BONUS HUNDRED POUNDS.' But the message Sayle appreciated most came from Richard Hughes, the Australian who represents The Sunday Times in Hong Kong. Hughes, doyen of correspondents in the East and an almost legendary figure for Sayle's generation of Australian journalists, cabled 'CONGRATULATIONS ON AN HONEST-TO-GOD OLDFASHIONED SCOOP'.

There is a sad postscript to this part of the Chichester story. Sayle flew from Punta Arenas to Buenos Aires, where he handled Chichester's own story, 'How I beat the Horn'. While in Buenos Aires he was interviewed by the local representative of Time magazine for a piece in the March 3 issue called 'Derring-do off Cape Horn'. Luton and Beggin objected to certain parts of the Time account and began a legal action against the magazine which was eventually settled out of court. (There was also an objection to entering the photograph which appeared in The Times in the News Photographer of the Year competition on the grounds that it was a team effort.)

Sayle went off to Bolivia to look for Che Guevara. Chichester sailed on for home and the tumultuous reception that was being prepared for him.

Early in May Evans and the BBC decided to pre-empt some of their rivals' plans by sending out a boat to meet Chichester as he rounded the Azores on the last lap of his voyage. Lady Chichester did not like the idea. She wrote Evans: 'I am sorry you have decided to send a boat out after him. . . . I am not trying to be awkward but I am considering Francis's safety and the intrusion into his privacy until he gets to the Western approaches.' Lest other newspapers had the same idea as The Sunday Times Lady Chichester wrote to editors: 'Rendezvousing with a small boat in the Atlantic is a hazardous business and if my husband has the extra burden of keeping constant watch for such boats there is no doubt it would throw an enormous strain upon his mental and physical powers at a time when he needs them most.'

The Sunday Times–BBC boat, *Sea Huntress*, with reporter Peter Dunn, news desk assistant Rachel Moodie, photographer Stanley Devon, American navigator John Thompson ('I want to satisfy my vanity by finding that small piece of wood riding out in the Atlantic') and the BBC team spent ten days scouring the area off the Azores without a sight of Chichester and then had to put back for fuel, water and food.

The second time out proved more successful. With only a $2\frac{1}{2}$-day-old fix on Chichester to go on, Thompson navigated *Sea Huntress* to where, by dead reckoning, he estimated Chichester to be and at 3 am on Thursday, May 18, the look-out on *Sea Huntress* picked up the light of what at dawn turned out to be *Gipsy Moth*. Chichester was far from happy to see them. He and Lady Chichester had taken to exchanging their messages in code to prevent amateurs picking up *Gipsy Moth*'s position, and Chichester had been fairly confident no one would have been able to locate him before he came within range of the 'live' television teams with their helicopters, converted minesweepers, light aircraft and Diesel yachts all waiting for him in the Western approaches. The *Sea Huntress* had caught him by surprise, although he had known that a motor vessel was near by during the night and he had been keeping watch on it through the last hours of darkness. He declined gifts which The Sunday Times team tried to deliver by rubber dinghy and warned them not to come too close. Over the ship-to-ship radio he explained, 'People aren't normal when they've been alone a long time and you've got to humour me to a certain extent.'

Dunn still had a story and Devon had taken an excellent picture. They raced it back to London where, after a dash from the airport, it arrived in time for Evans to stop the presses and in the final editions use the photograph splashed across eight columns.

The meeting in mid-Atlantic brought to a head dissension between The Sunday Times and Chichester which had been simmering for some days. Sayle had returned from South America early in May and on Thursday the 11th had spoken to Chichester by radio telephone from the G P O building in Brent. Extracts of the conversation had been provided for broadcast over B B C television news on the following Sunday and by I T N on the Monday. Greenfield had reminded The Sunday Times that their rights did not extend to television or broadcast material, and Lady Chichester had informed her husband of what had occurred. The meeting with *Sea Huntress* apparently reminded Chichester of the resentment he felt over this, because the same day he sent off a telegram to Evans: 'I protest my talk with Sayle being supplied to B B C without my consent or knowledge. I sent you a long message from Buenos Aires by Sayle explaining why I asked not to be interviewed or questioned on this voyage due to the effects of a long period – now four months – of solitude. As for Sayle not only disregarding my request but broadcasting my replies without my knowledge that is the end of Sayle for me.'

Evans and Sayle did their best to heal the breach. Evans wrote to Lady Chichester apologising for 'the absurdly long time' *Sea Huntress* had spent with *Gipsy Moth*: 'I am sure that this had nothing to do with our people, who had instructions not to be a party to anything to which Francis might object and to be guided entirely by his views.' He assured her that the BBC and ITN broadcasts of Chichester's talks with Sayle had been due to a misunderstanding, and 'I guarantee there will be no further contacts with either BBC or ITV'. Sayle also wrote. 'From my point of view,' he said, 'this is a rather sad way for a professional asso-ciation which appeared to be rapidly developing into a personal friendship to end. I am sure I do not need to tell you that I personally did not broadcast anything anywhere . . . no one consulted me about any broadcast . . . I will always remember the many happy, if a trifle hectic, evenings we all had together in Sydney, and the bond of the moments of danger and achievement we shared off Cape Horn. These, unfortunately, were in happy days when the interest of this paper and the voyage of the *Gipsy Moth* IV seemed to us all to run more closely together.'

It was all cleared up on May 29. Chichester had returned to the welcome he deserved and all the pressures and anxieties of the voyage had soon faded. Lady Chichester had agreed that many of the misunderstandings had arisen through lack of communication and had stressed that her concern had been to safeguard her husband's privacy as long as possible. Sayle had arrived at Plymouth with a giant enlargement of the photograph of Chichester rounding the Horn and, as Greenfield put it, 'from then on he could do no wrong with Sheila – or, later, with Francis either'. Lady Chichester had some pleasant things to say about Evans, and after a quiet dinner with his sailor-author and family Greenfield reported to The Sunday Times: 'All's well that ends well – and after the ups and downs of the last few weeks it is good to know that a very cordial atmosphere has been re-established.'

On September 28 The Sunday Times participation in Chichester's project reached its final stages when Evans sent Greenfield a cheque for £16,500 for the first British serial rights to the highly-successful book 'Gipsy Moth Circles the World', eventually serialised in the paper in four parts the following month.

From what had originally appeared a relatively unimportant

venture the Chichester saga had proved highly rewarding for everyone concerned. Chichester had the satisfaction of his achievement and of having earned a considerable amount of money. Murray Sayle had made a resounding success of a difficult assignment against powerful opposition, thus launching himself as The Sunday Times 'fireman' or 'trouble-shooter' correspondent, a rôle which he still successfully fills. Evans had proved that in an impersonal, mechanical age a good old-fashioned adventure story of man against the elements would find an enthusiastic readership, and although the paper's later sponsorship of another round-the-world sailing event brought tragedy, he still feels that it is part of a newspaper's function to help unusual men like Chichester attempt these triumphs of the human spirit.

III

On Monday, June 5, 1967, when Evans had been editor for only five months, war broke out in the Middle East. At Hamilton's encouragement The Sunday Times had taken a close interest in Arab–Israeli affairs for some years. Giles had made a tour of the area in the winter of 1963–4 and had written two long Review front articles. What he had learnt there had helped him influence the paper's editorial line. This was to recognise Israel's right to exist as a state and her need for security, but at the same time to express understanding of the Arabs' grievance, particularly the Palestinians, who had been the original sufferers from the foundation of Israel. Above all, the paper had been at pains to point out the folly of Israel's thinking that she could live for ever surrounded by a host of enemies.

So when United Nations troops withdrew from their peace-keeping rôle in May, 1967, and war appeared likely, three Sunday Times teams went off immediately to Tel Aviv, Cairo, and Damascus. But after filing on Saturday, June 3, with the danger of war apparently receding, they all received instructions to return to London. (One was actually in the air between Israel and Rome when news of the war was announced by their airline captain.)

In London, Evans heard of the outbreak of war on a radio newsflash and rapidly began arrangements to get The Sunday Times back into the area. Without any staff men in the Middle East he realised that the only hope of making up the initial disadvantage was to use the team approach and to send off as many men as possible. Colin Simpson, who had just returned from Damascus, set about organising aircraft reservations while Evans and Frank Giles got a team together. When it left London later that night for Cyprus – the nearest airport still open – it consisted of Colin Simpson, Murray Sayle, Anthony Cowdy, Donald McCullin, photographer, Neil Libbert, photographer, and Simpson's wife, Jane, to act as telex and telephone operator. (Later in the week David Leitch, Cal McCrystal and photographer Steve Brodie joined them, making a team nine strong in all.)

With no flights into Cairo or Tel Aviv, the idea was to try to hire a boat in Cyprus and make for Haifa, but boat owners were unwilling to make the trip under £8,000 per boat or had already been chartered. Cowdy managed to get on a fishing boat heading for Beirut, from where he planned to go by car to Syria and Jordan. (He found the Syrian border closed and was forced to sit out the war in the Lebanon.) The others approached the Israeli consul to locate telex facilities, and when they mentioned their unsuccessful search for transport to Israel he offered to arrange a plane. Late that night a small Israeli aircraft arrived and – at £20 a head – flew The Sunday Times team and other pressmen to Tel Aviv. Thus in the early hours of Wednesday morning, the third day of the war, The Sunday Times was finally on the scene.

Back in London the Tuesday conference had discussed how best to present the coverage everyone hoped would emerge when the Middle East team got into action. All agreed that a consecutive narrative and high-class maps were needed. Evans later suggested a section with no advertisements, backfolded into the paper, but Hamilton was against this. The decision was for the centre twelve pages – p. 5 to p. 16 – with a rearrangement of advertisements so as to leave eleven pages principally free for the war.

In Israel the team had split up. Simpson and McCullin went with Israeli troops storming the Old City of Jerusalem. Sayle and Libbert got into a taxi and said, 'Take us to the front'. The driver stopped off at his house to pick up his revolver and then drove them to the Gaza Strip, where Sayle found an Israeli tank general who willingly unfolded for him the entire Israeli strategy. Sayle spent two days in Sinai and then returned to Tel Aviv to write his copy and try to get it through to London.

Simpson and McCullin were in the middle of the battle which wrested the sacred Old City of Jerusalem from the Arab Legion. McCullin saw an Israeli soldier in front of him shot and killed and a few seconds later the one behind was killed too. 'I knew I had some good shots but if I was to really make a hit with them I had to get them to London for that Sunday's paper. I didn't want any censorship problems so on Friday I just caught the El Al flight to London. I figured that the Israeli authorities wouldn't imagine anyone with anything worth while would be leaving before the war was over.'

McCullin was correct. No one checked his film and he arrived at London airport in the early hours of Saturday with some of the best photographs of the war. One, the first of actual front-line fighting, occupied half the first page of The Sunday Times special section on June 11, and, with other pictures, won McCullin the Granada Press Photographer of the Year award.

Simpson, who had split up from McCullin, was convinced that McCullin had been shot in the fighting and spent some hours looking for his body. He found McCullin before he left for London and gave him various maps and plans to help The Sunday Times illustrate the area of action. He then wrote his story, filed by telex on Thursday night, and went off to cover the attack on Syria. His main story 'Into Jerusalem with the first platoon: how the Holy City Fell' was used under McCullin's photograph.

Sayle, to whom credit must go for compiling the first account of how the Israelis had won the war, ran into worrying communications problems when he tried to send his story on the Friday night. The telephone circuit to London kept breaking down and it took him hours to dictate a few hundred words. He switched to telex on Saturday morning; his last copy reached the office at 5 pm and was rushed straight into the page.

The section – put together by Bruce Page and laid out by Mike Randall – took the war day by day, and it all emerged better than anyone had dared to hope. But it was not until the following weeks that it gradually became clear just how successful an effort it had been. In the first days after the war Israel could not obtain enough copies of The Sunday Times special section. Some exchanged hands at inflated prices; others were pasted up as wall newspapers.

Then as the dust settled the six-day war was examined at leisure, and the definitive accounts written. Placed against these The Sunday Times special report emerged largely unaltered. Working in danger – three pressmen were killed during the war – and under extreme pressure, the paper's team had not only produced the first full account of the campaign but had, overall, got it right.

Looking back, Evans has one regret. 'The week after the war Randolph Churchill rang to congratulate me on our coverage. Then he said "Now, my son and I will do a book on the war for you. We want £15,000". When I said no Randolph went to The Sunday Telegraph, who serialised the book and did very well out of it. I should have bought it, but I thought the price was too high and I underestimated the continuing interest in the war.'

IV

The Six-Day War had interrupted the progress of a project for which Evans had great hopes and one which was also to demonstrate the success of the team approach – the Philby conspiracy.

The story, the painstaking unravelling of the life of H. A. R. Philby, the officer in British Secret Intelligence Services who was actually working for the Russians, was a landmark in Evans's career. It demonstrated the extent to which sheer luck operates in journalism and the importance of risking money and manpower on what can only be called a hunch, or as Bruce Page says, 'sensing the presence of the lode'. It showed that in investigatory journalism, publication often stimulates further revelations, and, finally, it sparked off a furious row as to whether the story endangered national interests.

It began with two more-or-less chance meetings. The first was at lunch between Evans and an old friend, Jeremy Isaacs, then head of current affairs at Thames Television. Isaacs remarked how interesting it was that Burgess, Maclean, and the other 'minor defector', Kim Philby, were all educated at Cambridge about the same period. Evans thought it would be interesting to trace the careers of the three men and see if this would identify the Cambridge recruiter. He asked Bruce Page to organise this. Then a chance meeting some months later transformed the idea. Michael Frayn wrote to Evans that a Cambridge friend of his working with the Foreign Office – even today it would be unfair to name him – was thinking of trying journalism. Evans lunched with the man, went to a party at his house and generally got to know him fairly well. He invited him to meet the foreign editor, Frank Giles, who, with a few direct questions, winkled out of the man that he was at that time working for SIS and had done so for some years previously. Giles told Evans that he was flatly against appointing the man to The Sunday Times on the grounds that once an SIS man, always an SIS man: that SIS might seek to benefit from the man's cover as an overseas correspondent.

At one of their later meetings Evans mentioned to the SIS man that The Sunday Times was looking into the career of Kim Philby. The reaction was dramatic. 'You'll never be able to print it,' the man said. 'Philby was a copper-bottom bastard. They'll never let you tell it. It goes to the highest in the land.'

As far as Evans was concerned this was all he needed to be convinced that a lode existed and that it could be uncovered. He immediately assigned Hugo Young, leader writer and political correspondent, to join Bruce Page and by the time these two had completed a quick feasibility study, everyone knew that the story would cost a considerable amount of money (in the end £20,000) and manpower (at one time eighteen reporters). However, there were also sufficient indications that the project would be well worth doing.

The present author went off to Washington to look into Philby's relations with the CIA and the FBI and to examine the damage Donald Maclean had caused to the Anglo–American atomic energy programme. David Leitch concentrated on Philby's early life; Hugo Young sought out friends and colleagues of Philby in Britain and the United States; Bruce Page directed the operation, did some crucial interviews, and kept a running memorandum of the story as it slowly emerged. Evans acted as commander-in-chief, doing one or two interviews, reassuring Hamilton as to the accuracy of the material, and dealing with reactions from various members of the Government, and finally from SIS itself.

How The Sunday Times engaged Philby's youngest son, John, to go to Moscow to photograph his father, how it was forced into publication before it was ready by The Observer's rushing in with Mrs Philby's story, a book in which it held the serial rights, and how The Sunday Times series led to the writing of the book 'Philby, the Spy Who Betrayed a Generation', an international best-seller, has been told at length before, both in the newspaper and in the book itself. But there are several aspects of the affair that have not been revealed.

One illustrates the fact, mentioned earlier, that luck plays a large part in investigatory journalism. Page gave the present writer the task of following up a lead that appeared both a bore and unlikely to produce anything worth while. It was to trace and interview the author of a book called 'British Agent' (William

Kimber, London, 1966). The book gave rather innocuous accounts of the author's thirty-five years as a member of sis, but there were publishing rumours of years of vetting before it was finally cleared under the Official Secrets Act. If the rumours were true, then the author had obviously been in a position to know a lot about the activities of sis. Perhaps he had even known Philby. It was a long shot, an enquiry born of some desperation rather than knowledge, but worth the effort.

It did not take me long to discover that the author's name, John Whitwell, was a pseudonym for A. L. (Leslie) Nicholson (it is presumably safe to name him, since he died in 1969). Nicholson was living in somewhat reduced circumstances over a café in the East End of London. At lunch he clearly enjoyed recalling his days with 'the Old Firm', as he insisted on calling it, and my questions, at first deliberately oblique so as not to reveal my own ignorance, became progressively more direct. Finally it became clear to Nicholson that although The Sunday Times knew that Philby had been in sis while actually working for the Russians, it had no idea what Philby's sis job was, and the delightful irony of it. Nicholson, an amiable and unassuming man who probably knew then the serious nature of his illness, took great delight in revealing the fact, and The Sunday Times team learnt for the first time that Philby, a Soviet agent, had been head of the anti-Soviet section of sis.

Another vital piece of information emerged as a result of the publication of the first part of the series. Throughout the inquiry Page came across tantalising references to something in which Philby had been involved in mid-career, something in retrospect so suspicious that his loyalties should immediately have been suspect. Concentrated attempts to discover what this was produced nothing except the vague hint that the incident had occurred early post-war and somewhere in Asia, probably Turkey.

Two days after the publication of the first article on September 30 a letter reached Evans from an address in the North of England: 'I am wondering,' it said, 'whether next week's issue will mention an incident which occurred in Istanbul in August '45 and in which both Philby and I were involved. If so, and I am mentioned by name, I should be grateful for a preview of the text before it is published. The incident convinced me that Philby was either a Soviet agent or unbelievably incompetent and I took what seemed to me at the time appropriate action.'

The present writer set out the next day to interview the author of the letter and obtained from him the details of the Volkov incident – the story of how Philby, sent by SIS to arrange the defection of Volkov, a senior NKVD officer who had offered to bring 'names of three Russian agents operating in London', arranged instead Volkov's one-way ticket to Moscow and a fate which remains unknown to this day.

With breaks like these, plus Page's painstaking following up of the flimsiest of leads and hunches, a picture of Philby's career emerged, together with an indication of the immense damage he had caused to Western intelligence operations. Early in the enquiry Evans had had a drink at the Garrick Club with Lord Chalfont, Minister of State at the Foreign Office, and had told him of The Sunday Times plans. 'Go ahead,' Chalfont had said, 'We won't stop you.'

But as the investigation progressed it became increasingly clear that The Sunday Times planned not merely a story of Philby's treachery but an examination of the state of the country's intelligence services, in order to explain how it was that Philby had been able to get away with his double rôle. This was a different matter. The Foreign Office began a campaign to try to convince The Sunday Times not to publish, or at least to persuade it to alter the tone and approach of its articles. There were personal appeals to various Sunday Times executives. Bruce Page, it was said, was a communist; the whole business was somehow masterminded by the KGB; Philby was not important and his story not worth telling; Philby was so important that to tell his story would endanger national security. The Sunday Times was, according to Mr George (now Lord) Wigg, then Paymaster-General and adviser to the Prime Minister, Mr Wilson, on security, 'raising the traitor, whose activities resulted in imprisonment and death for many men, to the status of a James Bond folk hero'.

As The Sunday Times was about to publish, two 'D' notices from the Services, Press and Broadcasting Committee went out to all national newspaper editors reminding them that no reference should be made to the names of British secret departments, to their responsibilities, or to their past actions. Further, no mention should be made of the names of people who had worked for such departments.

Evans decided to disregard these notices. He discussed it with Hamilton and agreed that while security arguments must carry great weight with any conscientious editor there could be no conceivable security details the Russian and American intelligence –

but not the British people – did not already know. The story, if anything, was reassuring, because it was intended to trace the reforms in SIS which had followed the Philby disaster. And above all, none of the information used in the story had come from Philby himself. Hamilton supported this view. Evans then went secretly to see the former judge, Lord Radcliffe, who had chaired security inquiries, and took advice on naming various SIS people.

Despite these precautions the risk Evans was running was considerable. Naturally, much of the information on which the story was based was covered by the Official Secrets Act and Evans could have been prosecuted and sent to jail for several years for publishing it. How strongly some sections of the Foreign Office felt about that matter was revealed after publication, when Philby offered his own book to The Sunday Times. The paper informed the Foreign Office of this approach and said that it was considering it. At a dinner for visiting US businessmen the same week, the then Foreign Secretary, Mr George Brown, publicly told Lord Thomson: 'It is about time you shut up. Some of us think it is about time we stopped giving the Russians half a start on what we are doing, and, my dear Roy, I ask you and The Sunday Times to take this into account and for God's sake stop.' Thomson, well capable of handling this sort of attack, told his guests, 'We don't always take George very seriously and now you have a very good picture of the man who is Foreign Secretary of this great country.' Brown continued his attack after dinner, and at 11 pm Hamilton, upset, telephoned Evans to tell him, 'George Brown has accused you of being a traitor to your country.'

Looking back on the affair, Hamilton says Brown's outburst, alarming at the time, was 'all baloney'. Hamilton says that through his contacts in Whitehall he had been secretly discussing The Sunday Times Philby story with high-ranking FO men. 'I wanted our material vetted for accuracy and, in particular, for risk. I didn't want our stories to endanger anyone's life. And I wanted SIS to have a chance to put its case. Brown ought to have been aware of what I had been doing so his outburst was, to say the least, uncalled for.'

Apart from deciding not to print the name of one serving SIS officer, a former friend of Philby's, Evans decided to publish the series largely as written. He also agreed that Murray Sayle, then in Moscow on a scientific assignment for the magazine, should try to interview Philby after the series had appeared and the paper could not be accused of using a traitor as a source. Sayle got in touch with Philby by the simple method of waiting inside the main Post Office until Philby showed up to collect his mail. When Sayle had introduced himself Philby said, 'I've been expecting you. Where are you staying? I'll get in touch.' There followed bizarre meetings: in a bare hotel room over a brief-case which held a pistol, a bottle of vodka and two glasses, and in a number of restaurants over vodka, brandy and caviare. Sayle wrote about the conversations he had with Philby, and these appeared as a front-page story in The Sunday Times on December 17, 1967. (Philby wrote to Sayle from Moscow – 'I want to thank you for a very fair piece' – and to explain a small point of fact, adding what a pleasant memory he had of their meetings.)

Philby made it clear to Sayle that he had decided to publish in the West his own version of his career – subsequently called 'My Silent War' – because of The Sunday Times investigation. Evans had been aware of the existence of Philby's manuscript for some time and had, in fact, written to Philby expressing interest in publishing it. He now decided not to do so. 'There were several reasons. After our series I felt everyone had had enough of Philby. And to present his story not knowing which parts of it were true and which parts were motivated by the KGB would have clouded and shamed our own achievement. Also Philby wanted money for his manuscript and I would have been very worried about paying him money.'

Philby's book was, of course, eventually published both in the United States and in this country and serialised by The Sunday Express. It was the final act in an episode which looks strange today, particularly the near-hysteria of some critics of The Sunday Times.

Five years later Evans is convinced that he made the correct decision in ignoring attempts to persuade him to drop the Philby investigation. 'The story didn't damage British security. It revealed that class was no longer a satisfactory basis for trust – think, for example, of what Guy Burgess got away with – and it showed that too much secrecy perpetuates error and inefficiency.'

The best postscript to the Philby affair comes from Sayle, who dines out on the following story. Over one of their lengthy dinners in Moscow Philby asked Sayle, 'By the way, Murray, when's your birthday?' Sayle told him it was January 1. Philby looked amazed. 'Good heavens! What a coincidence! So is mine.' The two of them spent the next five minutes commiserating with each other over the sad results of being born on New Year's Day: no one gives you a present because it is too soon after Christmas, no one comes to your party because of a heavy time the night before, and so on.

Sayle didn't write anything about this conversation – 'it was just a personal little thing between Philby and me' – and forgot all about it until two or three years later when he found himself sharing a pre-dinner drink at Da Nang, Vietnam, with Clare Hollingworth, of The Daily Telegraph. They began chatting about Philby and after a while Clare said, 'You know, Murray, I have a little personal link with Philby, a tenuous one admittedly, but it is a link: Kim discovered once that he and I have the same birthday.' 'Really?' Sayle said, his suspicion growing rapidly. 'When's that?' 'Why, Murray,' Clare said, watching the sunset, 'October the tenth, of course.'

V

In February, 1967, the original Insight ceased and its place was taken by Spectrum, basically Ron Hall's idea. The Philby investigation launched the new Insight with an international sensation. Spectrum was just settling down when an unfortunate caption to a photograph of the British Black Muslim leader, Michael X, resulted in Evans's being charged with contempt of court and leave being sought to commit him to prison. Although the High Court judgment in this case was of great importance to the legal position of newspapers and their editors, it has been widely misunderstood.

Michael X had appeared at Reading Quarter Sessions charged under the Race Relations Act with having used words likely to stir up hatred against a section of the public distinguished by colour. He had pleaded not guilty. Because of a legal hitch the case had been adjourned to be heard before a fresh jury. While Michael X was awaiting retrial Spectrum carried on October 29 a feature on race relations. The caption to the accompanying photograph of Michael X read: 'Michael Abdul Malik, 34, W. Indian. Came to U K 1950, took to politics after unedifying career as brothel-keeper, procurer, and property racketeer . . .' The article was drawn to the Attorney-General's attention by the Director of Public Prosecutions, who in turn drew Evans's attention to it, at the same time indicating that proceedings would be considered.

On November 8 Evans wrote accepting responsibility for the article but stating that he had not been personally concerned with it. (He had, in fact, not seen it until Sunday morning.) He said the caption had been published only after legal advice had been taken on it and it had been approved for publication by a practising member of the Bar. 'I understand that in this case the barrister concerned took the view that it could not constitute contempt of court because it did not have any bearing on any issue arising in the proceedings to which you refer.'

The Attorney-General instituted an action, and in the High Court on November 17, 1967, he was given leave to seek the committal to prison of Harold Evans. It must be emphasised that at this stage the likelihood of Evans actually going to prison was very real, and it was no consolation for him to hear that in the 1820s the editor-proprietor of The Sunday Times had been sent to prison for three months, for libelling the Prince Regent. There was even one well-known 'contempt' precedent. In 1949 the then editor of The Daily Mirror, Silvester Bolam, served three months in Brixton prison on a contempt of court charge.

The High Court hearing was on November 27 before Lord Chief Justice Parker, Mr Justice Widgery and Mr Justice Chapman. Through his counsel Evans expressed profound regret and pointed out that this was the first time in its 145 years that The Sunday Times had been accused in this manner.

The Lord Chief Justice said the court was satisfied that the newspaper had devised an elaborate and reasonable system to avoid contempts: as a responsible newspaper they were fully alive to their obligations. At the same time any system was liable to break down owing to the human element and did so in this case. It was quite clear, the Chief Justice said, that having regard to the seriousness of the contempt the publisher would have to be penalised. Times Newspapers Limited was fined £5,000. 'So far as Mr Harold Evans is concerned, he as editor takes full responsibility. On the other hand, when one is considering culpability one must consider his personal knowledge of what was going on. It is quite clear that he knew nothing about this, and that an editor in his position could not be expected to know everything that was happening. The court has come to the conclusion that it is unnecessary to impose any penalty on him.'

The comments which followed the case showed that the court's attitude to the editor of The Sunday Times had been widely misunderstood. The case did *not*, as many people inferred, mark a departure from the tradition that the editor is responsible for the contents of his newspaper. In fact, that Harold Evans took full responsibility as editor for the content of The Sunday Times was admitted and was never an issue. What the case did demonstrate was that the courts were prepared to recognise that in modern conditions, and with newspapers being much larger – the issue in question was sixty-four pages – an editor in Evans's position could not possibly be expected to read everything still less know everything that had led up to the publication of the offending caption. Since he knew nothing about the caption before publication and had devised a system to prevent as far as was humanly possible such a thing happening, it was quite unnecessary to impose any penalty on him. In short, the principle of editorial responsibility was preserved but the court recognised that mitigating circumstances were relevant to whether or not an editor should be punished personally.

VI

Throughout the latter stages of Evans's first year as editor there had been board-room rumours of a great serial coup – the purchase of sensational memoirs which would add thousands of readers to the paper's circulation. Evans was naturally intrigued, but early in 1968 he learnt that the project had suddenly collapsed. On February 18 it was The Sunday Times itself which broke the story of what had happened.

The project had been the purchase of the wartime diaries of Mussolini, and the manner in which the Thomson Group was misled over the matter must rank among the great publishing disasters of history. A full account of how a Polish-born arms dealer and an Italian businessman collected more than £100,000 as part payment of an agreed £250,000 for what turned out to be brilliant 'historical recreations' will probably never be told: secrecy has concealed the real rôle and rewards of those involved only too well.

Here it is enough to point out that after The Sunday Times disclosed the essential facts the rest of the British press followed up the story with some glee. Yet the early evidence the vendors presented justified the gamble, and if the risks of chasing world scoops occasionally result in fiascos like the affair of the Mussolini diaries, the fiascos have been more than outweighed by the successes, one of which was the Philby book – the result of further investigation following the Philby articles.

Evans had emerged by now as a first-class editor with his own ideas of how the paper should be developed. The challenge facing him was daunting. The paper had come a long way in eight years, and during this expansion the traditional rôle of an editor had altered radically. It was no longer sufficient to be a skilled and experienced journalist with a keen eye for news and make-up and a sound political judgment. Now an editor of The Sunday Times has to be a TV figure when called on, a speaker at international conferences, and conversant with management, marketing and finance. The reasons for this have to do with the changing nature of the press.

Today a national newspaper requires a huge amount of capital investment, and an editor who wants to get the most from his paper must understand how to use this money to the best advantage. As Hamilton has written: 'Far from being tied to his desk writing the night's leader, the modern editor should be up to his neck in the fight for solvency, having a strong say when investment in machinery is in contemplation, watching costs in every department, thinking out ways of making use of certain services, whether from his own organisation or newspapers and publishers abroad. He should know almost as much about advertising as his own advertisement manager.'

Hamilton had just this sort of relationship with the highly professional management team Thomson had built up over the years, and the whole onward march of The Sunday Times from 1959 had been made with the help and encouragement of all departments – 'everyone from chairman to office boy felt involved in our success.' But as the Thomson Organisation became more and more an industrial conglomerate it was important that The Sunday Times had a separate board to look after its special welfare and that its directors did not have their attention distracted by the Organisation's multiple outside interests. The formation in 1964 of The Sunday Times Limited, of which Hamilton was chairman at the same time as being editor, achieved this.

Then in 1967 after the merger of The Sunday Times and The Times had been approved by the Monopolies Commission and the Board of Trade, a new company was formed: Times Newspapers Limited, and a new board was set up consisting of five Thomson and four Astor nominees, the editor-in-chief, C. D. Hamilton, and the general manager, G. C. Rowett. Since it was necessary for financial reasons for this board to have a link with the main board of the Thomson Organisation, two directors, James Coltart and Gordon Brunton, sat on both.

Thus again Hamilton was filling two rôles – at first editor-in-chief and chief executive, and later editor-in-chief and chairman. In practice the system worked well. Hamilton says that being chairman and editor-in-chief is like being the admiral of the fleet who, although he sails in a particular ship, is responsible for all. His job was overall strategy, the watching of appointments, the forward planning. As far as The Sunday Times was concerned he saw this as 'making certain that the paper did not lose its authority, that it maintained its steady judgment, kept its sense of responsibility, and managed to develop new writers and sympathies without losing too many of our older readers.'

Yet it was important that Evans, executive director and editor, should have freedom to develop the paper as *he* saw fit. Thomson had given the Monopolies Commission assurances about the preservation of the separate identities of The Sunday Times and The Times and the maintenance of the independence of the respective editors. And Hamilton had appointed Evans, among other reasons, because 'I wanted an editor who would take the paper a stage further than I had done, someone who would be innovative and who would take chances. . . .'

Fortunately, Hamilton and Evans got on very well. Evans consulted Hamilton frequently and the line the development of the paper would take under its new editor soon emerged. The best of The Sunday Times would be sustained. In the literary and arts section, for example, changes of staff were minimal, a deliberate policy decision. 'When you've built up a reputation over a long period,' Evans says, 'you have to consider the weight of your reviewers' standing and experience against change for change's sake. No matter what surface alterations you make, the review section is for reviews, and when you have people like Cyril Connolly, Harold Hobson, Dilys Powell, Raymond Mortimer, John Russell and Desmond Shawe-Taylor you don't start shuffling artists like a vaudeville manager.'

Evans did make more space available to this section of the paper, brought in Alan Brien from The Sunday Telegraph, got Edwin Taylor to work out a new, cleaner, more unified design and introduced a regular front page commentary, with Kenneth Pearson doing a weekly column of news in the arts. J. W. Lambert remained as literary and arts editor (and also became a member of the Arts Council). Michael Ratcliffe moved to become literary editor of The Times. John Whitley, half-French and half-Yorkshire, joined, and in 1967 John Peter arrived. Peter, a refugee from Budapest at the time of the 1956 revolution, had been to Campion Hall, Oxford, under an arrangement whereby in return for his fees and expenses he worked as a part-time college servant. At the end of one year he was given a grant, and after taking a B. Litt. in Renaissance English Literature he worked for three years at The Times Educational Supplement before joining The Sunday Times.

Lambert's team has one of the more difficult jobs on the newspaper. Every year about 8,000 books arrive at the literary department but there is space to review only about 1,200. How are these selected? 'Our choice, not only of books but of reviewers, reflects our own beliefs and tastes,' Lambert says:

But that point of view must be, as a matter of prudence as well as courtesy, not too arrogantly remote from that of our potential readers – yet a little ahead of them as well. Our reviewers can and do, for all the arts, influence public taste. They do so not necessarily by campaigning or preaching but by offering one side of a conversation between intelligent people. They have to be able to inform those who don't know and do so without condescension, remind those who have half forgotten, yet manage not to irritate the many other experts who will be reading them.

One thing they are positively required not to do: use other people's desperate efforts as a springboard for self-display. Bad works when they cannot be ignored must get a thumbs down sign. But that is not the same as treating honest failure as a pretext for an outburst of abuse, however stimulating.

Primarily it is our job to point to what is worth paying attention to. I should like to think that anyone who regularly reads our pages will not only get news of what is most interesting in current books and arts, but the company of some remarkably fine, witty, and stimulating minds in our wide range of reviewers. At the risk of sounding priggish I believe that they will also get a rewarding perspective of the past through reviews of the classics, history, and biography, and of the present through reviews which at least outline the ferment of new ideas – artistic, philosophical, psychological, sociological, political, scientific, or what you will – as they are expressed in new or newly interpreted works discussed from week to week. If that declaration of faith gets me into Pseuds' Corner, it can't be helped.

Evans endorsed this credo, even if his own crusading temperament occasionally makes him prod the literary department for a more demonstrative approach, 'a blast or two on the siren', as well as Lambert's 'quiet but unrelenting pressure of the helm with which to alter unobtrusively the course of public understanding.'

What else would continue basically unchanged? The search for serials would go on, with Evans signing people as diverse as George Brown and the famous American humorist, S. J. Perelman. As Hamilton put it, 'For all the fun poked at us we can claim to have taken consistently, at the flood, tides of public interest. Our serials have done more than offer interesting reading. They have sparked off much controversy and almost always stimulated rather than satiated interest in the books from which they were taken. They have, moreover, never been chosen merely for sensation's sake at the expense of truth in its widest sense.' The paper's reputation for solid political comment and criticism would be maintained, and the staff of political correspondents – the veteran Lobby man James Margach, and leader writer Hugo Young – was strengthened when Evans engaged Ronald Butt from The Financial Times to be political editor and John Whale from ITN, where he had been Washington correspondent. Butt began a column of political comment while Whale began to specialise on Ireland.

Under Evans's influence the paper's political line began to change. Although offering no doctrinaire allegiance to the Labour Party it began to present radical views from the whole political spectrum, often because Evans considered that their sheer irritant value would help jolt political apathy. One of his early decisions, for example, was to offer the two most controversial back-benchers, Enoch Powell and Michael Foot, contracts to write a political column on alternate weeks. Unfortunately, both refused.

In the general election in 1970 the paper remained uncommitted until the last minute. Although The Sunday Times had never supported the Labour party the line of its editorials led many of its readers to believe that now it might do so. Evans had a series of discussions with his executives at which everyone advanced two views – his personal one and the one he believed the paper should present. In the end, over bitter opposition from some of the younger executives, Evans decided to support the Conservatives and wrote a final editorial explaining – in far from enthusiastic terms – why the paper had come to this decision. Evans said in 1972: 'We decided that the Labour party had not told the electorate enough about its policies and we thought that the Conservatives would be better for growth. So far, we have been proved wrong about that, but at the time it was the way it looked.'

Evans saw The Sunday Times as leading public opinion on a whole range of libertarian issues, from race relations to penal reform, from Vietnam to Ulster, standing firm against pressure from all sources. Two facts best illustrate his attitude. When he became editor and could write his own leaders without reference upwards, the first one he wrote advocated a law which eventually became the Race Relations Act; the second supported abortion law reform. When the paper criticised Enoch Powell for his statements on immigrants, Powell sued for libel on the grounds that the criticism imputed to him Nazi-style 'fantasies of racial purity'. Evans mustered a team of reporters and researchers under Lewis Chester and in two months thay had documented virtually every Powell utterance on the immigrant issue. The action was settled, The Sunday Times withdrawing any charge of a Nazi-style philosophy, which it had never in any case intended. Evans then returned to the attack on Powell's stance on the immigrant question which he had originally intended. Yet Evans would defend vigorously Powell's right to express his opinions.

'I think it is very important to be independent and to see that in a paper of our size many different points of view are represented. I don't *personally* decide what our policy will be on, say, scientific research or the disestablishment of the Church of England. I have an editorial conference on Fridays with Frank Giles, Ronald Butt, Hugo Young, John Whale, any of the senior people who want to come along. We argue a hell of a lot before we decide what our stance will be. But that stance is taken in the light of the continuing tradition of The Sunday Times as an independent paper, as one which believes in giving dissent an opportunity to be voiced, and which stands very strongly for individual liberty.'

Opinion at these editorial conferences can be sharply and some-times trenchantly divided. As Evans says, 'They're a sort of cross between All Souls and the Blue Lion [The Sunday Times pub]'. An issue like Biafra split the paper into two camps. Evans, Giles and Carroll held firmly to the pro-Federal line. They believed that to encourage secession in black Africa would lead rapidly to its Balkanisation with a general lowering of political and economic prospects, and they had no confidence in General Ojukwu, the Biafran leader. Butt, Young, Godfrey Smith, and some other senior men were pro-Biafran and, it is said, got a certain amount of pleasure from watching London's Biafrans come marching down Gray's Inn Road shouting for Evans's head.

On Rhodesia there was general agreement on the line which

Tuesday morning conference, 1972. Left to right: Duncan Gardiner (back to camera), Bruce Page, Ron Hall, Ma

470

klater, Harold Evans, Edwin Taylor, Nicholas Carroll, Nicholas Faith, Cal McCrystal, Frank Giles, J. W. Lambert.

Giles had traced out early on: that the paper should be squarely on the side of racial and human justice and thus emphasise the excesses and shortsightedness of the Smith regime. But there were disagreements over the significance of negotiations: after the HMS *Fearless* talks between Harold Wilson and Smith, Giles and Young split on what the paper should say and Evans flew home from a foreign visit to write the leader himself.

Evans believes that to encourage his executives in this frank expression of opinion on the paper's editorial policy can only help its vigour. 'We all say what we think – with information, I hope – but with no inhibitions. In a heated moment John Barry [Insight editor] told me I was guilty of morally dishonest journalism in my final 1970 election leader. But if the paper believes in free expression then it is only right that it should practise this belief in its own decision-making processes.'

On many matters the line Evans and his colleagues adopted for The Sunday Times was different from that of The Times. Although this eased the minds of the critics of the merger of the two papers – they had foreseen a monochrome editorial voice – it was not done deliberately. So The Sunday Times supported abortion law reform and The Times was against it. The Sunday Times was pro-Federal Nigeria (except the magazine, which Evans allowed to follow its desire to promote the Biafra case) and The Times was pro-Biafra. But it happened to fall that way and there is no contact on editorial policy matters between Evans and Rees-Mogg.

What was Lord Thomson's view on the way Evans was shaping the paper's policy? Evans does not know. Before he became editor Evans had heard that Thomson did not interfere in editorial matters, but he confesses to being surprised to find that this was unqualifiedly true.

He has never commented on a single editorial policy. In fact, I don't even know of his detailed views on any political issue. Not a week passes that he doesn't get letters from friends and people he has never heard of, all complaining about the editor or the paper or both. He is absolutely scrupulous about them. He replies saying that he never interferes in editorial matters and then he passes the letter to me to handle. Of course, he takes an interest when we have a libel action. As a businessman he does not like libel actions. But as a newspaper proprietor he likes successful newspapers and he realises that a successful newspaper pushing aggressively into new areas will inevitably collect libel writs. So he has become used to them.

VII

In this early period of Evans's editorship The Sunday Times hummed with argument, activity and purpose. Evans was forever searching for fresh ideas, some expressive or witty writing, some new means of presentation, a surprise on every page, and his excitement became infectious. Two stories will serve to illustrate what was going on at the paper in 1968: George Brown's resignation, and the start of the special books scheme.

On Friday, March 15, George Brown, then the Foreign Secretary, suddenly resigned. Evans conferred with Hamilton, who advised what the paper might do, and then dictated a letter to Brown and sent it and a message by an intermediary: The Sunday Times would like Brown to tell its readers of his period in office and his plans for the future. If he was agreeable Evans himself and the foreign editor, Frank Giles, would call at Brown's convenience.

On Saturday at 11 am Evans had a telephone call. 'Mr Brown will see you now. Please come to the side entrance.' So while the main door of the Foreign Office remained surrounded by journalists and cameramen, Evans, Giles, and two secretaries went in by the side entrance and were shown to Brown's office. Brown was clearing up his desk, helped by a couple of sad-faced assistants. But he was in good form, and after questioning him for an hour Evans and Giles went back to the office and put together his quotes to make 'My Future, by George Brown' which appeared exclusively in the paper on the Sunday. Brown, who had signed his approval of the page proofs, was impressed with the initiative of The Sunday Times and the trouble it had taken to get the article right. He met Evans on other occasions and when his book, 'In My Way', was published in 1971 it went to The Sunday Times for serialisation.

After the war The Sunday Times had published books, brochures and wallcharts under its own imprint or through various publishers, the ideas for them often coming from Leonard Russell, or Peter Wolfe, now a successful publisher on his own account but at one time head of the book publishing department of The Sunday Times (Jim Lee was also an active figure in many of these enterprises). The special books project dates from 1966 and Henry

Brandon's 'In the Red – the Struggle for Sterling, 1964–6' (Deutsch, London), to which Hamilton had contributed a lot of vital information obtained from his political contacts. But it was Evans, encouraged by Hamilton and advised by Russell, who launched The Sunday Times on an entirely new venture into the book-writing business. When the Philby series began in the paper Tony Godwin of Weidenfeld and Nicolson telephoned Russell to suggest a Sunday Times book on Philby. But for some reason Godwin lost his early enthusiasm, and Russell then turned to Deutsch. After a two-minute talk on the telephone Deutsch guaranteed an advance of £10,000, which was twice what Russell had asked Godwin. Evans needed no more encouragement, but he insisted on a real book and not a mere expansion of the original articles. He nominated a team of three to write it: Bruce Page, David Leitch, and Phillip Knightley.

Strictly speaking, Evans could have detached these three from their normal duties, told them to write the book, and have paid them no more than their normal salaries. But he decided that the authors would have more interest in the success of the project, and that it would generally be more just, if they received a share of the book's income. Accordingly, a division was drawn up whereby the paper would first recoup its expenditure; income from advances in excess of this would be split 60 per cent for the authors and 40 per cent for the newspaper, and any income in excess of the initial advances would go entirely to the authors. In any event, the authors were each guaranteed £1,200.

As it turned out, the Philby book was a runaway success. Published in ten languages, it earned in royalties more than £40,000, the paper taking £20,000 and each author about £5,500. At Evans's suggestion, and with full agreement from the authors, £5,000 from further money due to them was divided instead among fifteen other reporters who had at some stage or another helped on the project. Each of these received amounts ranging from £50 to £900.

Everyone was naturally delighted, but as it became clear that Philby was only the beginning of a series of Sunday Times book projects Evans came under some pressure to put the scheme on a more rewarding basis for the newspaper. Why, for example, had the paper ceased to participate in the Philby income after the book had earned its original advances? The answer was simply that no one – not even Leonard Russell – had foreseen that the book would be quite so successful. But clearly some scheme fair to all – includ-

The political bench, 1972: Left to right: John Whale, Ronald Butt, H. V. Hodson, Frank Giles,
Eric Jacobs, Hugo Young, Harold Evans.

ing the paper – would have to be devised.

Evans declined to reduce the authors' financial participation in a book's success. In the policy document on which all Sunday Times book projects are now based he set out the principles. 'The objects are to recompense the newspaper, reward the writers, and enable the whole staff, in some modest degree, to share whatever success we have.' Under the new scheme the paper provides the risk capital, legal indemnities, legal fees, salaries, all overheads, its world-wide network of correspondents, its prestige for negotiation and promotion, and its advice and encouragement. The authors, their normal salaries paid and guaranteed an extra £500 each even if the book should lose money, receive as well 15 per cent each of the net profit when there are three authors, 20 per cent when there are two, and 40 per cent when there is only one. The paper's share is either 45 per cent or 50 per cent, depending on how many authors there are. The remaining 10 per cent of the profit goes to a staff bonus fund which the editor uses at his discretion to reward anyone who worked on the book but who was not an author, and to provide special bonuses for any good work by any member of the staff on any assignment. This has been the policy on 'An American Melodrama', by Lewis Chester, Godfrey Hodgson and Bruce Page (Deutsch, 1969); 'The Secret Lives of Lawrence of Arabia', by Phillip Knightley and Colin Simpson (Nelson, 1969); 'Journey to Tranquillity', by Hugo Young, Bryan Silcock and Peter Dunn (Cape, 1969); 'The Strange Voyage of Donald Crowhurst', by Nicholas Tomalin and Ron Hall (Hodder & Stoughton, 1970) and 'Do You Sincerely Want to be Rich – Bernard Cornfeld and 10s: an International Swindle', by Charles Raw, Bruce Page and Godfrey Hodgson (Deutsch, 1971).

Each of these books began from some unusual form of journalistic initiative. The Lawrence book, for example, had its origins in a document which had been hawked around Fleet Street and the publishing world for years but which, because it sounded so improbable, no one had bothered to check properly before dismissing it. Russell spotted its possibilities. The 10s book grew out of the professional scepticism of Charles Raw, then of Business News, at a time when most of the British press had accepted Cornfeld's operation as a new style in international finance. Raw had written about the 10s London operation, International Life Insurance, from its start in 1964. Most of his articles were critical and a running exchange developed between him and ILI management. In 1966 Insight, at the suggestion of

Murray Sayle, who had once worked for Cornfeld, took a close look at ios in a piece called 'The Geneva Syndicate', which made it clear that it had certain reservations about Cornfeld's control of so much money with so little restriction.

In 1970, when the ios empire began to sag, it was not surprising, therefore, that a publisher met Raw to discuss a book about Cornfeld. After thinking about the scale of the operation it would require to investigate the affairs of ios in its many guises in its many countries, Raw replied that he would prefer to make the project a Sunday Times one. Evans agreed and contacted Sterling Lord, the New York literary agent; in three days he was offered an advance of $60,000 with more promised. It was needed. Page and Hodgson joined the team, and with assistance from fourteen reporters made enquiries in thirty-eight cities of the world. From the human and documentary débris of ios scattered over its field of operations they slowly pieced together their story. Since the legal difficulties were so great a leading Queen's Counsel worked with them virtually full-time for three months. The book, serialised in the paper, explained in laymen's terms, and with absolute clarity, financial affairs so complicated that some leading ios executives learned only when reading it what had been going on in their own organisation. It appeared on the best-seller lists in Britain (André Deutsch) and the United States (Viking Press) and remains a model for this form of financial investigation.

Apart from their success, these books marked a significant development in both newspaper and publishing worlds. At least three of them – 'Philby', 'Melodrama', and the ios book – could not have been attempted without the resources of a newspaper: 'Philby' because of the world-wide nature of the investigation, 'Melodrama' because of its cost, and the ios book because its legal problems would have deterred any publisher. ('If you're going to stand up to the bully boys of this world,' says Evans, 'then you need the muscle of a big newspaper.') Equally it is easier for The Sunday Times to embark on an expensive journalistic project if it knows that it can offset some of the costs by producing a book.

The 'Melodrama' book, which was an essential part of the paper's coverage of the 1968 Presidential election, is a case in point. The idea came from Godfrey Hodgson, then editor of Insight. He was supported by Page, who believed that big projects which enabled the paper to compete at an international level were an important part of The Sunday Times development. Evans was enthusiastic but worried about the cost: 'If I had known in advance that it was going to cost £40,000 I would never have done it.' But a major part of this was recouped by the book, which was not only a success of esteem but a Book of the Month club choice in America, and Evans still believes that, all in all, the project was well worth doing. 'It established our reputation in the United States and set the level for advances on later books.'

Evans adds, 'This whole book business is one of the most interesting things to occur in newspapers in years. Not only have we enriched The Sunday Times, produced a series of bestsellers, and discovered a lot of brilliant new writers, but we've opened a new field of newspaper-publisher co-operation which we intend to explore further.'

VIII

The third year of Evans's editorship found The Sunday Times riding high. Profits for 1968 had been a record £1.7m. With money available, and confidence gained from his early successes, Evans now went ahead with a programme of expansion, a lot of which he had set out in the memorandum he had written for Hamilton when he was still a candidate for the editorship. 'Current advertising and editorial is too slim for a separate women's section,' he wrote in 1966. 'But it might be viable as a family section including children, linked with everything we call leisure.' Evans believed that such a section would not in any way intrude on Ernestine Carter's territory. He fully recognised her contribution to The Sunday Times. Not only had she dominated the reporting of the international high fashion scene since the war but she had been a member of the council of the Royal College of Art, a member of the National Council for Diploma in Art and Design, a member of the selection panel for the Duke of Edinburgh's Prize for Elegant Design, an author, and a patron of promising young designers. In 1964 she had been awarded an OBE in recognition of her services to journalism. As Women's Wear Daily, the American bible of the fashion industry wrote: 'London is Ernestine Carter of the London Sunday Times.'

So Mrs Carter was given a high fashion page of her own and promoted to associate editor, and 'Look', the eventual product of Evans's 'family section', was launched in the Review Section of the paper on October 13, 1968 – 'two pages on modern living edited by Mark Boxer and Moira Keenan'.

To keep 'Look' different, Evans decided to rotate editors at short intervals, so in May, 1969, Hunter Davies and Molly Parkin took over. Davies, born in Scotland, brought up in Carlisle, had been with The Sunday Times since 1960, had made a very successful Atticus, and had become rich and famous as author of the official biography of the Beatles. Molly Parkin, a professional painter for twelve years, came to the paper from Harper's Bazaar.

Evans was happy with all their efforts. 'They really got the section away. It took on an irreverent freshness and rapidly became one of the most successful parts of the paper. Being editor of 'Look' isn't an easy job and I don't think anyone should do it for too long. So when Hunter felt he had had enough George Darby had a spell and then I brought in Allan Hall from The Sun.'

It was Evans who first spotted the wider possibilities of the controversial columnist of 'Look', Jilly Cooper. Godfrey Smith had met her at a dinner-party and had commissioned her to write a piece for the magazine. Evans read it. 'It was on seven years of marriage and it read so much like half my own marriage that I decided to hire her. She didn't hit her stride for a while – you've got to give writers time to settle in – but when she did I knew we had made a good choice. Half our readers love her, half think she is disgusting.' (Signing the author of 'The Female Eunuch', Germaine Greer, was more difficult. Evans confessed to masculine apprehension as to what the exponent of female sexual aggressiveness might do at their first meeting. Miss Greer, on the other hand, was physically ill with nervous anxiety at the thought of meeting what she imagined must be the very tough editor of The Sunday Times. They were both pleasantly surprised.)

'Look' was designed by Edwin Taylor, hired the previous month in one of Evans's most productive decisions as editor. 'As I moved around the paper examining various sections I realised that it was almost as important to give them a new appearance as a new content and, indeed, that a designer could make as great a contribution to the context as Peter Sullivan did when he drew his diagrams of the Aberfan tragedy. Peter, who does art work for us on Fridays and Saturdays, recommended Edwin. Leonard Russell and I met him. He came along with a portmanteau of books, bricks, tricks, toys, games for children . . . dozens of different things he had designed . . . and spread them out on the floor. It was a very unusual interview, but we spoke the same language, and after getting him to do one or two freelance commissions I hired him to head a design department.'

Taylor, who had been with Time–Life for four years working on the Life Science Library, was attracted by the challenge: 'Although newspapers are one of the oldest forms of communication, the business has a threshold feeling about it, a raw sense of urgency that is a refreshing change from the tired, phony scholasticism of the publishing business. Oscar Turnill explained some of the mysteries of newspapers to me and then I was left to get on with it.' Taylor's department grew to three full-time designers – Derek Alder, David Gibbons and Rosalind Newcomen – and four part-time artists.

Taylor proved a valuable revolutionary. Coming as an outsider he was able to challenge in his gentle manner a whole range of newspaper practices which had always been taken for granted. Although this aroused resentment – 'in some cases I was taking away what some executives regarded as untouchable: the right to lay out their own pages' – by working through Evans and being prepared to illustrate his point he usually won his case. Why, for example, Taylor would ask, does every article in the paper have to begin from a textual origin? Why could not some pieces start from a visual basis. So the 'Look' pages began to use features like 'What do you do with your fireplace now that you've got central heating', and 'How would you dress your country cousin'. Taylor remains aware that, in the end, a newspaper is a vehicle for words, but he feels that 'sometimes we have more words than sense'.

IX

Bigger and bigger papers in this period meant more editorial space to fill. Where should the expansion take place? Specialist sections offered limited opportunities for change. (Although the motoring section, in charge of Max Boyd, had taken on as a contributor Judith Jackson, wife of former racing driver, Peter Jopp. When she and Boyd started a new motoring column, Judith Jackson became the first woman to write regularly on motoring for a national newspaper since the war.) But obviously news, features, and the paper's authoritative political coverage could now receive whatever space the circumstances of the week demanded. Foreign reporting expanded, with more emphasis on sending a London-based writer to trouble-spots instead of relying totally on the local man.

Foreign editor Frank Giles says that there were several reasons for this: 'We found in the Six-Day war that a multilateral coverage from London got us out of a rather desperate position. In Czecho- slovakia in 1968 we sent out several men in the hope that one would get through. And in a war like the Bangladesh trouble, vast distances made it essential to have as many men as we could spare. Improvements in communications mean you can fly a man from London to practically anywhere in the world within a day. Even if he doesn't leave London until Wednesday that still gives him two or three days to work up his story. And you have the added advantage of bringing a fresh eye to look at a problem.'

Thus Giles himself made tours of Vietnam, the Middle East, Far East and India. Nicholas Carroll went to Vietnam and Nigeria. David Holden, the paper's Middle East expert, went several times a year to the area. Murray Sayle, Nicholas Tomalin and David Leitch made tours of Vietnam, producing fine descrip- tive and analytical despatches. Sayle followed the war more closely than the others, spending three or four months there at a time, while Leitch's picture of besieged Khe Sanh and Tomalin's piece about the American general wo went out 'zapping Charlie Cong' have become part of the journalistic history of the war. Hardly a week in this period passed without a reporter leaving London for an assignment as close as Paris or as distant as Tokyo. Sayle, easily the most travelled of Sunday Times correspondents – he spends only three or four months a year in London – says that as a result of this policy a major international crisis saw seven newspapers *always* represented: The New York Times, The Los Angeles Times, The Washington Post, Time, Newsweek, Le Monde – and The Sunday Times.

This concern for informed foreign coverage greatly helped the paper's reputation, especially in the United States, where it had a name for inside reporting from its Washington correspondent, Henry Brandon. Brandon's coverage of presidential elections, his face-to-face interviews (reprinted in two books), his long investiga- tion articles on the Sterling crisis, Vietnam, and the Skybolt missile were, in Hamilton's words, 'brilliant contemporary history'. Giles agrees on Brandon's contribution to The Sunday Times. 'It is no exaggeration to say that Brandon enjoys probably a greater degree of confidence and access to the sources of power in Washington than any foreign correspondent in any paper in any capital anywhere.'

In the early sixties this unique position had been attributed to

Brandon's personal friendship with the Kennedy family. But after the Dallas assassination Brandon showed that his contacts extended further than anyone had believed. 'It is hard not to be impressed by the guest list at a Brandon dinner party,' Harold Evans says. 'You're likely to find yourself sitting next to Dr Henry Kissinger [Nixon's special security adviser], Richard Helms [head of the CIA], the British ambassador, Teddy Kennedy, or any one of a dozen famous people.'

The only area where the paper's foreign coverage was not up to standard was in Eastern Europe; its reporting of communist affairs was poor. In the early 1960s Hamilton and Giles had discussed appointing a resident man in Moscow but nothing came of it, partly because of the high cost. But despite this disappointing situation the paper scored a fine coup in January, 1969, with the publication of a series of anonymous articles about life in the Soviet Union. Unlike many such articles these avoided generalisations and concentrated on the author's personal experiences of living among the Russian people, talking to them in Russian, working, and relaxing with them.

The articles created quite a stir, and the Foreign Office and the KGB spent a lot of time and effort to try to learn the name of the author. Since he no longer plans to return to Russia the whole story can now be told and his identity revealed. Evans and Giles had been fascinated to know how an event as important as the invasion of Czechoslovakia could have taken place without any reported intellectual reaction in Russia.

At a Tuesday conference the idea of doing some grass-roots reporting from Russia to try to find out how an apparent return to neo-Stalinism had affected the lives of the ordinary Russians was discussed at length. After the conference Godfrey Smith took Ron Hall aside and said, 'There is a young American called George Feifer who has done some stuff for us. He's a good writer and he has just spent a year or so at Moscow University. Why don't you try him?'

Hall talked to Feifer but found him very reluctant to become involved. He correctly foresaw that he would be harassed by the Russians and that when they finally learnt that he had written the articles he would be banned from Russia. 'He took a lot of persuading,' Hall says, 'and he was very nervous about the whole business.' Eventually Feifer produced a manuscript. He had changed the order of places he had visited and changed the descriptions of people he had met so as to protect them from reprisals. He insisted on delivering the manuscript in Evans's house rather than in The Sunday Times office and throughout the period only Evans and Hall had any contact with Feifer, or indeed knew that he was the author.

(This technique of looking for an expert and persuading him to write for the paper worked also with China. Giles retained Neville Maxwell, a colleague from his days on The Times but now a free-lance writer and an authority on Indian–Chinese affairs, to write for The Sunday Times while Maxwell was in China at the Chinese Government's invitation. Maxwell produced two long articles, including an interview with Chou En-lai which the paper pub-lished on the eve of Nixon's visit to Peking.)

This expansion of foreign coverage did not overshadow develop-ments in the newsroom. When Michael Randall, editor of The Daily Mail and 1965 Journalist of the Year, lost his job in 1966, Evans had telephoned him. 'I was shocked by his being sacked after what he had done with The Mail. After I became editor I had lunch with him and with Hamilton's agreement offered him what I had been when I first joined the paper – chief assistant to the editor. He said, "Can't you manage a title a bit better than that?" So we made him managing editor, news.'

Randall's job is to supervise news and pictures, plan their presentation, and to take charge of the budgets for the news and picture desks. He started slowly, playing his way into the paper's rather tricky power structure. By 1969 his influence had become marked. Under his direction, and with the design expertise of Robert Harling, the news pages had taken on a distinctive appearance – Randall is a marvellous headline writer – and the display of photographs had never been better. There was still, as No. 1 staff photographer, the long-serving Stanley Devon, a prodigious award winner, regular Royal Tour photographer and, in 1970, an MBE for his services to his craft. Now Randall had Jack Hallam as picture editor, and six freelances – Frank Herrmann, Steve Brodie, Bryan Wharton, Michael Ward, Peter Dunne and John Hodder.

Insight, Spectrum, book projects, and the features department had a habit of swallowing the best of the newsroom reporters, and more were now needed. Evans decided to try an idea he had had for some time. In common with most Sunday newspapers The Sunday Times had from its very beginning employed casual sub-editors on Saturdays. Evans's idea was to replace them with staff sub-editors. But since there would be no work for these subs early in the week, the new men would work as reporters from Tuesday to Friday and then become subs.

'I thought that we could develop reporters who would write more acceptable copy and subs who would understand the problems of reporters.' Over a period during 1968–9 Derrik Mercer, Peter Pringle, Tom Davies, Denis Herbstein, John Fryer and Derek Humphry were engaged for these dual jobs. The scheme failed. On a practical level it did not always prove possible for a reporter to finish his story by Friday night. On an emotional level the new men felt that the division of their duties made them second-class reporters and second-class subs. Evans abandoned the scheme. 'I was sorry, but it hadn't worked out.' The best of the Saturday casual subs were re-engaged and the reporter-subs became straight reporters.

All this expansion to service the bigger 72-page papers meant a strain on the paper's production, administrative, and service sides. James Dow had handled editorial administration and production, but with bigger papers, earlier press times, and the introduction of editorial budgets, this became too big a job for one man. 'Production alone became a bit like launching a battleship,' Evans says. 'Everything had to come together at exactly the right time or you missed the tide. So John Carr was appointed production editor and this freed Jimmy for the extra administrative and financial duties that all our new projects entailed.' Dow continued with this job but Carr moved to The Times. His place was taken by Duncan Gardiner, the chief sub who had rejoined The Sunday Times in 1967 after being assistant editor of Thomson's Western Mail in Cardiff.

On the service side the library found itself under heavy pressure. With an editorial staff of more than a hundred to look after, the library found it could barely cope with enquiries. On the retirement in 1967 of Wally Squires, who had been with the company for fifty years, Fred Brazier became head librarian. Brazier now added two librarians, extended the library area to accommodate the 150,000 packets of newspaper clippings which date back to the first world war, and began micro-filming the newspaper files to gain more storage space.

In the Review section, the travel pages were ripe for development. Evans noted the change which package tours had brought to the industry. 'Travel in Ian Fleming's day was for the middle classes and linked with adventure. Now everyone can travel and it is linked with the family and thus with consumer interest. Jean

Robertson and Ian Nairn became available at about the same
time and I hired them both – Jean to be travel editor and Ian both
to write travel and to join Nicholas Taylor, our environment
correspondent.' Jean Robertson quickly embarked on ambitious
plans. 'I got from Harry a proper travel budget, so that I could
pay to send writers to places and not rely on invitations. I improved the level of writing by commissioning professional writers
who enjoyed writing about travel. And because my earlier work
was as a consumer journalist I try to bring a strong consumer
interest to the pages.'

Gradually this section became a platform for Sunday Times
staff (who were paid for their contributions), for three or four
specialist writers with subjects like cruising, and for writers with a
passion for a particular area, such as Jeremy Rundall has for the
north. Since research showed that 90 per cent of readers of the
section did not travel beyond Europe and the Middle East, Jean
Robertson concentrated on this area, with only an occasional
article on far horizons.

The section expanded from one writer and a secretary to three
full-time writers (Brian Jackman became the third), three secretaries and up to eighty contributors. The 1971 Christmas travel
section ran to twenty pages and readership grew remarkably. Anything about France, for example, brought such a response that it
became standard practice for The Sunday Times to notify the
French Tourist Office in advance so that it could prepare to meet
the extra business – 'otherwise they were suddenly swamped.'

X

The picture, then, of The Sunday Times throughout 1968 and
1969 was one of a steadily developing newspaper, strong in its
traditional fields like politics, serials, reviews and haute couture,
but pushing new ideas, new presentations, and new theories of
journalism in order to expand its readership. There appeared to
be no limit to the paper's prospects. But in mid-1970 the outlook
changed dramatically. The country's economic recession began to
bite; markets shrank, unemployment grew, job opportunities contracted, advertising declined. The average size of the paper, which
had gone from 42 pages an issue in 1962 to 67 in 1969, fell back to
61, and the acute overflow of advertising in 1969 now became a

serious shortfall. This decline and its effect on the size of the paper coincided, because of escalating costs, with a series of the biggest price rises the paper had ever instituted: from 9d in 1967 The Sunday Times went to 1s 3d in 1970.

The economic situation was not as great a surprise to the paper as it might have been. Evans, an economics graduate, sensitive to unemployment from his days in the mining north-east, claims that from 1967 The Sunday Times had been consistently right about the state of the economy. 'We had said that Jenkins had done too little to reflate. We made a prediction that it would be hard to restore confidence, and without computers or information available only to the Ministries, the editorial column and Malcolm Crawford [economics editor] got our judgment of the state of the economy closer to the mark than the Government.'

The paper's problem was how to cope with smaller issues made necessary by declining advertising on the one hand, with the higher cover prices made necessary by rising costs. If the reader could not be offered any greater *quantity* of material then the increased price would have to be carried on the basis of better *quality*.

So in this period of economic concern, editorial development actually accelerated as Hamilton, Evans, and their colleagues sought new and attractive ways of improving the editorial content of the paper. A critical television guide was introduced, a venture bound to be resented by publications like The TV Times. The idea – and the decision to risk a confrontation – was Evans's:

I had always been keen on more television coverage. I wanted to print the week's programmes but knew that the companies and the BBC had always claimed the copyright. Then early in 1970 a friend told me that he knew a way around the problem. I went to James Evans and got him to take counsel's opinion. A plan was worked out. I had cleared the back page of the Review section to do a leisure page but it seemed a better place for the new guide. Just at that moment Elkan Allan wrote saying that what the paper needed was a four-page television guide and that he was the man to do it. A scheme was devised to turn the page on its side. Oscar Turnill got over the technical problems in doing this. Edwin Taylor did the design. Hamilton gave it the boardroom push it needed.

Soon after the first guide appeared The TV Times threatened action for breach of copyright but did not proceed. Then The Sun began its own television guide, from content to layout remarkably similar to that in The Sunday Times. Evans was still musing over this coincidence when Rupert Murdoch, the Australian proprietor of The Sun, telephoned. 'Harry, I've got a bit of a problem – I reckon you might be able to help. You know we've started this television guide? Well, we've had threats of writs. How did you get on?' Evans told Murdoch that he could not answer for The Sun guide but he was confident that The Sunday Times was not in breach of copyright. Murdoch was relieved. 'Then we're okay too,' he said, 'because we pinched the bloody idea off you.'

The guide was quickly accepted by the television companies and the B B C as a means of increasing viewer interest. (It did not interfere with the television critic's duties. Evans made the division clear: the guide would concentrate on providing the reader with information to help him decide his week's viewing; the critic, then Maurice Wiggin, would concentrate on writing reflective comment on selected programmes.) By the time the guide had been going a year it had a readership of over one million and had been followed not only by The Sun but by The Daily Mail and the weekly, Time Out.

Some of Evans's innovations were snap decisions. When he learned that the Consumer Council was to close he reasoned that a consumer column would have strong reader interest. When he heard that The Observer and the B B C were negotiating to link up with the Consumer Council and to take over its files, he quickly hired Patrick Foreman, the Council's chief legal officer, moved Adam Hopkins from assistant news editor to head a new section, and at Ron Hall's suggestion called it the Insight Consumer Unit. The unit now employs Peter Kellner, who moved from Business News, Patrick Foreman, and Caroline Ritchie, a researcher who came from the features department.

The paper's interest in sponsoring adventure continued. After Chichester it had promoted the Golden Globe, a round-the-world single-handed yacht race in which Donald Crowhurst tragically lost his life. It had been involved in the British Trans-Arctic expedition, led by Wally Herbert which had crossed the polar ice cap in 1968–9 and which had been reported by Peter Dunn and Tony Dawe. And, as we have seen, it took part with the B B C in the International Everest Expedition which failed to climb the south-west face of Everest in 1971. This was the old adventure school of journalism, yet a lot of what was happening on the paper in this period was an attempt to break away from safe and traditional formulas. As Edwin Taylor told Evans at one of their early meetings: 'I know you melt down the metal of last week's paper but how do you break down the mould. If you can re-make the paper for big events why can't you re-make it week by week.'

Evans was interested but cautious. He had run into heavy opposition in taking the classified advertisements off the back page of the Review section and using the space for the T V guide. His aim was to use the back page of each section in some striking way. The T V guide had worked well. Business News had fenced a back page with news and a column of comment written by Peter Wilsher or deputy editor Nicholas Faith.

Now Evans began to experiment with the back page of the news section. Traditionally this had been reserved for the paper's sports coverage, but in June 1969, half on hunch, half on the results of reader research, Evans moved sport inside. The theory was that since sports coverage is a certainty the reader would not mind turning a page to find it. This proved true and helped by John Lovesey whom Evans had brought in from Sports Illustrated to be sports features editor, readership of the sports pages actually increased.

Evans had met Lovesey in 1966, introduced by The Sunday Times football writer Brian Glanville, and had been impressed by Lovesey's ideas for developing the features and analytical side of sports coverage as opposed to straight reports. Now, nine months after moving sport inside, Evans made Lovesey sports editor with Derek Collier his deputy. With vivid graphics to help comprehension, Lovesey and his team expanded the scope of their pages so that anything from a series on how to teach children to play tennis to a mountain climber writing about his agonising re-examination of his motivation after the death of a fellow climber could find a place in the sports section.

With the back page now free, Evans at first used it for more news, but this did not really work and Evans swung to the idea of making it another platform for comment. What he wanted was a change of pace from the urgency of the front page, something entertaining, unpredictable, startling . . . 'a mixture of The New Statesman, Miscellany and Private Eye.'

To those who said he already had this with Atticus (Michael Bateman) Evans replied: 'I see Atticus as a man who went to a party, met four people, and got trapped. I wanted another columnist, one who had been to a party, flitted all over the place, and gathered everything that was shocking, vivacious and intriguing.' Alan Brien was engaged to do a weekly column written in diary style, and before he succeeded Maurice Wiggin as television critic endeared himself to some readers and infuriated others. Evans now tried a column called 'People', then a short pithy profile written by Peter Lennon and a gossip column called 'Private Ear', written by Peter Dunn. He is still not sure that this is the right mixture for this page and the experiment could well continue for years.

An obvious way of saving money in this period of economic concern would have been to have cut back on the foreign department, which has the largest single budget on the editorial side of the paper. But as we have seen, a paper's prestige depends on the strength of its serious coverage of politics and home and foreign news. So all that happened was that Giles decided that there was no longer any need for separate staff posts in Germany and France. Antony Terry, ex-British Army intelligence officer and ex-POW, a fluent German speaker and contributor to all parts of the paper, had been in Bonn many years and was the obvious choice for the new position of European correspondent based in Paris. But apart from this merger foreign coverage continued at strength. Giles put a new man, Eric Marsden, into Jerusalem and when Anthony Mascarenhas, Sunday Times correspondent in Karachi, walked into Thomson House on May 19, 1971, with a horrifying story of Pakistan Army massacres in Bangladesh, there was no hesitation about cost. 'I saw Nicholas Carroll. He listened and then took me to see Frank Giles and Harry Evans. Within forty minutes of entering the building I was heard, accepted, and ready to go back to Karachi to bring out my wife and children. There was immediate recognition of the story and I am still spellbound by the journalistic instincts and integrity of those responsible for that decision.' Mascarenhas received a special award from IPC and from 'What the Papers Say' for the article he wrote for The Sunday Times after successfully smuggling himself and his family out of Pakistan. (Once the war started Nicholas Carroll, Nicholas Tomalin and Phil Jacobson were sent to India and Murray Sayle to Pakistan. After the cease-fire Carroll obtained the only interview in the British press with Mrs Gandhi.)

On the emotive subject of Ulster, too, The Sunday Times did not allow anything to deflect it from what it saw as its duty: to report the situation impartially, to try to get at the roots of the tragedy, and to set the new situation in its political and historical perspective. Bruce Page suggested that the paper should attempt an operation to tell the whole story of British military involvement in Ulster: 'The aim would be to produce a historical reconstruction taking events right through to the last few hours of the week in which we write . . . this should be a piece of traditional campaigning journalism – but campaigning in the first instance not so much for any particular viewpoint as for a more serious level of political awareness . . . This is something of a test case for the kind of journalism The Sunday Times has been trying to develop for the past few years.'

A basic team of Page, John Barry, editor of Insight, his reporters John Fielding and Phil Jacobson, and reporters Denis Herbstein and Peter Pringle, was supplemented from time to time by chief reporter Tony Geraghty, political correspondent John Whale, and specialist writers Muriel Bowen and Peter Lennon. Their investigation took four months, in the course of which it produced news stories most weeks, culminating in the controversial account of the British Army's 'in-depth' interrogation techniques at Holywood, published on October 17, by Insight and John Whale. Despite a Stormont statement that this story was 'substantially untrue' and charges that the paper had fallen for a clever IRA propaganda trick, the official enquiry conducted by Sir Edmund Compton found that as far as interrogation procedures were concerned, The Sunday Times report had, if anything, under-stated the situation. And on March 2, 1972, the Prime Minister, Mr Heath, announced that five of the interrogation techniques used on the Ulster internees would be stopped for good – final and complete justification of The Sunday Times story.

The paper received a 'What the Papers Say' award, in part for the interrogation article – 'a model of how such journalism should be conducted' – and when the results of the main investigation were published in two parts on November 14 and 21 as 'A Perspective on Ulster' it created world-wide comment. Reaction ranged from charges of giving comfort to the enemy to the decision of the US Congress that the articles should be read into the record as 'an extremely valuable record of the development of the tragedy in Ulster'.

John Barry and John Whale as principal authors, with Geraghty, Jacobson and Fielding assisting, now expanded the material into a book which was published simultaneously in hardcover (André Deutsch) and paperback (Penguin) in Britain on February 24 and later in the United States (Random House). The book was widely and favourably reviewed. Roy Hattersley, the Shadow Minister for Defence, writing in The New Statesman, said 'Insight have done more than record the facts of what happened. *Ulster* conveys the spirit of the place . . . thanks to the Insight team, The Sunday Times knows what it is talking about.'

It is difficult to recall an issue that has brought on the paper as much criticism as its reporting on Ulster. Evans sees this as a predictable result of his determination that the paper should stick to its independent line, even though this might at times make it appear unpatriotic. Hamilton, who because of his position has had to absorb a lot of the higher-level criticism, is equally philosophical: 'It is the rôle of a great newspaper to be attacked.' It could well be that when emotions over Ulster one day cool, and historians come to set down how Britain's involvement was reported, The Sunday Times will emerge as one of the very few newspapers which kept its head.

XI

In many ways The Sunday Times had never been better than in 1972. Under Lords Camrose and Kemsley, for all their struggles to make it a political force, its reputation rested largely on its criticism of the arts and the humanities. Now its scope and its influence were infinitely wider. It had attracted to it some of the best writers inside and outside journalism and had found new and interesting ways of developing and presenting their talents. Its serials and memoirs satisfied the intense need of the ordinary citizen to know what had happened during crucial periods of recent history. It campaigned for just causes, brought an irreverent independence to its politics, and defended the individual against the State and 'the bully boys of the world'. It reported the issues of the day, both in Britain and abroad, with courage and concern. It informed, instructed, entertained, and amused four million readers a week. On its 150th anniversary its claim to be 'one of the world's great newspapers' is clearly a just one. But what does its future now hold?

An estimate of the paper's possible market in the 1980s proved very encouraging. Increased opportunities would mean a larger pool of more highly-educated readers. Greater leisure would mean more time – and more demand – for reading matter. Expenditure on newspapers would increase and a large part of this increase would be spent on serious newspapers. As a result of inflation consumers would be very value-conscious, and quality in a newspaper would therefore be important. The content of papers would tend more towards features and news comment, with more emphasis on foreign – especially European – news and scientific topics. The trend for a more percipient explanation of current affairs, for a probing analysis of why events had occurred, would continue.

For these and other reasons Lord Thomson is confident that The Sunday Times can continue to develop. He says: 'In an ideal world there would be some form of a moratorium on inflation, some system under which there would be no cost increases or price increases for periods of, say, three years. The Sunday Times went from 1 million to 1.5 million. If it had not been for inflation, which made newspaper prices higher and thus solidified the circulation graphs, then we would have made 2 million. One day we will.'

Denis Hamilton sees development as not only desirable but essential. 'A newspaper is a living organism and it must change and expand or die. The Sunday Times has been changing constantly. Politically I helped change it from an inflexible right-wing newspaper into an independent one. This was done without it losing its accuracy, authority, truth, and balance. To maintain this in the coming years we shall have to be more self-critical of our performance and try to find some source of independent criticism. Given this I am sure that The Sunday Times can continue to push forward still further the frontiers it helped pioneer.'

Harold Evans expects the influence of The Sunday Times to increase. 'The world will shrink because of satellites and television and supersonic planes and it will grow hideously and fascinatingly more complex. The speed of electronic communication will stimulate but it won't satisfy. To adapt Cordell Hull, a lie will get three-quarters of the way round the world before truth can pull its trousers on. Journalism of the printed word will have to find and record the truth, to make sense out of an excess of sensory perception, to elucidate what is supposed to have happened in news, art, business, science, and to anticipate, if we can, what may be about to happen. The diversities, frustrations and excitements of our civilisation cannot be understood on a few minutes, or even a few hours, of film clip. Only the marvellous mosaic of the newspaper is sufficiently flexible and convenient. Of course, if we are not to confuse ourselves and bore the reader, we shall require more skill and a better technology. With them, The Sunday Times will flourish – or fall – with the printed image.'

Appendix

Times Newspapers Limited was incorporated on December 22, 1966, as the controlling company of The Sunday Times and The Times. The board of Times Newspapers Limited, as at May 31, 1972, comprised:

PRESIDENT: Lord Astor of Hever

CO-PRESIDENT: The Hon. Kenneth R. Thomson

CHAIRMAN AND EDITOR-IN-CHIEF: C. D. Hamilton

MANAGING DIRECTOR AND CHIEF EXECUTIVE: M. J. Hussey

DIRECTORS:

Sir Donald Anderson	Sir George Pope
G. C. Brunton	Lord Robens
J. M. Coltart	Sir Eric Roll
Sir Kenneth Keith	Lord Shawcross

Index

497

Doctors switch man's blood

A YOUNG American Air Force sergeant was placed in bloodless suspended animation for about 10 minutes while surgeons. completely drained his blood before pumping in a new supply, it was revealed in San Antonio, Texas, yesterday. The operation was on March 31 —and yesterday the patient said he felt " just fine."

The surgeons said they used a heart-iung machine to pump a clear salt solution into his arteries as they drained his blood. They then pumped fresh donor blood back into his body. " Unlike blood transfusions, which simply augment or replace lost blood, the saline solution also completely flushed diseased blood from the patient, enabling the liver to regenerate sufficiently to resume its blood filtering process."—*AP.*

Vietnamese retreat before Red offensive

THE 31-DAY North Vietnamese offensive rolled southward unchecked yesterday, enveloping large areas of South Vietnam's two northern-most Provinces, laying siege to Quang Tri city and threatening the old imperial capital of Hué from both the north and west.

The South Vietnamese also gave up more ground on the central coast, abandoning the district headquarters of Bong Son in Binh Dinh Province, the most populous in the country with over one million people. " The Vietnamese are running away like you've never seen before." declared one American advisor in Binh Dinh.

Three high-ranking Soviet officials visited Hanoi just after Henry Kissinger's Moscow visit to assure the North Vietnamese of continuing Soviet support, the official Tass news agency said yesterday.

'Drop charges' call in university crisis

LANCASTER UNIVERSITY'S Senate has been recommended to drop proceedings against students involved in disturbances there last month by a special committee set up under Prof. John Bevington to investigate student unrest at Lancaster.

But after the committee's report had been considered at a Senate meeting yesterday student spokesman Mr Paul Howard said he was not optimistic about the outcome. Nine students still face disciplinary charges after troubles arising from the possible dismissal of Mr David Craig, a lecturer in English.
Tom Shaw

New 'hidden' planet

THE EXISTENCE of a tenth planet, far beyond Pluto, has been predicted by American astronomers. It is nearly 6,000 million miles away, three times as large as Saturn, which is about 70,000 miles in diameter, and orbits the sun once every 600 years. The prediction is based on a computer analysis of unexplained irregularities in the orbits of Halley's and other comets. The search for Pluto, after its existence had been predicted from peculiarities in the orbit of Neptune, took 15 years.—*Bryan Silcock.*

Sadat cu?? visit

Listener's corner at Speaker's Corner: William Craig in London ye

Two union lea their cases to

IN SPITE of their vigorously expressed opposition to the Industrial Relations Act, union leaders are finding themselves increasingly drawn into co-operating in vital areas of the Act's operation in order to defend their members' interests. This week Mr Clive Jenkins, general secretary of the Association of Scientific, Technical and Management Staffs—ASTMS—

By Vincent Hanna and Eric Jacobs

The implications of these moves will be reviewed by the TUC finance and general purposes committee tomorrow. Mr Jackson will tell the committee that he intends to appear before the Industrial Court whatever the TUC may say. Mr Vic Feather, in a speech at Cardiff yesterday, semed to be expressing the growing doubts of union lead-

has anoth members the Tribu

TSA w Office fo name of phonists, withdraw of its me with Mr guild's r